THE PSYCHOLOGY OF WOMEN:

PSYCHOANALYTIC PERSPECTIVES

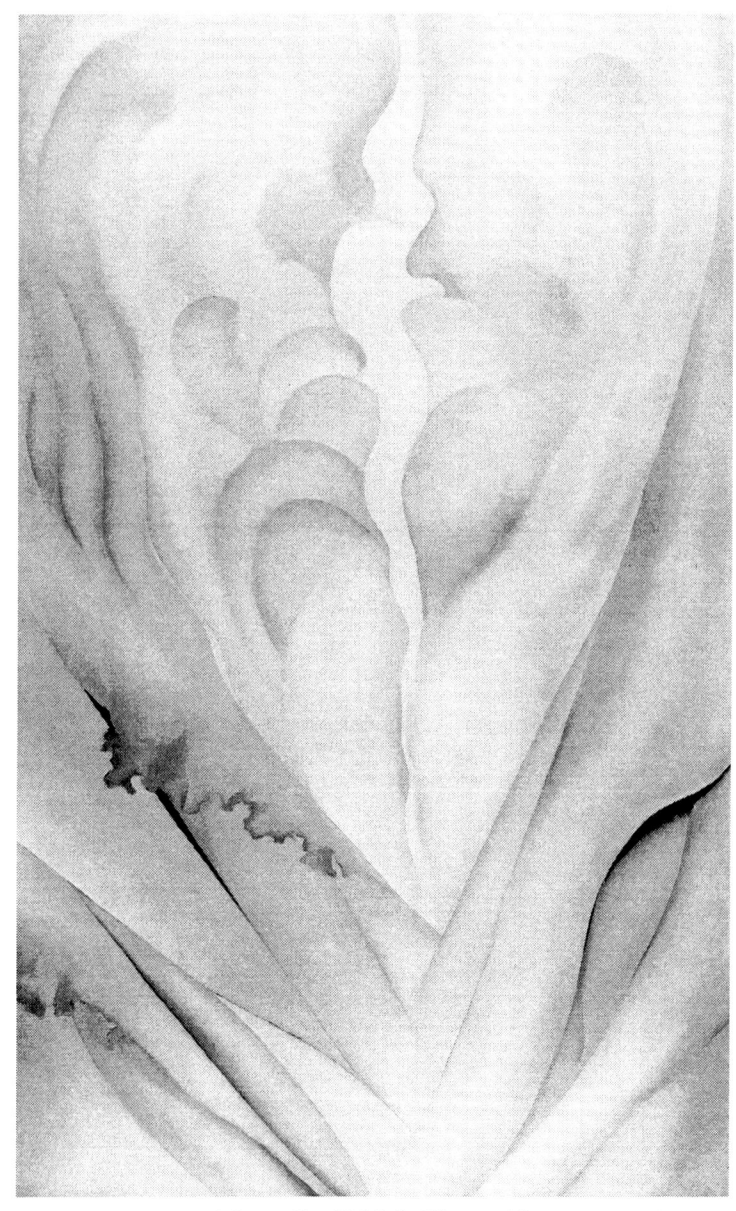

Figure 1. Georgia O'Keeffe (1924) *Flower Abstraction*. Photograph Copyright © 1996: WHITNEY MUSEUM OF ART, NEW YORK

THE PSYCHOLOGY OF WOMEN:

PSYCHOANALYTIC PERSPECTIVES

edited by

Arnold D. Richards
Phyllis Tyson

INTERNATIONAL UNIVERSITIES PRESS, INC.
Madison   Connecticut

Copyright © 2001, International Universities Press, Inc.

INTERNATIONAL UNIVERSITIES PRESS ® and IUP (& design) ® are registered trademarks of International Universities Press, Inc.

All rights reserved. No part of this book may be printed or reproduced or utilized in any form or by any electronic, mechanical or other means, now known or hereafter invented, including photocopying and recording, or in any information storage or retrieval system, without permission in writing from the publisher.

Library of Congress Cataloging-in-Publication Data

The psychology of women: psychoanalytic perspectives / edited by
  Arnold D. Richards, Phyllis Tyson.
     p. cm.
  Includes bibliographical references and index.
  ISBN 0-8236-5588-1
  1. Women and psychoanalysis.   2. Women—Psychology.   3. Femininity (Psychology) I. Richards, Arnold D. II. Tyson, Phyllis, 1941-   .
BF175.P795   1997
155.3'33—dc21   97-784
                                                                                                  CIP

Manufactured in the United States of America

Contents

Acknowledgments ix

A Note on the Illustrations

CONTEMPORARY IMAGES OF WOMEN IN CONTEMPORARY WOMEN'S ART:
CONCURRENT TRENDS IN ART AND PSYCHE
Janice S. Lieberman xi

Introductions

FEMALE PSYCHOLOGY IN PROGRESS
Harold P. Blum 3

FEMALE PSYCHOLOGY: AN INTRODUCTION
Phyllis Tyson 11

I. Freud and the Feminine

FREUD AND FEMININE SUBJECTIVITY
Leon Hoffman 23

FREUD AND THE REPUDIATION OF THE FEMININE
Shelley Orgel 45

II. The Theory of the Psychology of Women

FEMINIST PSYCHOANALYTIC THEORY: AMERICAN AND FRENCH
REACTIONS TO FREUD
Helen Rosen and Elaine Zickler 71

NATURE, NURTURE, AND CORE GENDER IDENTITY
Michael Robbins 93

UNCONSCIOUS REPRESENTATION OF FEMININITY
Dana Birksted-Breen 119

Contents

A Reconsideration of Object Choice in Women: Phallus or Fallacy
Rhoda S. Frenkel — 133

Beyond the He and the She: Toward the Reconciliation of Masculinity and Femininity in the Postoedipal Female Mind
Donna Bassin — 157

From "Nothing" to "Something" to "Everything": Bisexuality and Metaphors of the Mind
Barbara Stimmel — 191

Theoretical Gender and Clinical Gender: Epistemological Reflections on the Psychology of Women
Nancy J. Chodorow — 215

III. The Body in the Psychology of Women

The Meaning of Perineal Activity to Women: An Inner Sphinx
Anna Burton — 241

Primary Femininity and Female Genital Anxiety
Arlene Kramer Richards — 261

Castration Anxiety or Feminine Genital Anxiety?
Denise Dorsey — 283

Nevermore: The Hymen and the Loss of Virginity
Deanna Holtzman and Nancy Kulish — 303

Masturbation Fantasies in a Prelatency Girl: Early Female Body Fantasy Conflicts as a Major Determinant in the Experience of Primary Femininity
Jack Pelaccio — 333

A Revised Psychoanalytic View of Menopause
Sandra Bemesderfer — 351

IV. Motherhood

Pregnancy—Procreative Process, the "Placental Paradigm," and Perinatal Therapy
Joan Raphael-Leff — 373

Contents

THE PREGNANT MOTHER AND THE BODY IMAGE OF THE DAUGHTER
Rosemary H. Balsam — 401

ON MOTHERHOOD
Erna Furman — 429

TWO WOMEN AND THEIR MOTHERS: ON THE INTERNALIZATION AND DEVELOPMENT OF MOTHER-DAUGHTER RELATIONSHIPS
Anni Bergman and Maria Fahey — 449

V. The Psychology of Female Homosexuality

TOWARD FURTHER ANALYTIC UNDERSTANDING OF LESBIAN PATIENTS
Eleanor Schuker — 485

VI. Women and Training and Research

HEARING WHAT CANNOT BE SEEN: A PSYCHOANALYTIC RESEARCH GROUP'S INQUIRY INTO FEMALE SEXUALITY
Harriet I. Basseches, Paula L. Ellman, Susan S. Elmendorf, Elizabeth Fritsch, Nancy R. Goodman, Fonya L. Helm, and Shelley Rockwell — 511

CAN WE BE BOTH WOMEN AND ANALYSTS?
Sallye Wilkinson, Mary Jo Peebles-Kleiger, Bonnie Buchele, Alice Brand Bartlett, Sharon Nathan, Regine Benalcazar-Schmid, Michelle Mintzer, and Deborah Everhart — 529

Name Index — 557

Subject Index — 565

Acknowledgments

In 1994 a call went out in the *Journal of the American Psychoanalytic Association* (*JAPA*) and in *The American Psychoanalyst* (newsletter of the American Psychoanalytic Association) for submissions to this volume on the psychology of women. In response, we received forty-five papers. Each of these was evaluated by members of the editorial board and, where appropriate, by outside readers. The selection process was often a difficult one, and in the end, twenty-one papers were accepted. Many of the papers not selected were returned to their authors with suggestions for revision, and we expect that many of these may eventually appear in *JAPA* or in other journals. We recognize that not having a paper accepted can sometimes be painful, but we are at least pleased that this project may ultimately have an impact extending beyond the pages of this volume. We are grateful to all those who submitted papers, to the many readers who participated in the review process, and especially to the authors who worked with us to revise their manuscripts for final publication. We are also grateful to Martin V. Azarian for his willingness to support publication and to Margaret Emery for her tireless efforts to coordinate production. We thank Irene Guttman for willing, timely, and helpful editing of the manuscripts; Andrea del Conte, Paula Osheroff, and Lawrence Schwartz, our secretaries, who, among other things, coordinated what at times seemed an impossible cross-country effort of processing papers. Without their help, the publication of this volume would have been impossible.

Arnold D. Richards
Phyllis Tyson

Contemporary Images of Women in Contemporary Women's Art: Concurrent Trends in Art and Psyche

Janice S. Lieberman

In this fin de siècle issue of the *JAPA*, re-formulations and more innovative new formulations of Freud's major theories of female psychology are presented. Concurrent with these developments in psychoanalytic thinking about women have been developments in other fields. In the art world, for example, women artists have increasingly come into prominence during recent years and the works and writings of many of them have reflected an awareness of psychoanalytic concepts, whether latent or manifest. Many of today's artists if not psychoanalyzed themselves, are at least psychoanalytically informed.

The works of art chosen to illustrate the various sections of this issue range from those done prior to 1940 to post-1990, quite serendipitously reflecting the time when Freud was alive and developing his ideas about women and the time when the papers that comprise this journal were written! The painting by Georgia O'Keeffe (1924) (fig. 1) is typical of her flower abstractions. The shapes of the female genital and the wave-like experience of the female orgasm are conveyed in this sensuous libidinal work. Mcrct Oppenheim's (1936) (fig. 3) surrealist fur-lined teacup and fur-lined spoon (without the artist's conscious intent) presents the psychoanalyst-reader with a delightful dream image that condenses the female genital with the female nurturing function.

Frida Kahlo's (1940) (fig. 2) tormented life, injured and crippled body, and conflictual sexual identity are reflected in this self-portrait in which she depicts herself in an oversized man's suit holding the pair of scissors with which she has cut her hair. After having had polio as a child, an accident in her teens fractured her spine, shattering her pelvis and crushing her foot. Her vagina was impaled with a steel handrail. Judith Shea (1991) (fig. 4) casts a one-armed bronze Venus de Milo and gives her a silk garment, speaking to the issues of covering up and uncovering. Themes of castration are taken further in Kiki Smith's (1993) (fig. 5) life-size plaster and glass sculpture of "Daphne," who is headless, armless, and leg-less, but who nevertheless has a fulsome, competent body.

The abstraction of the weaver Lenore Tawney (1995) (fig. 6) extolls motherhood and fertility. Without apparent conflict, it presents woman as whole, as balanced and as full, a fitting introduction to the section on Motherhood. The middle-aged and robust artist Florine Stettheimer (1923) (fig. 7) painted herself as an ageless, flat-chested flapper. A feminine feminist antagonistic to male domination, she saw men as interfering with a feminized Eden. Her sexual object choice was never clear. Finally Deborah Kass' (1992) (fig. 8) Warholian humorous depiction of Barbra Streisand as Yentl portrays the dilemma of women who wish to function as serious professionals and yet believe that they must symbolically or even quite literally behave like men in order to do so.

These art works for the most part show women still in conflict at fin de siècle, not completely resolved as to the acceptance of their bodies or roles. Wolfflin (1932) wrote that "art is the mirror of life" (p. 226). If that is so, it will be the task of psychoanalysis to lead women to more adaptive solutions to these issues in the next century.

REFERENCE

WOLFFLIN, H. (1932). *Principles of Art History*, trans. M.D. Hottinger. Mineola, NY: Dover Publications.

INTRODUCTIONS

Figure 2. Frida Kahlo (1940) *Self Portrait with Cropped Hair*. Oil on canvas, 15 3/4 x 11" (40 x 27.9 cm). The Museum of Modern Art, New York. Gift of Edgar Kaufmann, Jr. Photograph © 1996 The Museum of Modern Art, New York.

Female Psychology in Progress

Harold P. Blum

It is a privilege to be able to introduce this second volume on female psychology and to survey the many relevant theoretical changes that have occurred in the last twenty years. At the time the first volume (Blum, 1976) was conceived, it was apparent to me that the so-called classical formulations and propositions of female development, "The Psychology of Women," were, in many respects, questionable both within and outside psychoanalysis. What had been learned and then taught by the earlier generations of psychoanalysts had, in very large measure, been based on the initial theories and limited experience of Freud and of psychoanalysts during his lifetime. Identified with classical teachers and teachings, analytic literature and analytic education perpetuated the authority, formulations, and cultural bias of the past. Many basic psychoanalytic discoveries had been confirmed, but the time was ripe for a critical reevaluation of classical theory, for testing new observations and ideas, and the implications arising from modifications of initial propositions and models. The growth and sophistication of psychoanalytic theory and developmental knowledge provided the background for the reconsideration and revision of older theory.

Freud had listened to and learned from his first female patients. He recruited brilliant women into the fledgling psychoanalytic movement, encouraged their psychoanalytic development, and anticipated and sometimes participated in their valuable contributions to psychoanalysis. The investigations and expositions of the pioneers, including several female analysts, led to what appeared to be rather definitive tenets and texts on female psychology. Historically, many of the pioneer contributions may be regarded as first approximations. To be sure, there were early psychoanalytic critics who questioned these formulations and who dissented on various points and

---

Former Editor (1973–1983), *Journal of the American Psychoanalytic Association*.

Harold P. Blum

issues. The formulation of the first Supplement provided the opportunity to explore inconsistencies, oversights, and errors, and to introduce fresh perspectives and propositions.

There was controversy within the Editorial Board. Was the challenge to "established" theory actually anti-theory, a capitulation to the critics of psychoanalysis, and a regression from a correct psychoanalytic position rather than a progressive development? The Supplement proposed an open analytic investigation of an important area of analytic controversy. The Program Committee accepted the Editor's recommendation for a series of panels on female psychology, but in the process certain problems appeared in bold relief. The Editor's initial invitations to participate in a panel on Female Psychology were, for the most part, answered with a willingness to write on the subject of "female sexuality." Female sexuality was substituted for female psychology by the majority of analysts of different ages and sexes. It was as though female psychology and female sexuality were equivalent topics. This represented an extraordinary *pars pro toto* overweighting of sexuality, probably predictable in retrospect. It was necessary to send second letters indicating an interest in a variety of contributions, encompassing female development; female aggression; sadomasochism; feminine values, standards, and ideals; girls at play and women at work; female creativity; the psychology of pregnancy and motherhood, etc.

The panels, presentations, and published papers were remarkably successful, and the *Journal* Supplement became a landmark in the changing views of the psychology of women and female development. This succeeded in stimulating further investigations of female development leading to new clinical evaluations of countertransference and the intrusion of possible selective observation, theoretical bias, and value judgments, not only in analytic work with women, but by extension into all analytic work. What is perhaps surprising is that some of the issues of that era and the impassioned controversies of prior times have now receded with theoretical change—not that the issues have simply disappeared. The baby has not been thrown out with the bathwater, but there has been much remodeling of theory and developmental models. Gaps have been filled in, inconsistencies clarified, unsupported assumptions challenged and

Female Psychology in Progress

changed, criticisms seriously considered and tested in the crucible of clinical work. Freud changed his own theory in the light of new knowledge, and contemporary psychoanalysis is, in many respects, far removed and far advanced from its pioneer period.

A male developmental model for both sexes and a phallocentric bias in which mothers were eclipsed by fathers and in which female genitals were devalued are no longer issues that are generally debated and contested. The female superego is not now regarded as weaker or deficient, and sex differences in structure and function are not given value judgments. Libido is not masculine, neither are passivity, narcissism, and masochism regarded as essentially feminine traits. Penis envy is no longer considered the bedrock of a woman's disappointment and necessary renunciation, but has been subject to major reinterpretation. Neither masochism nor envy is confined to women or necessarily related to the absence of a penis. Envy is an important affect with many sources and sequellae in both sexes. Both little boys and girls envy each other and grownups. Few analysts would any longer propose to derive femininity from penis envy, or consider women as suffering from a deficiency disturbance in which having a baby would represent compensation for an inherent sense of defect and disappointment. Past notions of the repudiation of femininity as bedrock represent a theoretical bias. Today's ideas would include constitution and development, narcissistic and preoedipal problems. Contemporary developmental theory takes into account the vast importance of early identifications and the internalization of social attitudes and stereotypes. Penis envy may be conceptualized as a reaction to castration fantasy, as a developmental organizer for the girl's masculinity, as a disguise for other losses and disappointments, as a metaphor for a wide variety of additional infantile wishes, and as a means to both possess mother and separate-individuate from mother. Penis envy may be a complex compromise formation which represents all of the above, as well as overdetermined envy of the male.

Boys have complementary envy—"womb envy" of the mother's obvious reproductive, procreative capacity. Historically it may have taken countless generations for the male role in reproduction to be understood. It may be noted here that little has been said of the comparative importance of penis envy in the male, although the

Harold P. Blum

little boy is envious of the father's larger penis as he is of the father's greater prowess, power, and, of course, possession of mother. Penis envy in the male is an important subject in its own right. Female penis envy may be projected onto the male and vice-versa. However, the boy's fear of losing his penis cannot be the same as the girl's fantasy of having and losing or having lost a penis she never had.

The phallic woman fantasy of both sexes is an important universal fantasy that denies castration and represents bisexuality as a composite of the parental couple. The fantasy that the girl has "nothing" and that "nothing" refers to the female genital is an infantile misconception and not a reality. The unconscious notion and social myth of the girl having nothing or having lost what she had, becoming a chronic loser, or being inferior and deficient because of what she lacks, was linked to fantasies about her anatomy. However, anatomy is only one determinant of destiny. That a girl is more confused about her external genitals than a boy whose genitals and urination are more clearly visible, defined, and named, does not in itself compromise ego function in the female. Cognitive capacities overlap and are not significantly sex-linked, despite stereotyped notions about genius and gender. The capacity for critical and creative thinking is evident in the original contributions of many female analysts. As more women enter medical and graduate schools and become psychoanalysts, women will have an ever more prominent role in our field and in other professions.

Femininity is primary because of a girl's biological endowment, and the primary experience of her own body. Appropriate labeling, parental discrimination of the infant as a girl, and response by the parents to a daughter which supports and complements her innate disposition appear to be critically important in feminine development. Parental fantasy, attitude, and behavior can apparently override innate endowment and disposition in vulnerable, passive infants. Primary femininity is not a secondary biopsychological formation, nor is it secondary in value. The historical (his-story), cultural, social, and linguistic representations of and attitudes toward women are internalized and reciprocally influence unconscious fantasy in a circular process.

Considering past emphasis on what girls lack, there is now much greater clinical and theoretical awareness of what girls do have in

Female Psychology in Progress

terms of their earliest life experience. In early theory the girl did not discover her vagina until after puberty and the onset of menstruation. The rhythmicity and organizing functions of female adolescence are now well recognized. Current emphasis is on the integration of genital structures rather than a theory of change from activity to passivity and transfer of the erotic zone from clitoris to vagina. The clitoris was devalued in theory as vestigially masculine and oft unacknowledged by parents. The significance of virginity has undergone vast cultural change in many areas, but unconscious fantasies concerning virginity and virgin mothers are ubiquitous. Some societies have retained archaic traditions associated with mutilating, dangerous initiation rites. Actual clitoridectomy is of vast psychosocial, legal, and medical importance and warrants further analytic investigation.

Parallel to primary femininity, the mother-daughter relationship now has a primary position in current psychoanalytic thought. While the importance of preoedipal development was first emphasized for girls, later theory incorporated a balanced view of preoedipal development for both sexes. Within psychoanalysis, the rise of object-relations theory as well as observational studies of infants and children coalesced with the clinical contributions of many child and adult analysts. Developmental theory advanced with new research, clinical, and interdisciplinary contributions. The experiences of adolescent pregnancy, rampant divorce, parent loss, reconstituted families, and single-parent families have further stimulated long-term developmental and outcome studies.

New concepts have emerged, and older concepts have been modified. Bisexuality, based on the model of innate, vestigial structures of both sexes, and object relations and identifications with both sexes did not account for gender identity. Gender identity apparently develops in the first 18 to 24 months of life and thereafter tends to be relatively irreversible. Psychosocial gender orientation and attitudes as well as the gender choice of object are influenced by nature and nurture. The father has been seen to be quite important, complementing feminine gender development, both directly and as part of the gendered complementary opposite-sex parents. Greater participation of father in infant care and child rearing today may lead to changes in preconscious attitudes about gender. Bisexuality is currently understood in a much more sophisticated appreciation of meaning and function. Bisexuality was related to the formation and resolution of the Oedipus complex and to the twofold positive and negative oedipal configurations. However, bisexuality is not simply an oedipal phenomenon. It is a component of a complex ongoing developmental process with potential influence on fantasy, identity, and behavior. Feminity develops and unfolds through the life cycle.

Psychoanalysis itself has undergone a complex developmental process since Freud (1905) found female psychology "veiled in an impenetrable obscurity" (p. 151). If the girl's erotic object choice is complicated by change from mother to father, she is perhaps also more secure in her gender identity. Her identification with her mother's femininity is less conflict-prone than the boy's. The girl's femininity is further shaped by education and her life experience through adolescence to senescence. Girls form concepts of their ideal self and ideal objects in relation to their parents and their culture. The expectations, attitudes, and feelings of parents toward each other and about women have a major influence on gender roles and attitudes. In societies where female babies are considered less desirable or unwanted, development may be just as stunted as the feet of girls that were formerly bound. Social and cultural forces influence development and unconscious fantasy. Expectations in analysis have also changed, and there is current analytic exploration of issues of pregnancy—the pregnant analyst as well as the pregnant patient. Prior to World War II, pregnant women were considered relatively unanalyzeable; the transference-countertransference issues were submerged in pregnant silence. Today, the analysis of a pregnant woman may be very rewarding, with major beneficial impact on the mother-child relationship.

To the impossible question of what does a woman want, there is no simple answer. A woman may want to be her own respected person, with appreciation of her individuality, gender, and achievements in many spheres of life. All of her hopes and fears will be related to her unconscious conflicts and developmental challenges. It is in this area that psychoanalysis can continue its unique contributions while benefiting from contributions and critiques from other disciplines. In the circular process of stimulating and integrating further investigation and innovative ideas, *Psychoanalytic Perspectives*

Female Psychology in Progress

on the Psychology of Women updates the psychology of women in the general context of the expansion of psychoanalytic knowledge.

REFERENCES

BLUM, H.P., Ed. (1976). *Female Psychology.* New York: Int. Univ. Press.
FREUD, S. (1905). Three essays on the theory of sexuality. *S. E.*, 7.

FEMALE PSYCHOLOGY: AN INTRODUCTION

Phyllis Tyson

In 1976, the *Journal of the American Psychoanalytic Association* published a landmark supplement on female psychology (Blum, 1976) that brought together the theories of female psychology held by the major American psychoanalysts at that time. As Blum's introduction to this volume indicates, that volume reviewed Freud's theories about the mind of the female and compared and contrasted Freud's views with the then contemporary ones. That volume has become a classic, shaping the psychoanalytic theories of female psychology held by clinicians of the 1990s. After 20 years, it seemed fitting to revisit the subject of female psychology.

Interest in the psychology of women is not new. Indeed, to the extent that myth and fairy tales can be recognized as expressive of individual and social concerns, we can trace interest in the psychology of women to preliterate times. The folklore of every society is filled with stories depicting young girls and women in various situations, assuming various roles, facing familiar dilemmas. Some of the earliest surviving artifacts from prehistoric times are representations of fertility goddesses. Such artifacts suggest that women were thought to hold the very key to survival. Depicted as the womb of the earth, woman ensured survival of the generation by her sowing and reaping of the grain; as childbearer and mother, she ensured survival of the human race.

Classical Greek civilization has left us a wealth of myth, ritual, and compelling imagery about women. These suggest an unprecedented clarity of thought regarding individual and societal concerns. Mythology provides graphic depictions of human dilemmas and often poignantly conveys the psychological agony and struggles of its heroines and heroes. Rituals, on the other hand, process, point the way toward resolution or even sometimes resolve the dilemmas portrayed in the myths. Study of Greek myths and rituals therefore can teach us a great deal about the ancient concerns of women and concerns about women. Although the Greek poets and artists were predominantly male, the voices of ancient Greek women can be heard across the page, or through the artist's depiction. The objects women dedicated in sanctuaries or those created to please them, such as wedding gifts, depict the rituals that were observed exclusively by women. These myths and rituals were, as far as we can tell, perpetuated voluntarily by women because the rituals spoke directly to their needs. The myths so specifically address female dilemmas that women surely transmitted and drew comfort from these stories, even if ultimately they were written down by male poets or depicted by male artists. Although no scientific articles or case studies survive to convey what the ancients thought about the psychology of women, the story of Demeter's loss and recovery of Persephone, exploring a mother's loss of her daughter in marriage, is a poignant depiction of a central psychological dilemma of the young woman. It conveys the prototypical bond of affection between two individuals, and the painful dilemma and inherent resistance of both mother and daughter toward moving beyond the mother-daughter bond. It speaks as clearly as does the case of Dora (Freud, 1905) about the psychological dilemmas women face.

In the latter part of the last century, Freud sought to unravel the mystery of hysteria. In so doing, he had the privilege of looking into the mind of a woman in a way that had never been available to the poets and storytellers of the ancient world. The lens of his mental microscope revealed the world of the unconscious. From his explorations of the unconscious, Freud gained the conviction that biology did not automatically determine psychology. A sense of femininity or masculinity was not a given, determined by biological sex. Rather, a sense of femininity or masculinity was a psychological achievement; he thought that various factors influenced the configuration of each person's individual sense of masculinity or femininity. But whereas Freud could draw on his knowledge of his own inner world to help him unravel the mind of a man, he had no such resource with regard to the mind of the female. He proposed several theories, but finally had to admit that his understanding was limited. For him, the sexual life of adult women was a "dark continent" (Freud, 1926, p. 212). He referred us back to the poets and storytellers, and to future generations, especially of women analysts. As we all know, Freud's theories

Female Psychology: An Introduction

sparked immediate debate which abated during the years of World War II and its aftermath, but it was revived again in the early sixties. The feminist movement in particular focused attention on this unresolved nexus of issues in psychoanalytic theory.

The Supplement on female psychology (Blum, 1976) was largely devoted to this debate. It brought Freud's theories together with contemporary thinking on the subject, and new theories with new directions for further research were forged. The volume was a landmark because never before had so many different American views on the psychology of women been brought together in one publication.

It was a landmark also because of its revolutionary focus on female *psychology* rather than female *sexuality*. Freud (1933) cautioned: "But do not forget that I have only been describing women in so far as their nature is determined by their sexual function. It is true that that influence extends very far; but we do not overlook the fact that an individual woman may be a human being in other respects as well" (1933, p. 135). Blum's conviction, as he has so eloquently stressed in his introduction to the present volume was that female psychology is rich in nuance and variety of interrelated issues, not all of which are directly related to sexuality. His intention was therefore to distinguish psychology and sexuality and to flush out the salient issues, in addition to sexuality, that contribute to the concerns of the female mind.

The distinction between psychology and sexuality had limited impact, however. Discussions about the mind of the female continue to be labeled as female sexuality (Panel, 1994), and even the Blum supplement is sometimes referred to and discussed in terms of female sexuality (e.g., Breen, 1993). Clearly these seems to be a great deal of resistance to a shift in focus. As this present volume is also intended to address a wide array of female psychological concerns, not simply those relevant to sexuality, or only sexuality, it will be helpful to clarify areas of misconception, to understand the resistance and to place it in its historical context.

We must begin with Freud's theory of sexuality. Freud was convinced that "the most significant causes of every case of neurotic illness are to be found in factors arising from sexual life" (1898, p. 263). His libido theory (1905) became a cornerstone of psychoanalytic theory, and concerns about the effects of sexuality and related unconscious conflicts on psychic functioning were central to all models of the mind that Freud proposed. Although Freud wrote the only two articles devoted solely to the female *after* the introduction of the structural model (1931, 1933), his theory of femininity was also formulated for the most part within the topographical model according to his 1905 libido theory.

Yet with thoughts on whether "anatomy is destiny," and that "physical sexual characters" are different from "mental sexual characters" Freud (1924) seemed also interested in understanding the ways in which anatomy, anatomical distinctions, and associated unconscious fantasy and conflict contribute to self-concept and to character formation.

The structural model Freud (1923) proposed suggested at least three intertwining but separately developing and separately functioning systems of the mind. Contemporary structural psychology has further elaborated the ways in which various developmental lines simultaneously influence each other yet develop and function separately (A. Freud, 1965; Tyson and Tyson, 1990). I think of the structural model as providing a broad organizational framework wherein a number of simultaneously emerging and functioning elements can be examined separately but in the context of the many other elements influencing psychic life. This framework permits consideration of one psychic issue without being misunderstood to disregard others.

As the papers in the first supplement, and now in this publication indicate, many forces simultaneously influence behavior. No two individuals are affected by the same forces in the same ways, at the same times, and in the same proportions. To make sense of behavior, many interacting developmental lines must be considered, and we must also consider the ways in which they interact and influence each other. No model of the mind is adequate to explain every clinical situation or psychic issue. Furthermore, some psychoanalysts are more at home using topographical theory, whereas others include structural theory. Topographical theory is particularly useful clinically, as psychoanalysts try to uncover the unconscious elements in their patients' communications. The structural theory had mixed reviews from the beginning. Many analysts in Europe and in South America have never been fully comfortable with it, feeling that it

Female Psychology: An Introduction

compromised the role of the unconscious and libido theory. Other analysts feel the opposite. That topographical concepts and the libido theory are too narrow a focus, and that it is reductionistic to confine explanations of psychic life to libido theory and the unconscious. These analysts are more comfortable using a structural framework and considering many psychic elements. They do not abandon libido theory and the unconscious, but consider it alongside other psychic systems.

In the late 'fifties and early 'sixties, Stoller and some of his colleagues began to study masculinity and femininity. He soon concluded that erotic excitement, unconscious sexual fantasy, preoedipal and oedipal unconscious conflict, and conflict resolution, i.e., Freud's libido theory, did not seem sufficient to explain the aberrations of masculinity and femininity he was seeing in his consulting room. He suggested that sexuality first should be considered in relation to sex—maleness, femaleness, i.e., a biological realm. Sexuality also implied erotic excitement—physiologically based motivations and behavior, hence also biologically grounded but with psychic consequences. Masculinity and femininity, on the other hand, implied self-concept, one's identity, the shape of one's self representation; identifications with others were crucial developmental factors, as the young child compared the shape of his or her self-representation to the shape of an object representation. These issues belonged to the realm of psychology (see Stoller, 1964, 1968a, 1968b, 1975, 1985). According to the structural model, the two also seemed to belong to two different psychic systems: erotic excitement and unconscious sexual fantasy belong to the realm of the id; formation of self-concept is more a function of the ego. Gradually the self-concept aspect of Freud's theory of sexuality became a separate study, and an entire new field of inquiry developed, that of gender identity.

Gender identity has come to refer to any one individual's sense of self, combined with biological sex, psychological reactions to biological distinctions, conscious or unconscious erotic fantasies and related conflicts, and identifications made with same- and opposite-sex parents and their attitudes. These combined influences result in a personal sense of masculinity or femininity.[1] This personally

---

[1] Even the terms masculinity and femininity have been heavily criticized in recent years, some feeling they too heavily reflect cultural stereotypes. Indeed, these are

Phyllis Tyson

constructed sense of gender identity represents a complex system of unconscious fantasy and personal myth that individual has formed in relation to anatomy and anatomical distinctions. Whether it be a sense of masculinity or femininity or combination thereof, a person's sense of gender identity may or may not be consistent with biological sex (Stoller, 1976, 1985).

It is in regard to female gender identity that contemporary theories differ most dramatically from those of Freud. Gender identity is also a concept often misused and misunderstood. Because of this, communication about new ideas of femininity and masculinity across international borders often breaks down. This may be due in part to Freud's failure to revise his theory according to the structural model and to consider the role of many elements that might simultaneously affect development.

Psychoanalysts working primarily from a topographical framework hold tenaciously to the term *female sexuality* when discussing any aspect of female psychic life. In response to the loss of sexual centrality in some discussions, they question if sexuality has a place in psychoanalysis (Green, 1995). Breen (1993) worries that in the concept of gender identity we have lost the unconscious.

I do not agree that sexuality or the unconscious are absent from discussions of female gender identity. It is simply not always understood that analysts working within a structural framework consider many elements simultaneously. Even though the focus in a given discussion may not be sexuality, or unconscious fantasy and conflict, this does not mean that it has been eliminated or disregarded. It may simply be taken as a given, and so not be the central focus. However, that such impressions exist confirms the misunderstanding I noted. This, I think, is part of a more general transatlantic rift among psychoanalysts. For decades, psychoanalysis in North America has been associated with so-called ego psychology. I have never fully understood or agreed with this narrow and somewhat pejorative connotation, for it implies that psychoanalysts utilizing the structural model have lost the id, the superego, perhaps even the unconscious.

---

somewhat problematic, as they are complex, composite terms, with significances relating to anatomical givens and psychological meanings, dispositional attributes (activity or passivity), and cultural stereotypes. However, the alternatives suggested, femaleness and maleness, refer to biological sex and do not reflect psychology. Therefore the terms masculinity and femininity represent the best choice.

Female Psychology: An Introduction

This perception has encumbered international dialogue. The history of this difficulty in communication can be traced to what I see as a misunderstanding of Hartmann's (1958) "conflict-free" sphere. In asserting that certain ego functions have "primary autonomy," he maintained that their appearance is not a product of conflict, but genetically predetermined. Unfortunately, primary autonomy has been interpreted to imply that these functions *operate* in isolation, independent of any other part of the mind, free of ambiguity and conflict. No part of the mind operates in this manner, and any function, even those that are not a product of conflict, can become secondarily compromised by conflict.

Gender identity, a concept conceived of and elaborated by psychoanalysts in North America (in particular Stoller, 1964, 1976) is looked upon by many in the same way. It is sometimes misunderstood to be leaning more toward biological, social, cultural, cognitive, and learning factors instead of a psychoanalytic focus on the unconscious and conflict (Breen, 1993). This misperception may be partly due to Stoller's also widely misunderstood concept of "primary femininity" (1976). Disagreeing with Freud that femininity is a compensatory measure, a product of sexual differentiation, penis envy, and unconscious conflict, he suggested that the potential was inborn. In his theory a confluence of factors (neurophysiological fetal brain organization, sex assignment at birth, parental attitudes and early interactions with the infant, bodily sensations, early maternal identification, self-categorization, and learning) forms a complex nucleus around which a mature sense of femininity will become organized. He labeled this first step "primary femininity" because, like certain ego functions, it is not simply a product of conflict. Despite some views to the contrary, this does not imply that the early female self-image emerges and operates outside of and free of ambiguity and conflict. It also does not imply that primary femininity is the finished product. Rather, a mature sense of femininity begins with primary femininity, but conflict (conscious and unconscious) and conflict resolution, as well as identifications made with both parents over the course of development, determine the ultimate form.

With the concept of gender identity, we acquired a new lens through which we view women. Fueled also by advances in the field of psychoanalysis as a whole, leading us to recognize many interacting factors, derivatives of many developmental lines influencing every clinical picture, we are now asking different questions and we are asking these in an extended field of inquiry. As we ask different questions, we are better able to identify and interpret a wider range of answers. This leads us to conclude that there will be no one universally held theory of femininity; there are many possible stories, many possible contents to unconscious fantasy; conflict may be organized around more than simply unconscious erotic fantasy, hence there will be many possible outcomes (Tyson, 1991). I think this is an important influence on the kind of papers appearing in this volume. In contrast to the last volume, where new theory was forged, these papers are "from the trenches," so to speak. They are largely clinically based, and they come from the questions and clinical issues facing psychoanalysts every day in their consulting rooms as they work with women, or as their understanding about women influences their thinking about men.

This volume begins with two papers on Freud. These papers explicate thoughts about the man and ways in which Freud's own psychology, his personal views and unresolved conflicts, may have influenced his theories about women. Next we have a section on theory. This section begins with a review of contemporary feminist writers, psychoanalysts or those informed by psychoanalytic theory in the United States and in France. The authors' review of the psychoanalytic traditions of the two countries interestingly informs us about certain writers who use Freud and psychoanalysis only to attack it, in contrast to those who would see themselves as guardians of the new psychoanalysis, the psychoanalysis of Lacan. Then follow several other papers considering and reconsidering theoretical issues, demonstrating that the theory of the psychology of women remains alive and vibrant. The role of the body in the psychology of women is the subject matter for the third section. These papers represent a sampling of the thoughts of clinicians as they share their clinical work and clinical ideas that emerge during the course of the daily work of analyzing young girls and women. Another central theme in the analysis of young girls and women must certainly be pregnancy and motherhood, which is the subject matter of section four. We then turn to the subject of female homosexuality, a much neglected area of investigation in work with women. The volume concludes with challenges to the future as psychoanalysts sharing some of their

Female Psychology: An Introduction

thoughts, experiences, and struggles working with, thinking about, and being women in this field.

A wealth of ideas and insights are shared in this volume. The breadth and depth of the observations and formulations demonstrate that in forging a conceptualization of woman, psychoanalysis has begun to shake the influence of Freud in that we are no longer on a quest to solve *the* riddle of femininity. No longer are we, like Raiders of the Lost Ark, seeking the true map so that we can unearth *the* hidden treasure and resolve the mystery of the dark continent. More and more psychoanalysts recognize that just as no two people look alike on the outside, no two people look alike on the inside. Different issues are important to different people. Recognizing that a multitude of factors contributes to every clinical picture, we are more accepting of ambiguity and conclude that there may not be one story of female psychology but many stories, many intertwining themes, and many possible outcomes. Although mysteries remain as they do in any science, the papers in this volume show that we are less likely to feel nowadays as Freud (1926) did, that the psychology of women is a "dark continent."

REFERENCES

BLUM, H.P., Ed. (1976). *Female Psychology.* New York: Int. Univ. Press.
BREEN, D. (1993). *The Gender Conundrum: Contemporary Psychoanalytic Perspectives on Femininity and Masculinity.* New York: Routledge.
FREUD, A. (1965). *Normality and Pathology in Childhood: Assessments of Development. The Writings of Anna Freud,* Vol. 5. New York: Int. Univ. Press.
FREUD, S. (1898). Sexuality in the aetiology of the neuroses. *S.E.,* 3.
——— (1905). Three essays on the theory of sexuality. *S.E.,* 7.
——— (1923). The ego and the id. *S.E.,* 19.
——— (1924). The dissolution of the Oedipus complex. *S.E.,* 19.
——— (1926). The question of lay analysis. *S.E.,* 20.
——— (1931). Female sexuality. *S.E.,* 21.
——— (1933). New introductory lectures on psycho-analysis. *S.E.,* 22.
GREEN, A. (1995). Has sexuality anything to do with psychoanalysis? *Int. J. Psychoanal.,* 76:871–883.
HARTMANN, H. (1958). *Ego Psychology and the Problem of Adaptation.* New York: Int. Univ. Press.
PANEL (1994). Contemporary theories of female sexuality: clinical applications. L. Grossman, reporter. *J. Amer. Psychoanal. Assn.,* 42:233–241.
STOLLER, R. (1964). A contribution to the study of gender identity. *Int. J. Psychoanal.,* 45:220–226.

——— (1968a). *Sex and Gender,* Vol. 1. New York: Science House.
——— (1968b). A further contribution to the study of gender identity. *Int. J. Psychoanal.,* 49:364–368.
——— (1975). *Sex and Gender,* Vol. 2. London: Hogarth Press.
——— (1976). Primary femininity. *J. Amer. Psychoanal. Assn.,* 24 (Suppl.): 59–78.
——— (1985). *Presentations of Gender.* New Haven: Yale Univ. Press.
TYSON, P. (1991). Some nuclear conflicts of the infantile neurosis in female development. *Psychoanal. Inq.,* 11:582–602.
——— & TYSON, R.L. (1990). *Psychoanalytic Theories of Development: An Integration.* New Haven, CT: Yale Univ. Press.

I.
FREUD AND THE FEMININE

Figure 3. Meret Oppenheim (1936) *Object* (Le Dejeuner en fourrure) Fur-covered cup, saucer and spoon; cup, 4 3/8" (10.9 cm) diameter; saucer, 9 3/8" (23.7 cm) diameter; spoon, 8" (20.2 cm) long; overall height 2 7/8" (7.3 cm). The Museum of Modern Art, New York. Purchase. Photograph © 1996 The Museum of Modern Art, New York.

FREUD AND FEMININE SUBJECTIVITY

Leon Hoffman

I have delineated a factor, subjectivity, to account for the difficulty in the psychoanalytic understanding of feminine sexuality, particularly the nature of feminine sexual pleasure. This factor has been unappreciated hitherto by psychoanalysts. Subjectivity is a notion that refers to the capacity of a person to posit him- or herself as an independent agent who determines or controls his or her own thoughts and actions. The construct feminine sexual pleasure, and by extension feminine subjectivity, was difficult for Freud and others to posit because of the implicit association among several mental phenomena. Subject, active, and libido (i.e., the source of active sexual pleasure) were, and to some extent still are, considered masculine attributes; whereas object, passive, and, by implication, the absence of an independent actively desirous state were considered feminine attributes. Freud's difficulty in accepting aggression in the mental life of women interfered with his gaining an implicit understanding of feminine subjectivity.

Subjectivity is a notion that refers to the capacity of a person to posit him- or herself as an independent agent who determines or controls his or her own thoughts and actions. This concept, which has been conceived as a fundamental property of language (Benveniste, 1971), implies the presence of a mental state in which a person thinks of him- or herself to be an active, desirous individual. Although subjectivity is an idea that connotes conscious self-

---

Training and Supervising Analyst, New York Psychoanalytic Institute.

I am grateful to the colleagues who have critically read previous versions of this manuscript, especially to members of The New York Psychoanalytic Institute's Colloquium, "Current Views of Female Development and Sexuality," chaired by Marianne Goldberger, M.D., The New York Psychoanalytic Institute's Colloquium on "The Writing of Psychoanalytic Papers," chaired by Charles Brenner, M.D., and to Anne Golomb Hoffman, Ph.D. A version of this paper was presented to The New York Psychoanalytic Society Extension Division: The Psychology of Women, May 1, 1993, and at the Fall Meeting of the American Psychoanalytic Association, December 18, 1993.

Presented to The New York Psychoanalytic Society, February 13, 1996, and to the Philadelphia Psychoanalytic Society, February 21, 1996.

reflectiveness (see Berger, 1993), a person's sense of self includes both conscious and unconscious fantasies.

The conception of subjectivity derives from a post-Enlightenment philosophical tradition that presumes man to be an independent, active agent who determines the course of his life. This presumption of activity was not automatically extended to include women. Following the French Revolution, for example, both men and women debated the nature of women's desire and whether women could be active participants in the social order (Laqueur, 1990, pp. 194–207). For the purposes of the present study, it is instructive to examine Freud's letters from his adolescence (Boehlich, 1990). The letters can be considered precursors to Freud's theoretical contributions to the psychoanalytic debates regarding the nature of feminine sexuality. They demonstrate that Freud's philosophic and intellectual roots include the assumption that subjectivity is to be considered possible only for men.

The adolescent Freud states that a man could allow himself to lose control of his passions and to slacken his morality because a man is "his own legislator, confessor, and absolver." In contrast, a woman has "*no inherent* ethical standard." Therefore, a woman can only act correctly if she keeps within the bounds of convention; she can never be forgiven if she rebels against convention (Boehlich, 1990, p. 92). In other words, as an intellectually gifted young man, Freud seems to express the cultural presupposition that a *man* is the independent *agent* of his actions, who can allow himself the gratification of passions, even to excess, because he has an *internal* agency with which ultimately he can control himself. A woman, by contrast, is *not* an independent agent because she lacks such an internal agency. This idea forms an obvious precursor to the psychoanalytic construct that women have deficient superegos. As an adolescent, Freud clearly believed that as a result of internal deficiencies a woman is compelled to follow social norms. Women's passions have to be controlled by outside convention because rebellion by the woman, that is, indulgence in passions, can lead to catastrophe. One can infer that the adolescent Freud believed that ideally women's passions should disappear completely. The adolescent Freud's conviction that women need to be controlled by others because they lack their own independent agency became an undercurrent in the

Freud and Feminine Subjectivity

adult Freud's psychoanalytic theories of feminine psychology (cf. Silver, 1991). He came to conceptualize that normal men are active, independent agents, in contrast to normal women who have to cede their sense of independent agency to the man.

Many have continued to argue that, in fact, the idea of subjectivity has not been yet extended to include women (Benjamin, 1988; Kulish, 1993, unpublished). Irigaray (1985) debates both Freud and Lacan and maintains that theories of the subject have always been conceptualized as masculine (pp. 133–146). The concept of subjectivity, and feminine subjectivity in particular, has been examined extensively by feminist scholars (see Irigaray, 1977, 1985, and particularly Butler, 1990, who provides an excellent summary and critique of studies dealing with the nature of the feminine subject). Benjamin (1988, 1991), influenced by Winnicott (1966), has examined the notion of subjectivity from a relational perspective; she describes the intersubjective point of view as complementary to the intrapsychic point of view. Recently, Loewenstein (1994) has discussed this topic from a Lacanian perspective. However, subjectivity as an organizing concept has yet to be explored psychoanalytically within a conflict model.

In order to understand the concept of subjectivity from the perspective of psychic conflict, I shall examine the evolution in Freud's consideration of women's sexuality. Freud's changing view of women occurred within the context of the psychoanalytic debate regarding the nature of feminine sexuality during the 1920's and 1930's. Although many authors have reexamined this early debate, studying the debate retains contemporary relevance because of the ongoing dialogue regarding the nature of feminine sexuality (cf. Benjamin, 1988; Chasseguet-Smirgel, 1964; Fliegel, 1973, 1986; Lacan, 1977; Lacan's Followers, 1968; Mitchell, 1982; Schafer, 1974; Young-Bruehl, 1991). In contrast to the primary nature of masculinity, Freud (1925, 1931, 1933) eventually contends that femininity is a secondary construction in development. Horney (1924, 1926, 1933) and Jones (1927, 1933, 1935), the major early psychoanalysts whose disagreements with Freud's hypotheses about women were forgotten by the mainstream psychoanalytic community until recent years, consider that masculinity and femininity develop along more or less parallel lines. Although analysts debated whether a woman

Leon Hoffman

"is born" or "made," no one questioned whether a man is born or made. Masculine psychology was, and to some extent still is, the standard against which female psychology was considered. Although it is beyond the scope of this paper, studying this early debate, including Jones's idea that the phallic phase is a neurotic compromise formation in *both* sexes (1933, p. 27), also can help further the analytic understanding of male sexuality and the development of a boy into a man.

An examination of the arguments and subtexts in the early debate demonstrates that the arguments continue to be applicable to recent psychoanalytic discussions. For example, some psychoanalysts have begun to question the value of the concept of primary femininity. Elizabeth Mayer states that this concept has had a "corrective effect" on the male-centeredness of psychoanalytic theory. However, she and others also agree with Francis Baudry's idea that both constructs, primary femininity and primary masculinity, have the untoward consequence of limiting psychoanalytic observations (Panel, 1994, p. 238). Only if one considers masculinity and femininity to be compromise formations *can* one analyze the conflicted components that contribute to an individual person's sense of sexual or gender identity. On the other hand, if one conceptualizes primary masculinity and primary femininity to be fixed, stable, irreducible binary oppositions, one has created a new reductionism, a modern version of bedrock, that cannot be understood psychoanalytically (cf. Butler, 1990).

In this paper I shall demonstrate that Freud does underscore the importance of considering the ambiguities and paradoxes of sex and gender. This is particularly true after 1914 when he alternately constructs and deconstructs clinical phenomena that fall under the rubric masculine and feminine. Freud's clinical psychoanalytic insight at this time reflects his conception that masculinity and femininity are not static, independent constructs; rather he maintains that in all individuals one finds many permutations of sexual life based on the interrelations among the person's physical sexual characteristics, mental sexual characteristics, and kind of object choice (1920, p. 170). However, he does not continue this radical course and does not elaborate further the seemingly subversive idea that sexual life in both men and women can only be understood if one

Freud and Feminine Subjectivity

appreciates its ambiguities and paradoxes. Instead, in the 1920's and 1930's he becomes dogmatic and formalizes a concrete view of the girl's development. Horney and Jones, on the opposite side of the debate, adopt a perspective riddled with the hazard of biological reductionism (cf. Grossman, 1986; Lacan, 1977; Lacan's Followers, 1968, pp. 99–122).

I shall lift out and articulate an important subtext—the nature of subjectivity—in the early psychoanalytic debate which can help explain why Freud recedes from his emphasis on the ambiguities and paradoxes in the sexual life of both men and women. Understanding this subtext can help explain why he becomes stuck in a seemingly masculine-centered view of feminine sexuality, as feminists and others have demonstrated (e.g., Horney, 1926; Irigaray, 1985). Furthermore, an appreciation of this subtext also can help us to discover a source of the difficulties that many theoreticians have encountered which has prevented them from attaining a full psychoanalytic understanding of feminine sexual pleasure.

Theoretically diverse authors, as a matter of fact, share the common impression that women's passion or desire, in contrast to men's, is mysterious, puzzling, and complex. For example, Freud notes that there is an enigma to femininity that derives from women's bisexuality (1933, p. 131). Benjamin (1988) points to the difficulty of symbolically representing feminine desire to counterbalance the phallus as the representation of masculine desire. She maintains that although "the image of woman is associated with motherhood and fertility, *the mother is not articulated as a sexual subject, one who actively desires something for herself—quite the contrary*" (p. 88, italics added). Lacan, in his linguistic frame of reference, considers the phallus to be the privileged signifier of desire and, although he maintains that the feminine implies the absence of desire (Rose, 1982), he also writes of women's mysterious jouissance (Lacan, 1972–1973, p. 147). Irigaray (1977, p. 350) discusses women's inability to possess others or themselves, and Chodorow (1978, p. 193) describes an inner object world in women more complex than that in men.

These theoretical conundrums can be understood by appreciating several factors. Both men and women consciously and/or unconsciously often link masculinity with active desire and the sense of oneself as an active subject. They also often link the converse attributes: femininity with the absence of active desire and the sense of oneself as a passive object. In addition, one has to appreciate the important role played by aggressive drive derivatives in a person's consideration of him- or herself as an active subject. These factors account for the difficulty in conceiving the construct "feminine subjectivity." I shall argue that this difficulty interfered with Freud's understanding of feminine sexuality during the early psychoanalytic debates and has been an important source for the continued perplexity about feminine sexuality.

Psychoanalysts have appreciated Freud's association of three concepts with one another—masculine, active, and libido (pleasure). However, they have not recognized that Freud also associates the concept, subject, with them. I will show that the link among subject, masculine, active, and sexual pleasure plays a significant role in Freud's investigation of the nature of libido in general and feminine desire in particular. Freud and others come to the conclusion that a normal little girl has to transform her sense of herself. The girl has to renounce the sense of herself as an active, desirous subject and become a passive object whose aggression has to be controlled.

In order to investigate psychoanalytically the concept of subjectivity, that is, the capacity of a person to posit him- or herself as an independent active agent who determines or controls his or her thoughts and actions, and feminine subjectivity in particular, I shall divide the remainder of the paper into three sections. In the first I shall examine the subject/object polarity and the active/passive polarity. I shall discuss their transformations and their connection to the masculine/feminine polarity. In the second section, I shall discuss the equivalence among the terms subject, masculine, active, and sexual pleasure and, in symmetrical fashion, the equivalence among object, feminine, passive, and, by implication, the absence of active sexual pleasure. In the third section, I shall consider the central role of aggression in subjectivity and the theoretical sequellae of Freud's difficulty accepting the direct expression of aggression in the mental life of women.

THE SUBJECT/OBJECT AND ACTIVE/PASSIVE POLARITIES

In common psychoanalytic discourse the terms subject and object refer respectively to the "person in whom an instinct (or other state

Freud and Feminine Subjectivity

of mind) originates and the person or thing to which it is directed" (Freud, 1915). However, in several instances, Freud also uses the term *subject* to designate the person who plays the active role in the relationship between two people (1915, pp. 127–128n). He discusses three antitheses: sadism/masochism, scopophilia/exhibitionism, and loving/being loved. He demonstrates that the transformation from sadism to masochism is a result of a change in the instinctual aim so that the wish to hurt changes into the wish to be hurt. The masochistic person seeks out another individual who has "*to take over the role of the subject*" (p. 127; italics added). Similarly, in the transformation from scopophilia to exhibitionism, Freud describes a stage where a person finds "a new subject" to whom he displays himself "in order to be looked at by him" (p. 129). Freud states that the antithesis of loving/being loved undergoes the same transformations as the other two polarities (pp. 139–140).

According to this view, the person who is active is by definition the subject and the one who is passive the object. Thus, *the person with the passive fantasy*—the one who is masochistic, exhibitionistic, or the one who is loved—relinquishes his or her sense of being a subject and considers the other person to be the subject. Freud maintains that "the narcissistic subject is, through identification, *replaced by another*, extraneous ego" (p. 132; italics added). In other words, the person with the passive fantasy considers the outside person (the one who is active) to be the subject and considers him- or herself to be the object (p. 130).

It is extremely important to note that the Freud of the mid 'teens demonstrates an acute awareness that the concepts of active/passive and subject/object are not fixed categorical essences. Many times he vacillates, alternately defending and challenging the hierarchical dualisms of masculine/feminine, subject/object, and ultimately, normal/abnormal. His investigations of the paradoxes and ambiguities of these dualities are at their height after 1914, perhaps as a result of the theoretical investigations stimulated by Adler's and Jung's challenges. In several publications he communicates an exquisite sensitivity to the ambiguities and paradoxes of mental life ("On Narcissism: An Introduction," 1914a; "Instincts and Their Vicissitudes," 1915, and the revisions prompted in "Three Essays on the Theory of Sexuality,"1905b). While he attempts to differentiate normal from abnormal, he rebuffs the assumption of a discrete categorization of sexual behavior and comes to argue, for example, that homosexuals cannot be differentiated unequivocally from "normal" people because everyone has a considerable amount of unconscious homosexuality (1920, p. 171).

However, Freud comes implicitly to associate the masculine with the subject and activity and the feminine with the object and passivity. This association emerges most fully in his discussions of women (e.g., 1905a, 1920). But, one can infer the connections in his discussions of men. For example, Freud states that the Wolf Man, who was a boy with a strong feminine side, had repressed his tender, passive impulses which had been directed toward his father. Although Freud concludes that castration anxiety triggers the phobia in both the Wolf Man and Little Hans, he maintains that the Wolf Man's situation is more complicated than that of Little Hans because the Wolf Man's intense wish to be loved passively by the father "was not able to subsist in the face of his masculine revolt" (1926, pp. 106–108). In other words, as a little boy the Wolf Man responds symptomatically when he surrenders the active role to the father. In the little boy's fantasy, the father becomes the lover (i.e., the active subject) while the little boy himself becomes the beloved (i.e., the passive object, the woman). This fantasy is intolerable for the boy because it implies that he accepts castration.

Freud underscores the pathological significance of the Wolf Man's need to relinquish to his father the active role and, by implication, the sense of being the subject. In contrast, however, Freud comes to stress that it is both normative and normal for a girl to renounce her sense of activity as well as her sense of herself as a subject. He maintains that women cannot develop an active (that is, a masculinelike) relationship to a love object because of the intensification of their narcissism at puberty (1914a, p. 88). Within this perspective only men can develop true object choice. Therefore, Freud supports Lampl-de Groot's (1927) conclusion that "the woman who is truly feminine does not know object-love in the true sense of the word; she can only 'let herself be loved' " (1931, p. 241) (cf. Fliegel, 1973, p. 394). A man who relinquishes his sense of active agency is abnormal, whereas the truly feminine woman acknowledges giving up her sense of activity or subjectivity to the man. In contrast to normal men, normal women are not their own independent agents. A normal woman cannot be the lover but the one who

Freud and Feminine Subjectivity

is loved. This sharp differentiation between men and women can be understood in the light of the implied equations of subject with activity and object with passivity.

Freud repeatedly asserts that masculinity equals activity, and by implication the sense of oneself as a subject, and femininity equals passivity, and by implication the *giving up* of the sense of oneself as a subject. Yet, Freud also appreciates the pervasiveness of the ambiguities in sexual life as when he states that "we far too readily identify activity with maleness and passivity with femaleness" (1930, p. 106). Furthermore, even though seemingly fixed assumptions about the nature of feminine sexuality were eventually transmitted to subsequent generations of analysts, he also foreshadows current social theories of gender role assignment. He maintains that the sociological meaning of masculine/feminine refers to the observation that individuals display a mixture of the character traits of both sexes, including a mixture of activity and passivity (1905b, pp. 219–220).

SEXUAL PLEASURE, THE ACTIVE/PASSIVE POLARITY, AND THE SUBJECT/OBJECT POLARITY

In this section I shall demonstrate that in addition to the link of active and subject with masculine (and the converse with feminine), Freud's equation of libido with active and masculine implies that feminine is equated with the absence of sexual pleasure. This conclusion can be reached if one bears in mind two of Freud's key theoretical concepts: bisexuality and the active/passive polarity. Although Freud always considers bisexuality to be a concept riddled with "obscurities" (1930, pp. 105–106n), he continually stresses its importance in mental life. Furthermore, he considers libido to be masculine because of the consideration that an instinct is always active, even if it has a passive aim (1905b, pp. 219–220n; 1915, p. 134). In other words, masculine, active, and libido (i.e., the source of sexual pleasure), are equivalent concepts. Therefore, although he argues against the too-frequent equation of active with masculine and passive with feminine, it seems justifiable to conjecture that since the concept "feminine" is equivalent to the absence of activity or active desire, one can consider that "feminine" is equivalent to the absence of libido. Since Freud considers bisexuality to be universal and libido masculine (active), logically one could deduce that *masculine aspects* of mental life motivate both men and women toward pleasure. An example of this theoretical construct can be found in Bonaparte's idea that a woman's erotic capacities can function only because of her residual virility (1953, p. 166).

In fact, and in stark opposition to Horney and Jones, Freud comes to conclude that the fundamental sources of sexual pleasure in both boys and girls are active or masculine wishes which the little girl has to renounce (1933, p. 243). Freud maintains that a girl's activity manifests itself very early in life when she wishes for a baby and plays with dolls. This wish, however, is not an expression of the girl's femininity but an expression of her identification with her active mother, who is "active" only in the sense of actively ministering to the child. In the doll play, the little girl does to her doll what the mother does to her. This play is not a feminine activity because the little girl is active, i.e., masculinelike. The girl identifies with an active mother, that is, a mother who acts in a masculine and not in a feminine way. In contrast, the wish for a penis is the central feminine wish; the feminine situation is established only when the girl's wish for a penis is replaced by one for a baby *from* father (1933, pp. 128–129). In other words, wishing for the male organ *is* the feminine activity *par excellence*. The later wish for a baby is a substitute for the wish for father's penis.

Freud's early considerations reflected a view that these masculine desires in women are to be considered pathological compromise formations as a result of oedipal conflict and defense. For example, in the analysis of a homosexual young woman (1920) he understands that the homosexual girl is disappointed by her father when her mother (the rival), rather than the girl herself, bears the father's child during the girl's early puberty. As a result the girl becomes dominated by a need to repudiate men. She assumes the characteristic of the masculine lover and turns to women. She repudiates her wish for a child, changes into a man, and no longer competes with mother for father. Freud maintains that when a girl turns away from a genital incestuous love for father, she abandons her feminine role easily and becomes *active* out of a desire to be a boy (1919, p. 191).

Freud and Feminine Subjectivity

Moreover, he underscores the likelihood that a girl might *defensively* remove herself from *all* erotic activity and become a *spectator* of the displaced sexual act (p. 199).

As his view of women's sexuality evolved, Freud came to the conclusion that such an abandonment of direct gratification is not a pathological phenomenon, but a normal occurrence for a girl. Young-Bruehl (1989) argues that Freud's two analyses of Anna Freud shaped the theoretical conclusions he reached in "A Child Is Being Beaten" (1919) and shaped the development of his theories of feminine sexuality. Furthermore, Young-Bruehl contends that Anna Freud's first paper, "Beating Fantasies and Daydreams" (1922), is an autobiographic account of her analysis with her father. In that paper Anna Freud maintains that the analysis of a fifteen-year-old girl's daydream illustrates Freud's ideas about beating fantasies. She describes early beating fantasies accompanied by sexual excitement and masturbation, but without conscious awareness of oedipal strivings for father. Subsequently, the girl fantasizes about "nice stories," but without autoerotic activity and therefore without guilt. The nonerotic love in the nice stories is a sublimation of the repressed oedipal sensual aims which reemerge in the anal-sadistic organization of the beating fantasy. Anna Freud's report of the analytic work demonstrates that as a result of intrusive daydreams the girl turns to writing as a defense in order to master her conflicted sensual feelings. The writing enables her to abandon *direct pleasure* and, instead, to gratify her ambitious tendencies by regarding the *reader's reaction* as the source of her pleasure. By objectifying the material, she renounces private pleasure in favor of the *indirect pleasure* of pleasing the audience. In other words, direct gratification of pleasure, an active, or one could say masculine, state is abandoned. Freud had reached a virtually identical conclusion in "A Child Is Being Beaten" (1919). Anna Freud's adolescent girl's fantasy reflects a transformation from active to passive. She renounces direct pleasurable gratification in order to identify with the pleasure of her audience. (Is that her father/analyst?) The audience becomes the subject or the active agent who admires the productions of the girl. The girl becomes the object or passive recipient of the subject's (audience's) love.

Renunciation of direct sexual gratification by a girl in favor of the man continued to be an important theme in Anna Freud's writings. She stresses, for example, that altruistic surrender is a method employed by girls in order to overcome their narcissistic mortification. She maintains that with this mechanism girls surrender their instinctual wishes to the man. Thus, in an altruistic attachment the woman expects the man "to carry out the projects in which she believes herself to be handicapped by her sex." Anna Freud maintains that in these altruistic attachments a true object relation does not occur and the altruistic woman renounces her own ambitions (1937, pp. 131–132). Whether or not Young-Bruehl (1989) correctly identifies the autobiographical nature of Anna Freud's adolescent case, certainly one can observe Freud's theoretical influence on Anna's ideas about women. One can imagine the personal significance to her of Freud's evolving theory that a woman's renunciation of direct sexual gratification is an appropriate, "normal" solution to conflicted sexual desire because direct or active sexual gratification is considered to be a masculine trait.

For Horney, in contrast to the late Freud, the masculinized version of the feminine castration complex is *not normal but rather a symptomatic defensive compromise formation* triggered by conflicted incestuous fantasies with guilt, fear of punishment, disappointment by father, and aggressive and revenge fantasies (1924). These ideas are similar to Freud's earlier ideas as in his analysis of a homosexual woman (1920). Horney argues that the wish for motherhood is an innate feminine formation (1933). She maintains that the girl's pleasurable wish to be penetrated by father's penis is repressed and transformed into a fear that the father's large penis would cause internal injury. In order to protect herself the little girl defensively denies the vagina's existence (1933, p. 160) and converts her fearful fantasy that she would be hurt by father into a fantasy of castration in masculine terms. The concrete idea that she is already castrated produces less unpleasure than the anxiety generated by the "uncertainty of her expectation of punishment" (1926, p. 67).

Fliegel (1973) concludes that perhaps Freud found Horney's theories unacceptable because Horney's ideas imply that there is "*an intrinsic pleasure-oriented feminine sexuality.*" Fliegel maintains that despite Freud's stress on the importance of sexuality, the notion of an intrinsic pleasure-oriented feminine sexuality was alien to him (p. 388). Grossman (1993, unpublished) disagrees with Fliegel's conjecture stating that Freud did not need to make specific reference to

Freud and Feminine Subjectivity

pleasure in his ultimate formulations of either feminine or masculine sexuality because Freud believed pleasure to be intrinsic to sexuality.

It seems to me that Fliegel's conclusion is credible if one considers the implicit link between sexual pleasure and the sense of oneself as a subject. The thrust of Freud's work leads him to consider that the transformation in a girl from active to passive is a normal phenomenon. He maintains that this transformation requires the girl to renounce her active or masculine wishes, which results in the injury to *all* of the little girl's sexual trends (1931, p. 239). Therefore, since libido (i.e., the source of sexual pleasure) is considered to be a masculine attribute, it seems logical to conclude that the little girl attempts to compensate for her renunciation of masculine wishes by attempting to acquire the masculine attribute for herself, that is, the penis, which is the source of pleasure or to use Lacan's phrase, the privileged signifier of desire (1977, p. 82). The girl or woman also can obtain pleasure by obtaining a penis surrogate (a baby) or through a proxy (by identifying with the active male subject as in altruistic surrender). Both the sense of oneself as a subject as well as the source of pleasure belong to the man. In other words, since subjectivity—the sense of oneself as an active desirous subject—is considered to be a masculine attribute, in her fantasy the girl has to cede the sense of herself as an actively desirous subject to the man while she becomes the object. It follows logically that this is the normal route for a girl to become a woman. Within this frame of reference, in her fantasy a normal woman could achieve pleasure only via the man who is the subject. Thus, the constructs "feminine pleasure" and "feminine subjectivity" are essentially oxymorons.

As a matter of fact, Freud argues that a woman who *acts* like a subject, such as the eighteen-year-old homosexual girl (1920) or Dora (1905a), is to be considered nonfeminine. He maintains that the homosexual girl appropriates the masculine role in her behavior toward her love object and becomes the lover rather than the beloved (1920, p. 154). In a similar vein, he states that Dora's love for Frau K. and jealousy of her father are emotions that might have been felt by a man. In his view such masculine feelings are typical of the erotic life of hysterical girls (1905a, p. 63). In short, a normal woman can only allow herself to be loved as an object by the man who becomes the active subject. The normal woman relinquishes active pleasure.

Riviere (1934), in her review of the *New Introductory Lectures*, concludes that it is inconceivable to imagine that a woman's sexual character and sexual function remain latent and almost nonexistent "from birth until such time as the accidental trauma of discovering that she has no penis takes place" (p. 127). She is critical of Freud's (1931, p. 239) conclusion that the road to development of normal femininity includes the dampening of *all* desire. In the next section I shall demonstrate that Freud's difficulties to fully encompass the role of aggression in mental life, especially in women, prevents him from perceiving the dilemma posed by his conclusion that normal femininity requires the dampening of desire.

VICISSITUDES OF AGGRESSION

The role of aggression in mental life, especially in women, poses a theoretical conundrum to Freud that he does not confront and explicate fully. As late as in "Civilization and Its Discontents" (1930), Freud wonders why he has overlooked the ubiquity and importance of nonerotic aggressivity and destructiveness (p. 120). In 1937, he tells Marie Bonaparte that whenever one performs an activity that results in rearrangements or changes, a certain amount of destructiveness occurs with a redirection of the destructive instance. He states that the sexual instinct cannot act without some measure of aggression, and maintains that curiosity or the impulse to investigate is a "complete sublimation of the aggressive or destructive instinct" (Jones, 1957, p. 464).

Freud's difficulty with the development of a clinically useful theory of aggression seems to have been tied to his theoretical disputes. Stepansky (1977, pp. 112–142) discusses the impact of the conflict with Adler on Freud's ideas about aggression. When Freud acknowledges the need for an aggressive instinct for psychoanalytic theory, he differentiates his instinct from Adler's by calling it the destructive or death instinct (1909, p. 140n). Eventually Freud does stress the importance of defense against aggression in the development of Little Hans's phobia (1926, p. 102).

Freud also rejects Jung's (1913, p. 154) attempts to conceive of a parallel between the boy's and girl's triangular jealous conflict.

Freud and Feminine Subjectivity

He dismisses Jung's term Electra complex (which connotes Electra's passionate desire to take vengeance on her mother Clytemnestra for murdering Agamemnon, Electra's father) because he feels that only in the boy does one observe the "fateful combination of love for the one parent and simultaneous hatred for the other as rival" (Freud, 1931, p. 229). Freud maintains that a girl's hostile feelings toward her mother are not a result of an oedipal rivalry; instead, he stresses that the girl's hate of the mother is a result of her feeling that the mother did not provide her with a penis (1931, 1933). He maintains that a boy surmounts his Oedipus complex and develops a superego because of his intense aggression and fear of retaliation by castration from his rival. A girl, on the other hand, who has no castration anxiety because she is already castrated, does not develop an adequate superego because she does not surmount her Oedipus complex. Instead, she escapes *to* the Oedipus complex for an indeterminate length of time, "as though into a haven of refuge," in order to escape from her extreme preoedipal hostility toward the mother (1931, p. 230; 1933, p. 129).

The theoretical dispute of Freud and Anna Freud with Melanie Klein is another source of theoretical conflict which may have led Freud to overlook the importance of the vicissitudes of aggression in the girl's oedipal situation. Although he acknowledges Klein's influence in understanding that suppressed retaliatory aggression toward a frustrating object plays an important role in the formation of the superego (1930, pp. 124–130), he continues to view the intense hostility of the oedipal period as characteristic only of boys. On the other hand, Klein (1945) maintains that the oedipal struggles of both girls and boys contain intense passions, both love and hate. Although Klein's oedipal constructions of the first year of life seem mythical, her theory includes a crucial focus on the importance of analyzing aggression in triangular situations. Chasseguet-Smirgel argues against Freud's notion whereby he maintains that the oedipal situation is a haven of safety for the girl. She affirms that the oedipal situation is as threatening to the girl as it is to the boy (1964, p. 127). She maintains that a girl's prolonged relationship to her father is in actuality a childlike relationship so that the girl avoids the dangers of becoming a woman and taking the mother's place.

Freud's difficulties with accepting and analyzing the expression of aggression in women may have contributed to his idea that the development of normal femininity requires the dampening of *all* desire, including the renunciation of the woman's sense of herself as an active desirous individual. His difficulty with women's aggression is evident in his analytic work with both Dora and the homosexual girl. He distances himself from them when they direct their intense hostility at him, and states that it is difficult to make patients aware of latent, strong hostility without endangering the treatment (1920). Freud rejects Dora's attempt to return to treatment and concludes that she is "not earnest over her request" (1905a, p. 120–121). Although he seems aware of the meaning of the homosexual girl's anger, including the defensive meaning that consuming love could be masked by hate (1920, p. 164), Freud dismisses her and tells her parents to take her to a woman. Can we conjecture that Freud presumes that a woman analyst would feel safer than a man when confronted by a woman's aggression?

If one hypothesizes that subjectivity, which after all refers to the capacity of a person to consider him- or herself as an independent agent who determines or controls his or her own thoughts and actions, requires an expression of sublimated aggression, it is easy to understand why Freud would conclude that the renunciation of subjectivity and the renunciation of aggression in women are normal rather than symptomatic defensive compromise formations. It seems as if Freud continued to theorize in a manner consistent with his adolescent conception that women's passions are dangerous and need to be controlled or damped. Women's aggression, with its inevitable role in subjectivity, has to be denied and avoided, both by the man who might doubt a woman's capacity to sublimate and control her aggression and by the woman *herself* who is frightened of retribution if she becomes an active or aggressive subject.

This construction can be observed in "The Taboo of Virginity" (1918). Freud demonstrates his awareness that the man may project his own aggression onto the woman and then consider her to be the source of danger, especially at the first act of intercourse (p. 200). However, throughout the paper Freud stresses that a man has *good reason* to avoid a woman's aggression. He emphasizes that a woman's hostility may be triggered by loss of her virginity because defloration activates her conscious and unconscious wishes to castrate the man who deflowers her and keep his penis for herself (p. 205). The hostility in the woman, unleashed by her defloration, may express itself in inhibitions in the woman's erotic life with the man who deflowers her. Freud understands that the woman's aggression toward the man who deflowers her heightens the man's anxiety and reinforces his sense of danger as a result of the projection of his aggression onto the woman (p. 201). However, he concludes that the man is fully justified in fearing and avoiding the act of defloration (p. 208). In short, a woman responds to her aggressive feelings by inhibiting her passions, and a man avoids the woman because she is potentially destructive.

In other words, *both men and women* have fantasies that women's passions can be terrifying because of the dangers of unbridled aggression. This aggression has to be avoided or suppressed (cf. Chasseguet-Smirgel, 1964, p. 127). Reviere (1929, 1932, 1936) carefully spells out the clinical and theoretical importance of these problematic reactions to aggression by women. She demonstrates convincingly that the masking of desire in women includes a *defense against frightening aggression.* Her concept of womanliness as a masquerade, which Lacan eventually appropriates, underscores the defensive nature of a woman's renunciation of her aggressive wishes in favor of fantasies in which those wishes are denied *by the woman herself.* This denial might take the form of ideas such as, "I must not take, I must not even ask; it must be given to me" (1929, p. 101). In a similar vein, McDougall discusses the common belief among some women, especially homosexual women, that they have no right to any erotic or narcissistic pleasure that is independent of the mother's will and pleasure (1991, p. 568). In essence women masquerade as guiltless, innocent, and "castrated" in order to avoid punishment for active or aggressive desires (Riviere, 1929, pp. 93–94).

CONCLUSIONS AND IMPLICATIONS

I have delineated a factor, subjectivity, to account for the difficulty in the psychoanalytic understanding of feminine sexuality, particularly the nature of feminine sexual pleasure. This factor has been unappreciated hitherto by psychoanalysts. Subjectivity is a notion that refers to the capacity of a person to posit him- or herself as an independent agent who determines or controls his or her own thoughts and actions. The construct feminine pleasure, and by extension feminine subjectivity, was difficult for Freud and others to posit because of the implicit association among several mental phenomena. Subject, active, and libido (i.e., the source of active sexual pleasure) were, and to some extent still are, considered masculine attributes, whereas object, passive, and, by implication, the absence of an independent actively desirous state were considered feminine attributes. Furthermore, Freud's difficulty in accepting aggression in the mental life of women interfered with his gaining an implicit understanding of feminine subjectivity.

Freud embarked on a radical course which included the seemingly subversive idea that the sexual life of both men and women can be understood only if one appreciates its ambiguities and paradoxes. This was most clearly demonstrated after 1914. In the 1920's and 1930's he retreats from fully applying this understanding. He becomes dogmatic and formalizes a concrete view of the girl's development, including the idea that a normal girl relinquishes her desires and cedes them to the man.

The supposition that masculine is associated with subject, active, and sexual pleasure, and feminine with object, passive, and by implication the absence of sexual pleasure has had untoward consequences in theory and technique. Both men and women may still assume that normally active desire and active aggression are masculine traits which need to be suppressed in women. Clearly, if one conceptualizes that a woman has to "retire from competition" (Freud, 1920) in order to become feminine, one cannot analyze the conflicting feelings and fantasies that lead to such a pathological compromise formation. Kalinich (1993) demonstrates the impact on women's analyses of psychoanalytic formulations in which the female genital, especially the vagina, is described in terms of what it is *not* rather than in terms of what it *is*. In such formulations activity is denied and passivity is stressed.

Freud broke with Adler and Jung because he felt they abandoned the central role of infantile sexuality and the Oedipus complex. Jones was concerned that Freud's diminished emphasis on the girl's oedipal conflicts in favor of the preoedipal would influence some analysts to proceed in a one-sided manner (Paskauskas, 1993, p. 689). Freud's scorn of Melanie Klein led him to think that Jones

Freud and Feminine Subjectivity

was influenced too greatly by Kleinian interpretations (p. 690). However, as Jones predicted, analysts did come to concentrate more and more on conflicts between the girl and the preoedipal mother. The active oedipal situation in women and the inevitable role of aggression in the triangular situation came to be underemphasized.

It seems to me that Freud's undervaluation of the role of intense, active oedipal wishes, conflicts, and compromise formations in girls has had the unintended consequence of contributing to attempts by some psychoanalysts to diminish the centrality of the Oedipus situation in the mental life of both boys and girls. Brunswick's (1940) report of her conjoint work with Freud stimulated a study of the preoedipal period in both boys and girls and contributed to the evolution of object-relations theories. These theories have emphasized the difficulty or ease with which children deal with separation and autonomy, sameness and difference, and closeness and distance, especially from mother (Chodorow, 1978, 1980). Although it is beyond the scope of this paper to elucidate this hypothesis, it seems to me that in some very important respects object-relations theories are heir to the early controversies regarding the nature of feminine sexual development (cf. Mitchell, 1982, p. 22). Stress on the theoretical importance of both boys' and girls' preoedipal struggles with mother has contributed to a diminished appreciation by some analysts of the cardinal importance to the development of compromise formations of the conflicted, passionate, active oedipal struggles. Freud's difficulty recognizing women's subjectivity (with its active sexuality and aggression) inadvertently has contributed to the many attempts to abandon the central role in mental life of infantile sexuality and the Oedipus complex. This is what Freud feared most.

REFERENCES

BENJAMIN, J. (1988). *The Bonds of Love: Psychoanalytic Feminism and the Problem of Domination.* New York: Pantheon.
——— (1991). Father and daughter: identification with a difference—a contribution to gender heterodoxy. *Psychoanal. Dialogues,* 1:277–300.
BENVENISTE, E. (1971). *Problems in General Linguistics.* Coral Gables, FL: Univ. Miami Press.
BERGER, L.S. (1993). Review of *The Bonds of Love* by Jessica Benjamin. *Psychoanal. Books,* 4:220–236.
BOEHLICH, W., Ed. (1990). *The Letters of Sigmund Freud to Eduard Silberstein: 1871–1881.* Cambridge, MA: Belknap Press.

BONAPARTE, M. (1953). *Female Sexuality.* New York: Int. Univ. Press.
BRUNSWICK, R.M. (1940). The preoedipal phase of the libido development. In *Essential Papers on the Psychology of Women,* ed. C. Zanardi. New York: New York Univ. Press, 1990, pp. 43–64.
BUTLER, J. (1990). *Gender Trouble: Feminism and the Subversion of Identity.* New York: Routledge.
CHASSEGUET-SMIRGEL, J. (1964). Feminine guilt and the Oedipus complex. In *Essential Papers on the Psychology of Women,* ed C. Zanardi. New York: New York Univ. Press, 1990, pp. 81–131.
CHODOROW, N. (1978). *The Reproduction of Mothering: Psychoanalysis and the Sociology of Gender.* Berkeley, CA: Univ. Calif Press.
——— (1980). Gender, relation, and difference in psychoanalytic perspective. In *Essential Papers on the Psychology of Women,* ed. C. Zanardi. New York: New York Univ. Press, 1990, pp. 420–436.
FLIEGEL, Z.O. (1973). Feminine psychosexual development in Freudian theory. *Psychoanal. Q.,* 42:385–409.
——— (1986). Women's development in analytic theory: six decades of controversy. In *Psychoanalysis and Women: Contemporary Reappraisals,* ed. J. L. Alpert. Hillsdale, NJ: Analytic Press, pp. 65–88.
FREUD, A. (1922). Beating fantasies and daydreams. *The Writings of Anna Freud,* Vol. 1. New York: Int. Univ. Press, 1974, pp. 137–157.
——— (1927). Four lectures on child analysis. *The Writings of Anna Freud,* Vol. 1. New York: Int. Univ. Press, 1974, pp. 3–69.
——— (1937). The ego and the mechanisms of defense. *The Writings of Anna Freud,* Vol. 2. New York: Int. Univ. Press, 1966.
FREUD, S. (1905a). Fragment of an analysis of a case of hysteria. *S. E.,* 7.
——— (1905b). Three essays on the theory of sexuality. *S. E.,* 7.
——— (1909). Analysis of a phobia in a five-year-old boy. *S. E.,* 10.
——— (1914a). On narcissism: an introduction. *S. E.,* 14.
——— (1914b). On the history of the psycho-analytic movement. *S. E.,* 14.
——— (1915). Instincts and their vicissitudes. *S. E.,* 14.
——— (1918). The taboo of virginity. *S. E.,* 11.
——— (1919). "A child is being beaten": a contribution to the study of the origin of sexual perversions. *S. E.,* 17.
——— (1920). The psychogenesis of a case of homosexuality in a woman. *S. E.,* 18.
——— (1924). The dissolution of the Oedipus complex. *S. E.,* 19.
——— (1925). Some psychical consequences of the anatomical distinction between the sexes. *S. E.,* 19.
——— (1926). Inhibitions, symptoms and anxiety. *S. E.,* 20.
——— (1930). Civilizations and its discontents. *S. E.,* 21.
——— (1931). Female sexuality. *S. E.,* 21.
——— (1933). New introductory lectures on psycho-analysis. *S. E.,* 22.
GROSSMAN, W.I. (1986). Freud and Horney. In *Psychoanalysis: The Science of Mental Conflict,* ed. A. D. Richards & M. Willick. Hillsdale, NJ: Analytic Press, pp. 65–88.

Freud and Feminine Subjectivity

Horney, K. (1924). On the genesis of the castration complex in women. In *Feminine Psychology*, ed. H. Kelman. New York: Norton, 1967, pp. 37–53.

——— (1926). The flight from womanhood: the masculinity complex in women as viewed by men and by women. In *Feminine Psychology*, ed. H. Kelman. New York: Norton, 1967, pp. 54–70.

——— (1933). The denial of the vagina: a contribution to the problem of the genital anxieties specific to women. In *Feminine Psychology*, ed. H. Kelman. New York: Norton, 1967, pp. 147–161.

Irigaray, L. (1977). The sex which is not one. In *Essential Papers on the Psychology of Women*, ed. C. Zanardi. New York: New York Univ. Press, 1990, pp. 344–351.

——— (1985). *Speculum of the Other Woman*. Ithaca, NY: Cornell Univ. Press.

Jones, E. (1927). The early development of female sexuality. *Int. J. Psychoanal.*, 8:459–472.

——— (1933). The phallic phase. *Int. J. Psychoanal.*, 14:1–33.

——— (1935). Early female sexuality. *Int. J. Psychoanal.*, 16:263–273.

——— (1957). *The Life and Work of Sigmund Freud*, Vol. 3. New York: Basic Books.

Jung, C.G. (1913). The Oedipus complex. In *C. G. Jung: The Collected Works*, Vol. 4. London: Routledge & Keegan Paul, 1961, pp. 151–156.

Kalinich, L.J. (1993). On the sense of absence: a perspective on womanly issues. *Psychoanal. Q.*, 62:206–228.

Klein, M. (1945). The Oedipus complex in the light of early anxieties. In *Essential Papers on the Psychology of Women*, ed. C. Zanardi. New York: New York Univ. Press, 1990, pp. 65–87.

Lacan, J. (1972–1973). God and the jouissance of the woman. A love letter. In *Feminine Sexuality: Jacques Lacan and the Ecole Freudienne*, ed. J. Mitchell & J. Rose. New York: Norton, 1982, pp. 137–161.

——— (1977). The meaning of the phallus. In *Feminine Sexuality: Jacques Lacan and the Ecole Freudienne*, ed. J. Mitchell & J. Rose. New York: Norton, 1982, pp. 74–85.

Lacan's Followers (1968). The phallic phase and the subjective import of the castration complex. In *Feminine Sexuality: Jacques Lacan and the Ecole Freudienne*, ed. J. Mitchell & J. Rose. New York: Norton, 1982, pp. 99–122.

Lampl-de Groot, J. (1927). The evolution of the Oedipus complex in women. In *The Psychoanalytic Reader*, ed. R. Fliess. New York: Int. Univ. Press, 1948, pp. 180–194.

Laqueur, T. (1990). *Making Sex: Body and Gender from the Greeks to Freud*. Cambridge, MA: Harvard Univ. Press.

Loewenstein, E.A. (1994). Dissolving the myth of the unified self: the fate of the subject in Freudian analysis. *Psychoanal. Q.*, 63:715–732.

McDougall, J. (1991). Sexual identity, trauma, and creativity. *Psychoanal. Inq.*, 11:559–581.

Mitchell, J. (1982). Introduction. In *Feminine Sexuality: Jacques Lacan and the Ecole Freudienne*, ed. J. Mitchell & J. Rose. New York: Norton, 1982, pp. 1–38.

Panel (1994). Contemporary theories of female sexuality. L. Grossman, reporter. *J. Amer. Psychoanal. Assn.*, 42:233–241.

PASKAUSKAS, R.A., Ed. (1993). *The Complete Correspondence of Sigmund Freud and Ernest Jones: 1908–1939.* Cambridge, MA: Belknap Press.

RIVIERE, J. (1929). Womanliness as a masquerade. In *The Inner World and Joan Riviere*, ed. A. Hughes. London: Karnac, 1991, pp. 89–101.

——— (1932). Jealousy as a mechanism of defence. In *The Inner World and Joan Riviere*, ed. A. Hughes. London: Karnac, 1991, pp. 103–115.

——— (1934). Review of Sigmund Freud, New Introductory Lectures on Psycho-Analysis. In *The Inner World and Joan Riviere*, ed. A. Hughes. London: Karnac, 1991, pp. 117–131.

——— (1936). A contribution to the analysis of the negative therapeutic reaction. In *The Inner World and Joan Riviere*, ed. A. Hughes. London: Karnac, 1991, pp. 133–153.

ROSE, J. (1982). Introduction. In *Feminine Sexuality: Jacques Lacan and the Ecole Freudienne*, ed. J. Mitchell & J. Rose. New York: Norton, 1982, pp. 27–57.

SCHAFER, R. (1974). Problems in Freud's psychology of women. *J. Amer. Psychoanal. Assn.*, 22:459–485.

SILVER, D. (1991). Freud, Gisela, Silberstein, and the repudiation of femininity. *Psychoanal. Inq.*, 11:441–456.

STEPANSKY, P.E. (1977). *A History of Aggression in Freud.* Psychological Issues Monogr. 39. New York: Int. Univ. Press, pp. 223–230.

WINNICOTT, D.W. (1966). Creativity and its origins. In *Essential Papers on the Psychology of Women*, ed. C. Zanardi. New York: New York Univ. Press, 1990, pp. 132–145.

YOUNG-BRUEHL, E. (1989). Looking for Anna Freud's mother. *Psychoanal. Study Child*, 44:391–408.

——— (1991). Rereading Freud on female development. *Psychoanal. Inq.*, 11:427–440.

Freud and the Repudiation of the Feminine

Shelley Orgel

> This paper begins with a discussion of Freud's central ideas on the feminine in his landmark paper, Female Sexuality (1931), written within months after his mother's death. It then traces the evolution of these ideas from the perspective of his own history from childhood to old age. Using some of his letters and clinical papers as reference, one sees that his experience of the feminine in himself, and especially his repudiation of the female components of his own identity, contributed to his belief that such repudiation of the feminine in males was a universal, biologically rooted phenomenon. His personal evolution, enriched by self-analytical insights, is reflected in changes in the nature of his understanding of, and in his ability to accept, his women patients' representations of him as feminine and maternal.

When his ninety-five-year-old mother died in September 1930, Freud confessed to Ferenczi: "It has affected me in a peculiar way, this great event. No pain, no grief . . . at the same time a feeling of liberation, of release which I think I also understand. I was not free to die as long as she was alive, and now I am" (in Lehmann, 1983, pp. 238–239). After his mother's death, Freud finally achieved some sense of permission to join her. In facing this loss, her final departure in a box, he could allow himself to reverse the developmental path depicted in the famous screen memory in which the three-year-old boy was devastated that his mother was nowhere to be found and believed she had been boxed up (encased, pregnant), and then remembers her returning to him slender and beautiful. When he was a boy, Freud's lost preoedipal mother (associated with and represented by the "heart-breaking" departure of his

---

Training and Supervising Analyst, New York University Psychoanalytic Institute.

Shelley Orgel

nurse when she was sent away to jail), was replaced wishfully, defensively by the beautiful, slender (not pregnant) mother who returned to him as the object of his oedipal desire.

In Freud's construction of his childhood, the phallic boy has now become a little Oedipus. He urinates, boylike, in the primal scene, no longer wanting to suck at the breast or its various equivalences (like Dora), or defecate in passive anal surrender to Father (like the Wolf Man), or have Lumpf babies (like Little Hans). Having shown us that the loss of desired others is overcome by identification with them, Freud had to interject as a biological principle the *most* compellingly powerful reason why the multiple childhood experiences of loss of *his* mother *did* not, *could* not, at the pain of death, cause him to take *her* inside him, at least consciously. He would not *become* her in a true identification with her. It is the strength of the boy's (biological) masculinity, he will write, that will enforce his refusal to surrender to passive sexual aims which require him to relinquish the penis he will need later to reenter the maternal womb as conqueror. And to accept *her* inside *him* would be to accept not just castration, but his own death. Only with his mother's actual death could Freud finally surrender himself to the last of the three Fates, the one he identified as "Death itself, the Goddess of Death" (Freud, 1913, p. 296), about whom he wrote more than thirty years earlier (Freud, 1900).

Yet, the surrender even of the old man, remains incomplete. His letter to Ferenczi continues: "I did not go to the funeral; Anna represented me there, too." (in Lehmann, 1983, p. 239). Appignanese and Forrester (1992) write: "A woman, rather than a doctor or a priest, would always be for Freud the 'silent Goddess of Death.' At the end of his life it was Anna who gave the signal to [Max] Schur [to end her father's life]. It was Anna—his Cordelia, the last of the three Fates, who cut the thread of life—into whose arms he entrusted himself." In spite of his stated "feeling of liberation, of release" (Lehmann, 1983, p. 238), he would not gaze upon his mother in her coffin. He sent Anna to his mother's funeral. Anna, his female self, his Athena-Antigone, would be his eyes. She could bear to look and take his mother in—*for* him, *as* him.

Upon the death of his father, Freud tells us about his childhood wish to be rid of his father, to become him and *have* his woman. These, he boldly declares, with the sure inspiration of genius, must

Freud's Repudiation of the Feminine

also be *our* wishes, if we, too, had once been little boys. Back then, the first two Fates, "the woman who bore him, the woman who is his mate" (Freud, 1913, p. 301) occupied him more. He was in the middle of his journey into the unknowable, the navel of the dream that can never be penetrated by the boy with a phallus, any more than one can breach the unconscious by charging the "gates of reason." The way is open only to someone who has surrendered to nothing, who accepts amounting to nothing, as Shengold (1991) has written so movingly. Not this path, back *then*, for Freud the conquistador, explorer, ravisher of dark continents, seeker in the underworlds.

I

Upon the death of his mother, Freud's mourning offering to her and us was his paper "Female Sexuality," the first draft of which was written in the months following his mother's death. The uncertain tone of the paper, described by Young-Bruehl (1990) as "contentious, abrupt, and sometimes annoyed" (p. 322) suggests Freud's partially externalized struggle with himself; but its fresh perspectives also reveal new directions in his never finished self-analysis. The living, real mother could appear in it as never before, no longer in the guise of death, the third Fate, the silent daughter to whom one chooses, in a "triumph of wish-fulfillment," to surrender (Freud, 1913 p. 299). The death of his mother seemed to ease his dread of identifying with her, to free him to acknowledge heretofore neglected aspects of the little boys' early relationships to their mothers and women; he could begin to consider in new ways how the subjective experience of girls and women overlapped those of boys and men. The maternal figure of Death to whom he now could imagine surrendering in final reunion became more recognizable as the beckoning figure of his own maternal self.

In this paper I shall consider where Freud arrived in 1931—and then go back to review his journey to this point by touching on a few highlights and milestones. My main focus, the repudiated female components of Freud's identity, will lead me to look particularly at his difficulties in understanding and working clinically with his women patients' representations of him as feminine and maternal.

Shelley Orgel

I also want to consider how examining his experience of the feminine in himself can be inferred from his letters and scientific papers.

Let us first look briefly at some parts of this surprising 1931 paper. It is as if on the death of his mother, Freud can begin to wonder again about the preoedipal relation to the mother, consider the universal inevitability and durability of *every* child's reproaches against her, and fear of her, and he can conclude, therefore, that she is not to be held solely responsible for them. He can examine his lifelong attachment to her and acknowledge his ambivalence while reaching a deeper level of reconciliation with his father as a recipient of hostility originally intended for the mother. Although his paper focuses on *female* sexuality, the discovery of the centrality of the preoedipal phase applies equally to the boy. And although Freud states that the girl's strongest motive for turning away from the mother is her "reproach that her mother did not give her a proper penis" (p. 234), he does not stop here. Behind the first reproach is a second. The girl accuses the mother of not giving her enough milk, of not suckling her long enough. But, of course, this is a statement about *all* children, and about the greed of their libidos. In fact, he wonders if children of primitive peoples, suckled for two or three years, would not bring the same complaint if analyzed. (Perhaps "two or three years" alludes to his age when he lost his nurse, the recipient of his oral greed and the displaced object of his cravings for maternal care.) In a conclusion that must be equally true for boys, Freud says: "Perhaps the real fact"—one senses his struggle and overcoming of resistance in this emphasis—"is that the attachment to the mother is bound to perish, precisely because it was the first and was so intense [i.e., unquenchable]" (*ibid.*). In other words, what he once called the "heartbreaking" loss of his nurse at two or three represented an occurrence that was bound to happen and is eventually to be accepted without heartbreak just as the seventy-four-year-old man seems to accept his mother's final departure.

The girl's attachment is forced away from her mother, he writes, "in consequence of a *general* characteristic of infantile sexuality" (italics added). How, then, can boys keep their attachment to their mothers intact? Freud's reply is that they displace their hostility onto their fathers. Freud suggests that for some boys, at least, it must be as we speculate it was for *him*. Serious disruption of the attachment

Freud's Repudiation of the Feminine

to the mother may be hidden in the thrust, both progressive and defensive, of positive oedipal development. He indicates that he is just beginning to become acquainted with these processes, with the "gray area" of earliest attachments into which "it is probably more prudent in general to admit that we have as yet no clear understanding" (p. 235).

One consequence of this dawning awareness is that Freud seems to be listening to his patients in new ways as he acknowledges past misconceptions. He says that girls are sexually *active* toward the mother, with oral, sadistic, and finally even phallic trends directed toward her. He acknowledges that these trends appear in disguised forms in analysis where he has seen them as "transferences onto the later, father object where they do not belong and where they seriously interfere with our understanding of the situation" (p. 237). Women in analysis with him, he says, cling to their father attachments in which they had taken refuge from the earliest phase (as he had taken refuge in the activity and potential for success of the oedipal phase). As the mother assumes her rightful place as first love, first seducer, first to threaten castration, and prime depriver, previous attributions of these to the father as primary stand corrected.

It is the little girl's oral aggression toward her mother that is turned into a fear of being killed by her. In men, where Freud had previously found the fear of being eaten by the father as a regressive expression of castration, he now adds that it is probably also the result of a transformation of oral aggression directed toward the mother from whom the child had its nourishment. Freud, it seems, in what I suggest is a wonderful burst of self-analytic work at the age of seventy-five, is enlarging his appreciation of his own and his patients' continuing wishes for the forms of love given by the mother of their first years. He is understanding his and their hatred of her, and the proliferation of vengeful fantasies both direct and projected, as she inevitably disappointed these desires. This is the mother he feared was "boxed up" and sent away by his brother Philip, as his nurse had been sent away to jail. In other words, bearing the loss, knowing mother is gone (*fort*) and will never be there again (*da*), he can now experience some of the previous feelings of immense need, ambivalence, rage, and the loss, and the incorporation of this

Shelley Orgel

mother into himself.[1] Insofar as he accepts such wishes in himself ("I can now die"), he can avoid having to look away from the maternal transference fantasies his patients, male and female, have in common, and he no longer must insist as vigorously and proudly as in years past on his masculine, paternal identity in their transferences to him.

II

Freud (1931) gives an example to illustrate that the intensity with which the child converts passivity to activity indicates the "relative strength of the masculinity and femininity it will exhibit in its sexuality" (p. 236). His example: "When a doctor has opened a child's mouth, in spite of his resistance [the generic child has become *he*], to look down his throat, the same child, after the doctor had gone, will play at being the child himself, and will repeat the assault upon some small brother or sister who is as helpless in his hands as he was in the doctor's" (*ibid.*). This illustration evokes the manifest content of the Irma dream and leads us directly to the struggle in Freud (1900) between what he called masculine and feminine strivings.

My emphasis in this paper is on *Irma* as one of the two leading characters of the dream, both of whom represent the dreamer; on Irma as female victim of doctors' attempts to cure through their scrutinies, probings, and poisonings; Irma as pregnant; as the intestinally incontinent child of the primal scene; as sufferer from symptoms in the left chest (and shoulder); as embodying the geography of the body and mind, the penetration into which will be consummated in an analysis of self which will be transformed by genius into the psychoanalysis of others; and as representing the necessary feminine "Other" in a duality only death unifies. Irma is Freud, the dreamer.

In sharp contrast to Freud's expressed readiness to surrender to the last of the three Fates after his mother's death, the "I" of the manifest content of the Irma dream concentrates on overcoming

---

[1] His daughter Sophie died in January 1920; I think Freud was writing of, and *as*, her grieving child in the famous "*fort-da*" passage in "Beyond the Pleasure Principle" (1920a).

Freud's Repudiation of the Feminine

"recalcitrance, unwillingness, resistance" (Appignanese and Forrester, 1992, p. 121) in his woman patient. His stance continues to be that of the *Studies in Hysteria* in which he wrote: "We force our way into the internal strata, overcoming resistance all the time" (Breuer and Freud, 1895, p. 294). (We shall see that this was his stance as well in the Dora case.)

Freud in the 1890's, Oedipus redux, dared to grapple with the riddle of the Sphinx by attempting symbolic phallic penetration into and possession of the body of the mother, and he resisted learning that it was not to be done. If, as Anzieu writes (1986), the dream represents the body of the mother, complete knowledge of it or her is not possible for the phallic child. Hannibal did not reach Rome, nor Moses, the promised land. Always remaining is the unplummable "navel," the path to the unknowable inside, the dark continent—to the heart of the mystery of who we are, where we come from, where we go when we die. We traverse it only in surrender—in birth, and finally in death. Or one can do as Freud learned to do at this crucial time in his and our history and as we analysts still do. One can recapture "first loves" by remembering them, by becoming a patient in analysis and reinterpreting their meanings.

The Irma dream of July 23-24, 1895 contains it all—the arrogance of the conquistador and the astounding realization that what has been impossible to satisfy in action becomes the ground of our psychological being in warded-off wish, and compromise which can be owned as insight.

What Freud was demanding of his dream self-representation in relation to his "female Other" portrayed as the women, mothers and daughters, who are condensed in and associated with the figure of the young widow Irma, was that he should "have" them, deflower them, satisfy their erotic longings, impregnate them with "germs" from "the dirty syringe," open them up (leaf by leaf, as it were) to see what is inside, deliver them of their "anal" babies, observe their return (like his mother in the famous screen memory) slim, beautiful, and healthy, with no more babies inside. What Freud was demanding of Irma was that she should represent him (without his having to know it), ill in the throat (displaced from the nose, of course), the heart, the intestines—ill from hysteria, he hoped, not really dangerously ill, just "poisoned" temporarily, burdened by the

Shelley Orgel

chemicals of pregnancy, like Martha in her third month, with the new Anna, his analyst child to be. Meantime, *he* had also been made pregnant-ill by his masculine *Other* (Fliess), having "opened his mouth properly" for him in February of that year for cauterization of his turbinal bones for empyema, and he was expecting another nasal surgical intervention (the delivery?) in September.

This illness of Irma-Freud would "pass" when the labor of dysentery, the cathartic "cure" supervened. Dysentery had ominous connotations as a cure for unwelcome pregnancies. His baby brother Julius had died of it. There is much evidence that Martha's sixth pregnancy in 1895 was not so welcome either. But first, she (like him) had to open her mouth properly to the masterful male doctor, just as he had done and would do, and reveal the truth of her false (detachable) teeth. By being identified in his dream with his male Other, Fliess, Freud felt strengthened in his membership in "the strong sex," as one Irma, Emma Eckstein, observed when he became ill at the sight of her near exsanguination[2] after *she* had been operated on by Fliess.

Freud needs to call upon his identification with Fliess, the "physician above all others," the possessor of the magical phallus that penetrates into and deciphers the secrets of nature, sharing between them, as boys do, what Horney called "the typical ideas the boy has of the girl" (Horney, 1926). No, he must *not* be identified with his female incarnations, Irma and the women, the mothers and the daughters who lack the penises they need to cure their—celibate widowhood, their neuroses, and their inability to create and procreate. Freud needed his fusion of object relationship and identification with Fliess ("I can barely do without the other—and you are the only other, the alter"), he wrote to Fliess in 1894 (Masson, 1985, p. 73). With Fliess as his alter ego, he could identify with a *man* in the act of conception, pregnancy and birth—and assert that mutual creation between males is possible and does *not* mean he must become a "castrated" woman (see also Blum, 1990).

In the Irma dream, accepting psychoanalytic interpretations is the means to achieve this "cure," and Freud depicts himself as both

---

[2]It frequently happens in dreams that the analyst represents the patient's male self in conflict with or in erotic connection to the dreamer-subject who represents the feminine identity of the patient.

Freud's Repudiation of the Feminine

phallic instrument and feminine object of it, just as he is the analyst and patient of his self-analysis. Anzieu (1986) names the dream: "A Child Is Being Conceived." He suggests that the double child about to be born—Anna Freud and Robert Fliess, representing the doubles of self-analysis and psychoanalysis—is shared between Freud and Fliess. Each has made it with the other, through the intermediary of the other's wife. Freud is, then, the patient, equivalent to the unconscious—which contains the repudiated feminine, the repressed—that he himself examines in the dream.

Unlike Irma, he will control his recalcitrance, resistance—and skepticism. Freud will allow Fliess to cauterize his turbinal bones in September as he had the previous February. Fliess will examine a dull area in his left chest (as Freud examines Irma) and will declare him free of a possibly fatal cardiac illness; his paroxysmal tachycardia and angina are the result of a poison, nicotine, which can be eliminated. But, *like* Irma, he also *does* question Fliess's solution—as she had refused to accept *his* interpretations—and he does start smoking again. Identified with Fliess the physician, he notes that it is *her* fault (i.e., his own fault) if she still gets pains. Freud seems to have decided that the consequences of smoking, a habit requiring deception and self-deception, is the price he must pay to work, to deliver himself of his psychoanalytic child. (We note his identification with the "deceptive" Martha of his associations here.) Still, he has not heard from Fliess in a while and, guilty and anxious about the results of his "rebellion," he writes to Fliess on July 24th, the day before the dream, "Why have you not answered me?" He still needs regular injections of Fliess's magical omnipotence to sustain his great labor. He must have worried that Fliess, impatiently hungering for glory, might replace *him* as he wished to replace the recalcitrant widow of his dream with someone more to his liking, someone who would accept his explanations and prescriptions unhesitatingly. One possible male judge or physician after another is brought into the dream as a potential substitute for Fliess, and all are dismissed. Only Fliess's gifts can supply the necessary injection of "life." As he wrote in May 1898 to Fliess: "I shall change whatever you want and gratefully accept contributions. I am so immensely glad that you are giving me the gift of the Other, a critic and reader—and one of your quality at that. I cannot write entirely without an audience, but do not at

Shelley Orgel

all mind writing only for you. . . . The most difficult task—the unraveling of the psychic process in dreaming—is still ahead of me and will be tackled only after I have been *revived* by our congress" (in Masson, 1985; italics added).

Freud certainly could not turn to the pale, limping, impotent Dr. M. (Breuer) to deliver psychoanalysis to the world. Breuer not only attributed Freud's cardiac symptoms to the more alarming diagnosis of myocarditis, but was terrified by the first symbolic announcement of the birth of psychoanalysis by Anna O., the inventor of the talking cure (Bertha Pappenheim). When she had said, "writhing in abdominal cramps," to her therapist, "Now Dr. B's baby is coming," Breuer "abandoned the patient to a colleague." He hid the fantasy baby, and Freud, writing about the incident to Stefan Zweig fifty years later, still scorns him for his cowardice (in E. L. Freud, 1970, pp. 408–409). It was Freud who had the courage to recognize the import of the event when Breuer told him about it in 1883. And eventually it was Freud who could acknowledge the timeless power of infantile sexual desire as his own. The plaque Freud proposed to announce his successful interpretation of the Irma dream is a birth announcement calling to my mind the shared completion of Walther's Prize Song in *Die Meistersinger*, about which Hans Sachs proclaims, "*Ein Kind ist hier geboren.*" Psychoanalysis is the child fathered by Wilhelm Fliess, born to Sigmund Freud on July 23–24, 1895.

Psychoanalysis comes into being from Freud's need to discover and reveal himself in each of the members of the primal scene, to "know" each of the participants without destroying either of the sexual pair, and without becoming lost in *being any* of them irretrievably. The stresses inherent in the attempt and the inevitable failure to maintain this equidistance, this fluidity of identities, in the face of conflicted erotic and aggressive passions, and the self-observation thereby stimulated in analysts ever since its origins have formed an essential basis for the vitality of our discipline. These delicately balanced tensions are, I believe, always evident in analyses when they come alive. In his self-analysis after the death of his father, Freud recreated and remembered the curious, excited child, mainly in his dreams; he found *himself* in the murderous struggle of Oedipus and Hamlet with the father he wished to replace and become. The knowledge of what it might feel like *to be* the mother, however, *what the*

Freud's Repudiation of the Feminine

psychological experience is of being a woman eluded him, and this troubled him (see Schafer, 1974). In 1895, he could wish to be cured (rescued=impregnated) by Fliess as he wished to cure Irma. What *Doctor* Fliess forced on *Patient* Freud whose feminine side, he said, needed such a relationship, Freud forced on patients like the Irma figure or Dora. He could, in other words, gradually come to know in this period about his unruly homosexual wishes to love and be loved by another man.[3] But in those years when Freud felt the passions—love and hate—derived from identifications with women or when patients imagined and desired him as a woman, he turned away. Perhaps to the end, this remained *his* bedrock. It took awesome courage to admit the wish to *have* mother, but it remained painfully difficult for him to wish to *become* her, or to be fused with her in a sealed world. The representation of mother in his memory emerges, begins to exist, only when she is reborn (emerges from the void of her absence) in her oedipal form, and the little boy, in identification with father and brothers, begins to wish to possess her sexually. Freud could not help believing that one had to *be* female to truly accept being the object of maternal transferences. Eventually he concluded that only women analysts could discover and map the child's earliest relationships and identifications with the mother of the first years. And even in the 1931 paper, he concludes: "We see, then, that the phase of exclusive attachment to the mother, which may be called the *pre-Oedipus* phase, possesses a far greater importance in women than it can have in men" (p. 230).

Only at the end, in the 1930's, as we have seen, will there be some shift in the bedrock. In *Analysis Terminable and Interminable* Freud (1937) disputes Ferenczi's statement made in 1927 that two complexes must have been mastered by the time of termination: the wish for a penis in a woman, and the struggle against passivity in a man. Freud writes: "At no other point in one's analytic work does

---

[3]Except for the last phrase which speaks of *exclusive* homosexual object choice, Freud (1920b), in this passage could be writing out of self-awareness. He seems to find a way out of a difficult dilemma in postulating an independence between masculine or feminine attitude and object choice. He writes: "Experience proves . . . a man writes with predominantly male characteristics and also masculine in his erotic life may still be inverted in respect to his object, loving [only] men instead of women." So, one *can* repudiate the feminine in oneself and still experience a desire for a man, presumably as a defense against castration anxiety consequent to a sexual relationship with a woman.

Shelley Orgel

one suffer more from an oppressive feeling that all one's repeated efforts have been in vain, and from a suspicion that one has been 'preaching to the winds' as when one is trying to persuade a woman to abandon her wish for a penis on the ground of its being unrealizable or when one is seeking to convince a man that a passive attitude to men does not always signify castration and that it is indispensable in many relationships in life" (p. 252).

Believing, though, that a woman is a castrated man and that passivity is equated with the feminine, that "the vagina is precisely the wound the father leaves after castration" (Chasseguet-Smirgel, 1976, p. 279), how can he truly convince others—or himself—to "master these complexes?" It is striking that in this passage Freud abandons an analytic attitude and speaks unguardedly of preaching and persuading. He fails to note that such a "phallic-penetrating" approach to the passive patient—"I know this; can't you see it?" —would produce, in males, *or* females, for that matter, what he called "one of the strongest transference-resistances" (Freud, 1937, p. 252). Retreating from psychological reasons, Freud concludes: "The repudiation of femininity can be nothing else than a biological fact, a part of the great riddle of sex." As Schafer (1974) puts it, "... anatomy had become Freud's destiny" (p. 476).

He will turn over to Anna and women analysts, "suitable mother substitutes," as he called them (Freud, 1931, p. 227), the study of what it means to be a woman. In his last years, she, especially, will be the "Other," as Fliess had been in the beginning. The women can speak of the experience of being "Mother" *for* him, and he will accept their solutions.

III

To understand something about the entangled theoretical position and personal stakes with which Freud approached the analysis of Dora in 1900, let us consider the Dora case in relation to relevant theoretical assumptions expounded in the contemporaneous *Three Essays* (1905b).

Having given up the seduction theory by autumn of 1897, almost simultaneously with his formulation of the Oedipus complex, the

Freud's Repudiation of the Feminine

essential elements of the *Three Essays* were already in Freud's mind, even though both this monograph and that on the Dora case were not published until 1905. In December 1897, Freud wrote to Fliess: "The insight has dawned on me that masturbation is the one major habit, the 'primary addiction,' and it is only as a substitute and replacement for it that the other addictions—to alcohol, morphine, tobacco and the like—come into existence. The role played by this addiction in hysteria is enormous; and it is perhaps there that my major, still outstanding obstacle is to be found, wholly or in part. And here, of course, doubt arises about whether an addiction of this kind is curable, or whether analysis and therapy must come to a halt at this point and content themselves with transforming hysteria into neurasthenia"(in Masson, 1985, p. 287). Among other things, it seems Freud is continuing to justify and explain his own inability to be cured of his addiction to cigars. This "habit" will appear meaningfully in the pages of the Dora case.

In the *Three Essays* there is a related passage. In some children, Freud writes, there is "a constitutional intensification of the erotogenic significance of the labial region. If that significance persists, these same children when they are grown up will become epicures in kissing, will be inclined to perverse kissing or, if *males*, will have a powerful motive for drinking and smoking. If, however, repression ensues, they will feel disgust at food and will produce hysterical vomiting. . . . Many ["All" in the first edition] of my women patients who suffer from disturbances of eating, globus hystericus, constriction of the throat and vomiting, have indulged energetically in sucking during their childhood"(1905b, p. 182). It is as if he is saying: If such a child is *male*, I can see that he could be *me*; if female, she may grow up to become, not me, but Dora. If so, the addictive component in her hysteria will ultimately be unanalyzable.

I would speculate, therefore, that a warded-off tendency to identify with this girl, attracted to both mother and father and their substitutes, ready to transfer onto Freud her wishes to be reunited with the maternal breast in a regressive resorption of object relationship into fusion, contributed to his misunderstanding and his rejection of her and to his strengthening belief, after a much too optimistic beginning, that she was unanalyzable. Her profligate use of her mouth to tell off her parents (*she* opened her mouth, but

Shelley Orgel

not properly) finally convinced him that she was not interested in more analysis.

To return to the beginning, Freud's happy "position" as psychoanalytic burglar and deflowerer of Dora becomes evident from her first appearance as we learn from a letter to Fliess dated October 14, 1900. "It has been a lively time and has brought a new patient, an eighteen-year-old girl, a case that has smoothly opened to the existing collection of pick locks" (in Masson, 1985, p. 427). If there is any doubt about what this says about Freud's countertransference equation of psychoanalytic interpretation with phallic penetration at the outset, he enlightens us in a footnote explaining her associations to her first dream of locking and unlocking her room (the *Zimmer* = *Frauenzimmer* equation). "It is well known, too," Freud writes with something of a wink, "what sort of 'key' effects the opening in such a case" (1905a, p. 67).

Freud writes that when he first saw Dora at age sixteen, she refused treatment for her coughing and hoarseness, "ridiculing all doctors who, as a class, aroused her resistance," and Freud adds, "it was only her father's authority," a mantle Freud easily assumed, "which induced her to come to me at all." Because he had successfully treated Dora's father four years earlier for symptoms of tertiary syphilis, the father "handed her [Dora] over to me for psychotherapeutic treatment," asking Freud to bring her to reason after giving him a detailed case history. Her agreement to go for treatment followed the death of her aunt of whom she had been very fond, an abdominal attack diagnosed as appendicitis, and her parents' discovery of a note in which she took leave of them because she could no longer endure her life. In addition, she had an attack of loss of consciousness after "a slight passage of words" between her father and herself. (Interestingly, in view of the central theme in this case of the erotization of conversation, Freud says nothing more about this last episode.)

I assume that the basic "story" Dora told is fairly well known: Her father's physical relationship with his "nurse" Frau K., which probably was largely played out in oral sex because of his impotence; Herr K.'s erotic kiss when Dora was fourteen (Glenn, 1993, notes that thirteen is the correct age) and her reaction of disgust rather than arousal, a response Freud, with notable lack of empathy with

Freud's Repudiation of the Feminine

this child, called already fully hysterical, a symptom he related to her childhood thumb sucking; Frau K.'s relationship with Dora who took care of the K.'s children, a relationship that included their sharing a bedroom at the lake where her husband "proposed" to Dora when she was sixteen. This bedroom was where she was sleeping when she had her dream of summoning her father to help her escape from the burning house. Frau K. had confided to Dora "all of the difficulties of her married life," while Dora told Frau K. about the sexual knowledge she had acquired through reading—also erotized conversation, this time therapeutically turned. Dora felt she had been "handed over to Herr K." (the very words Freud used to describe her father's bringing her for treatment) as barter to quiet her opposition to her father's affair. Finally, we must recall Dora's relationship with her governess, "her teacher in sexual matters," who was a truth teller concerning the affair between Dora's father and Frau K. and encouraged Dora to become one too. Dora had the governess fired when she learned of the latter's interest in her father rather than her, echoes of which will reverberate in the analytic transference.

Freud could not accept that *he* could represent this governess, a woman, in the transference any more than he could accept himself as Dora's mother, or Frau K. Yet, was he not her sharp-eyed confidante and participant in erotic conversation who seemed to be interested in her, while supporting the covert interests of her father and Herr K., *insisting*, as he did, that she erotically desired these men rather than the women she loved and needed?[4] Appignanese and Forrester (1992) write insightfully about the lesson Dora was teaching Freud "that psychoanalysis could as easily be a hothouse for the erotization of language, for taking pleasure in knowledge, as an enclave protected from it . . . the model for this erotic conversation was Ida's [Dora's] intimate friendship with Frau Zelenka [Frau K.]: the scene of two women talking . . . psychoanalysis could be an erotized conversation in which Freud played the part of a woman" (p. 115).

---

[4]This bias may well illustrate Schafer's (1993) argument that Freud generally heated up the heterosexual, apparently paternal transference to ward off recognition of the analysand's maternal transference (p. 86).

Shelley Orgel

Freud insisted to Dora that she was in love with Herr K. After all, he was "young and prepossessing," and his proposal to the sixteen-year-old girl was, Freud insisted, "neither tactless nor offensive." In fact, it resembled Freud's own interpretations. Freud analyzed her largely as suffering from a positive oedipal conflict, identified "both with the woman her father had once loved and the woman he loved now" (1905a, p. 56). Her intense wishes to suck on a penis *were* interpreted as a substitution for the original object, a nipple. But this nipple is not part of a person. In 1901 Freud does not really "know" about the original longing for a mother. Such wishes were labelled "prehistoric"; only the little girl's death wishes toward her mother are reconstructed (p. 57). He explains Dora's remembered thumb-sucking while tugging on her brother's ear until her father broke her of the habit when she was four or five as "a complete form of self-gratification by sucking" (p. 51), not, as we now would understand it, as a way of achieving comfort in the aftermath of separation from a mother. In other words, he postulated a kind of weakness in object-relatedness, reversion toward primary narcissism, with a heightened and lasting erotic cathexis of the oral zone. This cathexis then predisposes such girls to "subsequently become anaesthetic and hysterical" (*ibid.*), and less differentiated as female. Freud recognizes Dora's homosexual love for Frau K., seeing it as typical of hysterical women and as the result of energetic suppression of "the sexual libido which is directed toward men." This is a dynamic he will explore further in the case study of the homosexual woman (1920b).

I believe that the neglected side of Dora's transferences to Freud evoked his intense discomfort with accepting the maternal position including Dora's preoedipally and negative oedipally determined homosexual wishes toward him. He needed to repudiate his own femininity with the inevitable castration (and, as we have seen, surrender to primal abandonment and "death") that he believed, against all attempts to persuade himself otherwise, would be required. He was surprised that he became the governess dismissed with two weeks' notice. I do not think he could know he was also Frau K., "the main source of her [Dora's] knowledge of sexual matters," and behind this figure, the mother to whom the little girl clung in her addictive oral and masturbatory "habits" and symptoms

Freud's Repudiation of the Feminine

while everyone, including her analyst, worked to turn her "appropriately" toward the pleasures inherent in women's surrender to men.

To consider a brief but telling example of these transferences and of how Freud responded to them, let us look at her first dream. Recall the fire in the house, etc., Father standing by her bed, Mother wanting to stop to save her jewel case, Father refusing to let himself and his two children be burnt for its sake, their hurrying downstairs and outside, and then her waking up. Freud saw, of course, the fire of her sexual excitement (the dream of Chapter 7, including its famous entreaty: Father, Can't You See I'm Burning? provided a compelling linkage). But about the fire and smoke of his cigar, and his fantasies about and pleasures in sucking, chewing, taking the smoke into his mouth and throat and lungs, he is silent. Her turning from her mother to her father as rescuer from the dangers of prolonged frustration is depicted in the dream. Freud missed her rage and envy of *him* for enjoying the gratifications she, "the little thumbsucker," as he called her, was deprived of and intensely craved, from which they both escaped defensively to a positive oedipal position. I have speculated that this sequence recreates a parallel progression, at this time repressed, in Freud himself as a very young child.

Freud puts himself comfortably in the position of Herr K., also a smoker, and he concludes that Dora's transference wish is for a kiss from him. Dora had smoked at the lake, in the quarters she shared with Frau K., one presumes, but Freud cannot conclude that she wanted to use her mouth to smoke herself, even though it is in the same paragraph as he notes her wish for a kiss from him that he refers to her as "the little thumb-sucker."[5] He is aware of the power of the instinctual aim such desires express, but then fails to link them with their objects—the mouth, breasts, and genitals of a woman. He could not allow himself to become conscious of identifying himself as constituting such part objects even though unconsciously he could and did play the part of the woman Dora loved, "the secret source of her sexual knowledge," as Freud characterizes Frau K. in his postanalytic footnote. And he fails to appreciate as well her identification with her father and Herr K., the lovers of Frau K., and therefore Dora's rivals.

[5]Dora became a chain smoker as an adult (Rogow, 1978).

Shelley Orgel

Freud wrote up this case in 1901, then withheld publication for several years (probably until he learned Dora had herself become a mother). On January 30th, 1901, a month after Dora broke off the analysis—Freud rather coldly summed up the case in a letter to Fliess: "It is a hysteria with tussus nervosa and aphonia, which can be traced back to the character of the child's sucking, and the principal issue in the conflicting thought processes is the contrast between an inclination toward men and an inclination toward women" (in Masson, 1985, p. 434).

His awareness of Dora's homosexuality is most directly stated in a passage long after the analysis is over and the subsiding countertransference pressures have permitted further self-analysis. Freud (1905a) writes: "The longer the interval of time that separates me from the end of the analysis the more probable it seems to me that the fault in my technique lay in this omission: I failed to discover in time and to inform the patient that her homosexual (gynecophylic) love for Frau K. was the strongest unconscious current in her mental life" (p. 120). Even in this extraordinarily self-revealing and insightful statement, *after* he has recognized the crucial importance of transference as resistance in this case, Freud does not recognize his own position as object of Dora's negative oedipal and preoedipal desires for her mother, and he fails to consider her reproaches and vengeful fantasies as rooted in these thwarted first attachments. It required the scientific work and self-reflection of 30 years to make it possible for him to take into account and to write about how such desires of early childhood inevitably present themselves in the transference in every patient's psychoanalysis (Freud, 1931).

IV

The case of a homosexual woman is Freud's (1920b) other detailed report of an analysis of a woman, and I shall consider it just briefly here. Freud's attitudes show similarities to the ways he approached the analysis of Dora, but also differences, which convey the clinical experience and growth in self-awareness of 20 years. Freud now recognizes how unfavorable it is for analysis when someone else brings in the patient. The failure of the treatment becomes a way of thwarting parents and relatives while satisfying oneself that one has tried

Freud's Repudiation of the Feminine

to change, he says. He also realizes it is unfavorable prognostically "that the task to be carried out did not consist in resolving a neurotic conflict but in converting one variety of the genital organization of sexuality into the other" (1920b, pp. 150–151). So Freud, now less encumbered by unwarranted confidence in his powers, did not hold out to the parents any prospect of fulfilling their hope that their eighteen-year-old daughter would renounce her infatuation with an older woman, and seek a heterosexual life. The basic facts of her history Freud learned were that when her mother gave birth to her youngest brother when she was sixteen, she lost all interest in becoming a mother herself and began to take an interest in older women "substitutes for her mother," a development that "soon brought upon her a severe chastisement at the hands of her father."

Freud's explanation: "She changed into a man and took her mother in place of her father as the object of her love. Her relationship to her mother had certainly been ambivalent from the beginning, and it proved easy to revive her earlier love for her mother" (1920b, p. 158). This direction, "retiring in favor of her mother" (there are intimations of Anna Freud's "altruistic surrender" here) left the field free for her mother to enjoy sexual conquests of men with whom the girl could identify and thereby achieve vicarious satisfaction, as well as removed some basis for her mother's dislike of her. Her homosexual direction, furthermore, "could wound the father and take revenge on him." It was this latter intention that Freud recognized in the transference. "In reality, she transferred to me the sweeping repudiation of men which had dominated her ever since the disappointment she had suffered from her father.... As soon, therefore, as I recognized the girl's attitude to her father, I broke off the treatment and advised her parents that if they set store by the therapeutic procedure it should be continued by a woman doctor" (1920b, p. 164).

Freud's dilemma is quite explicit: He begins and ends as the parents' agent. He himself is by no means as shocked and disapproving of the girl's homosexual longings as the father; he seems to believe she has the right to choose, and his tolerance, if anything, resembles the mother's. But seeing himself as the paternalistic physician entrusted with her care by them (see Stone, 1961, p. 13), he did not feel permitted ethically or by temperament to explore the girl's wish to "attempt to gain my interest and my good opinion—perhaps in order to disappoint me all the more thoroughly later on" (Freud, 1920b, p. 165). (This "perhaps" is important; the certainty of 1900 that he is right is gone.) In this treatment, Appignanese and Forrester (1992) suggest Freud is "playing the role of a father of whom he does not quite approve" (p. 187). Hired to force her to be heterosexual, he "abdicates from this position of responsibility, this position infused with fantasies of paternal omnipotence; he defends the rights of homosexuals to be considered normal, he defends the rights of patients to lie and deceive." What he could not do was "play the part of the mother in the transference" (p. 188). He was, as it were, too protective of his core phallic self-representation to permit that. This patient's mother, though, was recognized as an individual and regarded with far more sympathy than he could muster for the women in Dora's life in 1900. By this time he could consider it compatible with ideal femininity in some women he admired and even envied that they shared qualities of intellect and moral courage he ordinarily attributed to men. And this patient influenced him to consider the central importance of female figures in the lives of his patients, male and female. He could write that her homosexuality was "probably a direct and unchanged continuation of an infantile fixation of her mother" (1920b, p. 168), pointing to further exploration on this realm and era of life.

During this period, Freud was analyzing his daughter Anna. I think it must be meaningful that not long after reviewing the case of this patient, he retired from that analysis and "handed" Anna "over to" just such an idealized woman (exquisitely feminine, he called her), Lou Andreas Salomé. I wonder if he believed that with *her*, Anna might work out that part of her maternal transference displaced onto him and labeled paternal. We have reviewed his formulation of this dynamic in the 1931 paper discussed earlier. In it he concurred with Lampl-de Groot's apt statement in her classic 1927 paper, "For it is difficult for a female patient to enter into rivalry with the father-analyst, so that possibly treatment under these conditions cannot get beyond the analysis of the positive Oedipus attitude. The homosexual tendency, which can hardly be missed in any analysis, may then merely give the impression of a later reaction to the disappointment experienced at the father's hands" (p. 222).

Freud's Repudiation of the Feminine

In addition, Freud may have wanted his daughter to love and to take *such* a woman as her ego ideal and model for identification. This would enable (or direct?) her to follow the path he had in mind for her. As with his young patient, with Anna he retired temporarily in favor of a woman, but one who, above all women, could *be*, and help his daughter to *become*, the woman he might aspire to be.

CONCLUSION

By the time of Freud's analysis of Hilda Doolittle (H.D.) in 1933–1934, he no longer consciously repudiated the identity of mother which she assigned him, although he was not comfortable with it. When she told him how she felt him to be a woman, " . . . he said he suspected it, then he said, in the best small-dog manner, 'but—to be perfectly frank with *you*—I do not like it—I feel so very, very, very MASCULINE.' He says he always feels hurt when his analysands have a maternal transference. I asked if it happened often; he said sadly, 'Oh, very often' " (March 10, 1933, in Friedman, 1990, p. 314).

As Friedman (1990) has shown in her definitive study of H.D.'s analysis, H.D., like the homosexual woman of Freud's 1920 paper, "had never, in her passage through the Oedipus complex and its partial repetition in puberty, altogether transferred her feelings from her mother to her father; and the loved woman for her was still the whole woman imagined in infancy, the phallic, uncastrated or masculine woman, the ideal woman with whom, in her homosexual loves, she recreated the mother-child relationship" (Friedman, 1990, p. 390). Freud seemed to know this by the time of her analysis. He acknowledged sadly that in his old age—no longer "young and prepossessing" like Herr K.—he could not expect to "convert" such a woman toward her oedipal father through the power of his masculine appeal. So he told her in his widely quoted comment: "The trouble is—I am an old man—you do not think it worth your while to love me." But these poignant words mean so much more, I think. He was saying, with the sadness and clarity of Lear, that she, daughter now become mother, another Cordelia, could neither love him as a male nor with the joyful pride with which his mother had once greeted the arrival of her golden son. He has had to understand and accept that ultimately each is mother and child to the other, that oedipal triangularity, with its sharp boundaries between male and female, adult and child, inevitably regresses at the end of life toward a diadic intermingling. Lear's last words to his "silent" daughter incomparably evoke that sense of reciprocal duality in a world that has shrunk to a womblike enclosure:

> Come, let's away to prison.
> We two alone will sing like birds ith' cage.
> When thou dost ask me blessing,
> I'll kneel down and ask of thee forgiveness."

Freud now knew that active possession of Mother was impossible, and that surrender to her, to her in himself, was the only path toward reunion left to choose.

REFERENCES

ANZIEU, D. (1986). *Freud's Self-analysis.* Madison, CT: Int. Univ. Press.
APPIGNANESE, L. & FORRESTER, J. (1992). *Freud's Women.* New York: Basic Books.
BLUM, H.P. (1990). Freud, Fliess and the parenthood of psychoanalysis. *Psychoanal. Q.,* 59:21–40.
BREUER, J. & FREUD, S. (1895). Studies on hysteria. *S. E.,* 2.
CHASSEGUET-SMIRGEL, J. (1976). Freud and female sexuality. *Int. J. Psychoanal.,* 57:275–286.
FREUD, E.L., Ed. (1970). *Letters of Sigmund Freud 1873–1939.* New York: Basic Books.
FREUD, S. (1900). The interpretation of dreams. *S. E.,* 4 & 5.
——— (1905a). Fragment of an analysis of a case of hysteria. *S. E.,* 7.
——— (1905b). Three essays on the theory of sexuality. *S. E.,* 7.
——— (1913). The theme of the three caskets. *S. E.,* 12.
——— (1920a). Beyond the pleasure principle. *S. E.,* 18.
——— (1920b). The psychogenesis of a case of homosexuality in a woman. *S. E.,* 18.
——— (1931). Female sexuality. *S. E.,* 21.
——— (1937). Analysis terminable and interminable. *S. E.,* 23.
FRIEDMAN, S.S. (1990). *Penelope's Web.* Cambridge, Eng.: Cambridge Univ. Press.
GLENN, J. (1993). Dora's dynamics, diagnosis and therapy: old and modern views. *Annual Psychoanal.,* 21:125–138.
HORNEY, K. (1926). The flight from womanhood: the masculine complex in women, as viewed by men and by women. *Int. J. Psychoanal.,* 7:324–329.
LAMPL-DE GROOT, J. (1927). The evolution of the Oedipus complex in women. In *The Psychoanalytic Reader,* ed. R. Fliess. New York: Int. Univ. Press, 1948, pp. 207–222.

LEHMANN, H. (1983). Reflections on Freud's reaction to the death of his mother. *Psychoanal. Q.*, 52:237–249.
MASSON, J.M., Ed. (1985). *The Complete Letters of Sigmund Freud to Wilhelm Fliess.* Cambridge, MA: Harvard Univ. Press.
ROGOW, A.A. (1978). A further footnote to Freud's "Fragment of an analysis of a case of hysteria." *J. Amer. Psychoanal. Assn.*, 26:331–356.
SCHAFER, R. (1974). Problems in Freud's psychology of women. *J. Amer. Psychoanal. Assn.*, 22:459–485.
────── (1993). Five readings of Freud's "Observations on transference love." In *On Freud's Observations on Transference Love*, ed. E.S. Person & A. Hagelin. New Haven, CT: Yale Univ. Press.
SHENGOLD, L.L. (1991). *Father, Don't You See I'm Burning?* New Haven, CT: Yale Univ. Press.
STONE, L. (1961). *The Psychoanalytic Situation.* New York: Int. Univ. Press.
YOUNG-BRUEHL, E. (1990). *Freud on Women.* New York: Norton.

II.
THE THEORY OF THE PSYCHOLOGY OF WOMEN

Figure 4. Judith Shea (1991) *Midlife Venus*. Michael Bliss

FEMINIST PSYCHOANALYTIC THEORY: AMERICAN AND FRENCH REACTIONS TO FREUD

Helen Rosen
Elaine Zickler

> Ever since Freud's observations on women and their psychology were published, there have been revisions, expansions, and reactions to his ideas. Most recently, feminist psychoanalytic theorists from the United States and France have been fertile in producing revisions to traditional psychoanalytic theory about women. Reviewing the disjointed psychoanalytic traditions of the two countries provides a context for understanding the different approaches to feminist thinking that each country has produced. American feminist psychoanalytic theorists tend to stage reversals of traditional Freudian theory, while the French feminist psychoanalytic theorists have had to position themselves intellectually and politically with reference to the teachings of Lacan. This paper examines selected contemporary theorists from these two countries—Jean Baker Miller, Nancy Chodorow, and Carol Gilligan from the United States and Julia Kristeva, Luce Irigaray, and Helene Cixous from France—and discusses the difficulties of constructing a theory of sexual difference that avoids the pitfalls of either biological essentialism or its reverse, social constructionism.

Freud's observations on women and their psychology were controversial almost as quickly as they were published. Since then, through more and less active periods in the development of psychoanalytic theory concerning women, a large body of psychoanalytic theory that continues to question and expand upon Freud's ideas has evolved. But a specifically feminist psychoanalytic theory has also developed within the context of particular intellectual and national

---

Dr. Rosen is on the faculty of the Institute of the Philadelphia Association for Psychoanalysis; Dr. Zickler has a Ph.D. in English from Bryn Mawr College and has written psychoanalytic articles on James Boswell and John Donne's poetry and prose. The authors would like to express their appreciation to Elisabeth Young-Bruehl, Ph.D., for her helpful suggestions during the preparation of this article.

traditions, influenced not only by differences in culture, but also by differences in the ways psychoanalysis itself was first introduced and then incorporated into a country's psychiatric, as well as political, social, and intellectual, practices. This paper will look at selected contemporary feminist psychoanalytic theorists from the United States and France, two countries that have been fertile in producing revisions to traditional psychoanalytic theory about women. A brief review of their disjoint psychoanalytic traditions will help provide the background for understanding the major concepts proposed by the feminist theorists of each country.

Psychoanalysis was imported to the United States in 1909, the year of Freud's historic trip across the ocean. In general, it was enthusiastically embraced by the burgeoning field of psychology, leading Ferenczi (1927) to write, "Now, visiting America again after almost twenty years, I had occasion to observe how lasting and far-reaching an influence Dr. Freud's teachings exert on all strata of American society. . . . Time and again, I have noticed that it seems fairly impossible to listen to a conversation for any length of time, without hearing problems of psychoanalysis and the name of Freud mentioned" (p. 17). When European analysts such as Karen Horney immigrated to the United States in the 1930's, debates about Freud's views on women came with them. Ferenczi's analysand and student Clara Thompson joined the discussion and helped bring American analysts to it. But this tradition was largely eclipsed during the war.

In the late 1920's and throughout the war period, the endorsement of psychoanalysis in the United States became intertwined with "the struggle of various learned professions in America to secure respect and recognition for expert knowledge and the training needed to acquire it" (Jones, 1961, p. 469), in this case, medicine and the specialty of psychiatry. In 1925 A. A. Brill wrote an article published in a New York newspaper expressing his disapproval of "lay analysis," and in 1926 the New York Legislature passed a bill making the practice of lay psychoanalysis illegal. While Freud supported lay analysis, it was a battle he did not win in the United States. Thus, until quite recently, psychoanalysis in the United States had been practiced exclusively by physicians, a province of the medical specialty psychiatry, and a male-dominated profession in which critical questions about female psychology seldom arose.

Feminist Psychoanalytic Theory

In France the beginnings of psychoanalysis were quite different. According to Oliner (1988) psychoanalysis in France began relatively late, and had a rather unorthodox introduction into the country. The initial enthusiasm for psychoanalysis came from literary figures, especially the surrealist poet, André Breton. Breton apparently learned about Freud in 1916, initiated a correspondence with Freud in 1919, and paid him a visit in 1921. Later, Breton was disillusioned with Freud, as he found the father of psychoanalysis lacking in the revolutionary political stance he assumed would be present in someone with such revolutionary ideas about the human situation (p. 24). The Paris Psychoanalytic Society, founded in 1926, was largely the result of the efforts of Marie Bonaparte, an analysand of Freud and a nonmedical analyst, and the Paris Psychoanalytic made no distinction between medical and nonmedical analysts. Later, when the Society was reestablished after World War II, Lacan was an important influence on the development of French psychoanalysis. Lacan, who, like Freud, was a physician by training, was determined to claim Freud's teachings as his own, by rereading them through the modern linguistic anthropologists, but also through Hegel, Aristotle, Plato, and the early Church Fathers.

As a result of their historical legacy, psychoanalysts in France tend to think of themselves as the guardians of Freud's intellectual heritage. Because French psychoanalysis developed outside of medical psychiatry, it can be neatly contrasted to American psychoanalysis in several crucial aspects. Whereas American psychoanalysis developed within the medical model of disease and cure, and is consequently pragmatic in its aims, French psychoanalysis tends to be less concerned with outcome and more illustrative of the uncertainties and potential interminabilities of the process of analysis itself. American psychoanalysis emphasized, particularly in the post World War II era, the normalizing aspects of psychoanalysis, the need and ability of the ego to adapt to external realities, thus opening the door for psychoanalysis to be used by some as an ally to conservative ideologies. By contrast, French psychoanalysis always allied itself with the intellectual left, with the Marxists and then the feminists, reading Freud against the biologism of the medical psychiatric tradition. Consequently, American feminist psychoanalysts found themselves reacting against psychoanalysis in a global way, focusing on the figure of Freud, of course, but in his particular incarnation within the tradition of American psychiatric psychoanalysis and ego psychology. French feminist psychoanalysts, on the other hand, never rejected Freud, but have produced their own readings of Freudian psychoanalysis, reinventing it from within instead of, for the most part, enacting a reversal.

These very different backgrounds, then, inevitably resulted in very different approaches within the two countries to understanding the psychology of women. In what follows, we hope to explicate what some of these differences are, and how both approaches provide valuable challenges to orthodox psychoanalytic views.

FEMINIST PSYCHOANALYTIC THEORY IN THE UNITED STATES

In 1963, Betty Friedan wrote about "the problem that has no name." Over and over, throughout the text of *The Feminine Mystique*, she indicted Freud and American psychoanalysis for contributing to the problems of women:

> The feminine mystique, elevated by Freudian theory into a scientific religion, sounded a single, overprotective, life-restricting, future-denying note for women. Girls who grew up playing baseball, baby-sitting, mastering geometry—although independent enough, almost resourceful enough, to meet the problems of the fission-fusion era—were told by the most advanced thinkers of our time to go back, and live their lives as if they were Noras, restricted to the doll's house by Victorian prejudice [p. 116].

In the ensuing feminist movement in America, issues of male control and dominance, both in a woman's everyday life and in the development of theories about women, were given prominence. Theory-building for the new, liberated age had a political as well as a scientific mission.

As a result of this context, much of the thinking developed by American feminist psychoanalytic writers tends to be in the form of "reversals," i.e., traditional theories about the nature and causes of women's problems are challenged by reversing either the label

Feminist Psychoanalytic Theory

placed on women by the traditional theoretical point of view or the cause of the problem as stated by traditional theorists. The effect of this reversal is to demonstrate phallocentrism in the prevailing theories of personality that have defined both mental health and mental illness for women. Specifically, American psychologists have taken Freud's (and others') characterizations of women as more childish, dependent, less moral, and needing to be loved more than men, and redefined these criticisms as positive, normative, and desirable. They have taken the idea that women's problems are the result of internal "dysfunction" and redefined the cause as "external," i.e., women have emotional problems in a society which, because it has been designed by men, fails to value, support, and encourage women's greater wish for connectedness and attachment. This method of reversal as a way of rethinking the psychology of women can be seen in the work of three of the most influential American feminist psychologists, Jean Baker Miller, Nancy Chodorow, and Carol Gilligan. Miller's *Toward a New Psychology of Women* (1976), *The Reproduction of Mothering* (1978) by Nancy Chodorow, and Carol Gilligan's *In a Different Voice* (1982) represent most clearly the direction American feminist psychoanalytic theory has taken. The theories of these three women are not psychoanalytic in the traditional sense in that, for the most part, they are not concerned with intrapsychic reality at all (Chodorow's work comes closest to developing a model of the mind). But they have been embraced by the feminist community as appropriate answers to the need for a theory of women that corrects the "misunderstandings" of psychoanalytic theory.

Jean Baker Miller

When Miller's *Toward a New Psychology of Women* was published, Jessie Bernard was quoted on the blurb as saying, "It also shows how women can come to recognize their own value and thus overcome the crippling fears and insecurities bred into them and rationalized by classic psychoanalysis." The task that Miller and others of this period set for themselves was to examine so-called differences between men and women, and to challenge traditional definitions of normalcy and deviance. In this book, Miller examines existing theories of development and their assumptions concerning what is "normal" and what is considered "pathological" in male-dominated psychologies. She points out that existing theories of development have largely been based on the concept of development as a process of separating oneself from others. The goals of being predominantly independent and autonomous are held to be almost universal in these psychologies. She goes on to posit that women and their development do not easily fit this mold; women tend to be more "relationship-oriented" than "separation-oriented." She criticizes traditional theory for failing to address the capacity for relatedness as an indicator of mental health. Miller draws on recent advances in infant research that support the importance of an innate need for interrelatedness. She proposes that the earliest mental representation of the self is one whose emotional core is attended to by others and who begins to attend to others. She also proposes that this early interactional self is the same for boys and for girls; however, as they grow up, she believes that girls are encouraged to expand these skills while boys are discouraged from doing so.

According to Miller a woman's sense of self as well as her mental health is based on her ability to function as a "being-in-relationship." The nature of her relationships are seen to be more important to her mental health then they would be to a man. When woman's so-called greater dependency, or need for relationships, is viewed as normative and desirable, rather than as immature and pathological, different conceptions of the causes of mental illness must follow. From Miller's perspective, woman's inner turmoil, depression, and other emotional ailments are the result of living in a society that disregards her normal needs. Men, who have most of the power within society, are socialized not to value relationships and connectedness in the way women do; thus women are unable to have the kind of affiliations in relationships with men that are necessary for their mental health.

> It is not that men are not concerned about relationships, or that men do not have deep yearnings for affiliation. Indeed, this is exactly what people in the field of psychodynamics are constantly finding—evidence of these needs in men as well as in women, deep *under the surface* of social appearance.... Men have deprived themselves of this mode, left it with women. Most important, they have made themselves unable to really *believe* in it.... Men are led to cast out this faith, even to condemn it in themselves, and build their lives on something else. *And they are rewarded for doing so* [pp. 87–88].

Feminist Psychoanalytic Theory

By contrast, a woman's sense of self develops in the context of making and maintaining affiliations and relationships. "Women have different organizing principles around which their psyches are structured. One of these principles is that they exist to serve other people's needs... Women are taught that their main goal in life is to serve others—first men, and later children" (p. 61). Problems occur, however, when women are *forced* or expected to do so rather than when they are responding out of their own felt need.

Miller sees female development as reaching a critical stage of conflict in adolescence, when a girl's burgeoning sexuality is treated by society as bad and wrong. The adolescent girl, who has up to this point been intensely engaged in relationships of all kinds, becomes passive and frustrated by the social message that her own perceptions of her sexual and bodily experiences are bad. "Doing for others" becomes an acceptable solution to maintaining relationships while avoiding sexuality. In heterosexual relationships she experiences conflict over her own desires: on the one hand she wants to and feels she should be attuned to the needs of others, but on the other hand excluding her own perceptions and desires from the relationship causes her conflict and frustration. "At adolescence the girl is seeking fulfillment of two very important needs: to use herself, including her sexual and all her capacities, but seeking to do so within a context that will fulfill her desire to be a 'being-in-relationship' . . . She wishes that the other person(s) will be able to enter into a relationship in this fashion" (Miller, 1990, p. 447).

Miller's ideas revived a set of ideas originated by Karen Horney and Clara Thompson that view female pathology largely as a result of conflict with a society that fails to appreciate and support what women need for a satisfying life. As was true in Horney's day, Miller also believes that women's needs are not easily attainable in today's society.

Nancy Chodorow

Nancy Chodorow is the author of *The Reproduction of Mothering* (1978), *Feminism and Psychoanalytic Theory* (1989) and *Femininities, Masculinities, Sexualities: Freud and Beyond* (1994). The first book was an important attempt at questioning traditional psychoanalytic theory, and became a frequently quoted resource for later feminist writers. In this book, we also see a "reframing" of women's supposed greater need for relationships as a positive and healthy developmental achievement rather than as a negative, pathological developmental deviation. For Chodorow, however, women's psychology is neither a biological given nor solely the result of culture. Chodorow asserts that much of the psychology of men and women can be traced to early development and the fact that women are the primary caretakers of children of both sexes. Little girls can grow up wanting to be like mother, identifying with her and with her caretaking and nurturing behavior. As a result, they tend to be less differentiated from their mother than boys and to experience a longer preoedipal attachment. Little boys, on the other hand, learn that they are *not* the same as mother, that they must differentiate themselves from her and from what she signifies. Thus, Chodorow explains, little girls develop more flexible or permeable ego boundaries than boys, which serve them well in their future role of mother. In Chodorow's theory as in Miller's love and relationships come to have very different meanings for men and women. For example, little girls do not ever experience an exclusive change of object from mother to father. When the little girl turns to father in the oedipal phase, it is "in addition to," not "in place of" the relationship to mother. Little boys, however, repress their attachment to mother and seek to replace her in later life by someone "like mother." In consequence, they retain an exclusivity in their relationships with women (which remains dyadic) whereas little girls' relationships with men move into the realm of triadic relationships. When the little boy and little girl replicate their early family dynamics in their adult relationships, he looks for exclusivity, which he both yearns for and fears. She is more "inclusive" in her relationships and is less conflicted concerning her needs for love and attachment.

In essence, Chodorow's (1978) thesis is that women's mothering is the *cause* of male dominance. Because mothers are the prime nurturers of children, they perpetuate a society in which daughters may become substitutes for mothers and develop "insufficiently individuated senses of self" and "sons may become substitutes for husbands, and must engage in defensive assertion of ego boundaries and repression of emotional needs" (p. 212). In the introduction to her more recent book, Chodorow (1989) enlarges her perspective to argue for a broader understanding of women's inequality, seeing

Feminist Psychoanalytic Theory

women's mothering as only one factor, albeit an important one, in the political situation of women. She understands her own emphasis on the role of mothers as a "reaction to and dialogue with the nearly exclusive Freudian focus on the father and the Oedipus complex" (p. 6). Her current views are more complex and multidetermined in that they encompass a broader range of factors than male dominance.

Carol Gilligan

Carol Gilligan has been a major player on the American feminist psychology scene ever since her work on the moral development of girls in the early 'eighties. Faludi (1991) considers Gilligan's (1982) book, *In a Different Voice*, "one of the most widely quoted and influential feminist works of the '80's." Reacting to both Freud and the work of her mentor, Kohlberg, Gilligan examined the basis on which evaluations of moral judgment (or superego development) were being made, rather than accepting the standard criteria, which seemed to find women lacking in that sphere. She describes a long history in Western tradition in which the representation of the self as separate and autonomous has dominated. As a result, definitions of morality have privileged conceptions of "duty" and "responsibility"—approving actions guided by an internalized conscience. At the same time, she writes, women have been viewed as failing to meet definitions of autonomy and individuation because they have a different orientation to the world, one that values connection and commitment. This orientation results in a different kind of morality for women. The male "moral voice" exemplifies what has been traditionally labeled "morality": decision-making based on ideas of impartial justice, rules, and rights. Women's morality is based on ideas of nonviolence, the wish not to hurt others, as well as on the values of nurturance and caring. Gilligan sees these two "predispositions" as resulting from the parent-child experience, in which everyone "has been vulnerable to oppression and to abandonment" (1990, p. 481).

Looking at adolescence, as Miller did, Gilligan sees teenage girls as resisting the detachment embedded in traditional views of morality and mental health, while struggling for inclusive solutions to the problems of conflicting loyalties they face. She writes: "Psychological development is usually traced along a single line of progression from inequality to equality, following the incremental steps of the child's physical growth. Attachment is associated with inequality, and development linked to separation. Thus the story of love becomes assimilated to a story about authority and power" (1990, p. 15).

For both Gilligan and Miller, women's sense of identity and morality is embedded in the context of relationships. Further, the message is that we must discard the old criteria of mental health and healthy development, giving up the old norms by which we judge the behavior of others. Those norms are only applicable to men. While initially Gilligan (1982) does not characterize these "voices" as belonging to only one gender, as she proceeds through her argument, she does indeed draw stereotypical generalizations about her findings, asserting that men make moral judgments based on an "ideal of perfection," while women make determinations based on an "ideal of care." She does not address the issue of whether or not these differences are inherent, or based on socialization in a gender-biased society.

Both Gilligan's and Miller's theories emphasize differences between the sexes and make a plea for appreciation of the attributes of each. Their ideas can appeal to both feminist and antifeminist forces because, while acknowledging sexual differences (and the underappreciation of feminine attributes) can sensitize us to the potential biases inherent in theory, they can also supply the seeds of a new kind of stereotyping that can have a different kind of "retro," antifeminist appeal. A theory of "normal development" based on behavior of women raised in our society (which is, admittedly, gender-biased), risks doing a disservice to women in exactly the same way Freud is criticized for—it fails to take into account the role of socialization and adaptation to the culture.

FRENCH FEMINIST PSYCHOANALYTIC THEORY

Any introduction to French feminist psychoanalytic theory must begin with Lacan and with Lacan's rereading of Freudian theory through the insights of linguistic theory, especially the structural linguistics of Jakobson (1960) and de Saussure (1959), and the linguistic anthropologist, Lévi-Strauss (1967, 1969). The three major

Feminist Psychoanalytic Theory

French women analysts and feminist writers whose works we shall examine—Kristeva, Irigaray, and Cixous—have had to position themselves intellectually and politically with reference to, and often in contradistinction to, Lacan's influential teachings.

Jacques Lacan

Lacan offers neither a biological nor a sociocultural theory of sexual difference, but a linguistic one. This is a crucial distinction which must be grasped before his difficult theorizing can be approached. According to de Saussure, difference is a structural necessity in language; binary oppositions at the most basic units of speech, between vowel and consonant, sound and silence, presence and absence, enable us to distinguish phonemes, morphemes, words, and larger units of language. Similarly, according to Lacan, it is sexual difference which constitutes culture and social structures, and not the other way around.

Language inscribes sexual difference in its vocabulary and syntax (this is more obvious in a language like French that employs the masculine and feminine article, for example). Lacan's most often cited visual aid is the cartoon of the two identical doors, side by side, one marked men (*hommes*) and the other women (*femmes*). To take up a position as a man or a woman in this system is to be subjected to a basic *binary* opposition (like the binaries that govern the production of sounds) that reduces the *polymorphous* nature of human sexual desire to a choice between two opposites whose social and cultural constraints are already in place within a hierarchy that values the man. Lacan specifically refutes biological essentialism in thus under scoring the cultural and linguistic structuring of sexuality, that is, masculinity and femininity are not psychological constellations that form naturally at the site of male or female sexuality. Rather, the psychological states of masculinity or femininity in any culture derive from this arbitrary duality; from the visible difference in the sexes, the presence or absence of the penis, a cultural ordering of sexuality is constructed.

For Lacan, it is neither culture nor biology that imposes sexual difference on men and women so much as it is sexual difference which is the founding moment of culture. This was Freud's (1913) insight about the cultural significance of the castration complex in *Totem and Taboo*. It is Lacan's central insight as well, but recast in terms of the subordination of every human subject, male and female, to the castrating effects of access to language itself. Language, conceived broadly as the symbolic order, castrates to the extent that it restricts and fixes meaning for the human speaking subject; it cuts off play and imposes a symbolic law. According to Jakobson, we use language in a lawful manner in ordinary language; poets play with the limits of form and meaning in language; but the psychotic speaks outside its limits. Therefore the speaking subject, as Lacan describes him, is both the subject of, and subject to language. One must first submit to the law before one has access to the privileges of its order.

The phallus, as Lacan theorizes, cannot be conflated with or reduced to the male penis because both men and women are subject to the castrating effects of language. According to de Saussure, the phallus, as Lacan conceives of it, is a privileged linguistic signifier. It comes to symbolize the sexual division at the foundation of the symbolic order; as such, it symbolizes the penis as well as the clitoris. But, as Freud observed, the female remains less "spectacular" than the male. That is, for obvious, or at least more easily observable, reasons, the elision of phallus and penis is too easily accomplished. This conflation of the signifier of sexual pleasure and power with the male organ has become perpetuated by cultural practices and beliefs, whether religious, scientific, or literary. An illusion arises that the male, by virtue of having a penis, has or is the phallus. Therefore, according to Lacan, patriarchal governments and religions, essentialist psychologies based on biological difference, literary conventions of courtly love and romance, as well as certain varieties of feminist theory, all share in this illusion. Lacan's aim is to sever the binary polarity of masculine-feminine by interrogating the connection between the fantasy of the complementary other that is the underpinning of any possible sexual relation at all, and the symbolic structures—political, scientific, religious, literary—which tend to support the fantasy. Like Freud, then, Lacan would say that there is only one sex, one sexual pleasure, and it is phallic; however, it is not determined by biology, by ownership of a penis, but by a linguistic relationship to the symbolic phallus. Lacan's theorizing persistently subsumes the body into discourse and refuses any recourse to biological essentialism. He places psychoanalysis squarely in the realm of language.

Feminist Psychoanalytic Theory

Lacan's project is not to assume *a priori* a difference and a natural sexual relation already determined by anatomy and to conduct his investigations along the lines of this difference, but to analyze the discourse of sexual difference itself. How do human beings, as speaking subjects, whether male or female, position themselves in relation to the phallus? What is the importance of the castration complex to human subjects? And what can be said about femininity, and specifically about feminine sexual pleasure?

The problem for feminist theory, for women in the world and in analysis as well, is that Lacan, for all his analytic rigor and elegance, seems to have solved the woman problem by proving that the Woman (*la femme*) does not, theoretically, psychoanalytically, exist, except as an exclusion from language (Lacan, 1982, p. 144). Placing a line of erasure through the definite article *la*, Lacan graphically emphasizes the arbitrary assignment of "Woman" to anyone not possessing the penis/phallus. He stresses that, far from being a category filled with linguistic meaning, Woman is defined as the absence of Man, as the negative of Man, as all that is beyond or in excess of Man. For women who find themselves relegated to this empty set, to this exclusionary zone outside of phallic language, it is clear on the one hand that the symbolic phallus does not separate from the actual penis without great pain and protest, and on the other hand that language itself seems to be at issue, and not just feminine sexual pleasure.

For Lacan, the pleasure that the sexes take in each other, or, more precisely, that speaking beings derive from whatever sexual act with whatever sex, is strictly in the realm of fantasy and *jouissance*. This French word for enjoyment encompasses and then surpasses orgasm, especially as the orgasm is defined in phallic terms: erection, ejaculation, detumescence. Lacan asks the question about a *jouissance* specific to women and offers the mystifying answer that she comes but knows "nothing about it" (p. 147). The language accommodates only one libido, the male. The woman (who does not exist as such, as a universal) exists only as a fantasy of complementarity to the male; she exists as a support, a supplement to phallic language and phallic sexuality. Consequently, the woman becomes Other, the site of all that is mysterious, unsayable, even mystical in the language of love.

Lacan's theory initially offers a way out for feminist psychoanalytic theory—out of biological essentialism into the realm of structuralism. Lacanian feminists point out the ways that Lacan has deconstructed vestiges of biological determinism in Freudian theory; for them, he makes a return to Freud possible. But Lacan, like Freud before him, poses challenges to women theorists attempting to articulate a psychoanalytic theory for feminist writing and political action. If women are subjected to and excluded from the cultural order, and if language perpetuates the subjugation of women, then it seems insufficient to uncover the illusion of the phallus/penis. The French feminist reaction to Lacan's phallocentric and phallologocentric theory has been both passionate and varied in its attempt to theorize woman, to find a place for her in language and culture that is not ordered by the phallus.

Helene Cixous

Cixous has been, not surprisingly, most accessible to and most attractive to American feminist psychoanalytic circles because she utterly rejects the phallicism of Freud and Lacan, assigning primary value to feminine *jouissance*. Cixous (1981) retains from Lacanian theory the refusal "to confuse the biological and the cultural" (p. 245), that is to fit the categories "masculine" and "feminine" neatly atop "male" and "female." She constructs what amounts to a feminist utopian polemic.

Cixous demonstrates her abilities to write in what she would define as the "masculine" or phallic mode, deftly exhibiting her analytic and critical facilities in her readings of Freudian and Lacanian texts. In the same essays, she then proceeds to write in the "feminine," to model an *écriture feminine* for her readers, a writing replete with word play, syntactical and logical reversals and excesses, a writing that she claims attempts to include the voice, the drives, the body of the woman who writes it. Indeed, Cixous prophesies that such a woman's writing will take the body of woman from its exclusionary exile, and return it "against" the logos (p. 250). The question remains, of course, whether any writing that succeeds at communicating can be said to be against the logos, against reason, logic, and syntax, and so not participating in the phallic economy after all.

Cixous' manifesto of feminine desire urges women to resist the diagnoses and the "psychoanalytic closure" (p. 263) foisted upon

Feminist Psychoanalytic Theory

them by Freud and Lacan. Like her American sisters cited earlier, Cixous sees in psychoanalysis a theory that first excludes, and then pathologizes women. Countering this phallic gesture, she envisions a "maternal, feminine utopia," a "writing" that rejects castration, rejects the death drive, and reflects a "gestation drive." Cixous acknowledges no threat in the fusional maternal presence she extols. The revolutionary possibilities can only work to the good; likewise, the mother is ever the one "who makes everything all right, who nourishes, and who stands up against separation" (p. 252). Again, the question remains as to whether such a total gesture of idealization does not work to marginalize and mystify the woman as "Other," as site of all that is not only repressed and unconscious, but true and good as well. If Cixous accuses Freud and Lacan of eliding and conflating the phallus with the penis, is she simply conducting a reversal of terms in her writing, conflating the *jouissance* of the mother with the female and infusing this gesture with positive ideological value? Certainly, Kristeva (1990) hints at such a danger in "Women's Time," in which she labels such feminist yearnings for maternal utopias a "phantasms" capable of mobilizing forces of terrible violence "unless one challenges precisely the myth of the archiac mother" (p. 390).

Feminist theory must struggle with the realities of the political and economic status of women in the world. A theory as powerful as psychoanalysis, capable of effecting its own world view, both seduces and repels women as they search for the theoretical underpinnings of political action and of social reconstruction of themselves. While Cixous's writings can be read as an essentializing gesture, equal but opposite to the ones she accuses Freud and Lacan of performing, it is nevertheless true that we somehow "see" what she is doing far more clearly than we "see" it when Freud or Lacan do it. That is, to the extent that phallicism has become naturalized in our discourse and in our practices, Cixous's "feminine" counterreading and counterwriting allow us to see a discourse of biological essentialism in the process of construction.

Luce Irigaray

Irigaray, a psychoanalyst and feminist writer and theoretician, performs perhaps the strongest "misreadings" of Freud's and Lacan's writings on female sexuality, in the process forcing the reader to begin to think differently about sexual difference. In the midseventies, Irigaray, then on the faculty of the school of psychoanalysis at the University of Vincennes, was prevented by Lacan from teaching a course on her own theoretical project based on her writings in *Speculum of the Other Woman* (1985a; Turkle, 1992). Placed on the margins of the psychoanalytic establishment that trained her, Irigaray used her position to read the major male psychoanalytic theorists as well as the major Western male philosophers—Plato, Aristotle, and Hegel—on the subject of woman and on woman as speaking subject.

Irigaray's project, indeed, cannot be grasped narrowly, in the realm of the consulting room. What she proposes is no less than an analysis that reaches to the sexualized assumptions of Western metaphysical discourse itself. To the extent that psychoanalysis does not examine the "historical determinants of its discourse . . . it remains caught up in phallocentrism, which it claims to make into a universal and eternal value" (1985b, p. 103). To this end, then, Irigaray rereads philosophy and psychoanalysis, demonstrating that sexual difference is everywhere absent in these discourses; what she finds are discourses of mimesis, of the "flat mirror," of sameness, oneness, of binary oppositions and hierarchies (the presence or absence of the penis/phallus) that place the male in the subject position and the female in the object position. Irigaray diagnoses phallicism as a symptomatic denial of real difference between the sexes, a denial amplified in Western metaphysics into an obsession with oneness, wholeness, and unity at the expense of plurality, fragmentation, and diffusion. Truth, like phallic sexuality, assumes a unitary nature in philosophy; the polymorphic nature of desire and the body of the woman are systematically denied entry into the language of metaphysics.

In the Kleinian language of object relations, one could say that, according to Irigaray's analysis, the Western male is historically in the schizoid position in relation to the female. She exists for him always and only in parts, and subject to his projections and introjections. In Freudian terms, the woman is fetishized, made to stand in for a lack, an absence that is denied. That is, for the man, the woman is the phallus that he, in turn, can possess. Irigaray thus agrees with Lacan's conclusion that there is no possibility of a sexual relation in

Feminist Psychoanalytic Theory

this discourse, but only of use, of mastery and submission. Relation, after all, presupposes the existence of two different and equal subjects.

Irigaray's goal is the discovery and articulation of the feminine, not as the complement of the masculine, its negative underside, its imaginary waste, its nurturing "matter"; nor as a simple reversal of terms, claiming a feminine power that is identical to its masculine counterpart, enacting a simple displacement of terms; but as a true difference as yet unexplored, unexperienced, and unarticulated.

The risk Irigaray takes, of course, is that in attempting to imagine the unimaginable, to lift a historical repression, to articulate what has remained absent from discourse, she necessarily reverts to a new set of binaries and reversals, even while disclaiming this strategy as inadequate to her project. If the masculine is identified with solidity and formal, univocal truth, then the feminine might (or must) be conceived of as fluid, amorphous, and polyvocal. If the discourse of masculinity requires that the feminine hold the zero-place of absence and negativity, then the discourse of femininity might (or must) be more connected to all that we relegate to the "unconscious." Irigaray puts Antigone in the place of Oedipus, as mythic model for woman, overtly tying her to blood, earth, and divinity. This is a "difference" that begins to sound and look the same.

And yet, Irigaray clearly intends to keep the subject open, if only by admitting that she is just as caught up in the logic of "phallocratic power" and the "circularity of its discursive economy" (p. 157) as any man speaking from a position of philosophical mastery. The conundrum remains that she cannot really escape the discursive system that she claimed as object of her critique. This is not to say that such a critique cannot be mounted, only that closure is somehow to be avoided. It is at this point that deconstruction becomes relevant to feminist theory as a way of, in Elam's (1994) words, keeping "the category of women incessantly in question, as a permanently contested site of meaning. Therefore, no history of progress should be allowed to suggest a final goal, an end or solution, to the question of women" (pp. 41–42).

When asked about her own practice of psychoanalysis, Irigaray makes a number of assertions, suggesting that she wishes to conduct an analysis of psychoanalysis first of all, to examine its "historical determinants" and sexualized assumptions, to interrogate its hierarchical practices, to once again make it a "plague" (in Freud's words) instead of the socially conforming institution she claims it has become (Irigaray, 1985b, p. 146). Psychoanalysis, after all, is a profoundly deconstructive practice as Freud theorized it; Irigaray would take his theory to the next horizon, that of sexual difference.

Julia Kristeva

Julia Kristeva, herself a linguist and a psychoanalyst trained by Lacan, concentrates on the semiotics of language, an area neglected by Freud and Lacan. For Kristeva the semiotic refers to the preoedipal stages of life, before the child has acquired language. The centrality of the Oedipus complex in Freudian theory with its focus on the father's prohibition against mother-son incest tended to keep the preoedipal and the maternal in the dark regions of psychoanalytic theory and practice, at least until Melanie Klein and the object-relations theorists moved it forward. Kristeva offers a linguistic revision of object-relations theory. Where the logos, or the word, assumes phallic power in Freudian and Lacanian theory, Kristeva explores the preverbal beginnings of speech and finds them in the undifferentiated stage of infant development which she calls the preobjectal or "abject" regions of the maternal body. These preverbal beginnings emerge linguistically in what structural linguists define as the suprasegmental phonemes—rhythm, intonation, gaps, pauses. These comprise the nonverbal parts of speech. According to Kristeva, the woman, specifically the mother, is not completely renounced when the human subject enters into the symbolic order and acquires language, but is always present as its enabling background, its spaces, its melodies and repetitions. While the symbolic law of the father, or the phallus, may govern the logic and syntax of speech, the semiotic mother still "holds" language in place or, conversely, disrupts its meaning, erupting in the various "poetics" of speech, including psychosis. It is important to note that Kristeva does not use the terms "maternal" and "paternal" in a sexualized way; the semiotic, being preverbal, is not a gendered space, not yet divided up into male and female.

Kristeva, like Lacan, produces texts at once political, literary, and clinical in scope and implication. In *Powers of Horror* (1982), the power of the archaic maternal enigma is her subject as she analyzes

Feminist Psychoanalytic Theory

cultural texts of contamination and purification from Leviticus to Celine. In doing so, Kristeva renews the power of psychoanalysis to apply itself to a wide range of cultural texts and practices, from religious dietary restrictions to anti-Semitism and fascism. Subsequent studies of the varieties of erotic love (*Tales of Love*, 1987a) and of depression and melancholy (*Black Sun*, 1987b) exhibit the same impressive range of scholarship and discerning eclecticism.

Perhaps the strongest music that emerges and erupts through Kristeva's own linguistic expertise, however, is that of forgiveness, compassion, ethics, and individual human rights. She has been accused of a lyrical humanism by her more radical feminist critics because of her refusal to embrace a politics of violent opposition. It is certainly the voice of the analyst that comes through her writing over and above the voice of the politician. But it is neither a soft voice nor an irrational one, even as it argues for the necessity of a language beyond reason, a "poetic language" that resists and pushes at the totality of rationalist "meaning." It is not insignificant that Kristeva has also been accused of advocating continual revolution, or anarchism, of validating maternal *jouissance* over paternal law. It is in the realm of speech, language, and writing that Kristeva envisions the possibility of revolution. In fact, she has written that women long for the father, for the law; she has also written that "modern society . . . can no longer afford to impose its laws without bestowing upon the demented drives that underlie the speaking being an analytic benevolence, without introducing the psychoanalytic experience into the conception of human rights and laws and in this way, saving them from abstraction and a pretentious universality" (1993, p. 174).

The notion that the "psychoanalytic experience" can rescue something individual and unique "from abstraction and a pretentious universality" seems to be a large claim, larger than the current purview of psychoanalysis, especially in America, would seem to grant it. Kristeva (1990), in her essay, "Women's Time," takes on the project of analyzing the women's movement, literally the movement of women through time, both mythical and historic time. She negotiates, in psychoanalytic terms, the territory of second-generation feminism, "the terrain of the inseparable conjunction of the sexual and the symbolic, in order to try to discover, first, the specificity of the female, and then, in the end, that of each individual woman" (p. 382). Kristeva never abandons the rigors of her analytical stance, never gives in to the seductions of temporary closures to the questions she asks. Addressing herself to the politics and the ethics of various brands of feminist thought, European and American, giving a balanced assessment of their "contributions and dangers," she concludes her essay by appealing to a "new ethics," obtainable only by moving on past this feminist "moment" in which we find ourselves now (p. 396). This "moment" seems threatened by a reversion to universalist and essentialist thought; she implies that the next moment might be able to contain the full expression of human sexual difference.

CONCLUSION

Feminist psychoanalytic theories that focus on reversals of terms, whether to valorize, normalize or pathologize particular traits conceived of as particular to one gender or the other, run the same risks and dangers as the old theories they set out to overturn and replace. As Young-Bruehl (1994) has pointed out, " . . . emphasizing sex or gender differences seems to be a function of a disposition or a need to identify with a single sex or gender and usually to valorize it by asserting that the other sex or gender is lacking" (p. 386). Both American and French feminist theories fall, at times, into the polarity of reversals and gender stereotyping. Psychoanalysis in the United States has a tradition of pragmatism, of goal-setting, and, at times, of evaluations cast in terms of adjustment to existing reality. American feminist psychoanalytic theorists tend also toward an emphasis on outcomes, and toward the creation of new definitions of masculine and feminine, health and pathology. The French have a tradition of philosophic inquiry for its own sake, and of using intellectual disciplines for the purpose of subverting social and political realities. French feminist psychoanalytic theorists tend more consciously to ideology and to the relations between language, thought, and the unconscious in shaping individual subjectivity. The clinician is rightly concerned with practice and outcome, the theoretician with intellectual foundations of thought and practice. But clinicians cannot ignore the theoretical underpinnings and ideological biases of their

Feminist Psychoanalytic Theory

practice any more than theoreticians can ignore the practical implications of their theories.

The fact that each of these theorists subjects psychoanalytic theory to such vigorous clinical and philosophical interrogation, and insists that its practice is worth remaking and has effects that transcend but in no way subsume the clinical setting, makes them worthy of our attention. In the writings and the practice of these women, feminism and psychoanalysis are subjected to close reading, to radically other ways of thinking and writing. We must be grateful to them for raising the questions that they raise. With regard to understanding the psychology of women, the subject is opened.

REFERENCES

CHODOROW, N. (1978). *The Reproduction of Mothering: Psychoanalysis and the Sociology of Gender.* Berkeley, CA: Univ. California Press.
——— (1989). *Feminism and Psychoanalytic Theory.* New Haven: Yale Univ. Press.
——— (1994). *Femininities, Masculinities, Sexualities: Freud and Beyond.* Richmond, KY: Univ. Press of Kentucky, 1994.
CIXOUS, H. (1981). Sorites. The laugh of the medusa. In *New French Feminisms,* ed. E. Marks & I. de Courtivron. New York: Schocken Books, pp. 245–264.
ELAM, D. (1994). *Feminism and Deconstruction: Ms. en abyme.* New York: Routledge.
FALUDI, S. (1991). *Backlash: The Undeclared War Against American Women.* New York: Doubleday.
FERENCZI, S. (1927). Introduction to Freud, S., *The Problem of Lay-Analyses.* New York: Brentano's.
FREUD, S. (1913). Totem and taboo. *S. E.,* 13.
FRIEDAN, B. (1963). *The Feminine Mystique.* New York: Dell.
GALLOP, J. (1982). *The Daughter's Seduction: Feminism and Psychoanalysis.* Ithaca, NY: Cornell Univ. Press.
GILLIGAN, C. (1982). *In a Different Voice: Psychological Theory and Women's Development.* Cambridge, MA: Harvard Univ. Press.
——— (1990). Remapping the moral domain: new images of the self in relationship. In *Essential Papers on the Psychology of Women,* ed. C. Zanardi. New York: New York Univ. Press, pp. 480–496.
IRIGARAY, L. (1985a). *Speculum of the Other Woman.* Ithaca, NY: Cornell Univ. Press.
——— (1985b). *This Sex Which Is Not One.* Ithaca, NY: Cornell Univ. Press.
JAKOBSON, R. (1960). Linguistics and poetics. In *Style and Language,* ed. T. Sebeok. Cambridge, MA: MIT Press, pp. 350–377.
JONES, E. (1961). *The Life and Work of Sigmund Freud.* New York: Basic Books.
KRISTEVA, J. (1982). *Powers of Horror: An Essay on Abjection.* New York: Columbia Univ. Press.
——— (1987a). *Tales of Love.* New York: Columbia Univ. Press.

——— (1987b). *Black Sun: Depression and Melancholia.* New York: Columbia Univ. Press.
——— (1990). Women's time. In *Essential Papers on the Psychology of Women,* ed. C. Zanardi. New York: New York Univ. Press, pp. 374–400.
——— (1993). The speaking subject is not innocent. In *Freedom and Interpretation: The Oxford Amnesty Lectures 1992.* New York: Schocken Books, pp. 147–174.
LACAN, J. (1982). *Feminine Sexuality: Jacques Lacan and the ecole freudienne,* ed. J. Mitchell & J. Rose. New York: Norton.
LÉVI-STRAUSS, C. (1967). *The Structural Study of Myth and Totemism.* London, Eng.: Tavistock.
——— (1969). *The Elementary Structures of Kinship.* Boston: Beacon Press.
MILLER, J.B. (1976). *Toward a New Psychology of Women.* Boston: Beacon Press.
——— (1990). The development of women's sense of self. In *Essential Papers on the Psychology of Women,* ed. C. Zanardi. New York: New York Univ. Press, pp. 437–454.
OLINER, M. (1988). *Cultivating Freud's Garden in France.* Northvale, NJ: Aronson.
SAUSSURE, F. de (1959). *Course in General Linguistics.* New York: Philosophical Library.
TURKLE, S. (1992). *Psychoanalytic Politics: Jacque Lacan and Freud's French Revolution.* London, Eng.: Free Association Books.
WHITFORD, M. (1991). *Luce Irigaray: Philosophy in the Feminine.* New York: Routledge.
YOUNG-BRUEHL, E. (1994). What theories women want. *Amer. Imago,* 51:373–396.

NATURE, NURTURE, AND CORE GENDER IDENTITY

Michael Robbins

>Literature about gender differences and their possible origins, and contemporary psychoanalytic formulations of gender, is reviewed. There is a broad consensus among investigators from different fields, and among psychoanalysts of different theoretical persuasions, that the modal female personality tends to be more sociocentric, and the modal male personality more self-centric. These modal personality differences may be qualitative rather than quantitative. The concept of core gender identity, which articulates the psychological root of these differences, is reexamined in the light of contemporary research into constitutional differences in the organization and activation of the brain, and an interactional model of core gender identity as a dynamic evolving phenomenon over the course of the life cycle is proposed.

While there is general consensus that typical male and female personalities differ, it is only relatively recently that a serious effort has commenced, ideologically in the women's movement, and with at least the pretension of objectivity in the human sciences, including psychoanalysis, to formulate the differences in a way that is not nullifying or devaluing to one sex or the other, and to ascertain whether they are superficial products of acculturation or more profound reflections of constitution, or both. After critically reviewing some of the social science and psychoanalytic literature about gender differences, I shall redefine the concept of core gender identity in a way that takes into account contemporary findings in neuroscience about differences in the brain related to genetic factors and to the intrauterine environment.

Assistant Clinical Professor of Psychiatry, Harvard Medical School.

Michael Robbins

SCIENCE AND CULTURAL CHANGE

The great debate of recent decades among conventional psychoanalytic constitutionalists who have concretely interpreted external genital differences as rationalizations for judging females to be inferior, and revisionist feminist culturalists, at least some of whose theoretical positions represent thinly disguised judgments on the male-dominated society they hold accountable, probably has as much to do with the longstanding dominance-submission struggle between the sexes as it does with scientific issues. With the benefit of hindsight we now know that Freud (1925, 1931) confused gender with one of its attributes, male sexuality. He substituted fantasy for reasoned inquiry when he went directly from gross anatomical observation to the conviction, embodied in his now infamous assertion that anatomy is destiny, that females are genitally defective males. He believed (incorrectly, in the light of current biological findings) that gendered aspects of personality emerge from a common (primordially male) matrix. From this fantasy it was but a few short steps to the conclusion that females are incapable of experiencing and resolving a normal Oedipus complex, and are therefore defective with regard to ego (sublimations) and superego (moral or ethical) development (Freud, 1925, 1931). Freud (1930) felt that, because of their presumably untamed sexuality and emotionality, women are especial enemies of culture and civilization. At a more subtle level, Freud's theory of sexuality or libido, including such things as pleasurable tension discharge and a phallic developmental stage, appears to be a projection or abstraction of male phallic physiology. He articulated a modal development endpoint for both sexes in which interpersonal and intrapsychic conflict is a central element, consisting of separation, objectification, and the quest for intimate knowledge of and control or domination over the animate and inanimate worlds, which seems in some respects an expression of then-predominant male traits.

Female analysts, initially and notably Horney (1933, 1939) and Thompson (1943, 1950), suggested that Freud's ideas about women were products of his cultural bias, and proposed that there is a primary female gendering which is entirely separate from that of males. In the ensuing theoretical debate it is sometimes difficult to distinguish useful hypotheses from polemics and to specify and objectify

Nature, Nurture, and Core Gender Identity

the data that might support or refute them. Some (e.g., Miller, 1976) have attempted to rewrite psychoanalytic theory and demonstrate that females are superior and males are deficient. Others have adopted the radical culturalist position that gender differences are either real products of cultural mandate or are entirely culturally fostered illusions (Maccoby and Jacklin, 1974). In the throes of reaction against naïve biological reductionism the tendency has been to overlook differentiating effects of constitution entirely (Blier, 1991).

DATA RELATING CULTURE TO GENDER

I do not intend to minimize the influence of culture on the shape of personality. It is so great that seemingly contradictory gender attributes and behaviors are encountered in personalities typical of different cultures. LeVine (1973, 1981, 1990) notes the existence of cultures where females occupy what are stereotypically thought to be male roles. In any given culture there is more communality than difference with regard both to innate potential and typical outcome to male and female personality. And it is certainly true that, regardless of gender, all humans develop capabilities for autonomy and separateness as well as relatedness or connectedness. These are not polar differentiating features of gender (Berlin and Johnson, 1989).

Turning first to psychology, most studies are limited by the fact that the subjects are from Western cultures. Among neonates the female sensory apparatus seems more sensitive, for example to sounds and to touch (Garai and Scheinfeld, 1968; Korner, 1974; Maccoby and Jacklin, 1974). Psychophysiological studies of dichotic listening patterns, which would seem to approach measures of pure brain functioning, show consistent differences between males and females (Gorski, 1991). Female infants seem more interpersonally responsive. They smile more, are less irritable and easier to calm. They vocalize both earlier and more frequently than their male counterparts. Males manifest more total body activity. Around one year of age female infants tend to look and vocalize more toward the same sex parent (Lewis and Weinraub, 1974; Spelke et al., 1973). Maccoby and Jacklin (1974, 1980) and Parke and Slaby (1983) claim that gender differences in aggressiveness and assertiveness are observable from very early in life in almost all cultures. Among adults, males have been observed to require more interpersonal space and females to manifest more nurturant behavior. Females tend to be more empathically attuned to personal and interpersonal nuances and to be more dependent on their social and interpersonal environment (Tyler, 1956; Witryol and Kaess, 1957).

Gilligan (1982) investigated Freud's belief that females are morally inferior because of superego weakness consequent to failure to negotiate and resolve an Oedipus complex. It is her observation that female morality is simply different from that of the typical male—not so impersonal and abstract, but structured in a more personalized and contextual way around specific caring human relationships.

Witkin and his associates (Witkin et al., 1962) have proposed a schema capable of differentiating members of cultures of varying degrees of complexity (hunter-gatherer through urban industrial) based on perceptual and spatial tests of field dependence. These tests have been given to males and females in a variety of sociocultural groups including New Guinea Telefomin, Cree and Athapaskan, Nigerian and Nsenga Africans, Fiji Islanders, Japanese, Indians and Mexicans; in every instance females have been found to be more field-dependent (less differentiated) than their male counterparts (Witkin and Berry, 1975; Maccoby and Jacklin, 1974). The overall difference between the genders is small in comparison to the range of variation within each gender, however, and there is much overlap. The difference appears to be greater in more stratified societies where females tend to assume more dependent roles in contrast to less stratified societies where they are more independent (Berry, 1966, 1971; MacArthur, 1967). While these tests seem to differentiate styles of relating, some have speculated that the difference reflects innate male superiority in perceptual-spatial ability, the measure chosen for field dependence. Moreover, the very terms chosen to describe the variable being discriminated (dependence and independence) have unfortunate value connotations and do not embrace the possibility that what is being measured is a different kind of sensitivity in females. The reader wishing to pursue the literature on gender difference further is referred to excellent reviews by Ember, 1981, and Notman and Nadelson, 1991.

Nature, Nurture, and Core Gender Identity

EFFORTS TO DIFFERENTIATE THE EFFECTS OF CONSTITUTION FROM THOSE OF CULTURE

Anthropological studies of primate societies indicate that male chimpanzees of all ages tend to be more aggressive than females. For example, Hamburg and van Lawick-Goodall (1974) and Bygott (1974) report that females rarely attack one another, and they tend to be more passive and submissive toward males except in situations where their young appear to be threatened. In the presence of hostile conflict among other chimps, mother chimps will collect their infants and move away. When their infants exhibit rageful and destructive tantrums, mother chimps rarely retaliate, but tend to initiate comforting and remediating activity. Hrdy (1981), in contrast, observes that aggressive competition among females for resources is one of the most striking and consistent findings in primate cultures.

INTERPRETING THE FINDINGS

It is difficult to know how to interpret these various behavioral and psychological studies of humans and primates. Behavioral communalities do not necessarily imply similar underlying psychological and neurobiological processes. Moreover, data that elucidate the relation of gender and personality are most difficult to distinguish from representations of bias. The culture, gender, and personality of the observer-theoretician determines, in ways that are at once powerful and obscure, the nature of his or her hypotheses about gender differences, the design of studies, and the interpretation of data. As the title of her book *The Woman That Never Was* suggests, Hrdy (1991) believes that some of the currently popular feminist conceptions of women as more caring, affiliated, interrelated and nurturing, and less aggressive and seeking of power and control, may be mythical (p. 190). She speculates interfemale aggression may have escaped observer attention because its manifestations may be less blatantly obvious than intermale aggression. It is possible that female aggression, rather than being quantitatively less than male, may be contextually confined to important relationships, ones that are often private, whereas male aggression, being more indiscriminate, may be more readily apparent to the casual observer. There has also been a tendency, which is debatable, to assume that gender differences observed in primates are expressive of constitutional differences in the brain. But who is to say that chimps do not create cultures of their own?

Turning to the human studies, most have been conducted by Western males (Divale, 1976). Critics have suggested that their "findings" of gender difference are simply reifications of existing bias (Blier, 1991; Notman and Nadelson, 1991). Studies that purport to verify stereotypic gender differences often select paradigmatic experimental situations in which males tend to be more practiced and involved, rather than ones more typically involving females (such as family situations). Were males and females compared in situations in which females are more experienced, the direction of the observed gender differences might well be reversed. Moreover, if there are personality differences between males and females their significance remains unclear, for many studies have now documented the differential treatment afforded to male and female infants by their caregivers, starting at birth. For example, male infants in Western culture typically receive more attention and vigorous stimulation than females (Korner, 1974; Maccoby and Jacklin, 1974; Moss, 1974).

Keller (1988) has gone so far as to suggest that science itself, the traditional bastion of masculinity from which not only psychoanalysis but other disciplines that study gender originate, may be a reflection of the male mental apparatus. With it, "man" attempts to distance himself from the natural world, to objectify it and to struggle to conquer it, make it reveal its inner secrets, and ultimately to possess and control it. Her ideas raise the most profound questions about the validity and interpretation of scientific methodology, observations, and conclusions.

PSYCHOANALYTIC STUDIES OF GENDER DIFFERENCE

I turn now from the behavioral observational data of psychology and anthropology and the inferences derived from them, to the data and

Nature, Nurture, and Core Gender Identity

theory of psychoanalysis, which focuses more on personal meanings. Overall, there has been a gradual evolution away from Freud's male model of gender, based on an economic theory of psychosexual maturation and the epistemology of genital awareness, and their dynamic (conflictual) and structural (superego) consequences, and toward dichotomous conceptions of identity and relationships involving autonomy, separateness, impersonality and abstract objectivity, conflict, power and control on the one hand, and emotional interrelatedness, subjectivity, and contextuality on the other. Contemporary concerns are remarkably similar to Fairbairn's position of half a century ago (1944). He not only discarded the concepts of separate drives and psychosexual stages, but proposed a theory of dyadic relationship commencing with a primary undifferentiated dependency on mother, initially experienced as a part object (the breast). Fairbairn maintained, in contrast to Freud, that basic human identity is female: "It is more than doubtful, however, whether the child at first appreciates the genital difference between the two parents. It would appear rather that the difference which he does appreciate is that his father has no breasts . . . " (pp. 122–123). He believed that the oedipal conflict is not so much a determinant of personality structure as it is determined by the endopsychic configuration resulting from the infant's dyadic experience with its mother.

Before describing some of the newer psychoanalytic models, it is worth noting some of the problems encountered in psychoanalytic efforts to revise accounts of gender. As Benjamin (1988) has pointed out, some of the most vociferous proponents of equity in gender theory have, in disguise, advocated models that stereotypically devalue one gender at the expense of the other. For example, Clower (1981) emphasizes such "female" characteristics as subjectivity, interdependency, and loose boundaries, but subtly devalues them in contrast to "male" characteristics by likening the female mind to a primitive, borderlinelike organization. Similar bias with a reverse twist is found in the writings of Chodorow (1978), Miller (1976), and some of her colleagues at the Stone Center. Miller idealizes (or to use an expression common in contemporary feminist writings, "valorizes") the very "female" traits Clower has devalued (relatedness, caring, empathy, and nurturance) by constructing a countermodel of relative female maturity in relation to male personality, which is conceived of as the product of deficiency and defense (Benjamin, 1988; Hrdy, 1981). The movement to model the emancipated woman around the very "masculine" characteristics women have found objectionable and felt themselves victimized by is another example. Most of these representations probably fit the criterion of sociopolitical ideologies formulated by a revolutionary minority group more than they do psychoanalytic theories.

One of the newer concepts in the psychoanalysis of gender is core gender identity. This is a differentiating bedrock of identity postulated to exist from very early in life, before gender role identity and sexual orientation, which develop later. Horney (1933, 1939) was one of the first to advance the concept of primary femininity based on genital sensations. This core of gendered differences in personality is generally believed to develop within the first two years (Amsterdam, 1972; Lewis and Brooks-Gunn, 1979; Emde, 1983), probably antecedent to or independent of most, if not all, of the differentiating influences of culture. It cannot be accounted for by a primordial male model and secondary responses in infants of both sexes to an awareness that one of them is missing something. Female core gender identity is generally thought to commence with the earliest sensory-perceptive-enteroceptive-cognitive-affective awareness of her body, mirrored in primary relationship with the same-gender mothering person (Erikson, 1968; Kestenberg, 1968; Mahler et al., 1975; Stoller, 1976; Roiphe and Galenson, 1981; Mayer, 1985; Person and Ovesey, 1983), and shaped through gender-differentiating early object relations, normal developmental conflicts, and selective identifications (Panel, 1994; Tyson, 1994).

Although derived from different schools of psychoanalytic thought and history, most of the newer theories of female personality share a model of female identity as interpersonal or socially collective, in contrast to male identity, which is perceived as individualistic, autonomous, or self-centered.

Over four decades investigators from three areas separately developed models employing the concept of intersubjectivity, which is now commonly used in contemporary writings about female gendering. The first of these is the interpersonal school of psychiatry, founded by Sullivan (1953), and currently represented by Hoffman (1983, 1987, 1991) as social constructivism. Levenson (1985, 1991),

Nature, Nurture, and Core Gender Identity

writes that "The interpersonal matrix is a self-perpetuating and self-equilibrating system that depends not on the fuel of fantasy for its viability, but on repetitive interactions" (1991, p. 219). The psychic realities of the participants in a relationship continually shape what the interpersonalists call the interactional field, and more traditional analytic constructivists would describe as the intrapsychic worlds of the participants.

Quite independent of one another, two other groups committed to a relationship model of personality also constructed hypotheses around the concept of intersubjectivity. One group (Stolorow et al., 1978; Atwood and Stolorow, 1984; Stolorow and Atwood, 1992) came to the concept through Kohut's self psychology, and have not applied it to gender. The other, beginning with the work of Dinnerstein (1976) and Miller (1976), was influenced by the theory of Margaret Mahler, and drew also on the work of Stoller (1964, 1968), Greenson (1968), and Lynn (1969). Others who have contributed to this model include Gilligan (1982), Lykes (1985), Sampson (1988), Keller (1988), Benjamin (1988), and Flax (1990).

Perhaps the best known proponent of this interpersonal or collective identity model, Chodorow (1978, 1989), employs Mahler's theory and proposes that mature women, more often than mature men, may achieve an advanced state of separation-individuation, requiring a higher level of differentiation and integration and including a more mature form of dependency which she calls intersubjectivity, defined as the recognition of another subject similar to the self. She suggests that such modal female personality traits as affiliation, empathy, nurturance, and contextual morality, hitherto derogated in our male-dominated society, may actually indicate a higher level of female maturity. This has led to speculation that it is the male and not the female whose development may in some respects be defensively crippled. Characteristics such as separateness, autonomy, objectivity, impersonal and logical thinking, and firmness of boundaries are socially valued because they are prototypically masculine, but if viewed from a different perspective, as fear of intimacy, rigid boundaries, objectification, alienation, and domination, they may not be so mature after all. These ideas are suggestive of Fairbairn's (1944) schema of a normal developmental line for dependency, from less to more mature forms.

Michael Robbins

Expanding on Greenson's (1968) work, Chodorow (1978, 1980) postulates a primal conflict in male gender identity development between primal identity and relatedness with mother and more mature identity as a male. Normal male development is hypothesized to involve repudiation of relatedness to mother and shifting of identification from mother to father. She believes such conflict is exacerbated because mothers tend to treat their male children as different from themselves, thus promoting a sense of alienation (1980). In female development, by contrast, development of core gender identity is hypothesized to be enhanced by mirroring relatedness to a same-sex person. It does not require repudiation of relatedness with mother. Keller (1988) and Flax (1990) propose similar ideas.

The use of Mahler's theory as a framework for their intersubjectivity models is problematic, however. Mahler's very model is based on a modal personality structure, for both genders, characterized by such traits as separation, autonomy, and objectivity. This reifies the very Western male bias that intersubjectivity theorists deplore.

Chodorow's model is gender-prejudicial in addition to being gender-differentiating, for it is now the female who is considered to be a more mature species. It is based on the belief that relationships between females, including mother and daughter, are qualitatively different from those between males—characterized less by aggression and conflict and more by relatedness and intersubjectivity. Hrdy (1981), who has made extensive studies of primate societies, believes that such ideas are fantasy. Studies of same-sex relationships have tended to focus on more traditionally masculine-competitive realms, outside the family. But it is commonplace to observe aggression and conflict, overt or covert, in intergenerational relationships among females (in-law or mother-daughter). While male *gender* identity formation may require some degree of aggressive repudiation of relatedness to mother, female *personal* (as contrasted with gender) identity and boundary formation out of a primary identification matrix might also require a degree of interpersonal aggression. In my own clinical experience, predominantly with severely disturbed patients whose primitive thinking and early experiences are highlighted, I have found that while female patients may be more adaptable than their male counterparts, they have roughly comparable problems around dependency, conflicts with mother, identity, and capacity for intimacy and recognition of otherness.

Nature, Nurture, and Core Gender Identity

Benjamin (1988) and Keller (1988) propose similar schemata for gender-related identity development which are less prejudicial than Chodorow's. Along with Winnicott (1971), Stern (1985), Ogden (1989), and Blatt and Blass (1990), they view separateness and intersubjective connectedness as poles of a dialectic process. Benjamin suggests the need for simultaneous complementary but qualitatively different one-person and two-person psychologies or psychoanalytic models in order to comprehend each of these poles or dimensions. Whereas the more primitive intrapsychic states of domination and submission can be conceptualized adequately with an intrapsychic model, she believes that a two-person psychology is necessary to conceptualize the mature intersubjective state. Recognition of the Other and the wish to be in harmonious relationship with her is a gradual process requiring maintenance of a state of intersubjective tension and mutuality. This is in dynamic conflict or tension with a more fundamental motivation toward a state of identification with the powerfully perceived nurturing person, which may take the form either of sadistic obliteration of the otherness of the object, or masochistic submissiveness to that person and consequent self-obliteration. Benjamin's two-person model stresses the importance of a circular, self-reinforcing process in which societal perception of mothers (and all females) as static objects of use, not as human beings, is both a reflection of primitive or infantile forms of thinking and a force perpetuating them.

Gendering of the male mind emphasizes difference, autonomy and separateness, and cognitive skills of abstraction and objectification. It involves development of polarized concepts of self/object; masculine/feminine; separation/connection; autonomy/intimacy; and power, domination, and control/submissiveness and love. As a consequence men tend to treat women as objects of use and domination rather than as people (Chodorow, 1978; Flax, 1990). Female gendering, in contrast, is based on closeness to and subjective involvement with others, as this reinforces rather than threatens their identity-based sense of gender. For this reason Benjamin believes that the alternative of submission is more typical for females, and that of dominance for males.

Possibly Benjamin has confused the important distinction between the state of psychological identity fusion or undifferentiation,

Michael Robbins

whether selfless (submission) or other-less (domination), and the state of differentiation that allows for awareness of the Other and intersubjectivity, with the equally important distinction between the power and scope of intrapsychic and interpersonal models of personality. An intrapsychic model ought to be capable of representing both states, differentiation and undifferentiation. What it *cannot* do is serve as an adequate model of an identity sense that is interpersonal or collective.

Keller's (1988) ideas are similar to those of Benjamin. She contrasts dynamic and static qualities of autonomy associated with intersubjectivity and objectivity, respectively. Static autonomy involves sharp boundaries between self and other. When the subject is dominant, he stands in opposition to an object, that is, another who is not perceived as being alive; when the subject is submissive she relinquishes her aliveness. In both of these static states aggression, conflict, and dominance-submission characterize relationships. In contrast, dynamic autonomy involves flexible boundaries between self and other: a Winnicottian subjective-empathic transitional area. According to Keller, far from being flawed because of its subjectivity, such typically female thinking may actually allow a more authentic knowledge experience.

The models of Benjamin and Keller, which emphasize the contrast between solipsistic, boundary-less relationships and ones characterized by flexible, mutually interpenetrating boundaries, appear to be very similar to Melanie Klein's more immature paranoid-schizoid (splitting) position and her more mature depressive position, respectively. Klein, however, included an important dimension of emotional development and regulation which these newer theories do not, involving integration of drive derivatives and achievement of the capacity for intrapsychic conflict and toleration of ambivalent feelings about others. Klein was also an epistemologist. She was less concerned with the firmness or flexibility dimension of boundaries than with their developmental transformation from a solipsistic state of self-splitting, which creates through projective identification, the fantasy of relatedness in a kind of power struggle, to a more mature cognitive-affective differentiation of self and other enabling true mutuality.

Perhaps the new feminist theories tend toward concreteness insofar as they confuse the capacity to differentiate and establish

Nature, Nurture, and Core Gender Identity

boundaries between conceptions of self and other with walls or barriers to sensitive relatedness and caring. When they refer to the rigid boundaries which seem more characteristic of males, perhaps they are referring to barriers against relating with appropriate empathy and affect, and not to the capacity to perceive self and other with relative accuracy and express and modulate affects accordingly. Whereas Keller utilizes Winnicott's (1971) transitional object concept as a new model for mature intersubjective relations and perhaps for science itself, Winnicott himself was conceptualizing an area of private or shared illusion, not of reality.

Fast (1984) points out that gender differentiation may or may not become confused with separation-individuation issues, and the two issues may become imbedded in conflict for females as well as males.

For the most part, these newer psychoanalytic accounts of gender tend to paint personality in broad brushstrokes. With some notable exceptions such as Gilligan's (1982) work they do not appear to be anchored in specific clinical data, but seem to have originated from scholarly anecdotal group discussions among women. What constitutes data, and how are we to differentiate data from ideologies in revolution? What emerges most clearly from them is not so much a new theory of personality and gender, as a general agreement, even among persons with different ideological biases and scientific and theoretical orientations, that there are important and probably qualitative differences between modal male and female mind and personality. I shall designate these typical gendered differences in personality, arising under average expectable circumstances, sociocentric (female) and self-centric (male). These are overlapping, not clearly dichotomous typologies, because all human beings are much more similar than different. Moreover, all of us grow up in proximity to both kinds of thinking, self- and sociocentric, and tend to be dually gendered from birth. What I shall consider next is a possible neurobiological basis for these gender typologies.

NEUROBIOLOGY OF GENDER DIFFERENCE

It is more than likely that the brain, affected by the endocrine secretions, and not the genitalia, is the major sex- and gender-differentiating body part. Hormonal effects on the brain are of two types:

organizing or structuring and activating or motivating. Hormones organize the sex-specific differentiation of the central nervous system in utero and in the neonate in patterned ways and at so-called "critical periods" of development, which themselves differ for each gender (MacLusky and Naftolin, 1981; Jacklin et al., 1983). At conception sex is determined by the presence of the second X chromosome which produces ovarian tissue, or the XY combination which produces testicular tissue. Testicular tissue, in turn, produces fetal testosterone and Mullerian duct-inhibiting hormone. The undifferentiated fetus is proto female, a finding more consistent with Fairbairn's theory than with Freud's belief that females are aborted or defective males. In the genotypically male fetus testosterone secretion stimulates male organization and differentiation, and Mullerian duct hormone suppresses development of female characteristics. In the genotypically female fetus testosterone is not secreted and feminization proceeds unimpeded. The masculinizing activational pathway has been studied in rats, and there is no reason to believe it is fundamentally different in humans. It involves conversion of fetal testosterone to estrogen. The female fetus is not masculinized by the high levels of maternal estrogen found in neonatal rats because of the presence of a specific fetal protein (McEwan, 1983, 1991; Meaney, 1989; Meaney et al., 1983).

It is in three areas of the brain that permanent structural sexual differentiation occurs. These areas—the cortex, the amygdala, and the hypothalamus (particularly the anterior portion)—contain sexually dimorphic nuclei, that is, nuclei that are differentially responsive to testosterone (Swaab and Fliers, 1985; Fuxe et al., 1988; Seeman and Lang, 1990; Kopala and Clark, 1990). These structural differentiations include that the male brain has larger groupings of nuclei INAH 2 and 3, SDN-POA, and BNST; and the female brain has midline structures that are larger (surface area of the midsaggital anterior commissure and massa intermedia) and differently shaped (a bulbous shaped splenium, or midsaggital section of the corpus callosum) (Gorski, 1991).

Studies of rats indicate that these sexually differentiating organizational changes in the brain are accompanied by development of a wide range of behaviors and functions, including ones that go beyond those ordinarily associated with sexual and reproductive activity. These include: specific sexual posturing and behavior, aggressive

Nature, Nurture, and Core Gender Identity

behavior, taste preferences, food intake patterns and body weight and weight-distribution, urination posturing, playfulness and other social behaviors, including rough play characteristic of males; territoriality, cognitive learning attitudes, maternal behaviors, and patterns of peptidase secretion (Phoenix et al., 1959; Goy and Goldfoot, 1974; Meaney, 1989; Gorski, 1991). It is worthy of note that the rough peer play that characterizes males of all species, and appears to be the developmental route to adult male dominance patterns, commences in juvenile relationships among peers *prior* to the pubertal activational effects of testosterone. That these patterns and the sequence of their development appear to be universal in males of many species suggests that they are organizational or neurostructural in origin (Meaney, 1989). The amygdala appears to be the locus of this response (Meaney et al., 1981; Meaney and McEwan, 1986; Meaney, 1989; Maccoby, 1990).

Organizational changes in the brain are not totally confined to the intrauterine and neonatal periods, however. Witelson's human studies (1976) of pre- and postpubescent males and females suggest that hemispheric specialization continues to develop through adolescence and is completed earlier in males, whereas the female brain retains plasticity until later in development. As with the finding that the fetal brain is intrinsically female, this is also at odds with Freud's belief that females are more rigid and their superego development tends to arrest at an early age because they do not experience and resolve an Oedipus complex.

The second category of hormonal effects is activational or motivational. Complex feedback loops are involved. The sexually differentiated areas of the brain, including hypothalamus and amygdala, both regulate hormonal secretion and are differentially responsive to it.

The hypothalamus depends on the amygdala for its connection to the cortex and to the sensory-perceptual world. The amygdala is believed to be responsible for stimulus-response learning patterns, both their establishment and their evocation in response to subsequent stimulation (MacLean, 1990). From this we may infer that intactness of the amygdala is crucial to continuity of learned control over emotionality. Amygdalectomy in male primates diminishes aggressiveness, whereas in females it enhances aggressive assertive behavior (Haber, 1981). If one thinks of this in terms of the learning function of the amygdala with regard to regulation of aggressiveness and assertion, it suggests that amygdalectomy, functionally conceived of as unlearning, leaves the female less submissive and the male less aggressive.

In rodent species hypothalamic control of progesterone secretion regulates aggressiveness in females. In humans estrogen is thought to be protective against affect disturbance and psychosis (Sherwin, 1988; Seeman and Lang, 1990; Kopala and Clark, 1990). Lowered estrogen levels are found in the late luteal phase of the menstrual cycle, postpartum, and in menopause, and they seem to have some relation to emotional disturbance.

The role of androgens (especially testosterone) with regard to aggression is complex. Experiments with neonatal female mice and rhesus monkeys given testosterone, and "natural" experiments with female human infants who for reasons of individual pathology or maternal exposure have sustained elevated testosterone levels, show that as these females grow they continue to be more aggressive than normal female controls (Leventhal and Brodie, 1981; Bronson and Desjardins, 1968; Joselyn, 1973; Rose et al., 1971). Studies of primates by Rose et al. (1971) and Mazur (1976) reveal a bidirectional correlation between testosterone levels and social status. For example, subsequent to conflict resolution and social status change within the group, newly dominant rhesus monkeys show elevation of testosterone levels, whereas those demoted to subordinate status show diminution. In adult male primates including humans, however, there is no simple correlation between testosterone levels and aggressive behavior (Leventhal and Brodie, 1981). Aggressive adult males do not always have elevated testosterone levels, and administration of testosterone to adult females does not necessarily make them more aggressive. As mentioned earlier, social learning patterns, structured through the amygdala, appear to play an important role and to have the potential to override activational effects of testosterone.

The combination of the organizational and activational effects of hormones on the brain with interpersonally activated modifications (according to the principle of neural plasticity) results in clear-cut patterns of difference in male and female brain function. The new neuroimaging technology is beginning to demonstrate the nature of these differences in humans. Positron emission tomography

Nature, Nurture, and Core Gender Identity

(PET) scanning of metabolic activity (Gur et al., 1995) reveals that males have a higher level of metabolism than females in temporal-limbic structures and cerebellum and a lower level in the cingulate gyrus. Small but significant differences in hemispheric functioning were found during performance of typical "male" skills (spatial, mechanical, and motor) and "female" skills (abstract, verbal, mental flexibility). One interesting and unexpected finding in this study relates to stereotypes about crossover or empathy. Men were much more likely to possess "female" brain characteristics than vice-versa. Shaywitz et al. (1995) presented phonological tasks (involving rhyming of unfamiliar words) to males and females, and found that males processed them exclusively in the left frontal gyrus, whereas females employed more diffuse neural systems including both frontal gyri. Such findings in adults further reinforce the widespread belief that there are differences between typical male and female patterns of thinking, although it must be emphasized that, taken by themselves, they do not allow us to distinguish constitutional effects from environmental ones.

What can we conclude from these studies? Certainly there is evidence to support the hypothesis that gender-stereotypical traits, such as masculine motivation to master the external environment, and feminine social relatedness and adaptability, are not simply expressions of differential cultural forces. In the male there are the aggressive, environmental-manipulative aspects of constitution, and in the female those constitutional elements suggestive of primary adaptability or relatedness, not only the neurobiology related to conception and pregnancy, but the postpartum lactation responses to sensations and perceptions of the infant. In the female there is one striking finding that suggests a constitutionally heightened sensitivity to biologically unrelated others, and that is the observation first made by McClintock (1971) and anecdotally confirmed by many others, that women who live primarily in close or intimate proximity to other women tend to attune their menstrual cycles to one another.

THE CONCEPT OF CORE GENDER IDENTITY

I should like to synthesize the hypothesis of qualitative differences in modal male and female personality, and the data of gendered differences in the brain dating from neonatal life, by proposing that we redefine the concept of core gender identity. As I read the literature, the commonly accepted definition seems more focused on the sensory-perceptual-affective experience of one's body, from the beginning of life, in the context of the primary relationship. It does not sufficiently take into account constitutional differences in the brain. Moreover, it is held to be a process involving the creation of self-object-affect representations which is completed in infancy and very early childhood. Tyson (1994), for example, writes, "... with an awareness of the sense of self and sense of bodily zones, a basic sense of belonging to one sex and not the other, and having certain characteristics of that sex accrues" (pp. 451–452). While the sensory-perceptual significance of the sexually distinctive body configurations and parts is an important *dimension* of core gender identity, it is constitutional differences in the brain and the endocrine system in relation to differently designed and functioning bodies that, in the context of culturally average or expectable early interpersonal interactions with caregivers, leads to a gender-differentiating organization and functioning of mind.

I think it is no accident that the importance of these neuroconstitutional factors is insufficiently appreciated. To illustrate my point I compare the current sociocultural attitude about the etiology of schizophrenia (that it is an organic illness) with the popular bias about the origin of gender differences (that they are largely sociocultural artifacts). In so doing, I do not mean to imply that gendering is a disease. Genetic factors appear to account for slightly more than a third of the variance in schizophrenia (Robbins, 1993), but despite that fact, and the absence of clearcut evidence of differentiating brain abnormality, it is now generally accepted that schizophrenia is an organic disease of the brain and the effects of the cultural and interpersonal environment on development of the illness are negligible. In contrast, genetic constitution accounts for much of the variance in sex, and there is much more definitive evidence for brain differences between males and females than between schizophrenics and nonschizophrenics. While it is not possible to make definitive morphological distinctions between single male and female brains, or schizophrenic and "normal" brains, and differences are encountered only when one statistically averages large groups, there is much

Nature, Nurture, and Core Gender Identity

more substantial agreement about the nature of gender differences. And there is a much higher probability that one can successfully ascertain, using neurochemical tests, whether a given individual is male or female than whether he is schizophrenic or normal.

My point is that powerful social attitudes and values are at play in determining what we view as data and how we construe it. In the instance of schizophrenia the predominant sociocultural belief that it is an organic illness leads people to discount the absence of definitive organic findings. In the instance of gender, reaction against the cultural bias that led people to concretely misconstrue organic (gross anatomical) differences in support of a theory devaluing of females tempts us to ignore the differentiating neurobiological findings.

There is little doubt that there is a constitutional predisposition to being typically gendered, and that the concept of core gender identity should be redefined to take this into account. Under ordinary circumstances of parenting, constitutional elements lead to the emergence of those aspects of personality we characterize as gender-related. Under unusual circumstances of parenting these developments may be thwarted or altered. The interaction of neurobiological and social-interpersonal experiential forces that constitutes gendered development is not a static process, but one that evolves over the course of the life span of the individual. Organic gender-specific changes in the brain and mind characterize puberty, mature adult procreativity, aging and senescence, every bit as much as the more readily apparent gross somatic changes do. We may conclude that core gender identity comprises constitutional gender-related differences which have qualitative consequences for how personality is constituted, and which evolve throughout the life cycle as part of a reciprocal interactive process with the environment.

CONCLUSION

Core gender identity formation is but one element of the evolution of gendered aspects of personality. Others include developmental interactions with parents and with one's culture as mediated through caregivers and social institutions. These may elaborate, alter, or abort the usual and typical gender developmental sequences. Culture not only influences structural development, it ascribes meaning as well; hence some of the confusion between "real" differences and culturally created beliefs or *illusions*. Part of the complexity stems from the fact that the constitutional-organic factors and the interpersonal-cultural factors, far from being static forces, are each evolving at the same time they are interactive. Cultural, social, and interpersonal experience modifies the brain (neural plasticity), and the brain, probably the temporal-limbic system whose role is perpetuation of learned patterns, both evolves and shapes the cultural and interpersonal worlds.

In a broad sense, gender can serve as an example of a range of conditions in which qualitative variability of constitutional neurobiological substrate may be a critical initial determinant of differences in personality organization that may be qualitative and not simply quantitative (i.e., more or less, or presence or absence of something). Other examples include typologies we consider extraordinary (schizophrenia; Robbins, 1993), statistically unusual (homosexuality; Friedman, 1994; Friedman and Downey, 1993), and not out of the ordinary at all (temperament). Taken together, the idea that core gender identity, a broadly dichotomous variable, is powerfully influenced by constitutionally determined neurobiological configurations, and the idea that culture is a creation of personalities, male and female, lead to the question of whether there is a broad dichotomy in the culturally determined aspects of personality.

REFERENCES

AMSTERDAM, B. (1972). Mirror self-image reactions before age two. *Devel. Psychol.*, 5:297–305.
ATWOOD, G. & STOLOROW, R. (1984). *Structures of Subjectivity: Explorations in Psychoanalytic Phenomenology.* Hillsdale, NJ: Analytic Press.
BENJAMIN, J. (1988). *The Bonds of Love.* New York: Pantheon.
BERLIN, S. & JOHNSON, C. (1989). Women and autonomy: using structural analysis of social behavior to find autonomy within connections. *Psychiat.*, 52:79–95.
BERRY, J. (1966). Temne and Eskimo perceptual skills. *Int. J. Psychol.*, 1:207–229.
––––––– (1971). Ecological and cultural factors in spatial perceptual development. *Canad. J. Behav. Sci.*, 3:324–336.
BLATT, S. & BLASS, R. (1990). Attachment and separateness: a dialectical model of the products and processes of development throughout the life cycle. *Psychoanal. Study Child*, 45:107–127.

Nature, Nurture, and Core Gender Identity

BLIER, R. (1991). Gender ideology and the brain: sex differences research. In *Women and Men*, ed. M. Notman & C. Nadelson. Washington, DC: Amer. Psychiat. Press, pp. 63–73.

BRONSON, E. & DESJARDINS, C. (1968). Aggression in adult mice: modification by neonatal injections of gonadal hormones. *Science*, 161:705–706.

BYGOTT, J. (1974). *Agonistic Behavior and Social Relationships among Adult Male Chimpanzees*. Doctoral Dissertation, Cambridge University.

CHODOROW, N. (1978). *The Reproduction of Mothering: Psychoanalysis and the Sociology of Gender*. Berkeley, CA: Univ. Calif. Press.

——— (1980). Gender, relation, and difference in psychoanalytic perspective. In *Essential Papers on the Psychology of Women*, ed. C. Zanardi. New York: N. Y. Univ. Press, 1990, pp. 420–436.

——— (1989). *Feminism and Psychoanalytic Theory*. New Haven, CT: Yale Univ. Press.

CLOWER, V. (1981). The acquisition of mature femininity. In *Women and Men*, ed. M. Notman & C. Nadelson. Washington, DC: Amer. Psychiat. Press, pp. 75–88.

DINNERSTEIN, D. (1976). *The Mermaid and the Minotaur*. New York: Harper & Row, p. 126.

DIVALE, W. (1976). Female status and cultural evolution: a study in ethnographic bias. *Behav. Sci. Res.*, 11:169–211.

EMBER, C. (1981). A cross-cultural perspective on sex differences. In *Handbook of Cross-cultural Human Development*, ed. R.L. Munroe, R.H. Munroe & B. Whiting. New York: Garland, pp. 531–580.

EMDE, R. (1983). The prerepresentational self and its affective core. *Psychoanal. Study Child*, 38:165–192.

ERIKSON, E.H. (1968). *Identity: Youth and Crisis*. New York: Norton.

FAIRBAIRN, W.R.D. (1944). *Psychoanalytic Studies of the Personality*. London: Tavistock, 1952.

FAST, I. (1984). *Gender Identity: A Differentiation Model*. Hillsdale, NJ: Analytic Press.

FLAX, J. (1990). *Thinking Fragments: Psychoanalysis, Feminism, and Postmodernism in the Contemporary West*. Berkeley, CA: Univ. Calif. Press.

FREUD, S. (1925). Some psychical consequences of the anatomical distinction between the sexes. *S. E.*, 19.

——— (1930). Civilization and its discontents. *S. E.*, 21.

——— (1931). Female sexuality. *S. E.*, 21.

FRIEDMAN, R. (1994). Homosexuality. *New Eng. J. Med.*, 331:923–930.

——— & DOWNEY, J. (1993). Neurobiology and sexual orientation: current relationships. *J. Neuropsychiat. Clin. Neurosci.*, 5:131–153.

FUXE, K.; AGNATI, L.; HARFSTRAND, A.; CINTRA, A.; ARONSON, M.; ZOLI, M. & GUSTAFFSON, J.-A. (1988). Principles for the hormone regulation of wiring transmission and volume transmission in the central nervous system. In *Neuroendocrinology of Mood*, ed. D. Ganten & D. Pfaff. New York: Springer-Verlag, pp. 1–53.

GARAI, J. & SCHEINFELD, A. (1968). Sex differences in mental and behavioral traits. *Genet. Psychol. Monogr.*, 77:169–299.

GILLIGAN, C. (1982). *In a Different Voice: Psychological Theory and Women's Development.* Cambridge, MA: Harvard Univ. Press.
GORSKI, R. (1991). Sexual differentiation of the endocrine brain and its control. In *Brain Endocrinology,* ed. M. Motta. New York: Raven Press, pp. 71–104.
GOY, R. & GOLDFOOT, D. (1974). Experimental and hormonal factors influencing development of sexual behavior in the male rhesus monkey. In *The Neurosciences: Third Study Program,* ed. F. Schmitt & F. Warden. Cambridge, MA: MIT Press, pp. 571–581.
GREENSON, R. R. (1968). Dis-identifying from the mother: its special importance for the boy. *Int. J. Psychoanal.,* 49:370–374.
GUR, R.C.; MOZLEY, L.; MOZLEY, D.; RESNICK, S.; KARP, J.; ALAVI, A.; ARNOLD, S. & GUR, R.E. (1995). Sex differences in regional cerebral glucose metabolism during a resting state. *Science,* 267:528–531.
HABER, S. (1981). Social factors in evaluating the effects of biological manipulations on aggressive behavior in nonhuman primates. In *Biobehavioral Aspects of Aggression,* ed. D. Hamburg & M. Trudeau. New York: A. R. Liss.
HAMBURG, D. & VAN LAWICK-GOODALL, J. (1974). Factors facilitating development of aggressive behavior in chimpanzees and humans. In *Determinants and Origins of Aggressive Behavior,* ed. W. Hartrup & J. deWit. The Hague, Netherlands: Mouton, pp. 59–85.
HOFFMAN, I. (1983). The patient as interpreter of the analyst's experience. *Contemp. Psychoanal.,* 19:389–422.
——— (1987). The value of uncertainty in psychoanalytic practice. *Contemp. Psychoanal.,* 23:205–215.
——— (1991). Discussion: toward a social-constructivist view of the psychoanalytic situation. *Psychoanal. Dial.,* 1:74–105.
HORNEY, K. (1933). The denial of the vagina: a contribution to the problem of the genital anxieties specific to women. In *Feminine Psychology.* New York: Norton, 1967, pp. 147–161.
——— (1939). Feminine psychology. In *New Ways in Psychoanalysis.* New York: Norton, pp. 101–119.
HRDY, S. (1981). *The Woman That Never Was.* Cambridge, MA.: Harvard Univ. Press.
JACKLIN, C., MACCOBY, E. & DOERING, C. (1983). Neonatal sex steroid hormones and timidity in 6–18–month–old boys. *Devel. Psychobiol.,* 16:163–168.
JOSELYN, W. (1973). Androgen-induced social dominance in infant female rhesus monkeys. *J. Child Psychol. Psychiat.,* 14:137–145.
KELLER, E.F. (1988). *Reflections on Gender and Science.* New Haven, CT: Yale Univ. Press.
KESTENBERG, J. (1968). Outside and inside, male and female. *J. Amer. Psychoanal. Assn.,* 16:457–520.
KOPALA, L. & CLARK, C. (1990). Implications of olfactory agnosia for understanding sex differences in schizophrenia. *Schiz. Bull.,* 16:255–261.
KORNER, A. (1974). Methodological considerations in studying sex differences in the behavioral functioning of newborns. In *Sex Differences in Behavior,* ed. R. Friedman, R. Richart & R. Vande Wiele. New York: Wiley, pp. 197–208.

Nature, Nurture, and Core Gender Identity

LEVENSON, E. (1985). The interpersonal (Sullivanian) model. In *Models of the Mind*, ed. A. Rothstein. New York: Int. Univ. Press, pp. 49–67.

────── (1991). *The Purloined Self: Interpersonal Perspectives in Psychoanalysis*. New York: William Alanson White Institute.

LEVENTHAL, B. & BRODIE, K. (1981). The pharmacology of violence. In *Emotion: Theory, Research, and Experience*. Vol. 3, *Biological Foundations of Emotion*, ed. R. Plutchik & H. Kellerman. Orlando, FL: Academic Press, pp. 85–106.

LEVINE, R. (1973). *Culture, Behavior and Personality*. Chicago: Aldine.

────── (1981). Psychoanalytic theory and the comparative study of human development. In *Handbook of Cross-cultural Human Development*, ed. R. L. Munroe & B. Whiting. New York: Garland, pp. 63–72.

────── (1990). Infant environments in psychoanalysis: a cross-cultural view. In *Cultural Psychology*, ed. J. Stigler, R. Schweder & R. Herdt. Cambridge, Eng.: Cambridge Univ. Press, pp. 454–474.

LEWIS, M. & BROOKS-GUNN, J. (1979). *Social Cognition and the Acquisition of Self.* New York: Plenum.

────── & WEINRAUB, M. (1974). Sex of parent X sex of child: socioemotional development. In *Sex Differences in Behavior*, ed. R. Friedman, R. Richart & R. Vande Wiele. New York: Wiley, pp. 165–189.

LYKES, M. (1985). Gender and individualistic vs. collectivistic bases for notions about the self. *J. Personal.*, 53:356–383.

LYNN, D. (1969). *Parental and Sex-Role Identification: A Theoretical Formulation*. Berkeley, CA: McCutchan.

MACARTHUR, R. (1967). Sex differences in field dependence for the Eskimo: replication of Berry's finding. *Int. J. Psychol.*, 2:139–140.

MACCOBY, R. (1990). Gender and relationships: a developmental account. *Amer. Psychol.*, 45:513–520.

────── & JACKLIN, C. (1974). *The Psychology of Sex Differences*. Stanford, CA: Stanford Univ. Press.

────── ────── (1980). Sex differences in aggression: a rejoinder and reprise. *Child Devel.*, 51:964–980.

MACLEAN, P. (1990). *The Triune Brain in Evolution*. New York: Plenum.

MACLUSKY, N. & NAFTOLIN, F. (1981). Sexual differentiation of the central nervous system. *Science*, 211:1294–1302.

MAHLER, M.S., PINE, F. & BERGMANN, A. (1975). *The Psychological Birth of the Human Infant*. New York: Basic Books.

MAYER, E. (1985). "Everybody must be just like me!" Observations on female castration anxiety. *Int. J. Psychoanal.*, 66:331–347.

MAZUR, A. (1976). Effects of testosterone on status in primate groups. *Folia Primatologica*, 26:214–226.

MCCLINTOCK, M. (1971). Menstrual synchrony and suppression. *Nature*, 229:244–245.

MCEWEN, B. (1983). Gonadal steroid influences on brain development and sexual differentiation. In Reproductive physiology IV. *Int. Rev. Physiol.*, 27:99–145.

────── (1991). Sex differences in the brain: what they are and how they arise. In *Women and Men*, ed. M. Notman & C. Nadelson. Washington, DC: Amer. Psychiat. Press, pp. 35–40.

MEANEY, M. (1989). The sexual differentiation of social play. *Psychiat. Devel.*, 3:247–261.
——— DODGE, A. & BEATTY, W. (1981). Sex dependent effects of amygdaloid lesions on the social play of prepubertal rats. *Physiol. Behav.*, 26:467–472.
——— & MCEWEN, B. (1986). Testosterone implants into the amygdala during the neonatal period masculinize the social play of juvenile female rats. *Brain Res.*, 398:324–328.
——— STEWART, J., POULIN, P. et al. (1983). Sexual differentiation of social play in rat pups is mediated by the neonatal androgen receptor system. *Neuroendocrinol.*, 37:85–90.
MILLER, J.B. (1976). *Toward a New Psychology of Women*. Boston: Beacon Press.
MOSS, H. (1974). Early sex differences and mother-infant interaction. In *Sex Differences in Behavior*, ed. R. Friedman, R. Richart & R. Vande Wiele. New York: Wiley, pp. 149–163.
NOTMAN, M. & NADELSON, C. (1991). A review of gender differences in brain and behavior. In *Women and Men*, ed. M. Notman & C. Nadelson. Washington, DC: Amer. Psychiat. Press, pp. 23–34.
OGDEN, T. (1989). *The Primitive Edge of Experience*. Northvale, NJ: Aronson.
Panel (1994). Contemporary theories of female sexuality. L. Grossman, reporter. *J. Amer. Psychoanal. Assn.*, 42:233–241.
PARK, R. & SLABY, R. (1983). The development of aggression. In *Handbook of Child Psychology*, Vol. 4, ed. P. Mussen. New York: Wiley, pp. 547–642.
PERSON, E.S. & OVESEY, L. (1983). Psychoanalytic theories of gender identity. *J. Amer. Acad. Psychoanal.*, 11:203–226.
PHOENIX, C., GOY, R., GERALL, A. et al. (1959). Organizing action of prenatally administered testosterone propionate on the tissues mediating mating behavior in the female guinea pig. *Endocrinol.*, 65:369–382.
ROBBINS, M. (1993). *Experiences of Schizophrenia: An Integration of the Personal, Scientific and Therapeutic*. New York: Guilford.
ROIPHE, H. & GALENSON, E. (1981). *Infantile Origins of Sexual Identity*. New York: Int. Univ. Press.
ROSE, R., HALADAY, J. & BERNSTEIN, J. (1971). Plasma testosterone, dominance rank, and aggressive behavior in rhesus monkeys. *Nature*, 231:366.
SAMPSON, E. (1988). The debate on individualism: indigenous psychologies of the individual and their role in personal and societal functioning. *Amer. Psychol.*, 43:15–22.
SEEMAN, M. & LANG, M. (1990). The role of estrogens in schizophrenia gender differences. *Schiz. Bull.*, 16:185–194.
SHAYWITZ, B.; SHAYWITZ, S.; PUGH, K.; CONSTABLE, R.T.; SKUDLARSKI, P. et al. (1995). Sex differences in the functional organization of the brain for language. *Nature*, 373:607–609.
SHERWIN, B. (1988). Affective changes with estrogen and androgen replacement therapy in surgically menopausal women. *J. Affect. Dis.*, 14:177–187.
SPELKE, E.; ZELAZO, P.; KAGAN, J. & KOTELCHUCK, M. (1973). Father interaction and separation protest. *Devel. Psychol.*, 9:83–90.

Nature, Nurture, and Core Gender Identity

STERN, D. (1985). *The Interpersonal World of the Infant: A View from Psychoanalysis and Developmental Psychology.* New York: Basic Books.

STOLLER, R.J. (1964). A contribution to the study of gender identity. *Int. J. Psychoanal.*, 45:220–226.

——— (1968). The sense of femaleness. *Psychoanal. Q.*, 37:42–55.

——— (1976). Primary femininity. *J. Amer. Psychoanal. Assn.*, 24(Suppl.):59–78.

STOLOROW, R. & ATWOOD, G. (1992). *Contexts of Being.* Hillsdale, NJ: Analytic Press.

——— ——— & ROSS, J. (1978). The representational world in psychoanalytic therapy. *Int. Rev. Psychoanal.*, 5:247–256.

SULLIVAN, H.S. (1953). *The Interpersonal Theory of Psychology.* New York: Norton.

SWAAB, D. & FLIERS, E. (1985). A sexually dimorphic nucleus in the human brain. *Science*, 228:1112–1115.

THOMPSON, C. (1943). Penis envy in women. *Psychiat.*, 6:123–125.

——— (1950). Some effects of the derogatory attitude toward female sexuality. *Psychiat.*, 13:349–354.

TYLER, I. (1956). *The Psychology of Human Differences.* New York: Appleton Century Crofts.

TYSON, P. (1994). Bedrock and beyond: an examination of the clinical utility of contemporary theories of female psychology. *J. Amer. Psychoanal. Assn.*, 42:447–467.

WINNICOTT, D.W. (1971). *Playing and Reality.* London: Tavistock.

WITELSON, S. (1976). Sex and the single hemisphere: right hemisphere specialization for spatial processing. *Science*, 193:425–427.

WITKIN, H. & BERRY, J. (1975). Psychological differentiation in cross-cultural perspective. *J. Cross-Cultural Psychol.*, 6:4–87.

——— DYK, R.; FATERSON, H; GOODENOUGH, D. & KARP, S. (1962). *Psychological Differentiation.* New York: Wiley.

WITRYOL, S. & KAESS, W. (1957). Sex differences in social memory tasks. *J. Abnorm. Soc. Psychol.*, 54:343–346.

Unconscious Representation of Femininity

Dana Birksted-Breen

> This paper sets out some of the main differences in approaches to the study of female sexuality, in particular in terms of the place of the body and biology in the construction of femininity. It illustrates a dual aspect of femininity in its reference to lack and in its more immediate bodily reality, suggesting that it is the interplay of these two which traces a woman's sexual position.

Both inside and outside the psychoanalytic community, Freud's ideas about female sexuality and femininity have attracted criticisms ever since he first wrote "Some Psychical Consequences of the Anatomical Distinction Between the Sexes" (1925).

It is often assumed that these ideas have been discredited, particularly in regard to the central place Freud gives to penis envy in initiating femininity. If we take an international perspective, the situation is not so simple and the debate is still alive, at least implicitly if not always explicitly. What the passage of time has highlighted is complexity rather than resolution.

The issue of whether femininity is biologically determined or whether it is constructed independently from biology still polarizes perspectives, as it did at the time of the original "Freud-Jones debate," as it came to be known. The importance of this issue goes beyond the topic of femininity to the conceptualization of psychoanalytic theory in general.

Very roughly (though schemas cannot do justice to the complexity of ideas) the approaches divide geographically. British psychoanalysts have, on the whole, not been very interested in the topic since the original debate (notable exceptions being Gillespie, 1969; Balint, 1973; Burgner and Edgcumbe, 1975; Mitchell and Rose, 1982; Laufer, 1982, 1986; Pines 1993—all of whom are outside the Kleinian

---

Training Analyst, British Psychoanalytical Society.

group). Implicitly they tend in the main to follow Klein's original position according to which there is always an unconscious knowledge of the vagina and natural heterosexual strivings from the beginning of life. While Freud stressed the relative independence of the development of masculinity and feminity from biological sex, Melanie Klein regarded natural masculinity and femininity as negotiated through defensive impediments to its expression.

In France, Lacan and his followers question, as Freud before them, the assumption of a natural heterosexual drive. For them there is no such thing as a pregiven male or female subject, but the human subject is constructed within the terms of language—that is, from a logic that comes from outside the individual. Lacan's emphasis on the aspect of Freud's work which wants to keep psychoanalysis separate from biology and within the area of mental representation, and which gives a central place to the castration complex in the unconscious and in promoting development along masculine or feminine lines, has been very influential in France even amongst those who are not followers of Lacan. Within this perspective, Freud's notion of phallic monism, and the foundation of feminine development on the discovery of lack, still hold an important place today.

Positions are becoming increasingly complex if we consider the recent view of those French psychoanalysts for whom the body is considered outside the realm of psychoanalysis and for whom phallic monism is accepted and central, but who nevertheless make reference to a feminine outside the opposition phallic-castrated (Cournut-Janin and Cournut, 1993). There are of course also other perspectives in France, notably that of Chasseguet-Smirgel (1964) who considers penis envy to be essentially defensive rather than primary, and the knowledge of the vagina repressed because of "incorporation guilt."

In the United States, great interest in the topic has lead to many and varied papers. On the whole, biological influences are deemed important in shaping femininity. The role of female anatomy and physiology on the development of ego functions (Erikson, 1964; Bassin, 1982) and in the elaboration of specific female genital anxieties (Bernstein, 1990) have been described. Penis envy tends to be considered either as defensive (Lerner, 1976), or as a metaphor for other more general narcissistic injuries (Grossman and Stewart,

Unconscious Representation of Femininity

1976). When it is considered to occur "naturally" as part of development, it is seen as an impediment to femininity (Blum, 1976; Parens et al., 1976) rather than initiating femininity as in the classical theory. Some even consider that penis envy and the castration complex exert crucial influences on feminine development, but this comes on top of an early feminine phase involving the genital zone and does not initiate femininity (Galenson and Roiphe, 1976).

Specific to the American perspective is the concept of gender identity first put forward by Stoller (1964) and later refined by Tyson (1982) who proposes a developmental line divisible into core gender identity, gender role, and sexual partner orientation. Core gender identity is the most primitive sense of belonging to one sex and not the other. It is understood in this perspective to be a conflict-free source of femininity prior to the perception of sexual difference. This notion of a nonconflictual "primary femininity" (Stoller, 1976) contrasts with the view of both British and French psychoanalysts for whom there is no area of cognition free of ambiguity, conflict, and unconscious fantasy. While Klein also describes an early femininity, hers is a view of feminine development as continuously challenged by projective and introjective mechanisms, and in no way simply related to biological and social reality.[1]

The concept of primary femininity put forward by Stoller entails the notion that the girl develops a mental representation of genital femaleness at an early age. This view has lead to the description of anxieties about the body which are comparable to but different from the boys' experience of castration anxiety (Bernstein, 1990) and to a "female castration anxiety" as a fear of the loss of the *female* genitals (Mayer, 1985). Melanie Klein also writes about a feminine form of castration anxiety but, while for Mayer the anxiety stems from the

---

[1]For Klein unconscious fantasies permeate the psychic life of the human being from birth. They color the child's relationship to others and to her own body from the start because fantasy is the invariably present psychic representative of instinctual drives, libidinal and destructive. Unconscious fantasies relate in the first instance to the mother's body as the seat of both male and female part objects. While Freud noted the privileged place of the penis and the envy it engenders in shaping mental structures, for Klein primary envy is directed to the maternal breast and womb and its fantasied contents. Both however rely on a notion of innate fantasy. For Freud it is not the perception of sexual difference in itself that is meaningful, but the primal fantasy of castration which gives meaning to the perception and propels development along masculine or feminine lines.

girl's early perceptions of the male being without her kind of genitalia and the fear of losing that which is specific to her sex, for Klein the anxiety is more rooted in fantasy than in perception and has to do with the girl's fears of retaliation (to the inside of her body and her female organs) for her own wish to invade, spoil, and rob her mother's body and its contents. For both authors castration anxiety can be associated with fears of punishment for oedipal wishes.

Klein's view on femininity is perhaps more in agreement, at least in part, with those American psychoanalysts who stress the anxieties connected with the "inner genital" sensations of the "early genital phase" (Roiphe and Galenson, 1981; Kestenberg, 1980) although for Klein there is no nondefensive phallic stage.

In spite of these theoretical differences, the need has been felt, on both sides of the Atlantic, to understand and conceptualize a feminine "before" language, or "outside" language, or "early" or "primary," or before penis envy. Another recent meeting point can be found in thinking about the psychical representation of the body as a body of drives that are felt rather than a body that is objective and located according to anatomical space so that the role of vision which was central in Freud's thinking about the development of masculinity and femininity from the organization of the castration complex, is now considered by some to be secondary (e.g., Gibeault, 1988, in France and Bernstein, 1990, in the USA).

These are some rapprochements, but there still remains an important difference in a basic tenet of an influential French approach that adheres to the notion that from a psychoanalytic point of view the (real) body does not count. This marks the radical difference between an approach that anchors itself in biological difference and an approach that considers "the feminine" and "the masculine" within a fantasy system that lies outside the sexed reality of the individual.

The complexity of Freud's own position on the relationship of mind and body is reflected in the fact that his theory has been seen by some as ascribing an inescapable biological destiny to man and woman—"anatomy is destiny"—while others have understood him to uphold the revolutionary belief that, psychologically speaking, we are not born man or woman and that masculinity and femininity are constructed over a period of time and are relatively independent of

Unconscious Representation of Femininity

biological sex. I suggest (Breen, 1993) that this opposition is there not because Freud was inconsistent or changed his mind, but because this opposition is at the heart of the matter. For Freud the ego is foremost a bodily ego and psychic phenomena are rooted in the drives, while at the same time, psychical events do not simply parallel biological determinants. This duality is at the heart of femininity in the contradiction between what I call negative femininity, which is based on the experience of lack as described by Freud, and positive femininity, which refers to the wealth of experiences connected to having a female body (Breen, 1993). By "positive" I do not mean that this will be necessarily experienced in a positive way, and the experience itself may be steeped in negative feelings. I refer to positive as opposed to negative simply to mean femininity in its reference to more than absence (of the penis), a reference to the experiences, anxieties, and conflicts relating to the internal female organs and to specific female experiences and fantasies. This includes the fears described as fear of penetration (Horney, 1926; Bernstein, 1990), fears of loss of the pleasure-giving function (Jones, 1935; Richards, 1994), fears of loss of reproductive function. I follow Klein in understanding these fears of internal damage as resulting from anxieties and projective mechanisms in relation to the mother and also the father. It is important to note that both positive and negative femininity take their meaning within the relationship to the parents. Even Freud's description of penis envy is rooted in the girl's relationship with her mother and her dissatisfaction and jealousy.

It is in relation to women that the issue of the place of the body came to the forefront since it is for the girl that Freud postulated a construction of her femininity that did not parallel her biological sex, whereas the boy's development follows in Freud's account a biologically syntonic path. Freud speaks of the "repudiation of femininity" in both men and women as bedrock (1937). For the woman it is her own biological sex that she is rejecting. With the advent of feminism and greater equality between men and women in the Western world, women can celebrate their femininity, and yet analyses still reveal a denigrated image of the feminine. Freud wrote that this repudiation is a biological fact, and Lacan understood it as transmitted through language ("the symbolic order"). This rejection of the feminine can also be understood as an envious denigration of the mother with all her riches (Klein, 1932), and a desire to triumph over the omnipotent primal mother (Chasseguet-Smirgel, 1976). It has been suggested that depressive feelings are considered to belong to a feminine part of the personality because they have developed in identification with the mother and her function as a container of the infant's anxieties and depression, and therefore the refusal of femininity is a fear of depression (Bégoin, 1994). It can frequently be observed how a phallic attitude is used as a defense against depressive and also psychotic anxieties. The phallus refers to a state of wholeness and completion. It is represented by a penis in never-ending erection. Penis envy is often phallus envy, the wish to have or be the phallus which, it is believed, will keep at bay feelings of inadequacy, lack, and vulnerability (Birksted-Breen, 1996). The characteristics of the female genitals, open to invasion, make them an easy representative of vulnerability, while lack belongs to the "phallic logic" along the lines of having and not having, being and not being (Gibeault, 1988).

This dual aspect of femininity, in its reference to lack and in its more immediate bodily reality, is what I shall illustrate and explore clinically with the analysis of Ms. C., a vivacious, irascible, at times violent woman in her late thirties. Her parents emigrated from overseas not long before her birth, and there is evidence that this had a disturbing effect on her mother such that she was unable at times to respond sensitively to her baby. Ms. C.'s actual experience of her mother is of a moody, "exciting," and sometimes cruel person. Ms. C. in turn tormented her younger brother on whom she felt were bestowed all natural gifts and successes. For her father, she has only utter contempt, although she will admit to a close relationship with him before puberty.

Crippled by severe anxieties and emotional problems, Ms. C. never achieved her academic potential at school but eventually, developing her drawing skills and using her imaginative abilities, she got a good job in a design company for which she still works.

The picture that unfolded in her analysis was of deep-seated anxieties revolving around a terror of death and of disintegration. Ms. C. had dealt with her anxiety, among other ways, by attempting to control her body with anorexia nervosa and compulsive exercising. The female body represented death to her because of its

Unconscious Representation of Femininity

monthly reminders of the passage of time and finite reproductive possibilities. Menstruation itself was linked with death and decay as the following dream during a menstrual period revealed:

> I was in my old flat and there was a dead woman on the floor. I told the police but they didn't come and said I'd have to live with it for a few days. I thought I couldn't possibly live with this dead, decaying woman stinking up the place and told my mother, but she didn't seem to care either.

Putting on weight was frightening because it is a literal expansion of boundaries and thus entails the threat of falling apart. Ms. C. believed that, in contrast, the male body showed unity and timelessness. Therefore not only did she envy the male body, but she liked to experience herself as having the body of a young man. All her life she had done that. As a child she had been a tomboy, carrying a gun on a belt around her waist and refusing to wear dresses. Once, when she indicated that she thought her vagina and rectum were linked, and I interpreted her dislike of the little girl she thought of as ugly and smelly, she became upset and shouted, "I've got a great body you know, I could have a harem and fuck them all," but then she calmed down and said she did not want to make links with the past, with the smelly, ugly little girl. "I didn't like myself except when I had the gun" she said, and then turned away from the little girl altogether by adding, "I've always thought of myself as a boy, ever since I can remember." This fantasy also allowed her to feel in charge. When she played with her brother she would make him be the mother while she would be the father. As a young woman Ms. C.'s sexual passions had been for women, although she also had sexual experiences with men. We could see in her analysis how this experience of herself as a young man made her feel more unified, less vulnerable and more in control. It also gave her a sense of identity to make up for the little sense of who she was. At times, Ms. C. also liked to think that she could be whoever she wanted to be, that she was really neither man nor woman, which meant that she was everything. I understand this refusal of the very basis of the human condition of belonging to one sex and not the other as encompassing both her terror of death and her hatred of any limitations. Mortality itself was a limitation that she could not accept.

In her analysis, Ms. C. enacted an erotized masculine attitude. In the early years, she fantasized being a young man in a sexual relationship with her female analyst. This phallic stance enabled her to feel tough and kept at bay all the feelings she associated with the feminine position, in particular feeling small, helpless, lacking, or ashamed. The feminine position also meant leaving herself open to attack and invasion, and she protected herself from that. "I'm afraid you'll force things into me . . . you'll fill me up and there will be nothing left of me. . . . You will tear out my insides and my brains." She experienced me, at this point, as forcing her into a submissive and hated feminine position while extracting her potency (both masculine and feminine). So instead she wanted to be the man. She engaged in homosexual relationships in which she felt herself to be the man and thus strong, while her partners were meant to be vulnerable and needy.

After a comment I made about a little girl in her who felt abandoned (which I thought, on this rare occasion, she had given me a glimpse of), she exploded in rage: "That's balls, I'm he-man, Tarzan, and you're wancky Jane." She kept depression at bay by becoming omnipotent when she felt threatened by internal collapse. Ms. C. also felt that as a man she could be more separate from me, have "contours"; otherwise, she complained, she would be "smudged" and there would be nothing left of her. Being the man with me was also a retreat from oedipal rivalry. She wanted to be my husband, my "number one," as she once put it, because that would mean neither rivalry for me nor rivalry with me. Once, when she had meant to speak of herself as a man trapped inside a woman's body, she made a slip and said a woman trapped inside a man's body. What she kept trapped was the vulnerable, mortal, desirous woman.

When, after some time, Ms. C. made moves in a feminine direction, she expected a maternal, envious, retaliatory attack. She believed that the gynecological problems she developed were proof that I was destroying her internal organs, ruining her life—that I wanted to stop her being a woman like myself. Nevertheless, over the years of the analysis, Ms. C.'s relationship with me and to her body began to change. She began to think of herself more often as a woman. The change first occurred in her relationship to a homosexual partner. She seemed to be searching for a mother who wold cherish the little girl in her. "You know, you *are* a girl," she reported her older woman partner to have said. But still she struggled against

Unconscious Representation of Femininity

the vulnerable position and the fear of invasion she felt the feminine position placed her in. Her partner became a phallic mother she could not get "out of her hair" (she dreamed of her as a "witch with a broomstick putting glue in my hair"). With another partner, she became frightened at the loss of boundaries between them when they were "the same." Some time later Ms. C. had the following dream:

> I was going to a Freudian clinic. It became a brothel and I was waiting to choose a woman, wondering what a woman does with a woman prostitute. Then this group of men came and I was terrified of them, that they would rape me. Then I was going up the hill to the clinic again; there was this mad girl being brought there by her parents.

I thought the "mad girl" whom she brought to psychoanalysis was her terror of the feminine, receptive position, now for the first time expressed directly in relation to men. In her analysis it was possible to see very clearly how, when she had been able to be more receptive to my interpretations, she suddenly became suspicious and secretive. This dream in fact followed a session when she had been more open to hearing what I had to say.

When her fear of the feminine position abated, Ms. C. wished to be a woman in relation to a man. This started in a concrete way. She imagined and hoped that the gynecological operation she had to have would turn her into a woman. She dreamed that she had to make a journey in which she had to be a black stallion and he would be cut open. A friend said it would be all right because the horse would die but she wouldn't. She did not want to, but thought she had to make that bit of the journey. The surgeon and I were seen as her hope of transformation by cutting out her maleness, the stallion. In the hospital, she dreamed that her surgeon was in love with her and, as his wife was infertile, he wanted to marry her. She felt her "insides" were like a flower opening up, and she cried about her father whom she had always despised. A few months later she again dreamed about the surgeon, that he was in love with her and would leave his wife. She then told me that in the dream she wanted him inside her, though normally she was not interested in a man's penis.

As Ms. C. began to feel more feminine, this brought problems: "Life was much easier when I felt I was one of the men." She had a terrifying dream that she had a stake driven through her head for being herself, like being a heretic. It was only days later that she could explain to me more fully that by "being herself" she had meant being a girl and pleased about it, and the stake driven through her head was a punishment for this. I understood that she had been a heretic to a part of herself that forbade her to be a woman.

Becoming more aware of her feminine body was difficult. She had never known she had "an inside" she said, until the surgeon/father had named her body parts (cervix, ovaries, etc.). She was pleased to discover this but was disturbed by the surgeon's words after the operation: "You now have a perfect cavity." She said she would rather have fibroids than a cavity. The thought of a cavity was terrifying; it made her think of Munch's painting "The Scream," or coffins going in to be cremated. For her the female body was not only representative of the passage of time and death, it was the source of death and destruction (her own wish to cremate or swallow up the penis, and her fantasy of the primal scene).

In spite of this, Ms. C. was beginning to feel that her body was more a part of her. She stopped being so obsessed with it, and her compulsive exercising diminished. She no longer felt attracted to women, and her homosexual relationships stopped. She said she felt herself to be a woman, that her gender had changed and that she did not want to be a man anymore. She could admit to me that "as a child I was always the prince. As a prince you didn't have to yearn for a prince." Now in the feminine position she was yearning for a prince, but no ordinary man would do. Yearning still felt so humiliating to her that it spoiled any potential relationship.

One day Ms. C. told me: "I don't think of myself as a boy anymore, now I think of myself as a girl—even when I'm jogging." But then she went on to say that she still felt she had something missing, "I haven't got that special thing that you have . . . all women have it, even ugly women." What was now missing was no longer the penis, but something feminine. The next session brought Ms. C. talking about fears that her gynecological problems were starting again and how she despised her sister-in-law. Thinly disguised was her envy of her pregnant sister-in-law. She had wanted to ask her sister-in-law advice about "what to do," meaning how to meet a man. It seemed that what was missing was not just the baby, but the feeling of having

Unconscious Representation of Femininity

an attractive feminine body and the capacity to attract a man (brother/father). When she was able to have a pleasurable and satisfying sexual experience, Ms. C. felt relieved, but this was followed by pains in her pelvis and the fear that "it's going wrong inside again, and this time it will be the last time" (meaning she would become sterile). When I interpreted that she felt she would be punished for her pleasure, the pains went away and she said she thought she was all right inside after all.

What I want to bring out with this clinical description is the bipolarity of femininity. Giving up the phallic position was not enough to make Ms. C. feel feminine. Although without the fantasy penis she felt she was a girl, something was still missing when the "cavity" she had been denying was felt to be a hole of death and destruction. Femininity would only be confirmed if she could feel that her internal sexual organs were intact and benign. Both her femininity and her masculinity were experienced as subject to envy: "If I'm feminine you'll be envious; if I'm masculine you'll feel threatened." She spoke of my scratching out her insides with my fingernails and making her stupid. She felt her "insides" and her mind to be "going wrong." I was threatening both her masculine and her feminine attributes. While I understand this to relate to her own envious and jealous attacks on the mother, the father, and on their relationship (particularly at a part-object level), I do not think envy of the penis is simply a displacement for envy of the mother's breast and of her womb and its contents. I think each exists in its own right, but of course the patient who cannot manage envy in relation to the breast will also find this problematic in relation to the penis, especially insofar as it represents the link of the parental relationship. Women who most envy men are those who, like Ms. C., are not able to value their femininity because it is closely tied up with oral or anal aggression. In the case of Ms. C. the unconsciously damaged object (father) and her own damaging organs became a source of unconscious guilt and persecution and consequent hatred. When she no longer felt herself to be a man, something was still missing of her femininity as long as it remained a source of extreme anxiety.

I have found with other women, too, that during their analysis, giving up a masculine stance did not automatically equal feeling feminine, although, as in the classical theory, it did initiate a movement toward femininity which then confronted them with rivalry and envy of the mother, something previously defended against. While for Freud there is a primary nonrecognition of the vagina and womb, I found that my patients' "missing" female organs, which they reported when they accepted the missing penis, were keeping at bay severe anxieties about the damaging potential of those organs. Ms. C. had an incinerating cavity, while another patient described feeling that there was a waste disposal in her abdomen that ground everything up into waste (this was in the context of talking about a fear of having damaged her mother's womb and babies, and expressed a confusion between reproductive organs and intestines). Without the penis and without the frightening internal organs, these women feel left with nothing. As one woman put it: "I think of my mother and you and other women as having a shape even though my mother is old and bent, but I feel shapeless. . . . I could put up with having a masculine shape or a feminine shape, but the problem is having neither."

Masculinity can be an attempt to have a "shape," as it was for Ms. C., but the feminine shape is more than the absence of penis. Penis envy hides a fear of feminine lack and intense oedipal anxieties. The phallic attitude is an escape from lack—both masculine and feminine, and an escape from the frightening feminine. The feminine which is felt lacking, which "other women have," is an image of the mother able to find pleasure and value in her own body, and able to attract father. Their own body cannot be thought about because it has in fantasy damaged the parental couple and the father's penis, and is feared to be in turn under attack. This is especially problematic when reality seems to confirm these fears. The negotiation of these two dimensions, acceptance of lack (and difference) and acceptance of the feminine body (with the complex anxieties rooted in the relationship with the mother and father) and their interplay trace a woman's sexual position.

REFERENCES

BALINT, E. (1973). Technical problems found in the analysis of women by a woman analyst: a contribution to the question "what does a woman want?" *Int. J. Psychoanal.*, 4:195–201.

BASSIN. D. (1982). Woman's images of inner space. *Int. Rev. Psychoanal.*, 9:191–205.

BÉGOIN, J. (1994). Eléments masculins et éléments féminins de la croissance psychique. *Rev. Franç. Psychanal.*, 5:1707–1711.

Unconscious Representation of Femininity

BERNSTEIN, D. (1990). Female genital anxieties, conflicts and typical mastery modes. *Int. J. Psychoanal.*, 71:151–67.
BIRKSTED-BREEN, D. (1996). Phallus, penis and mental space. *Int. J. Psychoanal.*, 77:649–659.
BLUM, H.P. (1976). Masochism, the ego ideal, and the psychology of women. *J. Amer. Psychoanal. Assn.*, 24(Suppl):157–193.
BREEN, D. (1993). *The Gender Conundrum.* New York: Routledge.
BURGNER, M. & EDGCUMBE, R. (1975). The phallic-narcissistic phase. *Psychoanal. Study Child*, 30:161–180.
CHASSEGUET-SMIRGEL, J. (1964). *Female Sexuality.* London: Virago, 1981.
—— (1976). Freud and female sexuality. *Int. J. Psychoanal.*, 57:94–134.
COURNUT-JANIN, M. & COURNUT, J. (1993). La castration et le feminin dans les deux sexes *Revue Franç. Psychanal.*, 57.
ERIKSON, E.H. (1964). Woman and inner space. In *Identity, Youth and Crisis.* New York: Norton, 1968, pp. 261–294.
FREUD, S. (1925). Some psychical consequences of the anatomical distinction between the sexes. *S. E.*, 19.
—— (1937). Analysis terminable and interminable. *S. E.*, 23.
GALENSON, E. & ROIPHE, H. (1976). Some suggested revisions concerning early female development. *J. Amer. Psychoanal. Assn.*, 24(Suppl.): 29–59.
GIBEAULT, A. (1988). Du féminin et du masculin. *Les Cahiers du Centre de Psychanalyse et de Psychotérapie* No. 16–17.
GILLESPIE, W.H. (1969). Concepts of vaginal orgasm. *Int. J. Psychoanal.*, 50:495–497.
GROSSMAN, W.I. & STEWART, W.A. (1976). Penis envy: from childhood wish to developmental metaphor. *J. Amer. Psychoanal. Assn.*, 24(Suppl.):193–212.
HORNEY, K. (1926). The flight from womanhood. In *Feminine Psychology*, ed. H. Kelman. London: Routledge & Kegan Paul, 1967, pp. 54–70.
JONES, E. (1935). Early female sexuality. *Int. J. Psychoanal.*, 16:263–273.
KESTENBERG, J.S. (1980). The three faces of femininity. *Psychoanal. Rev.*, 67:313–336.
KLEIN, M. (1932). The effects of the early anxiety-situations on the sexual development of the girl. In *The Psycho-Analysis of Children.* London: Hogarth Press, 1980, pp. 194–240.
LAUFER, M.E. (1982). Female masturbation in adolescence and the development to the relationship to the body. *Int. J. Psychoanal.*, 63:295–302.
—— (1986). The female Oedipus complex and the relationship to the body. *Psychoanal. Study Child*, 41:259–277.
LERNER, H.E. (1976). Parental mislabeling of female genitals as a determinant of penis envy and learning inhibitions in women. *J. Amer. Psychoanal. Assn.*, 24(Suppl.):269–285.
MAYER, E.L. (1985). Everybody must be just like me: observations on castration anxiety. *Int. J. Psychoanal.*, 66:331–349.
MITCHELL, J. & ROSE, J. (1982). *Feminine Sexuality.* London: Macmillan.
PARENS, H., POLLOCK, L., STERN, J. & KRAMER, S. (1976). On the girl's entry into the Oedipus complex. *J. Amer. Psychoanal. Assn.*, 24(Suppl.):79–109.
PINES, D. (1993). *A Woman's Unconscious Use of Her Body: a Psychoanalytic Perspective.* London: Virago.

RICHARDS, A.K. (1994). Primary femininity and female genital anxiety. *J. Amer. Psychoanal. Assn.*, 44(Suppl.): 261–281.
ROIPHE, H. & GALENSON, E. (1981). *Infantile Origins of Sexual Identity.* New York: Int. Univ. Press.
STOLLER, R.J. (1964). A contribution to the study of gender identity. *Int. J. Psychoanal.*, 45:220–226.
——— (1976). Primary femininity. *J. Amer. Psychoanal. Assn.*, 24(Suppl.):59–79.
TYSON, P. (1982). A developmental line of gender identity, gender role, and choice of love object. *J. Amer. Psychoanal. Assn.*, 30:61–86.

A Reconsideration of Object Choice in Women: Phallus or Fallacy

Rhoda S. Frenkel

> Within the context of Freud's theory of instinctual drives, analytic data from three female patients are presented which refute his concept that penis envy is the basis for female object choice. Contrary to Freud's theory, these patients did not feel their genitalia or genital arousal were inadequate. Rather, they believed their genital sexuality and fantasies were powerful and gratifying, but dangerous and bad. Their subsequent guilt and fears led secondarily to their defensive wish to have a penis to avoid their core conflicts; their penis envy was pathological. The data unequivocally demonstrate that the clitoris is *not* an inferior organ, but is the locus for the initiation of intense pleasure and occasional orgasm as early as ages four to six, when vaginal awareness also is present. In addition the material provides evidence that girls choose fathers to feel loved and valued, and that their wish for a baby is not a substitute for a relinquished wish for a penis. Observational studies and a vignette suggest that the instinctual drives of the genital phase coalesce with a change in object relations, forming an important motivation for a girl to switch her primary love object from her mother to her father.

> I made you take time to look at what I saw and when you took time to really notice my flower you hung all your own associations with flowers on my flower and you write about my flower as if I think and see what you think and see of the flower—and I don't.
> Georgia O'Keeffe (Eldredge, 1991, p. 83)

Almost a century has passed since Freud introduced his phallocentric view of female sexual development, and his subsequent explanation of why women reject their primary object, mother, and turn their affection and sexual longings to father. Freud (1905) was

---

Training and Supervising Analyst, Dallas Psychoanalytic Institute; Clinical Professor of Psychiatry, University of Texas Southwestern Medical Center at Dallas, Texas.

convinced that little girls' autoerotic and masturbatory manifestations were entirely masculine, involving only the clitoris, which he said was homologous to the male glans penis. Thus he concluded that girls, having only a small penis, have inadequate sexual pleasure and must be envious of boys. Over the next 30 years he expanded but never altered this basic position. He maintained that girls had no early vaginal sensations and that both sexes remained ignorant of the vagina until puberty. Kleeman (1976) has an excellent review of these views. Freud's explanation of the origin of the Oedipus complex in little girls was based on the girl's penis envy. In 1925, Freud wrote that realizing "she cannot compete with boys ... she gives up the idea of doing so ... she gives up her wish for a penis and puts in place of it a wish for a child: and with that purpose in view she takes her father as a love-object. Her mother becomes the object of her jealousy" (p. 256). From the beginning, within his own group, this formulation of female development was not accepted; it activated the Jones-Horney-Freud debates of the 1920's and early thirties. Freud's (1931) definitive paper, *Female Sexuality*, according to Fliegel (1973), resulted when "threatened with his [Freud's] survival, shaken in his trust of his closest collaborators, worried about ... the survival of his life's work, [he] responded to the alien thoughts emanating from Horney and Jones as a threat to the integrity of his theory" (p. 406). Because of this, he took a dogmatic stand in spite of his often reiterated awareness of his limited insight and understanding of women. Despite the intensity and duration of this controversy, Fliegel observes, a historical record of this debate has largely disappeared. In the face of Freud's illness and fears that the totality of Freud's thought would be obscured by disputes over some aspects of his theory, the debates also faded; the conflict was repressed.

Half a century later the concepts that, in women, persistent penis envy probably was a secondary defense, that female sexuality could be innately pleasurable (Horney, 1924, 1926), or that intrinsic femininity had a separate maturational path (Jones, 1927) resurfaced. Yet it was Freud's genius that laid the foundation for the flowering of psychoanalysis in the 1950's, which stimulated the burst of psychoanalytically relevant research from multiple disciplines in the 1960's and 1970's exploring female development, femininity, and the nature of female sexuality. The new data challenged Freud's

Object Choice in Women

thesis and offered clinical and observational research studies refuting his hypothesis that penis envy was the bedrock of female development. Synthesizing this new information led to a series of panels reassessing female development from infancy to womanhood and subsequently the publication of this journal's first supplement on female psychology (Blum, 1976a). Although Freud anticipated these changes, he could not tolerate them during his lifetime. He was a product of his time, his philosophical and social culture, his gender, and his own particular intrapsychic struggles. Makari (1991) argues that Freud's inability to be objective about women resulted from his own unanalyzed countertransference. Freud (1925) acknowledged that his findings were based only on a handful of cases which might not be typical and "would remain no more than a contribution to our knowledge of the different paths along which sexual life develops" (p. 258). In 1927 he wrote about transformations in scientific opinion as developments and advances, not revolutions. The validity of a universally accepted law "proves to be a special case of a more comprehensive uniformity, or is limited by another law, not discovered until later; a rough approximation to the truth is replaced by a more carefully adapted one, which in turn awaits further perfectioning" (p. 55).

The past two decades have seen an explosion of data from multiple disciplines and analytic viewpoints on human development which contradict Freud's beliefs concerning women. Nevertheless, we have not yet developed a sufficiently cohesive theory of female development, that is to say, a theory that would incorporate the advances in research and theory without abandoning the concepts that remain the cornerstones of psychoanalysis. This may contribute to the fact that, despite the tide of evidence to the contrary, many analysts give lip service to concepts of primary femininity (Stoller, 1985), but in practice they maintain Freud's phallocentric emphasis on the inadequacy of women, and castration anxiety (Brenner, 1991; Rangell, 1991). Because the female lacks a penis, many men view women's genitalia as being nothing rather than being something different (Mayer, 1995). Thus, personal perceptions and the trend to disregard libido theory and the Oedipus complex in favor of self psychology, object-relations theory, exclusive emphasis on preoedipal development, and/or reliance on observational studies, rather than analytic data, keep alive the belief that in women penis envy is bedrock. There has been a rush to debunk Freud. What his followers feared would happen in the 1930's is occurring now, dispensing with Freud's contributions as anachronistic and irrelevant in our current world. While sharing frustrations with libido theory, I feel it needs to be updated rather than discarded. This paper reemphasizes the importance of drives while integrating them with object relations. Observational studies have added enormously to our understanding of development in both men and women (Masters and Johnson, 1966; Kleeman, 1971, 1976; Money and Ehrhardt, 1972; Stoller, 1973, 1976) and much of it refutes some of Freud's theses, particularly concerning women. Nevertheless, a true refutation, revision, or augmentation of his theoretical position should come from analytic data. We know more about what women want, but we do not know why they want men, why or how they switch objects from mother to father. We do know it is multiply determined, a complex mixture of biology, intrapsychic forces, and familial and cultural attitudes.

The following cases demonstrate the importance of the instinctual drives, and how unconscious conflicts of the preoedipal phase contribute to and are integral in making it more difficult to resolve the later oedipal-phase conflicts. While preserving much of libido theory, these cases illustrate the fallacy of believing penis envy is the normal foundation of female development or femininity. While penis envy is present in all three cases, it is pathological and defensive. We need to revise, not abandon, libido theory. Case one will be presented in more detail because of the pervasiveness and implacability of her penis envy, and its unusual and ironic origin, which to my knowledge has not been previously reported in the literature.

CASE ONE

Evaluation and initial assessment. Ms. T., a single twenty-seven-year-old, sought psychiatric help stating, "The problem is not in my personal life... it's kind of overwhelming... I'm licensed in [her career], but I hate it." An attractive woman, her demeanor was nonintellectual, nonprofessional, and nonurbane. Wearing only pantsuits and occasionally jeans, she appeared as an incompletely differentiated

Object Choice in Women

latency-age child. While she alluded to a lonely childhood in a large southern city, her core issue, her self-hatred for being female and feminine, appeared only indirectly in her clothes and her denial of current social and personal problems.

Moving from her hometown the previous year, Ms. T. began a partnership with an ex-neighbor, an older married man who not only had been a childhood neighbor, but one of her heroes and a close friend of her father's. She rapidly established a respected and financially successful career. One evening, after drinking too much at a professional gathering, she asked her partner to drive her home. Despite stating, "It never entered my mind," they ended up in a motel bed, where she promptly rebuffed his advances. Later, rationalizing that working together would be impossible due to her partner's bruised ego, she agreed to have an affair with him. Prior to this she claimed she was unaware of any sexual interests. While her first experience of sexual intercourse was enjoyable, she was not orgastic. Subsequently, she became anxious and insecure at work. Complaining of an inability to tolerate office pressures, she first quit work, then ended the affair with the excuse that she knew her partner's wife. Some months later she decided to practice solo, but after several months she became even more symptomatic and sought treatment. She complained of crying uncontrollably over trivial work-related issues, but did not connect her recurring problems to her involvement in yet another triangular relationship. Stating that her former good self-image was now replaced by a sense of failure, she emphasized this was only in her professional dealings. While in the past she could handle any situation, no matter how pressured, "with cool," she now questioned her ability to handle any work and wondered if she ought to abandon her career.

Dynamically, she presented characterologic and neurotic features of a hysterical and an obsessive nature. Given her initial history of triangular relationships, unresolved oedipal conflicts with marked sexual repression and inhibition appeared to have prevented her normal progression through adolescence. Thus, although living in a different city, Ms. T. was unable to separate emotionally from her struggles with her parents; in her partnership, she essentially moved in with and won a paternal surrogate. Caught in latency, she had been unable to modify her superego, establish a nonincestuous object choice, and appeared to be having an identity crisis.

Rhoda S. Frenkel

Early treatment years. In her new practice she shared office space with a close girlfriend, who worked in another field. However, her friend's husband, B., also shared the space and was in the same profession as the patient. In order not to offend her girlfriend, she was amicable toward B., described as a male chauvinist pig, and on occasion worked with him. One evening, after a long day in the office, they went for dinner. Repeating, "It never entered my mind at all and I did nothing, absolutely nothing, to encourage it," Ms. T. related that she and B. found themselves sharing a motel bed. Although she walked out on him, she could not understand why he continued to pursue her. This history, hard to believe except as a put-on, was Ms. T.'s honest perception. Once more she quit work, complaining she could not tolerate the pressure and wanted to preserve her friendship. Shortly, however, Ms. T. ended the friendship, complaining her friend was domineering, like her mother. She then began to understand that her problems were more than professional. What emerged after several months of analysis was that while she could do well in school, when told to perform, on her own she could not accept success or responsibility for behaving in an independent, sexual, aggressive, or authoritarian manner. Behind her "city cool," was a naïve, romantic, sensitive little girl who was very afraid of her impulses.

In the early years of the analysis, profound oral and anal conflicts emerged rapidly; they dominated our work and helped to explain her impaired capacity to resolve oedipal issues. A strong therapeutic alliance allowed Ms. T. prolonged periods during which we were able to analyze her intense negative transference feelings. Guilt, intensified by her mother's current and earlier severe physical and emotional illnesses, motivated her behavior both in and out of analysis. Throughout these years she maintained that her father was one of the greatest people she had known. If not quite brilliant, he was highly intelligent, respected for his work, friendly, well liked and a VIP in their city. She commented wryly that due to his importance, others credited him with the many honors she had earned on her own merit. Nevertheless, she felt he had been "super" to her, was a fine person whom she adored. He was her hero, a designation she also used to describe his friend, her first business partner. By contrast, she expressed contempt for her mother's critical, cold, and

Object Choice in Women

duplicitous nature. As an undergraduate, she became a female activist; she realized that her mother had always been dissatisfied and disliked being female.

In the third year of analysis, struggling with oral rage and retaliatory fears that I, like her mother, might destroy her, Ms. T. began to complain of a sensation that I was going to hit her head with a frying pan. This led to memories of her mother battering her with fists and frying pans in the first four years of her life. Ms. T. also learned from a relative that she had a failure-to-thrive syndrome around three months of age and medical intervention was needed to force her mother to feed her adequately. Her mother claimed that Ms. T. had toilet-trained herself before the age of one. In fact, her mother gave her daily enemas. Subsequently, Ms. T. became chronically constipated, for which she took daily cathartics. Moreover, her mother now told her that, as Ms. T. had been the meanest kid the mother had ever seen, she had been forced to beat her three to four times a day. Actually, relatives had feared for her life, and her aunt told her that she had tried to adopt Ms. T., but was told not to interfere. During these years her father remained blameless. At work, ignorant of her mother's brutality, he was the knight in shining armor who came home every evening to save her.

Middle treatment years. It took many years to work through most of her preoedipal conflicts. For the first time in her life she was able to eat a variety of foods with ease and pleasure, and she stopped using cathartics. To her amazement, she felt better, had more energy and time for work and friends. Though still working below her potential, she allowed herself to get a reasonable job and better living accommodations. Although, after the first month of analysis, Ms T. stated that under no circumstance would she ever again discuss her sexual feelings, after five years, she changed her mind. Ms. T. had entered analysis as a very militant female activist and spent many hours preaching to me (really, to herself) about women's "lib." Gradually what surfaced was her hatred of women in general and herself in particular. Despite her progress and her professed feminist views, she was ashamed, but adamant about what she wanted. The only thing she considered would make her life tolerable was to be male. She was bitterly disappointed in me for not giving her the proper equipment. Being female was tantamount, in her mind, to

Rhoda S. Frenkel

having a life not worth living. She rationalized that her sexual feelings were not worth talking about because she only wanted to be rid of them. Moreover, marriage, child-bearing, child-rearing, even being around children were anathema to her. She felt nothing but contempt for anything labeled feminine. She became aware that, from the age of six, she had wanted to be a boy, and that she had hated her body for as long as she could remember. She hated her breasts, and dressed to disguise their presence. She not only wanted a penis, she wanted to be taller, to have male muscles, male power. Since adolescence, she had taken birth control pills. At first it was to regulate her periods and control her acne. Now she related that since she could not defend herself against rape, she could at least prevent a pregnancy. She quit analysis on several occasions because I was not helping her become male. She returned hoping I could help her tolerate being female.

After several years of celibacy, she decided to try dating single men her own age. While enjoying being held or cuddled, she disliked more specific foreplay and was anesthetic and nonorgasmic with intercourse or masturbation. After one date, she became depressed and disorganized. Several days later she was able to tell me that her boyfriend awakened in the middle of the night and tried to masturbate on her back. She became inordinately upset and refused to see him or speak to him again. Gradually, with agony, she recalled that it was not only her mother who had abused her, but that her father had held her down while her mother gave her enemas. Her memories of her father rescuing her at night, in fact, turned out to be her father seducing her at night. Between the ages of three and five, he regularly slept with her, with the excuse that she needed him to go to sleep. After pleasurably recalling that their hugging and cuddling had helped her to sleep, she remembered that she often woke up in the middle of the night with the backs of her legs wet. Her father would shame her for being eneuretic. Ms. T. became increasingly agitated and in one session asked angrily, "How could the back of my legs and pajamas be wet if the front wasn't?" She then had the sensation of a sticklike pressure on her back, and recalled it was similar pressure that had awakened her. Tremulous with rage, she recalled more. She realized now that her father had an erection and used her back to masturbate on. She realized what she had washed

Object Choice in Women

off was not urine but an ejaculate. Moreover, other times, when they were alone, if she was wearing a dress, he would put his finger in her vagina and use his other hand to tickle her. While these episodes began with pleasurable excitement, they ended with intolerable overstimulation causing Ms. T. to urinate on herself. She was humiliated further by her father shaming and laughing at her. This helped clarify why, after the one occasion when she wore a skirt in an earlier session, she had become acutely depressed with suicidal ideation for several days.

When the patient was five, for reasons that remained unclear, Ms. T.'s father stopped playing and sleeping with her, resulting in a severe depression of many months, relieved only when she was given a puppy. She then remembered, in kindergarten, developing a crush on a male singing teacher who gave her private lessons. Following one of her recitals she remembered seeing her father and her teacher embracing. At the time she believed her father was trying to punish her by taking away someone she loved. But as other memories followed, many involving seeing her father passionately involved with her teacher and later other men, it became clear that her father was homosexual. Her oft-repeated litany against women, her contempt for her body, in fact, was an identification with her father's hatred of women and fear of their sexuality. Her insistence that she *had* to be male was her very feminine wish to get her father's love. Her father loved men, not women, so she wanted to be male. Unconsciously, she felt obliged to collude with him in a constant denigration of her mother. She believed the basis of her parents' marriage had been her mother's lack of femininity and pathological need to be punished. Importantly, despite this knowledge, Ms. T. continued to crave a relationship with her father or someone like him. She was appalled at herself for what she viewed as her disgusting feminine need to be degraded. Recalling that by the age of six she knew she wanted to be a boy, she also remembered that at that time her mother had a series of breast biopsies. After each one, her mother would show Ms. T. the wound while commenting that if she had not gotten pregnant, she would not have had breast disease. Later, her mother had bilateral mastectomies. Ms. T. now questioned if these mutilating procedures were, in fact, medically indicated or more the result of her mother's need to be abused and to denigrate her sexuality. Confidant of her oedipal triumph that she had won her father,

Ms. T. believed her concomitant wish to get rid of her mother had caused the latter's illness. She believed that the punishment she had received throughout her childhood and that she maintained as a young adult, was deserved. It still took many months for her to realize that, indeed, she had not won her father, that he had used her and her mother to gratify his own narcissistic and sadistic needs. In fact, she had been the victim, not the victor. Her fantasy of winning made her feel less helpless and more in control. It also maintained the only decent sense she had of herself in that it enabled her to feel love for someone. Without that, she felt there was nothing to her except "wasted protoplasm and rage." Her capacity for love, if only in fantasy, made her feel human. Finally, she came to understand that this fantasy maintained her guilt, which inhibited her capacity for pleasure or success and prevented her from loving others.

CASE TWO

Detailed psychoanalytic process data from the opening to early midphase and pretermination through termination phases on this patient have been reported previously (Frenkel, 1991a, 1991b). Several issues highlight her difficulties with object choice and penis envy. Entering adolescence, Ann was so frightened by her sexuality that, unsuccessful at repressing her conflicts, she developed serious psychosomatic illnesses that led to agoraphobia and withdrawal from school. Indifferent to these symptoms, at sixteen, Ann entered analysis to find out why she was always the "third person," repeatedly won other girls' boyfriends, but soon lost interest in them claiming, "I'm not much for physical expression." She denied ever masturbating. During her only attempt at sexual intercourse she felt mild genital arousal, which dissipated with nausea and led to the onset of her illness.

The youngest of three, Ann was very jealous of her siblings. She envied her mother's exclusive devotion to her older brother. Also, confused by her mother's preference to read the bible rather than sleep with her father, she asked why sex after marriage was wrong. She felt rejected by her father who seemed to prefer her older sister, a nonrebellious high academic achiever. By contrast, Ann and her

Object Choice in Women

father frequently deprecated one another. This behavior was ultimately understood as a mutual unconscious defense against incestuous feelings, as Ann's exceptional physical endowment and high drives clearly surpassed both her sister's and her mother's. This became conscious following an episode when an acquaintance identified Ann as her father's mistress.

As the analysis progressed Ann's agoraphobia alternated with promiscuity. Penis envy emerged as an intermittent theme following failed "third-person" encounters when Ann questioned her sexual orientation. She wondered if she was a lesbian, but thought probably she wanted to be male, as having a penis would permit her to enjoy sex. Disturbed by these thoughts, she occasionally imagined being the admired mother of a male toddler; this alleviated her feelings of being unloved and unlovable. In the first part of the analysis Ann developed and aborted a pseudocyesis in response to my vacation. Although the baby-penis equation was present, it was evanescent and reparative. What she wanted was my return and interest. After being promiscuous, Ann complained of feeling low and unlovable. Initially blaming her ugly body and genitalia, later she understood that it was her genital feelings and fantasies she abhorred. Ann's response depicts Horney's (1926) concept that penis envy develops when girls flee from a sense of guilt to a sense of inferiority.

Ann's penis envy was a secondary phenomenon, a defense against tender erotic feelings which she associated with oedipal triumph and subsequent rejection by her parents, siblings, and God. An excellent illustration is a dream in which she saw herself with an erect penis while Christ reached out to hug her. The analysis uncovered her belief that if she had a penis, sexual excitement was acceptable; she could love and be loved by Christ, and no longer need her parents' love or feel inferior for being sexual. Later she admitted hating being a girl; having a vagina made her feel dirty. She recalled, at age six, being punished for masturbating in bed. She realized, that since then, unconsciously she had used the water pressure from a shower to have orgasms. Finally, after recalling that at age six her male baby sitter had fondled her vaginally, she remembered her fantasy that the baby sitter was her father and that she had gotten rid of her mother. She was able to connect this to her school phobia and her fear of harming her mother if she separated from her. As her earlier dream indicated, she wanted to be male because then Christ would love her. Ann's penis envy was not primary; it was a secondary defense, a fantasy to compensate for the loss of love she experienced from her entire family, which she blamed on her libidinal strivings and fantasies.

CASE THREE

Detailed developmental history and extensive analytic process data from the analysis have been presented previously (Frenkel, 1993). Erica, at six and one-half, was psychologically unable to enter latency until she was nine. Her analysis offers an unusual opportunity to view in *statu nascendi* many of the vicissitudes of the instinctual drives, as well as their modification by object relations. Because her mother, Mrs. G., had been in psychotherapy with me during and after her pregnancy with Erica, I had the rare opportunity to have in-depth information about Erica's parents, extended family, as well as the emotional climate and details of her development prior to analysis. The following material briefly reviews the relevant factors in Erica displaying her capacity for intense genital pleasure and orgasm during her sessions, as well as her wish to have a penis, expressed as a wish to be a "boy-girl."

Erica entered analysis because of her oppositional behavior at school and at home. Nearing the end of a bitter divorce, Mrs. G. was distraught, felt incapable of stopping the accelerating battles with Erica, and feared she would abuse Erica physically, repeating her own childhood. Mrs. G. was unaware that the increase in Erica's belligerence paralleled the increase in her own irritability and withdrawal following spiraling friction and physical fights with her husband. Erica's father, Dr. G., the scion of three generations of proud male chauvinists, angry at not having a son, became increasing hostile at home and at work after the birth of his third daughter. Inability to maintain his practice coupled with his refusal to be at home, except to fight with his wife, led to the divorce. On weekends, when Erica and her two younger sisters visited their father, Erica would share her father's bed while her sisters slept in another room. While ignoring his wife and two younger daughters, Dr. G. encouraged

Object Choice in Women

Erica to be a tomboy and enjoyed roughhousing with her. Unfortunately their roughhousing frequently escalated to overt sexual play which both aroused and overwhelmed Erica.

After six months of analysis Erica began to portray her sexual conflicts affectively. In connection with plans to celebrate her father's birthday, she became very excited, wiggled in her chair, and then rolled on the floor calling herself a monkey. Later she told me her father called her his monkey. Following his birthday, she said she did monkey dances for him. Gradually, over the next months, she showed me the details of the monkey dance, a precociously erotic dance that ended with her on the floor displaying her capacity for intense genital pleasure and orgasm by manual stimulation of her clitoris and vaginal introitus.

This clinical material is significant because Erica's masturbation fantasies and activity on several occasions led to orgasm during her analytic sessions. Although, in part, it was a reenactment from recent memory and a report of activity outside the analysis, its primary importance was that it occurred as part of the analytic process, so that the exact nature of the activity and its accompanying fantasies were analyzed and understood. Erica demonstrated dramatically that her clitoris was not physically inferior but rather was the locus of the beginning of intense, pleasurable genital arousal, which she called the "jeebies." Moreover, Erica's perception of her genitalia and jeebies was the opposite of what Freud (1925) proposed. Erica imbued her erotic capacity and fantasies with a magical potency so powerful and dangerous that she believed her successful conquest of her father had caused her parents' divorce, her mother's hostility and withdrawal, and her ultimate abandonment and rejection by both parents.

When Dr. G. remarried and left the country, Erica, convinced that her jeebies had driven him away, stopped all overt masturbatory activity in her sessions. Penis envy then became the focus of our work. Since Erica observed accurately that in her family boys were loved and girls were not, she was convinced that boys did not have jeebies. She desperately wanted a penis to get rid of her jeebies or at least to diminish their power and destructiveness so that she could be loved and valued. She never expressed a wish to be a boy, but rather a boy-girl. Clearly aware of her vagina and its erotic connection to her clitoris, she enjoyed her jeebies and did not want to lose them or her genitalia. Her solution was to have a penis inside her vagina. Aware that some girls and women got affection, she imagined that they must have hidden penises in their vaginas which somehow made their jeebies acceptable. Thus, her persistent intense penis envy was pathological and occurred as a secondary phenomenon in response to her perception that being *only* a girl was intolerable because of her unacceptable genital drives. This was reinforced by the thinking and behavior of her family in which throughout three maternal and paternal generations, women were both feared and degraded.

DISCUSSION

The analyses of Erica, an early latency age girl, Ann, a mid-adolescent girl, and Ms. T., a young adult woman, document that their penis envy was not normal or primary. Rather, it emerged as a secondary defense against fears of their genital drives and fantasies. Contrary to Freud's theory, by the ages of four to six, all three were aware of their vaginas and were capable of such intense pleasure with masturbation that, occasionally, it overwhelmed their ego functioning. While Ann described masturbating to orgasm, Erica reported, but also showed me how she achieved orgasm. Ms. T. recalled that her father tickled her while manually stimulating her vagina until she urinated, a loss of control that can be interpreted as an orgastic equivalent as well as an outlet for anger. Nearing termination, all expressed in their own unique fashion the opposite of what Freud postulated. They did not feel that their genitalia or their genital arousal was inadequate. Quite the contrary, they felt their genital sexuality and fantasies to be wondrously strong and gratifying, but dangerous and bad. Their subsequent guilt and fears of harm to themselves and others led secondarily to their defensive wish to have a penis in hopes of eliminating their core conflicts. The exaggerated wish to be male was more persistent in Ms. T. due to the unusual complication that her beloved father was a homosexual.

Analytic studies of vaginal awareness and the capacity for orgasm in young girls has been reported previously (Bornstein, 1953; Kramer, 1954; Barnett, 1966; Kestenberg, 1968; Fraiberg, 1972). Barnett (1968) reports that little girls are not only aware of their vaginas

Object Choice in Women

but, unlike boys, physiologically capable of orgastic release. The addition of the present analytic data provides evidence refuting the notion that women are biologically inferior due to their small clitoris and limited orgastic potential. The vitality and force of female genital arousal may frighten both sexes, leading to its suppression and the misbelief that it is weaker in women.

These cases validate the contemporary view that persistent penis envy in females is pathological and defensive, a complex intermingling of intrapsychic conflicts reinforced by familial and cultural biases (Applegarth, 1976, 1988; Blum, 1976a, 1976b; Grossman and Stewart, 1976; Karme, 1981; Tyson, 1982; Tyson and Tyson, 1994; Chehrazi, 1986; Lax, 1990). They also answer criticisms of these current theories as presented in a recent panel (1994) on female sexuality. There is some justification in objecting to the theory of primary femininity or to theories that only consider the biological, cultural, and personal factors in female development. These concepts are important but too often ignore the potency of psychic reality, intrapsychic conflict, and compromise formation, and the necessity of validating our theories from analytic, not observational data.

It is notable that all three cases recalled parentally induced trauma and sexual abuse long before the current focus in the lay press. Recently, there has been great emphasis on the role of incest and trauma (Dewald, 1989; Levine, 1990; Kramer and Akhtar, 1991; Person and Klar, 1994; Simon and Bullock, 1994). These cases also illustrate that as harmful, and in some instances horrendous, as these occurrences are, other factors are equally important in their emerging psychopathology, ego weaknesses, and general limitation in growth and development. Moreover, to varying degrees in each case, both parents were abusive. Therefore, their penis envy, while clearly influenced by a patriarchal society, is not solely a wish to identify with masculine power.

Integrating a wide range of data and concepts including instinctual drives, structural theory, object relations, self psychology, affect, cognition, and gender identity, the Tysons (1990) maintain that the epigenesis of the intrapsychic is central to psychoanalytic theory. While I agree with most of Tyson's (1982, 1994) formulations of female development, the present three cases illustrate that greater emphasis needs to be placed on the instinctual drives and the potential for intrapsychic conflict in infancy. Despite their respected public demeanor, both of Ms. T.'s parents had physically, sexually, and psychologically abused her throughout her infancy and early childhood. Psychopathology was present as early as three months when she developed a failure-to-thrive syndrome. While she had no memory of this, she developed intermittent dissociative states, psychosomatic symptoms such as constipation, anorexia, weight loss, and/or depression when she felt overwhelmed by unconscious preoedipal and oedipal conflicts. By age six she hated her body and longed to be male. It is both poignant and germane that Ms. T. did not hate her parents' horrible behavior. She thought the abuse was the result of her unacceptable oral, anal, and genital drives and fantasies, which arose from her body, an unacceptable female body. Erica's mother, rejected by her husband for being fat, had conflicts over being pregnant. In addition, she had her own conflicts over being a mother, not only from her own past, but also from the moment Erica was born, when her husband rejected her for having a girl. While initially rejecting, Erica's father, under the guise of affection, was overstimulating and abusive, imitating his father's behavior to women. However, Erica blamed herself, all of her drives, but especially her "jeebies," for the rejection and abuse she received. Ann's mother, who probably had a latent psychosis, fondled Ann anally until the child was eight. Also, she had an unnatural attachment to her son, whom she preferred over her husband or her daughters. Ann prematurely sought nurturing from her father and older brother, which augmented her early sexual strivings for them. She blamed her body and her needs for her family's rejection of her.

Each case illustrates a generational transmission of abuse and a failure of attachment due to deficiencies in the abuser's empathy (Steele, 1994). All three came to know their gender and role in a hostile environment. Normally sex assignment affects the different patterns mothers and fathers have in handling their infants and in their infants' responses to them (Money et al., 1957; Lamb, 1976). All parents have some degree of apprehension or ambivalence which infants sense. Thus core gender identity and primary femininity may be the bedrock of female development, but we do not as yet know that they arise without conflict, only that, as they coalesce in the second and third years, they appear nonconflictual. While none of the cases questioned their core gender identity and each developed

Object Choice in Women

primary femininity, their preoedipal and oedipal instinctual drives brought about conflicts through their interaction with their disturbed primary objects who reflected familial and cultural biases. Internalization of their perceptions of these interactions with their drives formed the basis for their unconscious fantasies, conflicts, and symptomatology.

In each of the analyses, months to years of work on preoedipal conflicts preceded the analysis of oedipal conflicts. Remarkably, what emerged as their primary problem was fear that their genital drives and fantasies, far from being inadequate, were extremely potent and perilous. Having a penis was a retreat from these oedipal wishes and fears. Only Ms. T. rejected her entire body and wanted to be totally male. Her wish to be a man was not to have greater sexual pleasure, but was the only way to obtain her father's love. With her father's love, she felt she could love. The capacity to love, not a penis, made her feel human, made her life worth living. In Ann's dream she had to have a penis in order for Christ to love her. While she believed that male genital strivings were acceptable, in her dream she pictured herself as a woman, with breasts and a vagina as well as a penis. Erica, on the other hand, never wanted to give up her "jeebies." They were far too pleasurable for her to relinquish them. In her mind having a penis up inside her vagina would make her "jeebies" less hazardous and onerous, thus enabling others to love her. The bedrock for Ms. T., Ann, and Erica was the wish to love and be loved for themselves: for being female, for being feminine, for having valued and enjoyable libidinal drives (Frenkel, 1991a, 1991b; Richards, 1992).

Freud (1925) postulated that, relinquishing their wish for a penis, girls substituted the wish for a child and therefore changed love objects to their fathers. If penis envy is not the bedrock of female development, why do girls shift their love from their mothers to their fathers? In these three cases genital arousal occurred after the shift to father. Preoedipal pathology, primarily maternal hostility, prematurely drove these girls to their fathers. The fathers became the preoedipal diadic focus for their affections and already were in place for the triadic oedipal conflicts.

What happens in normal female development? It is generally accepted that in the preoedipal years boys and girls experience transient penis envy, as well as breast and baby envy. Everyone wants to have it all. When envy of anything is tenacious and pervasive, we now assume pathology is present. In my experience penis envy lingers longer in boys, while breast envy is more important to girls. The first wishes for a baby appear in both sexes prior to entry into the oedipal phase (Barglow and Schaefer, 1976). Early in Ann's analysis, she developed a pseudocyesis while I was on vacation. While the baby-penis existed in her fantasy, that is, having a male child by a father surrogate would make her feel loved and lovable, she had an even more powerful fantasy of a nurturing relationship with a loving child which would not only eliminate both her positive and negative oedipal longings, but equally important, would free her from the dependency needs of the diadic preoedipal phase. If she had really wanted a baby, since she was sexually active and neither she nor her partner were using contraceptives, she could have become pregnant. Actually, I briefly believed she was pregnant, until it was clear she was trying to upset and hurt me, denying she had missed and needed her analysis. Contrary to Freud's thesis, she was not angry with me for not giving her a penis. She was hurt and angry with me for abandoning her, reliving her rejection by her parents. She believed that her libidinal strivings, preoedipal and oedipal, as well as her promiscuity had made me reject her. However, as what she really wanted was my return and interest, several weeks after resuming her analysis she aborted the pseudocyesis. Similarly, in her sessions prior to a vacation, Erica acted out a fantasied pregnancy. Silently lying on my couch, she regressed into a blissful symbiotic union with a female baby doll, seemingly unaware of me or her surroundings, denying her feelings of loss. Ms. T.'s complex, severe conflicts about having a child have been discussed previously in detail (Frenkel, 1992). Her wishes and fears permeated all levels of development. These cases provide more analytic illustrations that early wishes for a baby arise from an identification with a maternal ego ideal (Blum, 1976b) and a wish for loving reunion with the nurturing mother.

It is still unclear why, in normal development, a girl shifts objects in the oedipal phase. Here instinctual drives seem to become intertwined with object relations. Early theory proposed that a child progressed from fear of loss of the object, to loss of the object's love, to castration anxiety mirroring the progression from oral to anal and oedipal phases. This presents a contradiction in our field. While we

Object Choice in Women

believe that an individual who only has part-object relations has not fully developed, we make the highest level of development the fear of injury or loss of a part object. While genital loss or injury is clearly a source of intense anxiety, a reformulation is needed to explain the gender differences in the experience and meaning of this anxiety. There is ample evidence that castration anxiety in boys contributes to resolving oedipal conflicts and superego development, but loss of love may contribute more than has been acknowledged. I disagree with Rangell (1991) that loss of love is just an extension of separation anxiety. I believe separation-individuation has more to do with safety and survival, while loss of love is more involved in secondary narcissism and self-worth. Girls take an entirely different path. There is general agreement that loss of love is a primary concern of women. There is no evidence to support Freud's formulation that girls, missing a penis, lack the motivation to develop as strong a superego structure as boys. As first-grade teachers will attest, girls are much better behaved than boys and seem to develop a strong superego earlier than boys. Some data indicate that considerable superego *anlagen* are needed for the girl to enter the triadic relationships of the oedipal phase (Tyson and Tyson, 1990; Tyson, 1994). A positive identification with the mother is insufficient to explain the girl's shift in object.

Lamb's observational research (1976) plus a vignette may contribute to our understanding of the shift in objects and the development of triadic relationships in the Oedipus complex. He shows that while mothers, as caretakers, held infants more often and longer than fathers, infants had a more positive response to being held by their fathers for the purpose of play. By the second year, as the exciting other, the father is an important aid to toddlers in the separation-individuation phase (Abelin, 1971). Love for the father does not arise *de novo*. However, Freud may have been on to something when he assumed that a narcissistic injury drove a little girl to her father. The following vignette is germane.

Seeking advice, a neighbor, a loving mother of a three-year-old girl, an only child, told me the following story. One morning, after her husband had left for work, her daughter interrupted their breakfast angrily demanding to know why her mother liked boys better than girls. The mother denied that she preferred boys and went into

Rhoda S. Frenkel

a long discourse of how girls and boys were both special, but in different ways. The daughter, who was somewhat precocious, said she knew all that: Mr. Rogers had explained that boys were special outside and girls were special inside, but she knew who her mother liked best. The mother reviewed their recent activities, a play group, a birthday party, and a visit to a neighbor, a new mother of an infant girl. Her daughter agreed that she had not shown any preference for boys, but that was not the point. The mother asked what was the point. By now the girl, crying, had wiggled out of her chair and ran from the room yelling that the mother was lying because if she really loved girls more, she would have married one.

One interpretation of this episode could be that the little girl was upset that, lacking a penis, she could not replace her father. This would ignore the daughter's real complaint. As I explored and followed this scenario with the mother, we learned that her child felt betrayed because she no longer felt she was the center of her mother's world, while the mother had remained the center of the daughter's world. Moreover, the girl realized that even growing up would not restore the specialness she had felt with her mother; her mother had a separate life with interests that did not involve her daughter. Shortly thereafter, the daughter became openly seductive with her father. The narcissistic injury was her perceived loss of importance to her mother which felt like a loss of love, a major change in her world and her view of herself. This is a narcissistic loss that most children experience in some form, often with the birth of a sibling, or if mother leaves for a vacation. We often see this in our analytic work when analysands complain over canceled sessions, vacations, jealousy of other patients, or just awareness that the analyst has other interests. My vacation precipitated Ann's pseudocyesis and Erica's fantasied pregnancy and birth of a baby girl. With these cases, as well as with other analysands, the complaint is not that I have not given them a penis, since at least half of my patients are male, but that they feel hurt and sad that my outside interests exclude them. This initially painful transference later becomes a path for autonomy and success after analysis.

In the vignette, as the little girl's instinctual drives moved into the infantile genital phase, they combined with her increased cognitive skills to change her perception of her object world. This caused

Object Choice in Women

her to shift from her mother to her father, who was already in place as an exciting other love object, and thus began the triadic relationships of the oedipal phase. This is but one example, and there are no analytic data to substantiate it. What happens in single-parent families or homosexual families needs further study. There may be many stories of female development (Tyson and Tyson, 1990; Richards, 1992; Mayer, 1995) and object choice (Tyson, 1982; Tyson and Tyson, 1990). The interaction of the instinctual drives of the genital phase with a change in object relations may represent an important motivation in a girl's changing her primary love object from mother to father.

CONCLUSION

Using Freud's criteria emphasizing the importance of all developmental levels of the instinctual drives, this paper presented three female analytic cases to demonstrate from intrapsychic data that the phallocentric view is a fallacy. All three cases illustrate the development of penis envy as a defense against genital drives and fantasies. This adds analytic data to the growing body of evidence that penis envy can no longer be considered the bedrock of femininity. While it may exist transiently, persistent penis envy in a woman is pathological and defensive. Furthermore, these cases illustrate that the clitoris is not an inadequate organ for sexual excitement. Quite the opposite, the clitoris is the locus for the initiation of intense, pleasurable, and often overwhelming sexual excitement. The cases demonstrate that the belief that girls are unaware of their vaginas until puberty is equally untenable. In fact girls have equal if not greater sexual pleasure from their genitalia than boys, and are capable of orgasm almost a decade ahead of boys. Perhaps the intensity of female sexual responsiveness has frightened both sexes, leading to its repression and the mistaken perception that it is weaker. Furthermore, present analytic data do not support the belief that the primary reason a girl switches love object from mother to father is to have his baby as substitute for her relinquished wish for a penis.

The question of why a girl switches love objects is still not fully understood. While multiple factors influence female development, loss of love is generally agreed to be important for women, and in the present cases was the predominant motivation for their shift in object. Guilt over the potency of their genital sexuality and fantasies made them feel unloved and unlovable. Sociocultural, environmental, and interpersonal influences critically influenced their intrapsychic conflicts, secondarily reinforcing, amplifying, and validating their belief that their instinctual drives were not only bad but dangerous, resulting in their rejection by others and themselves. Analyzing their preoedipal and oedipal conflicts enabled normal developmental progression that resulted in pride and pleasure in their sexuality, in being female with a capacity to love and be loved.

While these cases can inform us, they do not represent normal development. Using observational studies in conjunction with analytic experience, a vignette was presented to illustrate the proposal that the coalescence of the instinctual drives of the genital phase with a change in object relations may represent an important motivation in a girl's changing her primary love object from mother to father.

REFERENCES

ABELIN, E.L. (1971). The role of the father in the separation-individuation process. In *Separation-Individuation: Essays in Honor of Margaret S. Mahler*, ed. J. McDevitt & C. Settlage. New York: Int. Univ. Press, pp. 229–252.

APPLEGARTH, A. (1976). Some observations of work inhibition in women. *J. Amer. Psychoanal. Assn.*, 24(Suppl):251–268.

——— (1988). Origins of femininity and the wish for a child. *Psychoanal. Inq.*, 8:169–176.

BARGLOW, P. & SCHAEFER, M. (1976). A new female psychology? *J. Amer. Psychoanal. Assn.*, 24(Suppl.):305–350.

BARNETT, M.C. (1966). Vaginal awareness in the infancy and childhood of girls. *J. Amer. Psychoanal. Assn.*, 14:129–141.

——— (1968). "I can't" versus "He won't." *J. Amer. Psychoanal. Assn.*, 16:588–600.

BLUM, H.P., Ed. (1976a). *Female Psychology*. New York: Int. Univ. Press.

——— (1976b). Masochism, the ego ideal, and the psychology of women. *J. Amer. Psychoanal. Assn.*, 24(Suppl.):157–192.

BORNSTEIN, B. (1953). Masturbation in the latency period. *Psychoanal. Study Child*, 8:65–78.

BRENNER, C. (1991). A psychoanalytic perspective on depression. *J. Amer. Psychoanal. Assn.*, 39:25–43.

CHEHRAZI, S. (1986). Female psychology. *J. Amer. Psychoanal. Assn.*, 34:141–162.

Object Choice in Women

Dewald, P.A. (1989). Effects on an adult of incest in childhood: a case report. *J. Amer. Psychoanal. Assn.,* 37:997–1014.

Eldredge, C.C. (1991). *Georgia O'Keefe.* New York: Harry N. Abrams.

Fliegel, Z.O. (1973). Feminine psychosexual development in Freudian theory: historical reconstruction. *Psychoanal. Q.,* 42:385–408.

Fraiberg, S. (1972). Genital arousal in latency girls. *Psychoanal. Study Child,* 27:439–475.

Frenkel, R.S. (1991a). The early abortion of a pseudocyesis. *Psychoanal. Study Child,* 46:237–254.

——— (1991b). Termination in the analysis of an adolescent girl. In *Saying Goodbye,* ed. A. Schmukler. Hillsdale, NJ: Analytic Press, pp. 211–229.

——— (1992). An unexpected abortion controversy: some observations from an analytic session of a single nonpregnant woman. *J. Clin. Psychoanal.,* 1:583–599.

——— (1993). Problems in female development: comments on the analysis of an early latency-age girl. *Psychoanal. Study Child,* 48:171–192.

Freud, S. (1905). Three essays on the theory of sexuality. *S. E.,* 7.

——— (1925). Some psychical consequences of the anatomical distinction between the sexes. *S. E.,* 19.

——— (1927). The future of an illusion. *S. E.,* 21.

——— (1931). Female sexuality. *S. E.,* 22.

Grossman, W.I. & Stewart, W.A. (1976). Penis envy. *J. Amer. Psychoanal. Assn.,* 24(Suppl.):193–212.

Horney, K. (1924). On the genesis of the castration complex in women. In *Feminine Psychology,* ed. H. Kelman. New York: Norton, 1967, pp. 37–53.

——— (1926). The flight from womanhood: the masculinity complex as viewed by men and women. *Int. J. Psychoanal.,* 7:324–339.

Jones, E. (1927). The early development of female sexuality. *Int. J. Psychoanal.,* 8:459–472.

Karme, L. (1981). A clinical report of penis envy. *J. Amer. Psychoanal. Assn.,* 9:427–446.

Kestenberg, J.S. (1968). Outside and inside, male and female. *J. Amer. Psychoanal. Assn.,* 16:457–520.

Kleeman, J.A. (1971). The establishment of core gender identity in normal girls. *Arch. Sex. Behav.,* 1:103–129.

——— (1976). Freud's view of early female sexuality in the light of direct child observations. *J. Amer. Psychoanal. Assn.,* 24(Suppl.):3–27.

Kramer, P. (1954). Early capacity for orgastic discharge and character formation. *Psychoanal. Study Child,* 9:128–141.

Kramer, S. & Akhtar, S., Eds. (1991). *Trauma and Transgression: Psychotherapy of Incest Victims.* Northvale, NJ: Aronson.

Lamb, M.E. (1976). Interaction between eight-month-old children and their fathers and mothers. In *The Role of the Father in Child Development,* ed. M. E. Lamb. New York: Wiley, pp. 307–327.

Lax, R. (1990). An imaginary brother. *Psychoanal. Study Child,* 45:257–272.

LEVINE, H.B., Ed. (1990). *Adult Analysis and Childhood Sexual Abuse.* Hillsdale, NJ: Analytic Press.
MAKARI, G.J. (1991). German philosophy, Freud, and the riddle of the woman. *J. Amer. Psychoanal. Assn.,* 42:183–213.
MASTERS, W. & JOHNSON, V. (1966). *Human Sexual Response.* Boston: Little, Brown.
MAYER, E.L. (1995). The phallic castration complex and primary femininity: paired developmental lines toward female gender identity. *J. Amer. Psychoanal. Assn.,* 43:17–38.
MONEY, J. & EHRHARDT, A. (1972). *Man and Woman, Boy and Girl.* Baltimore, MD: John Hopkins Univ. Press.
——— HAMPSON, J.G. & HAMSON, J.L. (1957). Imprinting and the establishment of the gender role. *Arch. Neurol. Psychiat.,* 77:333–336.
PANEL (1994). Contemporary theories of female sexuality. L. Grossman, reporter. *J. Amer. Psychoanal. Assn.,* 42:233–241.
PERSON, E.S. & KLAR, H. (1994). Establishing trauma: the difficulty distinguishing between memories and fantasies. *J. Amer. Psychoanal. Assn.,* 42:1055–1081.
RANGELL, L. (1991). Castration. *J. Amer. Psychoanal. Assn.,* 39:3–23.
RICHARDS, A.K. (1992). The influence of sphincter control and genital sensation on body image and gender identity in women. *Psychoanal. Q.,* 61:331–351.
SIMON, B. & BULLOCK, C. (1994). Incest and psychoanalysis: are we ready to fully acknowledge, bear, and understand? *J. Amer. Psychoanal. Assn.,* 42:1261–1282.
STEELE, B.F. (1994). Psychoanalysis and the maltreatment of children. *J. Amer. Psychoanal. Assn.,* 42:1001–1025.
STOLLER, R.J. (1973). The impact of new advances in sex research on psychoanalytic theory. *Amer. J. Psychiat.,* 130:241–251.
——— (1976). Primary femininity. *J. Amer. Psychoanal. Assn.,* 24 (Suppl):59–78.
——— (1985). *Presentations of Gender.* New Haven, CT: Yale Univ. Press.
TYSON, P. (1982). A developmental line of gender identity, gender role, and choice of love object. *J. Amer. Psychoanal. Assn.,* 30:61–86.
——— (1994). Bedrock and beyond: an examination of the clinical utility of contemporary theories of female psychology. *J. Amer. Psychoanal. Assn.,* 42:447–467.
——— & TYSON, R.L. (1990). *Psychoanalytic Theories of Development.* New Haven, CT: Yale Univ. Press.

Beyond the He and the She: Toward the Reconciliation of Masculinity and Femininity in the Postoedipal Female Mind

Donna Bassin

> This paper concerns a postoedipal psyche organization in the female mind whereby early overinclusive body-ego representations and cross-sex identifications are recuperated symbolically in the context of a differentiated female identity. This reintegration allows the female to symbolize what has been "lost" upon awareness of sex differences, play out masculine aspects without there being a threat to her core, primary feminine identity, and by linking rather than prohibiting cross-gender representations, provide imaginative elaboration and empathic access to another as a subject. This state does not reflect a denial of difference; rather, it reflects a psychic organization that uses symbolization to play with differences. Bisexual conflict can be mastered rather than repressed. Such mastery transcends normative, rigid, polarized sexual positions and gender conformity, perversions, and disturbed gender identity. Within the classical discourse, this mastery is suggested as an expansion of our limited and archaic notions of a genital stage specifically for the female. A new elaboration of a specific female genital stage can deepen our understanding of adult femininity and the development of cross-gender transference.

In my discussion I focus on the role of the symbolic process in transforming and using early body-ego experiences in the service of the reconciliation of masculinity and femininity in the postoedipal female mind. It is my observation that symbols, with their transitional bridging functions, can reunite such early, now-polarized component instincts as active and passive, and dichotomous images of genitals. I also address some of the intrapsychic and interpersonal

---

Member, Institute for Psychoanalytic Therapy and Research. Earlier versions of this paper were presented to Division 39 of the American Psychological Association.

difficulties that ensue when cross-sex representations are repressed in the body or projected onto the Other in the name of gender consistency. I describe a particular postoedipal psychic organization in the female mind, showing how transitionality and symbolization may develop in cases that allow a recuperation of early, overinclusive body-ego representations—representations that are undifferentiated as to gender—and those that allow an integration of cross-gender identifications originating in the oedipal drama, which can mitigate rigid polarized gender identity.

Fast (1984) speculated that the earliest experiences of girls and boys are undifferentiated and overinclusive as to gender; that is, that early in development children do not categorize themselves or their experiences in terms of gender. She pointed out, for example, the commonalities of organ actions, in which both girls and boys share similar action schemas (later transposed to a symbolic level). These organ actions, like Erikson's organ modes (1968) and Kestenberg's descriptions of organ objects (1975), are modes of relating or going at objects based on early body experiences, e.g., grasping, receiving, penetrating, and inserting. These organizers are experienced in the bodily world and get their underlying structure from the corporality of the body, but they develop into psychic metaphors that do not properly belong to either biological sex. They are transitions to symbolic behaviors, or flexible sets of categories in which the mind experiences the body and organizes its making and perceiving systems.

Erikson (1982) suggested that the infantile genital stage is dominated in both sexes by combinations of intrusive and inclusive modes and modalities that become differentiated only during puberty. Considering this differentiation, however, he asked the question I am concerned with: "What becomes, in either sex, of the countermodes?" (p. 39). I argue that these early body representations do not drop out or become totally eclipsed by later developments. Rather, as Rose (1980) demonstrated in his discussion of the creation and appreciation of the arts, and in particular, music and dance, they may be "stored" and can be reconstituted or reexperienced. These early overinclusive structures or cross-sex representations, I suggest, are used not only metaphorically in the service of self-definition in an adult female organization, but are necessary for the optimal transcendence of sexual polarities and rigid gender identities. Overinclusive body ego representations afford the raw material, or foundation, for the imaginative elaboration of the Other. Furthermore, this organization provides the female with the capacity to understand or conceive her male counterpart, allowing her to see him as a subject and not a male object. With Fonagy (1991), I offer that understanding or conceiving the Other requires the ability to imagine temporarily that one is the Other and the capacity to distinguish between this pretense and reality.

Despite the rather politically radical and utopian flavor of Reich's declaration (see Bergman, 1988) that "the genital character is not resigned, but rather rebellious to gender norms" (Reich, 1929, p. 161), his comments provoke a reexamination of the organization of the mature female genital position in light of gender identity.[1] In viewing the complexity of genital experience from a gender-neutral position, I am suggesting that the reconciliation of femininity and masculinity in the genital stage depends in part on the extent to which the self is able to generate a transitional space and to use true symbols of cross-sex representation. It is by means of symbols that early overinclusive body ego states and cross-gendered representations can be reintegrated within a *predominately* gendered self. These symbolic representations serve as a bridge between the dichotomies articulated as gender. Lasky (1989) suggests that the analyst's work requires an integration and acceptance of bisexual substrates; I argue that obtaining genitality requires them as well.

The idea of bisexuality certainly assuages castration anxiety on both sides and provides, as Blos suggests (1979, 1985), the idea of limitless possibilities. Yet within the context of a postoedipal differentiated self, the infantile fantasy of realizing a perfect gender completeness can be modified into what Blos (1985) calls a tolerance of self-limitation and a push for self-determination and possibilities. Regarding Jacobson's (1964) resistance to the idea of the containment of development, we can conceive of this capacity of the female mind as a process of potentiality, allowing for an ego that assimilates cross-sex representations simply for their value in internal and external mastery rather than for their with-or-without-penis status. Essentially, these observations provide a way to separate Kubie's (1974)

---

[1]Perhaps it was Erikson (1950) who first attempted to describe genitality in terms of life tasks other than mutuality or orgasm, citing the ability to regulate the cycles of work, procreation, and recreation.

understanding of the pathological wish to be both sexes or the hermaphroditic omnipotence of classical Greek tales from the adaptive use of symbolic transcendence of gender differentiation. The task, then, might be to articulate a series of character types or organizations, ranging from phallic or vaginal characters to genital characters, that would reflect mixtures of masculinity and femininity with varying abilities for symbolic and imaginative use. There is ultimately no normal psychic organization, only certain organizational types and certain paradoxes to be resolved. A series of possibilities in sexual organization would allow each type its own pleasures, anxieties, and resolutions.

Chodorow (1994) challenges the normative models of one modal boy or girl and suggests that we should find a wide variety of heterosexuality (as well as homosexuality) clinically and that we should treat all "sexualities as problematics to be accounted for." In this version of the female genital mind, the woman is tied to her core sexual identity yet is simultaneously able to draw on bisexual fantasies. She can symbolize relatively freely from overinclusive body ego representations. Her integration of bisexual components in the psyche makes it possible for her to transcend normative, polarized sexual positions and gender conformity—an appropriate goal for psychoanalysis, which should aim not for normative behavior, but for psychic health. This kind of female psychic organization allows for the symbolic integration of masculine strivings and body ego representations and of cross-gender identifications, without recourse to a disturbed gender identity. It reflects a dynamic, synchronic development of personality as opposed to a linear sequential axis in which one phase builds on the other (Ogden, 1986).

Through the efforts of feminist psychoanalysts, psychoanalytic clinical theory has illuminated a phallocentric logic that affects the way we perceive gender, mature object relations, and heterosexuality. The critique I refer to is not a mundane, simplistic attack on male domination, but rather the theory of a mind that makes order out of inconsistency and chaos by reducing the plurality of experiences. The word phallic and its erroneously literal tie to the male genital distract us from articulating the limitations of the phallic order for both sexes. Unduly privileging male gender, that order ignores the complex variability within the same sex and provides a

Beyond the He and the She

fixed, normative, and rigid gender identity by polarization and repression.

The resolution of the oedipal stage should mark an end to the division of the world into the phallic and the castrated, but this is rarely accomplished fully, thus giving normative male and female sexuality an unduly phallic cast. Lacan, as cited by Gallop (1982, p. 34), suggests that the phallic order, the logic in which genitality has been conceived theoretically, represents "a failure to reach the Other." Because the phallic order cannot account for femininity, it closes back on itself, and any real sexual relation between the sexes is doomed to failure. As Benjamin (1988) argues, where gender relations are organized around domination and polarity, gender splitting occurs and one part of the self disowns another part. As normatively construed within this psychosexual logic, heterosexuality is a sexual organization that knows only one active sexuality: a phallic one, one that refuses the vagina. Chodorow (1994) suggests that psychoanalysis provides a normative story that ties heterosexuality to male dominance and sexuality to gender. In broad strokes, the following clinical vignettes illustrate two women's struggles with the possibilities, failures, and complexities of cross-sex representation.

CLINICAL DATA

Miss A

The patient, Miss A, a beautiful twenty-eight-year-old single woman, initially presented with anxieties about penetration during intercourse and an intense fear of driving a car. She was very much in love with a man; they were moving toward marriage, and yet she was distressed by her inability to enjoy intercourse. She felt close to her father and was aware of the guilt she experienced regarding her loyalty to another man. Miss A felt anger over what she perceived to be her lover's invasion of her body and his penetration into her emotional life. She felt resentment and contempt toward the legitimate owner of the penis, but also felt positive about her own sensuality and identity as a woman. She reported a history of good early body closeness with the mother, who supported Miss A's developing relationship with her own body. Despite having loving feelings for her fiance and knowing that he cared deeply for her, she felt he was demanding too much of her, that he was impatient, selfish, and unwilling to take her needs into account. Although initially she was excited by the sight of his erect penis, Miss A's sexual excitement quickly abated at penetration and was replaced by an uncomfortable sense of floating. She felt safe in this floating state but frightened by a loss of sensations and an emotional emptiness. During those moments she could not relate to her lover; she felt detached and alienated. She experienced his penis as an inert object, one that was "sticking itself into places where it did not belong."

She found her work gratifying insofar as it called upon her ability to be generative; her colleagues appreciated this generativity and her vitality. However, she reported moments of intense anxiety about not being able to come up with creative solutions to problems at her job. Moreover, her fear of driving a car—specifically, of losing control of the car and killing an innocent bystander—interfered with the necessary independence and mobility she needed to develop her career.

Over time, in the transference, Miss A began to experience me as an intrusive Other who was sticking my analytic structure into what she previously experienced as a warm, safe, comforting, and generative space. Manifestly, she began to disagree with the structure of the sessions, in particular with their length, complaining that her free associations were being disrupted by my need to end the sessions at an appointed time. She objected to my bringing up her not paying me at a previously agreed-upon time as an intrusion into her analytic session, and claimed that I was disrupting and controlling the content of her sessions. During this period, Miss A often met my questions and interpretations with sensations similar to those she had felt during intercourse. She would float off, much to her dismay, as she had during her orals for an honors Master's degree and as she occasionally did during problem-solving situations at work. She claimed she liked the "old me" better, namely, when I let her free-associate and did not comment. She wanted to be left alone to float quietly away into the room, somehow held in space but free from the intrusive disruptions of my voice. The warm floating feelings were eventually transformed into feelings of immobilization whereby she could

Beyond the He and the She

watch and listen but not act; she felt safe and protected, as when she was held by her mother, from what she now experienced as demanding and intrusive. In addition, by floating away, untouched by my comments, she could render me helpless to touch her psychically. I told her that this was a way to castrate me as her analyst, just as she wished to do with her lover. Rendering us both impotent, she robbed me of my analyzing tools and her lover of his means of getting inside her.

Some months later, during another phase, seemingly triggered by a lengthy visit from her mother, Miss A began to express an active preoccupation with my personal life. She had seen my male office mate and discussed with me her fantasies that he was my husband; she wondered whether we got together between sessions. She asked me many questions: How did I feel about men, really? Did I still have an active sex life? What were my sexual fantasies? Although she wanted me to respond because she thought my answers might be important for her progress, she was ambivalent. She felt they would be intrusive and dangerous. Miss A saw her mother as a successful women, still very sexy and beautiful, despite her age, and extremely competent as a mother. She felt she was like her mother in many ways and that her mother had given her many gifts, including her creativity and warmth. She recalled childhood memories of sneaking to look through her mother's closet. The closet was filled with beautiful women's things, such as silky nightgowns and lounge wear. The garments were soft and pliable and were saturated with her mother's perfume. She remembered many such visits to her mother's closets, touching the wonderful fabrics, and stopping herself from trying on the garments. She had been frightened that she would be caught doing something or looking at something she was not supposed to.[2]

Her wishes and fears regarding knowledge about me as a woman intensified. The comparison between her wish to know the inside of her analyst and her wishes to know about the inside of her mother's body/closet evoked a memory of being punished for her curiosity, for her intrusion into her mother's space. She thought that perhaps her mother had "slammed" or slapped her. Miss A was shocked by this memory; she had never thought of her mother as physically

---

[2] The primal scene material was noted but not explored at this time with the patient.

hurting her. The memory of being slammed led to Miss A's recollection of her banging her head against her closet door when she was a child. The head banging was her response to frustration over not getting what she wanted; it felt powerful and soothed her. At those times her mother would attempt to comfort her by sitting Miss A on her lap. The slam-slap, as we reconstructed it, might have been her childhood distortion of a psychic narcissistic blow by her mother experienced as an assault on her body, as well as a projection of her own frustrated aggression. Her head banging was an aggressive response to feeling shut out. Multidetermined, it represented her futile attempt to understand what went on inside a woman; he wishes to harm her mother for depriving her of softness and guilt; and reparation for her envy of the imagined intimacy between her parents.

The recall of memories of childhood head banging led us into the analysis of her fear of driving. Driving was associated with her father, who had taught her to drive and who had communicated his pleasure at her new mobility. It represented an oedipal victory over the mother, who had never learned to drive despite her husband's efforts to teach her. Miss A remembered the sense of power and exhilaration of chauffeuring her father. The analysis of her fear of driving led to a fantasy wherein she would inadvertently press the gas pedal rather than the break at a red light. Instead of stopping, in compliance with traffic rules, she feared feeling overwhelmed by her wishes to push forward, to use the car as an expression of her power. She feared her driving would lead to her or someone else's death. The unconscious wish to thrust the car and smash into others was a derivative of her early frustrated intrusive mode for getting into mother's body. It seemed it was impossible for her to express the exhilaration and power of motion without hurting herself or others.

Gradually, she was able to see the connection between her fear of penetration by her lover and her projection of her aggression in wanting to penetrate her mother's and analyst's insides. In addition, penetration represented a mastery of facing things and knowing them from having been inside. She experienced her little-girl disappointment over her inability to get to know her mother as she imagined her father had as an inadequacy on her part and perhaps even as a punishment for her aggression. I suggested to her that she

Beyond the He and the She

wanted to be free "to stick her nose into my affairs," to penetrate my secrets, to find how I felt, and to use her curiosity and aggression. Yet she hid behind her floaty softness for fear she was too intrusive and that she would hurt someone. An unconscious masturbation fantasy was eventually revealed in a series of dreams. Miss A found the following dream significant:

> It was my head inside his body. I am making love to a woman, but it is really him. I can feel the sensation of penetration. I am myself, and then I am him. I have an erection, and it is obvious to him how I feel.

She felt joyful and liberated by this dream. Her associations to the dream, however, were initially blocked by her concerns that I would misinterpret it and interpret, superficially, her sexual confusion. When I pressed her about her fantasy about my interpretation, she suggested that I might think her problem with her lover was based on some deep homosexual wishes, and furthermore that her wish to love a woman might mean that she really must wish to be a man. Was a woman who wished to be inside a male body not a woman, I asked. I then suggested that she could not imagine that I could understand her wishes to know what it was like to be a man inside a woman or a woman inside a man without denying her her sexuality or identity as a woman.

Further associations deepened the meaning of the dream. She recalled leafing through a book of poems by Anne Sexton. Miss A could not understand, given Sexton's ability to put her fantasies to literary and imaginative use, why the poet had felt the need to kill herself instead of symbolically destroying or transforming the parts of herself that distressed her or that she no longer needed. She said she wished in part that she could let herself have a breakdown as Sexton had. For Miss A, a breakdown was associated with an ability to lose control, to break out of the rules of behavior that were causing her to behave like a good girl—passive, disembodied, and floating around in her life. She claimed that following the rules of analysis was like conforming to what her father and mother wanted for her. She experienced herself as a wolf in sheep's clothing. The sheep is quiet and passive, taking only what is given, as opposed to the wolf, a hunter able to pursue what it wants actively. She remembered discovering "rubbers" in her mother's closet, thinking about her parents having sex, her mother wanting her father and encouraging him with her beautiful nightwear. I suggested that finding the rubbers and understanding that her mother had a sexual desire for her father had made Miss A feel she had violated their privacy with her excitement.

In later sessions there was a surge of oedipal material when the patient was a good, passive girl who followed rules. I suggested that her feelings must have been overwhelming in light of her felt attachment to her mother and her needing at that time to deny her active sexuality and be good. Going limp with her lover at the moment of penetration was to deny her own excitement and keep herself from remembering exciting, forbidden feelings and guilt, as had the child in her mother's closet. She experienced the choice she made between hiding the feelings and allowing herself the feelings as a defeat. In a sense, every aspect of her life had represented a loss of part of herself as a result of that choice. I further suggested that being a sheep was her way of hiding the wolf inside, whom she both envied and feared. She felt she had to conceal those aspects of herself, that she wanted interpretations as she desired the penetration even though to her it meant something forbidden, something she was not entitled to have. Miss A then revealed that the "he" in the dream was her lover; it was also her finger. It was her curiosity and her sexual power. It was a part of her, like the little unselfconscious girl who danced vigorously through the house. In her childhood fantasy she could enjoy those feelings and escape punishment. These aspects of Miss A, which enabled her to fulfill her desire—concretely, using her finger during masturbation, and symbolically, using her mind inside her lover's body in her dream—had been cast. Her denial of her own wishes led her to resent me, the male-female analyst, and her lover for being free to get into things and penetrate and to be sexually alive, and caused her to be frustrated by rage. She feared that her mother, like her analyst, would either deny her, punish her, or not recognize her own sexuality (telling her she was sexually confused) because of her wishes both to love and be like her father and know the inside of a female. Miss A was striving to reclaim an aspect of herself, represented symptomatically by her childhood head banging and her current fears of driving a car and being intrusive and too curious. She had found symbolic expression

Beyond the He and the She

for her active sexual desire in her male lover's body and erection. She had described childhood wishes and physical attempts to penetrate her mother's closet, to get inside her mother's clothes/closet/body in order to be part of the sexually exciting experience she imagined between her parents, but felt that it was forbidden. Instead, she contented herself to sit passively on her mother's lap and on the analyst's couch.

The patient saw Sexton as a representation of her own defeated self, but as someone with the tools to transcend her situation through imagination and creativity. Miss A's anger toward herself was comparable to her anger at Sexton for having killed herself rather than using her imagination and creativity to transcend difficulty. This anger was now available to be transformed into initiative. She could allow herself to put fantasies to imaginative use and to experience her pervasive need to be a woman in a male body temporarily, without feeling she was a wolf in sheep's clothing. Erection for her had to do with her own tools. She could give them form, she suspected, through her lover's penis; perhaps it was something that could be shared.

Miss A began to realize that her use of the penis in her dream was symbolic rather than the reflection of a wish for the anatomical part itself. With the assistance of the visible form of the penis and a borrowing of her lover's male body, Miss A could imagine and represent her abilities to penetrate previously closed-off parts of her mind without having to negate her female experience. She began to understand the construction of sexuality as something to which she had given meaning rather than something given to or taken from her. Her envy of her lover and her contempt for him were gradually transformed into an appreciation of her somewhat aggressively tinged wishes to penetrate. The reclamation of her representations of penetration and thrusting promoted empathy for her lover and for his expression of desire, rather than power and aggression. She understood both his vulnerability and his need for her and knew that she was not giving herself over to an image of herself as her own lover. As Segal suggests, "The symbol is the result of psychic work, and therefore the subject has the freedom of its use" (1991, p. 96).

Donna Bassin

Miss B

The patient was a thirty-five-year-old highly educated obese woman unable to lose weight or find a job commensurate with her intellect. She was clearly disappointed with her current life situation but experienced little manifest anxiety. She was not married, despite her persistent and conscious wishes to be involved with a man and mother many children. Her work with me was her second attempt at treatment. Although she felt kindly toward her first analyst, she broke off treatment, claiming that her analyst lacked competence and empathy. She did have doubts about my effectiveness as an analyst because I was a woman and wondered whether she would be better off with a man. She presented with a well integrated but hypermoral, rigid, and tyrannical superego. Her highly developed characterological defenses were manifest in her body with its erect, stiff posture and a constrained quality to her movements. She found her relations with others frustrating. Her unconscious feelings of humiliation and dependency, accompanying aggression toward the rejecting and frustrating Other, and a need for revenge for instinctual frustrations were covered by a pseudomaturity, sadistically tinged caretaking behavior, overcompensatory kindness to friends, exaggerated sense of morality, and exacting intellectualizations.

Her discussions of her parental relations were minimal but revealed oedipal disappointments. Her view of her mother was that of an inadequate wife who was always too tired to be available to her husband. Miss B thought her father preferred her—the adoring little girl who always had time for him when he came home from work. Ultimately, she felt abandoned when he chose to support his wife in mother-daughter conflicts. Her contact with her family was frequent but obligatory and was fraught with criticism regarding their lack of emotional development. She described her father as rigid and authoritarian and her mother as hysterical and incompetent. She experienced her mother as emotionally distant, except when the children were sick and required physical care. She said that her mother described Miss B as being born an adult and proudly praised her for toilet-training herself at eight months.

Miss B reported that at fourteen she was extremely sexually aroused by a boy with whom she was having sex and who then humiliated her. Although in the midst of her adolescent passion, he commented that she was like a hungry animal and rejected her. After

Beyond the He and the She

this rather traumatic first sexual experience, which was later understood as a rejection by father for her sexual feelings, she became devoutly religious and, in accordance with the laws of her faith, decided not to have sex until she married. She described herself as slowly detaching herself from her body. She fed others and herself ritually, substituting food for emotional support. Yet she felt the food was destructive in that it removed her from the feminine body she also wanted. While consciously attempting to date, she refused to lose the weight she believed stood in the way of a man being sexually aroused by her. Miss B rejected many potential suitors, dismissing them based on descriptions of them by others as inadequate. The few dates she did have ended with Miss B's critical rejection of their limited intellectual capacities or superficial emotional development. After a date she would spend part of her session disparaging the man, thus allowing her once again to defend against her own longings and vulnerabilities. She squelched her sexuality through the years of overeating and covered her femininity with layers of fat. In fact, she experienced her enlarged body, muscular and impenetrable, as a walking powerhouse, without need of another and able to manage life by herself. She fantasized that her body weight created a masculine shape. She could become the humiliator, the boy who had rejected her scornfully, the father who had ultimately chosen her mother despite her excitement about him.

Her analytic experience was based on her intellectual efforts. She dismissed the analyst's interventions, claiming she needed the analytic hours essentially as time for herself and that she needed to do the therapeutic work alone. Her competition with the analyst in the transference interfered with her getting empathy and support. As Miss B stated, however, she was as competent in her treatment as she was in her everyday life. She was someone without need, and no one could give her anything she did not already have. She believed in the magical power of words and logic to overcome emotions and the events that aroused emotions; the master in life was the "one who knows." Her transference enactments revealed the depth of her feelings of being exposed and defeated. Instead of talking about her feelings about me, which were focused on her fantasy that I was cold and detached, she generalized and abstracted about therapeutic relations in general. She fended off all new situations, quickly countering intervention with a retort. For Miss B, therapy was simply another ritual to be followed; she would follow the rules and comply with the treatment situation, but without true involvement. She would recite a dream and interpret it, leaving no room for surprises. I was the Chinese laundry: she would give me her dirty laundry; she wanted it returned to her cleaned and pressed. Self-observation was to be used in service of control and self-criticism rather than understanding. She wanted to remain essentially sealed over—as she perceived men to be—with no bodily or psychic openings. Men were safe; their pants allowed them to be covered up. By analogy she suggested that she felt uncomfortable in women's clothing; stockings and high heels made her feel exposed and vulnerable and detracted from her being powerful and self-assured.

She fantasized that she could master what she considered her residue infantile impulses by holding on to them. As these fantasies were slowly interpreted (without retaliation for her incessant anal-sadistic attacks on the analyst), Miss B could finally associate to what I have since called her breakthrough dream. She dreamed of a Miss K, a friend of hers she often identified with.

> Miss K had a penis. It was not a normal penis but actually a part of her stomach that had pushed through. I stared at her in amazement, and thought, "It has been there all along."

Miss B associated to her bitter, envious feelings about Miss K's psychological strength. Despite her conscious feelings of self-sufficiency and power, she perceived Miss K to be even stronger, without any needs and able to negotiate the intricacies of her job without stress. She resented what she perceived as Miss K's self-containment, her ability to tolerate the frustrations of their shared nonmarried status. Miss B felt that Miss K did not really need a man. She stood tall and independent. The penis inside (which was inside all along) was finally pushed out for Miss B and myself to see. It came out of her intestines, suggesting that it was full of dirty bowel movements, but it was part of her and therefore in her control. By owning the anal phallus she could control her father and mother as she controlled situations, by being at once mother and child, analyst and patient. She had control over men, suggesting the way she seduced, by craftily evoking desire and need and then rejecting the Other through humiliation. The dream suggested her awareness of the anal phallus bodily protection against longing, but her intense need for revenge interfered with giving up this position. She could defeat us

Beyond the He and the She

all in a way that she had felt bodily and emotionally defeated. She now held the sense of mastery over her body and bodily impulses.

I return to Erikson's question regarding the fate of the female's use of the countermode of penetration and intrusion. With different levels of object relations and psychosexual development, and a different capacity for symbolization, Miss A and Miss B illustrate the variation in the psychic use of early body ego representations and cross-sex identifications. Miss B protected herself from the premature cut-off from maternal dependency at a critical point of separation by sealing herself off psychically through the use of the anal penis, a concrete barrier to her feelings of invasion and strain during anal-phallic development. In response to her feelings of being out of control over a body that was experienced as vulnerable and exposed, Miss B became the defensibly exaggerated anal penis to protect herself from loss and humiliation. As the self-sufficient penis she could evoke desire and need from others yet ultimately deny them, as she felt had been done to her. Her defensive autonomy was experienced as an abandonment and loss of the mother. Miss B felt the intestinal, anal penis in her dream, not as the symbolic representation of an internal fantasy of mastery and activity and a companion fear of loss and emptiness, but as the actual missing piece. Also, because it was difficult for her to realize that an underlying fantasy and fear were causing the disturbance, she placed false hope in the penis as the object that would rectify the lack. Memories of power and activity written on the body were not available for Miss B's symbolic use. For Miss B, the self experience was confused with the object, and the symbol the ego created was confused with what was symbolized. The intervening link, in Loewald's (1988) understanding of symbolization, is the fantasy and the fear, which in Miss B's case were unknown to her.[3]

Miss B's defensive use of the penis to support her inability to contain, own, or represent drive experiences contrasts with Miss A's use of cross-sex representation to elaborate imaginatively on an aspect of self and to form a bridge to her partner. Miss A's good, solid

---

[3]Later in treatment we were able to tie the dream image of the penis emerging from the stomach to an infantile construction of her father's penis when she sat on his lap. She eventually came to realize not only that she, as penis, had identified with the perceived aggressor, but that she could now be self-sufficient and feel desire without humiliation.

body ego and the use of a containing symbolizing mode of the ego capable of integrating overinclusive body representations and cross-gender identifications are in contrast to Miss B's fragmented body ego. Miss A's "borrowing" of her lover's body can be seen as a regression in the service of ego integration. Miss A saw the penis representation as a symbol that contained her desires to penetrate and to thrust. For her, the revival of childhood overinclusive body representations and modes of intrusion and penetration enabled her to reclaim and make use of activity and initiative. She wanted use of the symbolic penis not to be a man, but rather to develop and enrich her predominately feminine identifications. Furthermore, it provided a shared bodily experience that linked her to her lover and enabled her to empathize with his sexual experience. This in turn provided a new way of object-relating.

WHAT CONSTITUTES THE NORMAL MIND?

Jones (1942) argues that the normal mind can be defined only in relation to specific cultural norms. The healthy mind, however, can be evaluated by its flexibility, its ability to frolic and roam, accommodating contradiction and conflict. Jones's conception of the healthy mind as one that accepts conflict without undue polarization or repression may be utopian, but it is nevertheless generative in its attempt to understand how we can transcend the norms of gender conformity. Winnicott (1966) is similarly helpful: he portrays psychic health as a state in which male and female elements in intercourse bring forth creative progeny. In contrast, in the model of domination and submission one part of the self represses the Other. Both Jones and Winnicott refer to what Mitchell (1974, p. 45) calls the "uneven relationship between the two sexual possibilities [of masculinity and femininity] within a person as well as between persons." For Mitchell, it is the exploration of this relationship that was Freud's true project.

As many researchers today note, much of the classical theory of female development is now interpreted as reflecting conformity to culturally normative gender roles and compliance with the biological needs of reproduction. Since the 1950's, with relatively restricted,

Beyond the He and the She

rigid gender roles and the accompanying war between the sexes, American culture has been trying to open itself up to more permeable notions of gender.[4] The psychoanalytic literature reflects this change. Note, for example, the shifting position on the cacophonous duet of femininity and masculinity within the psyche: in the 1930's, Boehm (1930) argued that the goal of analysis was to free the male of his feminine wishes and the woman of her masculine ones. By the 1980's, Bergman (1988) suggested that the psychoanalyst had the dual goal not only of uncovering repressed countergendered wishes, but of increasing the superego's tolerance of these wishes. Our analytic commitment to understanding female sexual organization and our analytic responsibility of neutrality (which Poland defines as the "technical manifestation of respect for the essential otherness of the other" (1984, p. 289), require an ongoing push against the tide of conscious gender ideals. American culture, in some ways still in its adolescence in its intolerance of gradation, may reinforce society's restraints on the flexibility of gender roles. But the task of psychoanalysis, as Jones (1942) poetically describes it and as Grossman and Kaplan (1988) and Kaplan (1990) argue powerfully, is to treat gender roles and their normative values as manifest content. We need further elaboration of the ways in which social norms may be transcended without undue conflict and regression. Kaplan (1990) suggested that conformity to a certain moral code ensures a subjective experience of normality.

The norms of conformity in gender role behavior hinder the psyche in its attempts to imagine a reconciliation of masculinity and femininity as something other than narcissistic pathology. They obscure the diverse sexual identities within the psyche and the admixture there of the active and passive, subject and object, and masculine and feminine. The limitations of our language force categorizations that level out the complexities of nonlinear experiences. As Wisdom (1983, p. 161) suggests, "We have difficulty in specifying what a man is when he is part female and in specifying what a woman is when she is in part male."

There are alternatives to the female's acceptance of castration and to the repression or dissociation by both men and women of

---

[4]Much contemporary art and film, for example, "The Crying Game," has concerned itself with an attempt to interpret and deconstruct the pleasures of the male and female into a less politically oppressive form.

the limitless bisexual wish to be both sexes. These alternatives will be overlooked, however, unless we are able to elaborate a transitional resting space, a mastery mode in which the fact of castration and the differences between the sexes are not lost but transcended through true symbolization.[5]

Analysts' increased attention to cross-gender identifications in the development of the transference, indeed, to their necessity there (Lasky, 1989; Bernstein, 1991) makes further investigation of more flexible and elastic sexual identities a clinical essential. Freud's (1930) emphasis on renunciation and his predilection for hierarchical development—carried through in much of the classical literature—forecloses the wishes of bisexuals for symbolic and imagistic modes of realizing themselves.

TOWARD NEW MODELS OF ORGANIZATION AND INTEGRATION

To suggest revised alternatives requires more than a simple disassembly of polarized positions. New models of organization and integration are needed to assist in the arduous task of pushing forward content latent in the female narrative. Winnicott's (1971) appreciation of how the intermingling of fantasy and reality leads to an adaptive playing with reality and Loewald's (1988) refusal of a fixed, linear model of development provide the theoretical context for an integration and reconciliation of cross-sex representations. Ego states of transitionality and fluidity suggest conceptual structures within which the developmental progression of the female mind might be understood not as a hierarchical stabilization of sexual component instincts, but as an integration and dynamic application of deep early ego states—in this case, the recuperation of early bisexuality in the context of a postoedipal differentiated self (see also Benjamin, 1995).

---

[5]This position is different from Norman Brown's (1959) position in *Love's Body*. Brown argues that boundaries such as male and female are problematic to human fulfillment and suggests the preferable alternative of an androgynous or hermaphroditic body that contains both sexes. Unfortunately, however, he polarizes childhood play and the reality principle.

Beyond the He and the She

Here, I believe, we have theoretical guides for understanding how each sex integrates components of the opposite sex into its psyche without compromising its core gender identity, which Person and Ovesey (1983) define as a sense of belonging biologically to the male or female sex. One's core gender identity provides a frame for self-identity and self-continuity, but it can also drop into the background as the situation requires. The female's cross-sex identification with paternal figures, as well as her same-sex synthesis with maternal figures, is a significant dimension in her adult ego organization. Kestenberg (1968), McDougall (1980), Mendell (1988), Winnicott (1988), and Benjamin (1991) discuss the desirability of cross-sex identifications in the empathic understanding of the Other.

Classical theory has it that the Oedipus complex directs bisexuality into a clear dichotomy between masculinity and femininity. Alongside the classical view are other clinical narratives of the development of gender and of the female psyche. Contemporary gender theory continues to debate the place of the body and the impact of the Oedipus resolution in the construction of gender identity and fantasy. Freud's omission of a female body ego organization skewed our understanding of sexual development. It did not allow for a specific elaboration of how the female's body affected her character other than her preoccupation with loss.

Counterbalancing the monistic view of the female as simply nonmale, revised contributions describe a uniquely female body ego and an early, primary sense of femaleness for the girl child. This vision of a truly active female subjectivity, surfacing in part from the female body ego, was foreshadowed in the work of Horney (1926, 1933) and Jones (1935) and was theoretically detailed later by Bassin (1982), Bernstein (1983, 1990), Irigaray (1985), and Lord (1991, unpublished). Bernstein's elaboration of a gender-specific body ego has illuminated a female subjectivity and fostered clinical interventions that help the female subject understand her particular bodily interiority, anxiety, and modes of mastery.

In my earlier work (Bassin, 1982) I explored the relation between woman's experience of inner space and her construction of a category of experience or metaphor that serves as a structure for knowing and creating the world. This symbolic organization, based on a uniquely female body ego schema, provides a specific mode of activity, self-knowledge, organization, and subjectivity as a counterpoint to phallic modes. The illumination of symbolic possibilities for the female ideally provides interpretive alternatives or "conditions of possibility" (Foucault, 1978) in the clinical narrative. Unfortunately it has also resulted in theoretical positions that have led to the creation of new norms of female development, or new versions of the essentialism Freud strove to deconstruct. These new norms of female behavior—for example, "women's ways of knowing" or "self-in connection" may pose as great a threat to psychoanalytic work as did those of the *fin de siècle* (see also Grossman and Kaplan, 1988). A normative model of female behavior and fantasies that excludes the presence of masculine wishes and strivings may represent just another fantasy of gender consistency to normalize characteristics of interiority, relatedness, and connectedness at the psychic expense of competition, assertion, and aggression (Harris, 1987). A normative model of female behavior and fantasy would negate the underlying multiplicity of the sexual organization and create a female version of a phallocentric theory. The terms have merely been reversed.

Compelling experiences of gender overinclusiveness make distinct and invaluable contributions to the female mind. In my view, the apparent conflict between the narratives of the classical position, with its monistic body ego, and those of the revised theory, which posits a specifically female body ego, is reconcilable. The overlap of these two narratives might be seen as the "duality at the heart of the feminine" (Breen, 1993, p. 36). Breen, in her extensive analysis of the Freud-Jones debates and the subsequent arguments for both sides, concludes that the narratives of a "positive femininity" and the experience of lack coexist in the female. These two aspects of femininity together present a paradox of sameness and difference within and between the sexes, or, as Dimen suggests (1991), a gender multiplicity whereby the recuperation of split-off aspects of the self occupies a transitional space. We can envision a body ego experience that is both differentiated and overinclusive. Two strands of development affect this female organization: one moves toward firm gender identity based on anatomy, identification with the same-sex parent, and resolution of the positive oedipal drama; simultaneously, another allows the psyche to move away from the comforting but containing limitations of gender based on early overinclusive body ego experience with nongenitalized parents, identifications with opposite-sex parents, and resolution of the negative oedipal in adolescence. This paradoxical conception of a simultaneous identity and multiplicity of a self that is differentiated yet fluid and elastic has developmental support. First (1994), for example, details it empirically in her observation of cross-identifications in toddler play. She suggests that although self-Other boundaries are consolidating, they also move in the direction of being more fluid and imaginatively exchangeable. (Thus we can understand the girl child simultaneously mapping a specifically female body ego while integrating multiplicity through memorial symbolization of an earlier, overinclusive body ego.)

BODY EGO AS ORIGIN AND CONTAINER FOR SYMBOLIZATION

Although the two contributions of the body ego cannot be divided functionally, to help us understand cross-sex representations in an adult female psyche I shall discuss the body ego first as an origin and generative source in the creation of metaphoric and symbolic representation, and second as a container for experience.

As an origin for the content of symbols, the contested relation between anatomy and sexuality has presented a thorny problem for the psychoanalytic claim that sexuality is not based on biology. When Freud laid out his well-known arguments regarding the ego's development from the body in "The Ego and the Id" (1923), he suggested that the ego is first and foremost a *body ego*—a structure that represents its psychic activities as equivalents of bodily activities (p. 173). The conception of the body ego as the *imaginative elaboration of the body* (Winnicott, 1988) allows sufficient play for indeterminate contributions from both the body and psyche that are elaborated in affect-laden object relations (e.g., identifications from significant Others arising from separation-individuation, primal scene, and oedipal drama). The body ego has a symbolic and metaphoric relation to the body; we might say that what we have here is an imaginary anatomy (Lacan, 1953). The radical disjunction between anatomy and sexuality rests in that these representations are not veridical imitations or accurate representations of the body and its relations, but rather are interpretations based on object relations and representational abilities.

The body ego incorporates representations of sex and gender that are both differentiated (specifically related to anatomy) and undifferentiated (i.e., overinclusive). From the vantage point of symbolic processes, then, the body is actually elastic rather than "given." The body ego can shrink, expand, take parts of the outside world into itself, and give parts of itself to the outside world (Schilder, 1935). It is this flexible entity that constitutes the self's elemental representations of experience. The body may be a significant origin of experience and a model through which other experiences are understood, but this model is not simply given. It requires interpretation and symbolic mediation. The body ego cannot be reduced to anatomy, nor can anatomy be seen as an obstacle to the imaginative elaboration of cross-sex representations. Body ego organizers originating from the early, overinclusive stage contribute to the body ego's imaginative symbolic representations of the opposite sex and are ready for access when necessary. The physical impossibility of cross-sex behavior does not prevent the mind from playing with reality, creating imaginative elaborations of the Other, empathic identifications that serve as an internal bridge between gender polarities. The interaction of the body ego with the outer world provides for the development of a self that becomes firmer and fuller as it enriches itself through isomorphic structures. Also, the outside world takes on a sense of familiarity as it is processed through the self (Bassin, 1982). Through this interactive process we build bridges from inside and out, enriching both realms of experience.

The containing function of the body ego in relation to significant others serves as a boundary for the self and notself. It is crucial in the self's use of symbolization and differentiation of fantasy. A secure and activated body ego provides the space in which adaptive functions can thrive and good contents reside. As a containing structure, it is an organizer of drive activity. Instinctual experiences focus and organize infants' sense of themselves as authors of their experience (Winnicott, 1966); their integration of body parts and libidinal zones, in part a function of the mastery of discharge, reflects the achievement of the container function of the body ego. The well-developed body ego allows children to recognize themselves as initiators of actions that have effects on the external world (Grand, 1982).

Beyond the He and the She

This in turn contributes to their development of intentionality, instrumentality, and self-competence.

White (1963) argues that the self's feelings of efficacy originate in the activity of the body, not just from the specific consequences of our actions, but from activity itself. Discussing ego passivity and activity, Rapaport (1950) describes the ego's ability to defend against and control the discharge of id demands. From this perspective, both passivity and activity—unduly associated, respectively, with femininity and masculinity—have more to do with ego autonomy, specifically body ego integrity, than with gender. Indeed, Benjamin (1988) argues that it is the ability to be a container of the drives and not the drives' direction per se that creates a feeling of subjectivity. Subjective self experiences of passivity and activity need to be ferreted out from both those states as theoretical constructs related to the aims of instincts. During toilet training, for example, physical letting go can be experienced passively in regard to the body, but actively in response to the mother's request.

In fantasy life, similarly, both the male and the female subject take the active and the passive position. On the one hand, the assumption that all the characters of the dream or fantasy are the dreamer reveals the oscillation between the active and the passive position within unconscious fantasy. On the other hand, the ideal of gender polarity, manifestly assuming exclusive predominance of active or passive aims toward the object, masks this underlying oscillation. In fact, I postulate an interchangeability of positions within fantasy, which Freud discusses in "Instincts and Their Vicissitudes" (1915), as necessary for reconciliation of masculinity and femininity. Whatever the individual choice, the opposite aim is simultaneously being realized and gratified in the unconscious. What appear to be dichotomies are merely defensive surface splits.

Fast (1984) observes that as children become aware of sex differences, they renounce early, overinclusive representations and identifications they find physically impossible or incompatible with gender. Her epigenetic model posits a developmental progression, suggesting the child's need to relinquish this state of overinclusive and bisexual completeness in order to develop gender identity. This confrontation with limits becomes the foundation for what the child accepts as self and what he or she repudiates and consigns to the

Other. Yet Fast's own Piaget-influenced notions of levels of cognitive development, and specifically her idea of "mature event-centered thought," suggest how the rich, original overinclusive representations may be integrated within the child's acceptance of the limits of reality. Mature event-centered thought is a mode of symbolic process, a primary process occurring on a sophisticated level. As in Noy's (1969) articulation of a tertiary process, in which primary process is oriented to adaptive alterations of reality, the subject does not confuse thought and referent. We are perhaps most aware of this process in the creation and appreciation of art, music, dance, and poetry. As Rose (1980) argues, artists are able to regress to early body images in a controlled fashion, which protects them from languishing there and allows them to return to objective reality with an expanded awareness.

SYMBOLS: LINKS BETWEEN POLARITIES AND MEMORIALS TO LOST OBJECTS

Ogden's (1986, 1989) interpretation of Melanie Klein's depressive stage provides further clarification of the possibility of a differentiated adult female organization that transcends the rigidity of masculinity and femininity in adult life. For Ogden, psychic growth is not simply a result of the modification of unconscious psychological contents; it is a shift in the psychological matrix within which fantasy is experienced. As Segal states (1991), the great achievement of the depressive position is the individual's capacity to use symbols and to know that he or she is creating them to differentiate among the symbol, what is symbolized, and the interpreting subject. As a clinical example of this, Chertoff (1989) suggests that although the patient's biological sex may influence the specifics of the transference fantasy, the patient's ego strength may allow him or her to let go of the analyst's biological sex in order to work through the cross-gender transference. This psychological matrix allows for the as-if relation that is necessary if the patient is to transcend the reality of the analyst's sex and thus tolerate a full range of parental transference.

It is the advent of the depressive position, with its experience of separation and loss, that brings true symbolic representation into play: symbols can now be used to overcome loss. Imaginatively elaborated cross-sex representation may be seen, for example, as an elegiac emergence from the ashes of the earlier, overinclusive body ego—a kind of mourning of lost bisexuality. In opposition to the repression of gender-incompatible fantasies and images (a repudiation that inevitably leads to a return of the repressed in symptom formation or in love relationships in which incompatible polarities prevail), we can envision a mastery of loss that is accomplished through memorial symbolization. The penis, for example, a useful symbol of penetration, may be experienced not concretely but metaphorically and can link the female to her experience. This link, I believe, is what is restored in treatment and through true symbolization.

Older formulations of symbolization, as, for example, Jones's model (1938), require repression between symbol and fantasy in which symbolization has a defensive cast. In Loewald's (1988) model, symbolization is part of ego development, without the traditional emphasis on defense. Here the creation of a symbol emphasizes a hidden linkage and restores the breach between primary and secondary process. These memorial symbolizations are to be differentiated, then, from the fetish—another memorial to castration—in that they do not disguise what is symbolized. Kaplan (1991, p. 73) suggests, for example, that the "fetishist brings a misperception of anatomical difference to the theme of absence and presence that belongs to early infancy."

CONTRIBUTION TO A FEMALE GENITALITY: TRANSITIONALITY OF MASCULINITY AND FEMININITY

The concept of genitality, which the classic psychoanalytic literature posits as the provocative and rather utopian culmination of psychosexual development, can be reexamined. Although the idea of a genital stage has largely been relegated to the archives of classical psychoanalytic thought, it can still help to deepen our understanding of adult femininity and can help address the psychoanalytic problems of polarities, such as homosexuality and heterosexuality, and conformity.

Donna Bassin

As Benjamin (1988) suggests, we have come to realize that psychoanalytic theory's failure to elaborate a postoedipal stage is powerful testimony to the theory's limits. In addition, Chodorow argues for the necessity to articulate—as we have already done with the development of various homosexualities and perversions—a clinical and developmental account of the various heterosexualities. We have, in Chodorow's (1994) observations, been blind-sighted in theorizing about the variations and complexities in heterosexuality and have assumed masculine and feminine to be single rather than multiple, owing in part to the overarching division of sexual orientation in our culture.

The classical conception of the genital stage has always implied a postoedipal resolution of gender polarities and object love, but the idea has never been extensively developed. Novey (1955) argued that in Abraham's (1926) understanding of the capacity for postoedipal ambivalence, relatedness toward the partner was part and parcel of the psychoanalytic ideal of the genital character, but the lack of theoretical differentiation between heterosexual functioning and genitality (Ross, 1970; Hershey, 1989) has opened this sketchy aspect of psychoanalytic theory itself to infantile fantasies of a gendered polarity. Most relevant to this discussion are Ross's questions about the achievement of genital levels in the face of immature functioning in object relations and ego development. The impossibility of maintaining a true symbolic functioning, in which symbols are always differentiated from what is symbolized, is reflected in the difficulty we have as theorists and clinicians in staying with the metaphoric and symbolic relation to the body in our clinical writings and readings about the clinical data of our patients.

The rather sketchy classical model assumes that in the genital phase proper cross-sex representations are conceded to the Other for gender consistency. It is thought that in many traditional heterosexual relationships, this loss of the bisexual fantasy is assuaged by the exchange of cross-gender and cross-sex behavior. Bergman (1988), for example, suggests that love can be seen as the benign outcome of the bisexual conflict: to find one's other half in the safety of a heterosexual relationship frees one from the need to repress countergender wishes. In addition, Kernberg (1991) has written extensively on the dynamics of the couple, suggesting that a function

Beyond the He and the She

of coupling is an "attempt to overcome boundaries between the sexes" (p. 58) as well as a "repository of both partners' conscious and unconscious sexual fantasies and desires" (1993, p. 653). Yet the discovery of the repressed in the Other, while appearing to provide what one lacks oneself, can result in each partner relating primarily to his or her projective identifications. Thus, neither person can understand the other's experience (Goldner, 1991). In this normative mind, then, repudiation of opposite-sex characteristics within the psyche, while fueling the fire of erotic desire for the Other, also contributes to the antagonism of the interpersonal relationship between the sexes. The female's passive surrender of her masculine components to her male partner may result in an unconscious, coercive enlistment of the male lover to portray a role in her unconscious fantasy. As Lord (1991, unpublished) states eloquently, "Male libidinal objects [are asked] to perform what should be an inner symbolic function." The Other cannot really be imagined or loved as a subject if he or she is asked to provide a sense of the completeness of one's own self (Benjamin, 1988, 1990; Goldner, 1991).

The project of articulating a route to the transcendence or breakdown of gender polarities has been a major task of Benjamin (1988, 1990, 1991). In her understanding of intersubjectivity, the transcendence of opposites occurs through the reformation of the relation between them. Her deconstruction of the polarity between difference and Otherness with respect to identification also illuminates the difficulties psychoanalytic theory has in understanding what allows us to love the Other not merely as an object, but as a subject. The endeavor to understand "difference without constituting an opposition" (Gallop, 1982, p. 93) has led me to articulate a mature genital-stage female organization that is an alternative to the traditional heterosexual either-or of phallocentric logic. This organization posits transitionality as a central aspect of the female genital-stage psyche. Gender polarity might usefully be seen as a stage-appropriate fantasy—a concept extrapolated from Grossman's (1982) notion of self as fantasy—necessary for the development of self-identity, object relations, and social requirements, but requiring transcendence later in development. Polar gender identity, perhaps even a rather rigid gender identity, as Lasky (1989) discusses, has its functions in development, providing needed stability, consistency, and differentiation. Recalling Goldner's (1991) provocative description of gender as not only a solution but a problem, however, we can clinically understand rigid gender identity in postadolescent life as a defensive character structure, an unfortunate fixed solution to a conflict.

GENDER AS CHARACTER

Baudry (1989) comments that when one approaches an understanding of the problems of masculine and feminine sexuality, one is close to understanding character. Identity, as May observes (1986), can be a sustaining delusion when it is used as protection against the various conflicting wishes and aspects of the self. Yet this protective identity, which may serve to smooth over contradictory inner wishes and fantasies, can also lead to shame and doubt. Kaplan (1991) argues that socially normative gender stereotypes serve to mask cross-gender wishes and desires. She further proposes that female perversions reflect distress in coming to terms with this underlying inconsistency (p. 16). Character as a solution to conflict may situate itself primarily through modes typical of the organ on which they are organized. (Here we may apply, for example, Erikson's [1968] description of the female's receptive way of holding and of the forceful linearity of the male.) Yet heterosexual functioning that fixates on one organ mode or one gendered identification at the expense of the other can result in an impoverishment. Although culturally "normal," such rigid gender roles may involve a developmental arrest or a defensive character structure.

NOTES TOWARD A REFORMULATION OF A MALE GENITAL STAGE

I have focused on the female mind in this discussion, but the exploration of the relation between genitality and transitionality may be equally usefully applied to male development. Although one might suspect that playful cross-symbolization symmetrically applies to "normal" male gender identity as well, the parallel set of challenges

Beyond the He and the She

for male development is beyond my supporting clinical data at this time. I can provide only a brief clinical illustration of its parallel potential in men. A male patient who prided himself on female conquests associated to being force-fed during a physical illness in childhood. Later in his treatment he recalled feelings of passivity, helplessness, and intrusion in relation to this event and his latest lover's ambivalence over his foreplay style. He had finally understood the difference between waiting for her to want him and forcing his way in. Thus he was able to tell her that she should lead more during lovemaking. The availability of an experience of force-feeding, which he used as a model of a feminine experience he needed to master, allowed him to empathize with his lover and to modify their lovemaking.

Many analysts have noted that female sexuality has greater latitude to accept masculine aspects than masculine sexuality has to accept female aspects (Blos, 1979, 1985; Wisdom, 1983; Harris, 1987). Lacan's work suggests that the male, who has always been associated with "having it" (because of his anatomical penis), is in fact more susceptible to confabulating the literal and the symbolic. This would make his entrance into the symbolic use of cross-sex representations that much more difficult. Winnicott (1988) as well comments on how female sexuality calls upon pregenital aspects in a way that male sexuality does not. In light of the undue synonymity between genital organization and the male phallic stage, however, a fuller understanding of the symbolic integration of early bisexual representations in the male lies dormant in our limited theoretical organizers. Gallop (1982) postulates that phallic order suppresses not only femininity but masculinity, pointing to a footnote in Freud's (1923) writings in which he muses on how remarkable it was that a small child could be so uninterested in the other part of male genitals, the little sac and its contents. Subsequently, others, e.g., Bell (1968) and Kestenberg (1968), elaborated on the boy's interest in his scrotum and the elaboration of his feminine components in his psychic development. Kestenberg, stressing the differences that inner and outer genitals play in the development of male and female children, also implied that boys go through a feminine stage. The awareness of this inner genital stage is terminated by a repudiation of the inside, which Kestenberg claims is required for the phallic stage. Later in development, however, with the onset of male emissions, there is proof of the existence of an inner genital structure, and the opportunity for reintegration is possible.

CONCLUSIONS

The polarization between core gender identities, the biological sense of being female, and the ability to symbolize freely and draw upon cross-gender fantasies and representations do not signify obligatory choices. The physical impossibility of cross-sex behavior does not prevent the mind from playing with reality, symbolizing, and creating imaginative and empathic identifications. Symbols serve as intrapsychic bridges between rigid gender polarities and help the self to reconcile the dilemma of bisexuality and of disappointment over castration and other limitations, without recourse to repression or perversion. The troublesome resolution of bisexuality as a rigid, one-sided sexual identity contributes to the phenomenology of gender as dualistic and based on repression, splitting, and projection. The alternative is the possibility of a more mobile, flexible sexuality under the control of a symbolizing ego.

Freedman (1985) proposes that the formation of symbols reflects a psychic structure in which antagonistic component wishes, previously held apart by splitting, are assimilated in a new context. When one side of a polarized conflict is not brought into awareness in symbolic form, or united through an image, projective identification occurs, such as the perception of the Other as castrated or as dominating phallus. In the model I am suggesting, however, it is crucial to understand that cross-sex representations are developed and facilitate the capacity to know the Other as a mutual subject. We can also see how this would apply in homosexual relationships, perhaps even more symbolically.

Entrance into the female genital stage requires integration, acceptance, and symbolic elaboration of the body ego genitals of both sexes within the psyche. To the extent that a woman cannot call upon her early overinclusive body ego experiences and use them in playful symbolic representations, she will be dominated by a vaginal world, her inner generative space, or an empty hole. Finding herself surrounded only by this vaginal world, she forecloses a true object relation with a man.

For the female, the wishes and activities of her male counterpart, such as the desire to penetrate, must be familiar desires. The tender feelings of mature relationships require temporary empathic identifications. Cross-sex representations assist in the construction of an inner image of the lover, an image like a flexible working hypothesis, open to amendment through feedback and observation. As Freedman remarks (1985), the "familiar is found in the unfamiliar." The resolution, integration, and acceptance of physical impossibility need not impair the mind's ability to symbolize, to make imaginative elaborations and empathic identifications. Accepting biological reality does not preclude a transcendence of that reality in fantasy and play.

The mastery and symbolic use of cross-sex identifications contribute to the ability to play beyond gender-normative structures, as in the musician's ability to improvise after mastering the basic musical technique. In this context, one can know but can supersede the reality of one's gender-specific identifications and overinclusive body ego representations, as a jazz musician can play on tempo and as a dancer must respect gravity and space but is not tied to them.

REFERENCES

ABRAHAM, K. (1926). Character formation on the genital level of libido development. *Int. J. Psychoanal.*, 7:214–232.

BASSIN, D. (1982). Woman's images of inner space: data towards expanded interpretive categories. *Int. Rev. Psychoanal.*, 9:191–203.

BAUDRY, F. (1989). Character, character type, and character organization. *J. Amer. Psychoanal. Assn.*, 37:655–686.

BELL, A.I. (1968). Significance of scrotal sac and testicles for prepuberty male. *Psychoanal. Q.*, 34:182–191.

BENJAMIN, J. (1988). *The Bonds of Love.* New York: Pantheon.

——— (1990). An outline of intersubjectivity: the development of recognition. *Psychoanal. Psychol.* 7(Suppl.):33–46.

——— (1991). Father and daughter: identification with difference—a contribution to gender heterodoxy. *Psychoanal. Dial.*, 1:277–299.

——— (1995). *Like Subjects and Love Objects: Recognition and Sexual Difference.* New Haven, CT: Yale Univ. Press.

BERGMAN, M. (1988). Freud's three theories of love in the light of later developments. *J. Amer. Psychoanal. Assn.*, 36:653–672.

BERNSTEIN, D. (1983). The female superego: a different perspective. *Int. J. Psychoanal.*, 64:187–201.
——— (1990). Female genital anxieties, conflicts, and typical mastery modes. *Int. J. Psychoanal.*, 71:151–165.
——— (1991). Gender-specific dangers in the female/female dyad in treatment. *Psychoanal. Rev.*, 78:37–48.
BLOS, P. (1979). The genealogy of the ego ideal. In *Adolescent Passage*. New York: Int. Univ. Press, pp. 319–369.
——— (1985). *Son and Father: Before and Beyond the Oedipus Complex*. New York: Free Press.
BOEHM, F. (1930). The femininity complex in men. *Int. J. Psychoanal.*, 11:444–456.
BREEN, D., Ed. (1993). *The Gender Conundrum*. London: Routledge.
BROWN, N. (1959). *Life Against Death*. Middletown, CT: Wesleyan Univ. Press.
CHASSEGUET-SMIRGEL, J. (1981). Loss of reality in perversions, especially fetishism. *J. Amer. Psychoanal. Assn.*, 29:511–534.
CHERTOFF, J.M. (1989). Negative oedipal transference of a male patient to his female patient during the termination phase. *J. Amer. Psychoanal. Assn.*, 27:687–713.
CHODOROW, N. (1994). *Femininities, Masculinities, Sexualities: Freud and Beyond*. Lexington, KY: Univ. Press of Kentucky.
DIMEN, M. (1991). Deconstructing difference: gender, splitting, and transitional space. *Psychoanal. Dial.*, 1:335–352.
ERIKSON, E.H. (1950). *Childhood and Society*. New York: Norton.
——— (1968). Womanhood and the inner space. In *Identity, Youth, and Crisis*. New York: Norton, pp. 319–369.
——— (1982). *The Life Cycle Completed: A Review*. New York: Norton.
FAST, I. (1984). *Gender Identity: A Differentiation Model*. Hillsdale, NJ: Analytic Press.
FIRST, E. (1994). The leaving game, or I'll play you and you play me: the emergence of the capacity for dramatic role play in two-year-olds. In *Clinical and Developmental Approaches to Symbolic Play*, ed. A. Slade & D. Wolf. New York: Oxford Univ. Press, pp. 11–132.
FONAGY, P. (1991). Thinking about thinking: some clinical and theoretical considerations in the treatment of a borderline patient. *Int. J. Psychoanal.*, 72:639–656.
FOUCAULT, M. (1978). *History of Sexuality*, Vol. 1. New York: Random House.
FREEDMAN, N. (1985). The concept of transformation in psychoanalysis. *Psychoanal. Psychol.*, 4:317–340.
FREUD, S. (1915). Instincts and their vicissitudes. *S. E.*, 14.
——— (1923). The infantile genital organization. *S. E.*, 9.
——— (1930). Civilization and its discontents. *S. E.*, 2.
GALLOP, J. (1982). *The Daughter's Seduction: Feminism and Psychoanalysis*. Ithaca, NY: Cornell Univ. Press.
GOLDBERGER, M. & EVANS, D. (1985). On transference manifestations in male patients with female analysts. *Int. J. Psychoanal.*, 66:295–309.
GOLDNER, V. (1991). Toward a critical relational theory of gender. *Psychoanal. Dial.*, 1:249–272.

Beyond the He and the She

GRAND, S. (1982). The body and its boundaries: a psychoanalytic view of cognitive process disturbances in schizophrenia. *Int. Rev. Psychoanal.*, 9:327–342.

GROSSMAN, W.I. (1982). The self as fantasy: fantasy as theory. *J. Amer. Psychoanal. Assn.*, 30:919–929.

—— & KAPLAN, D. (1988). Three commentaries on gender in Freud's thoughts: a prologue to the psychoanalytic theory of sexuality. In *Fantasy, Myth, and Reality*, ed. H.P. Blum, Y. Kramer, A.K. Richards & A.D. Richards. New York: Int. Univ. Press, pp. 339–370.

HARRIS, A. (1987). Women in relation to power and words. *Issues in Ego Psychol.*, 10:29–38.

HERSHEY, D.W. (1989). On a type of heterosexuality and the fluidity of object relations. *J. Amer. Psychoanal. Assn.*, 37:147–172.

HORNEY, K. (1926). The flight from womanhood. *Int. J. Psychoanal.*, 7:324–339.

—— (1933). The denial of the vagina. *Int. J. Psychoanal.*, 14:57–70.

IRIGARAY, L. (1985). *Speculum of the Other Women*. Ithaca, NY: Cornell Univ. Press.

JACOBSON, E. (1964). *The Self and the Object World*. New York: Int. Univ. Press.

JONES, E. (1935). Early female sexuality. *Int. J. Psychoanal.*, 16:459–472.

—— (1938). Theory of symbolization. In *Papers on Psychoanalysis*. Baltimore, MD: William Wood, pp. 55–68.

—— (1942). The concept of a normal mind. *Int. J. Psychoanal.*, 23:1–12.

KAPLAN, D. (1990). Some theoretical and technical aspects of gender and social reality in clinical psychoanalysis. *Psychoanal. Study Child*, 45:3–24.

KAPLAN, L.J. (1991). *Female Perversions*. New York: Doubleday.

KERNBERG, O.F. (1991). Aggression and love in the relationship of the couple. *J. Amer. Psychoanal. Assn.*, 39:45–70.

—— (1993). The couple's constructive and destructive superego functions. *J. Amer. Psychoanal. Assn.*, 41:553–678.

KESTENBERG, J. (1956). On the development of maternal feelings in early childhood. *Psychoanal. Study Child*, 11:257–291.

—— (1968). Outside and inside, male and female. *J. Amer. Psychoanal. Assn.*, 16:457–510.

—— (1975). From organ-object imagery to self- and object representations. In *Children and Parents: Psychoanalytic Studies in Development*. New York: Aronson, pp. 215–233.

KUBIE, L.S. (1974). The drive to become both sexes. *Psychoanal. Q.*, 43:349–426.

LACAN, J. (1953). Some reflections on the ego. *Int. J. Psychoanal.*, 34:11–22.

LASKY, R. (1989). Some determinants of the male analyst's capacity to identify with female patients. *Int. J. Psychoanal.*, 70:405–418.

LOEWALD, H.W. (1988). *Sublimation: Inquiries into Theoretical Psychoanalysis*. New Haven, CT: Yale Univ. Press.

MAY, R. (1986). Concerning a psychoanalytic view of maleness. *Psychoanal. Rev.*, 73:175–193.

MCDOUGALL, J. (1980). *Plea for a Measure of Abnormality*. New York: Int. Univ. Press.

MENDELL, D. (1988). Early female development: from birth to latency. In *Critical Passages in the Life of a Woman: A Psychodynamic Perspective*, ed. J. Offerman-Zucherberg. New York: Plenum.

MITCHELL, J. (1974). On Freud and the distinction between the sexes. In *Women and Analysis: Dialogues on Psychoanalytic Views of Femininity*, ed. J. Strouse. New York: Dell.
NOVEY, S. (1955). Philosophical speculations re: concept of genital character. *Int. J. Psychoanal.*, 36:88–94.
NOY, P. (1969). A revision of the psychoanalytic theory of the primary process. *Int. J. Psychoanal.*, 50:155–178.
OGDEN, T.H. (1986). *The Matrix of the Mind*. Northvale, NJ: Aronson.
—— (1989). *The Primitive Edge of Experience*. Northvale, NJ: Aronson.
PERSON, E.S. & OVESEY, L. (1983). Psychological theories of gender identity. *J. Amer. Acad. Psychoanal.*, 11:203–226.
POLAND, W. (1984). On the analyst's neutrality. *J. Amer. Psychoanal. Assn.*, 32:283–300.
RAPAPORT, D. (1950). On the psychoanalytic theory of thinking. *Int. J. Psychoanal.*, 31:161–178.
REICH, W. (1929). The genital character and the neurotic character. In *The Psychoanalytic Reader*, ed. R. Fliess. New York: Int. Univ. Press, 1948, pp. 7–68.
ROSE, G. (1980). *The Power of Form. Psychol. Issues*, Monogr. 49. New York: Int. Univ. Press.
ROSS, N. (1970). The primacy of genitality in the light of ego psychology. *J. Amer. Psychoanal. Assn.*, 18:267–284.
SCHILDER, P. (1935). *The Image and Appearance of the Human Body*. New York: Int. Univ. Press, 1950.
SEGAL, H. (1991). *Dream, Phantasy, and Art*. London: Routledge.
WHITE, R. (1963). *Ego and Reality in Psychoanalytic Theory. Psychol. Issues*, Monogr. 11. New York: Int. Univ. Press.
WINNICOTT, D.W. (1966). The split-off male and female elements to be found in men and women. In *Psychoanalytic Explorations*, ed. C. Winnicott, R. Shepherd & M. Davis. Cambridge, MA: Harvard Univ. Press.
—— (1971). *Playing and Reality*. London: Tavistock.
—— (1988). Interrelationship of body disease and psychological disorder. In *Human Nature*. New York: Schocken, pp. 19–24.
WISDOM, J.O. (1983). Male and female. *Int. J. Psychoanal.*, 64:159–168.

From "Nothing" to "Something" to "Everything": Bisexuality and Metaphors of the Mind

Barbara Stimmel

> Psychoanalytic understanding of female sexuality has continued to evolve since Freud presented it as a central and abiding question in psychoanalytic theory. This paper is an attempt to demonstrate that much of what we have learned and added to our theory is based in part on the classical thinking which remains a foundation of psychoanalytic wisdom about human sexuality in general, male and female. And this foundation rests on the cornerstone of the human longing for completeness, for "everything"—a bisexual core. A clinical case, the basis of psychoanalytic data, demonstrates, primarily through the analysis of a dream, the neurotic derailments that follow upon a disavowal of the need for the little girl to identify with the metaphorical representation of male genitalia. The theoretical underpinnings of this perspective are presented as well as a correction of a common misreading of Freud's ideas about anatomical "bedrock."

> > In psycho-analytic treatment it is very important to be prepared for a symptom's having a bisexual meaning ... The bisexual nature of hysterical symptoms, which can in any event be demonstrated in numerous cases, is an interesting confirmation of my view that the postulated existence of an innate bisexual disposition in man is especially clearly visible in the analysis of psychoneurotics [Freud, 1908, pp. 165–166].

Psychoanalysis is in the midst of an exciting phase in its development as a theory and a technique. Partial and mistaken ideas from the past are being completed and corrected, particularly having to do with making more accurate sense of the sexual and psychological lives of women. (As we continue to make clearer sense of female psychology we find, unsurprisingly, that many of the theoretical

---

Training and Supervising Analyst, The New York Freudian Society; Assistant Clinical Professor, The Mount Sinai School of Medicine, Department of Psychiatry.

Barbara Stimmel

points are overlapping and true for both sexes.) One of the aims of this paper is to help us keep several things in mind while we go about the important business of unlocking more doors to the truth about women.

Foremost among these things is that in the quest for needed revisions in our understanding of female sexuality we remember that although cultures and their mores may change, some basic desires do not. We know that neurotic troubles brew when there is a clash between culture and desire, and it is important that we not ignore that the neuroses in our society reflect the individual neuroses of our patients. Cultural symptoms (e.g., androgyny in art and advertising, food faddism, weight obsessions, consumerism) come and go, but the universal fantasies which underlie them do not.

Among the most complicated psychological tangles psychoanalytic theory continues to grapple with is the differences between the sexes—concrete and abstract. Bisexual cohesion is a universal fantasy which in part helps people contend with these differences. By this I do not mean simply(!) the wish for a penis in women or the wish to have a baby in men, but rather the more fundamental shared wish men and women have to possess both female and male genitals. This fantasy of bisexual completeness has important meaning for creativity of any kind. It is this core idea around which the paper is developed.

I am neither alone nor the first in addressing the interaction between bisexuality and creativity (see especially Kubie, 1974). One of the most stimulating examples of such a study is to be found in a paper by McDougall (1988) in which she traces a different but significantly relevant path. She highlights the constancy of bisexual wishes, particularly in the face of our "ineluctable monosexuality." McDougall's focus is on the narcissistic and homosexual fantasy inherent in creative activity given that "in such production, every one is both man and woman at the same time" (p. 221).

This paper takes a different turn and follows in little girls (and boys) the "normal" developmental vicissitudes of identification with male and female genitalia and the subsequent symbolic possession of their attributes. I shall demonstrate, with the help of a clinical vignette, how a fused image of *both* male and female anatomy helps convey the experience of the mind; it is after all not possible for the experience of one's mind to be represented by only her or his

Bisexuality and Metaphors of the Mind

anatomy.[1] An essential point to be made is that phallic strivings in women do not necessarily reflect the longing to have a penis *per se*, but rather the qualities it reflects (see Renik, 1990, for a variant on this idea; see also Shaw, 1995). I shall describe how this unconscious self-representation of possessing both male and female genitalia lends itself to versions of the mind that, when unconflicted, lead to productive and pleasurable intellectual and artistic endeavors.

The wish for everything (for bisexual completeness) is not in itself a problem; rather it is the disruption of bisexual symbolization, in men and women, which follows the guilty disavowal of such a wish. This disruption is at least one possible determinant of the neurotic inhibitions of intellect, creativity, and ambition in women—and men (Soll, 1984–1985). The consequent unrealized solutions to oedipal and other dilemmas of self-representation then become a subset of psychic disarray. The necessary integration between the reality of what one has and the wish for all that one wants becomes derailed by this guilty diavowal, the linking of bisexual fantasies with the adaptive aspect of the defense of displacement upward goes awry, and neurosis follows.

CASE

Much could be said from many perspectives about Dr. L.'s analysis. The sexualization of her mental processes was an important character trait that found its way into the transference. This sexualization also became a resistance to the working through of Dr. L.'s abiding fantasy of bisexual completeness. However, I shall focus on one major component of the analytic work which brought forth an unconscious infantile fantasy in the context of a dream. It is my contention that the fantasy of bisexual wholeness is both limitless in its form and universal. The following clinical vignette presents just one of an infinite number of ways we might discover our patients weaving a bisexual fantasy.

[1] I am exploring a different phenomenon from that which Lax (1977) described so well when discussing the critical need for girls to identify with their fathers. As difficult as it may be to separate nature from nurture, I am interested in studying the imago of the genitals almost as a biological given in that there is a universal and primordial impact which they have on psychic life.

Barbara Stimmel

Dr. L., an anthropologist with a faculty appointment at a leading university, sought psychoanalysis during the completion of her Ph.D thesis. Although she had always enjoyed a variety of social and intellectual successes, she discovered that publicly presenting her ideas resulted in struggles that inhibited her academic success. It was this inhibition that brought Dr. L. to analysis.

Dr. L. is one of three children, having a younger brother and an older sister. Her mother was a homemaker and her father a professional who was the dominant member of the family and certainly the marriage. Her mother had suppressed aspirations having to do with the theater although these were never expressed overtly, at least during Dr. L.'s younger days. Dr. L.'s marriage was a good one with an active and meaningful sex life in which she experienced not having children as a reasonable choice.

Dr. L. was a good student who enjoyed school both academically and socially. It was during preparation for her Ph.D oral examinations that she encountered, for what seemed to be the first time, an overwhelming sense of anxiety at presenting what she knew, of going on stage. This was heightened during her thesis defense when she had to present what she had created, namely her research, its hypotheses, and its findings.

In the same way that Dr. L. was not ashamed of her genitals during sexual activity, she was ordinarily not ashamed of her mind during intellectual activity. There was a certain kind of situation, however, in which she found herself almost paralyzed with anxiety, so that her ordinarily flexible and receptive mind became frozen and immobile. Such a situation would always include an actual or imagined man in the room who would see her for the fraud she believed herself to be. This led to her anticipation of being unable to participate intellectually or retain the thoughts stimulated in her mind. Dr. L. had no doubt that an unavoidable and shameful outcome would occur if she but dared to open her mouth.

The image of opening her mouth led us to extend the fantasied boundaries of Dr. L.'s mind to include the properties of her oral cavity. We spent time deciphering the aggressive nature of the act of thinking itself as well as its representatives in language. She feared her oral aggression along with her wish to devour all things intellectual; she wanted to spit out ideas and feed others with her mind and,

Bisexuality and Metaphors of the Mind

as she said, she had an appetite for knowledge. The idea that her mouth (and its characteristics) was used by Dr. L. as a metaphor for her mind was a critical first step in the analysis of her inhibition. It was the analytic work of dealing with her conflicts in relation to oral aggression that released her from the vise of her symptom of overeating; she then lost a fair amount of weight, a goal that had eluded her. As helpful as this analytic work was, her academic inhibitions persisted.

Dr. L. went on, however, to uncover a set of ideas during analysis which astonished her and which were pivotal in the working through. In addition to consciously experiencing her mind as simply a space, a repository, in which many "things" (images, words, sounds, and colors) coexist, she learned that her mind also moved! It could travel to different parts of Dr.L.'s body, as a sort of free-floating organ. She understood this movement to be a kind of checking up on what was going on in the universe, that is her body, of which her mind was the center. This fantasy is not as strange as it first might appear. In a sense it is related to the hysterical fantasy of a phantom limb or, more pointedly, a wandering uterus. Dr. L.'s version is different in that rather than something being there, which in reality was not, her organ, thing, mind was quite there, just not where she always expected to find it.

We uncovered this unusual image through the analysis of Dr. L.'s long-standing wish to become a race car driver. In her musings she would imagine herself seated in the car with the wheel in her hands. In analysis, however, Dr. L. always returned to this conscious fantasy with the experience that there was another piece to it. This other "piece" was initially understood by us, through her associations, to have phallic properties, particularly since car racing is stereotypically a male activity. Yet Dr. L. remained unsatisfied in her understanding of this sense of unfinished business. This feeling was interpreted in the light of anatomical realities, particularly the notion that something was missing and that she herself was unfinished.

Then Dr. L. fell asleep on the couch. Her waking fantasy about my activity during her sleep included the idea that my mind left my body in order to explore hers. This led us to the idea of a roving eye/mind, which resulted in the lifting of the repression of her unconscious fantasy that her mind traveled, too. Movement through space, quickly and powerfully as in a race car, became linked with sexual union, hers and mine. The availability of this formerly repressed fantasy opened the way for Dr. L. to explore her complex view of her genitals.

When we continued to string together the elements of her conscious and unconscious fantasies, we began to perceive the central pattern of her mind as possessing properties usually assigned to the female genitalia. It was a passive receptacle for all kinds of entering objects which was mostly experienced as a pleasurable occurrence by Dr. L. She loved receiving new ideas, as she loved the secret spaces to her mind from which she frequently withdrew novel perceptions and creative imagery. She understood her mind to be fertile and creative and something of which she was typically proud. The anal and vaginal references to this space and the activities within were not lost on Dr. L. But the mystery remained as to why she could not exhibit, in a particular kind of public forum, the intellectual products her mind both created and stored. Dr. L. was curious also as to why her mind was described in anatomical terms.

These metaphoric allusions to female anatomy became fuel for the resistance to further understanding of Dr. L.'s inhibition. Our focus on her unconscious fantasies gratified some exhibitionistic-voyeuristic aims in her relationship with me. This act of my "looking at" her fantasies allowed Dr. L. to stimulate and excite my mind, my quasi sexual organ, which she then got to "see at work." The mutuality of looking and being looked at was a central theme of the transference—one that captured the sexual underpinnings of her conflict around demonstrating what was in her mind. This was most clear when Dr. L. described the pleasure she took in her metaphors, a pleasure she assumed I shared. What analyst would not enjoy the way Dr. L. so readily reflected different conceptualizations she had of her mind and its functions, such as space, creativity, passivity, and secrecy? The mirroring of her genitals was reflected in these metaphors.

As we continued the analysis of the resistance and the transference we accomplished some important work. We learned a great deal about Dr. L.'s defensive (and perhaps, primary) fears regarding damage to her inner space, namely her vaginal and anal cavities, which intersected with her strongly defended-against guilty wish to have a baby.

Bisexuality and Metaphors of the Mind

Analyzing associations to her cloaca as well as pregnancy and childbirth led Dr. L. to thoughts about the origins of the universe. Theories of the "black hole" and the "big bang" led her to thoughts of the garden of Eden and childhood ideas about heaven. Before too long her abiding unconscious fantasy that she had a garden inside her in which many little babies lived while waiting to be born was lifted from repression. Sometimes this garden was in her abdomen, at other times in her uterus, and at still others it was a garden in her mind. Her psychological difficulty lay not in the idea of the garden, but with her conflict exhibiting it. This garden was filled with an intertwining of oral, anal, and genital derivatives which became apparent when Dr. L. described the dirt, seeds, and nutrients necessary for it to grow. We came to see that, in a sense, Dr. L.'s mind was the psychic correlative of her cloacal anatomy, which for her was the site of all things having to do with creation.

The oedipal competition with her mother also emerged as she connected her mother's frustrated wish to be on stage with her own anxiety when performing. As we did the analytic work of linking past to present, we came to understand that the babies in her inner garden were condensations of body parts (breasts, clitorises, penises) and body products (feces and thoughts). Her conflicted wish to show off her fertile garden/creative mind was guiltily transformed into its opposite, so that Dr. L. found herself unwilling to have a baby and unable to defend her thesis. As these compromises unwound, Dr. L.'s conflict eased and she became pregnant.

One of the oedipal threads which ran throughout the transference was manifested in the conviction Dr. L. had of my hidden disdain for her intellectual strivings. Although she had the conscious belief that I admired her thinking and the thing by which she produced thoughts, it was clear that there was another level of reality for Dr. L. The seductive nature of the intellectual dance she did for me was compelling. She continually displayed her intellectual wares for my viewing pleasure in the hope that I would finally come to appreciate her impressive mind. We both knew that something was being hidden within this grand parade. After a short vacation, Dr. L. returned with the following dream.

> I was in a locked room, the living room, and wanted desperately to get out. But I was afraid of what I would find in the next

room. I knew a man had entered and I hadn't seen him leave. When I entered what I found astonished me—it was a fat, dead man in an easy chair. But I could not solve the mystery of who had committed the murder since all the doors were locked from the inside; as a matter of fact, double-locked!

All dreams are essentially small mysteries. Part of the lure of dream analysis is the intellectual challenge of solving a puzzle. That Dr. L.'s dream was itself presented as a classic mystery—the murder in the locked room—reminded me of what is often obscured by the intellectual excitement of understanding the dream, that is, its possible use as a resistance to understanding the transference, a kind of locked door to throw the detective off the track. What one learns from reading such mystery stories is that the author is often inviting the reader to look at the scene as though it were a map of something else—namely, the criminal's mind.

With this possibility in mind, I invited Dr. L. to consider the spaces in which the dream took place. The picture that emerged from her associations was of Dr. L. herself locked in the living room; her body surrounded the smaller locked room, her mind. A man had entered this smaller room never to be heard from again—he was dead. As a matter of fact, he was a stiff! We were beginning to make sense of Dr. L.'s inhibition. It included a notion of herself which comprised fused versions of male and female genitalia. The space within the space, her mind, was creative, fertile, and receptive. An aspect of what was in it, however, was hard, aggressive, and possibly dangerous to her. We began to see the multiple versions of her mind as an organ of receptivity and an organ of penetration.

The man in the dream betrayed the crime hidden in her mind, that of her secret possession of and identification with the erect male organ. The act of displaying her mind at work in ways that Dr. L. as well as much of her culture defined as male—scientific, factual, measurable, and even philosophical[2]—left her in dread of discovery (see also Laqueur, 1990; Wisdom, 1983).

In the manifest content Dr. L. was locked in a frightening yet exciting puzzle. How did the murderer get out of the locked room?

---

[2]There is an ongoing feminist debate over the capacity of women for objectivity, reason, and logic. The Society for Analytical Feminism is one of its fora; for a book germane to this topic, see Antony and Witt (1993).

Bisexuality and Metaphors of the Mind

The only way for the dreamer/murderer to get away with such a crime was to remain ignorant of what was inside. Her associations suggested the probability that this man was not dead but resting, or detumescent. We learned that if the phallic, projective aspect of her intellect emerged, Dr. L. would be lost.

Her analyst (and her mother) would be enraged with Dr. L. for coveting and possessing father's penis; for maybe having something that she did not; and for abandoning her for another. The detumescence, or castration embodied in this ultimate act of aggression, murder, directed toward a man, had the perhaps stronger function of offering Dr. L. protection from an act of aggression by a woman. The oedipal (positive and negative) nature of her wish to impregnate as well as be impregnated with everything from sperm to ideas had become increasingly clear. That the fatness of the man was a condensation of Dr. L. herself as overweight and of her pregnant mother when the patient was three years old reinforced the observation that fusion of male/female was complete.

Also, the narcissistic pleasure in being independent of the object so that she was complete unto herself, both male and female, was an unconscious gratification Dr. L. was loathe to give up. In this context, the detumescence effectively shrinking her secret had more to do with protecting narcissistic supplies than with avoiding warring sexual and aggressive aims. The pathological narcissism Dr. L. paid for by her masochistic abdication of intellectual pleasure slowly gave way to appropriate narcissistic enjoyment of her mind and its possibilities.

Most of this work was accomplished in the context of the transference in the here-and-now, particularly vividly in Dr. L.'s interest in and fantasies about my mind and my body. As she described the room within a room, it began to sound more and more like my office, my space. The analyst, as a woman with the same metaphorical male part to her mind, according to Dr. L., would perhaps know Dr. L.'s secret. Yet she longed to identify with her analyst as she expressed, within the analytic encounter, the complexity of her female/male mind. This identification would thus allow Dr. L. secret pleasure in her own male identifications. The inhibition of her intellect was a form of autocastration so that submission to the male/female analyst was complete. This submission also carried within it the great and guilty pleasure of forbidden sexual activity with me, her analyst. This maneuver, aimed at disarming her analyst, at the same time protected Dr. L. from the aggressive (rape?) entry of the analyst's interpretations into her mind. And to the extent that I, the analyst, was represented in the office space of Dr. L.'s dream as the dead man, she rendered me passive and unharmful. This image of the castrated/dead analyst protected Dr. L while at the same time it conveyed a projected version she had of herself, of her mind.

DISCUSSION

One partial answer to the philosophical conundrum "how does matter (or, in our case, the mind) know itself?" might be found by reflecting on the facility of the mind to fashion itself after parts of its own extension in space, the body. These extensions represent one possible version of the mind which, in turn, then knows itself by assessing the body. The psychic and cognitive feats of displacement and metaphor are central to this question of knowing.

We know that one way children come to know the world and themselves is through their anatomy. Reciprocally, they make sense of their anatomy in part by observing the opposite sex. As we shall see, bisexual fantasies are an intrinsic part of that developing self-knowledge.

Conceptualizing the mind as a mirror of genital anatomy, though, tends to obscure the power of the idea of the mind as an organized reflection of the *self*. Theories of the self, sense of self, and self-representation offer a complex array of possible frameworks from which to think about how the child comes to know her sexual self (see Blum, 1982; Kernberg, 1982; Mahler and McDevitt, 1982; Rangell, 1982; Richards, A.D., 1982; Ticho, 1982). In particular, Grossman's (1982) view of the self as a constellation of organizing fantasies or "categories of experience" leads him and us to view the self as a "personal myth" (Kris, 1956). I am suggesting that this myth continues to develop from derivative images of all the bodily zones as the child continues to define herself along the developmental path of consuming interest in body part to body part.

There is a growing body of literature that calls attention to the impact of the vagina, the introitus, and the inner space of the female

Bisexuality and Metaphors of the Mind

genitalia to help explain psychosexual development of the young girl as well as her developing sense of self. Reference is made to these anatomical realities as explanatory organs in their own right, much as the penis has been used to explain male and female psychology in the past.

The early literature on the presence or absence of the penis and its impact on the development of the inner sexual life of the little girl is well known. Its problems have recently overshadowed its helpfulness, but they have stimulated clinicians to find new and creative ways of continuing to make sense of their female patients' problems and associations. The penis after all could not possibly explain "everything."

We also had to make serious sense of "nothing." There is a line in our literature, starting with Lewin (1948; see also Abrams and Shengold, 1974; Brakel, 1986; Shengold, 1989; Slap, 1979), which suggests that references to "nothing" in the patient's associations will lead to the vagina, in both men and women.[3] "Nothing" (the vagina) and "something" (the penis) have given us ways of understanding some of the fantasy elements people carry around with them regarding female and male genitalia.

But there have been several papers recently that enlarge our understanding of the more complex ideas and experiences girls have of their own genitals, beginning early in life. The vagina as "nothing" cannot be the only or even fundamental experience they have, especially since it is only a part of the female genitalia. There are too many spaces, folds, projections, and possibilities for sensory stimulation to maintain the idea that the female genital is nothing (e.g., see Lax, 1994; Richards, A.K., 1992); it is quite decidedly something (see Kalinich, 1993). Nonetheless, the *visibility*[4] of the penis/testicles compared to that of the labia/clitoris/vagina will lead all children

---

[3]Abrams and Shengold (1974) include the critical idea that "nothing" has different meaning to the child at different times in development so that it represents "the helplessness of separateness, flatus, and the absent phallus. Its inverse, "everything," also will have changing representations: "the omnipotent mother, the valued feces, and the envied penis" (p. 115). These ideas will have particular relevance to the unfolding of the case as well as to the formulation in this paper of developing self-representations.

[4]Krausz (1994) presents an interesting idea in her paper on "The invisible woman" having to do with the "experiential world of femininity as it moves from the invisible to the visible" (p. 59).

Barbara Stimmel

to answer the questions anatomical differences pose. Their theories and conclusions will provide unique possibilities as to how they will understand their bodies, and ultimately their minds.

For example, when a little girl considers that there is something wrong with a little boy's anatomy since he is "sealed over" and not "open" like her (Mayer, 1985), we immediately understand the internal logic of her incorrect thinking. As a matter of fact, this is a good example of how language, and metaphor in particular, lend a sense of meaning to the complex, confused, and nonlogical functioning of primary-process thought. "Sealed over" is a metaphoric description that may be one of those the little girl grown up will use as an anatomical descriptor to make sense of the psychological differences between the sexes.

It is hard though to ignore the negative/positive valence given by Mayer's patient to "sealed over" and "open." In that sense these two terms are analogous with "nothing" and "something"—now reversed in that the girl has a version of something and the boy has nothing. Additionally (and ironically), the girl now worries about losing her openness in light of the boy having already lost his!

In making this comparison there is at least one other thing Mayer's little girl undoubtedly has done; she has displaced her interest from one part of male anatomy (the penis) to another (the testes). This shift in attention brings the girl's eye to parts of the body which are morphologically related (labia and testes) in contrast to those (vagina and penis) which are vastly different. In this way the language of comparison between body parts helps her cope with the mind-boggling fact of difference. It helps her comprehend observable reality a little better and it adds to her sense of her own and a boy's place in the universe; a categorical imperative of sorts. It does not, however, explain internal reality in the form of a wish, to possess the penis as one example or to have a baby as another. For the purposes of analysis we must move from the descriptive, linking level of metaphor to the explanatory level of psychic experience in order to understand the possible frustration of such wishes.

The idea of "nothing" reminds us also of Freud's (1912) description of his repeated experience that when the patient's "free associations fail [p. 101] . . . all of which [associations] he has replaced by the word 'nothing' [1913, p. 138]," it most likely means

Bisexuality and Metaphors of the Mind

that the patient is thinking of the analyst. Conflating these two lines of thought, that the vagina is nothing and that the flow of associations turning to nothing refers to thoughts of the analyst, offers greater possibilities for clinical exploration which will include the object, the relationship to the object, and the fantasies upon which this object relationship is based.

Then, when the patient thinks of nothing, which the analyst interprets as an association to him- or herself, there is every reason to consider that this may be, at least on one level of analysis, a reference to the analyst and his or her representation as a person with a vagina—a woman, a feminized (or perhaps castrated) man, a masculinized woman, a phallic mother, or a true hermaphrodite. The salient point is that any one of these ideas is at once a metaphor of self- and object representation as well as an image based on wishes and defenses.[5] One of the most powerful wishes among them is that it is possible to be female and male at once. We then see that the phallic woman is not only a defense against castration anxiety (in men and women) but also a straightforward representation of an ideal.

This universal longing for bisexual completeness is a cornerstone of psychoanalytic theory. Freud developed his ideas in the context of his relationship with Wilhelm Fliess whose preoccupation with bisexuality is well known. The following are just several of many references Freud made to Fliess on the role of bisexuality in human behavior during their years of correspondence.

> In order to account for why the outcome [of premature sexual experience] is sometimes perversion and sometimes neurosis, I avail myself of the bisexuality of all human beings [in Masson, 1985, p. 212].

> To me, it seems to be as follows: I literally embraced your stress on bisexuality and consider this idea of yours to be the most

---

[5]Freud as a phallic woman, to take one possibility, seems to have had significant meaning in his analysis of Dora. One likely reason Dora's treatment was unsuccessful goes beyond Freud's obvious ability to theorize such a fantasy on Dora's part. Rather it must have had more to do with the transference use she made of this fantasy. He ignored this aspect of the object relationship as experienced by Dora in the transference so that her possible version of him as a female object carrying within it a number of fantasies and self-representations did not get analyzed. The embedding of the fantasy in the relationship also reflected, most assuredly, an image Dora had of herself.

significant one for my subject since that of "defense." If I had a disinclination on personal grounds, because I am in part neurotic myself, this disinclination would certainly have been directed towards bisexuality, which, after all, we hold responsible for the inclination to *repression* [p. 292; italics added].

But bisexuality! you are certainly right about it. I am accustoming myself to regarding every sexual act as a process in which four individuals are involved. We have a lot to discuss on this topic [p. 364].

Fliess was not the only early thinker, analytic or otherwise, to posit the ubiquity of bisexuality (see e.g., Freud, 1905, p. 143n). Ferenczi, before having met Freud and as early as 1906, was writing about human bisexuality (Brabant et al., 1993, p. xix). Freud and Ferenczi became colleagues, analyst/analysand, collaborators, and avid letter writers; bisexuality was among their topics of choice. Freud wrote, "The question will probably be answered with bisexuality and the knowledge that there are women who are capable of everything"(p. 122).

However, although Freud considered bisexuality a universal fantasy, he understood it to be pathogenic in its interference with one's acceptance of anatomical and psychological reality. Ferenczi, too, understood the central role bisexuality played in the development of neurosis. Ferenczi's main interest though was in the fluidity of choice of object rather than the "presence of male and female material in the organism" (p. 184), *à la* Fliess.

Freud of course was interested in both aspects of bisexuality—object choice and self-representation. Regardless of emphasis, Freud came to accept the inevitability of bisexuality, if only in fantasy, remaining a part of the human condition, analysis or no analysis. In "Analysis Terminable and Interminable" Freud (1937) elaborates on and corrects Ferenczi's postulation that in order for an analysis to be successful, the wish for a penis in the woman and the male's struggle against passivity (or the castration complex) must be mastered (p. 251).

Freud's response to Ferenczi contains the famous idea, often refuted, that penis envy is the bedrock of female sexuality (cf. Stoller, 1972). The popularization of this quote out of context, therefore typically misunderstood, overlooks Freud's belief that, "Something

Bisexuality and Metaphors of the Mind

which both sexes *have in common* has been forced, by the difference between the sexes, into different forms of expression [and that therefore Ferenczi] was asking a very great deal" (p. 252; italics added) from *both sexes* by expecting them to be able to renounce completely their preoccupation with possessing aspects of the opposite sex. The famous "bedrock" quote actually refers to men and women and is an indirect reference to the inherent bisexuality of both.

> We often have the impression that with the wish for a penis and the masculine protest we have penetrated through all the psychological strata and have reached bedrock, and that thus our activities are at an end. This is probably true, since, for the psychical field, the biological field does in fact play the part of the underlying bedrock [p. 252].

An embedded, and less discussed problem this quote poses is that upon reaching bedrock " . . . our activities are at an end." This is an illustrative point of interaction between "old" theory (worth keeping) and "new" technique. It is impossible not to accept that the hardwiring (our current version of bedrock) of the brain is the underlying network of the software called the mind. That a universal wish, in this case for "everything," has a direct line to the biological substrate should be completely noncontroversial. After all, we have no trouble believing in various other "bedrock" wishes—to merge with the breast, have sex with our parents, live forever! But bedrock, too, has strata. If we think of bisexuality in its broadest sense, much in the same way Freud advised us to think of sexuality itself, we discern its influence in these other well-accepted, ubiquitous fantasies.

The most important advance in our technique occurs here, where Freud stopped—at the uncovering of the wish, at bedrock. Now, after uncovering a guilty wish (even one at bedrock) we look forward to the unique exchange between analysis and synthesis, which occurs as we work through in the transference of the moment the multiplicity of compromises our patients make with their impulses. Given that the vicissitudes of our patients' wishes are the stuff of our activities, we do not stop at bedrock; here is where we begin. That we do this construction, reconstruction, remembering, and working-through in the context of a dynamic, multilayered relationship rather than under the lens of an electron microscope just demonstrates the transcendant power of the mind.

Barbara Stimmel

In this last quote we also encounter, implicitly, the too-often overlooked and criticized component instincts of passivity and activity which become concretized in the context of genital anatomy. But women want more than the penis. They want the abstract, active properties of power, prominence, and penetration attributed to it. And men, in addition to their masculine protest, which we understand to be a defense, in part, against the wish for a passive-receptive relationship with a man, also want the organs that nurture, envelop, and bring forth into the world, babies, the ultimate creative product (see Nunberg, 1949, and Rose, 1961, for extended discussions on male procreative fantasies). Activity and passivity are primary biological givens which comprise the psychology of both sexes. That their genesis is based on primordial wishes (the longing by both little girls and boys to impregnate mother and be impregnated by father) just reinforces psychic conflict and compromise.

> Such observation shows that in human beings pure masculinity or femininity is not to be found either in a psychological or a biological sense. Every individual on the contrary displays a mixture of the character-traits belonging to his own and to the opposite sex; and he shows a combination of activity and passivity whether or not these last character-traits tally with his biological ones [Freud, 1905, p. 220n].

This seems "metapsychological old-hat," but is it really? We may be able to and perhaps we should develop more acceptable descriptive terms than feminine and masculine and passive and active (see Chasseguet-Smirgel, 1976; Grossman, 1976; Meluk, 1976; Moore, 1976; Serebriany, 1976). We would still have a need though to find conceptual language to fit the phenomenology of human sexuality. And we would be left still knowing that there are psychological and biological differences between the sexes and that our work to a large extent revolves around helping our patients work through the wishes and frustrations stimulated by these differences. We know that many analysts are thinking through these problems as we encounter continuing attempts to understand the complexity of male and female sexuality in our increasingly international literature. When we move beyond the "classical" literature, at least in the United States, we are reminded that all of the familiar theoretical frameworks include at their core the oedipal configuration, even

Bisexuality and Metaphors of the Mind

amid an almost preoccupying interest in preoedipal issues, as well as a male/female dialectic.

For example, Melanie Klein, with her emphasis on neonatal object relations, places the oedipal dilemma and drama very early (even if imprecisely) in child development. The early superego, primitive though it is, is fundamental to her model of the mind. This superego must be a blend of both objects—mother and father. Even while disagreeing with Klein's idea that the fantasy of a combined parent figure is most likely frightening, the blend of the two has significance for the unconscious quandary of wanting and fearing possession of the genitals of the opposite sexed parent. The possibility of having two sets of genitals implies either a kind of rotating or alternating self-representation or a kind of fusion, which is what we find in iconic and religious depictions. The fused primal-scene couple comes close to one version of an anatomically complete individual in that lines of demarcation between the two are blurred so that they may become one in the child's fantasy.

Lacan, as another example, has given us the Law of the Father or the Phallus as he trumpets the use of language to move the child from the dyad with mother to the culture of father. In this sense the phallic properties of the father transcend his anatomy and transform him into a bridge between the perceptual, affective world of mother to the symbolizing world at large. The phallus for Lacan, however, is not a thing but a concept, one which spells power.

Father-as-bridge, although differently conceptualized, is implicit in the classic line of psychosexual development which also encompasses the Mahlerian lines of separation-individuation of infant from mother. It is also explicit in the literature on the role of the father in infant development and infant observation studies. It is particularly, at least historically, his connection to the world with its teeming array of possibilities, which lends father the phallic power of which Lacan and others speak.

We cannot avoid acknowledging the dramatic impact the *phallus* plays for everyone as he or she comes to grips with feelings of incompleteness and powerlessness. Several authors, while writing from a variety of perspectives, including those of Klein, Bion, Chasseguet-Smirgel, and Lacan, make related points. For example, and these are just a few, they are interested in the confusion of the "thing"

Barbara Stimmel

itself with the concept (Abelin-Sas, 1994), or how the power of the phallus offers a sense of completion so that one can exist "beyond the human condition . . . which exists in the unconscious as a basic position" (D. Birksted-Breen, 1995), as well as the father's sexual power (phallocentricity) over mother which " . . . ensures that someone is stronger than mother, who was once stronger than everybody" (Bernstein, 1993, p. 36).

Anatomy (actual or fantasied possession of the penis) may seem to compensate for these feelings of lack; but since the dilemma is existential, material reality offers illusory comfort. I am suggesting that it is the fantasied unity of female and male genitalia that gives the phallus its magnificence. In this sense, the phallus, with its potential for creative (and destructive) energy (see Torsti, 1994) is itself a metaphor—a metaphor of the ultimate sexual organ, neither male nor female but both.[6,7]

The idea that people create metaphors to explain what is ultimately ineffable is easily applied to our understanding of the human endeavor to understand female and male sexual anatomy and its morphological, physiological, and sensory differences. For example, when a woman complains of her mind being "spacey" she may be referring to her vagina and its defining interior space (Kalinich, 1993). This vaginal metaphor then can be plumbed to add to her experience of her mind as well as capture her use of anatomy to mirror her sense of herself. The imprecise nature of spaciness evokes

---

[6]The phallus as an anatomical term refers to the organ rudiment that emerges as the penis or the clitoris in embryonic development. In cultural and religious worship of the phallus, both male and female sexual organs are adored (e.g., the male *linga* and female *yoni* in India). See Heiman et. al. (1968) for a spirited discussion of bisexuality in response to Sherfey's attack on psychoanalytic theories of sexuality.

[7]It is beyond the scope of this paper, and of psychoanalysis itself, to explain the complex reasons that cultures transform one thing into another. The situation becomes confusing when the early infantile narcissistic pursuit of completion collides with sexual desire for the object, for mother, for father. It is perhaps here, with the penis as an overlay of the breast, that we find the determinants of the concrete representation of the phallus. To the extent that there is an unconscious process in the child which accounts for the confusion between the penis and the phallus it must in part be due to the overlapping borders between concrete and symbolic thought in children. The ability to create metaphors starts early; it is one of the fundamental ways we comprehend new realities. When the secondary or figurative system of the phallus is transferred to the primary or observational system of the penis/breast the child has created a condensed phallic metaphor.

Bisexuality and Metaphors of the Mind

imagery of floating disconnectedness, a common metaphor for a certain sense of self. Being "spacey" then is a wonderful example of the meeting of the mind, the body, and the self.

It is suggested that the displacement upward in the example of feeling spacey describes the genitalization of the mind. But it is important that we not remain content with one determinant, which currently also has a social-political function. We can certainly imagine the small girl using other spaces such as her mouth, anus, or urethra to metaphorize her mind. These possible and logical displacements reflect the impact of different developmental pressures on the unfolding sense of self. After all, some men, too, describe themselves as "spacey"!

This single and simple example reminds us of several important psychoanalytic tenets. A metaphor, like a dream or any other symbolic event, represents psychic reality on a manifest, transformed, and conscious level. It must be analyzed to understand not only what the metaphor represents, but why it is chosen in the first place. What are the wishes and defenses anatomical space evokes? How is the mind used as a symbolic representation of a compromise to the conflict? Much like the discussion of "anatomical bedrock," above, when we encounter the experience of being spacey, in a male or female patient, we know that this is a place to begin, not conclude, the work of analytic exploration of object and subject representation, fantasy, wish, and compromise.

CONCLUSION

The developmental march through various erotogenic zones—the pleasures, fantasies, and dangers inherent in all of them—implies that at each stage the child will know herself, her mind, and her world in part as she knows her own body. This self-knowledge continues to transform so as to include the most recently interesting part of the body which will also be a palimpsest of all that had been traversed before. Yet we also know that in normal development the genitals are the *ne plus ultra* in the line of the child's (proprio- and exteroceptive) sensory and (conscious or unconscious) fantasy fascination and preoccupation with parts of his or her body. And we know that children are fascinated with the genitals of the opposite sex as well.

This forward progression is the basis for averring that displacement upward is a generic activity that helps the developing child metamorphose instincts, organs, and self into a cohesive identity. One's identity depends on an experience of extension in space, namely the body, with the resulting implication that the mutuality of mind and body requires that each of them help define the other. These definitions are not bounded by the limitations of language and metaphor. Rather, they are ways of knowing, of experiencing. They are phenomenologically real in that they allow for the use of the body to make sense of the mind, of the self.

It goes without saying that language, our most significant symbolic creation, may be used defensively as well as being an element in the array of defenses and adaptations available to us all. Therefore, to the extent that one can in the process of analysis, language is parsed in order to get as close to its underlying images as possible.[8] It is the analysis of a patient's spacey mind-vagina condensation, for example, that will uncover the unconscious fantasies about the space that displacement upward helps to keep in check. We move beyond metaphoric disguise and display to analysis of the underlying psychic realities which must be gotten to no matter how many locks on the door.

There is a long theoretical line, going back to Horney and Jones, continuing to the present, which states that physiology and psychology come together in gender formation so that girls experience primary femininity and by implication, boys primary masculinity. Others argue "From the analytic point of view there is no concept of the primary (and therefore no primary femininity or masculinity)" (Grossman and Kaplan, 1988, p. 335). Regardless of the basic or derivative level on which one believes gender enters identity formation, it is not conceivable that either boy or girl could escape the pull of bisexual aims and biparental object ties. The combination

---

[8]In a classic paper on metaphor, Arlow (1979) highlights this point in the following way: "... the ubiquitous foreground character of metaphor drew my attention to its role as a derivative of the basic, persistent, unconscious fantasy life of the patient. Focusing on the phenomenon, it seemed to me that metaphor can regularly be seen as an outcropping of unconscious fantasy. Specific associations to the metaphor regularly lead to an unconscious fantasy typical for the patient" (p. 370).

Bisexuality and Metaphors of the Mind

of a universal wish with increasingly complex object identification becomes the mechanism of imbricating in the sense of self, in the experience of the mind, a multifaceted body representation with the genitals at center stage.

Psychic realities thus blur the edges of anatomy which has us all deal with the same few body parts, each in his or her own creative way. It is the integration between feminine/masculine—passive/active that helps account for unconflicted expressions of creativity. The wish to be both, to have both (Kubie, 1974) makes it very likely that the genitals which are displaced upward in order to be explored and explained include the genitals of the opposite sex. Genital displacement upward also offers another advantage—the mind becomes a hiding place. Finally, in the back-and-forth between self and object, the oedipal child successfully traverses this phase by identifying not only with both parents' superegos, but by incorporating their genital anatomy as well (see Bergmann, 1982, for a related point). They would have to in order to satisfactorily bring closure, such as it is, to the oedipal phase with its positive and negative object-related lures (Bergmann, 1995; Lax, 1995).

It is the unconflicted (to the extent this is truly possible) integration of these multiple anatomical and psychic identifications that allows for the fullest use and enjoyment of ego capacities, such as intellect and creativity. Women have to be able to bring their ideas forward, into space, and men must be able to nurture their thoughts and bring them to fruition.[9]

If we go back to Dr. L.'s garden we are reminded that this was a metaphor she had of her mind as well as an infantile unconscious fantasy of a real place in which the babies of her future resided. The unmistakeable link between the products of her mind and the products of her womb remind us that neither set of creations can be formed without combining, psychically and concretely, critical male and female elements. Neurotic compromises occur when there is guilt and shame over the need and wish to combine.

Here we see the complexity of bisexuality as a wish-fulfilling fantasy. It gratifies the narcissistic longing for completeness and freedom from need of the object. At the same time, contradictory as it

---

[9]Even here we cannot avoid noticing the mutuality of the descriptive language applied to each sex. Women bring their babies forth into the world; men fertilize, thereby helping bring to fruition, those very babies.

may seem, the necessary internal presence of the object, the other, is the closest we ever come to having everything. "Anatomy is destiny" perhaps means that the mind is the sum of all that is part of the human body, male and female.

And now we can perhaps solve the mystery of how the murderer got out of the locked room. She did not. The locked room was an illusion, a space that could be opened from the outside. Dr. L. had only to learn that her wish for "everything," while ultimately impossible to gratify, was not a crime, but rather an inescapable part of the human experience.

REFERENCES

ABELIN-SAS, G. (1994). The headless woman: Scheherezade's sorrows. In *The Spectrum of Psychoanalysis*, ed. A. K. Richards & A. Richards. Madison, CT: Int. Univ. Press, pp. 161–184.
ABRAMS, S. & SHENGOLD, L. (1974). The meaning of "nothing." *Psychoanal. Q.*, 43:115–119.
ANTONY, L.M. & WITT, C., Eds. (1993). *A Mind of One's Own: Feminist Essays on Reason and Objectivity*. Boulder, CO: Westview Press.
ARLOW, J.A. (1979). Metaphor and the psychoanalytic situation. *Psychoanal. Q.*, 48:363–385.
BERGMANN, M. (1982). The female Oedipus complex. In *Early Female Development*, ed. D. Mendell. New York: S. P. Medical and Scientific Books, pp. 175–202.
BIRKSTED-BREEN, D. (1995). Phallus, penis and mental space. *Int. J. Psychoanal.*, 77:649–658.
——— (1995). Observations on the female negative oedipal phase and its significance in the analytic transference. *J. Clin. Psychoanal.*, 4:283–296.
BERNSTEIN, D. (1993). *Female Identity Conflict in Clinical Practice*, ed. N. Freedman & B. Distler. Northvale, NJ: Aronson.
BLUM, H.P. (1982). Theories of the self and psychoanalytic concepts: discussion. *J. Amer. Psychoanal. Assn.*, 30:959–978.
BRABANT, E., FALZEDER, E., & GIAMPIERI-DEUTSCH, P., Eds. (1993). *The Correspondence of Sigmund Freud and Sandor Ferenzci. Volume I, 1908–1914*. Cambridge, MA.: Belknap Press of Harvard Univ. Press.
BRAKEL, L.A. (1986). "Nothing is missing . . . yet: two disturbances in the sense of reality and a woman's fantasied phallus. *Psychoanal. Q.*, 55:301–305.
BREUER, J. & FREUD, S. (1895). Studies on hysteria. *S. E.*, 2.
CHASSEGUET-SMIRGEL, J. (1976). Freud and female sexuality: some considerations of the blind spots in the exploration of the "dark continent." *Int. J. Psychoanal.*, 57:275–286.
FREUD, S. (1905). Three essays on the theory of sexuality. *S. E.*, 7.
——— (1908). Hysterical phantasies and their relation to bisexuality. *S. E.*, 9.

——— (1912). The dynamics of transference. *S. E.*, 12.

——— (1913). On beginning the treatment (Further recommendations on the technique of psychoanalysis). *S. E.*, 12.

——— (1937). Analysis terminable and interminable. *S. E.*, 23.

Grossman, W.I. (1976). Discussion of "Freud and female sexuality." *Int. J. Psychoanal.*, 57:301–305.

——— (1982). The self as fantasy: fantasy as theory. *J. Amer. Psychoanal. Assn.*, 30:919–938.

——— & Kaplan, D. (1988). Three commentaries on gender in Freud's thought: a prologue to the psychoanalytic theory of sexuality. In *Fantasy, Myth, and Reality*, ed. H. P. Blum, Y. Kramer, A. K. Richards & A. Richards. Madison, CT: Int. Univ. Press, pp. 339–370.

Heiman, M., Kestenberg, J., Benedek, T. & Keiser, S. (1968). Discussions of M. J. Sherfey: the evolution and nature of female sexuality in relation to psychoanalytic theory. *J. Amer. Psychoanal. Assn.*, 16:406–456.

Kalinich, L. (1993). On the sense of absence: a perspective on womanly issues. *Psychoanal. Q.*, 62:206–228.

Kernberg, O.F. (1982). Self, ego, affects, and drives. *J. Amer. Psychoanal. Assn.*, 30:893–918.

Krausz, R. (1994). The invisible woman. *Int. J. Psychoanal.*, 75:59–72.

Kris, E. (1956). The personal myth: a problem in psychoanalytic technique. *J. Amer. Psychoanal. Assn.*, 4:653–681.

Kubie, L.S. (1974). The drive to become both sexes. *Psychoanal. Q.*, 43:349–426.

Laqueur, T. (1990). *Making Sex: Body and Gender from the Greeks to Freud.* Cambridge, MA: Harvard Univ. Press.

Lax, R. (1977). The role of internalization in the development of certain aspects of female masochism: ego-psychological considerations. *Int. J. Psychoanal.*, 58:289–300.

——— (1994). Aspects of primary and secondary genital feelings and anxieties in girls during the preoedipal and early oedipal phases. *Psychoanal. Q.*, 63:271–296.

——— (1995). Motives and determinants of girls' penis envy in the negative oedipal phase. *J. Clin. Psychoanal.*, 4:297–314.

Lewin, B.D. (1948). The nature of reality, the meaning of nothing, with an addendum on concentration. *Psychoanal. Q.*, 17:524–526.

Mahler, M.S. & McDevitt, J.B. (1982). Thoughts on the emergence of the sense of self, with particular emphasis on the body self. *J. Amer. Psychoanal. Assn.*, 30:827–848.

Masson, J.M., Ed. (1985). *The Complete Letters of Sigmund Freud to Wilhelm Fliess* (1887–1904). Cambridge, MA: Belknap Press of Harvard Univ. Press.

Mayer, E.L. (1985). 'Everybody must be just like me': observations on female castration anxiety. *Int. J. Psychoanal.*, 66:331–347.

McDougall, J. (1988). Eve's reflection: on the homosexual components of female sexuality. In *Between Analyst and Patient: New Dimensions in Countertransference and Transference*, ed. H. Meyers. Hillsdale, NJ: Analytic Press, pp. 213–228.

——— (1991). Sexual identity, trauma, and creativity. *Psychoanal. Inq.*, 11:559–581.
MELUK, T. (1976). Discussion of "Freud and female sexuality." *Int. J. Psychoanal.*, 57:307–310.
MOORE, B. (1976). Freud and female sexuality: a current view. *Int. J. Psychoanal.*, 57:311–313.
NUNBERG, H. (1949). *Problems of Bisexuality as Reflected in Circumcision.* New York: Int. Univ. Press.
RANGELL, L. (1982). The self in psychoanalytic theory. *J. Amer. Psychoanal. Assn.*, 30:863–892.
RENIK, O. (1990). Analysis of a woman's homosexual strivings by a male analyst. *Psychoanal. Q.*, 59:41–53.
RICHARDS, A.D. (1982). The superordinate self in psychoanalytic theory and in the self psychologies. *J. Amer. Psychoanal. Assn.*, 30:939–958.
RICHARDS, A.K. (1992). The influence of sphincter control and genital sensation on body image and gender identity in women. *Psychoanal. Q.*, 61:331–351.
ROSE, G.J. (1961). Pregenital aspects of pregnancy fantasies. *Int. J. Psychoanal.*, 42:544–554.
SEREBRIANY, R. (1976). Dialogue on "Freud and female sexuality." *Int. J. Psychoanal.*, 57:311–313.
SHAW, R. (1995). Female genital anxieties: an integration of new and old. *J. Clin. Psychoanal.*, 4:315–330.
SHENGOLD, L. (1989). Further thoughts about "nothing." *Psychoanal. Q.*, 58:227–235.
SLAP, J.W. (1979). On nothing and nobody with an addendum on William Hogarth. *Psychoanal. Q.*, 48:620–627.
SOLL, M.H. (1984–1985). The transferable penis and the self-representation. *Int. J. Psychoanal. Psychother.*, 10:473–493.
STOLLER, R.J. (1972). The "bedrock" of masculinity and femininity: bisexuality. *Arch. Gen. Psychiat.*, 26:207–212.
TICHO, E.A. (1982). The alternate schools and the self. *J. Amer. Psychoanal. Assn.*, 30:849–862.
TORSTI, M. (1994). The feminine self and penis envy. *Int. J. Psychoanal.*, 75:469–478.
WISDOM, J.O. (1983). Male and female. *Int. J. Psychoanal.*, 64:159–168.

THEORETICAL GENDER AND CLINICAL GENDER: EPISTEMOLOGICAL REFLECTIONS ON THE PSYCHOLOGY OF WOMEN

Nancy J. Chodorow

> This paper points to problematic tendencies in psychoanalytic thinking about women and suggests approaches that might address these problems. Psychoanalytic theories about women tend to overgeneralize, universalize, and essentialize. Furthermore, they do not sufficiently explicate the inextricable cultural aspects in anyone's gender psychology, and they are often permeated with unreflected-upon cultural assumptions. I suggest that paying attention to clinical individuality and assuming that subjective gender has multiple components for everyone gives us better understanding of our patients and points us toward more accurate and complete gender theories. There are many psychologies of women. Each woman creates her own psychological gender through emotionally and conflictually charged unconscious fantasies that help construct her inner world, that projectively imbue cultural conceptions, and that interpret her sexual anatomy. By making some unconscious fantasies and interpretations more salient than others, each woman creates her own prevalent animation of gender.

Twenty years after the *Journal of the American Psychoanalytic Association* published its first special issue on female psychology (the first special issue on women published by any psychoanalytic journal) and about thirty years after the first stirrings of contemporary feminism, it is useful to reflect on where thinking on the psychology of women has gone, and where it now needs to go. Within psychoanalysis, as within psychoanalytic feminism, there have been generative theoretical and clinical writings too abundant to cite or

---

Faculty, San Francisco Psychoanalytic Institute; Professor of Sociology, University of California, Berkeley.
I am grateful to the National Endowment for the Humanities and to the Guggenheim Foundation for support during the year this paper was written.

Nancy J. Chodorow

summarize, on many topics and from multiple perspectives (for my own now-dated attempt to synthesize and summarize, see Chodorow, 1989c).

Yet, some tendencies cross many of these writings, and it is these tendencies that I wish to explore. In what follows, rather than directly addressing the psychology of women, I reflect upon and attempt to unpack some widespread epistemological and methodological problems in thinking about gender that I believe we need clearly to keep in view. My reflections take somewhat the form of a cautionary tale. First, our thinking on gender (and, inseparably within psychoanalysis, sexuality) tends to subsume individuality and difference to universality and similarity, in the process turning clinical observations of the fluctuating personal emotional meanings of gender into fixed developmental tasks. Second, this thinking tends not to be sufficiently cognizant of either the inextricable cultural aspects of gender psychology or the unreflected-upon cultural assumptions in our theorizing. As I shall suggest below, this second set of problems is partially responsible for the first.

The academic feminist critique of psychoanalysis has most clearly described these problems, but analysts learn of them firsthand in the clinical consulting room: I am proposing that there is a great gap between what we experience and observe transferentially, clinically, and empirically of gender identity, sexual and gender fantasies, and particular women's psyches and what most theoretical and developmental accounts claim about inevitable or necessary stages of development, "the" psychology of women, "the" role of gender in the transference, and other gender-related developmental or intrapsychic processes and tasks. In our clinical work, we find a changing constellation of transferences and countertransferences over the course of treatment. Likewise developmentally, each caregiver-child pair will form its own unconscious fantasy and emotion-imbued relationship, and each child brings her own capacities for the creation of intrapsychic meaning to every experience and perception (see, e.g., Stern, 1985; Winnicott, 1965, 1971; Trevarthan, 1979, 1980). These transference-countertransference constellations, unconscious parent-child communications, and any person's intrapsychic life include aspects of subjective gender and sexuality, and these are always in turn intertwined with other aspects of self, unconscious fantasy, and affect (Dimen, 1991). In my view, gender identity and aspects

Theoretical Gender and Clinical Gender

of the psychology of gender develop and are experienced in these personal, transferential, meaning-creating contexts. From such a perspective, it is apparent that gender, like selfhood, must be individually unique (see Chodorow, 1994, 1995).

However, I believe that psychoanalysts have singled out particular aspects of psychic functioning and treated these as less contingent, created, individual, and emergent than other aspects of psychic functioning. Psychologies of gender, and indeed most developmental theories, fall under this rubric (Chodorow, 1996). Contemporary as well as classical theories make universalistic claims about women as opposed to men and imply that they describe the core experience or essence of femininity or masculinity. This includes "primary femininity" theorists (e.g., Kestenberg, 1968, 1982; Mayer, 1985) and gender identity investigators (Tyson, 1982) as much as those psychoanalysts who hold an asymmetrical phallic/castration model (e.g., Roiphe and Galenson, 1981; Mayer, 1995). French theorists, whether Lacanian (Mitchell and Rose, 1982), anti-Lacanian (e.g., Irigaray, 1985), or mainstream (e.g., Chasseguet-Smirgel, 1985, 1986; McDougall, 1986), also make universal claims about gender identity and its psychobiological essence. Following more or less explicitly Freud's libidinal stage theory and theory of the Oedipus complex, all these writers discuss seemingly inevitable (or at least desirable) stages of development, developmental tasks, innate femininity and masculinity, "the" psychology of men or women, or what "must" in every analysis be discovered and analyzed. Like much of academic psychology and virtually all of popular psychology, the psychoanalytic literature has tended to overgeneralize, to oppose all men to all women, and to assume that masculinity and femininity and their expressive forms are single rather than multiple (for a notable exception to this generalization, see Applegarth, 1976, who discusses the many paths and patterns of conflict that may lead to work inhibitions in women. See also Tyson, 1991, p. 583, who suggests, "there may not be *one* story of female development, but many stories, many intertwining themes, and many possible outcomes," and Person, 1995).

I am talking about "mainstream" psychoanalytic theory. Relational psychoanalysts have criticized the still largely unchallenged Freudian assumption that, in the case of gender (and self), genital

Nancy J. Chodorow

anatomy and body ego come first, and they have argued for multiplicity, individuality, variability, and instability in the psychology of gender (see e.g., Goldner, 1991; Harris, 1991; Dimen, 1991; Benjamin, 1995).

By contrast, other critics of the traditional psychoanalytic point of view pose an alternate universalism. My impression is that self-in-relation theorists (Jordan, et al., 1991), women's ways of knowing theorists (Belenky et al., 1986), and theorists of women's voice or morality (e.g., Gilligan, 1982; Gilligan et al., 1991; Brown and Gilligan, 1992) increasingly cast their claims not just as clinically, observationally, or experimentally based findings, but as universal claims about how women are, and even, by implication, should be.

There is both a methodological and an epistemological disjunction here. Our case method focuses on the unique person emerging in the intersubjective analytic encounter, and our claims to knowledge rest on our clinical findings. Yet our theories in the case of gender and sexuality generalize and universalize regarding developmental lines and tasks, regarding the assumption that body functions initiate developmental phases, and regarding gender-differentiated aspects of character or pathology. Our epistemology has practical effects. Too often, the useful patterns we observe or believe in are held preconsciously, consciously, and unconsciously as normative or statistical expectations or as certainties about essential and universal truths. As such, they serve as blinders to clinical, empirical, and intersubjective seeing and recognizing. Epistemologically and methodologically, there is a conflict between essentializing, universalizing, and overgeneralizing and a clinical case approach; clinically, when we work with individuals, we find diversity, variation, and unique individuality.

Various unreflected-upon practices seem to lead to these outcomes (on generalization, false universalism, and false difference, see J. R. Martin, 1994). We begin with generalizations, acknowledged as such: women tend to feel more comfortable with intimacy and dependence than men; little boys are more physically aggressive than little girls; women tend toward hysteria, men toward obsessionality; boys act out, girls act in. Such generalizations are based on empirical observation, and they are, implicitly, statistical claims—claims for prevalence or typicality. With all statistical claims, there is variation;

Theoretical Gender and Clinical Gender

statistics assume variance, and claims cast in related terms must do so as well. Therefore, within these claims, it is always also implied that some little girls are more physically aggressive than some boys, that some men are more comfortable with intimacy and dependence than some women, that some men are hysterics and some women obsessive, and so forth.

But in the history of psychoanalysis, variance is often forgotten, as empirical generalizations seem to become first, overgeneralizations—allowed to stand beyond their empirical basis—and then, universalizations. We come to think that all little boys are physically aggressive and all little girls are not, that all men are uncomfortable with dependence, that all women need relationality. These overgeneralizations and universalizing claims have clinical consequences: clinicians begin to assume pathology when they find a boy who is not physically aggressive or a physically aggressive little girl; they notice hyperaggressive ambition in a woman patient in a way they do not notice it, or notice it differently, in a man. Exploitative sexual acting out or going from one sexual partner to another are thought to have different psychobiological roots in a man and a woman, whereas the dynamics might in both cases be very similar. By contrast, two men's behaviorally similar compulsive sexuality may have different dynamic meanings.

Universalizing is different from but can lead to essentializing—defining the essence of what it is to be masculine or feminine. Historically, psychoanalysts have tended to follow Freud's lead in assuming that anatomy in some way precedes or underlies gender identity or has a privileged weight not accorded to other components of gender or sexuality. For Freud, as for Galenson and Roiphe, the essence of feminine psychology is penis envy and its consequences and transformations; the essence of masculinity is castration anxiety and its consequences and transformations. Primary femininity theorists oppose this, defining femininity in terms of an inevitable developmental bodily-based primary cathexis of the female genitals and/or fears of injury and castration of these genitals. Rather than following the psychoanalytic methodological principle that the meaning of the body is never self-evident, but always imbued with individual fantasy and conflict, constructed as we construct all aspects of meaning, in the case of femininity we assume that female embodiedness inevitably generates particular meanings and that it is always salient in the construction of gender. In my own clinical experience, however, I have found that genital and reproductive anatomy, whether or not to become a mother, and other aspects of gendered and sexual embodiment, are extremely central to some women's sense of gender, psyche, and self and much less significant to the psyche, self, and gender of other women.

But essentialism is not limited to mainstream psychoanalysts: self-in-relation theorists imply that the essence of femininity or female psychology is the need for relation; for Winnicott (1971), the essence of femaleness is being, of maleness, doing. What is *essentially* female is penis envy and defenses against it in body imagery and fantasy, ego development, and object relations; or, what is *essentially* female is the desire to maintain connection and relation. Within the clinical literature, many other empirical observations of specific people have been overgeneralized, universalized, and then essentialized. As with universalizing, essentializing has consequences when you find, as any clinician must, a female whose psychology is not centrally about connection and relation, or centrally about how she experiences, fantasizes about, and reacts to her genital anatomy.

CULTURAL ASSUMPTIONS IN THINKING ABOUT WOMEN

Psychoanalytic essentializing and universalizing can be explained partially through another feminist insight (one first put forth by Karen Horney, Clara Thompson, and other interpersonalists), that into the role of culture in our conceptualizations of gender. As I have argued also in other work (Chodorow 1978, 1989a, 1994), psychoanalysts embed unconscious and preconscious, unthought and unnoticed, pretheoretical cultural assumptions about gender into our theories and into what we see and hear clinically. Schafer (1974) first noted a disjunction between psychodynamic explanation in most aspects of psychic functioning and what seemed to call for explanation and treatment in the case of gender and sexuality. Pretheoretical assumptions that I and others have pointed to include the assumptions that women are naturally maternal or that they are

Theoretical Gender and Clinical Gender

instinctually passive and masochistic; that heterosexuality can be taken for granted, but homosexuality needs explaining; that a masculine psychology centered on superiority over women, or based on traumatic fear of castration, does not need clinical unpacking and analysis; and that masculine aggressivity and violence do not call for special explanations, whereas feminine aggressivity and violence do.

Psychoanalytic accounts of mothers and fathers, whether or not directly about gender identity, also reflect taken-for-granted assumptions about normal gender that inform our theories and clinical work. I am thinking of theorizing and clinical accounts that pathologize nontraditional parental role patterns (active, managerial, aggressive mothers and passive fathers are more problematic than the reverse), as well as the plethora of assumptions, particularly in the object-relations and self-psychology traditions, we have about mothers, the breast, primary maternal preoccupation, and the mother-blame and psychoanalytic rescue fantasies these assumptions can generate (see Chodorow and Contratto, 1982; Phillips, 1993).

As contemporary commentators note repeatedly, within the history of psychoanalysis Freud's claims have been less subject to theoretical or empirical scrutiny than those of other thinkers. In the case of gender, this history, sustained by everyday culture, rests many unquestioned assumptions on putative biological reasoning. Freud and H. Deutsch, for example, explain much of female psychology as an outcome of "women's service to the species" (on Freud's teleology, see Schafer, 1974). As I describe elsewhere (Chodorow, 1994), part of the reason heterosexual object choice does not seem to need explaining in the individual clinical case, as do homosexual object choice and a variety of noncoital perversions, is that you need heterosexual coitus for species continuity. With the exception of Lacanian theory, which has influenced French psychoanalysis more generally, most post-Freudian branches of psychoanalysis (American ego psychology, object-relations theory, Kleinian psychoanalysis), even as they begin from the view that the psyche must be seen in terms that go well beyond the drive theory, continue to assume that gender is a matter of sexuality and genitals (Chodorow, 1978).

Our recent centering of attention on the here-and-now of the transference-countertransference, with its focus on the unique, contingent, emergent creation of intersubjective and intrapsychic meaning, does not seem to affect understandings of gender. Gender

Nancy J. Chodorow

remains a matter of sexuality, genitals, or body parts like the breast—at most, an early genital phase replaces the phallic-oedipal phase as criterial, or primary femininity replaces penis envy. Cutting-edge, radical, original, contemporary thinkers claim that we are hardwired to organize experience in terms of gender-inflected universal fantasies such as primal scene, castration anxiety, childhood seduction, and the Oedipus complex—fantasies that to the cultural or clinical observer are clearly culturally and individually specific. Although nonpsychoanalytic thinkers, in the case of gender as elsewhere, may be unwilling to acknowledge the noncultural, nonlinguistic, unconscious emotional and fantasy components of subjectivity, it is also the case that psychoanalysts need fully to recognize the inextricable cultural and linguistic contribution to constructions and fantasies of gender.

Instead, accounts imply that there is a precultural or noncultural core of femininity and masculinity, usually based in the body. Even accounts sensitive to the cultural determinations of gender imply that these determinations are superimposed upon a precultural essence, either a genitally determined subjective identity or some observed universal gender differences in psychic operation that we can "find" if we factor our culture. But the clinical and cultural evidence does not suggest that we can differentiate between something fixed (a basic universal core of psychological gender) and that which varies among individuals (for example, fantasies, the emotional tonality of gender, or identifications). Thus, it is not only that psychoanalytic theories of gender have unnoted cultural assumptions. It is also the case that everyone's sense of gender and sexuality has cultural as well as personal resonance and meaning. Because gender has cognitive components, we cannot think of gender entirely apart from language and culture. From earliest development, culture enters the gendered psyche, as nonverbal communications to children about their gender or about the gender of the person who is communicating help form a basis for the emotional resonance of cultural categories. From the time a child is spoken to, read to, or put in front of the television, myths, fairy tales, and stories contribute to unconscious as well as conscious fantasy about gender. Investigations of life histories, biography, autobiography, and fiction also make especially clear how much available cultural understandings and narratives shape any

Theoretical Gender and Clinical Gender

individual's unconscious self-understanding and any individual self-story (Person, 1995; Heilbrun, 1988).

Because of cultural assumptions that inform both psychological gender and theorizing about gender, there also seems to be a tendency among psychoanalysts to study the psychology of women by searching for differences in what defines or characterizes men as opposed to women, paying less attention to and occluding within-gender variation and between-gender similarities (a point made by Maccoby and Jacklin, 1984; and Bem, 1993, regarding academic psychology). There is an unquestioned assumption that we shall find the observable and clinical regularities of gender difference we expect. Indeed, it would be an interesting exercise to compare those clinical observations that become universalized and those that do not. To take recent examples, an article on envy and malignant envy (Shengold, 1994) and an article on how particular patient behaviors generate loneliness in the countertransference (Schafer, 1995), both stop with describing particular clinical instances; neither claims to describe a universal clinical or developmental manifestation. By contrast, a clinical case of penis envy leads to the suggestion that primary femininity and phallic-castration complexes are "necessary aspects of every girl's progress toward becoming a woman" (Mayer, 1995, p. 17).

I have argued elsewhere (Chodorow, 1996) that the anxieties of uncertainty in the clinical here-and-now lead psychoanalysts to rely on fixed causal-determinist theories. In order to sustain clinical unpredictability and the radically noncommonsense and anxiety-provoking understandings that underpin psychoanalysis—that motives are unconscious, that we interpret and construct the world and our lives in terms of unconscious, emotionally laden wishes, fears, and fantasies, that anxiety generates major aspects of human functioning (including our own)—we also defensively rely on some completely everyday and familiar assumptions. Gender and sexuality, I suggest, historically serve this role. Our first challenge, then, is to assume that gender and sexuality are as interesting and new for us as everything else we observe clinically and theorize about—to tolerate the uncertainty that comes from questioning some of our most taken-for-granted (since childhood) personal and cultural assumptions.

Nancy J. Chodorow

OBSERVED AND SUBJECTIVE GENDER

Several concepts can help us in this endeavor. I think particularly of Fast's distinction (1984, p. 77) between objective, or observed, and subjective gender. Objective gender refers to observed differences in features of psychic or mental life, or aspects of personality, character, or behavior that tend to differentiate or characterize the sexes, for example, the kinds of statistical differences in prevalent diagnoses or character traits I described earlier. We might find prevalent experiences in women's or men's life histories or developmental patterns, or, as some current research suggests, possibly in brain biology or hormone levels, that begin to account for these commonalities. Claims about women's self-in-relation, greater ease with dependence or intimacy, weaker superego, or ego fusion and empathy in the service of mothering, in contrast to men's, are parts of observed gender that might or might not be linked to an identity or sense of self as female. Depending on how central to the psyche we saw these to be, we might consider these part of (a still implicitly statistical) psychology of women. By contrast, subjective gender refers to personal constructions of masculinity and femininity—elements consciously or unconsciously linked to the sense of self as gendered. These personal constructions might include, for example, fantasies about one's gender, sexual fantasies consciously or unconsciously connected to sense of gender, bodily imaged gender, core gender identity, or gender identifications.

It is an empirical question whether an aspect of someone's identity, fantasy, self-construction, body ego, or character is subjectively gendered. For example, we observe that girls and boys tend to develop an attachment to and involvement with their mother, in the case where the mother is their primary caretaker. As observers, we know that the mother is a woman and that her breasts come with her biological sex, but at first her gender or biological sex is not subjectively relevant to her children's conceptions of mother, mothering, or breasts. If aggressivity is, as some think, hardwired in the male brain or in male hormonal patterns, then it is not necessarily part of subjective masculine gender, though there will certainly be a gender-related statistical difference in aggressivity. By contrast, if little boys consciously or unconsciously think or fantasize that big,

Theoretical Gender and Clinical Gender

strong men, other boys, their father, or the absent father whom they idealize act aggressively as part of their masculinity, that is part of subjective masculine gender. A *Jane Eyre* or *Rebecca* fantasy of submissive involvement with an aggressive man who turns gentle is part of many women's subjective gender, and we can observe it as a fantasy more prevalent in women than in men. But our traditional thinking is liable to conclude that a fantasy that is more prevalent, or even exclusively found, among women, even if among only a portion of women, characterizes "the" psychology of women or female sexuality.

Freud made claims about both subjective and observed gender. His account of how boys and girls develop penis envy or castration anxiety describes subjective gender, specifically, gendered subjectivity organized around the body. By contrast, his claims about gender differences in superego formation or narcissism are in the arena of observed gender: a woman's faulty superego is not an aspect of her subjective sense of her femaleness (though it may be a *result* of her subjective gender, that is, of her not fearing castration). Melanie Klein obviously makes observed gender crucial to her theory when she makes fantasies about the breast central to psychological life, but these fantasies (paranoid-schizoid splitting, depressive reparation, etc.) are cast mainly in nongendered terms. In her writings there are only scattered references to subjective gender in boys and girls, for instance, when she claims that idealization of the penis and the father in both sexes is a way to get away from the fear and overwhelmingness of the maternal breast, or when she describes the oedipal child's imaging of bodily gender differences in the fantasy of the father's penis and the mother's babies inside the mother.

The distinction between subjective and observed gender enables us to sort out the relation between individual uniqueness on the one hand and commonality, generalization, or universality on the other. For example, based on clinical observation, developmental research, or findings about human biopsychology, we might make the (to all intents and purposes) universal observation that everyone constructs a gendered and sexual subjectivity. However, each person subjectively constructs this gender and sexuality in unique ways. Neither anatomy nor core gender identity has automatic effects and, as Freud first noted, there is no single way that the psychology of women

Nancy J. Chodorow

proceeds (Freud theorized both one normal femininity and three typical female developmental patterns, and described a number of unique and complex individual cases [see Chodorow, 1994]). Everyone has unconscious fantasies about his or her gender and sexuality and projectively and introjectively animates a complex sense of gender, but the content of these fantasies and the particularity of this gender identity will be tied into that person's individual selfhood. Gendered subjectivity, gender identity, and gender-inflected sexuality, are personally constructed: there is no simple relation between gender identity and sexual orientation, and gender is intertwined with seemingly nongender-related aspects of self and with a personally unique emotional tonality (Dimen, 1991; Chodorow, 1994, 1995). We have here both universalizing—everyone constructs his or her own gendered subjectivity—and clinical individualizing—the particular construction, the particular unconscious and conscious fantasies, will vary. There is, then, no single femininity or masculinity, feminine or masculine identity, or way of constructing a sense of male or female self, but everyone will do so. Even so, Bem (1993) reports research finding that the centrality of gender to the overall sense of self varies: some people's sense of gender is highly significant, central to their overall self-schema, and invested with meaning and emotion; for others, gender is less significant and invested. This was my own reluctant conclusion (see Chodorow, 1989b) as I tried to get second-generation women analysts to claim that gender was as important to their sense of self and psychoanalytic identity as it was to mine.

Can we maintain this both-and stance, or are we left only with individuality and difference? What happens to generalizing theories? Here, I find useful the concept of pattern (see Frye, 1990). Clinically, there is a difference between, on the one hand, assuming that we are talking about how "the girl" or "the boy" will or must develop, what constitutes the essence of masculinity or femininity, or what are the universally necessary tasks to achieve these, and, on the other hand, keeping a wide variety of patterns of development and psychology in the back of one's mind. Such an approach is much truer to how we work clinically. We keep all sorts of potentially contradictory theories and generalizations (not just those about gender and sexuality) in mind, recognizing them as patterns as we find them in a

Theoretical Gender and Clinical Gender

particular moment. But if we have fixed developmental schemas, preconceived ideas about the meanings of particular fantasies or dreams, or assumptions about what in the wide spectrum of the analyst's action will be relevant to the patient, we cannot truly listen or hear.

In my experience, some women express "penis envy" (already in the literature a concept that covers many fantasies, wishes, and beliefs) during some of the time when they are talking about their body, sexuality, or gender. Yet this penis envy may or may not be central to these women's sense of gender or to their feelings and fantasies about their body or sexuality, and gender and sexuality may or may not be central to their construction of self or to the conflicts and fantasies that emerge in our work together. Some women construct a sense of pleasure, identity, or body integrity primarily from an image of and fantasies about their female genital anatomy. Some men experience women as terrifying engulfers; others fear humiliation or castration by other men. Some women are afraid that achievement will leave them alone and lonely; others feel that it gives them a welcome sense of autonomy and pleasure. But in each case, the same qualifiers and caveats that I suggest about penis envy apply. Knowing how Freud, Klein, Horney, Kestenberg, Mayer, Tyson, or other writers have described these and other dynamics situates them and makes them recognizable as patterns. By complement, when we find something we have never read about or experienced with another patient, that is also interesting: we may tentatively begin to elaborate from it another pattern. However, this kind of clinical stance and theory differs from claims that all girls or all boys must traverse certain experiences or fantasy organizations in order to achieve femininity or masculinity.

Such a formulation complements, rather than criticizes or dismisses, generalizations about gender psychology. We can probably generalize usefully about aspects of many women's (and men's) subjective sense of gender, about prevalent variations in subjective sense of gender, and about observed aspects of gender personality that may or may not be related to a person's subjective sense of gender. We can also generalize usefully about gender within particular cultural, racial-ethnic, and class groups and during different historical periods. In all such generalizations, however, we need to be careful that our claims do not go beyond our data base or that we specify the basis of our speculations that they can. As I note above, generalization, certainly about features of personality or psychology, is implicitly statistical and rarely universal. Overgeneralizing or universalizing are never accurate, and especially in a field so easily subsumed into unreflected-upon cultural assumptions, caution is especially warranted. In the area of observed gender, we need to guard against overgeneralizing from our observations, selectively searching out gender differences, and ignoring observations of commonality between the sexes and within sex variation. We need also to guard against allowing the various patterns of observed gender difference to stand as the essential psychology of women or men.

We can see how the concept of pattern enables us to draw upon ostensibly contradictory or mutually exclusive theories in the course of clinical work and theorizing. I am trying to have it both ways, but I also believe that this both-and stance is, finally, the only empirically and epistemologically legitimate way to have it. On the one hand, we do not want to pigeonhole our patients, as I believe we do if we think that all women and men follow particular developmental lines and have to deal with particular tasks to reach femininity or masculinity, or if we have a stated or unspoken assumption that there are normal women and normal men, with normative roles and normal sexual orientation, so that only deviations from these norms need explaining. On the other hand, we do want to understand them.

CONSTRUCTING SUBJECTIVE GENDER

I am taking the position that there is nothing noncontingent in female psychology, that subjective gender is always composed of multiple elements and stories that are themselves not fixed once and for all. This individual view of gender accords with contemporary clinical thinking, in which we pay attention to emergent, contingently created transferential meanings and unconscious projective fantasies in the here-and-now, to an unfolding psyche that is not fixed and given when a person enters therapy or analysis, and to the particularity of the individual analyst-analysand relationship. Clinical experience likewise documents the personal emotional and fantasy

Theoretical Gender and Clinical Gender

construction of individual gender and the individualized projective animations of cultural gender meanings. People create their sense of gender through emotionally and conflictually charging with unconscious fantasy recognizable cultural meanings, their personal experience, and their bodies. Gender meanings as we observe them are, finally, articulated in language, but this language only approximates an inner psychic reality that is emotional, partially conscious, fragmentary, and indicated by disconnected thoughts.

This does not leave us entirely at sea. Without thinking that all women differ from all men in certain ways or that all women must traverse the same necessary path to end up with the same necessary femininity, we can nonetheless point toward aspects of intrapsychic experience that with some regularity seem to go into constructions of gendered subjectivity. Clinical experience documents both the multiplicity and variability of individual constructions of gender and indicates some of the axes of definition and emotional castings that different individuals may bring to their own gender construct.

The Inner Object World

For most people, unconscious fantasies (I mean here the emotionally charged projective and introjective stories about self and object described most extensively by Kleinians and object-relations theorists) about aspects of self, mother, father, and other primary figures, observation of them, comparison of them to each other and to other women and men, seem an important primary ingredient in personal gender. To elaborate upon one example, my own early writing focused on the mother-daughter relationship and argued for the importance of the mother-daughter relationship in the female psyche (Chodorow, 1978). I noted patterns in mothers' unconscious experience of sons and daughters that helped to create differently constructed inner object worlds and differently formed self boundaries in men and women. But it is also possible to claim that the mother-daughter relationship, although almost always important in the female (daughter's *and* mother's) psyche, will be projectively and introjectively animated in individual, particularized ways. Unconscious fantasy constructions and symbolizations of self and mother are not all alike. For individual women, or at different times in a life cycle or over the course of an analysis, the mother can symbolize nurturance or its rejection, an angry or welcoming breast, intimacy or fear of intimacy, guilt at independence or resentment at dependence, passivity or activity, aggression or submission, attraction to or fear of female genitality or anatomy, and many other issues. These unconscious and conscious animations can link to cultural gender in many ways, through images of wifehood or motherhood, through fantasies about giving and the breast, through images of domination and submission or of purity and impurity. These are *some* aspects of the intrapsychic relationship that tend to be psychologically symbolized, accorded emotional and fantasy meaning, and entered into the sense of gender. I list them at some length to emphasize both prevalent patterns and the fact that we cannot predict or limit, when it comes to understanding anyone's inner object world and constructions of self in that world.

I do not think that "oedipal" or "preoedipal" does justice either to the overwhelming power of and individual variation within different daughters' guilts, rages, feelings of loyalty and disloyalty, wishes to protect and repair, or sexual desires for their mother or father, or to their relation to these parents and the way these relationships affect their sense of gendered self. Several of my patients, for instance, fear that if they make their own choices or act on their own desires, they will destroy their mother. But in each patient this fantasy is embedded in and related to an otherwise individually constructed psyche. Both the fantasy and the dominant feelings it evokes, whether of anxiety, anger, guilt, sadness, loss, or fear of falling apart, vary. This variability contrasts with psychoanalytic tendencies to reduce the mother to one particular symbolization, for example, "the" holding environment, or "the" breast, or "the" symbol of castration. It is not universally the case that the mother's lack is necessarily contrasted with the father's phallus, or her baby-gestating capacities with *his* lack. This variation also applies to the place of the father in intrapsychic gender, and to other people who have played a significant role in a person's life (I am thinking of patients who grew up with several primary female caretakers and of others who had many siblings).

The gendered meanings of family members go well beyond explicit or implicit gender messages. They derive from the totality of the mutual creating of inner and outer worlds and the defensive and creative splitting that go into development and selfhood. Affects

Theoretical Gender and Clinical Gender

significantly imbue the relationship to a parent and the gender imagery created in relation to that parent. If a mother seems depressed or ineffectual, this tonality lends partial meaning to femininity and to conscious and unconscious senses of and fantasies about womanliness. If a father is experienced as domineering, or exciting but absent, gender meanings develop accordingly.

The sense of femininity or masculinity does not come directly from the parent who is female or male, respectively. Daughters and sons can also experience their father's "femininity" or their mother's "masculinity," and this experiencing itself can take many forms, for example, the affective communication of unconscious parental cross-identifications or unconscious parental cross-labeling of or fantasies about the child. It might involve a conscious or preconscious sense that some parental behavior crosses traditional gender lines—say, a marine sergeant mother, a cross-dressing father, a father who does infant care, or two lesbian mothers. Children may also infer that others (teachers, neighbors, grandparents, clinicians) believe that a particular parent's personality or behavior crosses gender.

Any gender-related category (man, woman, mother, father, sister, brother, feminine, masculine) gains meaning not just from language, but from personally experienced emotion and fantasy in relation to a person of that label. Children first observe gender-specific behaviors, sexed anatomy, and genital difference in daily routines, before they understand gender categorizations (de Marneffe, 1993). Each of these observations and experiences, as well as the settings in which language develops, are themselves accorded fantasy meaning and have emotional resonance, and integrating and coordinating them help lead to primary gender categorizations. Gender and genital concepts are thus affected by the unconscious and conscious gender interpretations and identities of parents and caretakers and the child's interpretation and understandings of this. Any linguistic categorizations in this context will have a personal emotional meaning that varies widely and individually.

The internal gendered world is not fixed once and for all in early development. Gender transferences and fantasies and the emotional tonalities that accompany these in the clinical encounter demonstrate the life cycle, day-to-day, and even moment-to-moment

Nancy J. Chodorow

shifting of gender and its varying salience and complexity, as different elements in the gendered sense of self become important and as gender itself is more or less salient in a current period of transference. At one moment in an hour, an early experience of incest may be prominent, at another attachment to the mother, at another idealization of the father. In work with one women, now the controlling, intrusive mother may be central to the creation of gender, now the dominant father, now the excited little girl, now the one humiliated by her excitement. In treating a man, now the swaggering little boy expresses himself, now the fearful one; now the boy excited by his triumphant possession of mother, now the boy afraid of engulfment or longing for his father.

Sexual Anatomy

From infancy throughout life, classical psychoanalysis suggests, body experience and body changes, including and especially sexual-genital-reproductive experiences, are likely to be felt with some intensity—to, in a sense, demand psychological meaning. Gendered subjectivity for most people does seem to include feelings and fantasies about sexual anatomy. I have found, however, that we cannot predict what this meaning will be and that the centrality and content of these feelings in any person's overall construction of gender will vary. Again, we have universals, patterns, and individuality: all people make something psychologically of their bodies and body experience, and we can find prevalent patterns within this, yet there is nothing automatic or self-evident about what these meanings will be.

For Freud, subjective gender derived first and foremost from genital anatomy and centered on genital difference. Psychoanalytic theories of gender thus began from Freud's focus on the presence or absence of the penis. Almost immediately, other analysts made clear that a girl's and woman's fantasies of her own inner and outer genitals were extremely significant and not secondary to her fantasies about the penis. Later, analysts began to document the importance to many women of menarche, menstruation, and pregnancy. Each of these developments stays with bodily experience, but each expands and transforms what in bodily experience is significant, enabling, as with the internal object world of gender, a more contingent and individualized account of how fantasies and emotions about sexual anatomy and bodily experience might develop

Theoretical Gender and Clinical Gender

and change. Thus, although it seems hard to find a mother for whom pregnancy and lactation are not important, maternal identifications and fantasies vary widely. Among nonmothers I have seen, some feel their life to center on the question of pregnancy or not; for others, this question pales before other important issues and conflicts. It may be only with the great rise in rates of breast cancer that we begin to see how important breasts are to many women's sense of self and gender—to paraphrase (and turn on its head) a distinction made in the case of penis envy, between wanting the breast libidinally (orally) and wanting it as part of one's own body.

Within these particularized projective trajectories, gendered anatomical meanings do not necessarily create or oppose masculine and feminine. In a single woman patient, one day her breasts, and the next day her mother's, are a topic of rage or hope. The following week, pregnancy is on her mind. Two months later, she is preoccupied with thoughts and feelings about her vagina. Next, she dreams about her brother's penis. For any one patient, and across different patients, these anatomical preoccupations generate a variety of symbolizations and fantasy constructions and a number of axes of sexual difference. For example, fantasies about anatomical male and female may compare at one moment father to mother, at another penis and vagina. The comparison might be presence or absence: penis and no penis, or breasts and no breasts. For other patients' imaging of genital anatomy, small and big may be a more criterial difference than male and female. I think of one patient for whom the male-female anatomical difference was irrelevant in comparison to her sense of the intensely shameful comparison of her own little-girl genitals with her mother's large, womanly genitals, and another for whom her mother's body was a subject of great disgust in comparison to her own pleasurable little-girl body. Big and little and masculinity-femininity may fuse, in a man's sense of being a little boy with a little penis with his big woman analyst with big breasts, or in a woman's sense of being a little girl with a little vagina with a big man analyst with a big penis and hair on his chest.

This does not mean that body feelings are entirely without pattern or idiosyncratic. These patterns may emerge partially from anatomy itself (it may require less unconscious work to fantasy nursing if you have breasts, or taking in if you have a vaginal opening, but this

Nancy J. Chodorow

has not stopped some men from having nursing or bodily receptive fantasies, and has not led all women to have them), and they are certainly affected by parental treatment and unconscious parental messages. Culture also influences the construal of bodily processes (for example, anthropologist E. Martin, 1987, shows that middle-class and working-class American women have different conceptions and experiences of menstruation, and many non-Euro-American women writers describe the profound effect that white beauty standards have on even little girls' sense of feminine body). In cautioning Western analysts about cultural assumptions and norms concerning bodily gender, the Indian psychoanalyst Kakar (1995) contrasts Western classical statues of muscular, lean gods and men with Hindu and Buddhist images of rounded, plump masculine gods who have incipient breasts.

Prevalent Animations of Gender

Among the different factors of self, object, and body I have described, each women makes some factors more significant than others, creating what we might consider her own prevalent animation of gender. In any analysis, discovering (and creating) this personal animation of gender, the dominant axes and feeling tones around which a patient organizes her subjective gender, will be important. We shall also find, as I suggest above, that for some women, their femininity, however it is created, will be a central area of conflict and will be central to transference-countertransference, while for other women, it will be less significant. For some women (see Chodorow, 1995), being female contrasts with being male, whether a man or a boy, a father or a brother. For others, it evokes a desperate, driven hunger for men. In the latter case, the male-female contrast is still there, but the woman wants to have a man rather than to be one. For some, femininity predominantly signifies a mother who weeps or a mother who is yearningly longed-for; for others it contrasts being an adult woman with being a little girl. In none of these cases does gender have one and only one meaning: different gendered meanings can be animated at different times, but as an analysis progresses, gender will organize itself around more dominant and more subordinate fantasies and themes. Prevalent animations of gender also often involve particular affective constellations—emotions that may not be construed consciously or unconsciously as

Theoretical Gender and Clinical Gender

gendered, but nonetheless form part of gendered subjectivity. Global affects such as anxiety or depression may invest a woman's sense of gender (Mayer, 1995, makes this point), and I have also found that more defined emotions seem to imbue different women's predominant animations of gender. In my experience, for example, shame and guilt seem central to many women's feelings and fantasies about mother, self and gender, and shame and disgust often imbue women's sense of bodily self. Envy and anger may dominantly animate feelings and fantasies about mother and self or about father and self.

CONCLUSIONS

Since Freud, there have been within psychoanalysis tensions between universalizing and essentializing claims about theoretical women in the developmental theory and the varieties of observations about clinical women in all their difference, context, individuality, and specificity. Similarly, contemporary feminism points us to the differences among women and to the multiplicities and individualities of gendered subjectivity, as well as to the fragmented, contradictory, multiple, and contextualized partialities of any one person's gendered and sexual subjectivity. Clinical understandings of gender and feminist theory here come together to document individuality and variation against the overgeneralizing, universalizing, and essentializing of psychoanalytic theory.

The fluidity and changeability of emotionally cast transferences in clinical experience make clear the specificity of any person's gendered subjectivity, a subjectivity we cannot capture in terms of monolithic claims about genital structure and function or preoedipal and oedipal developmental patterns. By staying with the clinical, we remember that any particular woman's or man's gender is a continuously invoked project in which self, identity, body imagery, sexual fantasy, fantasies about parents, cultural stories, and conflicts about intimacy, dependency, and nurturance are constructed, and that for each person we need to give an individual developmental, a transferential, and a cultural account fully to characterize these creations and transformations. Each person's gender also has its own emotional tonalities that accompany particular conflictual, defensive, and reparative fantasies.

Nancy J. Chodorow

I suggest that there is not a psychology of women, but that there are many psychologies of women. We need to disentangle the incontrovertible observation that for our patients (and ourselves), gender is inevitably thought about, felt, and fantasied, and our observations of repeated patterns of gender construction, from our assumption that we always know what this thinking, feeling, and fantasy or its underlying basis will be. Exploring female development is not the same as outlining universally necessary developmental tasks or achievements against which we assess our patients. We want to hold on to the clinical and theoretical truths that gender remains a useful category for psychological thinking, so that gender does not disappear completely into other aspects of subjectivity, identity, and self, while also holding on to the clinically observed personal uniqueness of the individual. Continual attentiveness to our tendencies in the areas of gender and sexuality to overgeneralize, universalize, and essentialize and to allow preconsciously held cultural assumptions to infuse theory, along with continual attention to clinical individuality, will help to achieve these goals.

REFERENCES

APPLEGARTH, A. (1976). Some observations on work inhibition in women. *J. Amer. Psychoanal. Assn.*, 24(Suppl.):251–269.

BELENKY, M.F.; CLINCHY, B.M.; GOLDBERGER, N.R.; & TARULE, J.M. (1986). *Women's Ways of Knowing: The Development of Self, Voice, and Mind*. New York: Basic Books.

BEM, S. (1993). *The Lenses of Gender*. New Haven, CT: Yale Univ. Press.

BENJAMIN, J. (1995). *Like Subjects, Love Objects*. New Haven, CT: Yale Univ. Press.

BROWN, L.M. & GILLIGAN, C. (1992). *Meeting at the Crossroads: Women's Psychology and Girls' Development*. Cambridge, MA: Harvard Univ. Press.

CHASSEGUET-SMIRGEL, J. (1985). *Creativity and Perversion*. London: Free Association Books.

——— (1986). *Sexuality and Mind*. New York: N.Y. Univ. Press.

CHODOROW, N.J. (1978). *The Reproduction of Mothering*. Berkeley, CA: Univ. California Press.

——— (1989a). *Feminism and Psychoanalytic Theory*. New Haven, CT: Yale Univ. Press.

——— (1989b). Seventies questions for thirties women: gender and generation in a study of early women psychoanalysts. In *Feminism and Psychoanalytic Theory*. New Haven, CT: Yale Univ. Press, pp. 199–218.

——— (1989c). Psychoanalytic feminism and the psychoanalytic psychology of women. In *Feminism and Psychoanalytic Theory*. New Haven, CT: Yale Univ. Press, pp. 178–198.

Theoretical Gender and Clinical Gender

——— (1994). *Femininities, Masculinities, Sexualities: Freud and Beyond.* Lexington, KY: University Press of Kentucky.

——— (1995). Gender as a personal and cultural construction. *Signs,* 20:516–544.

——— (1996). Reflections on the authority of the past in psychoanalytic thinking. *Psychoanal. Q.,* 65:32–51.

——— & CONTRATTO, S. (1982). The fantasy of the perfect mother. In *Feminism and Psychoanalytic Theory.* New Haven, CT: Yale Univ. Press, pp. 79–96.

DE MARNEFFE, D. (1993). *Toddlers' Understandings of Gender.* Doctoral dissertation, University of California, Berkeley.

DIMEN, M. (1991). Deconstructing difference: gender, splitting, and transitional space. *Psychoanal. Dialog.,* 1:335–352.

FAST, I. (1984). *Gender Identity: A Differentiation Model.* Hillsdale, NJ: Erlbaum.

FRYE, M. (1990). The possibility of feminist theory. In *Theoretical Perspectives on Sexual Difference,* ed. D. Rhode. New Haven, CT: Yale Univ. Press, pp. 174–184.

GILLIGAN, C. (1982). *In a Different Voice: Psychological Theory and Women's Development.* Cambridge, MA: Harvard Univ. Press.

——— ROGERS, A.S. & TOLMAN, D. (1991). *Women, Girls, and Psychotherapy: Reframing Resistance.* Binghamton, NY: Haworth Press.

GOLDNER, V. (1991). Toward a critical relational theory of gender. *Psychoanal. Dialog.,* 1:249–272.

HARRIS, A. (1991). Gender as contradiction: a discussion of Freud's "The psychogenesis of a case of homosexuality in a woman." *Psychoanal. Dialog.,* 1:197–224.

HEILBRUN, C.G. (1988). *Writing a Woman's Life.* New York: Ballantyne.

IRIGARAY, L. (1985). *This Sex Which Is Not One.* Ithaca, NY: Cornell Univ. Press.

JORDAN, J.; KAPLAN, A.; MILLER, J.B.; STIVER, I.; & SURREY, J. (1991). *Women's Growth in Relation.* New York: Guilford Press.

KAKAR, S. (1995). Clinical work and cultural imagination. *Psychoanal. Q.,* 64:265–281.

KESTENBERG, J. (1968). Outside and inside, male and female. *J. Amer. Psychoanal. Assn.,* 16:457–520.

——— (1982). The inner-genital phase. In *Early Female Development: Current Psychoanalytic Views,* ed. D. Mendel. New York: Spectrum, pp. 81–125.

MACCOBY, E. & JACKLIN, C. (1984). *The Psychology of Sex Differences.* Stanford, CA: Stanford Univ. Press.

MARTIN, E. (1987). *The Woman in the Body.* Boston, MA: Beacon Press.

MARTIN, J.R. (1994). Methodological essentialism, false difference, and other dangerous traps. *Signs,* 19:630–657.

MAYER, E.L. (1985). 'Everybody must be just like me': observations on female castration anxiety. *Int. J. Psychoanal.,* 66:331–347.

——— (1995). The phallic castration complex and primary femininity: paired developmental lines toward female gender identity. *J. Amer. Psychoanal. Assn.,* 43:17–38.

McDougall, J. (1986). *Theatres of the Mind: Illusion and Truth on the Psychoanalytic Stage.* London: Free Association Books.

Mitchell, J. & Rose, J., Eds. (1982). *Jacques Lacan, Feminine Sexuality.* New York: Norton.

Person, E.S. (1995). *By Force of Fantasy.* New York: Basic Books.

Phillips, A. (1993). Playing mothers: between pedagogy and transference. In *On Kissing: Tickling and Being Bored.* Cambridge, MA: Harvard Univ. Press, pp. 101–108.

Roiphe, H. & Galenson, E. (1981). *Infantile Origins of Sexual Identity.* New York: Int. Univ. Press.

Schafer, R. (1974). Some problems in Freud's psychology of women. *J. Amer. Psychoanal. Assn.,* 22:459–485.

────── (1995). Aloneness in the countertransference. *Psychoanal. Q.,* 64:496–516.

Shengold, L. (1994). Envy and malignant envy. *Psychoanal. Q.,* 63:615–640.

Stern, D.N. (1985). *The Interpersonal World of the Infant.* New York: Basic Books.

Trevarthan, C. (1979). Communication and cooperation in early infancy: a description of primary intersubjectivity. *Before Speech: The Beginning of Interpersonal Communication,* ed. M.M. Bullowa. New York: Cambridge Univ. Press.

────── (1980). The foundations of intersubjectivity: development of interpersonal and cooperative understanding in infants. In *The Social Foundation of Language and Thought: Essays in Honor of Jerome Bruner,* ed. D.R. Olsen. New York: Norton.

Tyson, P. (1982). A developmental line of gender identity, gender role, and choice of love object. *J. Amer. Psychoanal. Assn.,* 30:61–86.

────── (1991). Some nuclear conflicts of the infantile neurosis in female development. *Psychoanal. Inq.,* 11:582–601.

Winnicott, D.W. (1965). *The Maturational Processes and the Facilitating Environment.* New York: Int. Univ. Press.

────── (1971). *Playing and Reality.* New York: Basic Books.

III.
THE BODY IN THE PSYCHOLOGY OF WOMEN

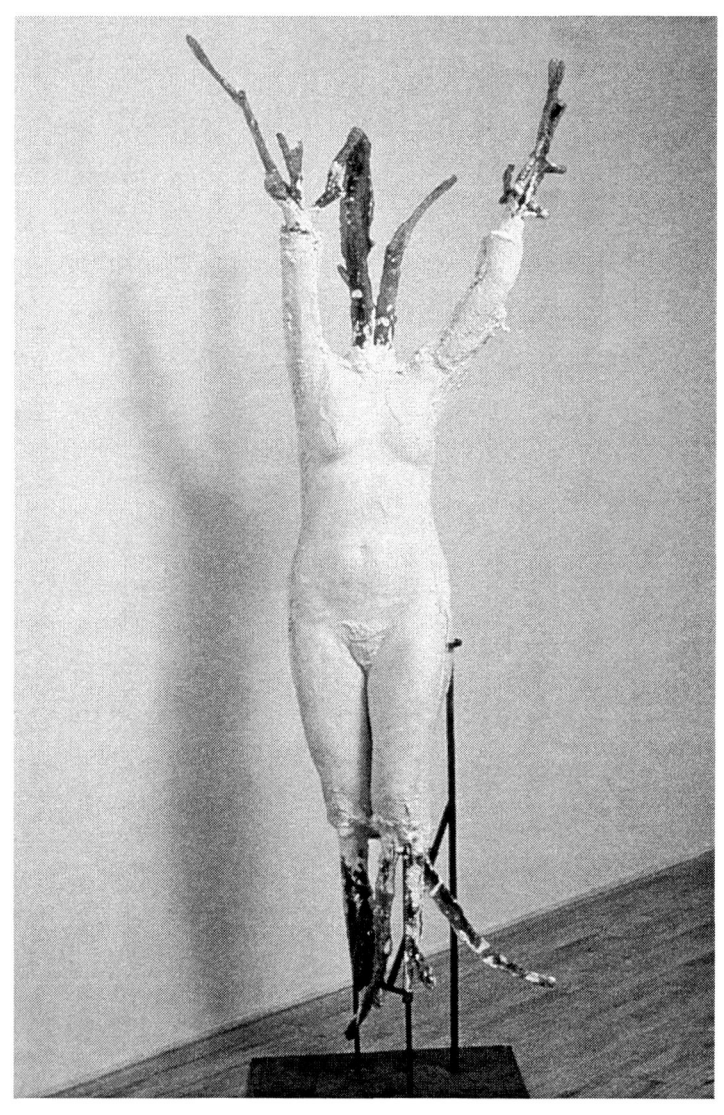

Figure 5. Kiki Smith (1993) *Daphne*. Plaster and glass, 83 × 32 × 17" Photograph courtesy of Pace Wildenstein.

THE MEANING OF PERINEAL ACTIVITY TO WOMEN: AN INNER SPHINX

Anna Burton

This paper is an inquiry into the close association of anal and genital functions in women and the background and meaning of that association. Excerpts from the analyses of two women with sexual and intellectual inhibitions illustrate aspects of erotic life deriving from anal-phase development, and the unconscious fantasy of an inner, erotic, and powerful "organ." Along with the lifting of their inhibitions, both analysands achieved integration of anal-sadistic and incorporative wishes with vaginal receptivity.

Female anatomy and physiology are so arranged that the action of perineal and sphincter musculature also stimulates the genital. This fosters overlapping mental representations of vagina and rectum which in turn affect body image and unconscious fantasy in women.

The experience of perineal contraction acquires complex psychic meanings with both libidinal and aggressive charge. The libidinal aspect is the largely covert erotic sensation that informs the mental representation of the genital and is destined to be integrated into female sexuality. The aggressive component may present as an unconscious fantasy of possessing an inner, powerful, and dangerous organ—a focus for conflict between anal-sadistic wishes and early elements of the superego.

It is now widely recognized that even in the first two years of life, psychosexual development in the female follows a different course from that in the male. Jacobson (1976), Greenacre (1952), Galenson and Roiphe (1976), and Kestenberg (1956, 1975, 1982) have explored the interaction between anatomy, object relations, and identification as the developing girl meets her preoedipal and oedipal tasks. More recently Bernstein (1990), Mayer (1985), A.K. Richards (1992), and Bass (1994) have discussed the effects of body structure on female development.

Faculty, New York University Psychoanalytic Institute.

Anna Burton

In this context, I call attention to a set of mental representations leading to an unconscious fantasy—that of an inner, erotic, and powerful "organ." This fantasy has roots in sphincter action and perineal anatomy, and becomes part of early psychic development and conflict. As the derivatives of this unconscious idea become easier to recognize, its frequency suggests that it may be a common fantasy in women. Writings by Chasseguet-Smirgel (1970) on feminine guilt and by A.K. Richards (1992) on sphincter control and the body image present clinical material consonant with such a formulation. My own interest in this topic began with the observation that analyzing the aggressive meanings of sphincter action in women brought forth something more than the expectable material relating to anxiety and inhibitions; many women also spoke of pleasure of a sexual nature, associated with masturbation. I also noticed that although women do not spontaneously describe anal sphincter and perineal matters, they easily acknowledge such sensations, and associate them with lingering confusions about their anatomy and sexuality.

Clinical material from two analysands (Marie and Frieda) indicates that the fantasy of an inner, aggressive capability was closely connected with their central conflicts. This led to the question of how frequently such a fantasy lies embedded in female inhibition, and whether it is to be considered as one strand in the weaving of female character and genitality.

That anatomy and function are silent co-shapers of character has been assumed in psychoanalysis from its very beginnings (Freud, 1905). Greenacre's (1952) work follows the approach that anatomical factors are "primary nuclear ones in determining early divergence in . . . development" (p. 149). In this spirit it is therefore appropriate to look once more at the anatomy of the perineum in an effort to more fully understand the course of development in the female.

There are anatomically based differences in the ways in which men and women experience the perineal region of their bodies. One difference is the greater separation of genital and urinary functions in the female. Another is in the distribution of erectile tissue. In both sexes, arousal occurs on the physiological basis of a direct response of vascular erectile tissue, a response mediated by known nerve pathways. All of the erectile tissue of the male genital is contained in two cavernous bodies or bulbs, and a third bulb (the *corpus*

Meaning of Perineal Activity to Women

cavernosus urethrae) which surrounds the urethra. These three structures form a bundle running the length of the penis.

In contrast, the shape of the female erectile organ is a divergent one, consisting of the three parts of the clitoral organ. Within the shaft of the clitoris lie the paired cavernous bodies, homologous with those of the male. The other two clitoral parts are the deeper structures, the right and left "vestibular bulbs." (This bifid arrangement, quite separate from the female urethra, is nevertheless the homologue of the third male corporum, the *corpus cavernosus urethrae*). Its two elongated masses of erectile tissue run longitudinally from front to back, deep to the labum on each side, from a point of anterior origin at the root of the clitoral shaft (Brash, 1953). This spread-apart disposition of erectile tissue provides separate sources of perceptual elaboration, and fosters the variety of ways in which female arousal is subjectively localized.

A third difference in the genital experience of males and females derives from the proximity of the lower vagina to the anal sphincter. In 1905 Freud noted that some unconscious confusion of vagina and anus always exists. He called attention to the common fantasy of a cloaca, which would conflate all three products—urinary, reproductive, and anal—and he juxtaposed this psychic confusion with the anatomical cloaca in animals and human embryos. As late as 1932, Freud held that "interest in the vagina is . . . essentially of anal-erotic origin" (p. 101) and he quoted Andreas-Salomé's (1916) idea that infantile genital erotism in women derives as though "on lease" from a cloacal entity (pp. 187, 196).

The vagina is a potential space within a perineal mass that contains and includes the sphincters. The anatomic relations make the sphincters relevant to genital sensation. As one would expect, some sexual sensations arising from sphincter closure are common to both males and females. These arise in the rectal mucosa and in deep pressure sensors, and are mediated by nerve plexuses surrounding the bladder, intestines, vagina, or, in men, the prostate, seminal vesicles, vasa deferentia and testes. In females however, the perineal compression that accompanies sphincter closure results in stimulation of receptors in the vestibular bulbs, as well as mucosal friction within the vulvae and around the clitoris. I wish to emphasize that *the action and release of perineal and sphincter musculature can stimulate all of the female's genital pleasure-mediating structures.*

Anna Burton

The functional anatomy dictates an experiential difference between women and men in the organization of sensual-erotic components. The difference is readily apparent in the observation that a woman enhances orgasm through tightening her perineum and sphincters, whereas a man's orgasm is incompatible with such sphincter tightening. In fact, voluntary clenching of the perineal muscles, which brings a mild genital pleasure, has been one means by which girls attempt to locate their genitals.

It follows that the achievement of bowel control must of necessity be registered differently in girls and boys. When the girl toddler strains to retain or expel, her perineal muscles become accessories, adding through pressure a genital component to the sphincter proprioception. Memory traces of these incompletely differentiated perineal experiences enter into body image and unconscious fantasy. Furthermore, the covert genital sensations (in contradistinction to direct stimulation of the external clitoris) do not result from handling by mother or self-handling by infant. They constitute an early autoerotic possibility, a self-discovery which remains unnamed and uncommunicated.

The above considerations provide a somatic foundation for observations that seem to support a special affinity between anal and vaginal in the mental representations of these organs. To illustrate this affinity, I offer a partial description of the analysis of Celia, and an excerpt from the analysis of Marie (about whom more will follow).

Celia was a bright, capable woman of twenty-seven whose progress in career and family life was at a dead stop because of anxieties and inhibitions. She told me of her habit of sitting on the toilet with her legs crossed in order to monitor her evacuations. This was one of several anal-masturbatory preoccupations which had generally eclipsed her genital-erotic life. She had a horror of seeing dead squirrels or other small creatures, a fear we had traced to hostile and envious feelings toward a sibling and also toward her somewhat infantile father—all the rivals for her mother's attention.

Some time later, Celia imagined that if she used the toilet after her father did, she could become sick or pregnant. Other oedipal themes as well as genital interests gradually entered the analysis. Her images of small, furry animals began to have life and movement. However, it was not yet possible for Celia to reach orgasm during

Meaning of Perineal Activity to Women

intercourse. Instead, perching again on the toilet, and using a vibrator, she programmed her vaginal orgasm very much as she had formerly done with her anal gratifications.

Celia's progression in analysis retraced a developmental path described by Kestenberg (1975) in which fear of self-injury and guilt feelings lead the small girl to deny the introitus for a period of time. The externalized representative of the genital (e.g., doll or animal) then loses its animated quality. While Celia was remembering and repeating in the transference her love and jealousy of her mother, she was beginning to allow herself genital discoveries. The introitus was no longer a place of fear and guilt, and orgasm was possible, albeit with stringent control. The small animals in her phobias became alive and benign.

The analysis of another woman's intellectual inhibition revealed an underlying conflict over her perineal competence. Marie came to analysis in her mid-thirties, demoralized by doubts about herself as a woman and a mother, and no longer sure of her ability to think effectively. Her character was strongly marked by the need for material gain and orderly habit. Control was essential to Marie in all her activities and relationships. For example, she would not swim or ride horseback for fear of being overwhelmed by external forces. In a marriage that had become a battlefield of mutual denigration and struggle for power, she felt trapped and helpless.

When her husband developed a gastrointestinal illness with diarrhea, Marie became very anxious. She herself had always "managed" her bowel movements through diet and suppositories. If menstrual flow was light, she took pride in having some control over that as well, claiming that she could stay "closed" for hours. (Lewin [1950] describes the same formulation in a woman who connected menstruation with anal loss.) In answer to my question, she explained that pregnancy exercises had taught her how to tighten herself "down there." These perineal exercises, she said, gave her a good feeling—in fact a sexual feeling. Marie had often thought to use those muscles during intercourse, but somehow she always forgot. I asked what effect the tightening might have, and she thought it would feel good, but wondered if it would please or anger her husband. She could never predict his reaction; sometimes at work he got angry just when she was thinking most clearly. I remarked on how she had shifted scenes, and asked whether the feelings at work were related to the physical feelings she had just described. It was true, she said, that in both situations—i.e., tensing her perineal muscles and thinking effectively—she feared her husband's anger as though in response to some hostile act on her part. She then made the connection between forgetting to "use her muscle" in bed and doubting her decisions at work.

The dynamics of Marie's inhibition resemble those of a woman whom Chasseguet-Smirgel describes (1970, p. 106) for whom sexual pleasure was lost through the flaccidity of her vagina. Both situations imply the unconscious fantasy of a sphincter within the perineum. Anatomically, of course, there is no vaginal sphincter; its absence is the basis of some specifically female anxieties about what may enter and do damage, and what may flow out that is valuable or shameful, as Barnett (1966) and Bernstein (1990) describe. However there are kinesthetic sensations that accompany sphincter action and become part of the mental representation of a contracting, lifting, or tightening of the pelvic floor. This is the complex perineal action for which Kestenberg (1982) identifies specific musculovascular structures, as background for her observations on bodily and psychic development. The effects of these kinesthetic sensations on the body image of adult women (as mentioned above) was taken up by Richards (1992). I am proposing that the sensory input from erectile organs, with these kinesthetic sensations from the sphincters, go to form the mental representation of a "perineal sphincter."

The act of tightening the "perineal sphincter" may have layers of meaning with libidinal and aggressive charges, parallel to the psychic elaborations of anal constriction. For instance, this "sphincter" might be felt as a defense against invasion as well as against loss, and as part of a defining body boundary. Referring to Abraham's (1927) second division of the anal phase, Shengold (1985) notes that "the registration of true transient experience of the anus holding on and closing down makes the registration of a closed system possible. The child can know what it is like to feel his body as an entity with boundaries and with doors that shut" (p. 52).

Psychic registration of perineal and sphincter control can be further elaborated as the ability to master overwhelming affect. A woman described by Richards (1992) illustrates this meaning. In

Meaning of Perineal Activity to Women

childhood she had clenched her sphincters to ward off feelings about her parents' quarreling. The same patient in adulthood took pleasure in ballroom dancing, while at the same time the controlled action of the dance served to master her fears of aggression. (This illustrates also how the idea of movement and control extends from an association with sphincters to association with large body musculature [Freud 1905, p. 198; Shengold, 1985]).

Frieda was a forty-five-year-old mother of grown children, who had turned to analysis because of depression and inhibitions. Like Richards' patient, she activated a muscular-kinesthetic response in the pelvic floor and large body musculature, which had a specific meaning and purpose. At social gatherings, in order to overcome feelings of inadequacy, she would tighten her perineum and stand very straight, while also imagining that she wore a tight waist-cincher. This maneuver, together with its associated fantasy, gave her a sense of pleasure and bolstered self-confidence.

Representations of a "perineal sphincter" may contribute to various unconscious fantasies, such as the fantasy of pregnancy, or the fantasy of an internal phallus. Quite graphic representations may occur with anal-incorporative fantasy. The idea of a perineal grasping organ, for instance, was expressed by Yvonne, a young woman who worked at a nursing home. She was ordinarily an empathic listener, but, one day she became annoyed with an elderly man's romantic reminiscences. She found herself rhythmically contracting her perineal muscles, an act which ordinarily gave her a mild pleasure, but this time was accompanied by the disturbing thought that she "had something like a hand there, and was choking him with it!" Yvonne's associations detailed a long-standing conflict over vengeful and erotic oedipal fantasies.

In these vignettes we find perineal muscle action to be associated with genital pleasure and aggressive, even sadistic impulses. The resulting conflict caused anxiety in Yvonne, whereas Frieda had established a compromise: she tensed her muscles as though to assert herself, but at the same time imagined that she was herself being tightened by a waist-cincher.

In its function as an active organ with aggressive tone, the perineal musculature can symbolically express the urge to grasp, to take, or to use or abuse the object. The fantasy of inner dangerousness provides focus for conflicts between anal-sadistic wishes and the early elements of the superego (Jacobson, 1976). Fantasy retributions for anal-sadistic wishes are modeled on expulsion (being cast out, dismembered, or devalued), retention (being tied up, choked, squeezed, or pinched), and control (being enslaved). It is striking to hear in clinical material the ways in which specific aggressive attributes of the perineal sphincter may be rendered as talion fears of being grasped, dismembered, or otherwise used. I shall offer further illustrations of these fantasies in the working through of inhibitions, which led to better integration of anal-aggressive with genital impulses.

The first theme in the analysis of Marie (the woman who needed to control her husband and her bodily functions) was her hostility toward this husband. In debasing and trying to manipulate him, she was very like her mother, who had "managed" her alcoholic father in the same way. Marie had seen her mother stealing father's money while he slept, and had felt guilt over her own implicit collusion. This was repeated in her present conflict over urges to steal from her husband. Her lovemaking was a joyless weighing of how much she "gave" and "got," and was disturbed by violent impulses to pinch, squeeze, or strangle him.

Marie's need to control included her choice of clothing; she wore stylized outfits that seemed tight and uncomfortable. She once wished to buy a long, smooth fur coat that would reach from chin to toe. The fur would be a warm, brown color, like that of the cover of the analytic couch. She then dreamed of gobbling down a whole tray of sticky candies, the way she had stuffed herself as a teenager. The thought of a particular kind of sausage came back to her, and she said, "I'd like to wrap myself around one of those right now!" I reminded her of the wish to wrap herself in a long coat, of the same color as the couch, and she responded warmly, "So then I'm the hot dog and you wrap yourself around me!" A brief affair at this time was giving Marie some gratification mixed with anxiety. She complained that her lover used his weight to immobilize her while he performed cunnilingus. Over time we made connections between her urges to take control and to devour, and interwoven ideas of herself being trapped, immobilized, or devoured.

Meaning of Perineal Activity to Women

Much later in the analysis, Marie detailed a startling coital fantasy: she was squeezing her husband in a vise, "harder and harder." While telling me this, she felt aroused "somewhere down there." The excitement came from imagining herself doing the tightening, while he became a "helpless blob." She would imagine releasing him a little and then beginning again. I connected this fantasy with the idea of controlling and releasing a bowel movement. Marie agreed, and after a short silence told me that while on the couch, she had covertly "tried out that feeling" by tensing her perineal muscles.

In our sessions Marie often felt she had me trapped: "I feel sorry for you having to hear all this; you must sit there and just take it until the time is up. You can't even speak until I stop and let you." I pointed out her sense of power in starting and stopping my words, and we traced the parallels to her coital fantasy and to her sphincter play with bowel movements. Marie then felt weak and helpless, as though my cruel interpretations had disarmed her. She could do nothing except lie helpless on the couch and tell her thoughts; I was the boss. As we analyzed her feelings about power and powerlessness with respect to me, her competitive attitudes softened. She was able to befriend a younger woman whose qualities she had envied; at the same time she regarded me in a new light as a kind of mentor.

During the last year of analysis, Marie regained a pleasure in "owning" her body, and freedom to enjoy physical activities. She began to redecorate her home, and in discussing rugs, curtains, and the like, she realized she was being more considerate and allowing her husband to share in the project. More important, the same welcoming and sharing attitudes were entering their lovemaking.

This analytic review of a woman with marked "anal" characteristics follows her emergence from intellectual and sexual inhibition. During the process, she elaborated fantasies of taking both the active and passive roles in such actions as squeezing, stuffing, and immobilizing the object; in a brief turn toward perversion, one of these fantasies became obligatory. Many transference repetitions were explored on the way to achieving a more mature genitality.

Frieda (briefly mentioned above), in her third year of analysis, was occupied with mourning for an infant who had been stillborn many years before. She rehearsed her old belief that sexual intercourse had killed the fetus, imagining that for the baby inside, orgasm would be like a destroying earthquake. During labor she had known that the fetus was not living, and yet with each contraction she worried about harming it.

A memory returned of one of Frieda's adolescent masturbation fantasies: she was in a disastrous earthquake, surrounded by fallen masonry and pinned down by a corpse that lay on top of her. The fantasy was that she screamed and "went crazy" until rescuers arrived. Meanwhile she had the exciting sensation that her "insides were shaking." Quite apart from its connection to the stillbirth, this fantasy turned out to be an entry to her lifelong fantasizing. I learned that her early daydreams were accompanied by practices of indirect masturbation such as pressing her thighs together to cause her "insides to shake."

She soon brought in a childhood dream which she had often recalled and puzzled over. The night following a nasal packing for a nosebleed, she had dreamed that she pulled from one nostril a long clot shaped like a string of sausages. Frieda then said she had just cooked sausages and felt uneasy when the strings dividing the sections came loose. How could the sausages retain their shape without the strings? Later, at dinner, she devoured a huge portion; it was the kind of eating she called "stuff-your-mouth eating" (which by now was recognized in the analytic work as coprophagic eating). She thought then of lead curtain weights, which have a similar shape, since they come as a string of lead shot encased in a thin fabric tube. The sausages and the weighted line reminded her, finally, of feces. Responding to a movement of mine, she then said, "You must hate listening to this. There you are; you can't stir out of here, or stop me. Too bad you just have to take it... " I said nothing, and we both listened to the sound of rain falling outside. Frieda thought, " 'Water, water everywhere, nor any drop to drink'—*The Ancient Mariner*... represents endless guilt... has an albatross around his neck because he broke the rule and shot it. The curtain weights doom the curtain to forever carry their weight."

To Frieda, rain also signified forgiveness by God, and this thought led her to tears. "What am I crying about? The lost child.... " Her guilt seemed to her to be misplaced. Was it more

Meaning of Perineal Activity to Women

about her husband? His unpredictability, his quirky, original thoughts were unsettling, and yet these were the very qualities that had made him so attractive. She decided that it was when she felt "out of control" that his surprises made her anxious. Frieda explained his character to me at length, and doing so, she began to behave as though I, too, were likely to take her by surprise. She began to speak "nonstop," closing out my words. It developed that my thought processes had to be predicted, categorized, and mastered, she felt, "or else you might suddenly penetrate my defenses; it would shake me to my foundations."

During analysis, Frieda's sexual pleasure had returned. However, she again became unable to reach orgasm during coitus without a new type of fantasy: a man is tightly bound "like a thing" and either pinched or penetrated in different ways. In order to remain aroused, she would alternately "be" the victim in this fantasy, and the woman directing the torture scene. Either way, she felt a burden of guilt in not feeling love toward her husband. She recalled something he had said about "lasting long enough," and only now understood that her own sexual difficulty was putting stress on him as well.

Shortly afterward, Frieda reported she had discovered a new position in which she could again reach orgasm: she wrapped her arms and legs around her husband in a close but loving embrace.[1] This solution was apparently made possible by our analysis of the "bound man" fantasy, through tracing connections between the early "shaking" masturbation fantasies, sadomasochistic transference feelings, and one positive, pleasant memory from childhood—that of being tightly tucked into bed by her mother. Afterward, Frieda enjoyed coitus with or without various fantasies of a less severely sadomasochistic nature.

Frieda, like Marie, needed to anticipate, order, and control her objects and her world. She was in conflict over repressed wishes to do harm, for example, by "shaking up" a fetus inside, or by imprisoning the object. However, in her recollected adolescent fantasies, she

---

[1]Grunberger (1974, cited by Oliner, 1982) describes a woman who reached "orgastic release for the first time ... by pressing and imprisoning [her partner's] penis between her thighs. In the ensuing coitus this sensation was transferred to the vagina: 'I held him in my power, as one holds a whole man by the scruff,' which reminded her of defecation (the sphincter surrounding and pressing against the fecal mass)."

was the passive member who experienced erotic pleasure mixed with retaliatory punishments. Her preoccupation with images relating to intestinal function were connected to sadistic impulses expressed in the transference and in her sexual fantasy.

I chose these excerpts to highlight material that points to the fantasy of a "perineal sphincter." Deriving from the unconscious idea of retention, stool, penis, and object were, in fantasy, grasped, pressed, bound, or imprisoned. Each patient became aware of guilt feelings. Marie's anxiety was intolerable when her husband became ill, and she devalued herself as viciously as she had disparaged him. She atoned for her acquisitiveness as though she were a thief, and was thrown into the same conflict with her husband that she had felt over seeing her father cheated by her mother. Fear and guilt were dominant affects, and her work was inhibited on the basis of the unconscious guilt explicated by Chasseguet-Smirgel (1970), in which any success is unconsciously equated with stealing the father's phallus. In addition, a coprophagic erotism appeared in Marie's memories of devouring sticky candies and sausages, while the idea of being devoured constituted the appropriate retaliation (Oliner, 1988). Marie's coital fantasy of having her husband in a vise was her temporary solution. It permitted orgasm but left her haunted by guilt feelings. The fantasy of the long fur coat, and the lover who weighted her down are examples of her combined gratification and atonement for anal-sadistic fantasies of squeezing her husband.

Frieda saw herself trapped and immobilized in identification with her stillborn infant, and before that in her earthquake fantasy. We know that she needed to stand tensed and straight in order to feel socially secure, and that this unspoken assertion was "paid-for" through the waist-cincher fantasy. Her genital competence and pleasure, lost through unconscious guilt, returned with the telling of the "bound-man" fantasy and the alternation of seeing herself as victim or torturer. This stark fantasy then became modulated to integrate with vaginal-incorporative wishes, so that she embraced and welcomed her husband's entry. (The associations of both Frieda and Marie bring to mind the concept of alternating identifications with "the container" and "the contained" [Chasseguet-Smirgel, 1970]. Marie's image of a long, wraparound coat suggests a fecal guise and

Meaning of Perineal Activity to Women

at the same time an expression of her need to trap and be trapped. She switched from being "contained" [ensconced in the long coat or pressed down by her lover] to "containing" [wrapping herself around a hot dog]. For Frieda the earthquake that buried her in fantasy, and her identification with the trapped fetus represented herself, both containing and being contained.)

Kestenberg (1982, p. 84) points out that the mother acts as the external organizing influence during the girl's passage through anal and early phallic phases. It is necessary for the analyst to play a parallel role. Marie's harassment of the analyst, and her opposite sense of being powerless on the couch were repetitions of these ambivalent power struggles. Frieda, on the other hand, initially took a masochistic position and "suffered" at the hands of the analyst. Each gained a more versatile ego, so to speak, capable of shifting back and forth between these power positions and eventually of integrating them with the expression of mature love. The general progress of both analyses was reflected in changes in object relations, which little by little transformed the tenor of life from struggling for control to one of mature sharing.

Cloacal or anal shadowing of infantile genital pleasure was first connected by Freud (1905) with an "archaic colouring," and with sadism and ambivalence in the sense of opposing instincts. His discoveries opened the way to later work on the characterological effects of anal sadism and masochism. Abraham (1927) identified retention and evacuation as sources of part instincts pressing for libidinal and aggressive release. He connected the aggressive component with wishes to cast off or destroy the object, and, with later psychic development, to keep and control the object.

The discovery of the cloacal fantasy by Freud gave word and image to a ubiquitous unconscious fantasy of the female genital's interior site and close anatomical relations. A distinction by sex was introduced by Ferenczi in 1923. His observations led him to contrast an anal influence on female genitality with the more urethral coloring of male genitality. Equipped with Freud's theory of the organ as source for instinctual drives, Ferenczi developed the term "cavity erotism," a feature of psychic representation common to all hollow organs, and the term "amphimixis," to convey the blending of instinctual urges:

> ... apparently considerable amounts of oral and anal erotism are displaced also upon the vagina, the unstriated musculature of which seems to imitate in its spasmodic contractions as in its peristalsis the oral pleasure of ingestion and the anal of retention.... For the leading zone of genitality, in which in the male the emphasis is definitely upon the urethral, regresses again in the female chiefly to the anal, in that in the sex act the accent is shifted to sheltering the penis and its secretion and also the fruit thereof (parental erotism) [p. 14].

The early analysts had seen a triple overlapping identification of mouth, anus, and vagina. In 1952, Greenacre's infant observations added clinical substance to the concept:

> In many infants a stimulation of the mouth through feeding produces a readily observed lower bowel stimulation.... In some instances there is a special linking of the activity of the musculature of the vaginal introitus with anal sphincter activity and with acts of suckling and swallowing [pp. 241–242].

Greenacre further connects rectal with vaginal sensations:

> In the female the greater connection between the vagina and the rectum may mean that the vagina is readily stimulated by anal discharges and, since this mechanism matures earlier than that of the clitoris, the vagina thus regularly borrows stimulation earlier... [p. 243].

One might expect this repeated, simultaneous stimulation to be reflected in an overlapping of anal-aggressive and genital impulses in girl toddlers. And indeed, some support for this expectation is found in the developmental observations that gave rise to a landmark study. Galenson and Roiphe (1976) observed toddlers as they developed mental representation of their perineal parts, progressing from the anal to urethral and genital areas. The authors' chief concern was to demonstrate the interweaving of object relations and preoedipal drive development, as reflected in ego function, especially during the period they establish as the "early genital phase." While they emphasize parental fantasies and behaviors concerning infant daughters, Galenson and Roiphe do not overlook the consideration that anatomical differences provide differing sensuous components to the tactile exchange between mother and child. Genital play became something more than infantile exploration under the influence of new anal and urinary awareness, and approached true

Meaning of Perineal Activity to Women

masturbation in its rhythmic pattern and rudimentary, symbolic evocation of the object.

> In the wake of castration reactions, we have seen marked oral-regressive behavior; anal-zone exploration and anal masturbation become markedly intensified, and there is reemergence of the fear of object loss and of anal loss, and a subsequent change in the pattern of genital masturbation in many girls... [becoming] indirect [pp. 47–48].

My focus here is less on the girl's regressive reaction to the anatomical difference, and more on the ease with which she registers anus and vagina as though parts of one system.

Kestenberg (1975), much influenced by Greenacre's body-oriented approach to psychic development, used detailed, longitudinal observations to study patterns of action and object relations in the developing infant and child. From externalizations in play and behavior, she derived the ways in which the child registers sensations in the lower abdomen and perineum, and arrived at the concept of an amorphous, vaguely localized "inner genital": "the activity of an organ enhances its localization and sharpens its boundaries, thus creating a foundation for its representation in conjunction with a passive object." However, for girls, "invisible activity... [and] lack of visual confirmation detract from its activity value" (pp. 6–7).

What is felt as vaginal swelling, due presumably to the engorgement of erectile tissue, cannot be localized. One aspect of this difficulty is that "vaginal sensations are merged with rectal sensations and experienced as one" (p. 11). The same admixture of inner-genital and anal elements is reflected, she notes, in the girl's object relations. Her characterization of the anal toddler casts light on Frieda's defensive need to stand straight and tensed. "The firmness of the standing infant's body helps him achieve a new 'one-piece' unity of his body self.... [The] anal toddler... begins to appreciate the mother as a solid but separate unit" (p. 218).

The girl toddler meets with the mystery of her sexual equipment and turns to her mother for support and identification. It is in the context of this ambivalent relationship that the beginnings of superego function appear. Kestenberg illustrates by analyzing the meaning of the doll:

> While the treatment of the doll is greatly influenced by the girl's identification with the real mother, it always shows

unmistakable traces of the anal-sadistic type of mastery.... We recognize derivatives of these sadomasochistic impulses in the much later fantasy of a powerful master driving the girl to continuous sexual acts without hope for deliverance.... This scene is subject to abrupt changes.... The doll becomes the victim and the girl mother the persecutor [pp. 13–14].

It does no violence to our appreciation of such landmark concepts as the early genital phase, or the inner genital, to shift focus to the overlapping and indistinctness of anal and genital elements. Mastery of sphincter function plays an important role in genital development, and the sphincteric element is a plausible source of female aggression. The child first learns control in the anal arena and that context determines the girl's chief model of exerting power, while the boy, through anal control and phallic provenance, has two models of power (Bernstein, 1990). Chasseguet-Smirgel (1970, p. 102) asserts that normal genital female sexuality requires an anal-sadistic component, and suggests that the wish to anally incorporate the penis is a forerunner of active female sexuality.

Jacobson (1976) reconsidered Freud's views on the female superego and explored an earlier dimension. The fear of genital impairment in girls "is not dictated by the oedipal relationship but develops during the preoedipal relation to the mother..." signifying punishment for phallic and negative-oedipal wishes (p. 527). The girl's notions about what might be damaged can range from a vague fear of internal destruction to a pointed anxiety about losing a fantasied internal penis.

The coupling of aggressive or sadistic fantasies with fears of talion punishment lies at the root of what is often termed an early, harsh female superego. Jacobson made this connection from observing breakthroughs of cruel, presumably more primitive superego demands in some women with weak or uncertain moral judgment (pp. 525–526). She saw the retaliative fears based on introjective and projective mechanisms as the foundation for the superego, rather than as an early form of that structure. However, she also recognized a "nucleus" or a "first maternal-phallic stage" in superego development, which she dubbed the "heir of the negative Oedipus complex."

Jacobson's contribution is important because she saw two pathways of superego formation. She looked backward in time and culture at the girl whose "fear of loss of the penis had been replaced

Meaning of Perineal Activity to Women

by fear of losing the phallic love object, thus establishing an orally determined, narcissistic and often masochistic attitude toward the latter" (p. 531). The girl's love object then serves, to some extent, as her superego. Looking forward to the development of girls in a less phallocentric culture, Jacobson expected that early valuation of the vagina would permit direct libidinal investment in the organ itself, with the fantasied internal penis serving as a bridge in the equation of the penis with the erotized female genital. The girl's "castration fear" at this point in development would be a fear of vaginal injury, rather than fear of losing the phallic love object. This would allow for development of a more independent superego.

There are talion fears deriving from the period of anal conflict and the experiences surrounding toilet training. Because unconscious fantasies of destruction or incorporation by sphincter action include a genital component, the feared retaliations in the form of being destroyed or incorporated are also aimed at the female genital. This fear of vaginal destruction may coexist with fears of inner destruction on an oral model, as well as with castration fear as defined according to the "male" model—i.e., the idea of having lost a penis.

Oedipal and postoedipal development require the integration of these attributes of the "perineal sphincter" into normal female genitality. Bernstein (1990) outlines the girl's complicated program to master castration anxiety: she becomes confused, she regresses, loses control, panics, and turns to others—and finally, there is resynthesis and emergence of genital pleasure. The girl progresses from control of defecation to control of the whole body and then of the genital. Bernstein's example of a woman who, after feeling helpless, "resurrected an anal position" in the stock market, shows how a return to anal issues can point the way to developing genital control and power. The analyst, like the mother, must welcome both the necessary "regression" and the subsequent turn toward mastering erotic interest.

The association in patients' productions of ideas of sexuality, aggression, and anatomical confusion originally suggested to me the image of the Sphinx. "Sphinx" and "sphincter" derive from the Greek verb "sphingein," meaning "to draw tight," or "to strangle" (*Oxford English Dictionary*, 2nd Ed.). In all studies of the Sphinx, the prominent features are her seductive and self-contained mysteriousness—and her ferocity.

Anna Burton

Kanzer (1950) took the riddle of the Sphinx as "an allegory of the problems presented by female sexuality. A full-breasted woman above, a lioness below, she combines the beloved and dreaded aspects of femininity which the boy must reconcile in order to achieve genital potency" (pp. 562–564). As a composite, the Sphinx's form and mythology bring together oral, anal, and phallic powers formidable to the male confronting them. One wonders, then, what the Sphinx means to females. The metaphor of an "inner Sphinx" is an apt one for all of the libidinal and aggressive impulses of oral, anal, and vaginal origin. Could it be that the male fantasy of a dentate vagina has its counterpart in the female's fantasy about her inner sphincter parts? Whereas the male would encounter the Sphinx outside of himself and fear injury, the female would sense the Sphinx within her, and fear talion injury.

To sum up, I have suggested first that the perineal sphincter experience in women combines or blends the awareness of anal sphincter function with erotic genital sensations. Second, the coupling of aggressive or sadistic fantasies with fears of talion punishment (the early, harsh female superego) carries long-range implications for women regarding conflict over empowerment, inhibition, and character.

REFERENCES

ABRAHAM, K. (1927). A short study of the development of the libido in the light of mental disorders. In *Selected Papers of Karl Abraham.* New York: Basic Books, 1953, pp. 418–502.

ANDREAS-SALOMÉ, L. (1916). "Anal" and "sexual." *Imago,* 4(5):249–273.

BARNETT, M. (1966). Vaginal awareness in the infancy and childhood of girls. *J. Amer. Psychoanal. Assn.,* 14:129–140.

BASS, A. (1994). Aspects of urethrality in women. *Psychoanal. Q.,* 63:481–517.

BERNSTEIN, D. (1990). Female genital anxieties, conflicts, and typical mastery modes. *Int. J. Psychoanal.,* 71:151–165.

BRASH, J.C., Ed. (1953). *Cunningham's Textbook of Anatomy.* London: Oxford Univ. Press, 1981.

CHASSEGUET-SMIRGEL, J. (1970), Feminine guilt and the Oedipus complex. In *Female Sexuality.* Ann Arbor, MI: Univ. Michigan Press, pp. 94–134.

FERENCZI, S. (1923). *Thalassa. A Theory of Genitality.* New York: Norton, 1968.

FREUD, S. (1905). Three essays on the theory of sexuality. *S. E.,* 7.

——— (1932). New introductory lectures on psycho-analysis. *S. E.,* 22.

GALENSON, E. & ROIPHE, H. (1976). Some suggested revisions concerning early female development. *J. Amer. Psychoanal. Assn.,* 24(Suppl.):29–57.

GREENACRE, P. (1952). Anatomical structure and superego development. In *Trauma, Growth, and Personality*. New York: Norton, pp. 149–164.

GRUNBERGER, B. (1974). Gedanken zum frühen Uber-Ich. *Psyche*, 28:508–529.

JACOBSON, E. (1976). Ways of superego formation and the castration complex. *Psychoanal. Q.*, 45:525–538.

KANZER, M. (1950). The Oedipus trilogy. *Psychoanal. Q.*, 19:561–571.

KESTENBERG, J.S. (1956). Vicissitudes of female sexuality. *J. Amer. Psychoanal. Assn.*, 4:453–476.

——— (1975). *Children and Parents: Psychoanalytic Studies in Development*. New York: Aronson.

——— (1982). The inner genital phase—prephallic and preoedipal. In *Early Female Development*, ed. D. Mendell. New York: Spectrum, pp. 81–125.

LEWIN, B.D. (1950). Smearing of feces, menstruation and female superego. In *Selected Writings of Bertram D. Lewin*, ed. J. Arlow. New York: The Psychoanalytic Quarterly, pp. 12–25.

MAYER, E.L. (1985). 'Everybody must be just like me': female castration anxiety. *Int. J. Psychoanal.* 66:331–347.

OLINER, M. (1982). The anal phase. In *Early Female Development. Current Psychoanalytic Views*, ed. D. Mendell. New York: Spectrum, pp. 25–60.

——— (1988). Anal components in overeating. In *Bulimia: Psychoanalytic Treatment and Theory*, ed. H. J. Schwartz. Madison, CT: Int. Univ. Press, pp. 227–253.

RICHARDS, A.K. (1992). The influence of sphincter control and genital sensation on body image and gender identity in women. *Psychoanal. Q.*, 61:331–351.

SHENGOLD, L. (1985). Defensive anality and anal narcissism. *Int. J. Psychoanal.*, 66:47–73.

PRIMARY FEMININITY AND FEMALE GENITAL ANXIETY

Arlene Kramer Richards

> Primary femininity implies that female development proceeds along lines that generate anxiety about damage and loss similar to the fears of castration that trouble males. The female fears are classified as fear of painful penetration, fear of loss of pleasure, and fear of loss of procreative function. The first two fears are illustrated with clinical material showing the ways in which they manifest themselves in adult women.

After Reading *Mickey and the Night Kitchen* for the Third Time Before Bed

My daughter spreads her legs
to find her vagina:
hairless, this mistaken
bit of nomenclature
is what a stranger cannot touch
without her yelling. She demands
to see mine and momentarily
we're a lopsided star
among the spilled toys,
my prodigious scallops
exposed to her neat cameo [Dove, 1989, p. 41].

The poet describes an intimate moment between mother and little daughter which might have been unmentionable a decade earlier. The little girl wants to see her mother's genital and the mother shows it to her. They compare. The education in sexual openness, in the permission to be curious and in the child's right to be in control of her own sexuality, is clearly delineated in a few lines. Are we up to this?

Training and Supervising Analyst, New York Freudian Society; Fellow, Institute for Psychoanalytic Training and Research.

I thank Dr. Leon Hoffman, the members of the RAPS Study Group on Female Psychology of the Society for Medical Psychoanalysis, Dr. Arnold D. Richards, Dr. Jules Glenn, and all the other readers of this paper who asked incisive questions and did not let me get away with easy answers.

Arlene Kramer Richards

We psychoanalysts have learned much about female psychology since Blum's (1976) major effort to update our views. Of particular interest to me is the new understanding of female sexuality as it relates to body image, self-esteem, and sense of productive possibility. Part of the new understanding is a sense that women have a genital which they value and which they can worry about losing. This idea is not a new one, but one which has been controversial. I want to support with clinical data the idea that female anxiety about genitals could be anxiety about loss of specifically female anatomical features, functions and sensations.

The other side of this debate in the early analytic literature (Freud 1905, 1908; Deutsch, 1930; Rado, 1933; Jacobson, 1936) developed the idea of penis envy as the bedrock motivator of female behavior. Associated with that idea was the belief that females suffered from castration anxiety in the form of fear of loss of a fantasied penis (Freud, 1924) or in the form of an idea that they have already been castrated (Freud, 1933, Brenner, 1982).

My special interest is to examine the received wisdom of the concept of castration anxiety as it is applied to normal female development and as it is used to conceptualize female experience when development goes awry and leads people to our offices for help with dealing with their symptoms. The idea that forms the basis of this paper is that girls, like boys, value pleasure and fear unpleasure. From this it follows that girls would value the pleasurable sensations arising from genital stimulation. It also follows that girls would not need to experience anything more complicated than genital pleasure to value that pleasure. Nor would they need to experience anything other than genital pain to fear that pain. The fear of unpleasure would have to be understood as fear of pain and fear of loss of positively pleasurable sensation. Once this stance is adopted, ideas of pain and of loss of pleasure would be evident in the analytic work with almost any female patient. If loss of pleasure is understood to include aphanisis and frigidity, it becomes a concept often reported in the analytic literature, and especially as a presenting complaint in neurotic women patients. Since fear of genital pain is almost always associated with fear of painful penetration in adult women, I have postulated the idea of painful penetration. Quinodoz (1989) puts the more inclusive idea this way:

Primary Femininity and Genital Anxiety

> This anxiety about losing the female function and organs is present in girls just as its counterpart is in boys (Klein, 1932), but has never been given a specific term. Freud reserves the term castration loss for loss of the penis and not even the testicles [p. 58].

Stoller (1968) delineates the idea of primary femininity that entails a belief that one is a female and values femininity and one's female genital. This idea of primary femininity rests on clinical evidence that women and girls have fears of genital damage. Since the term "castration anxiety" means fear of loss of the penis, these female fears are best labeled "genital anxiety" (Goldberger, unpublished; Lax, 1994).

This paper is both a critique and an elaboration of D. Bernstein's (1990) and other authors' idea that females have fears of genital damage. It presents new clinical material in support of this idea. Bernstein proposes that female genital anxieties can best be conceptualized as fears about access, penetration, and diffusivity. While I agree that fear of penetration is ubiquitous in female patients, I also believe that it overlaps with what Bernstein calls access. Thus, I have condensed access into the category of penetration. I differ from Bernstein in that I have not found diffusivity to be a felicitous concept in regard to female genital anxieties. Interpretations to my patients about such fears have led to surprise and interest, but not to psychic change. Unlike Bernstein, I have inferred loss of function as a primary fear in many women. This loss sometimes appears to me to be loss of the pleasure-giving function of the genital, and sometimes as fear of loss of the reproductive function. For these reasons, I shall modify her categories. The purpose of the clinical material in this paper is to illustrate these concepts. My hope is that this formulation will enable the reader to listen to patients differently from the way they listened before.

Female genital anxiety consists of many manifest fears: first, fear of painful penetration (Horney, 1926; D. Bernstein 1990); second, fear of loss of pleasurable sensation (Jones, 1927); third, fear of loss of reproductive function of the genital apparatus (Mayer, 1985; Bergmann, 1985). I shall not address the third category here. Little girls can have fears of any or all these calamities. In my clinical experience adult women clearly have one or more such fears. They also fear loss of love, loss of the object, and experiencing guilt and shame. In the material that follows, separation issues (Olesker, 1990) and other fears can be seen, and clinicians might choose to focus on one of these other issues. The question I address is whether female genital fears are worth interpreting or whether seeing the issues as related to penis envy, as had been done in the past, is sufficient.

PAINFUL PENETRATION

How are fears of painful penetration manifested? Some women fear being alone in their homes and hearing noises in the night; some fear dark streets and parking lots. They have realistic concerns about such dangers. Besides their realistic concerns, some women have fantasies about rapists under the bed or in lonely or deserted spots. These women may also wish for forceful or involuntary penetration, but their fears are more than mere repudiations of desire.

An example of such a fantasy comes from a woman who had put up with an abusive husband for several years rather than face her fears of being alone. She had always been compliant in the analysis, reporting dreams, telling of her current life, and recalling the events and feelings of her childhood. This behavior paralleled her behavior in her current life and what she reported of herself in her past. She often remained silent when she had been hurt, slighted, or snubbed, or when she believed she had been mistreated by her analyst. When confronted with her compliant and self-effacing manner and given interpretations about the covert aggression expressed by her creating a situation in which the other person was the bad guy and she was the good girl, she was able to explore the fantasy of the object's potentially explosive aggression and to modify her behavior. She was gradually able to talk more about her feelings that the analyst was hurting her, then about interactions in which her husband physically abused her. Gradually, she recognized that she enjoyed seeing herself as the analyst's passive victim rather than the person who had initiated the exploration of her pain and suffering. She began to recognize that she had needed her husband's abuse for displacement of her own aggressive wishes. Accepting how violent her interior life actually was, allowed her to ask her abusive

Primary Femininity and Genital Anxiety

husband to leave. Shortly after his departure, he forcefully reentered their home, ostensibly to collect his possessions. He shattered a mirror in the hallway in his rage over the end of the marriage. Her first dream after this violent intrusion was:

> Someone is flying a plane. It's a war mission. It's a secret mission. People are on the ground waiting for him. The gas leaked; the pressure was down. I felt like I could have stopped it. I closed my eyes. The back of his head began to explode. Blood started coming out and went all over his face. Then it switched to the ground. People were looking for him. They found things on the ground. A flare. A parachute case. Spread-out. It was a field, but overgrown. Then they found him. He was alive. I didn't really want to see him. I was afraid. I didn't know if he was alive at first. I didn't know if I wanted to see it. There was blood on his face. It was O.K. I wasn't in the dream. They went into the water. I was swimming around. This joined with the part of the dream I was in. I can't remember any of it. I'm trying to remember.

The patient's affect was muted. She said the dream had to do with her fear that her husband would crash and burn without her. She said she felt "sympathetic, painful, and curious." Her associations were to thoughts of a penis with blood coming out of it, circumcisions, and other dreams she had recently about drowning, floating, and swimming. What led me to ask whether she was the pilot was a series of remarks: her denial that she was in the dream, her remark that she felt she could have stopped it, her assertions that she closed her eyes and did not want to see, and her confusion about what she remembered. She hated that idea, but it seemed to me that she confirmed it when she responded thoughtfully that flying was like swimming underwater.

The dream took place in a war. We both knew that her father had been in a war. The idea of harming men's penises and of not knowing where the blood came from led to thoughts of seeing her father naked. He liked to swim naked and would not wear a bathing suit even when he was teaching her to swim when she was a little girl. This led to thoughts of having intercourse while menstruating, thus allowing herself to bloody her lover's penis in a way that did not hurt him. The idea that her father would let *her* fall in the water was linked with the pilot's crash in the dream. The most hidden

Arlene Kramer Richards

idea, the unconscious fantasy, was that she had been the one to bleed. Eventually she came to state that her genital was the damaged and painful one.

The fear underlying her apparently aggressive and destructive attitude toward men, and the male genital in particular, was only recovered when we got to the understanding that she was both the author and the protagonist of her dream. Because she was the author, the war was her war. The aggression was her aggression. Her fear of her own aggression was displaced onto the wartime enemies in the dream. Her fear that her husband would "crash and burn" if she left him was also a displacement of what would happen to her if she left him. She would be damaged. She had refused to talk to her father about paying my fee, which she would have to ask him to do if she were to continue her treatment when she no longer had a husband to share her expenses. She was sure that her father would "explode at her" if she asked him to help her. We reconstructed a childhood fantasy that her father damaged her in an explosive version of intercourse. The fear that she would be damaged did not simply serve as a defense against the wish to be penetrated by her father. That fear was defended against by her displacement onto the husband. She was afraid to be alone with her aggression toward the husband and men in general. Even though her analyst was actually a woman, the ideas she had about me were similar to those she had about men. I was the father in the transference, always to be fended off, guarded against, and placated. I often felt hesitant about making interpretations, as if I would hurt her by saying what I was thinking. The fear that she would be damaged had been elicited by the conviction that her father's penis had damaged her genital. Thus, her fantasy followed the pattern outlined by Devereux (1957), but with the important difference that she did not experience herself as having a fantasy penis. Instead, she fantasied that she had a female genital that had been damaged by penetration and could be damaged again in the same way. The difference may be attributable to the fact that she, unlike Devereux's patient, had not actually been raped.

Many other female patients imagine imminent danger whenever they are alone at night. Their manifest fantasies of being killed, robbed, mugged, and raped derive from infantile fears of genital

Primary Femininity and Genital Anxiety

damage like those of this patient. Even women who enjoy intercourse with their chosen partners imagine pain and suffering as consequences of their masturbation fantasies when they are alone. This pain is partly punishment for the wish to have sexual gratification from the stranger who represents the father. The infantile origin of the wish accounts for another part of the fear. The father's penis seems to the little girl too large to fit into her genital without damaging it. Therefore she believes that penetration must be painful.

What the concept of fear of painful penetration added to my understanding of this specific female patient was the specifically sexual component of her fear of recognizing her own aggression. Examples of her fantasy that she had no aggressive wishes were frequently found in the transference. She always paid for her sessions promptly, even when she had to deprive herself to do so. She used silence to efface her aggressive wishes toward me. Because she imagined that I would feel guilty about hurting her if she cried, she stopped herself from crying in sessions. The analysis of the sexual component of her fear of aggression—her fear that she would damage the penis and its associated fantasy of damage to her own genital—provided another link to her fear of leaving her husband.

Aggression, penis envy, castration wishes, fears of separation and loss as well as other themes could have been interpreted here. But thinking of the dream in terms of fear of painful penetration allowed the patient to see the part of her struggle that had to do with her own body and her own mind. This issue went beyond the present interaction with her husband and her present struggle with me. It went back to an earlier time when her father exposed himself to her in a swimming pool by teaching her to swim while holding her face down in the water, supporting her on his forearms while he wore no bathing suit. I believe that the unique value of the concept was that it allowed her to think about what she had fantasied about that experience, how she had organized it in her memory, and how she had used it in shaping her view of the world as a dangerous place and her own body as too small and too vulnerable to contain or express her aggression. I believe that our exploration of this fear contributed to her later being able to choose a lover who was gentle.

Arlene Kramer Richards

LOSS OF PLEASURE

How do fears of loss of pleasure manifest themselves? Women fear they will not find a sexual partner. Some believe they must marry early to avoid such a fate. Others make themselves available to men they do not desire to ensure that they will not be without a partner. Other women fear they will become frigid because of rape, masturbation, or failure to find the man they can love. The fantasy that there is only one "Mr. Right" clearly reflects their belief that pleasure can only be had with the man who was unique: the father. Their idea that this man only exists in the future reflects their understanding that the father they are looking for only exists in the past. In the childhood fantasy the father was the giver of sexual pleasure. As adults they still believe that they will never have sexual pleasure without him.

A fantasy of losing genital pleasure was inferred late in the analysis of a woman who had an unusually ascetic way of life. By the end of the analysis we came to the conclusion that her asceticism was a defensive maneuver, a way to allow herself the sexual pleasure she feared losing as a deserved punishment for having experienced sexual pleasure with a grandmother. Several years of analytic work had allowed her to take her first vacation since finishing college and beginning work. In the week following her vacation, she began a session by saying she had a curious dream about something that happened "in real life":

> *L.* It was last night or this morning. There were lots of people there. It was in the subway. All my friends were going to dance somewhere. Dana and Ellen were trying to decide what to do with their purses. I was going to put mine in a locker in the subway. I decided not to wear long pants because I would get really hot. Everybody else was wearing long pants. They were progressing. Men showed up. Robert was there. They were collecting money for something. They were, I don't know what . . . I am annoyed at myself for being so complicated. For making it complicated.
> Yet it happened in real life, too. It always happens. I always take long to get ready to go. I am amazed when my roommate gets ready so fast when we decide to go out.
> It was in a restaurant in the dream. I saw Harry, but in reality Harry is in Israel . . . with Pam. I was staying in her apartment in the dream.

Primary Femininity and Genital Anxiety

Last night I actually went back home to Connecticut. Sally is back but she wasn't there, she must have stayed at Bill's last night. He got an apartment in the Village so that will change Sally's plans. I drove my clothes to Sam's street. There was nowhere to park, so I went back to the garage, then walked back.

A. It sounds like you complicate your life with many people and many plans and activities.

L. In Phoenix there was no way to get to the Grand Canyon. The bus didn't work out, so I had to figure out a way to get to Phoenix before the plane left. I had to take a 10:00 a.m. bus to Flagstaff. I went to the Bright Angel Lodge. They are all owned by the same person. Joe had said I could use his phone. I had run into Jim. I was trying to make the phone calls. The phone ate my change. I said to Jim I was going to use Joe's phone. So in two seconds Jim had made a reservation on the plane. I feel I do things the worst way possible when I try to do them my own way. I complicate things. I see things as being really big problems when they really are not.

I didn't really talk with Sally about dividing our furniture. I can live with a few extra pieces of furniture until she has time to deal with it. She said all I have to do is call Goodwill and they'll come and take it. I see problematic solutions. It made me think of my father and the phone calls he doesn't make. The only time he called me in the past couple of years was to get my brother's phone number. But he sends me a card and money twice a year—on my birthday and Christmas.

A. I had not called so much either. I had said very little.

L. I agree.

A. I wonder why you had to do so much. You were putting all your change into the phone in our session also and not allowing me to respond to you. I admired your skill in showing me what you are telling me about.

L. I always felt other people could go straight to the point. Only I have to be complicated.

A. You had that problem in the dream when you were getting ready to go to a dance. You stood in the way of your own chance to have pleasure.

L. I understood that as a reprimand. You are saying that I didn't deserve to have fun because I always screwed things up.

This was typical of her way of understanding everything as proof that she should not allow herself pleasure. She believed that everyone around her wanted to deprive her of pleasure also. What she did not understand before her analysis was that her renunciation of other pleasures was in the service of protecting herself from the loss of sexual pleasure.

She said the image of putting her purse in a locker in the subway before going to a dance represented what she wanted to do with her genital. She did not want to wear long pants because she did not want to be "hot." She understood her dream as a representation of her defenses against sexual excitement and pleasure. As she saw it, she wanted to be safe and she sacrificed pleasure for safety. I suggested that she imagined external danger to ensure that she got no pleasure. The dangers she was protecting herself from were internal. One danger was of condemning herself for wanting sexual pleasures from her father. Another was losing her father's love by demanding more of him than he was willing to give. Although she understood the demand as wanting more frequent telephone calls and visits, she also came to understand that this represented her childhood wishes to sleep with him and have sexual pleasure from him.

She expressed the same idea when she told of her difficulty in arranging a part of her vacation trip. What made it so problematic for her was that it was a pleasure trip. She could not allow herself pleasure even in the sublimated sphere of travel. She had to spend her time and her change trying to arrange to go by bus when it was so easy to go by plane. In her view, her male friend had no trouble arranging things because he was a man. Women, she believed, are more fussy, more focused on details, more in need of being sure of what they are doing. Men are more willing to take a chance. Besides, the plane would cost more than the bus. In her view men are willing to spend more money than women are because men will pay for their pleasures when women will not.

Another theme of the session which I interpreted to her was her insistence on crowding her account with many names and her life with many friends. In this she was using a compromise typical of latency children. She had a gang so that she would not get too close to any one person. That fended off sexual intimacy. She had orgastic but casual sex, always at the price of having little or no pleasure in the rest of her life. Her college years had been spent with a group of other young women. She felt deserted as most of them settled into long-term relationships. Her last roommate, Sally, was now leaving the house they had all shared in the early years of their careers.

Primary Femininity and Genital Anxiety

She had to dispose of the extra beds and all the old furniture they had left. It was as if they had left her behind with all of their discards. They had gone on to live with sexual partners. Only she stuck with the shell of their life together. They had many parties. Each of them, including the patient, had dates with men, some of whom they had sex with. Yet as long as they lived together, she maintained the fantasy that their primary loyalty was to the group (Kernberg, 1980) and their current sexuality was *unimportant.*

As she mourned them, she also mourned the loss of her family when her parents divorced. She had never felt comfortable letting people go or letting old relationships end. That was part of why she had so many people in her life. She had several early caretakers and had formed special relationships with each of them. Her multiple early love objects seemed to have resulted in multiple love objects in her later life. She had experienced as forbidden her wishes for sexual pleasure with each of those early objects. Now she clung to many images of people with whom she was forbidden to have sexual pleasure.

One important precursor of her fantasy of a dirty and dangerous female genital was the circumstance of her birth. Her parents had been divorced before she was born and she had been told repeatedly, as part of the family lore, that it was because her father did not find her mother attractive when she was pregnant. Her own fantasy was that her mother hated having a female genital and found it dirty and disgusting, and that she should also. Her compromise was to enjoy her genital but deprive herself of other pleasures.

Shortly after the session presented here she recalled that she had been very sad when her father's mother died. She had masturbated while in bed with her grandmother when she was a little girl. Her guilt over this transgression haunted her. The "Bright Angel" in her story of making her reservations was important. Her grandmother had called her "Angel" as a term of endearment and was now with the angels herself. She believed that angels were like people, only better in that they were nonsexual. Angels had no sexual urges. Thus, her apparent asceticism had to do with defending herself from losing genital pleasure as a punishment for her early incestuous pleasure.

Transference fantasies were difficult for her to acknowledge. She rejected my idea that she involved so many friends in her life and names in our sessions as defensive shields against losing me. She did not like my inference that she was holding on to me by telling me stories in order to prolong the treatment. Her understanding of the analytic work was that I wanted her to get "hot" while I would keep "cool," thus humiliating her. Worse yet, she believed that I had many patients, all of whom loved me, and that she would be seduced into loving only me and thus be hurt by what she believed would be my inevitable rejection of her. We came to see that she believed I would divorce her as her father had divorced her mother. At the point in the treatment when she experienced me as dangerously leading her into temptation, I became the grandmother in the transference.

After months of continuing to work on this problem, I came to this formulation: she was describing the interference with pleasure that resulted from her fantasies about sexual greediness. Masturbation and its accompanying incestuous fantasies are universal. They lead to severe inhibitions only when accompanied by special circumstances. For this patient the experiences with her grandmother were crucial. For other women memories of early experiments with siblings, being forced to have sex with adults, and seductions can be such circumstances. What the focus on the concept of fear of loss of pleasure added to her treatment was the notion that she was depriving herself of pleasure of loving and being loved in the present because she believed she should be punished for experiencing sexual pleasure in the past. By punishing herself, she was preventing punishment from the outside. Her punishment was especially effective because it was a talion. As she experienced pleasure, so she must renounce pleasure. As she had many objects, so she should have none. Her understanding that she was doing all this to herself to pay for infantile sexual "crimes" made the punishment seem ludicrous to her, and she could give it up.

The experience of pleasure can be forbidden to such a degree that the taboo threatens or destroys the capacity to function sexually. This is true both for the process of menstruation and the capacity to bear children. Some patients have to suppress their menstrual function by starving themselves down to below the percentage of body fat needed to maintain it. Some manage this effect by dieting, purging, fasting, exercising, or combinations of these methods. Such

Primary Femininity and Genital Anxiety

suppression can only be fully understood when the component of punishment is considered. This category of fear adds another dimension to female genital fears, one that I hope to address at another time.

DISCUSSION

It is time to come back to the questions about the relationship of theory and clinical observation. It is for the reader to decide whether the concepts of primary femininity and female genital anxiety illuminate the clinical material in the cases sketched here. Painful penetration seems to me to fit the fears of the patient with the war dream. Fear of loss of pleasure seems to fit the patient with the prolonged reliance on a cast of friends and an inhibition about moving on to a more adult status. These descriptive concepts seem a closer match to what the patients were thinking and feeling than would ideas of penis envy, even if penis envy is understood as a metaphor for the social valuation of masculinity (Grossman and Stewart, 1976).

The clinical utility of this version of the concept of genital fears can be evaluated in each case. For the first patient the idea that what she is afraid of is damage to her own genital from painful penetration allows her to see the problem as her own. Interpreting her fear as fear of loss of a fantasied penis might easily have led to more concern about loss of the husband, and been understood as an injunction to stay with him and tolerate his abusive behavior because as long as he was around, she had a penis in the house. For the second patient, the interpretation of fear of loss of pleasure and conviction that she deserved to have no pleasure seemed to have worked because it encompassed her history of depriving herself of pleasure and addressed her symptom of holding on to outgrown patterns of life. An interpretation focusing on penis envy would not have had the same immediacy. Therefore, I believe it would have been less likely to change her behavior. For both patients and, I think, for women in general, the idea that penis envy is the motivator of their behavior only serves to support the idea that the penis is the only genital worth having, a notion contradicted by every experience of pleasure and functioning girls and women have.

Arlene Kramer Richards

Because the clinical material shows how the theory of primary genital anxiety changes the interpretations given to the patient, I think it may actually be validated by the clinical material. The theory gains validity as it explains the observations better than previous theory. It seems to me to have been more effective than the theory that regarded penis envy as primary in allowing these patients to understand themselves and change their behavior.

Functions of the female genital have been understood as important motivators of behavior ever since Horney (1926) postulated the wish for a baby as the little girl's premordial desire. Motherhood has been central to the image of woman in recent thinking. While Person (1986) advocates understanding motherhood as a limited part of a woman's role rather than as her entire identity and Welldon (1991) warns against the idealization of motherhood as a full-time career, their views show that the idea of motherhood is a currently powerful metaphor for womanhood. Freud (1917) believed that the wish for a baby was a secondary compromise formation. Deutsch (1944) and Erikson (1968) believed this longing for a baby led the developing girl to value the inner portion of her genital. Mayer (1991) has shown that little girls today still prefer structures containing enclosed spaces, while little boys prefer towers. While Mayer cautions against concluding that this preference reflects awareness of an inner genital, Bassin (1982) reasons that early experiences of inner space contribute to a schema that structures later cognition so that the girl constructs a world partly on the model of her inner experience. Ironically, Freud, in his insistence on the importance of the clitoris, had the kernel of the idea that the little girl was aware of her external genital all along. The possibility of viewing the little girl as valuing the vulva and the surrounding area had taken another 50 years (Richards, 1992). Now a new literature of neuropsychology (Damasio, 1994) points to the inextricable part bodily sensation and the resultant body image play in all of mental functioning. While bodily sensations of a steady state can only form a background for continuous mental functioning, it seems plausible that body sensations, which wax and wane dramatically as do genital sensations, must reach foreground early, and the pleasure and pain associated with such genital functioning would have to play an important part in the formation of body image as well as in the formation of fears of genital damage.

Primary Femininity and Genital Anxiety

Mayer's suggestion that the girl values the vulva and fears loss of openness seems to correspond with the fears of loss of pleasure and loss of function. If the opening to the female genital is lost, the possibility of the pleasure of intercourse is lost also. Similarly, loss of the opening implies loss of the capacity to menstruate as well as the capacity to bear children.

Why had psychoanalysts so long believed that little girls look at boys' genitals and see something enviable while believing that they themselves have "nothing"? Is it true that little girls think they have "nothing"? No. Why would analysts think so? It is my hypothesis that the idea that girls have "nothing" is a defense against the male fear of the female genital.

Representations of the female genital have struck fear in both men and women since ancient times. The Medusa image has been horrifying people (Hamilton, 1940) since the Greeks moved from an agricultural matriarchal society to an urban manufacturing patriarchy (Gimbutas, 1989; duBois, 1988). According to duBois the Greek representations of woman evolved as the social structure changed. Early representations of woman as all-giving mother-field gave way successively to various metaphors of: furrow, ploughed into fertility by man; stone enclosing a secret space from which life comes and into which mortality sinks; oven in which male seed is baked into food sustaining life, and tablet on which man inscribes his will on his property. All of these images coexisted in ancient times. Of them Medusa is the image most frightening because the sight of her turns men into stone. Her image was, according to Gimbutas (1989), the image of the earth goddess, an image, in turn, preserved in stone.

In contrast to Lacan and the Lacanian feminists, duBois thinks such a mother is not a phallic mother, but a mother empowered by her own fertility, a power that precedes and stands apart from that of the phallus. Her view coincides with Bergmann's (1985) description of the importance of motherhood in the empowerment of modern woman. It also intersects with Lax's (1994) view of primary femininity as emanating from the female experience. My own emphasis on the power of the sensations emanating from the entire genital and perigenital area (1992) and Bass's (1994) on the sensations of the urinary sphincter also support this position. Gilmore (unpublished) adds an object-relations perspective to Burton's

Arlene Kramer Richards

(1994) work on the anatomical roots of conflation of anal and genital sensations in the girl. Gilmore sees this conflation as a regressive fantasy "compensating for feelings of castration as well as fears of helplessness, penetration, and injury arising from oedipal fantasies of the paternal phallus, sexual intercourse, and childbirth." These feelings of castration correspond to what I am calling fear of loss of pleasure and fear of loss of function. The fantasies of the paternal phallus, intercourse, and childbirth correspond to what I am calling penetration fears. Fears of damage to the body from penetration are frequent in little girls, and fears of bodily damage from babies are seen both in adult women and little girls (Bonaparte, 1935; Luquet-Parat, 1970; I. Bernstein, 1976; Blum, 1976; Parens et al., 1976; Friedman, 1985).

In discussing a previous version of this paper, J. Glenn (unpublished) cited two cases of congenital absence of the vagina. One was a woman analyzed by Greenacre (1958), the other a girl who had been treated in psychotherapy by a colleague of Glenn. Both patients wanted to be more womanly, asked for plastic surgery to create a vagina, got it, and were very pleased with the result. He described a woman in treatment with him who had fantasies of damaging men's penises and fears of being damaged by her analyst. He analyzed these fantasies as revenge for molestation by a gang of boys when she was still in late latency, rather than primary envy. He believes that this evidence bolsters the case for the secondary and special place of penis envy in women. Like Rees (1987), he believes that masculine identifications and the vicissitudes of development complicate the fantasies of girls and make it impossible to attribute penis envy or castration fantasies to simple "castration shock" at seeing the penis.

IMPLICATIONS FOR FUTURE RESEARCH

Why had genital anxiety in women been studied so little between 1930 and 1970? Hoffman (1996) suggests that Freud and his followers could not understand feminine sexuality because they could not conceive of feminine subjectivity. He believes that the consequence of this was that Freud defined any active wish on a woman's part as masculine. Could primary femininity be frightening to men because

Primary Femininity and Genital Anxiety

the active woman is powerful? Why should a powerful woman frighten men? Chodorow (1978) believes that she evokes the image of the powerful mother of infancy, reducing the other to his or her passive helplessness of that stage of life.

Castration anxiety seems self-evident. No one asks what men are afraid of when they are afraid of being castrated. Abelin (1994) attributes extreme submissiveness and lack of aggressivity in women to their fear of eliciting castration anxiety in men. Fears of pain, of loss of pleasure, and of loss of function seem to be prominent components of castration fear. Reserving the term "castration anxiety" to fear of loss of the penis and/or scrotum and using the term "female genital anxiety" for fear of damage to the vulva and inner genital structures may help to clarify the differences between the experiences of the little boy and the little girl on the way from the anal to the oedipal stage. Goldberger (unpublished) proposes replacing the term "phallic" stage with "infantile genital" stage to make it clear that girls have their own fears and developmental line. Alternatively, such a stage could be called the "narcissistic-genital" stage. This would imply that boys and girls understand their own genitals as normative, experience fear of losing what they have and envy what they perceive or imagine the other sex to have. Infant observation like that of Galenson and Roiphe (1976) and Olesker (1990) as well as theory-building about infantile development (Tyson and Tyson, 1990) could add to our understanding of the genesis of the fears of this stage.

The research that could make a difference in this regard is not another look at observations made when penis envy was the only reaction thought to be noteworthy. In order to investigate whether little girls show evidence of enjoying, valuing, and fearing the loss of their own genitals, researchers would have to be looking specifically for such reactions at the time of gathering their data. Observations made in day care centers and infant nurseries would be relevant. So would anecdotal evidence from parents and other caretakers.

Evidence from adult analyses would have to be gathered by analysts who were open to the idea that girls, like boys, value pleasure and fear unpleasure. Reich (1964) has described the enormous effect of female genital pleasure in bolstering self-esteem. The fear of unpleasure would have to be understood as fear of pain and fear of loss of positively pleasurable sensation. The experience of genital pleasure can be renounced to such a degree that the taboo threatens or destroys the capacity to function sexually. This symptom can be seen as a compromise formation in which the fear of loss of feeling or the conviction that feeling has already been lost plays a crucial role. Although the wish may be for sexual pleasure with a beloved caretaker, the fear is of unpleasure, either through pain or through aphanisis.

But it is still the case, unfortunately, that students and seasoned analysts read papers that assert as facts such ideas as: (1) female genitals are internal and invisible; (2) female genitals are incapable of focused sensation or direct erotic discharge; (3) the girl becomes sexually awakened by a man; (4) women do not masturbate; (5) women prefer hugging and fondling to intercourse. There are many such ideas accepted as truth by otherwise rational analysts. In the course of our scientific work, I believe we have the responsibility to challenge the received wisdom, especially when it contradicts sensory experience and common sense.

Is the fear of genital pain or loss of pleasure always object-related? I believe so, and I believe that it is important for an analyst to take account of the object in understanding fantasy as well as conflict. But that is not the whole story. The idea of primary femininity is part of a view that shows female sexuality to have a complex development with strands woven from body image, object images, fantasy development, and interactions with the caretakers (Breen, 1993). Having a good mother does not protect from all of life's vicissitudes. Having an inadequate one does not necessarily presage disaster. One of the factors other than the adequacy of the object is experience with one's own body.

The body as a source of pleasure is rivaled by the body as a source of knowledge. As Piaget, Dewey, Montessori and many others have amply demonstrated, learning takes place on a sensorimotor level long before the language system is fully developed. As Vygotsky and others have shown, language-mediated learning is increasingly important with age. As many educators have known, motoric learning is more stable, less conscious, and more permanent than linguistically mediated learning. Once you know how to ride a bicycle, you

Primary Femininity and Genital Anxiety

are likely to know it forever. But you can easily forget the theorems of geometry is you have never learned them by pacing out the earth to make fields.

All of this is to say that the sensory experience a little girl has of her genital may not be one she can put into words, but it is deep, going back to her earliest life. It is permanent as the result of flexing and relaxing the sphincters and surrounding musculature, and it is valued as it gives a great deal of pleasure. By comparison, seeing a boy's genitals is a relatively transitory, usually purely visual and not necessarily formative experience. To base a whole theory of female development on that one experience while discounting the ongoing deep musculature sensation and the surface experience of clitoral and labial stimulation is, to my mind, not reasonable. I believe that the experience of female genital sensation and its importance in the developing girl's sense of her own body is a kind of experience Heinz Hartmann referred to as the body ego. It is basic to the experience of being female. Paying attention to it in analyzing female patients can only enhance the analytic experience for them.

REFERENCES

ABELIN, G. (1994). The headless woman. In *The Spectrum of Psychoanalysis*, ed. A.D. Richards & A.K. Richards. Madison, CT: Int. Univ. Press, pp. 161–184.
BASS, A. (1994). Urinary sphincter. *Psychoanal. Q.*, 63:491–517.
BASSIN, D. (1982). Woman's images of inner space. *Int. Rev. Psychoanal.*, 9:191–205.
BERGMANN, M.V. (1985). The effect of role reversal on delayed marriage and maternity. *Psychoanal. Study Child*, 40:197–220.
BERNSTEIN, D. (1990). Female genital anxieties, conflicts and typical mastery modes. *Int. J. Psychoanal.*, 71:151–165.
BERNSTEIN, I. (1976). Masochistic reactions in a latency-age girl. *J. Amer. Psychoanal. Assn.*, 24(Suppl.):589–607.
BLUM, H.P. (1976). Masochism, the ego ideal, and the psychology of women. *J. Amer. Psychoanal. Assn.*, 24(Suppl.):157–192.
BONAPARTE, M. (1935). Passivity, masochism and femininity. *Int. J. Psychoanal.*, 16:325–333.
BREEN, D. (1993). *The Gender Conundrum.* New York: Routledge.
BRENNER, C. (1982). *The Mind in Conflict.* New York: Int. Univ. Press.
BURTON, A. (1994). The meaning of perineal activity to women: An inner sphinx. *J. Amer. Psychoanal. Assn.*, 44(Suppl.):241–259.
CHODOROW, N. (1978). *The Reproduction of Mothering.* Berkeley, CA: Univ. California Press.
DAMASIO, A. (1994). *Descartes' Error.* New York: Putnam.

DEUTSCH, H. (1930). The significance of masochism in the mental life of women. *Int. J. Psychoanal.*, 11:48–60.
——— (1944). *The Psychology of Women*, Vol. 1. New York: Grune & Stratton.
DEVEREUX, G. (1957). The awarding of a penis as compensation for a rape. *Int. J. Psychoanal.*, 38:398–401.
DOVE, R. (1989). *Grace Notes*. New York: Norton.
DUBOIS, P. (1988). *Sowing the Body*. Chicago, IL: Univ. Chicago Press.
ERIKSON, E.H. (1968). Womanhood and the inner space. In *Identity: Youth and Crisis*. New York: Norton, pp. 261–294.
FLIEGEL, Z.O. (1973). Feminine psychosexual development in Freudian theory. *Psychoanal. Q.*, 42:385–409.
FREUD, S. (1905). Three essays on the theory of sexuality. *S. E.*, 7.
——— (1908). On the sexual theories of children. *S. E.*, 9.
——— (1917). On transformation of instinct as exemplified in anal erotism. *S. E.*, 17.
——— (1924). The dissolution of the Oedipus complex. *S. E.*, 19.
——— (1933). Femininity. *S. E.*, 22.
FRIEDMAN, L. (1985). Beating fantasies in a latency-age girl. *Psychoanal. Q.*, 54:569–596.
GALENSON, E. & ROIPHE, H. (1976). Some suggested revisions concerning early female development. *J. Amer. Psychoanal. Assn.*, 24(Suppl.):29–58.
GIMBUTAS, M. (1989). *The Language of the Goddess*. New York: Harper & Row.
GREENACRE, P. (1958). Early physical determinants in the development of the sense of identity. In: *Emotional Growth*, Vol. 1. New York: Int. Univ. Press, 1971, pp. 113–127.
GROSSMAN, W. & STEWART, W. (1976). Penis envy. *J. Amer. Psychoanal. Assn.*, 24(Suppl.):193–213.
HAMILTON, E. (1940). *Mythology*. Boston: Little Brown.
HOFFMAN, L. (1996). Freud and feminine subjectivity. *J. Amer. Psychoanal. Assn.*, 44(Suppl.):23–44.
HORNEY, K. (1926). The flight from womanhood. *Int. J. Psychoanal.*, 12:360–374.
JACOBSON, E. (1936). On the development of the girl's wish for a child. *Psychoanal. Q.*, 37:523–538.
JONES, E. (1927). The early development of female sexuality. *Int. J. Psychoanal.*, 8:459–472.
KERNBERG, O.F. (1980). Love, the couple, and the group. *Psychoanal. Q.*, 49:78–108.
KLEIN, M. (1932). The effects of early anxiety situations on the genital anxiety of the girl. In *The Psychoanalysis of Children*. New York: Norton, pp. 194–239.
LANGER, M. (1992). *Motherhood and Sexuality*. New York: Guilford.
LAX, R. (1994). Aspects of primary and secondary genital feelings and anxieties in girls during the preoedipal and early oedipal phases. *Psychoanal. Q.*, 58:271–296.
LUQUET-PARAT, C. (1970). The change of object. In *Female Sexuality*, ed. J. Chasseguet-Smirgel. Ann Arbor, MI: Univ. Michigan Press, pp. 84–93.
MAYER, E. (1985). Everybody must be just like me. *Int. J. Psychoanal.*, 66:331–348.

——— (1991). Towers and enclosed spaces. *Psychoanal. Inq.*, 11:480–510.
OLESKER, W. (1990). Sex differences during the early separation-individuation phase. *J. Amer. Psychoanal. Assn.*, 38:325–346.
PANEL (1970). The development of the child's sense of his own identity. V. Clower, reporter. *J. Amer. Psychoanal. Assn.*, 18:165–176.
PARENS, H.; POLLOCK, L.; STERN, J. & KRAMER, S. (1976). On the girl's entry into the Oedipus complex. *J. Amer. Psychoanal. Assn.*, 24(Suppl.):79–108.
PERSON, E.S. (1986). Working mothers. In *The Psychology of Today's Woman*, ed. T. Bernay & D. Cantor. Hillsdale, NJ: Analytic Press, pp. 121–138.
QUINODOZ, J. (1989). Female homosexual patients in analysis. *Int. J. Psychoanal.*, 70:55–63.
RADO, S. (1933). Fear of castration in women. *Psychoanal. Q.*, 2:425–475.
REES, K. (1987). I want to be a daddy. *Psychoanal. Q.*, 56:497–522.
REICH, A. (1964). Masturbation and self-esteem. In: *Annie Reich: Psychoanalytic Contributions.* New York: Int. Univ. Press, 1973, pp. 312–333.
RICHARDS, A.K. (1992). The influence of sphincter control and genital sensation on body image and gender identity in women. *Psychoanal. Q.*, 61:331–349.
STOLLER, R.J. (1968). The sense of femaleness. *Psychoanal. Q.*, 37:42–55.
TYSON, P. & TYSON, R.L. (1990). *Psychoanalytic Theories of Development: An Integration.* New Haven, CT: Yale Univ. Press.
WELLDON, E. (1991). *Mother, Madonna, Whore.* New York: Guilford.

CASTRATION ANXIETY OR FEMININE GENITAL ANXIETY?

Denise Dorsey

> Adherence to terminology that no longer reflects current theories of female development is explored and challenged. In particular, the concepts of castration anxiety and phallic phase are examined and an argument is made for the general usage of the terms, feminine genital anxiety and infantile genital phase. Relevant literature is reviewed and a case is presented to illustrate the concepts. Speculations are offered as to why we persist in keeping woman a "dark continent."

From the beginning of my psychoanalytic training and persisting to this day I see the term castration used to refer to two different phenomena in women. According to the most recent *Psychoanalytic Terms and Concepts* (Moore and Fine, 1990), castration is defined as "real or fantasized loss of or injury to the genitals of either sex" (p. 36). The threat of damage (producing anxiety) or belief that her female genital has already been damaged (producing depressive affect) is associated to oedipal fantasies and is a motive for superego formation in the female similarly as in the male (Jacobson, 1937; Lax, 1992). At other times, castration refers to the notion that the female genital *resulted* from damage—loss of the male genital. Moore and Fine (1990) continue with the definition of castration: "The girl may develop the fantasy that she has already been castrated because she lacks a penis; penis envy characterizes the female castration

---

Training and Supervising Analyst, New Orleans Psychoanalytic Institute; Clinical Associate Professor, Department of Psychiatry, Louisiana State University Medical Center at New Orleans.

I wish to offer special thanks to Drs. Edward Knight, Jacquelyn Robinson, and Vann Spruiell for their encouragement and thoughtful comments, and to acknowledge the support of my husband, Charles Lee, without which this paper would never have been completed.

complex. Penis envy is not simply a wish to have a penis; it has significant defensive and reactive aspects. Restitutive fantasies may include what is essentially an illusory penis" (p. 36).

Consequently, castration anxiety takes on two meanings. One is the fear of damage to the female genital and the other is fear of loss of an illusory phallus. The fantasy of having an illusory penis is a compromise formation that serves a defensive function against an image of the female as a mutilated male. This image, like a symptom, both defends against and expresses the ambivalence about recognition of the sexual difference. Later this image may serve additional functions during the phase of development traditionally referred to as phallic, when the child is in transition from dyadic to triadic relationships.

According to current usage, one meaning of castration is actually a compromise formation that defends against the other meaning of castration. I have always found this double use of the term castration confusing, because in the psychoanalytic literature there are many examples where the author never specifies exactly what is meant. The reader is left to infer, correctly or incorrectly, from the associated ideas just how the author is using the term at that moment.

I propose we separate the two meanings of castration anxiety and substitute the term "feminine genital anxiety" when referring to the fear of loss or damage to the female genital. Feminine genital anxiety is associated with the female's fear of using her genital for pleasure and procreation originating in both the preoedipal and oedipal phase. The term "castration anxiety" consequently would be limited to a fear of loss of an illusory phallus. Further, the "infantile genital phase," a gender-neutral term, should be used in place of phallic phase in both sexes, certainly when discussing this stage in the female.

I shall trace the evolution of these concepts and make a plea for a more unified and concise usage of terms reflecting the current level of sophistication of our thinking. I shall offer clinical material to illustrate the usage of the concepts and relevance for psychoanalytic education and conclude with speculations about why we persist in keeping the woman a "dark continent."

Feminine Genital Anxiety

II

The evolution of a theory of female development can be traced simply by reviewing *Female Psychology: An Annotated Psychoanalytic Bibliography* (Schuker and Levinson, 1991). The contributions of clinical material, child observation studies, and long analyses have resulted in a theory of female development vastly different from that conceived by Freud. Most analysts who were his contemporaries viewed penis envy as bedrock in the unconscious fantasy lives of women, consequently viewing women as castrated males and therefore inferior. In Freud's scheme of psychosexual development, the little girl is unaware of her female genital and upon recognition of anatomical sexual differences believes she has sustained a major loss. She blames the mother and turns in disappointment to the father. Initially wanting to possess her father's penis, the girl then substitutes a wish for a child from him in place of the original wish for a penis (Freud, 1932).

There were a handful of Freud's contemporaries as early as the 1920s who believed penis envy was to a great degree reinforced by the actual social subordination of women (Horney, 1926; Thompson, 1942). Others suggested the phallocentric version of female psychology represented a defense in men against fear and envy of women (Jones, 1927; Horney, 1932; Mueller, 1932). Women as well as men used this defense against a deeper layer of anxiety related to the infantile awareness of the female genital. From Freud's time to this day, many have written about this awareness (Barnett, 1966; Clower, 1976; Fraiberg, 1972; Horney, 1926; Kestenberg, 1968; Kleeman, 1976).

In 1926 Horney distinguished between penis envy and feminine genital anxiety. She identified a primary penis envy that originated upon recognition of anatomical differences, whereas the wish to be a man expressed by adult women in analysis represented "a secondary formation embodying all that has miscarried in the development toward womanhood" (p. 333). By this she meant that a large part of the strength of primary penis envy occurred by "retrogression" from the Oedipus complex. The female's resulting fantasy of herself as a castrated male would follow as a secondary formation.

Horney pictured the origin of these fantasies as follows:

> When the woman takes refuge in the fictitious male role her feminine genital anxiety is to some extent translated into male terms—the fear of vaginal injury becomes a phantasy of castration. The girl gains by this conversion, for she exchanges the uncertainty of her expectation of punishment (an uncertainty conditioned by her anatomical formation) for a concrete idea. Moreover, the castration-phantasy too is under the shadow of the old sense of guilt—and the penis is desired as a proof of guiltlessness [p. 337].

III

Many analysts now agree with the ideas contained in Horney's early papers (1924, 1926). Later in her career she abandoned the centrality of the infantile experience in determining personality and instead emphasized the influence of postoedipal cultural experiences. Perhaps because she abandoned mainstream psychoanalytic thinking regarding the origin of psychopathology, or because the majority of analysts simply did not share her views regarding female development, these ideas and the concept of feminine genital anxiety were lost in the sea of literature.

"Penis envy as bedrock" prevailed for the next 50 years following Horney. The phallic developmental stage with depressive affect and penis envy went unchallenged by the majority and informed the interpretive meaning of the depressive affect in some child observation studies (Galenson and Roiphe, 1976). The majority of authors focused on only one meaning of castration by illustrating the many ways in which women defended against penis envy and the consequent aggressive feelings toward men. Tyson (1982) notes:

> A girl's reaction to the discovery of genital differences has been referred to throughout the psychoanalytic literature as "castration anxiety," "castration reaction,"or "castration complex." This term, introduced by Abraham in 1920, was borrowed from the psychology of males and is a highly unsatisfactory one [p. 73].

Following the women's liberation movement in America, a large number of analysts began reevaluating female psychology. There was

Feminine Genital Anxiety

a reappearance of the concept that penis envy represents a compromise formation. A host of articles gave clinical examples of the defensive function of penis envy—sometimes expressive of pregenital conflicts, and at other times a regressive compromise of oedipal-level fantasies (Grossman and Stewart, 1976; Karme, 1981; Torok, 1970). Overall, the complexity and richness of meaning were elaborated allowing for deeper analysis to occur than was common previously. At this juncture castration anxiety again takes on multiple meanings in the literature, albeit, ambiguous meanings.

Papers written during the last 20 years on the infantile genital phase (phallic phase) in girls argue against the simplistic view of penis envy. That an argumentative tone was necessary is unfortunate. That the tone persists implies that authors *continue* to feel they must validate the evolved theory of female development.

Although the contemporary theory of female development appears to be generally accepted, I believe the adherence to terminology that no longer fits female development demonstrates a resistance to fully integrating these concepts into clinical theory. Why else would the misleading misnomer, phallic phase, remain a label for a particular developmental period in girls even though the concept of primary femininity (Stoller, 1976; Parens et al., 1976) has been well established? This persistant clinging to words that no longer accurately represent the concepts allows the feelings of debate to live on in psychoanalytic education through omission.

Schafer's (1976) comments regarding Freud's masculine-active and feminine-passive equations are pertinent. He states, "To designate is also to create and to enforce. By devising and allocating words, which are names, people create entities and modes of experience and enforce specific subjective experiences. Names render events, situations, and relationships available or unavailable for psychological life that might otherwise remain cognitively indeterminate" (p. 352).

IV

Infantile genital organization (Freud, 1923) and feminine genital anxiety (Horney, 1926) are terms that reflect concepts that have been around a long time and continue to be preferred by some (Parens, 1990; Roiphe, 1968; Tyson, 1994). However, clear definitions have still not found general agreement. A selected review of the pertinent literature will demonstrate the complexity of the confusion. The first group reviewed contains ideas similar to my own. The second group contains compatible ideas, but in confusing or different terminology. The third group reveals continued use of a simplistic definition of castration.

In 1986 Chehrazi addressed nomenclature in an article in which she compares early and recent psychoanalytic views of female development. With a knack for clarity, Chehrazi notes each point of discrepancy between the original concepts of female development and the current view. She, too, notes the problem of retaining nomenclature that ignores our current level of knowledge and distinguishes genital anxiety (p. 149) from castration anxiety (p. 155) in exactly the way I do. She defines genital anxiety as an oedipal-level anxiety, as I propose.

Informed by two decades of direct observation of young children, Parens (1990) suggests revisions of psychosexual theory. The first proposal is to adopt the general term, "first (or infantile) genital phase" (p. 745) in place of phallic or phallic-oedipal phase. Parens believes reconstruction and direct observational findings do not support the formulations pertinent to the use of "phallic" in girls.

His second proposal addresses superego formation. He argues against the narrow linkage of superego formation to the castration complex. Instead, he conceptualizes the motive for superego formation to be ambivalence. Parens' data challenge "Freud's 1925 hypothesis that the girl's entry into the Oedipus complex is a secondary formation which arises out of her castration complex" as well as the hypothesis that "the girl's wish to have a baby is secondary in origin, inherently reactive to her castration complex, namely her pained reaction to not having a penis" (p. 746). Parens' focus on ambivalence as a motive for superego formation is complementary to the formulation of feminine genital anxiety as a motive, for the little girl's fantasies of using her genital for pleasure and procreation fuels the ambivalence in her relationships.

Richards (1992) writes about the significance of genital sensation and sphincter control for gender identity formation in women.

Feminine Genital Anxiety

She writes, "... many psychoanalysts believe they know that when women are afraid of castration, they are afraid of losing a fantasied penis or they are afraid of their masochistic wishes in reaction to their wish to castrate a man." She presents "evidence for the idea that women believe they have an internal (and an external) sexual organ which is a source of pleasure and which they fear losing." She asks, "To what extent is the female's fear of castration a fear of loss of genital sensation?" (p. 332). This notion is similar to Jones's (1927) proposal of aphanisis. Richards presents clinical material demonstrating her thesis and the complex interplay of the development of sphincter control, gender, and sexuality in the girl. The fear of damage or loss of genital function Richards describes in her clinical presentation is an example of feminine genital anxiety.

Wilkinson (1993, p. 313) expands our understanding of "How the girl's genital awareness becomes integrated and synthesized into her sense of self at the oedipal threshold." Naming this phase the "genital dress rehearsal," she proposes, "The transition turns on the girl's paradoxical creation of her feminine sexuality through a playful phallic identification that is distinct from penis envy. The phallic identification serves a complementary rather than a compensatory function, which the girl employs temporarily to help establish her femininity." Wilkinson skillfully describes the nuances of genital individuation in a manner reminiscent of the differentiation model proposed by Fast (1978, 1979). Fast conceptualizes a matrix of bisexual completeness. While letting go of the attributes of the opposite sex during individuation, the child anticipates being able to experience these attributes through the relationship.

Whether we presume an undifferentiated matrix (Parens et al., 1976) from which gender evolves through identification or a matrix of bisexual completeness necessitating a process of loss experiences, the phase of transition from individuation to triadic relationships is referred to in girls and in boys as phallic. This is a misnomer for girls. Like Tyson (1994), I prefer to use the label, infantile genital phase. Wilkinson offers a reformulation of penis envy as a failure in the little girl's ability to use the phallus as a "displaced container for the penetrating, seductive, and overpowering aspects of the girl's sexuality" (p. 325). Wilkinson helps us appreciate the difference between a phallic identification that is integrated into feminine identity and an identification that serves a defensive function. She then applies her ideas to interpret, from a different perspective, the clinical material published by others. The female genital dress rehearsal is a lens through which to view the complex synthesis and integration necessary to navigate the infantile genital stage.

Tyson discusses the usefulness of contemporary theories of female psychology, and the inaccuracy of concepts such as phallic phase, castration complex, and bisexuality. Through clinical material, she demonstrates the complex interplay of sexuality, aggression, and object relations involved in the understanding of both preoedipal and oedipal object-related conflicts of early childhood. Tyson advocates the adoption of a gender-neutral term, infantile genital organization, in place of the term phallic phase. Penis envy, she states, represents "a complicated compromise formation involving aspects of gender identity, pathological object relations, defenses, narcissism, and self-esteem" (p. 456). Tyson also refers to the work of Fast (1979) and to Berstein's (1990) concept of feminine genital anxiety. Tyson's approach to understanding her patient's sense of inadequacy is consistent with the thesis of this paper.

V

Mayer (1985) calls attention to the confusion in the use of the term castration and distinguishes the "phallic castration complex" from "true female castration anxiety." She expresses the opinion that "Historically, the phallic castration complex has been elaborated to the exclusion of the identification of a true female castration anxiety" (p. 332). Unfortunately, her use of "castration" in naming both concepts is confusing. However, the concepts are consistent with the meanings I propose for castration anxiety and feminine genital anxiety. Mayer cites clinical material of several women who view men as emotionally closed, and missing something essential. She links this view to the little girl's fantasy that boys originally had a female genital and were "closed up" as punishment. This reconstruction is the mirror image of "phallic woman" imagery. The conceptualization of fantasies of bisexual completeness (Fast, 1979) or a desire to be both sexes (Kubie, 1974) arises from the child's struggle to further individuate genitally during the time of transition from dyadic

Feminine Genital Anxiety

to triadic relationships. It is at this point that children of both sexes must reconcile the limits of their sex. Fantasies of bisexual completeness defend against this recognition. Increased cognitive development of the three-year-old also allows for greater awareness of the subtle differences in gender roles which are incorporated into images of maleness and femaleness. These fantasies will represent a compromise of preoedipal and oedipal conflict.

Ten years later in the footnote of a paper on female gender identity, Mayer (1995) acknowledges that using the term genital anxiety may be preferable. "Since, however mistakenly, 'castration' remains irretrievably associated with the loss of a penis" making it "difficult for our field to integrate the idea of a true female castration anxiety defined as anxiety that is parallel in function to male castration anxiety but involves fantasies of danger to a specifically female genital" (p. 30).

Berstein (1990) proposes three terms: access, penetration, and diffusivity, representing "castration-like" anxieties which she subsumes under the umbrella of "female genital anxiety." These three "clusters of female genital anxiety" must be mastered by every little girl to some degree. Berstein defines "access" as the little girl's concern over control, or lack thereof, of her vaginal opening which increases vulnerability and shame. "Diffusivity" refers to the spread of sensation that can threaten to overwhelm ego boundaries and result in a motive for defense—a fear of the intensity of one's own desire. Her discussion of "penetration" is restricted to a girl's fear of damage to her little body at a preoedipal level.

Berstein demonstrates through clinical material some of the anatomic-biologic underpinnings of female genital anxiety. She views genital anxieties as coloring the "separation-individuation process which is played out in two directions—in relation to the girl's own body and in relation to her mother" (p. 154). I prefer to use the term feminine genital anxiety to refer to oedipal-level anxiety, and agree with Berstein that fears from every developmental level contribute like a watershed to influence the experience of the oedipal phase.

Lax (1994) examines "two types of genital anxieties that a little girl may develop as a consequence of her erotic feelings" (p. 271). She defines the little girl's primary genital anxiety as the fear of "losing access to or a part of the genitals she has, enjoys, and wants to continue enjoying freely." This anxiety is derived from "current overt or veiled threats directed toward girls' sexuality or measures taken to prevent their masturbation" (p. 283).

Secondary genital anxiety as defined by Lax develops toward the end of the negative oedipal subphase and is related to "a belief, or unconscious fantasy, held by the girl, that she was deprived of a penis. Consequently, she may fear the loss of her mother's love and possibly even the loss of her love object" (p. 288). Secondary genital anxiety, as defined by Lax, occurs as a feeling of inadequacy regarding the little girl's inability to gratify her mother genitally, this being the source of the girl's desire to own a penis.

The manner in which Lax uses the terms primary and secondary genital anxiety is different from that of the other authors. The actual prohibitions of caretakers during childhood would certainly influence the nature of the feminine genital anxiety. Lax's definition of secondary genital anxiety would seem to correspond with what most authors describe as the girl's childhood wish to own a penis. If this childhood wish evolves into an adult defensive fantasy of owning an illusory phallus, then castration anxiety would be experienced when this defense is threatened as defined in this paper.

VI

Another aspect of the problem under discussion is demonstrated by Brenner (1991) and Rangell (1991). Brenner elucidates his perspective regarding the role of depressive affect in triggering conflict. Although female dynamics are not the central focus of his article, a case presentation of a thirty-three-year-old unmarried woman is offered to elucidate his thinking. She sought treatment for unhappiness and lack of career direction. These symptoms began after her brother, five years junior, stepped into the family business in which she had been involved. Although she had been her father's right hand, "it soon became clear to the patient that it was not she, but her brother who was destined to be her father's close associate and eventual successor" (p. 39). Anger at gender roles is apparent within the description of the family context, but not acknowledged as contributing to the intrapsychic conflict. Brenner states, "this patient's

Feminine Genital Anxiety

conflicts centered about the fact that she was a girl, not a boy.... Her penis envy and her misery at having been born a girl, which to her as a child meant having been castrated, were intense." He acknowledges that "this outline of the patient's psychodynamics and pathogenesis is both abbreviated and oversimplified" (p. 41).

Although Brenner focuses on the psychic function of compromise formations, nowhere in the discussion does Brenner seem to view the construction of penis envy itself to be a compromise formation. Rather, he seems to see penis envy as the main motive for defense. He continues, "The patient's envy of men and her unconscious anger at every man for having the penis she so envies and wished for did not prevent her from enjoying sexual relations with men. It did, however, make it impossible for her to be happy with a man or to marry one. Marriage had the same significance for her as did her menarche. It meant being irrevocably a woman. To remain unmarried meant, unconsciously, to be a man, a gay blade with a stable of sexual partners to pick from and to exploit for her pleasure. To marry meant to be castrated, as numerous dreams and associations made clear" (p. 40).

Brenner formulates that this woman's central problem is her anger at having been born a girl and therefore deprived of a penis. However, he does not ask why she defines her femininity in this way, nor what intrapsychic function this image serves. He appears to ignore her anxiety regarding the genital she does own.

Many analysts today, including myself, would organize this material differently. In this situation, there would be more questions than answers. However, the type of questions the analyst formulates is influenced by our clinical theory. Different views regarding the role of penis envy in the development of psychopathology will result in different directions of analytic inquiry. Brenner reconstructs that at the birth of her brother, when his patient was five years old, she felt jealous rage, castrative and murderous impulses, and guilt. He formulates this reaction to her brother's birth as based on her feeling castrated—a second-class citizen.

Brenner does not suggest that there is more to this story. The complex dynamic situation of a five-year-old girl would have me wondering toward whom she felt jealous rage and castrative and murderous impulses. Was this felt toward her mother, father, and the baby?

Denise Dorsey

It seems overly economical to focus all rage, wounded narcissism, and ambivalence in relationships on having been born a girl. How did this complex constellation result in this little girl forsaking her primary feminine identifications and adopting a mutilated male image of herself, as Brenner reconstructs? Brenner interprets his patient's awkwardness with her body at menarche and her inability to marry as meaning she does not want to be a woman. This equation is not self-evident. It is not clear from the material that this woman actually wishes to be a man. It would seem just as plausible that she would like to be valued as an equally competent, first-class citizen.

Brenner explains his patient's psychopathology as stemming from her castration complex. The reader is left with the impression, correctly or incorrectly, that Brenner does not recognize the other meaning of castration, that a woman's focus on what she does not have—penis envy—often defends against her fear of punishment for using and enjoying the genital she does have. Her feminine genital anxiety is rooted in unresolved oedipal fantasies and contributes to the formation of character and neurosis. The depressive affect Brenner describes in his patient may ultimately be linked to the loss of her oedipal objects. While a change in terminology will not necessarily change clinical practice, it may raise consciousness and allow for clearer communication and allow for open debate.

Rangell (1991) writes a thesis on castration, a concept which he believes has lost centrality in psychoanalysis in the 90's. He defines castration anxiety as a fear of genital injury presumably in both sexes. Although he does have clinical material from both sexes illustrating castration anxiety, the examples of his male cases allows for a clearer picture of how Rangell defines castration. He proposes that the castration complex has a developmental history of its own and states, "There are early states, of an awareness of the genital, trial actions and thoughts of its use and application, renouncement of these, a stage of the sense of penis inferiority, all preceding the oedipal stage of the strong sense of its function and the vivid fear of its loss" (p. 11).

It appears that Rangell is describing a developmental schema which he applies equally to men and woman. As such, his schema implies that he uses only one definition of castration in women—the definition based on vaginal unawareness. Although he gives both

Feminine Genital Anxiety

male and female clinical examples, the bulk of his theoretical discussion is directed at an exploration of male psychology even though he does not explicitly limit the discussion to males. The reader is left with a confused conceptualization of castration anxiety in the female.

VII

In order to demonstrate the use of these terms as I propose, I shall present clinical material from the analysis of a twenty-four-year-old, single woman. Sue was brazen, feisty, sexually active, and vaginally anesthetic (orgasmic with cunnilingus only). She sought analysis because of a depressed mood and unsatisfying relationships with men. She was aware of wanting something from a man which she could not define, which resulted in repetitions of fighting, disappointment, and breakups. Sue was overtly envious of men who she felt had much easier lives. She described herself as a naughty child in constant strife with a mother who had always hated her, and felt guilty because of her "close" relationship to her father amidst much marital conflict.

Prior to the death of an idolized older brother (mother's favorite) when Sue was fourteen, she had romantic dreams of defloration and intended to remain a virgin until marriage. However, she dealt with the ambivalent loss of her brother by "stepping into his shoes and hotrodding around town." This included abandonment of her romantic fantasies and adoption of a "fearless, casual" attitude toward sex. Throughout Sue's history we shall see that she turns to sexuality to defend against loss. She began to think of her clitoris as a "little penis" and was orgasmic with cunnilingus only. Her vagina was either "dead" or a "stinky, steamy thing a lady tried to make dainty." This view of her genital alternated with an image of having "nothing"—a scar where her penis was, as if it had existed. During her analysis it became clear that her defective male view of herself and overtly stated wish to be male were never accompanied by a desire to give up her femaleness. What she wanted was to have "everything" so as to avoid feeling "vulnerable and needy" in relationships. Thus, she used fantasies of bisexual completeness to defend against both preoedipal and oedipal conflict. Lovers were used as part objects to fulfill this fantasy, resulting in power struggles and the repeated disappointments for which she initially sought treatment.

Denise Dorsey

Early in the analysis Sue's sexuality was coarse and aggressive. During analytic sessions she developed a conversion symptom of her leg alternately feeling "dead" or "tingly." Analysis of her dreams and associations indicated that this symptom defended against a blossoming erotic homosexual transference. Amidst much castration anxiety, Sue became aware of a desire to place her "little penis" in the analyst's mouth as a sign of "true love." However, she was filled with disgust by the thought of "returning the favor," by performing cunnilingus on the analyst. Integration of this insight resulted in the realization that *she* had denigrated her genital, not men as she had always thought. She became less anxious and therefore less controlling in relationships. Her anger at men softened and her pleasure from cunnilingus began to feel "immature."

At this point the analyst became pregnant, precipitating a crisis in Sue's analysis. She felt her world had ended. Sue messed up the analyst's office, wailed in despair, and railed at the injustice the analyst had dealt her. Through her fits of temper and misery, she hoped the intensity of her distress would cause the analyst to miscarry. The depth of Sue's despair, narcissistic injury, and rage were interpreted as meaning that her relationship to her mother had not always been purely hateful as she remembered, for one cannot experience such loss without having first possessed something precious. Instead, Sue eventually recognized a deeply gratifying, tender relationship with the analyst, likely reminiscent of the one with her mother before her sister was born, when the patient was two.

Her mother's betrayal of her by having another baby and not "loving her enough" when she was likely struggling with the recognition of anatomical differences provided the setting for this woman to use her penis wish defensively and metaphorically. Her view of her clitoris as a little penis was a concrete expression of dissatisfaction in maternal nurturing and screened feelings of shame and humiliation over the small size of her breasts. It was "little" as a measure of the little bit of love she felt she received, but it was imagined to be there as a salve to her wounded narcissism.

Sue's rage at two years old was blamed on her mother who had interrupted their blissful union with an intruder, and also on the fact that she herself could not have a baby: her breasts were too small! This was felt to be the core of her painful feelings of inadequacy as

Feminine Genital Anxiety

a woman and of her conscious shame over the small size of her breasts. The painful loss of what they once had, accompanied by murderous rage toward her mother and the baby, was repressed. The mother was denigrated as was Sue's wish to have a baby. This repression interfered with the individuation process and was bolstered by a defensive identification with her father in childhood and then again with her brother in adolescence. However, her maintenance of a solid observing ego and reality testing throughout the entire analysis indicated adequate individuation in all other respects.

Sue's overvaluation of and focus on what she did not have (a penis) allowed her to express her preoedipal injury and protect what she did have. She would often say "I have nothing to give because I do not have 'it' [a penis]." Thus she denied what she did have and what she wanted to do with it on an oedipal level. This defensive devaluing to keep safe what is most treasured inside is seen in Sue's comment, "I don't want to let anyone know what I do have for fear they'll take that too." Thus there was a defensive turn of attention to what she did not have to defend against anxiety aroused by thoughts regarding the genital she did have—feminine genital anxiety. This anxiety was manifested as a fear of genital damage in retaliation for oedipal wishes and preoedipal rage directed toward the mother's insides.

Consistent interpretation of her defenses against vaginal sensation and accompanying fantasies revealed her "secrets." In fact, Sue felt she had been robbed of the "joys of womanhood" because of her badness. She believed she had been given small breasts and a dysfunctional, "dead" womb incapable of pleasurable sensation or of carrying a child as punishment for her tender, erotic, incestuous masturbation fantasies. In fact, she punished herself with painful feelings of inadequacy and shame which interfered with her enjoyment of the beautiful body she actually did have.

As vaginal sensations were awakened, Sue became fearful of intercourse. She felt like a virgin, unsure of her ability to contain her desire. She initially feared she might literally explode. Practice and gynecologic examinations reassured her of her intactness. As her anxiety diminished, she experienced a new, fuller type of orgasm than was previously possible. Whereas her orgasm in cunnilingus was accompanied by a fantasy of placing her little penis in her lover's mouth, the accompanying orgasmic fantasy with intercourse was of being tickled deep in her womb by his "love stick." Evidently this change in location of focus and fantasy resulted in a change in the quality of her subjective experience of orgasm. The nature of her object relationships had shifted as she no longer needed to control her lover to contain her anxiety. Her sexual experience became a shared, mutual, and reciprocal trusting closeness.

Feeling sexually competent, Sue then struggled over whether or not to gratify her desire as fantasies of being powerfully irresistible entered the transference. A desire to hurt the analyst-mother by taking away her man gave way to sadness over the limits of her power to make all dreams possible. The ability to mourn all she could not have allowed Sue to then enjoy fully all that she did have. Sue's adolescent male view of herself with accompanying castration anxiety defended against even more frightening anxieties related to the use and enjoyment of her female genital—feminine genital anxieties. Sue's "inner genital" experience, to use Kestenberg's term, was defended against by externalization to the "outer genital," her clitoris. Penis envy not only helped to maintain the secrecy of her feminine genital sensations and fantasies, but also acted as an organizer of all pregenital deprivations.

VIII

It is noteworthy that 70 years after Horney, analysts are still feeling they must demonstrate the validity of the second definition of castration. Why is this? The confusion evolved from Freud's false assumption that the female genital is unknown to both sexes until puberty. If one begins with this schema of female sexual development, it invariably leads to the persistant belief that castration in women is synonymous with the loss of a penis. If, on the other hand, one begins with the established belief that an infant is aware of her genital, castration in females automatically takes on a meaning vastly different from that conceived by Freud.

Rangell (1991) states that castration is the most central conflict addressed in psychoanalysis. As such, we each have as our task the understanding of our own and our analysands' unique oedipal situation colored by the preoedipal experience.

Feminine Genital Anxiety

The adherence to confusing terminology stems from the conflict engendered in each of us by the infantile awareness of the vagina. The inner genital, vagina and womb, stimulates powerful fantasies that reflect and give rise to conflict from every developmental level. The vagina as interior space is the womb we come from—a symbol of union, security, and for some the illusion of a conflict-free existence. As a part of the individuation process, the child's taking possession of his or her own genital—penis or vagina—requires further demarcation of boundaries, control, and acceptance of limits. During the infantile genital phase, many threads of unresolved preoedipal conflict are woven into the fabric of the ascending genital experience. Because the child is in transition between dyadic and triadic object relations, his or her own genital or that of the opposite sex is often used as a container for defense.

It is at this crossroads that the recognition of sexual difference takes on even greater sophistication and genital narcissism is at stake. Feeling inferior and inadequate is unavoidable. Increased cognitive ability enables children of both sexes to be keenly aware of the subtle nuances of gender roles within their environment. These observations, even if inexact, will come to color the oedipal drama. Demeaned mothers can add to the daughter's feelings of inferiority and burden the process of feminine identification. Esteemed mothers offer strength in identification, but can enhance the feelings of smallness and undesirability in comparison. Children struggle with integrating gender roles, consolidating identity, and modulating drives. Feelings of inferiority can arise to the parent of the same or opposite sex. The phallus or womb can be used to explain and simplify the incomprehensible.

Naming acknowledges existence and diminishes irrational power by demystifying. Without this explicit acknowledgment, an experience is not fully available to be integrated cognitively although it may be known. Recognition of anatomical differences, and unifying definitions in psychoanalytic theory allow for greater clarity. Just as Lerner (1976) suggests that accurate naming of a little girl's genitals would facilitate cognitive development and reality testing, I believe more accurate identification of anxiety and conflicts is necessary to adequately understand our patients.

The desire to keep female psychology a dark continent is to avoid having to confront one's own conflicts fully, for one cannot clearly know another who is different without knowing oneself. The term feminine genital anxiety refers to anxiety during the infantile genital phase. This anxiety, associated with the female's fear of using her genital for pleasure and procreation, has both preoedipal and oedipal determinants. As part of the Oedipus complex, it plays a major role in the formation of character and neuroses.

REFERENCES

ABRAHAM, K. (1920). Manifestations of the female castration complex. In *Selected Papers of Karl Abraham*. New York: Basic Books, 1953, pp. 338–369.
BARNETT, M.C. (1966). Vaginal awareness in the infancy and childhood of girls. *J. Amer. Psychoanal. Assn.*, 14:129–141.
BERSTEIN, D. (1990). Female genital anxieties, conflicts and typical mastery modes. *Int. J. Psychoanal.*, 71:151–165.
BRENNER, C. (1991). A psychoanalytic perspective on depression. *J. Amer. Psychoanal. Assn.*, 39:25–43.
CHEHRAZI, S. (1986). Female psychology: a review. *J. Amer. Psychoanal. Assn.*, 34:141–162.
CLOWER, V. (1976). Theoretical implications in current views of masturbation in latency girls. *J. Amer. Psychoanal. Assn.*, 24(Suppl):109–125.
FAST, I. (1978). Developments in gender identity: the original matrix. *Int. Rev. Psychoanal.*, 5:265–574.
——— (1979). Developments in gender identity: gender differentiation in girls. *Int. Rev. Psychoanal.*, 6:441–453.
FRAIBERG, S. (1972). Some characteristics of genital arousal and discharge in latency girls. *Psychoanal. Study Child.*, 27:439–475.
FREUD, S. (1923). The infantile genital organization. *S. E.*, 19.
——— (1932). Female sexuality. *S. E.*, 21.
GALENSON, E. & ROIPHE, H. (1976). Some suggested revisions concerning early female development. *J. Amer. Psychoanal. Assn.*, 24(Suppl.):29–57.
GROSSMAN, W.I. & STEWART, W. (1976). Penis envy: from childhood wish to the developmental metaphor. *J. Amer. Psychoanal. Assn.*, 24(Suppl.):193–212.
HORNEY, K. (1924). On the genesis of the castration complex in women. *Int. J. Psychoanal.*, 5:50–65.
——— (1926). The flight from womanhood: the masculinity-complex in women. *Int. J. Psychoanal.*, 7:324–339.
——— (1932). The dread of woman. *Int. J. Psychoanal.*, 13:348–361.
JACOBSON, E. (1936). On the development of the girl's wish for a child. *Psychoanal. Q.*, 37:523–538.
——— (1937). Ways of female superego formation and the female castration conflict. *Psychoanal. Q.*, 45:525–535.
JONES, E. (1927). The early development of female sexuality. *Int. J. Psychoanal.*, 8:459–472.

Feminine Genital Anxiety

Karme, L. (1981). A clinical report of penis envy: its multiple meanings and defensive function. *J. Amer. Psychoanal. Assn.*, 29:427–447.

Kestenberg, J.S. (1968). Outside and inside, male and female. *J. Amer. Psychoanal. Assn.*, 16:457–520.

Kleeman, J. (1976). Freud's views on early female sexuality in the light of direct child observation. *J. Amer. Psychoanal. Assn.*, 24(Suppl.):3–27.

Kubie, L.S. (1974). The drive to become both sexes. *Psychoanal. Q.*, 43:349–426.

Lax, R. (1992). A variation on Freud's theme in "A child is being beaten"—mother's role: some implications for superego development in women. *J. Amer. Psychoanal. Assn.*, 40:455–473.

——— (1994). Aspects of primary and secondary genital feelings and anxieties in girls during the preoedipal and early oedipal phases. *Psychoanal. Q.*, 68:271–296.

Lerner, H. (1976). Parental mislabeling of female genitals as a determinant of penis envy and learning inhibitions in women. *J. Amer. Psychoanal. Assn.*, 24(Suppl.):269–283.

Mayer, E.L. (1985). Everybody must be just like me: observations on female castration anxiety. *Int. J. Psychoanal.*, 66:331–347.

——— (1995). Female gender identity. *J. Amer. Psychoanal. Assn.*, 43:17–38.

Moore, B.E. & Fine, B.D. (1990). *Psychoanalytic Terms and Concepts.* New Haven, CT: Yale Univ. Press.

Mueller, J. (1932). A contribution to the problem of libidinal development of the genital phase in girls. *Int. J. Psychoanal.*, 13:361–368.

Parens, H. (1990). On the girl's psychosexual development: reconsiderations suggested from direct observation. *J. Amer. Psychoanal. Assn.*, 38:743–772.

——— Pollock, L., Stern, J. & Kramer, S. (1976). On the girl's entry into the Oedipus complex. *J. Amer. Psychoanal. Assn.*, 24(Suppl.):79–107.

Rangell, L. (1991). Castration. *J. Amer. Psychoanal. Assn.*, 39:3–23.

Richards, A.K. (1992). The influence of sphincter control and genital sensation on body image and gender identity in women. *Psychoanal. Q.*, 61:331–351.

Roiphe, H. (1968). On an early genital phase. *Psychoanal. Study Child*, 23:348–365.

Schafer, R. (1976). Problems in Freud's psychology of women. *J. Amer. Psychoanal. Assn.*, 24:331–360.

Schuker, E. & Levinson, N. (1991). *Female Psychology: An Annotated Psychoanalytic Bibliography.* Hillsdale, NJ: Analytic Press.

Stoller, R.J. (1976). Primary femininity. *J. Amer. Psychoanal. Assn.*, 24(Suppl.):59–78.

Thompson, C. (1942). Cultural pressures in the psychology of women. *Psychiat.*, 4:331–339.

Torok, M. (1970). The significance of penis envy in women. In *Female Sexuality: New Psychoanalytic Views.* Ann Arbor, MI: Univ. Michigan Press, pp. 135–170.

Tyson, P. (1982). A developmental line of gender identity, gender role, and choice of love object. *J. Amer. Psychoanal. Assn.*, 30:61–86.

——— (1994). Bedrock and beyond: an examination of the clinical utility of contemporary theories of female psychology. *J. Amer. Psychoanal. Assn.*, 42:447–467.

WILKINSON, S.M. (1993). The female genital dress-rehearsal: a prospective process at the oedipal threshold. *Int. J. Psychoanal.*, 74:313–330.

Nevermore: The Hymen and the Loss of Virginity

Deanna Holtzman
Nancy Kulish

> A major milestone in a woman's life is the loss of virginity, "defloration," with the breaking of the hymen. Psychoanalysis has paid little attention to the meaning of defloration to either women or men, and virtually none to the hymen as a part of the female genitalia. The reasons for this disregard or avoidance are explored. Utilizing the few psychoanalytic writings, mythology, literature, and anthropological studies in addition to numerous clinical examples, the authors find that the unconscious meanings of the loss of virginity and the hymen emerge clearly. The common theme is that of negation, never, never again, never seen, known or named. Theoretical considerations regarding female sexuality are discussed. Technical implications for analyst-patient are presented.

> Maria's treasure chest was not too safe
> a place for that—indeed it could not be,
> For since the time the padlock was first broken,
> Her treasure chest has always been wide open.

This bawdy song of a medieval minstrel (Penman, 1991, p. 332) alludes to a major milestone in a woman's life—the loss of virginity, "defloration," with the breaking of the hymen. Yet psychoanalysis has paid little attention to the meaning of defloration to either women or men, and virtually none to the hymen as a part of the female genitalia. We propose to explore the reasons for this disregard or avoidance. We shall review briefly the few psychoanalytic

---

Dr. Holtzman is Clinical Assistant Professor, Department of Psychiatry, Wayne State University School of Medicine, and Training and Supervising Analyst, Michigan Psychoanalytic Institute. Dr. Kulish is Adjunct Professor, Department of Psychiatry, Wayne State University School of Medicine, and Lecturer, Michigan Psychoanalytic Institute.

This paper is an abridged and modified version of a book that is in preparation.

writings that bear on the topic, and then glean whatever help we can from mythology, literature, and anthropological studies. We shall focus primarily on examples from our clinical work in which the unconscious meanings of loss of virginity and the hymen emerge most clearly. We have found that all of these sources have a common theme, that of negation. The hymen is invariably introduced with the idea of "never"—never again, never seen, known or named. The famous refrains from Poe's "The Raven" are apt: "With such a name as Nevermore," or "Quoth the Raven, Nevermore."

The word "hymen" is derived from the Greek word for membrane (Partridge, 1958). The Greek word for bridal song, from which the word "hymn" is derived, is identical, although ethnographers are cautious about making inferences about a common link between the two words. The second meaning of the word comes from marriage customs. In ancient Greece, a bride was accompanied to her husband's home by wellwishers, who sang and cried, "O hymen hymenaii!" (Rose, 1959). Marriage was personified by Hymen, the god of marriage, represented as a male youth carrying a torch and veil (Bullfinch, 1979). Sissa (1990) tells us that Hymen died on his wedding night, as did Hymenaios, a mythical figure whose suggestive name inevitably turned him into an allegory for the dangers of nuptial deflowering and its connections to death. In one account, he was crushed under the walls of his house on his wedding day. Sissa concludes that, "In spite of such an obvious and unavoidable vocalic similarity, the relationship between the wedding song 'Hymenaie' and the hymen of histology remains obscure" (p. 352).

There is disagreement among classical scholars about whether or not the ancient Greek and Roman scientists knew of the existence of the hymen, anatomically. Sissa (1990), for example, argues that the early Greeks viewed defloration as the extension of a preexisting, but protected, fissure rather than the breaking of a closed barrier. She describes a common metaphoric view of the female genitals as closed by lips pressed together. Hanson (1990), in contrast, argues that there is evidence that during the second century A.D. popular anatomy pictured the uterus as sealed off—for example, as an upside down jug closed by a stopper. Only with later and more sophisticated anatomy and dissection was the knowledge of a hymeneal membrane

The Hymen and the Loss of Virginity

established definitively. What is especially interesting here is that the negation and doubt regarding knowledge of the hymen, which we shall demonstrate in our clinical examples, are also reflected in scholarly debate among classicists.

The word "virgin" in antiquity meant a woman who was not married, a woman unto herself. The Latin root carried the meaning of strength and skill as in "virile" and did not necessarily refer to sexual chastity or intactness. These connotations came with later Christian translations (Sjoo & Mor, 1987). Because the translations of the word virgin are unclear, anthropologists (Sissa, 1990) warn us that we should be careful about reading modern meanings and connotations into it, such as assuming that the ancient world knew of a bodily part like the hymen and its rupture. Yet interpretations of classical literature and mythology yield a concept of "parthenia," something translated as virginity, which is treasured and can be lost or taken (Sissa, 1990, p. 342). The origin of the word "defloration" is Latin, probably colloquial. Thus, the various contradictory and conflictual derivations of these terms are open to debate and conjuncture.

PSYCHOANALYTIC LITERATURE

Freud (1918a) examines the topic of virginity in "The Taboo of Virginity" as the third contribution to the psychology of love. He introduces this subject by saying: "Few details of the sexual life of primitive peoples are so alien to our own feelings as their estimate of virginity, the state in a woman of being untouched" (p. 193). He takes as axiomatic that a woman's virginity is highly valued by her future mate. Freud goes onto explain the practice among primitive people in which an elder, priest or holy man, and not the bridegroom, performs the defloration of the bride. Freud attributes the taboo nature of virginity to the horror of blood and its link with menstruation and ideas of sadism, and to neurotic apprehension of every new undertaking—"feeling on the threshold of a dangerous situation."

Freud states that frigidity is due to three factors: first, to the narcissistic injury from the "destruction of an organ" but not to the pain of defloration itself; second, to the infantile sexual wishes fixed on the father or brother which make the husband "only a substitute, never the right man"; third, to masculine envy from childhood which can produce "uncontrolled aggression" toward the husband after intercourse. Freud found that women frequently have a paradoxical reaction to defloration which may bind them enduringly to the man and at the same time unleash an archaic reaction of hostility toward him and a desire for revenge via castration. Freud also describes the ubiquitous and defensive fantasy of the child who denies the sexuality of parents and turns the mother into an "untouched virgin" or a perpetual virgin.

Throughout Freud's writings (1900, 1901, 1905, 1913, 1914, 1916a, 1916b, 1917, 1918a, 1918b, 1922) virginity, defloration, and their symbols are delineated. In dreams white and red flowers represent purity and innocence as well as their opposite (the word defloration itself employs flower symbolism). The dream element "violet" is connected to "violate" and "violence." Flowers represent virginal femininity, defloration by violence, and the sexual organs themselves (both male and female) just as blossoms are the sexual organs of plants. The gift of flowers between lovers may have these meanings. We shall also see these symbols reflected in myths and literature.[1]

An additional reference to the hymen occurs in "From the History of Infantile Neurosis" (1918b). Here the patient's fantasy of a torn veil is interpreted by Freud as a birth veil and in terms of a wish for rebirth. In a footnote, Freud adds: "A possible subsidiary explanation, namely that the veil represented the hymen which is torn at the moment of intercourse with a man, does not harmonize completely with the necessary condition for his recovery. Moreover it has no bearing on the life of the patient, for whom virginity carried no significance" (p. 101). It strikes us that this interpretation, which Freud considers and rejects, is indeed plausible, given the patient's

---

[1]Certain common rituals in current daily life which seem symbolically to represent defloration are: launching a ship by breaking a bottle prior to the maiden voyage, cutting a ribbon to inaugurate a new venture or building, ground-breaking ceremonies by an important man such as the mayor, the superstition that it is bad luck to cut the ribbons of gifts at a wedding shower, the wrapping of gifts to cover secret treasures, breaking the glass at a Jewish wedding or of crockery at betrothals, carrying the bride over the threshold, the veil worn by the bride, the custom of wearing virginal white or, in some cultures red, by the bride.

The Hymen and the Loss of Virginity

identification with the female. Striking also is the evidence of negation. It is puzzling to us that in his paper on "The Taboo of Virginity" Freud (1918a) stresses the importance placed on virginity, yet here clinically he disavows it.

Abraham (1922), in his essay on the female castration complex, states that menstruation and defloration are connected with the loss of blood and the idea of a wound. He agrees with Freud that defloration reinforces the sense of castration which promotes accompanying vengeful feelings toward the man.

In the most extensive psychoanalytic study on the subject, Yates (1930) notes the historical emphasis on virginity which swings between two polar opposites—that of a "high positive value" or a "negative value." Typically, virginity is prized as a function of the idea that women are regarded as property and must enter marriage undamaged. She agrees with Freud's explanations of ritual defloration but feels they are not sufficient. She also concurs with Freud's idea that avoidance of the woman's revenge may be a contributing factor but is not the most significant factor in explaining virginity taboos and rituals. Gathering material from psychoanalyses and primitive cultures, Yates examines the dynamics of the underlying attitudes toward virginity that differ between women and men. She suggests that for females the desire to preserve virginity for the "ideal man," God, the Father (the infantile incestuous wish) is accompanied by the idea that they would lose something precious. Defloration leaves a wound, they are "never the same again."

Yates explains that for males there is a double taboo—defloration and the first intercourse. With ritual defloration, the husband avoids causing blood to be shed and avoids having intercourse with a "dangerous" virgin. That there is almost always an actual injury to the hymen serves as the basis for the fear of the perpetration of a sadistic injury on the woman, equivalent to castration. The man's guilt feelings are aroused and therefore his own castration anxiety. In addition, the view that intercourse with a virgin may be seen as "with a woman who belongs to a god or spirit or other father substitute" revives the fear of father's revenge for the wish to take the mother away from the father—the infantile oedipal fantasy. The initiation rite allows the man to escape these guilt feelings and fears of castration, sadism, and death.

Deanna Holtzman—Nancy Kulish

Horney (1933) attributes one form of feminine genital anxiety as stemming from early attempts at vaginal masturbation where the little girl will "incur pain or little injuries obviously caused by infinitesimal ruptures of the hymen" (p. 68). We note that these obvious but infinitesimal ruptures can never be verified, nor have we found reports of these phenomena clinically. Deutsch (1945), in her study of femininity, states, "A painful bodily injury—the breaking of the hymen and the forcible stretching and enlargement of the vagina by the penis—are the prelude to woman's first complete sexual enjoyment" (p. 81). Thus pain which is secondarily linked with pleasure "endows the sexual experience with a masochistic character" (p. 81). The masochistic trend in females seen by Deutsch as an essential of femininity is organized around the breaking of the hymen. We believe that the assumption that a once-felt pain, that is, the breaking of the hymen, must lead forever to a commingling of pain and pleasure is an erroneous and unsubstantiated one. Once the way is opened to enable pleasure, it does not necessarily carry with it the connotation of pain. Pain can also be reinvoked as a defense against the forbidden aspect of sexual pleasure.

Freud, Abraham, Horney, and Yates all suggest a connection between the first menstruation and defloration, blood and injury or wound, castration and death.

In Female Sexuality (1953), Bonaparte describes the "perforation complex" which is the fear of penetration and a common cause of frigidity. "We may not be surprised then, when we turn to the human race, if we find that women react with anxiety and terror to their sexuality far more often than do men" (p. 186). She attributes this to the real dangers of female sexuality—by pregnancy and childbirth, and the pain that is a part of menstruation, defloration and childbirth. In keeping with our sentiments, Gardiner (1955) argues that except for defloration, intercourse is pleasurable for the woman and pain is an indication of conflict. We would also argue with Bonaparte's assertion that women's sexuality is more fraught with terror and anxiety than is men's.

Lerner (1977) points to incomplete and poorly differentiated knowledge of female anatomy as having serious psychological consequences such as penis envy and learning inhibitions in women. It is notable that among what she cites as unrecognized parts of the female anatomy, i.e., clitoris, vulva, she makes no mention of the hymen. It is striking to us that the hymen is omitted as a recognized

The Hymen and the Loss of Virginity

and named part of the anatomy in a psychoanalytic paper devoted to the psychological importance of the clarification of the female genitals.

CLASSICAL-LITERARY AND ANTHROPOLOGICAL WRITINGS

The image of deflowering is frequently associated with the loss of virginity in ancient myths and literature, even while scholars from various disciplines argue about the meaning of the term "virginity." In the well-known myth of Demeter and Persephone, for example, imagery of flowers is woven into a tale of loss of virginity by rape. Persephone, the daughter of Demeter, is a young girl on the verge of womanhood. The other name by which she is known, "Kore," is virtually synonymous with the Greek for "maiden" or "virgin." In the words of the Homeric Hymn " . . . she, Kore, was playing with the deep-breasted maidens of Okeanos, picking blossoms, roses, crocuses, and fair violets on the gentle meadow, agallis and hyacinth and narcissa . . . " (11, 1–23). She was suddenly snatched up by Pluto, who carried her off and raped her. According to Ovid's "Metamorphoses," "the loosened flowers fell and she in simple innocence, grieved as much for them as for her other loss" (5, 399–400). In vain, the girl called for her mother's help. Cyane, a water nymph, tried to save her and to stop Pluto. In anger he smote the pool of the nymph open with his scepter, and his chariot plunged down to Hades. Grieving for the violation of the girl and for her fountain, Cyane dissolved into tears, "And in her silent spirit kept the wound incurable" (5, 427–428). The incurable wound is a frequent unconscious representation of the female genitalia. As we will see, these are common themes—defloration as an irrevocable loss, the loss of virginity associated with rape, and the daughter turning to the mother for help.

The Greek poetess, Sappho, put these themes of defloration and loss into her verse, "Lament for a Maidenhead," from 600 B.C.:

> Like a hyacinth in
> the mountains, trampled

> by shepherds still
> only a purple stain
> remains on the ground . . .
>
> Why am I crying?
>
> Am I still sad
> because of my
> lost maidenhead?

In this verse the purple stain is an allusion to the blood which can mark the irrevocable loss of virginity.

Repeatedly in mythology and literature, blood from defloration is pictured as a stain that will not go away, a curse. In *The Choephoroe* by Aeschylus, Orestes, about to step over the threshold of the familial palace to avenge the killing of his father by his mother, gives voice to the fear of breaking a taboo marked by blood:

> As we who treads the virgin bower can find
> No cure, so too, though stream on stream should pour
> Their swift-cleansing waters on the hand of blood, the old
> Stain shall not be wiped away [69–74].

Loss of virginity is equated in the above with crossing over a forbidden threshold.

Similarly, in Christina Rossetti's poem, "The Convent Threshold," the speaker on the doorstep of the convent feels caught between sexuality and chastity. Choosing to become a nun because there is mysterious "blood" between her lover and herself, she looks down to see her lily feet "soiled with mud, / With scarlet mud which tells a tale." Again, we see the association between crossing over a threshold from which one cannot return and a forbidden love.

Bettelheim (1989), in his psychoanalytic study of popular fairy tales, also finds that themes of the loss of virginity are linked with ideas about forbidden thresholds. In the tales "Bluebeard" and "Fitcher's Bird," for example, a man instructs a young girl not to enter a forbidden space or secret room, but she betrays his trust and is discovered. In one story, it is a key that gives the woman away; in

The Hymen and the Loss of Virginity

the other, it is an egg—each object has blood on it that cannot be washed off. Bettelheim's interpretation is that the egg is a symbol of female sexuality which is to remain unspoiled. He goes on to associate the key with the male sexual organ, which is bloodied in first intercourse when the hymen is broken. We recognize the theme of irrevocable loss, that is, once over the threshold, into the forbidden room, the blood cannot be washed away—virginity has been ended forever.

In various primitive cultures the taboos against blood and virginity are often associated with fears of crossing thresholds. A successful paramour in Gambia (Ames, 1953) is admired and envied by other young men and thought to be very brave because in traveling from town to town on illicit adventures, he dares to pass the crossroads and other dreaded places where witches and malevolent spirits lurk at night. These beliefs may illustrate Freud's idea that fears of crossing thresholds represent fears of the female genital and breaking the incest taboo.

The blood from the breaking of the hymen has been used as proof of a bride's virginity in many societies across the world. The public display of the blood-stained bedclothes was a prominent custom in Arabic, African, Hebrew, and European cultures. A passage in Deuteronomy (22:14–20) perscribes that the garments of a Jewish bride are to be spread before the elders, as "tokens of virginity." If she does not pass the test, she is to be stoned to death. The test for virginity among Bedouins was done manually with the white toga of the groom wrapped around his fingers. Then the toga was displayed and the men, waiting outside of the tent, celebrated wildly and loudly. The bride is said to have cried out for her mother (Peters, 1965). Evidence of a Kurdish bride's virginity was obtained from the white bedclothes which were displayed, or the groom would smear a handkerchief with the blood and present this to his mother. If this proof was not obtained, the girl would be sent back to her family to be slain (Masters, 1953).

The custom of displaying the stained white bridal sheets is a centerpiece of a short story by Isak Dinesen (1983) called "The Blank Page." The nuns in a convent make the bloodied sheets of the royal houses of Spain into objects as sacred as altar cloths and read the stains as if they were hieroglyphs. Dinesen implies that the fact of blood must be taken into account before we can understand the nature of female art. We believe that the intrapsychic representations of blood and its many connections must be taken into account before we can understand sexual fantasies of women and men.

Hymeneal blood is often thought to have magical powers (Kemp, 1935). Lederer (1968) suggests that the danger in breaking the hymen for many peoples lies in the bleeding itself, which they equate with the blood of menstruation, often a taboo. Malinowski (1929) describes a Malanesian myth of virgin birth, in which the hero's mother sleeps in a cave and the dripping water pierces or opens her. Anthropologists argue about whether the language in this story should be interpreted as "piercing" or "opening." "Piercing" implies defloration and some kind of knowledge of a membrane or covering. This language was translated elsewhere (Austin, 1934) differently as a "hammering back of the menstrual blood," which does not imply a piercing of a membrane. Again we see the question among anthropologists as to whether or not a particular culture had explicit knowledge of a hymen.

Unopened versus unbroken are two common images of virginity cross-culturally which have different, conflicting connotations. White, unopened buds represent virgins in Tipopia in the South Pacific (Firth, 1936); white shells are commonly associated with virginity in the South Pacific and Africa (Abraham, 1933). "A pierced vessel" is another image used in the South Pacific to depict the flow of blood from defloration (Firth, 1936). Similarly, in one African society the bloodstained cloth shown to wedding guests is shown with the triumphant chant, "He has broken the silver bracelet" (Levine, 1965).

The doubts and arguments about the knowledge of the hymen in a particular context, be it literary, historical, or anthropological, represent the cultural and scholarly manifestation of what we have found in patients in our clinical practices. We have selected the following from numerous examples.

CLINICAL MATERIAL

Words such as "never," negations, denials, reversals, and doubting are characteristic when patients speak of the hymen. In addition,

The Hymen and the Loss of Virginity

bisexual imagery appears with regularity in the clinical material of both males and females. However, the content, feelings, and conflicts about the hymen and defloration differ between men and women. With the male patients, the material can be organized significantly around three major themes: oedipal conflicts, castration anxiety in multiple forms, and sadomasochism. With our female patients the material can be organized around several different themes: genital anxieties, damage, and vulnerability; protection and thresholds; guilt about masturbation; the role of mother; and menstruation, blood, and childbirth. Of course all of these themes are entwined, but we shall highlight each for the purposes of our discussion. The following are typical examples derived from male patients:

The Hymen and Positive Oedipal Themes in Men

A forty-year old married man, several years into his analysis, was beginning to experience intensely erotized feelings for the female analyst. He reported a dream in which he was standing at a big desk which looked like a rare and beautiful cherry wood desk he once owned. Someone "older and bigger" was getting many gifts. He associated to the analyst's desk which had cherry-colored cross bars. The cherry reminded him of virginity, purity, a great gift—"first prize because it means I'm the first. A cherry was something I never encountered. I'm supposed to have sex with my wife and never anyone else." Of their early premarital sex life, he said, "She did not have a hymen that I was aware of. Someone older and bigger must be my father." The dream represented his desire to be the first with his mother, the virgin. In another dream around that time he dreamed of a child with a hole in its forehead "where I put in a needle and fluid spurts out. Someone had already drilled the hole." His associations went to adolescent talk of drilling girls—drilling through the hymen. "I never had a virgin—I would not like to have to be the first and cause the pain." The dream, like the one above, expresses his denial of the oedipal wish to be the first with the mother/analyst.

A young man reported a dream about a dead-end street which he associated with birth, death, and female genitalia. "Beautiful ladies are a trap." His first thoughts went to Sharon Stone—the dangerous blonde in *Basic Instinct*, her going to take a shower and steaming up the shower doors. He recalled the famous scene from

Psycho in which a woman is murdered in the shower by a male killer dressed as a female. Then he described being in his apartment where people could not see in but he could see out. While looking through a half-open window at older women passing by, he would masturbate.

He thought of a slit, or a half-covered cavity. When the analyst asked about a covered cavity, he said, "I never found one; never found a hymen." He had had at least three virgins, but none had a hymen that he could detect. "I forgot that hymens exist because I never encountered one." He said that a hymen should be "an opaque, thin membrane through which one couldn't really see—like the shower door." He mused, "A young girl who has a hymen has a nice gift for someone . . . a certification that you are the first." With his first girlfriend, they did not talk about it. He felt he might have ruptured it digitally although he did not remember feeling it. Other girls said that he was the first but there was no evidence of the hymen, difficulties in penetrating, or blood. "It was not an experience I had," he concluded. Here the hymen is viewed as a gift, as the covering of a dangerous and exciting trap, and as a barrier that obscures vision and entry. Note the striking reoccurring use of negations, which are attempts to mediate underlying anxiety, throughout this material.

The Hymen and Castration Anxiety in Men

As one would expect, castration anxiety often accompanies positive oedipal strivings. The image of a dangerous trap, seen in the preceding case, reoccurred in the material of a divorced fifty-year old man, in treatment for the first time, a virginal experience for him. In his opening dream, which reflected anxieties about starting an analysis with a woman, he reported being in an office with a girl whose pants are suddenly down and her legs open. "Over her vagina is a black wire. I was able to penetrate through the hole and had a superlarge penis." He said the black wire was like the covering over a champagne bottle which "when you open it can surprise you—explode and spurt out." The wire reminded him of a cage, a trap. The office looked like the analyst's. The new experience of lying down led to pleasurable memories of lying in bed with his mother.

The imagery of a covering as a hymen was not elucidated until several years later. At this point in the analysis, positive oedipal longings in the transference were emerging in a clearer and more workable form. The patient recalled an image of his mother sitting on a

The Hymen and the Loss of Virginity

screened porch—which was all wire. He was reminded of the kind of wire on a champagne bottle "covering the hole." He said, "Popping the cork is like an ejaculation." He recalled his opening dream and thought of a covering of part of the woman's body—like a trap—the wire covering over the hole. "Wire mesh is like a screen." In response to the analyst's query for clarification, he replied, "It's like with a virgin—there is a covering. What's hidden in there, who knows? I never had sexual intercourse with a woman who was a virgin, where there was a hymen. For some reason I did not want to. I never chose to. I did not think it was important. My thought was that the girl wanted to save it until marriage." He reported recently being fascinated by reading about the abuse of women and the ritual removal of the clitoris. Abuse reminded him of some sort of bondage, and a "covering" or wire can produce abuse. "When you break and enter, then there is something bloody."

The bisexual imagery of "something popping out" from behind the screen or wire expresses an important dynamic in this case. The image of the bottle with "something popping out" represents the wished for and feared phallic mother. The fear of castration stems from retribution for oedipal impulses and sadistic impulses projected onto the analyst. It also reflects an identification with a virginal female—victim of the penetrating analyst. He often remarked how impressed he was by the analyst's "penetrating" comments.

The Hymen and Sadomasochism in Men

Early in his analysis, a young male patient was struggling with sexualized fears of being hurt by the analyst. He reported a dream which followed his having intercourse with his girlfriend who was "bleeding," that is, menstruating. In the dream a man was being operated on and his ribs were exposed, "but it looks kind of dry, not bleeding." Two men gestured with their arms as if in a sword fight. Ribs evoked associations of Adam and Eve. When asked about "not bleeding," he responded, "The only time anyone bleeds is if there is a period or if something is terribly wrong." The analyst asked, "What about the first intercourse?" He said, "Oh, I never thought about that, I never remembered that. I forgot that. That is when the hymen is broken." He then recalled another portion of the dream in which a woman surgeon inserted a long knife and the wound was gushing.

Deanna Holtzman—Nancy Kulish

The patient experienced the entire analytic process as a rupturing of the hymen by a penetrating analyst. He, like many patients beginning analysis and confronted with a new relationship with the analyst, fantasized being like an exposed, opened virgin. Anticipation of intimacy and closeness can become sexualized defensively. A major transference-countertransference paradigm in the case was the image of the analyst as the castrating, penetrating surgeon and the patient as feminine victim. In saying "anyone bleeds," the patient blurred over the gender distinction and betrayed his unconscious identification with the female. Here again, the fantasy of bisexuality is prominent. The above material demonstrates that conflicted sadomasochistic fantasies around defloration and penetration lead to the negation and denial of such events.

Such is the case with yet another male patient who reported a dream of hair coming out in patches. "The hair looked like pubic hair." He recalled seeing the genitals of a five-year old girl when he was about ten. Her genital area appeared to him like the skin which "covers the balls—only nothing is there." He compared the male and female genitals. "If one is a Jew, you circumcise although now there is a wave of anticircumcision feeling. A piece of skin is not necessary, or is it? The hymen in women reminds me of such a piece of skin. Circumcision makes a man like a woman—a piece is removed." Here we see an equation of foreskin and hymen in the service of maintaining the fantasy of bisexuality and denying the difference between the sexes.

In the following case the sadomasochistic imagery and fantasies are especially striking. A male patient had a history of overstimulation in childhood and of exhibitionism. In reaction to being excited and frightened by the analyst's attempts to understand his provocative use of what he considered dirty words, he had thoughts of exposing himself to her. He said, "My girlfriend told me the name of a certain type of flower which I forgot. I remember the book I bought for her—*My Secret Garden*, which told all about sexual fantasies. The cover is a picture of a woman with a flower in her pubic region. It's a very pretty picture." He thought of "deflower" but he did not have any words to put to it. "The hymen is not something that I consciously thought about. I don't think I knew anything about the hymen."

The Hymen and the Loss of Virginity

This material occurred in the context of the patient being stimulated by barely repressed sexual fantasies about his girlfriend's teen-aged daughter, whom he fantasized to be a virgin. He asserted "young girls are the instigators—they set up pursuit, and then they keep boys at arm's length." In the transference, he perceived the analyst as the dangerous instigator, as well.

As his thoughts returned to the desire to expose himself to the analyst, an image of an eagle claw came to mind. A bird of prey "picks up prey and rips parts of it into pieces and feeds it to the kids." The night before, he had watched a segment of "Mash." In an operating room scene, the nurse's face looked so pretty with "the bottom half masked, but when she unmasked it—it was structurally not as attractive." The hymen was a mask or a veil that covered the vagina made dangerous by projected sadomasochistic impulses. The analyst was experienced as a phallic "ripping bird of prey." The emphasis on aggression in defloration motivated his forgetting the name of the flower.

Another patient, a seventy-year-old man, spoke of having a "long and interesting" dream. In it, a young lady offered him an apple which he did not want and was afraid of. Nevertheless, he ate part and threw the rest away. The patient thought "it was long" sounded like talking about penis size. "The thought I have is of putting my penis in your mouth—and that is not certain." He was reminded of Adam and Eve who became aware of their nakedness and were embarrassed by it. After sharing the apple, they got sexual and God got mad at them. "I want to stay away from this topic. It arouses an erotic feeling. The thought of taking a bite—I'm not sure. I sliced it with my knife and threw away half. It sounds castrationlike."

The patient recalled how early in the analysis he had experienced the analyst "like a spider spinning a web," because it seemed to him that she had a veiled or disapproving look. Veiled reminded him of a hymen—"a membrane shaped like a cobweb, thick and translucent, not completely attached to the walls, with gaps in it. Hymie may be the plural—that's a joke." (The patient was aware that the analyst was Jewish and had a number of anxiety-provoking thoughts which he labeled anti-Semitic.) "Hymens come in different shapes, most are incomplete. I have never seen one. Maybe that's what half an apple means. I had named it the serpentine apple. The serpent encouraged them to partake, and a serpentine apple sounds like a red chili pepper. Dangerous—the thought of putting my penis in your mouth and maybe someone would take a bite. In California, therapists and patients get involved.... This could be a trap. It could be a way of getting people involved."

Here, with the analyst as a seducer, the hymen is represented as a trap, a spider web, as well as flower and fruit. The redness of the apple or red chili pepper—hot and phallic-shaped, is an interesting bisexual image. Again, we see the connection between the foreskin and the hymen. In this case, the imagery is dominated by oral sadistic fantasies. We turn now to clinical data derived from the analyses of female patients.

The Hymen and Genital Anxieties and Vulnerability in Women

A young woman dreamed of the analyst's entrance "across which someone is building something delicate and old." Old made her think of her mother's antiques. The patient described her favorite as "the best piece." She had gone shopping for rings for her upcoming wedding. Her thoughts went to the shape of the construction in the dream which reminded her of arches. She loved arches, which are "entries to rooms." Arcs were associated with penises. She then thought of sobbing or crying, which she would never—not ever—do in front of her mother. If she were to do so, her mother would be reminded of the patient's femininity. The patient would once again be vulnerable, open to hurt and rejection since mother preferred her brother. The delicate covering of an entrance also reminded her of losing her virginity which had made her cry. She contrasted this event with the extravagant and joyful celebration of the bris of her favored younger brother. Once again we see a link between the hymen and the foreskin.

Here, the delicate decoration across the entrance to the female analyst's office was seen as representation of the feminine permeability and vulnerability to pain (the breaking of the hymen). Females were seen as "open" and vulnerable. Tears (and other secretions) differentiate them from males who are "closed" and more prized. Arches and arcs became related bisexual images.

Another young woman, who also had just become engaged, reported that soon after getting her engagement ring, she lost sexual

The Hymen and the Loss of Virginity

interest in her fiancé. The ring had been presented to her in an elaborate set of boxes, placed on the finger of a long white glove. In this context, she dreamed that she was working for her father doing manual work and looked down to see that her ring was broken, scratched and "all mucked up." She went on to speak of her feelings of sadness and disappointment since her engagement. Now she lamented the earlier loss of her virginity and purity. Is her disappointment that she has not "saved" her virginity for her father? Does her sense of loss cover over a more dangerous, libidinalized attachment to her father? The broken ring would typically be interpreted as vagina. It is plausible in this context to see it as a "broken, scratched" hymen, encircling the vagina. We have found that the broken circle frequently stands for the hymen—intact or broken. There is an allusion, with the "manual" work, to worries about damage from manual masturbation as well. As we can observe in these two cases, and as we might expect, an upcoming marriage serves as a ready precipitant for the emergence of fantasies about defloration and virginity. We have found that this is the case whether the woman is actually a virgin or not.

The Hymen, Protection and Thresholds in Women

Expectations of being opened up, exposure, hurt frequently accompany the opening stages of analysis and can evoke fantasies about defloration and the hymen. A middle-aged woman in the beginning phase of her analysis was talking about a wished-for surgery—a face-lift and a brow lift. She had a fantasy that a bone would be found there that didn't belong—that was extra—"like an extra membrane. This may have something to do with my brain." She then remembered a dream in which her father, who had been dead for a number of years, was saying, "My daughter is not dumb." The patient spoke of how she feared and hated to get rid of things. "Having an extra part and needing to get rid of something is something I'm afraid to do. Once you take it out, it's gone forever. You can never get it back." The surgical removal of extra skin was linked with the idea that she would lose some of her intelligence—"They would take it out and then something that should have been there would leave a hole. What happens after you die? . . . "

Her thoughts went to a membrane—and wondering what it looked like. "Not paper-thin, but like a lump that was inside of me all those years." She thought of a hymen and said, "I used to think about it when I was little. That once it's gone you can never get it back again. It was so irreversible—once you had sex you could never go back to being the way you were before." She continued obsessionally negating and undoing the feelings about this event. "I remember I thought it would really be a big deal and at the time it wasn't. I wasn't so different. I was in high school. I can't remember much of it. I did not like the sex at all... I wished I hadn't done it... I had built it up to being such a big deal and it happened in a split second... It wasn't bad. Well, it was bad. It hurt me physically, but it was not that bad emotionally."

While this can be conceptualized in familiar terms of the displacement upwards of genital anxiety to the brain and intellect, there are other ways to view this material. The wished-for surgery may be a metaphor for the desire for the mind to be changed for the better (structural change) by the analyst and the analysis. In addition, there are unconscious, warded-off wishes for erotic pleasures. The negations in the patient's retelling of the time she lost her virginity, and the minimization of the experience—"no big deal"—are minimizations of the wish for and the experience of erotic pleasure.

She reported another dream in which there was one spot on the head. "There was a scab on it and it was yucky." It made her think of an earlier dream where her whole head was shaved. "It meant exposing everything in treatment and my fears about it." She said, "A scab is what covers over a wound. Usually there is blood. It protects the area from anything getting in. Bleeding reminds me of menstruation. The hymen is a covering that bleeds when it is ruptured. A scab may mean covering something up—like you were caught hiding something. A scab is someone who crosses over the line and goes where they shouldn't."

For this woman, there is a connection of the hymen with fantasized phallus and fecal phallus. In such instances, the loss represents castration of the inner phallus, evoking pain and death. Here the hymen is also seen as a protection from exposure and penetration, as a container of the fantasized hidden phallus, and as a line over which one should not cross—the forbidden threshold. The meaning of "nevermore" in this context is that nevermore can there be a return to the previous, unbroken, unopened state. The forbidden

The Hymen and the Loss of Virginity

threshold opens the way into adult sexuality and all its pleasures. Finally, a step across the threshold from childhood to adulthood is a step toward death.

The Hymen and Masturbation Guilt in Women

The breaking of the hymen, with the common reference to breaking the "cherry," is suggested by the following: In the midst of struggling with an awareness of homosexual feelings toward the analyst, a young woman remembered fighting with her mother as an adolescent. Then after a pause she said: "I remember that when I was about five, my dad brought home some chocolate-covered cherries, and I was sitting on his lap and I was eating one. Instead of just putting the whole thing into my mouth, I bit into it, and all the stuff squished out . . . and he was angry with me, and pushed me off. I was embarrassed and upset." In the same session, she went on to talk about her guilt about her childhood masturbation and her fear that she would damage herself. She had had the fantasy that she had "plugged up a hole," and that she had only two. She had heard some girls saying there were supposed to be three. Embarrassment and shame are associated here with forbidden erotic, oedipal wishes and pleasureful masturbation. A cloacal genital fantasy—"a hole" is evident.

The Hymen and the Role of the Mother for Women

Very often the affect associated with the loss of virginity is shame, as in the above, but another common feeling among women is disappointment and loss along with pain. Typically, in women's minds the mother is the object of these feelings of disappointment and blame.

An inhibited, frightened woman, who had memories of sexual abuse by an older male cousin, resisted the increasing evidence that her alcoholic father had also been involved. She reported having repetitive dreams after the previous session in which she insisted that Woody Allen could not be guilty of any crime. With a great deal of shame, hesitation, and reluctance, she recounted one of the dreams. "I don't know why it's so hard. You and I were in this place and I went to the bathroom, a shared bathroom. I had left in the sink . . . - why can't I say it . . . It's so horrible . . . a douche bag. I left the bathroom and realized you would go in and see it, and I was so embarrassed." The dream made her think of an incident she had never told to anyone. At the age of twelve, she had gotten what she now thought was a vaginal discharge. Her father, a physician, took her to the hospital where for some reason she did not understand, she was catheterized. The nurse in a harsh tone asked, "Are you active?" "Sexually active?" the analyst asked. "No, I think physically. I wonder if my hymen was broken." The girl was found to have a yeast infection, for which there was medicine to be applied vaginally with a plunger. The mother, in a ritualistic manner, applied the plunger. As she continued, the patient began to obsess about whether an aunt was always present. She complained to the analyst how "This was all humiliating." Then the patient recalled how she had first used pads, "not tampons," when she began to menstruate. When later in the session the analyst asked if the patient had any discomfort or bleeding with her first intercourse, the patient replied, "No. Never. Not at all. Never. It was nothing. I don't even remember when I had intercourse for the first time." She had made herself dead drunk every time she had sex in college. Obsessing, she recounted how the first time might have been with this boy, or perhaps it was somebody else. In this instance the doubting, denial, and negation surrounding the memory of the breaking of the hymen are clearly associated with protection against guilt-laden oedipal memories of traumatic familial experiences and fantasies, all with strong sadomasochistic meanings. Not to know who was the first lover both expresses and defends against incestuous masochistic wishes toward the father. The harsh nurse is the embodiment of the forbidding mother who denies the girl her desires. In the transference she recreated the scene with the analyst the passive onlooker to her humiliation, and cast her again as the forbidding mother.

In the above, bleeding from menstruation and from the breaking of the hymen are inextricably linked, as they are in this next case. A woman had been talking about her difficulties and feeling of inadequacy in being a mother and giving her prepubertal daughter guidance. In the transference, she had been expressing wishes that the analyst help her to be a woman, give her sexual guidance. Her lack of memories of her own mother she labeled a "black hole" or a "hole in my development." She mused about who had taught her to use tampons. Not her mother, certainly. In fact, her mother was strongly opposed to their use. It was the era. Again we encounter

The Hymen and the Loss of Virginity

the image of the mother who forbids the girl to be penetrated by the tampon/penis and holds her back from a readiness to enter sexual maturity. When the analyst questioned her about this, the patient expressed the idea that the tampon would interfere with the hymen. She added, "But I don't know about that stuff. What is the hymen? I don't know. I still don't know what it is." The analyst asked, "Did you bleed when you had sex for the first time?" "No! Not like a period. It wasn't vivid. . . . "

The Hymen and Menstruation, Blood and Childbirth

The indifferent, uncaring mother appears in the next case as well. A woman, in her ninth month of pregnancy, was dealing with fears of delivery. In this material were allusions to the breaking of membranes, which the analyst did not take up in terms of the hymen. This decision was made out of a wish not to impose her own interests onto the material. The feeling was that the more timely interventions needed to address the upcoming childbirth and issues in the transference. Retrospectively, however, we think that this decision also reflected the general unconscious inhibition that we find so frequently against mentioning the hymen. The language and the images in this patient's associations are clearly identical with fantasies about the breaking of the hymen and the loss of virginity.

She spoke of her fears of the water breaking—"would it hurt?" she asked. "Can I stop here? But there's no going back . . . " This idea of not going back is a central feeling about the loss of virginity—the idea of "nevermore" again. She continued, "Sometimes they do it to you (break the water) and it seems like a violation, breaking a membrane." The patient talked anxiously about how residents' hands are "up you all the time."

A few sessions later, she reported a dream and noted that she had been feeling guilty, as if she were going to be punished for all her past sexual behaviors. As she was to put it later, "I was a rotten kid and I would have to be punished." In the dream, she had gone to the bathroom and there was blood. She associated to her Lamaze class in which the dangers of childbirth were described. "In two medical conditions you'd start bleeding." The blood, she felt, was "like punishing myself for having sex." In her dreams during this time there were repeated themes of precariousness and danger, of being a victim of the elements, or of being broken or broken into, of violent attack, and of valuables being stolen. For example, she was in an upstairs room and the doors were unlocked downstairs. Her mother seemed indifferent and not concerned. Then two men on horseback came right into the house, upstairs, riding their horses into the room. The patient associated the scene with a kind of sexual attack and the men on horseback with the analyst. Thus, in the transference, the analyst was viewed both as the forbidding mother and as the mother who could not protect the girl against sexual attack. The patient longed for protection against her fears and the anticipated pain. Behind the fears was highly conflicted sexual excitement. Alternately, the mother was seen as an intrusive invader. "I need a barrier against my mother," she said. She thought of anesthesia as "like a barrier." The idea of a protective barrier may also be seen as a reference to the hymen. The principal dynamic was the fantasy of punishment for masturbation by genital damage, inflicted through childbirth in a sadomasochistic scenario; the subtext was the breaking of the hymeneal membrane, also seen as punishment. In both, there is a reality to the fantasies of painful rupture.

Women commonly blame their mothers not only for not protecting them, but also for keeping them ignorant sexually. A married woman described how surprisingly pleasureful sex was with her husband. She praised the analyst's sensitivity to and respect for her female concerns such as menstrual cramps, a first experience for her. She spoke of being the first in her class, the first time she menstruated and then her first intercourse at 15 which was "very, very, very painful. It was never any better; it never felt any good. He was as inexperienced as I. I knew nothing about the details of my body. I didn't know I had a clitoris. Later, I learned, took a mirror. I was so angry at my mother—enraged. Why didn't she tell me about this? All she said was 'Wear Kotex, don't use tampons, and don't get pregnant.' The real stuff she didn't tell me and I felt stupid." We see the connection for many females of their being "dumb or stupid" with their genitals as intellect is linked not only to a sense of the female genital as "inadequate" but even more importantly to inadequate knowledge of it and its capabilities. The mother's inadequate preparation of the girl also implies prohibition against sexual pleasure.

The Hymen and the Loss of Virginity

DISCUSSION

Contemporary revisions of psychoanalytic theories of female sexuality have emphasized a female line of development, a primary femininity, and the uniqueness of the female genitalia. These newer ideas have not, however, sufficiently taken into account the importance and the reality of the hymen as the representation of the entry into adult female genital sexuality. The representation of the hymen is frequently repressed and often suppressed, and serves as an organizing image around which fantasies and conflicts are elaborated.

The striking occurrence of the word "never" in connection with material about the hymen calls for explanation. Our curiosity about this was first aroused by the remarkable occurrence of "nevers," negations, and denials in our clinical material concerning the hymen or defloration. It was only afterwards, in researching the literature, that we discovered a strong, consistent concurrence of this phenomenon in some psychoanalytic writings, anthropological material, classical mythology, and many literary works and fairy tales. The psychoanalyst, Yates, spoke of defloration leaving the woman with a wound, "*never* the same again." Classical and anthropological scholars argue about whether the existence of the hymen was ever known to a given culture, that is to say, *never* known. Literature is replete with references to the loss of virginity as a stain that will *never* go away.

One explanation for the theme of "never" is that the loss of virginity represents a passage or a transformation in life that is irrevocable. Such a passage implies a step toward inevitable death, as in the refrain from Poe's "The Raven." In Peter Pan's "Never Never Land," children escape the step from childhood to adulthood—they *never* grow up to be adults. In the biblical story of Adam and Eve transgression from innocence into sexual knowledge led to being cast out of Eden forever. Breaking of the hymen is associated in many cultures with an irreversible crossing from closed to open, from clean to unclean, from treasured to devalued, as illustrated in marriage rituals in primitive cultures. Defloration, like birth and death, is a one-time occurrence which cannot be repeated.

The emphatic and exaggerated use of double negatives, like the dream within the dream, functions as an undoing, a denial of an unpleasant or traumatic reality. The reality in this case is the loss and the breaking of the hymen and what this means to the individual.

Deanna Holtzman—Nancy Kulish

Negation and doubting are characteristic of thinking about the hymen and represent defensive reactions to underlying conflicts and anxieties. We note that the hymen is a useful vehicle for the expression of and the defense against conflicts and wishes around bisexuality, an important dynamic in many of these cases. We found in our material with both males and females an equation between circumcision of the foreskin and the rupture of the hymen. This finding is different from the generally accepted notion in the psychoanalytic literature that vagina and foreskin are equivalents (Jaffe, 1976; Nunberg, 1947). The equation between circumcision and the rupture of the hymen is one important representation of the unconscious bisexual meaning attributed to the hymen.

Our material confirmed Yates'(1930) suggestion that the meanings of the hymen and defloration were different for men and for women, although we would elaborate these differences in the following way. In women, feelings of sadness, disappointment, and loss were associated with the end of virginity. The loss is twofold—loss of innocence or youth or purity and the loss of the mother's protection. The loss of virginity and the breaking of the hymen revive feelings from earlier stages of development. These feelings encompass loss of a fantasized penis, loss of female genital intactness, and feelings of genital damage and mutilation. Breaking of the hymen often evokes feelings of vulnerability and permeability, not the feared loss of openness, the "female castration complex" posited by Mayer (1985), but rather the fear of suffering a permanent opening, being exposed. With many females, the blame placed on an unprotecting mother who does not prepare her daughter for adult sexuality is clearly evident. We did not find this constellation in the material of our male patients. These feelings of anger and resentment toward the mother in the female patients could be seen as representations of oedipal or preoedipal ties which under stressful situations are re-evoked. The feeling of loss of mother's protection also reflects the unconscious sense of achievement over taking the mother's place as the girl moves into active rivalry with mother and into the pleasures of adult sexuality. The revengeful hostility and binding to the man who deflowers the girl, which was reported in the early psychoanalytic literature, was not present in our female cases. Rather, strong negative feelings seemed to center on their mothers.

The Hymen and the Loss of Virginity

The women also seemed to blame their mothers unconsciously for their feelings of undeveloped or lost sexuality and eroticism. That the female genital or parts of it have been unnamed is a cause for blame of the mother. This blame reflects the perception and/or reality of the mother's need to keep the girl a child, small and "dumb."

In the Judeo-Christian tradition, knowledge and carnality are linked in the Bible in the Adam and Eve story with the use of the verb "to know," as possession in a sexual sense. Part of the inhibition of verbalization and education about the female genitals is connected to the deep anxiety that to know means to act, in this case sexually—that thought equals the deed. Kulish (1992) argues that the non-naming of, and the practice of, excising the clitoris are attempts to curb female sexual appetite and desire. Similarly, the hymen's rupture means the pathway to adult female sexuality is open. The inhibition in verbalizing and knowing about the hymen is also enhanced by the ready perception of sadistic meanings in the event of defloration.

Other affects associated with defloration in females are those of shame and humiliation. Although both male and female patients claimed not to know of the hymen's existence, the narcissistic element of "feeling stupid" about it was characteristic only for the women. The various cultural traditions and traumatic situations that force exposure to others of the state of the girl's genital, as in the ritual deflowering ceremonies, produce or intensify these affects of humiliation and shame. We did not find clinically strong evidence of what others (Lupton, 1993) have reported about taboos about blood as representing feared power of the woman, that is, symbol of her fertility and her life-giving force. The need to humiliate and overpower women may underlie such public rituals.

Another prominent finding in women regarding the breaking of the hymen and the bleeding was the revival of guilt for masturbation and fantasies of having damaged the genitals. This phenomenon is linked intrapsychically with menstruation which induces similar fears. Some of the differences in meaning and affect between men and women about the hymen stem from the fact that the hymen and bleeding are real parts of the female genitalia and experience.

Deanna Holtzman—Nancy Kulish

With men, the affects associated with the hymen and virginity are somewhat different. The obsessional doubting in men was a defense against positive oedipal anxieties aroused at the idea of being "the first" with a woman (unless all of the reported women were lying about being virgins). We did not see in men the predominance of the sense of loss and sadness as with women. Rather, the feelings shift more to fears of castration and destruction by the retaliating father and the phallic woman. In addition, the doubting reflects anxiety about the unresolved dilemma of two conflicting images of mother—Madonna/virgin versus whore/used and fallen woman. There are indications that the idea of the perpetual virgin is motivated by many of these conflicts in men (and women).

These unconscious fantasies determine the multitudinous representations of the hymen that appear in the clinical material. The rather remarkable multiplicity of images in this selection of our cases were: as a semi-transparent surface—glass, a steam shower door, screen, veil; as some kind of trap—a spider web, or a wire; as something edible—an apple, chili pepper, cherries; as flowers, plants, tree; as coverings—a mask; as barriers of various sorts, both mental and tangible—a cork stopper, a block; as a gift, a treasure or a ring; as membranes of other sorts, open and closed; as foreskin, a scab, a Jew. The clinical material confirms and mirrors these images in literature, anthropology, and mythology.

A preponderance of both male and female patients presented material relating to the hymen in associations to dreams. We wonder, is the tendency for this conflict-laden anatomical fact to remain repressed the determinant for its emergence as latent dream content, or simply an artifact of our population or analytic styles? Or is there a connection between the fact that a dream is often presented as a gift to the analyst, just as virginity may be perceived as a gift?

Several clinical questions emerge from our research. Since this material was gathered by female analysts, we wonder if it was shaped in any way by our sex. For example, male patients frequently experienced the analyst as a seductive, dangerous temptress; female patients frequently saw the analyst as the silent, uncaring mother who was passive or forsook them in their danger, or the jealous rival who

The Hymen and the Loss of Virginity

appropriates sexuality for herself. The sex of the analyst seemed to facilitate these images. Would a male patient imagine "deflowering" his male analyst in the maternal transference and/or would the male analyst readily recognize such imagery?

Defloration and the breaking of the hymen can become a metaphor for the entire analytic process, as our clinical material illustrates. Like defloration, analysis is an opening up that can change one forever. Both men and women identify with the virgin in terms of opening up, exposing oneself in an intimate situation, being penetrated, and acquiring knowledge, that is, knowing or being "known." On the opposite side, patients often identify with the penetrator as with, for example, a wish to penetrate the veil of secrecy of the analyst.

While deflowering and its opposite, being deflowered, might appear as a central metaphor in some cases, their clinical importance is more generalized. The hymen and defloration constitute part of the reality of sexual relationships and the female's body. Thus the hymen revives and reoccurs in many mental scenarios. With its conscious signal "never," the hymen is linked to unconscious fantasies elucidating childhood and adolescent conflicts. (As Freud said, the unconscious knows no nevers.) Because of its dynamic and genetic importance, it is necessary that we be aware of and sensitive to its many appearances and meanings in clinical material. Ignoring or missing these meanings sacrifices understanding and empathy with our patients. An emphasis on castration/penis envy can lead to a one-sided, facile view of sexuality and a loss of a richer understanding that the concept of the hymen and its role contribute.

Our material emerged in most cases spontaneously or with little direct questioning. Like the physical reality of the hymen, the topic in our clinical material seems to lie just below the surface and requires little technical activity to allow its emergence. The paucity of analytic literature around this one-time happening or phenomenon may echo a mutual collusion or resistance by both patient and analyst to downplay its importance in the intrapsychic world. We have suggested some motivations for this resistance.

Anxieties about the physical reality of defloration have implications for education. The same tendency toward collusion between patient and analyst frequently exists between mother and child and educator and student. The facts of female sexuality and anatomy are not clearly recognized or delineated. Frequently, sexual education is held back from girls as if it would harm them. We wholeheartedly agree with Horney (1935) that, "These biological functions have in themselves no masochistic connotation for women, and do not lead to masochistic reactions; but if masochistic needs of other origin are present, they may easily be involved in masochistic fantasies . . ." (p. 232).

This paper is a beginning attempt to explore an area that has received little attention. Female sexuality as portrayed in early and classical psychoanalytic literature was distorted by attention to what was not there rather than what was there. Beginning with the general collusion about the notion of there being no knowledge of the vagina in the child, which became a crucial part of the psychoanalytic theory of female sexual development, followed by the overemphasized line of phallocentric interests, a clearer understanding of the female genital experience has been obstructed and delayed. A more complex and clear understanding comes from an appreciation of the importance of bisexuality and the contributions of both male *and* female genital experiences. This study represents an addition to a line of contemporary psychoanalytic thought which is attempting to reevaluate and articulate uniquely feminine genital experiences (Bernstein, 1990; Mayer, 1985; Richards, 1992; Tyson, 1989). We hope further data on these subjects will help to lift "the veil of secrecy surrounding the dark continent."

REFERENCES

ABRAHAM, K. (1922). Manifestations of the female castration complex. *Int. J. Psychoanal.*, 3:1–28.

ABRAHAM, R.C. (1933). *The TIV People*. Lagos: Government Printer.

AESCHYLUS. *The Oresteia of Aeschylus*, ed. G. Thompson. Cambridge, Eng.: Cambridge Univ. Press, 1938.

AMES, D.W. (1953). Plural marriage among the Wolof in the Gambia: with a consideration of problems of marital adjustment and patterned ways of resolving tensions. Unpublished Ph.D. dissertation. Evanston, IL: Northwestern University.

AUSTIN, L. (1934). Procreation among the Trobriand Islanders. *Oceania*, 5:103–113.

BERNSTEIN, D. (1990). Female genital anxieties, conflicts, and typical mastery modes. *Internat. J. Psychoanal.*, 71:151–165.

The Hymen and the Loss of Virginity

BETTELHEIM, B. (1989). *The Uses of Enchantment.* New York: Random House.
BONAPARTE, M. (1953). *Female Sexuality.* New York: Int. Univ. Press.
BULLFINCH, T. (1979). *Bullfinch's Mythology.* New York: Crown.
DEUTSCH, H. (1945). *The Psychology of Women: A Psychoanalytic Interpretation,* Vol. 2. New York: Grune & Stratton.
DINESEN, I. (1983). The blank page. In *Last Tales.* New York: Random House, pp. 99–105.
FIRTH, R. (1936). *We, the Tikopia: A Sociological Study of Kinship in Primitive Polynesia.* London: Allen & Unwin.
FREUD, S. (1900). The interpretation of dreams. *S. E.,* 4 & 5.
——— (1901). On dreams. *S. E.,* 5.
——— (1905). Fragment of an analysis of a case of hysteria. *S. E.,* 7.
——— (1913). Totem and taboo. *S. E.,* 13.
——— (1914). On the history of the psycho-analytic movement. *S. E.,* 14.
——— (1916a). Some character types met with in psychoanalytic work. *S. E.,* 14.
——— (1916b). Introductory lectures on psycho-analysis. *S. E.,* 15.
——— (1917). Introductory lectures on psycho-analysis. *S. E.,* 16.
——— (1918a). The taboo of virginity. *S. E.,* 11.
——— (1918b). From the history of an infantile neurosis. *S. E.,* 17.
——— (1922). Some neurotic mechanisms in jealousy, paranoia and homosexuality. *S. E.,* 18.
GARDINER, M. (1955). Feminine masochism and passivity. *Bull. Phila. Assn. Psychoanal.,* 5:74–79.
HANSON, A.E. (1990). The medical writer's woman. In *Before Sexuality: The Construction of Erotic Experience in the Ancient Greek World,* ed. D. M. Halperin, J. J. Winkler & F. I. Zeitlin. Princeton, NJ: Princeton Univ. Press.
HORNEY, K. (1933). The denial of the vagina. *Int. J. Psychoanal.,* 14:57–70.
——— (1935). The problem of feminine masochism. In *Feminine Psychology.* New York: Norton, 1967, pp. 214–233.
JAFFE, D.S. (1976). The masculine envy of woman's procreative function. *J. Amer. Psychoanal. Assn.,* 24(Suppl.):361–392.
KEMP, P. (1935). *Healing Ritual: Studies in the Technique and Tradition of the Southern Slavs.* London: Faber & Faber.
KULISH N. (1992). The mental representation of the clitoris. *Psychoanal. Inq.,* 11:511–536.
LEDERER, W. (1968). *The Fear of Women.* New York: Harcourt Brace Jovanovich.
LERNER, H.E. (1977). Parental mislabeling of female genitalia as a determinant of penis envy and learning inhibitions in women. In *Female Psychology: Contemporary Psychoanalytic Views,* ed. H. P. Blum. New York: Int. Univ. Press, pp. 269–283.
LEVINE, D.N. (1965). *Wax and Gold: Tradition and Innovation in Ethiopian Culture.* Chicago: Univ. Chicago Press.
LUPTON, M.J. (1993). *Menstruation and Psychoanalysis.* Urbana & Chicago: Univ. Illinois Press.
MALINOWSKI, B. (1929). *The Sexual Life of Savages in Northwestern Melanesia.* New York: Liveright.

MASTERS, W.M. (1953). Rowanda: a Kurdish administrative and mercantile center. Unpublished Ph.D. dissertation. Ann Arbor, MI: University of Michigan.

MAYER, E.L. (1985). Everybody must be just like me: observations of female castration anxiety. *Int. J. Psychoanal.*, 66:331–348.

NUNBERG, H. (1947). Circumcision and problems of bisexuality. *Int. J. Psychoanal.*, 28:145–179.

OVID (1955). *Metamorphoses*, trans. R. Humphies. Bloomington: Indiana Univ. Press.

PARTRIDGE, E. (1958). *Origins: A Short Etymological Dictionary of Modern English*. London: Routledge & Kegan Paul.

PENMAN, S.K. (1991). *The Reckoning*. New York: Ballentine Books.

PETERS, E.L. (1965). Aspects of the family among the Bedouin of Cyrenica. In *Comparative Family Systems*, ed. M. F. Nimkoff. Boston: Houghton Mifflin, pp. 121–146.

RATTRAY, R.S. (1927). *Religion and Art in Ashanti*. Oxford, Eng.: Clarendon Press.

RICHARDS, A.K. (1992). The influence of sphincter control and genital sensation on body image and gender identity in women. *Psychoanal. Q.*, 61:331–351.

RICHARDSON, N.Y., Ed. (1964). *The Homeric Hymn to Demeter*. Oxford, Eng.: Clarendon Press.

ROSE, H.J. (1959). *Religion in Greece and Rome*. New York: Harper & Row.

ROSSETTI, C. (1993). The convent threshold. In *Poems*. New York: Alfred A. Knopf, pp. 111–116.

SAPPHO. Epithalamia. In *Sappho*, trans. M. Barnard. Berkeley: Univ. California Press, 1958.

SISSA, G. (1990). Maidenhood without maidenhead: the female body in ancient Greece. In *Before Sexuality: The Construction of Erotic Experience in the Ancient Greek World*, ed. D. M. Halperin, J. J. Winkler, & F. I. Zietlin. Princeton: Princeton Univ. Press, pp. 339–364.

SJOO, M. & MOR, B. (1987). *The Great Cosmic Mother*. New York: Harper & Row.

STONE, M. (1976). *When God Was a Woman*. New York: Harcourt Brace Jovanovich.

TYSON, P. (1989). Infantile sexuality, gender identity, and obstacles to oedipal progression. *J. Amer. Psychoanal. Assn.*, 37:1051–1069.

YATES, S.L. (1930). An investigation of the psychological factors in virginity and ritual defloration. *Int. J. Psychoanal.*, 11:167–184.

Masturbation Fantasies in a Prelatency Girl: Early Female Body Fantasy Conflicts as a Major Determinant in the Experience of Primary Femininity

Jack Pelaccio

> Material from a child-analytic case is presented demonstrating the way in which a girl created erotic fantasies from her understanding of bodily sensations and used those fantasies in masturbation. The material shows how analysis of early fantasies of this nature helps us to understand and follow a line of development of primary femininity in which core conflicts involving urethral sphincter, periurethral, and bladder sensations combine with genital area sensations in the creation of anxiety over fears of genital injury. The clinical implication of anxiety as the dominant affect early in female development in this case is discussed.

The concept of primary femininity has gained wide acceptance in the psychoanalytic community. From an ego psychology perspective most would readily agree that a girl's sense of herself as female is rooted in her experience of her body. While few would eschew this preeminent importance of a girl's normal experience of conflict and anxiety inherent in the discovery of her female body, many analysts still view the impact on development by these conflicts of primary femininity to be less dramatic and intense than a girl's preoccupation with the desire to have a penis and coming to terms with depressive feelings at lacking one, i.e., the phallic castration complex. Others feel that the aforementioned tenets are not mutually exclusive. Renik (1992) and Mayer (1995) posit two separate lines of development that contribute to the attainment of female gender identity. Debate and discussion have been subject to speculation since it is not until a girl becomes verbal that she can communicate her experience of her body and her fantasies about it. The

---

Faculty in Adult and Child/Adolescent Psychoanalysis, New York University Psychoanalytic Institute.

evidence for differences of opinion between those who believe the female can develop without feeling depressed at lacking a penis and those who claim (Rangell, 1991; Brenner, 1991) that female development does not take place without the dominance of such feelings, has relied heavily on material from adult analyses to provide insights into this conundrum. While work with adult women (Mayer, 1995; Renik, 1992; Tyson, 1994) has furnished constructions and reconstructions of what patients as little girls must have experienced, felt, and fantasized, more information on how children think about their bodies is needed to test our hypotheses.

Material from my analytic work with Sarah, a prelatency girl, provides insights into a girl's way of experiencing herself that may help us in reformulating our theories of female sexual development, and in turn female psychological development. Of the many ideas and fantasies, conscious and unconscious, Sarah and I discovered in our work together, I shall focus on the exploration and analysis of Sarah's theories and fantasies about her body.

In my approach to the study of gender, I agree with Tyson's (Tyson, 1982; Tyson and Tyson, 1990; Tyson, 1994) suggestion to split the subject into gender identity, gender role identity, and sexual partner orientation. Within the area of gender identity we have what Stoller (1976) refers to as "core gender identity," or primary femininity in the girl. We have seen that it is during the latter half of the second year of life that a girl attains a sense of herself as belonging to one sex. This sense of a female self, which occurs so early in development, evolves in a complex, multidetermined fashion as a girl's core emerging ego is derived from her body matrix. Of the various determinants of primary femininity that have been discussed, little evidence has been provided about the nature of early genital area erotic fantasies. The difficulty in obtaining information about erotic fantasies from children is well known. Such fantasies are generally so buried in compromise formations and myriad defenses that only an analytic approach offers any hope of unearthing them. Child-analytic work is unique in its capacity to obtain some understanding of these fantasies.

When I worked with Sarah, my primary intent was to engage her in a progressive analytic process. The method used was the child-analytic technique of engaging her in play by following her directives

Masturbation Fantasies

and interpreting conflicts and defenses. Following the approach of being as nondirective as possible and staying close to the material, Sarah led the way to the exploration of her experiences of erotic bodily feelings which involved a particular interest in urethral sphincter and associated periurethral urogenital sensations. In sessions that involved masturbatory play, her description of these sensations provided a unique look at the way in which a child in stages of early development represents her understanding of her anatomy and bodily sensations in the expression of erotic fantasy. Fantasy and body sensations acted both reciprocally and in tandem in the production of erotic pleasure. Sarah's fantasies stimulated by her bodily feelings were joined by other fantasies/theories about whether she had had a penis and lost it or had one inside of her which would someday appear. Her response to her father's penis as an erotic object was also elaborated upon and explored.

Whether the nature of the fantasies Sarah reported are typical for girls her age is not known. We do not possess enough data on verbally communicated erotic fantasies of children to make a case for a general theory about the way in which a girl's fantasy life evolves early on in development. I think that my work with Sarah from age three years, seven months till six years, ten months contributes some understanding about how a girl experiences her body, has erotic fantasies about it, and applies this internal matrix of self-experience to complex oedipal fantasies. Sarah communicated certain consistent core fantasies and feelings which emerged as an ongoing nexus of ideas in which genital area conflicts involving anxiety at the threat of genital injury were a dominant influence on her development.

EROTIC FANTASY IN MASTURBATION

Masturbation combines experiences of stimulating body fantasies with stimulating object fantasies in the construction of the erotic event. The working definition of masturbation used in this paper is that suggested by Clower (1976), i.e., "stimulation of the genital zone with the conscious or unconscious aim of self-arousal, characterized by mounting excitement where seeking pleasure predominates over exploring." The practice of masturbation while essentially

Jack Pelaccio

driven from inside by the pleasure principle in response to the maturing body ego, can also be stirred by external erotic influences. The primal scene is such an influence as it conveys a stimulating erotic engagement to the observing child. While her parents stated that Sarah never witnessed their sexual activity, there was in the material a great deal of evidence to the contrary. It is most likely that episodes of overstimulation resulted in Sarah choosing primal scene-like fantasies at times in masturbatory play, but it is not clear how much she saw and how much she fantasized. Also unclear is to what degree her synthesis of what she witnessed directed or influenced her fantasies when combined with her understanding of bodily feelings and sensations from inside. It is probable that the reason Sarah made so much erotic material available for analysis was because she was an overstimulated child. Defenses against erotic bodily expression were overwhelmed. She fashioned many stimulating fantasies to respond to the drive to create pleasurable bodily sensations. Her masturbatory play was the enactment and expression of the excitement she sought.

The masturbation fantasies described by Sarah were a combination of anal and phallic phase fantasies. How commonly girls of her age combine urethral and anal sphincter conflicts with genital area sensations in the creation of a masturbation fantasy is a question that deserves further analytic study.

What did emerge as an important insight into early female development was the discovery of the way in which a child synthesizes erotic fantasies in terms of multiphasic determinants. When Sarah began masturbating by touching her genital area, it was not genital structures she described in her body fantasies. She summoned fantasies that involved familiar prephallic urethral and occasionally anal sensations which were of an erotic nature. Sarah masturbated by pressing her hands against her genitals while playing out the fantasy that she was holding back a powerful urge to urinate. The feelings she described were those created by first playing that she held back the urge to "pee," then almost releasing control against intensifying waves of urgency till she ultimately gave in as if she were releasing control of her urethral sphincter. Sarah's revelations direct us to think of the development of erotic sensations with accompanying conflicts and anxiety as an emerging mosaic of overlapping anatomical/physiological influences from different phases of development.

Masturbation Fantasies

This mosaic which develops in a multi-foci fashion, as its elements differentiate to maturity, accounts for the diversity of body sensations and erotic fantasies in the mature, adult woman.

Sarah's masturbatory play was the enactment of a fantasy. There was no evidence that Sarah actually had to urinate, nor did she do so following the play. Richards (1992) wrote about the contraction of urethral and anal sphincter and perineal musculature as a preferred method of masturbation in some girls. Bass (1994) in his illuminating paper about aspects of urethral erotism explores the many ways urethral stimulation is experienced in female development. Sarah employed as her body fantasy the erotic bodily feelings produced by the buildup of sensations, produced by (as she called it) "holding it in." She combined this fantasy with various others. These masturbatory fantasies were always enactments structured around or derived from intense feelings of urogenital pain and pleasure. Although it was not clear from which specific structure or location in her genital area Sarah actually derived the sensations, the source of the feelings she identified as causing the sensations were those she described as produced by "holding back" a full bladder; they were always the core of the fantasy. A thorough and detailed developmental history revealed what seemed to have been a normal toilet training experience. There were no indications that the training had been conducted in an overly demanding or traumatic manner.

The material of Sarah's analysis is presented as an assemblage of notions about her body as they appeared in more or less patchwork fashion during our analytic work. It is in chronological order so as to reflect her developmental advancement. Her masturbatory play, while present early in the analysis, became more explicit as the analysis advanced.

CASE PRESENTATION

Sarah, an intelligent and verbal girl, was in analysis for three years and three months. She was three years, seven months old when we started. Her parents brought her for treatment because they found her behavior intolerable and she had become "nearly impossible to live with." The shift to such behavior, highlighted by the absolute refusal to obey her parents, took place several months before the birth of her sister. Until that time Sarah had enjoyed the special position of the much desired first child.

Since infancy her mother had attended to her daughter's every need immediately, without fail. When Sarah woke up at night, her mother hurried to her, nursed her, and took her into her bed. Within her first few months of life Sarah started sleeping in her parents' bed nightly. In her second year, Sarah's father, an easygoing, amiable man, somewhat passive in his approach to family conflicts, began sleeping in another room, leaving Sarah and her mother to share the bed until the birth of her baby sister, Lisa. Sarah's father seemed content to accede to the mother's parenting decisions. He enjoyed a close relationship with his daughter, but often drifted to the periphery when Sarah and her mother engaged in some disagreement.

According to her parents they waited to institute toilet training until Sarah signaled she was ready. Toilet training was accomplished "without a struggle," just before age three, by talking to her about using the small potty placed in the bathroom and "encouraging" her to wear underpants during the day and diapering her at night. At the beginning of treatment, Sarah began to ask her mother to wipe her after bowel movements. Soon thereafter, Sarah cleaned herself without her mother's aid.

As the birth of Lisa approached and then after the baby's birth, when Sarah was three years, three months old, Sarah's relationship with her mother became increasingly dominated by struggles and standoffs. She insisted on doing "whatever she wanted," and if denied, had "screaming fits." These episodes were usually an escalation of some disagreement with her mother. Sarah's mother could no longer tolerate "giving in" to her daughter in order to avoid Sarah's apoplectic tantrums, and worried that she would ruin their relationship by having to punish Sarah constantly for misbehaving.

Sarah's family lived in a one-bedroom apartment with one bathroom. Both children slept in the bedroom, Lisa in a crib and Sarah sometimes in her own bed, but usually in bed with her mother. The parents felt privacy was important, and made efforts to keep bathroom use and sexual activity private. It was apparent though from what she reported that Sarah was witness to both.

Masturbation Fantasies

When we started our work Sarah was pressured and impatient. She had to have things her way without exception. She was always ready for a fight with me, just as she had been with her mother. The analysis of her struggles with her parents and me gradually led to the discovery of worries and conflicts involving control of her bodily sensations. First, we uncovered worries she had about "bad" feelings she got when we played that we were scared. We pretended we were afraid of being punished because we were "bad" for peeing on the floor. In subsequent sessions the police came when someone "peed" or "pooped" in their pants. As we talked about how kids might feel bad about these bodily experiences, I pointed out Sarah's worries about controlling her "peeing and pooping" feelings.

Three months into the analysis, when Sarah was three years, ten months old, she pointed out the anatomical differences between boys and girls. I played a boy and Sarah told me that I had a penis and was to use the boys' bathroom. She and a monkey puppet played girls. She said that they had vaginas and used the girls' bathroom.

A month later, we played that the big bad wolf ate my penis and I had to feel sad because I could not "pee pee or poopy." In addition to the implied sad feelings about losing a penis, I noted both the value Sarah placed on being able to urinate and defecate and her awareness of those bodily feelings. Next, Sarah played that she and the puppet lost their noses and were trying to find them. I thought at first that the play represented Sarah's belief that she had once had and then lost a penis. I found out later that this fantasy was only one of a number of theories she came up with to explain genital differences.

In the fifth month of analysis she created triangular play by having us follow the script of the Disney Film, *The Little Mermaid*. Sarah played Ariel, who was in love with Eric. She overcame obstacles posed by a maternal rival and seemed to be in a state of arousal as she kissed Prince Eric (played by the puppet). She pretended that she and Eric were married and that they shared the bathroom. She played that they had to urinate, and held their genitals to help them "hold it in." Sarah clarified their sexual differences, stating that Eric had a penis and she had a vagina. When they went to bed at night, Sarah swung her leg over the puppet and pressed her genitals against it before rolling off. These scenes were the first ones that combined in fantasy the sensations of having to urinate with genital area sensations. These bodily sensations were in turn linked with fantasies of being married and going to bed together.

After a break following the first six months of analysis, Sarah was angry at me for being away. We played that girls get spanked by their fathers when they cannot hold in their "pee." Sarah would lie on the carpet, press her genitals into it, and act as if she were in pain when trying to "hold it in"; then she would die when she could not "hold it" any longer. She repeated this play over and over. In a subsequent session we played repeatedly that a toy horse had to go "pee pee" because she "tickled" his penis. The horse "peed" on the floor because it could not "hold it" any longer. We also often played that Sarah tried to get to a toilet but "peed" on the front of the bowl before she could get on it. In dramatic fashion, she delighted in acting as a girl who felt intense pain (she moaned) and pressure to urinate and was about to lose control.

The aforementioned masturbation fantasies consistently involved sensations which Sarah implied as originating from the urethral sphincter and periurethral musculature. At times she pressed her hands against her genital area, but whether she were feeling clitoral, labial, or vaginal sensations was not clear. Perhaps some would regard Sarah's reports of urethral stimulation as a regressive form of masturbation or as a sexual perversion *in statu nascendi*. Yet, it seems more accurate in a girl of Sarah's age to understand what she labeled specifically as the "holding in and letting go" bladder/urethral erotic feelings as a multidetermined primary body fantasy, a mental representation constructed from the confluence of genital area sensations that precede later-stage identification of distinct anatomical structures as sources of these sensations. To call her masturbatory behavior "regressive" or a "perversion" would require that we subscribe to the notion that specific dynamic influences (e.g., intense anxiety from traumatic toilet training, possibly combined with threats of maternal abandonment) created an "erotization" of anxiety, which became attached to urinary-tract sensations resulting in a deviation from the path of normal development. Even if there were evidence of such specific dynamics in Sarah's case, which there did not appear to be, the concept of the erotization of anxiety involving fusion of exciting feelings with anxious ones that can be displaced from one body area to another, cannot be viewed in early

Masturbation Fantasies

female development as taking place between clearly delineated body areas in a fixed dynamic relationship. There is so much flux in the child's experience of genital area body sensations that it is more likely that many foci are primary sources of erotic or protoerotic sensations assembled in idiosyncratic fashion as a child's experience of her body becomes a fantasy that is reworked and reshaped during development. We do not know enough about the timing of the appearance of a child's body fantasies or the way in which body sensations become erotic mental representations at these early stages of development to accurately label an erotic fantasy as a regression or a perversion, or to predict whether a perversion will appear in the future. The kinds of ideas Sarah described might well be typical of the manner in which children put together mental representations in the normal progression of development. What was atypical about Sarah was that she was overexcited, overstimulated, and therefore unable to contain the intensity of her responses to erotic, pleasurable sensations. In a child not as stimulated we might expect more suppression of affect derived from erotic sensations, although the body fantasies about the sources of stimulation could be quite similar.

Around the time Sarah turned four, she told me again that "boys have penises and girls have vaginas." She was curious about the genital differences and offered various theories to explain it. She stated that in girls the penis was "inside," and that "some day it comes out." An idea she had was that the girls' "penis inside" might be located in her "culie" (Sarah's word for anus). When fantasies about being sick came up repeatedly in association with not having a penis, I commented that girls sometimes worry about something being wrong with them when they see they don't have a penis. I said that, because I thought at that point that Sarah believed she would someday grow a penis, but was losing confidence in her theory (we would call her theory a defense, a defense which was weakening). I thought she felt bad about not having a penis as her theory/defense was dissolving. While I could indeed see that Sarah worried about something being wrong with her, I think my interpretation was misleading. My comment focused on a missing penis as the cause of her worries about something being wrong with her, while the cause of her worries would have been more accurately described, as I later understood, as fear of genital injury. I believe this is true because I soon discovered that her interest in genitals included touching her own, which brought pleasure and consistently stirred guilt-driven fantasies of punishment of either being hurt (genitally injured) or dying. I do not think feeling sick represented feeling bad at not having something. Rather, feeling sick represented the anxiety Sarah felt at experiencing forbidden pleasurable sensations.

The fact that Sarah felt conflict over the erotic—or protoerotic—urethral sphincter feelings as the source of pleasure implies that unconscious erotic fantasies involving early-phase sphincter conflicts of holding back and letting go may play a role in later conflicts involving the female experience of genital pleasure and orgasm.

At eight months into the analysis (following my summer vacation) Sarah told me that I was bad for going on vacation. She punished me by having me play that she scared me so much I "peepeed" in my pants. We later played that we "peed" in our pants when "witches" scared us in the night. Having already established that "pee feelings" represented genital-area excitement, I now saw a link between being scared and being sexually excited.

Triangular relationships occurred increasingly in our play. We pretended that Sarah, playing "Mommy," sent me, the child, into another room while she slept with "Daddy." Sarah noticed my wedding ring and became jealous. We played that she came to my house and stabbed my wife with a sword, after which worries of genital injury emerged. Meanwhile, her mother reported that Sarah had become frightened of ghosts and of being alone in the bathroom. We played that the monkey puppet (cast as a girl) had to worry about genital injury as she was forced to sit on the toilet and "pee" while "sparks went up her vagina." I saw that the pleasurable bodily feelings of "holding it in" were linked with oedipal wishes, and that the punishment for these was injury while urinating, injury to the offender's vagina.

Sarah's ideas of injury to her genital at the time of heightening oedipal fantasies paralleled and seemed driven by heightened pleasurable urogenital sensations. It seems plausible that Sarah's ideas of injury to her vagina, seen in the oedipal phase, represented a developmental continuum of earlier-phase worries of urogenital injury as punishment for similar "bad" protoerotic sensations which were present before the appearance of triangular fantasies. It is in

Masturbation Fantasies

attempts at toilet training that the "badness" of the act of losing control of sphincters is linked to conflict represented by body fantasies derived from body sensations that are experienced as erotic by the child.

Sarah revealed some more ideas she had about her genitals when she became interested in playing a game in which we named different parts of the body. She told me that her vagina was "in front," adding, "the pee comes from there [she pointed]." She then said, "But where it is," and added, "It's inside."

Following a vacation break during which Sarah had been punished for having insisted on sitting between her parents in the front seat of the car, we played that Sarah was the "good child" who got everything she wanted, while another child interrupted parents and acted badly by going into the bathroom with "Daddy." When her parents decided to take a vacation (their first ever overnight separation from the children), Sarah experienced fears of abandonment. She was Alice as we played *Alice in Wonderland*. Our play was filled with worry about the consequences of "being bad."

With oedipal conflicts intensifying, Sarah turned her attention to birth theories. She became interested in studying a book written for children which used illustrations to explain the internal organs. She was curious about where babies came from. She played waking at night and exploring in the dark while worrying about running into ghosts and witches. She said, "I know babies grow in the mommies' tummies, but how do they get there? Do they crawl up there?" Sarah asked her mother, "When are you going to have another egg?" When we played "shadows in the night" with the lights turned out, everyone drank hot chocolate and "Mommy had a big cup and her tummy got very full." Sarah's understanding of the inside of her body and how it produced a baby was derived from her understanding of familiar bodily feelings.

We began playing that we had to go "pee-pee and poopy" and were not able to hold it in. The kids whispered back and forth about what they did. Then "Daddy" had to question them and asked them if they went in their pants. They denied it, but the progress in the analysis of defenses concerning ideas and feelings about her body led Sarah to reveal how "kids" sometimes touch themselves around where they "pee," and get "pee feelings" there. We played that it

Jack Pelaccio

"gets wet there," and that it "didn't feel good," so the "kids" had to go to the hospital to see the doctor. I pointed out that the "kids" worried that they had hurt themselves by touching themselves. The worry of genital injury as punishment for creating genital sensations was a conflict consistently repeated. We played out many versions of these masturbatory conflicts which had created intense anxiety. It was central in the working-through process of analysis.

Sarah expressed more theories about how she came to have her genital. She had us play that we were making up the boy puppet to look like a girl. She said that he now had a vagina instead of a penis. I commented that sometimes girls think they were boys first and then turned into girls. Sarah responded, "Yes they do!" She explained to me excitedly that first girls have a penis and then it goes away. "It just goes away," she smiled, "It's magic, it goes away by magic." In a subsequent session Sarah played that she "ate Daddy's penis" and grew her own. She said, "I'm a girl with a penis, not a boy." In this series of sessions Sarah stated that she wanted a penis because she "liked" penises. We played that "Mommy" gave her (Mommy's) penis to the puppet (who played a girl). When I told Sarah that I wondered about Mommy having a penis, she whispered in the manner of an aside that Mommy had a penis in her underwear. When I commented to Sarah that girls sometimes think that when they grow up that they will grow a penis, she replied, "Yes," rather matter-of-factly. I was impressed by the enthusiasm and excitement she demonstrated in her search for the right explanation.

Sarah next became intensely interested in seeing my penis. As we played, she asked me why I was sitting with my legs spread apart. She told me that her father sat that way when he wore shorts such that she saw his penis. She then pretended she had a penis. She took a nipple of a baby bottle, held it against her genital area, and pretended to urinate through the nipple in this position. She laughed, said she was a girl with a penis, and pranced around the room. I commented on the defense of reversal by saying that now I was the one interested in her "penis." She sucked on the nipple, commenting that it tasted good. Then she said that she had to run away from her mother because her mother would throw her in jail when she found out Sarah had a penis. Her interest in penises was intense and was expressed in play many times. She was particularly

Masturbation Fantasies

interested in creating exciting scenes in which the children could sneak a peek at Daddy's penis.

As we moved into the seventeenth month of analysis Sarah had her fifth birthday. She was increasingly interested in play that specifically involved bodily feelings associated with the act of holding back the urge to urinate. She experienced intense pleasure playing that she had to "pee" as she lay on the floor on her abdomen, writhing in pretend pain in an excited, exaggerated way. In a subsequent session Sarah's masturbatory practices became more explicit. She rubbed her genitals while leaning back on a pillow, moaning while she expressed both worries and excitement about not being able to "hold it in." Sarah created a scene where I, as father, was in the bathroom making her wait outside the door, while she had to urinate and strained to "hold it in." She held her hands on her genital and said she was touching her vagina. I pointed out to her that sometimes children touch themselves there because it feels good, even when they don't have to go to the bathroom. Not responding to my comment, she continued to press her hands against her genitals, telling me to pretend that the door of the bathroom was open and she could "see Daddy's penis." She smiled and said his penis was "very interesting." Another masturbatory scene included fantasies of being scared in addition to being excited in scenes that took place during the night. The play emphasized scary excitement associated with "holding it in." Sarah turned the office lights off and created a charged atmosphere in which she masturbated by pressing her hands on her genital area. I commented to Sarah that sometimes kids see Mommy and Daddy in the night. "They look like skeletons," she replied. I then pointed out that kids sometimes find getting scared kind of exciting and get feelings like they have to pee. Sarah then had me play "Daddy," who made her wait outside the door as she strained to "hold in" her "pee-pee." She pressed her hands against her genitals to "hold it in" as before, while "looking at Daddy's penis." Her father's penis was consistently the object of erotic stimulation in these masturbatory scenarios. The pain/pleasure of holding it in was an important component in heightening the intensity of the scene. This fusion of feelings of pain and pleasure of the urethral sphincter and genital area sensations gave a sadomasochistic quality to the erotic experience.

Jack Pelaccio

Sarah continued to create play in which she would get excited and feign anxiety. They were games of scaring and being scared. Again and again she played that she had to "poop and pee," but could not for some reason, and had to hold it in. In some scenes she held it in till she "exploded," died, and went to heaven where she was alone, separated from her parents. Then she would magically return and do it all over again. The intensity of Sarah's masturbatory experiences grew. Once she rubbed her genitals against the arm of the chair until she collapsed in exhaustion. I pointed out that sometimes girls get certain feelings when they have to go "pee-pee." She said, "in their vaginas, they're yucky feelings."

When Sarah's play returned to what seemed to be the repeated enactment of primal scene experiences, I asked Sarah if she had sometimes seen her parents doing the things she talked about. She said she had watched them "hugging and peeing and pooping on each other." She worried that "Mommy would be mad" at her. Sarah's worries about her mother being angry could be understood as an expression of her guilt at becoming excited by what she witnessed. Guilt and anxiety again were in evidence when she had us play that "Daddy peed and pooped" on the kids. In this incest fantasy, the kids died and went to heaven, and could not return till "Mommy and Daddy cried," and "Daddy promised that he would no longer be bad."

Primal scene exposure appeared to stimulate play in which "the kids" filmed "Mommy and Daddy" in their "private place" in the living room, where they "hugged and peed and pooped" while making moaning sounds. Sarah's description of sexual intercourse as "hugging and peeing and pooping on each other" was derived from the lasting impression of confluent erotic urethral, anal, and genital bodily sensations. Whereas she talked about defecation in her references to the primal scene ideas, in her masturbatory play Sarah usually talked only of having intense feelings from the urge to urinate. She never mentioned anything specifically about holding back solely the urge to defecate.

Sarah was five years seven months old as we entered the twenty-third month of analysis. We played that Sarah died after touching herself on the "vagina" and "peed." Her masturbation fantasies began to emphasize secrecy. She played out the fantasy that she was

Masturbation Fantasies

well hidden as she experienced intense pleasure/pain sensations by "holding it in" while observing her father expose his penis as he urinated in the bathroom. She said she had to make sure that her mother did not see her, since she would punish Sarah if she discovered these secret feelings. We played that while I, a little boy, slept, I urinated in my pants. I had to pretend I did not feel it, but woke up and felt wet. I commented that when kids touch themselves at night in bed sometimes it feels to them like they peed. Sarah replied, "Don't talk." A few sessions later Sarah wrote "private thoughts" (I was not allowed to see them) in her "girls' diary." She wrote down rules that prohibited "peeing in one's pants." Her struggles over masturbation pitted her excitement and pleasurable feelings against the "rules." The onset of latency-style defenses coincided with Sarah's parents' move to new, more spacious living quarters with increased privacy. There was a decrease in play having to do with ideas about masturbation and enactments of masturbation fantasies. Sarah's overall behavior improved greatly. She became cooperative with her mother, performed extremely well in school, and made many friends. We agreed on a termination date three months away and reached it as planned.

DISCUSSION

I have explored ideas that may help us to better understand the interplay of conflict and bodily feelings in early female development. Child observation studies of preverbal children have helped us put together a compelling theory of the way in which core gender identity emerges from early body experiences by the second year. These studies do not tell us, however, how a girl assembles mental representations of her body, body fantasies, and derives affects from conflicts involving these fantasies. As a girl acquires words to describe her experiences and fantasies of herself, analysis brings into view her unobservable psychic reality. Sarah had much to tell us. We saw the importance she placed on intense bodily feelings she perceived as originating from the act of "holding it in." She derived sexual pleasure from these feelings by fantasizing that she had to hold back the painful/pleasurable urge to urinate. Her placement in fantasy of

Jack Pelaccio

these bodily genital-area sensations in the urinary tract during the phallic phase of development is a finding that helps us conceptualize the manner in which girls interpret urogenital sensations and derive erotic fantasies from them in early development. What we learned from Sarah can contribute to a general theory of female development in orienting us to explore a female's body fantasies with new insight into their derivation.

The developmental importance in a female of the affect of anxiety generated by conflicts involving pleasurable urogenital sensations and fear of genital injury was consistently demonstrated in Sarah's analysis. From age three and a half to six, she demonstrated fear that her genital or genital area might be injured as she experienced conflict and guilt over urogenital sensations. From earlier anal-phase enactments of "pooping and peeing" to later-phase enactments of explicit oedipal masturbation fantasies, there was a predominance of anxiety attached to the aforementioned body conflicts.

It was notable that she did not demonstrate appreciable depressive affect at the idea of not having a penis. Sarah did not appear to feel diminished or depressed in her thoughts about not having a penis. She did appear intensely curious about the genital differences between the sexes, and presented many fantasies about her genital anatomy. She came up with various explanations of why she did not have a penis, like the idea that it disappeared by magic, or the idea that she had a penis inside that would someday grow out. She did not seem depressed by her conclusions.

Sarah regarded her father's penis as a stimulating erotic object to which she responded with intense erotic urogenital sensations. Her anxiety over guilt from these sensations, rather than depression at the notion of having been castrated, was the dominant affect that emerged in the analytic process. The material of Sarah's analysis points to the importance of exploring urinary/anal sphincter and genital-area anxiety in our female patients since both areas appear to be involved in creating this dominant affectual line of development in the conflicts of primary femininity.

Sarah's body fantasies were those of an overstimulated child. Children not exposed to overstimulation would express the experience of their bodies in a less intensely erotic fashion. I feel they would, however, be presented with the kinds of body sensations

Sarah described, and similarly construct psychic representations of conflicts derived from these perceptions. Because there is reason to believe that the developing female psyche is influenced primarily by such conflicts and concerns, an appreciation of this primary line of development should help orient our thinking in analytic work with women. I am not implying a diminution in the importance of the influence of conflicts and depressive affect that may be created by phallic castration fantasies in some or many females. My findings with Sarah, however, highlight the dramatic differences in the degree of influence on a girl's developing psychology between feelings and fantasies derived from a girl's body matrix and ideas and theories she constructs to explain why her body is different from a boy's. In every case we treat we may seek and explore the influence of these fantasies and theories informed by the data psychoanalytic work with children provides.

CONCLUSION

Child analysis enables us to unlock and explore the early fantasy world of the developing female. The fantasies of young girls are products of nascent egos derived from and responding to bodily feelings and sensations in the context of equally powerful influencing object relations. It is by discovering these fantasies that child-analytic work can test and confirm our theories of female psychological development. Only a thorough understanding of this early fantasy life will enable us to comprehend and analyze the derivative vestiges that make up conflicts and compromise formations which appear disguised and defended later in life.

REFERENCES

Bass, A. (1994). Aspects of urethrality in women. *Psychoanal. Q.*, 63:491–517.

Brenner, C. (1991). A psychoanalytic perspective on depression. *J. Amer. Psychoanal. Assn.*, 39:25–44.

Clower, V.L. (1976). Theoretical implications of masturbation in latency girls. *J. Amer. Psychoanal. Assn.*, 24 (Suppl.):109–126.

Mayer, E.L. (1995). The phallic castration complex and primary femininity: paired developmental lines toward female gender identity. *J. Amer. Psychoanal. Assn.*, 43:17–36.

Rangell, L. (1991). Castration. *J. Amer. Psychoanal. Assn.*, 39:3–24.
Renik, O. (1992). A case of premenstrual distress: bisexual determinants of a woman's fantasy of damage to her genital. *J. Amer. Psychoanal. Assn.*, 40:195–210.
Richards, A.K. (1992). The influence of sphincter control and genital sensation on body image and gender identity in women. *Psychoanal. Q.*, 61:331–351.
Stoller, R.J. (1976). Primary femininity. *J. Amer. Psychoanal. Assn.*, 24:59–78.
Tyson, P. (1982). A developmental line of gender identity, gender role, and choice of love object. *J. Amer. Psychoanal. Assn.*, 30:61–86.
—— (1994). Bedrock and beyond: an examination of the clinical utility of contemporary theories of female psychology. *J. Amer. Psychoanal. Assn.*, 42:447–468.
—— & Tyson, R.L. (1990). *Psychoanalytic Theories of Development.* New Haven, CT: Yale Univ. Press.

A Revised Psychoanalytic View of Menopause

Sandra Bemesderfer

> The traditional psychoanalytic view of menopause regards it as inevitably accompanied by reactive depression resulting from the loss of reproductive function. This view is grounded on a theory of female sexual development that stresses the centrality of the phallic castration complex. The inevitable menopausal depression involves a remobilization of this complex and a reexperiencing of castration fears. The new view, based on the concept of primary feminine identity, complements the concept of a phallic castration complex with the related concept of female castration anxiety. In this view menopause, though it typically involves physical discomfort and a reworking of maternal identification, involves an interplay of both types of castration fears. By understanding and analyzing these fears, progressive adaptation to menopause, including the opportunity for enhanced creativity and emotional fulfillment, is possible. A clinical case example is presented to illustrate these ideas.

Early psychoanalytic writers about menopause[1] such as Deutsch (1924) assumed that the end of child-bearing capacity was inevitably accompanied by depression. More recently, Lax (1982) presented a version of this idea as the basic psychoanalytic view of menopause. However, it is contradicted both by empirical data which establish that depression is more common among women in their twenties and thirties than among menopausal women (Rosenthal, 1983) and other studies showing that for a significant fraction of

---

Member, San Francisco Psychoanalytic Institute.

[1] I use "menopause" in its popular sense, as embracing the entire period from the onset of symptoms ("peri-menopause") through the complete cessation of bleeding (menopause in the literal sense). The less familiar clinical term "climacterium" denotes the *process* of psychological and biological change that occurs most commonly between the ages of forty-five and fifty-five. In this paper, when I refer to menopause I generally mean the entire process of change. Where I mean literal menopause, I believe the context will make it clear.

women, menopause is accompanied by an increased feeling of well-being rather than by sadness (Notman, 1984) and that perhaps as few as 10 percent of all women going through menopause find it an exceptionally stressful or upsetting experience (McKinlay et al., 1987). Other researchers respond that these studies fail to differentiate adequately between clinical depression and transient depressive mood; between natural and surgical menopause; and between life stressors such as aging, children leaving home, the death of friends and relatives, and hormonally induced mood changes (see, e.g., Tobias and Lewis, 1993). In summary, it appears that while transient depressive moods are common among perimenopausal women, clinical depression is rare among postmenopausal women.[2]

The early view has remained formative in psychoanalytic theory and clinical practice. This paper reconsiders menopause in light of new psychoanalytic ideas about primary feminine identity. I argue that menopause is a developmental phase during which significant changes in physiology imply concurrent changes in conscious and unconscious self-assessment and fantasy. In particular, the emotional experience of menopause typically involves two types of castration fears, both the classical phallic castration complex elaborated by Deutsch, and the feminine castration anxiety described by Mayer (1985). Finally, I suggest that for many women menopause represents an opportunity for expanded creativity and emotional fulfillment.

The aim of this paper is to show how the new ideas about female psychology modify the traditional view of menopause, and to illustrate with a case example how these ideas can be usefully applied in a clinical setting.

THEORETICAL BASIS OF THE TRADITIONAL VIEW

Existing psychoanalytic perspectives on menopause have been well summarized by Harris (1990), whose thoughtful discussion I paraphrase in the balance of this section. The traditional perspectives

---

[2]Most of the studies cited above have drawn their subjects from self-referred populations of middle-class women of European descent. While it is beyond the scope of this paper to consider menopause from a cross-cultural perspective, studies of women from other backgrounds suggest that the experience of menopause is, to

A Revised Psychoanalytic View of Menopause

assume that depression is an inevitable consequence of menopause. The classical view is epitomized by Deutsch's (1924) statement that "Woman's last traumatic experience as a sexual being, the menopause, is under the aegis of an incurable narcissistic wound." This view identifies menopause with the loss of childbearing capacity and, by implication, the corresponding loss of ability to create a penis substitute. Although Deutsch later revised some of her views, her interpretation of the meaning of menopause was based entirely on the stages of psychosexual development described by Freud (1905). The course of menopause was determined wholly by the vicissitudes of libidinal development. As Freud (1937) wrote:

> Twice in the course of individual development certain instincts are considerably reinforced: at puberty and, in women, at the menopause. We are not in the least surprised if a person who was not neurotic before became so at these times. When his instincts were not so strong, he succeeded in taming them; but when they are reinforced, he can no longer do so [p. 226].

These remarks summarized views Freud had first set forth in 1912:

> [M]ore or less sudden increases of libido . . . are habitually associated with puberty and the menopause—with the attainment of a certain age in women. . . . Here the damming-up of the libido is the primary factor; it becomes pathogenic as a consequence of a *relative* frustration on the part of the external world, which would still have granted satisfaction to a smaller claim by the libido. The unsatisfied and dammed-up libido can once again open up paths to regression . . . [p. 236].

Following the Freudian example, Deutsch broadly analogizes puberty and menopause, linking them both to the concept of regression to infantile libidinal positions. In contrast to puberty, according to Deutsch, the libido at menopause goes into reverse "because of the impossibility of genital 'catharsis.' " There is an extended struggle because of the forward thrust of the libido during puberty as compared with its backward movement at menopause, with the menopausal woman attempting to retain all the values of puberty just at a time when the ultimate "devaluation of the genitals as an organ of reproduction" is immanent. Fantasy productions are said

---

some degree, culturally determined. See, for example, the studies of menopause among South American Indian and Greek women by Beyene (1989).

to be similar at puberty and menopause, with fantasies of rape and prostitution occurring at both times. At menopause, depression is the result of the "irrevocable blow to female narcissism" induced by the "remobilized castration complex."

Lax (1982) views psychological dimensions such as self-image and ego interests in the light of "phase-specific psychological changes." During the climacteric, a number of interrelated factors will determine a woman's response to this phase of life. Lax writes:

> The manner and extent to which a woman responds to the climacteric will depend on the severity of her physiological symptoms, the nature of past experience, her internalized object relations, her psychic structure, the strength of her libidinal investments, the width of her conflict-free ego sphere, the nature and strength of her ego interests, the extent of her healthy narcissism, the nature of her current object relations, and the nature of her familial and social setting [p. 157].

Although each woman's reaction to menopause will differ based on the factors listed above, Lax argues that depression[3] is the "expectable" reaction to the climacteric. In contrast to Deutsch, for whom menopause necessarily implied clinical depression, Lax argues that menopause is typically accompanied by a decline in the sense of well-being caused by a woman having to accept a loss of function over which she has no control. Anger becomes directed toward the deflated, failing self with an accompanying loss of self-esteem and shame. A sense of loss is expressed in mourning for the youthful self of one's past. The awareness that one is no longer able to bear children frequently induces either a conscious or unconscious depression. However, Lax also introduces the idea of a positive outcome from this situation if the woman works through her mourning process. She may then develop an identification with an idealized matriarchal model, "whose characteristics of generativity, generosity and compassion become her own goals." Object relations are enriched by such a working through.

Benedek (1948) allows for the possibility that depression, while an aspect of menopause for some women, is not inevitable for all.

---

[3] In a personal communication to the author, Dr. Lax indicated that if she were revising her paper today she would replace the word "depression" with "sadness" or some equivalent term that does not carry the implication of clinical depression.

A Revised Psychoanalytic View of Menopause

Unlike Deutsch, Benedek takes note of empirical data that indicate that as many as 85 percent of women pass through menopause without undue distress. She also notes contemporary research on the effects of hormone production on emotion and concludes that "the woman reaches the highest level of her psychosexual integration at the height of her hormonal cycle." Like Deutsch, Benedek also finds analogies between puberty and menopause, advancing the idea that the climacterium causes a woman to reexperience "emotional tensions originating in the conflicts of feminine development." Although Benedek herself did not fully develop this linkage between the unavoidable natural changes in reproductive capacity and feminine identity, it constitutes a pathbreaking insight into the nature of menopause from a psychoanalytic perspective. Nonetheless, it requires updating in light of more recent understanding of normal female development.

THEORETICAL BASIS OF A REVISED VIEW

The new viewpoint begins by challenging the Freudian notion that normal female development is a reaction to the girl's discovery that she lacks a penis, i.e., that normal female development is actually and metaphorically derivative of male development. This account is increasingly being questioned on both empirical and theoretical grounds. Blum (1977) collected a volume of papers by a diverse group of authors who, while sharply disagreeing among themselves about the mechanism of female development, unanimously reject the traditional Freudian view. Stoller's (1975) studies of the development of gender identity in transsexuals led him to propose a primary feminine identity in both genders, an idea that accords with the observation that every child's first intense emotional relationship is with its mother. Mayer's (1985) insightful observations of female children led her to propose that girls have a "primary feminine identity" made manifest in what she terms "female castration anxiety," as distinguished from the classical "phallic castration complex." Female castration anxiety has its roots in the girl's belief that her genitalia are special and precious and that she might be deprived of them by having herself "sealed up" as she imagines boys are. The phallic castration complex, as elaborated by Freud, consists in the girl's belief that she has already been deprived of the external genitalia she observes in boys, i.e., she has been castrated. Although as Renik (1992) points out, these differing castration fears may alternate or coexist within one individual, female castration anxiety is present, to a greater or lesser degree, in all normal female development.[4]

From the classical standpoint, the fantasy of prior castration is a key determinant of female development. Imagining that she has lost her penis, the girl attempts to make up for that loss by identifying with her mother, acquiring a male companion, and ultimately acquiring a penis substitute in the form of a child. In the newer view of female development, the girl also identifies with her mother, not by joining her in an association of the maimed, but rather by observing the ways in which she increasingly resembles her mother. This identification is dramatically confirmed through the fact of menstruation, when the girl sees herself becoming like her mother in this very important way. A clear implication of this view is that the prototypical experience of the onset of menstruation is not a confirmation of the phallic castration complex (blood = evidence of having been mutilated) but rather a confirmation of primary feminine identity (blood = proof that everything is working as it should and fears of being asexual or defeminized are groundless). From this point of view, the onset of menstruation, though it may be accompanied by physical discomfort, is primarily a positive experience that validates the girl's prepubertal expectations of adult femininity and relieves her anxieties about her inner workings. Just as no woman goes through puberty without intense self-examination in the face of new experiences of her physical being, no woman goes through menopause without similar self-examination. Although the analogy can be overdrawn, the experiences of puberty and menopause have much in common. At both times, there are erratic changes in hormone production; labile emotional states; flushed skin; weight gain; changes in breast, hip, and buttock size and shape; and an intense

---

[4]Mayer also suggests that even when the girl is still too young to conceptualize a vagina and the other internal female organs, the ovaries and the uterus, she still experiences her genitals as having an opening and a potential inner space. Infant and toddler research reported by Roiphe (1981) has confirmed that girls discover their genitalia and their interior spaces by age two.

A Revised Psychoanalytic View of Menopause

dream life. Both phases are also most often discussed primarily in terms of these "symptoms."[5] Most important, from the present point of view, both menarche and menopause stimulate fantasies about one's sexual organs. A key difference between these fantasies is that the fantasies of menarche are stimulated by the acquisition of the reproductive function and those of menopause by the loss of that function. As noted above, from the standpoint of primary feminine identity, one prototypical fantasy in normal female development at menarche is that bleeding equals proof that one's organs are intact and that one will not in fact lose them or have them sealed up. Clinical data from my own patients and from other menopausal women I have interviewed, suggest that one prototypical menopausal fantasy is that one's ovaries are shrinking or shriveling and that one has a cavity or hollow space where the fully functioning ovaries used to be.

A key feature of this fantasy is its relation to the notion of a cycle. Women live with the biologically determined monthly cycle from adolescence forward. They are accustomed to measuring time in cyclical terms. The normal monthly cycle has a beginning, a middle, and an end. Bleeding and the cessation of bleeding are both part of it. On the larger time scale of a normal life cycle, this pattern repeats itself. Bleeding (the onset of menstruation) and the cessation of bleeding (menopause) are both part of it. More important for the understanding of the fantasy that often accompanies menopause, the monthly cycle consists of a filling followed by an emptying. When the ovaries empty each month, the space left behind contains the potential for fulfillment in the future. Menopause creates a space that will be permanently empty unless it is "filled" with something other than the swollen or impregnated ovaries. For example, a fifty-five-year-old childless menopausal woman had repeated dreams involving the emptying and refilling of a container such as an overflowing bathtub, a person's mouth, a water-filled balloon. These dreams

---

[5]By thus characterizing a natural part of the life cycle as if it were a disease process, we build into the discussion an unconscious bias. Although we no longer profess to find menstruating women "unclean" or afflicted by a "curse," our discussions of menopause continue to focus on perimenopausal symptomatology. This focus diverts attention from the *normalcy* of the process to its assumed pathology. It cannot be emphasized too often that menopause and puberty are normal developmental phases, not pathological processes.

were often interspersed with dreams of pregnancy. She understood the liquid dreams to represent the emptying and filling of her womb during her menstrual cycle. Confronting the reality that this cycle was ending, she began to fantasize about filling her inner space with new interests, specifically, new work productions, rather than with a child, real or imagined.

Another significant way in which menarche and menopause resemble each other is that each of these developmental phases is accompanied by an intensified maternal identification. Menopause typically involves both an explicit remembering of the woman's mother at the same time of life and an unconscious reworking of aspects of her maternal identification. Benedek states that the most significant factor in how a young woman reacts to menstruation is the nature of her mother's "emotional and psychological orientation to her own feminine functions." Likewise at menopause, when the middle-aged woman confronts the impending loss of her childbearing capacity, a significant factor in her reaction to this prospect is the memory of her mother at middle age and her mother's "emotional and psychological orientation" to her altered feminine functions. During this process of recalling and reworking, most women recognize that menopause, like menstruation, is an essential part of what it means to be a woman. Thus, normal menopause, like normal menarche, is a confirmation of primary feminine identity. Seen in this light, the fantasy of shriveling or shrinking ovaries is interpreted by these women as part of their natural life cycle. It would be unnatural and disturbing to them if this change did not occur.

But what of those women for whom menopause is significantly conflictful and who, in all likelihood, form a larger proportion of our caseload than of the population at large? I suggest that for them, menopause is likely to be experienced either as a remobilized castration complex with resulting depression, or as female castration anxiety focused on the possible loss of creativity and productivity; or as a mixture of both types of castration fears.

Testing of these ideas in practice is a task that remains to the profession. There are many reasons why there is so little reported clinical material dealing directly with the role of menopause in the lives of our middle-aged female patients. The main reasons seem to be these:

A Revised Psychoanalytic View of Menopause

1. The difficulty of separating the effects of menopause on the patient's emotional life from the effects of aging in general. It can be argued that menopause is, more than anything else, an indicator of aging; that the responses it evokes are nothing more than responses to the fact of growing older; and that, in any event, the importance of aging to the patient's psychology is so great that it overwhelms any independent significance that menopause may have. While I do not subscribe to this line of thinking, I have to acknowledge that attitudes toward aging are of tremendous importance to middle-aged and older patients. The task of separating out the specific effects of menopause on the emotional life of a patient is daunting. Nevertheless, I believe it not only can be done, it must be done if the analyst is to gain a clear view of the patient's mental life.

2. The reluctance of both analysts and patients to discuss menopause and its implications. In spite of the recent rash of popular books and articles about menopause, and the welcome appearance of Formanek's (1990) compilation of articles, menopause was not treated as a separate topic in a Panel (1986) on analyzing older patients, nor is it discussed in either of the two recent and influential works on feminist psychoanalytic theory, Chodorow's *Feminism and Psychoanalytic Theory* and Prozan's *Feminist Psychoanalytic Psychotherapy*. However, there are indications that the attitude of the profession is changing (see Panel, 1996). Patients who mention menopause in the course of their analyses almost inevitably do so by way of referring to its symptomatology. From a survey of the literature, it appears that with some notable exceptions (e.g., Renik, 1985, 1992) neither analysts nor patients initiate investigations of the psychodynamic fantasies and wishes related to the menstrual cycle in general and menopausal symptomatology in particular. I have asked colleagues whether and how the subject of menopause has come up in the course of their analytic work with middle-aged women. On the one hand, my colleagues acknowledge that menopause is "of course" an "important issue" in female development and that it comes up in associations to feelings about symptoms, and about aging in general. On the other hand, they do not display much interest in, or excitement about, menopause as a topic in its own right. Their answer is generally that they do not see the particular importance of menopause compared to other aspects of the patient's functioning. In this

way, the patient's denial combines with the analyst's blindness to keep the topic out of the analysis.

Menopause in this regard is like parapraxes and jokes before Freud: a universal, unavoidable aspect of (female) experience that is so common its importance is simply overlooked. Like Poe's "purloined letter," it is hidden in plain sight.

A CLINICAL EXAMPLE

Agnes D., a fifty-year old professor of education at a northern California college, had been in analysis for five years. For about six months, she had been complaining to me about headaches which, according to her internist, had no neurological basis. I had offered various psychological hypotheses to account for the headaches, but had not thought of menopause as a partial explanation. A friend invited her to an information session offered by a local nurse and a psychologist on dealing with menopause. Agnes was startled to discover that she had been having symptoms like those her friend described—headaches, night sweats, sleeplessness, reduced libido, and fluctuating body temperature—but had not, to that moment, connected them with menopause. Once she had acknowledged to herself that she was experiencing perimenopausal symptoms, Agnes asked her gynecologist to prescribe hormone replacement therapy (HRT), which significantly reduced the symptomatology.

After beginning HRT, Agnes reported this sequence of events with a mixture of annoyance at me for not understanding what she had been going through, and mild hopefulness as a result of obtaining symptom relief. When I asked myself why I had not made the connection between the patient's symptoms and her menopause, I realized that I had overlooked this relationship because of unconscious associations to my own beginning menopause. Recognizing these associations made it possible for me to respond more effectively to my patient on the many subsequent occasions when this topic came up.

Agnes has a history of personal trauma. Throughout childhood, she was told by her father that if she acted in a way that attracted sexual interest from a man, she had to bear the consequences, i.e.,

A Revised Psychoanalytic View of Menopause

she had to give the man whatever he wanted because she had aroused him. "If you swing your hips on the street, men can do anything to you." This idea was confirmed during her college years when she sought help from a social worker to overcome her severe sexual and work inhibitions. When he made advances to her, she complied out of the irrational belief that she had caused his misconduct. Before telling me about this incident, she had never revealed it to anyone.

Both parents enforced extreme passivity on her. Her father was a domineering individual with a violent temper who insisted on everything being done his way. Agnes had to conform to his schedule, agree with his ideas on any topic, even lose to him in competitive games like ping pong or checkers. Her mother was chronically ill and could not tolerate the slightest emotional or physical demands. Agnes learned to ignore signals from her body and tune out both pleasure and pain. As a result, anything that reminds her of the physical reality of her body is to some degree both anxiety-producing and relieving to her, including such things as night sweats and hot flashes, picking open scabs on her body, injuring herself by falling "accidentally."

Menopause forced her to more fully acknowledge the physical reality of her body. While she might be able to deny awareness of her level of sexual excitement, she could not deny drastic, sudden temperature changes and night sweats. Menopause also caused her to have vivid dreams and to wake in the midst of those dreams. By keeping what she called her "menopause dream book" at her bedside to record these dreams, she turned this change to her advantage. Menopause provided an avenue into her unconscious that was not previously available to her or to me.

Agnes is profoundly inhibited in talking about sexual fantasies. In her mind, fantasies are more dangerous than dreams. Dreams are "data," while fantasies might lead to acts that would threaten her. The enriched dream life brought on by menopause provided her and me with unconscious material that she could tolerate discussing. These dreams fell into several distinct categories: sexual dreams, dreams of depression and mourning, and dreams of envy toward other women.

As one early example of a specifically sexual dream, Agnes dreamt that a puppy had urinated all over her office. The dream

Sandra Bemesderfer

coincided with an episode of night sweats, so that Agnes had awakened wrapped in wet sheets. She gingerly associated to a memory of her early married life when her orgasms were often accompanied by a great deal of vaginal lubrication, sometimes including gushing liquid. She imagined that at those moments she might have lost control of her bladder and that she might actually have been urinating. As we discussed the dream and these associations, it became clear that Agnes wished to be more sexually out of control; feared humiliation if she let herself go; and also, in a sadomasochistic fantasy, wished for that humiliation. She associated to feelings of disgust about her own secretions and her husband's and to confusion as to whether she was attracted to those fluids or repelled by them. Because of the immediacy of the physical symptoms accompanying perimenopause and because of a sense of urgency in grappling with these symptoms, Agnes was much more receptive to exploration of her sexual feelings than she had been earlier in the analysis.

A recurring dream theme during this period involved Agnes being a passenger in a vehicle that loses its brakes and runs out of control. In a typical version of that dream, she is on a tour bus traveling through an exotic country she has never seen before. The driver abandons the bus and it begins to careen down the road. It is stopped by a band of young thugs who sexually assault her. In the analytic work that followed these dreams, Agnes began to deal with her father's irrational blaming her for provoking men, and with the sexual abuse she received at the hands of the social worker. Dreams like this one, expressing a wish to be bolder and explore new areas, were almost always accompanied by a crippling fear of failure and humiliation. I interpreted her self-defeating and punitive stance, pointing out that she seemed to decide on a poor outcome before she had even begun. I reminded Agnes of occasions in her childhood when her parents had quashed her strong creative drive by ridiculing her singing—even though she was a talented musician—and her correspondence with European pen pals. In connection with this shift from excited curiosity to immobilizing imagined humiliation, I made reference to a deeply troubling childhood experience about which Agnes had spoken briefly and with great difficulty several years earlier. At about age ten she revealed to her father that she was suffering from recurrent insomnia and asked for his help in dealing

A Revised Psychoanalytic View of Menopause

with the problem. Instead of responding with empathy to his daughter's utterly reasonable request, he accused Agnes of keeping herself awake by masturbating in her bed at night. Agnes experienced her father's accusations as betrayal of her trust in him, in part because she did occasionally masturbate and felt humiliated that he had guessed her secret. I suggested to her that the reason her wishes to engage in new endeavors were so often accompanied by fear of humiliation was that the wish to be expressive and reach out to others revived memories of this early traumatic betrayal by her domineering father.

Anxiety about potential humiliation was the first of two linked emotional responses Agnes had to the conscious desire to become more productive and creative. The second and more troubled response was to recall a persistent sadomasochistic sexual fantasy whenever she experienced anxiety about humiliation. Agnes has never been able to experience this fantasy directly in the hour, and has only been able to talk to me about it in the most general terms. It involves her being sexually passive and humiliated before she is permitted to experience sexual pleasure. My working assumption about this fantasy is that her inability to speak about it with full candor has multiple origins, including repeated humiliations by her father; her mother's masochistic stance toward life in general and toward her father in particular; and her sessions with the social worker, to whom she fully described the fantasy. He was aroused by her description and took advantage of Agnes as a direct result of her confiding this most intimate material to him. Since that time, she has been unable to reveal the details of the fantasy to anyone, including me. However, as we have worked on these issues in the analysis, she has become increasingly able to speak about the role this fantasy plays in her sexual life, and has also been able to recall and tell me about occasions on which she has had the fantasy. Progress in this area is slow, but eventually I believe she will be able to free herself of this perverse fantasy.

Within her birth family, Agnes was assigned the role of caretaker for her invalid mother. This role forced her to remain passive for long periods of time, waiting for her mother to express a need or demand some form of attention, and underscored the passive stance Agnes was also forced to take toward her father. As Agnes has struggled to achieve a more proactive and engaged life for herself, she has run into the difficult task of freeing herself from identification with her depressed and passive mother. This theme was also expressed in a dream: a good friend who in reality is unable to bear children, has a child in the dream. Agnes who in reality is a mother, has no children in the dream and is the friend's baby sitter. I pointed out to Agnes that she was taking on the role of the depressed woman, helping her friend feel better by depriving herself. I noted that this was Agnes's role in her family, sacrificing her own interests and talents for her mother's supposed welfare, acting as her mother's baby sitter. I also told her that I knew of women who had experienced increased vitality and greater sexual energy as a result of menopause. Since this is an explicit goal she has set for herself, my reference to other women who had achieved such a goal was relieving to her.

In her dream life and within the hours, Agnes has vacillated between themes of depression, loss, and mourning in relation to her mother (Agnes's mother died of a heart attack five years ago) and the themes of increased energy, ambition, and vitality. Indeed, one of the most striking features of her dreams at this point in the analysis is that dreams embodying these conflicting themes alternate almost on a nightly basis. A night in which Agnes dreams of regression, loss, or depression will be followed the next night by a dream of progression, gain, or optimism. Earlier conflicts around moving ahead and away from her family, most especially her mother, have been recurrent associations. Agnes and I have sought to understand the meaning to her mother of her going away to college and embarking on her career. Agnes has had a deep belief that such progress was at her mother's expense. A poem from her childhood expressed this thought:

> When I'm feeling great,
> There's an ambulance at the gate
> There's a policeman at the door,
> People lying on the floor.

The upwelling of her wishes to travel, write, etc. has heightened this conflict and offered an opportunity to focus on the irrationality of these ideas.

Since her mother's death, Agnes has been unable to mourn for her, and this failure has tormented her. We have come to understand that her difficulty in mourning for her mother is rooted in the very

A Revised Psychoanalytic View of Menopause

complex story she was told about her role in her mother's illness. According to both of her parents, her mother was a relatively healthy woman prior to Agnes's birth. Shortly after she was born, her mother was diagnosed with the serious heart condition which eventually killed her. Both parents blamed her for her mother's illness and justified their requirement that she care for her mother on this basis. When her mother died, Agnes blamed herself for the death. Only in the past year have dreams and associations come to the surface in which she has experienced mourning. This is a particularly dramatic example of such a dream:

> I am crying, going through my mother's closet. I smell her odor on her clothing. I keep crying to someone, "She's dead!" Somehow, going over and over her smell and thinking that my smell is changing with menopause. Something going brown. I'll put the black towels in the bathroom.

The patient's associations to this dream: "going brown" is blood drying; an anorexic friend has black towels in her bathroom; the movie *Indochine*, about loss of mother-daughter relationships; thoughts about when her daughter will go off to college.

When Agnes grapples with the reality of her daughter's impending departure from home, she recalls that her own departure for college was interpreted by her parents as a betrayal of her role as her mother's caregiver and, at the same time, as a dangerous step by which she exposed herself to unknown risks. In a dream, she is combing her daughter's full head of long auburn hair and resenting the task. She finds a bug or a tick in the hair, which her daughter asks her to remove. Agnes is repelled by the bug and refuses to remove it. In her associations to this dream, she compares her daughter's hair to her own thinning and graying hair—particularly to her thinning pubic hair. She experiences feelings of envy toward her daughter, and seeks revenge on her for being young and beautiful, by placing the disgusting bug in her hair. She recalls the wicked queen's envy of Snow White for being young and beautiful. She dislikes the picture of herself as an envious older woman and realizes that she is pleased by her daughter's vibrant youthfulness as well as envious of it. Associations to this and similar dreams have led Agnes to try to imagine what her own mother must have felt as she observed Agnes entering young womanhood. This effort at empathic understanding of her mother is in sharp contrast to Agnes's involuntary taking on of her mother's depressed affect both during her childhood and in her present struggles to lead a less conflicted life.

Earlier analytic work had focused on Agnes's anxiety about separation and loss when she recalled aspects of her childhood separation anxieties, especially her mother's sadness and worry about her when she moved away to attend college. Associations during this period to her own undeniable physical losses—her reproductive capacity, her thick hair, her youthful appearance, etc.—allowed us to begin to explore her feelings of envy and jealousy directed toward her sister, daughter, and mother. Agnes has stalwartly resisted interpretations about envy prior to this time. The immediacy of the narcissistic wound brought on by menopause forced her to revisit and more openly acknowledge her rivalrous, competitive feelings toward other women.

This patient's psychology illustrates graphically the way in which both the remobilized castration complex and female castration anxiety are shaping her emotional responses to menopause. On the one hand, Agnes experiences depression in connection with the loss of reproductive function and the related inability to create a penis substitute in the form of a child. The depression expresses her recognition of phallic loss. On the other hand, she experiences female castration anxiety when she contemplates engaging in new and creative endeavors to "fill the empty space" left by menopause, the anxiety that she will be shut up and rendered unproductive. As noted above, these differing types of castration feelings tend to alternate in controlling her dream life and, consequently, the content of her analytic hours. Successful treatment of this patient has required both a working through of the feelings of loss and repeated questioning of the reality of her anxieties. Finding the proper occasions to respond to the patient is a constant clinical challenge, since both types of castration feelings are typically expressed within a single hour, even if one is apparently predominant at a given moment in the session or in the prior night's dream productions.

As we explored the psychic material that menopause helped bring to light, Agnes began to experience significant positive changes in her work life. For several years prior to the advent of her menopause, she had wanted to write a paper in her field. She had numerous ideas for the content of the paper, but was unable to

A Revised Psychoanalytic View of Menopause

commit herself to organizing the ideas, reading the existing literature, or sitting down on a regular basis to write. During that first year in which we focused on her menopause dreams and her associations to them, she completed research for the paper, purchased a personal computer, learned how to use word processing software, and wrote the paper.

For years, Agnes has also avoided taking part in national meetings of education teachers, even though she is aware that such contacts would be valuable to her. As she was completing the paper, she agreed to deliver a version of it at a national meeting and to participate in a panel discussion of her ideas. While preparing this talk, she wrote to other scholars in her field, soliciting their comments on her paper, and discovered to her pleasure that they found her ideas provocative and interesting. It was clear that explicitly discussing her experience of menopause and its relation to her sexual and work inhibitions was central to her achievement of these previously frustrating professional goals.

In the sexual sphere, Agnes alternates between feeling empowered and more sexualized as a result of menopause and feeling inconsequential and desexualized. Although she has not yet been able to break the link between the specific perverse fantasy and her ability to have an orgasm, she has been able to be more spontaneous in her lovemaking and to encourage her husband, who had grown used to a predictable sexual routine, to do so as well. These changes in her attitude toward sex, while gradual, are cumulatively significant in moving her toward a freer and richer sex life.

Discussion

This period of Agnes's analysis, corresponding to her perimenopausal years, is a time of enhanced opportunity for analytic work. The clearest effect of menopause on the analysis has involved the relation between physical symptoms such as night sweats, hot flashes, hormonal shifts, and increases and decreases in libido, on the one hand, and her repression of feelings of excitement and liveliness, on the other. Specifically, as she passes through menopause, she finds it increasingly possible to substitute creative intellectual work in place of child bearing and child rearing and, to a lesser degree, free herself from a sadomasochistic sexual fantasy and the constricted sex life that has accompanied it. These changes have been accompanied by intensified anxieties about being more active, sexual, and exhibitionistic, and brought forth details about her sadomasochistic fantasy previously unavailable in the analysis. Her dreams have been characterized by repeated representations of active-passive conflicts and she has struggled with feelings of loss, loneliness, emptiness, and occasional despair. These alternating feeling states reflect the patient's alternating experience of a remobilized castration complex and female castration anxiety. The remaining work of the analysis is to help her work through her feelings of loss and liberate her creativity from its anxious bonds.

While the specific ways in which this patient has responded to the physical and psychological changes brought on by menopause are unique to her, they also represent a general phenomenon of reassessment of one's role as a woman that is forced on every woman undergoing this experience. The intensified feeling states and related fantasies about one's body and one's sexuality that accompany menopause provide fertile ground for analytic work, particularly in relation to castration fears. While other age-related issues such as children leaving home and parents dying clearly affect the emotional life of middle-aged women, menopause has an independent claim to analytic attention that, if appropriately responded to, will repay both analyst and patient for the effort.

REFERENCES

BENEDEK, T. (1948). Menopause as a developmental phase. In *Psychoanalytic Investigations.* New York: Quadrangle, 1973, pp. 322–349.

BEYENE, Y. (1989). *From Menarche to Menopause: Reproductive Lives of Peasant Women in Two Cultures.* Albany, NY: SUNY Press.

BLUM, H.P., Ed. (1977). *Female Psychology: Contemporary Psychoanalytic Views.* New York: Int. Univ. Press.

CHODOROW, N. (1989). *Feminism and Psychoanalytic Theory.* New Haven, CT: Yale Univ. Press.

DEUTSCH, H. (1924). The menopause. *Int. J. Psychoanal.*, 65:55–62, 1984.

FORMANEK, R., Ed. (1990), *The Meanings of Menopause.* Hillsdale, NJ: Analytic Press.

FREUD, S. (1905). Three essays on the theory of sexuality. *S. E.*, 7.

——— (1912). Types of onset of neurosis. *S. E.*, 12.

——— (1937). Analysis terminable and interminable. *S. E.*, 23.

HARRIS, H. (1990). A critical view of three psychoanalytic positions on menopause. In *The Meanings of Menopause*, ed. R. Formanek. Hillsdale, NJ: Analytic Press, pp. 65–77.

A Revised Psychoanalytic View of Menopause

Lax, R. (1982). The expectable depressive climacteric reaction. *Bull. Menninger Clin.*, 46:151–167.

Mayer, E.L. (1985). 'Everybody must be just like me': observations on female castration anxiety. *Int. J. Psychoanal.*, 66:331–347.

McKinlay, J., McKinlay, S. & Brambilla, E. (1987). The relative contributions of endocrine changes and social circumstances to depression in mid-aged women. *J. Health Soc. Behav.*, 28:345–363.

Notman, N. (1984). Psychiatric disorders of menopause. *Psychiat. Annals*, 14:448–453.

Panel (1986). The psychoanalysis of the older patient. N. E. Miller, reporter. *J. Amer. Psychoanal. Assn.*, 34:163–177.

——— (1996). Menopause. S. Bemesderfer, reporter, *J. Amer. Psychoanal. Assn.*, 44, in press.

Prozan, C. (1992). *Feminist Psychoanalytic Psychotherapy*. Northvale, NJ: Aronson.

Renik, O. (1985). An example of disavowal involving the menstrual cycle. *Psychoanal. Q.*, 54:523–532.

——— (1992). A case of premenstrual distress: bisexual determinants of a woman's fantasy of damage to her genital. *J. Amer. Psychoanal. Assn.*, 40:105–210.

Roiphe, H. (1981). *Infantile Origins of Sexual Identity*. New York: Int. Univ. Press.

Rosenthal, M. (1983). Psychiatric disorders and the menopause. *Psychiat. Annals*, 13:35–38.

Stoller, R. (1975). *The Presentation of Gender*. New Haven, CT: Yale Univ. Press.

Tobias, C. & Lewis, S. (1993). Menopause and depression: course, assessment and treatment. *Women's Psychiat. Health*, 2:1.

IV.
MOTHERHOOD

Figure 6. Lenore Tawney (1995) *Shrine*. E.M. Donahue Gallery

Pregnancy—Procreative Process, The "Placental Paradigm," and Perinatal Therapy

Joan Raphael-Leff

>Based on extensive clinical experience with childbearing women, a metaphor is suggested depicting psychic reality during pregnancy as a "procreative container," constituted through three intertwining systems—physiological-placental, intrapsychic-familial and socioenvironmental.
>
>Psychohistorically predisposed thresholds of tolerance are proposed, with each woman manifesting varying degrees of "permeability" or "psychological immunity" to engagement in the process of emotional gestation.
>
>A model illustrates variations in affective quality, fixity, and intensity of preconscious maternal representations underpinning defensive structures. This "placental paradigm" charts seven permutations of the combination of herself as mother to her fantasized baby (in relation to split aspects of herself as baby to her archaic mother) and effects of these imagined dyads on the postnatal exchange. The paper concludes with an exposition of unique features of psychoanalytic treatment during pregnancy and postnatally, and the impact of the procreative psychic reality on patient and analyst.

> ... and a threefold cord is not quickly broken
> —*Ecclesiastes, 4:12*

PROCREATIVE SYSTEMS

Pregnancy is a strangely disorienting process. An expectant mother in actuality recreates her origins within the internal space of her own body: heavy with child, she, like all pregnant

---

Member, British Psycho-analytical Society and International Psychoanalytical Association.

Joan Raphael-Leff

counterparts before her, carries a fetus within her womb as she herself was carried within her mother's pregnant body. Having conceived, a woman is thus catapulted into a paradoxical experience at one and the same time primordial and universal yet intensely individual, subjective, timebound and culturally specific. Entering the arena of maternity, she re-encounters there personal residues of childhood progenitive fantasies, riddles of sexual difference, oedipal jealousies and primal scene passions as well as generic anxieties about clashes between generational life forces and tyrannicidal powers and the age old female corporeal mysteries of formation, preservation, transformation and separation (Raphael-Leff, 1985). I suggest that three systems intertwine in the triple-stranded bond formation between the pregnant woman and the baby within her: (1) the physiological system—those involuntary bodily processes and symptoms which acquire emotional significance within the intricate bi-directional exchange of their conjoint bodies; (2) the psychohistorical system—constituting a powerhouse of fantasies feeding the woman's representations, predetermining her psychological experience of pregnancy, and, by means of maternal transmission, taprooting the baby to emotional forebearers and significant others in the expectant mother's inner world; (3) the sociocultural environment—the particular matrix of cultural beliefs and practices that defines parameters of each woman's normative expectations and definitions of childbearing, childrearing, and childcare in her society.[1]

Once pregnant, the woman can no longer maintain an illusion of being a monadic individual. Not only a link on the genealogical chain of mothers, she is literally cordlinked to her future child. Pregnancy confronts her with the bizarre situation of having two people in her body, one inside the other. Physically, her muscles, ligaments, and skin modify and stretch to accommodate the new person growing within her. On a psychical level, her inner reality, too, expands

---

[1]Elsewhere (Raphael-Leff, in press), reviewing some 250 anthropological studies of childbearing conducted by WHO worldwide, I have argued that perinatal care and practical provisions serve as an index of a given society's basic values relating to life, death and reproductive powers. These not only reveal local beliefs and perceived differences between women, men, adults, and male and female babies, and the negative influences against which childbearing/rearing practices serve as defenses. In turn, practices themselves cultivate and endorse cultural imagery of bodies in illness and health, and complex interconnections between psyche and soma, natural and supernatural, purity and pollution, sacred and profane played out in social attributions.

Pregnancy

and recoils with awareness that she is no longer a single entity bounded by her skin. Invasion by an other burrowed deep within her physical borders calls into question the fundamental *axiom of singularity*—personal separateness so laboriously and poignantly cultivated since infancy. Paradoxically, at this very time when she is quintessentially feminine, and *male/female distinctions* are at their maximum, they are also blurred, as a male substance, the sperm, penetrates her ovum, and an embryo, potentially male, begins to gestate within her body.

As pregnancy progresses, making its presence felt, the internal being emphasizes in tangible ways its very real possession of her interior, and (through movement and often conflicting rhythmicity) duplication of her body's inhabitants. How she relates to this occupancy will depend on many factors.

Genetically, the fetus is a partly foreign body. With recent scientific advances such as ovum donation, it might even be genetically unrelated to the maternal incubator. Nevertheless, for reasons as yet not fully understood, the pregnant body usually supresses its immunological urge to abort. I argue that psychic reality, too, operates its own "immunological" defense to otherness. Threatened by the emotional disequilibrium long noted by psychoanalysts such as Deutsch (1945), Bibring (1959), Benedek (1970), Pines (1972), and Kestenberg (1976), some women, through denial, do resort to "psychological abortion," remaining impregnable to the onslaught of internal "implantation." Many, more receptive, surrender to introspective reformulation of their integral stance, whereas yet others rigidify internal barriers, struggling defensively against potential breakdown of the continuity of self with the invasion of an other. Elsewhere I have linked degree of "psychic permeability" tolerated antenatally to parental orientations (Raphael-Leff, 1991, 1996).

In this paper I draw on thousands of hours of psychoanalytic work with over 150 women, seen one to five times per week in my clinical practice which over the past 20 years has been almost entirely devoted to referrals on reproductive issues. Treatment continues for anything between two and ten years, including, in cases of subfertility or psychological unpreparedness, a stretch preceding conception, during which time the woman may or may not be undergoing medical interventions. Other women are referred during pregnancy itself or postnatally; and in many cases treatment continues over the early years of motherhood, and sometimes spans two or more subsequent gestations. I shall expand on the specific nature of perinatal and postnatal psychotherapy toward the end of the paper.

In addition to psychoanalytic treatment of individual fertile and infertile women, my exposition here is also based on work with several hundred parents—in weekly therapy groups for pregnant women, couples, parent-infant therapy, and discussion groups with expectant parents and questionnaire surveys with some of these. In addition, my work is informed by thrice-weekly disciplined longitudinal observation of 23 mother/infant pairs in a large community center toddler group setting over a two-to-three-year period, and close contact with over a thousand primary care professionals in weekend workshops I have conducted in many countries worldwide.

On the basis of this experience, I suggest that wide variation among women in the way each emotionally assimilates both the foreignness and selfsameness of her baby during pregnancy and postnatally, will be determined by the *meaning* she herself attributes to specific cultural and psychosocial and constitutional-medical factors colored by her emotional relationship to her impregnator, and unconscious representations of this baby, of her baby self, of archaic figures in her inner world, and the unconscious significance of gestational processes and placental exchange. In other words, an individual woman's psychic reality of pregnancy is defined by and in turn defines the degree of her own particular "psychological immunity" or receptivity to the emotional upheavals of pregnancy and increased permeability between conscious and unconscious, inside and out, fact and fantasy, past, present, and future mothers and babies.

PROCREATIVE CONTAINMENT AND PLACENTAL EXCHANGE

Bion (1962) describes the maternal function as one of mental "containment"—holding, providing nurturance, and processing unmetabolized infantile anxieties which the mother "detoxifies" to be safely reintrojected by her baby. I propose that this metaphor has a precursor during pregnancy, when the expectant mother serves both

Pregnancy

psychically and physically as a "procreative container" systemically engaged in a material and emotional placental exchange with her baby.

Clearly, neither physiological nor psychological process is simple or unidirectional. Throughout the generations, pregnant women the world over have expressed concern about the interuterine exchange across the placental barrier. Many wonder about their own influence over the gestational process through potentially constitutive good and bad thoughts, dreams, feelings, or, more literally, the quality of nutrients and noxious substances they inadvertently pump with every heartbeat of oxygen-laden blood. Medical studies too numerous to cite have increased our awareness of the womb's permeability—to environmental toxins and technological hazards, to pathogenic effects of nicotine and alcohol intake, to viral infections, and indeed, to maternal emotional states transmitted to the fetus through heart rate acceleration, antibody formation, hormonal, vestibular, and temperature variations.

Similarly, the fetus itself is found to be influential: in addition to depositing waste products in the maternal body (such as carbon dioxide to be breathed out through her lungs and nitrogen compounds for excretion in her urine), when resources are scarce, the fetus actively and at times competitively demands a share, altering maternal biochemistry to accommodate to its needs, sometimes in a way that is detrimental to her health. Partly due to sonography, photoendoscopy, and other technological advances, we now recognize that each fetus differs on a range of responses much richer than previously imagined. Extraordinarily, some fetal capacities greatly exceed those of the newborn (Raphael-Leff, 1996)! Fetal research illustrates that the fetus not only reacts, but initiates, engaging in complex activity to maximize use of the intrauterine environment and responding to stimulation of all modalities, including tactile, auditory, visual, kinesthetic, vestibular, gustatory, thermic, and pain receptors (Chamberlain, 1987). In addition, the fetus may be seen to spend time "playing"—manipulating cord and placenta and relating to a twin where present (Piontelli, 1992); shows dream-type (!) REM and alpha rhythms, discriminates and learns, as can be demonstrated by postnatal preferences for antenatally familiar stories, songs, and sounds (DeCasper et al., 1987).

Joan Raphael-Leff

Paternal input also has its influence on gestation. Contact between expectant father and future offspring is mediated (or blocked) by the pregnant women, directly or emotionally. However, on a microlevel, he is present, and not only genetically. Some functional aspects of the gestatory provision are now thought to be derived from encoded information inherent in the sperm. Recent embryological studies (Wolpert, 1991) suggest that while development of the embryo proper is determined by guidelines contained in the nucleus of the fertilized mammalian egg, it appears that it is information contained in the male nucleus which controls development of extra-embryonic structures, such as the placenta. The biological father may or may not be in contact; he may not know of the pregnancy, or (in cases of sperm donors, rape, promiscuity, etc.) may be unknown to the expectant mother. She might have another (male or female) partner. But beyond social, genetic, or gestational input, on a *psychical level* his contribution takes root. Objective or imaginary, articulated or denied, the notion of the baby's biological father in the mind of the burgeoning woman contributes to the degree of her "psychological immunity" to pregnancy and to the nature of attachment to her fetus.

In sum, I suggest that in concrete form already during pregnancy (as later in infancy and in increasingly symbolic forms within the psychoanalytic process) a complex *triangular* structure may be postulated operating within the "procreative container"—the mind-body receptacle of the pregnant woman. Equally, we may say that although her idea of the baby has its roots in her own infancy, and although the actual social relationship with her baby becomes operative only postnatally, an *interactive systemic exchange* begins during pregnancy as the woman unwittingly receives and metabolizes her baby's products while transmitting bodily and psychic products of her own—investing her unknown inmate with derivations of her lifeblood and her innermost feelings.

To what degree these subtle influences of her desires, anxieties, wishes and fears, and concommittant preconscious fantasies and expectations are conveyed, transformed, and absorbed through the placental system is yet to be determined. However, that they form the seedbed of her own maternal stance is now evident. In addition, simultaneously, she herself is subject to subtle influences from the

Pregnancy

baby—unregistered biochemical changes, nausea, and other symptoms; kinesthetic movements she experiences and, with routine ultrasonic scanning, visual imaging of the baby. The mother not only sees her baby bearing facial features and performing intrauterine acrobatics, but she ineffably engages with previously mysterious areas—looking into her own intrauterine space, examining each chamber of her baby's heart, following patterns of growth, and possibly knowing her baby's sex well in advance of the birth.

While not suggesting isomorphism, I am playing here with the idea that the fertile womb as actual container of fetus, placenta, and amnion has an emotional corollary in the woman as "procreative container," in which three influential systems converge—intrapsychic-familial, physiological, and sociocultural. Stretching the metaphor to its limits, we may postulate that, within this generative crucible, an internalized ethos as influential as the genetic input of blood relatives contributes to the expectant mother's (and father's) psychic representations of the fantasy baby (see Raphael-Leff, 1991, 1992 on modification of unconscious contracts during the transition to parenthood). It is even conceivable to imagine their pooled parental residues as a kind of "transgenerational placenta"—a veritable powerhouse dynamically generating or filtering out transmission of unconscious or cumulative personal and ancestral emotional deposits—of unresolved conflicts, disavowed projections, fond aspirations, and unacknowledged residues of intergenerational transference, all situated within the cultural amnion.

PLACENTAL PARADIGM

Be that as it may, given the multifactorial constructs of psychosocial experience during pregnancy, variability among pregnant women is not surprising. In addition, each woman's psychic reality changes from pregnancy to pregnancy and during the course of a single gestation. Powerful forces released by pregnancy create emotional turbulence taking the woman by surprise and necessitating greater receptivity, constant reappraisal or intensification of defenses. The bizarre experience of dual unity often reactivates primitive fantasies about the inside of the maternal body as it triggers triple identification (of fetus, mother, and baby self), with attendant ideas of merger, exploitation, imprisonment, violation, and contamination. These fantasies, accompanied by damaging and reparative urges, may induce anxiety states, panic, phobic reactions, yearnings, idealizations, and heightened preoccupations with the archaic mother of her own gestation, birth and infancy add to the turbulence. An expectant mother who at times feels ecstatic about blurring of "intrapersonal" boundaries may at other times feel threatened by interpenetrating internal realities or find intolerable her paradoxical sense of existential isolation, essentially on her own while tethered to a partial stranger feeding off her internal resources and pumping its waste into her. I propose therefore that *this bidirectional placental system can serve as a metaphor for the imagined give-and-take within the affectively colored exchange.*

To illustrate variations among women and emotional oscillations in a woman between pregnancies and within the same pregnancy, I have constructed a simple paradigm of positive or negative preconscious representations and affects which intensify depending on the nature of a woman's current internal and external realities. The latter include fluctuations of self-esteem and physical health, changes in her support system and/or internalized emotional network, or confidence in her own creative resources. For simplicity's sake I am restricting the paradigm to the pregnant woman's representations of *herself as mother* (invariably paired or contrasted with her archaic mother) and her *fantasy baby* (paired or contrasted to her imagined baby self). Variations are therefore charted here as permutations of only two interdependent parameters, although clearly more elaborate versions of this paradigm could be expanded to include dynamics between herself, her internal mother, her partner and/or the baby's father, her own father, siblings, grandmother, etc.

This "placental paradigm" proposes that in her psychic reality, benevolent coexistence is possible if the expectant mother is able to tolerate her *ambivalence* toward the pregnancy as a source of both joy and discomfort. If her "threshold of immunity" allows her to incorporate the baby as both part object and different from herself, flexible oscillation among various positions (I–VI) and acceptance of the complexity of her own mixed emotions means that she can allow herself to treat the baby, too, as a mixture, sometimes seen

Pregnancy

TABLE 1
THE PLACENTAL PARADIGM

	Representations		Experience
	Mother	Baby	
	Mixed		
	GOOD & BAD +−	GOOD & BAD +−	"good enough"—coexistence (ambivalence)
	Fixed		
p	dyad I GOOD +	GOOD +	"symbiotic" exchange (idealization)
o	dyad II GOOD +	BAD −	mother's defense barrier vs. alien "parasite" (persecution)
s			
i	dyad III BAD −	GOOD +	maternal compensation (depression)
t	dyad IV GOOD vs. BAD	GOOD +	internal conflict (schizoid dilemma)
i	dyad V BAD −	BAD −	mutual barrier vs. contamination (detachment)
o	dyad VI GOOD/BAD +/−	GOOD/BAD +/−	compulsive thoughts (obsessional)
n	dyad VII GOOD or BAD + or −	NONENTITY 0	life as usual (denial)

Adapted from Raphael-Leff, 1996.
Abstract plus (+) and minus (−) signs have deliberately been chosen to emphasize that *content* of the fantasy is culture-bound, highly personal, and contextual, varying from woman to woman and in the same woman at different times. These signs serve as reminders that it is the *affective quality*, its fixity and intensity, that determines the nature of (perinatal) emotional experience.

innocently growing inside her, unaware of her contribution, at times seemingly communicative or playful, caring or ruthless, deprived and cunningly nudging her to notice, demanding, needy, willful or selfishly competitive, benign or competitively sapping her energies.

It is likely that a woman who through such flexible "primary maternal preoccupation" (Winnicott, 1956) can conceive of her good/bad self and baby coexisting during pregnancy, will have worked through early conflicts with her own mother and integrated an infantile polarized view of her baby self, and therefore will be able to continue after the birth to accept herself as an ordinary "good enough" mother (Winnicott, 1960) aware of her own hatred (Winnicott, 1947) as well as love toward a "good enough" good/ bad loving/hating baby, as the following clinical excerpt illustrates:

> It was quite frightening when she was born [says my once-weekly patient, holding her nine-day-old baby]. She looked exactly like

Joan Raphael-Leff

Sarah [older daughter] had, and for a little while I felt as if I was going mad, like the same baby reincarnated in another body. I felt relieved as I began noticing differences, but it shook me up. Made me realize how easy it could be to negate the reality that she is a different person, and just project my desires and expectations onto her. It was helpful having Sarah around, making her own feelings clear—quite unfriendly toward me and the baby at first, and coming in each morning asking hopefully: "baby gone?" My mother is staying with us and I find myself more aware of her not answering *my* needs rather than me afraid I'm not answering hers. Seeing more clearly what *she* can't give, I spend less time in mortal fear of letting her down and dreading her unhappiness and disapproval. In fact, to my surprise, I feel quite sorry for her—she seems to run her life by rules and is so utterly bound by her own rigid routines. She's not very good with Sarah, says she's never coped with toddlers—I think it's the naked honesty of need, and "unreasonableness"—but she's lovey-dovey with the baby, and although she seems threatened by us wanting time alone, she can be helpful if I explain what I want. Mum told me yesterday that her mother used to treat her like a doll and I think she can't bear seeing Sarah express her needs when she herself had to be so "good" and self-denying as a little child.

Some women do not have the psychic fluidity to sustain such simultaneity of multivalent feelings. Some "blossom" during pregnancy by highlighting only positive aspects of the prenatal exchange (fixed dyad I [+ +]). Psychic homeostatis is maintained by *denial of any negative feelings*. When this idealization extends to imagined fusion, an expectant mother indulges in fantasies of mutually enriching pooled resources ("we're in a constant state of communion"). Unconsciously, she not only regards herself as bountiful provider, but through primary identification (or triumphant competition) with both her own archaic mother and her baby, luxuriates by proxy in the rapturous intrauterine state of her fetus. Unless she recovers herself before the end of pregnancy by mourning the passing of their special intimacy, her defensive stance will necessitate reinstatement of the illusion of blissful "symbiotic" merger and its maintenance postnatally. In mothering, as in pregnancy, she will play out the imaginary part of perfect "placental" provider to the perfect counterpart of her own idealized baby self, an all-embracing omnipotently exclusive source of emotional nutrients enforced through projective identification and reinforced by cultivation of dependency.

Pregnancy

Clinically speaking, while facilitation promotes perinatal continuity and possible creation of an illusion of fusion *by the infant*, maternal overidentification may manifest in prolonged regressive mirroring, the mother gratifying her own projected infantile needs rather than intuiting those of the child, and failing to acknowledge the baby's individuality and thrust toward individuation. Furthermore, an idealized baby is expected to present a constant affable and appreciative response, and the infant's negative feelings may be ignored, forbidden, and inhibited. Denial of her own negative feelings may also inflate protectiveness, leading to maternal overindulgence with projection of malevolence beyond the magic dyadic circle, possibly inducing paranoid anxieties about the partner or others and/or social avoidance. Such idealization is maintained at great personal cost, involving denial of imperfection and underlying awareness of rivalry, hostility, anger, or envy. Unless treatment is available, in the face of inevitable disappointment, an overrating mother is liable to traumatic disillusionment and postnatal despair (dyad III).

Illustration I

Identifying herself with the fetus inside her, Angela resolved to spend her entire pregnancy "hibernating", curled up in a warm place to shield herself and her baby from any negative influences. Her previous late miscarriage has left her wary and she resists her partner's attempts to lure her out for walks. She remains indoors, studiously avoiding any social intrusions from friends and devoting all her energies to cossetting her baby, thinking "positive" thoughts, and daydreaming. She was referred for therapy by her doctor when she panicked after some minor "spotting," incessantly castigating herself for not having been sufficiently careful. In the initial sessions she gives the impression of being only half-awake. She speaks in a low drowsy story-telling voice, incorporating baby talk and fragments of nursery rhymes, seemingly expecting her analyst to be telepathically clairvoyant as she feels her mother (and baby) to be. Gradually the historical picture emerges of an adored little girl living out a balancing act of perfection. Caught between impossible loyalties to both parents, she had felt that to engage with her reserved austere father or even to enter invited into a corner of his manly world was to betray her beloved victimized mother (who has remained frozen in time, undefined and childlike, fearful and socially phobic,

Joan Raphael-Leff

brought up by a housekeeper, following inexplicable abandonment by her own idealized mother at a young age). Despite her considerable capacity for psychological awareness, Angela's parents' avoidance of disagreement as dangerous and her own unquestioned compliance with their ascriptions of "niceness" have left her with little realistic self-knowledge or capacity to appraise her own agency.

During the middle trimester of her pregnancy, Angela has repetitive dreams of a paradisal place in which one door is labelled "Sweet Nobody's room." Outside, beyond the ornamental railings fencing the old house, lurk unseen members of the sinister "Special Branch"; inside, behind a lace curtain, she knows there is a locked cupboard, full of secret messages on scraps of parchment. Egged on by the "deadline" of her delivery date, she begins in earnest to use her thrice-weekly therapy to explore her own feelings and desires, gradually differentiating from nebulous all-pervasive identifications with her mother.

Over the course of her pregnancy and early motherhood this young woman comes to piece together the narrative reality of her life history through powerful transferential emotions that enable her to delineate her own memories and subjective experience from the semimystical reconstructions her doting but controlling mother has imbedded in her over the years. Gradually, we come to recognize repetitive parapraxal patterns and puzzling concrete enactments as wordless "foreign body" implantations of her unknown maternal grandmother's disaffections unwittingly absorbed and unconsciously transmitted by mother to daughter to daughter.

Tentatively, Angela now begins to formulate her own growth needs. In one dream she chops and eats spinach she herself has grown to prevent her blood getting "thin." In parallel, the everyday reality of her life seems to gain substance, with negative feelings less hived off. She is able to confront an intrusive neighbor and, in addition to practical domestic preparations, has taken to buying baby items, despite her (understandable) superstitions and dislike of crowded shops. She begins to voice her fears, wondering whether the baby will be normal and what kind of a mother she herself will be, and at times complains of feeling drained and "fed up." Phobic tendencies have not been overcome, however the splitting is not as stark. In a dream toward the end of pregnancy she is in a gondola,

Pregnancy

propelling herself along with her feet in the water, avoiding the turds floating there. As she approaches term she is able to voice fears of having damaged her previous baby. Mourning his loss, she relives the fraught days around the late miscarriage. She expresses her guilt at having felt rejected by the dead baby and remorse at having been unable to grieve fully at the time.

Increasingly, she contemplates the reality, viability, and individuality of the child she is now carrying and foresees changes which parenthood will bring to their lifestyle. After consultation with her partner, Angela decides to reinstate the bricked-up Victorian fireplace in their home, saying she wants her baby to have a "real," live fire with direct knowledge of "mankind's greatest discovery." She attributes this idea to her own feeling of being "more directly part of the human race," and takes pleasure in the capacity to tame and creatively channel destructive forces, including her anger.

Nearing her due date and well prepared for labor, she is able to contemplate the possibility of complications and of a forceps delivery rather than the fervently wished-for-water-birth without feeling devastated. She no longer feels the need to sustain an illusion of perfect fusion: "She is lovely, but I realize I know my baby only as far as one person can know another," says my patient ten days after the birth of her daughter. "I even trust her now to continue breathing through the night without checking up on her. When I was so desperate to have a baby I used to think I would be Somebody once I was a mother. But I think the truth is I first had to become Somebody to *be* a real mother and to allow my baby to be a real person."

Conversely, when, rather than the ego ideal/ideal object of perfect breast and perfect baby, split-off malevolence is invested in the baby, a pregnant woman experiences herself as benevolent yet potentially exploited and internally *prey to a dangerous alien* greedily feeding off her resources or polluting her with its waste products. The fetus may be regarded as a concrete part of her impregnator or experienced as a menacing internal object, controlling her from within. Thus persecuted by her fetus, she feels compelled to establish a protective barrier to keep good things inside herself safe from parasitic exploitation (dyad II [+ −]). Unable to sustain this, panic may ensue: "I feel so frightened—day and night there is no escape from this uncontrollable thing scrabbling its way right inside my innermost 'shell,' " says one pregnant woman. Others come into therapy following precipitous (and often multiple) abortions, wanting a baby but terrified at being able to "stomach" the persecutory sense of being drained, poisoned, overwhelmed, and/or taken over by the powerful internal forces released by conception.

During pregnancy, such preconscious anxieties often manifest in rigidification of defenses, compulsive rituals or elaborate bodily care to claim the body back from the possessive fetus. Symptoms such as flatulence, heartburn, or constipation may be attributed to the baby's noxious or malign influence, or else to her own defenses against it: "I feel as though my whole body is in rebellion against this hijacking." Some women counter the threat of internal depletion by taking extra precautions, such as "eating for two" to counteract being "devoured," "emptied," or overwhelmed by the insatiable competitive fetus, or drinking vast quantities of fluids to avoid being "sucked dry" or to flush out the baby's contaminating waste products. Others may resort to anorexic abstinence to reestablish separateness and regain some control: "I'm physically disgusted by my body. In the mirror, I look huge . . . enormous belly like a snake with a whole rat inside. I was flat and lean until this baby crammed itself into me," says a pregnant woman whose starving herself has led to being tube-fed. Clearly these are overdetermined, desperate efforts to combat persecutory anxieties around femininity/maternity and revelation of repudiated shameful aspects of the self invested in the fetus. Other pregnant women display dangerous passive-aggressive resistance patterns, fetus-directed violence, or compensatory/punitive compulsive eating disorders and/or alcohol or drug abuse.

Where such "primary maternal persecution" (Raphael-Leff, 1986, 1996) remains unresolved, defensive measures may manifest postnatally in various degrees of emotional detachment and/or need for physical separation from the "dangerous" baby who can threaten to undermine the mother's sense of adult competence and hardwon independence by revealing her disavowed baby self or infantile neediness or rage. When defenses fail, "retaliatory" thoughts of punitive vengeance may erupt, with possible enactment of violence. "When that baby looks at me with his glittering eyes, I feel like sticking my scissors into him," confesses a mother who referred herself for therapy when her son was two weeks old. "He looks so evil, like a smug

Pregnancy

toad, just like my brother did when he was born. I can't stand the thought of him sucking at me, and when he starts making demands, I want to bash his head against a wall."

By contrast, a woman who feels herself to be a "bad" mother to a good baby (dyad III [− +]) has a predominantly *depressive* rather than persecutory experience. If she suffers from a chronic sense of inner poverty, during pregnancy she may try to combat her insufficient good resources or feeling of emptiness by manic activity, seeking to cosset the baby with sumptious food, beautiful sights, and lovely music to mitigate her poor self-esteem and maternal deficits. Unlike most expectant mothers who tend to feel guilty if they smoke or get the flu, in her self-recrimination such a woman will feel compelled to overcompensate for her blame-ridden remorse, resorting to amelioration of her internal "badness" by constantly monitoring her thoughts and vigilantly employing superstitious behavior to prevent "seepage" to the baby of her harmful ideas or bad habits. Others may engage in bravado to evade the full impact of despair: "Well, if it can survive my [alcoholic] drinking now, it means it's resilient enough to stand me later."

Postnatally, a woman who continues to experience herself as empty or full of badness will try to cope by erecting an emotional buffer aimed to shelter the vulnerable child from her own negative forces and herself from alleged criticism. Aligned with her own idealized mother, the infant is often ascribed judgmental motives, each cry deemed an accusation that she does not measure up. "I constantly guage my involvement with Nancy—feel I have to protect her from me," says Belinda about her three-week-old baby. "I try not to grab because I feel so hungry inside I could overwhelm her, almost devour her. . . . I try and work out what to do with her and what she wants from me, but I feel I've nothing to give her and I keep thinking how much better off she'd be without someone like Mummy."

As a solution she may hand the baby over for care by someone "superior" who can mitigate her deficiencies. A variation on this theme (dyad III) may also apply to an idealizing woman who, due to complications of pregnancy or birth or psychosocial deficits, feels she has failed to maintain the consummate [+ +] state of dyad I: "I'm devastated by my baby having to spend these days in an incubator . . . it's no use, it's all spoilt, can't ever be put right again."

Joan Raphael-Leff

Protective overindulgence, remorse, and compensatory reparations (Winnicott's "therapeutic" mothering) often follows nonfulfillment of the idyll. Depending on the mother's emotional assets, in a crisis, manic defenses may give way to self-accusatory melancholia and postnatal depression.

Equally poignant is the woman who regards her care as a potentially overwhelming numinous influence on the vulnerable baby. This mother may go to some lengths to avoid falling in love with the baby or exposing it to the full brunt of the potentially "smothering" force of her love, at times resulting in an internal conflict or schizoid withdrawal (dyad IV [+ vs. − +]): "When I found out I was pregnant, at first I was overjoyed. But then I started attacking myself, couldn't sleep and had terrible dreams. I'm afraid of inflicting myself on the baby," says a suicidally depressed woman, self-referred for treatment late in her pregnancy, suffering from anxiety attacks. She has spent her life alternately rebelling and trying to achieve some recognition from her flamboyant father and correct, ambitious, and critically undermining mother. She dreams of a cabbage rotting in the refrigerator. In another dream she watches her stupified dog drag itself out of the hot oven where she had left it all night. My patient says it proves what a "bad container" she is for the baby—she doesn't know whether she will do more harm by holding herself coolly aloof or "killing the baby with love." In time, as we come to recognize both the internalized split between her parents and the elaborate defensive rituals she has had to install internally, since childhood, to mitigate the experience of her mother's voiced displeasure in motherhood, rejecting dismissal of her baby daughter's loving advances, and overt disgust at her bodily functions.

> I'm a wreck [my patient says tearfully when her son is 10 days old]. The birth was wonderful and I was beginning to get used to the baby, but then my parents arrived and mother immediately said I was doing everything wrong. Father joked about my appearance and Mother kept saying things like: "Don't hold him that way!" and "Is the milk flowing too fast?" and the baby made these noises while feeding that sound like suffering. Have I already damaged him by being such a smothering mother? Sometimes I have sinister feelings like I did when my mother watched me feeding him, that my milk is poison and whenever he burps, vomits, or shits I feel it's proof something is wrong and it's my fault.

Pregnancy

Since Mother left I fluctuate between fear of overfeeding or cruelly abandoning him, poor little mite [she says a week later]. When he screams I think he'll die of colic—his crying really gets to me like an accusation that I am no good for him and I feel so guilty; I had a dream that he was allergic to breast milk. Summarizes everything.

Some weeks later she speaks with amazement of breast-feeding: "He can live off me and grow. I didn't think I had it in me." But she worries: "Am I denying him? Am I spoiling him?" having difficulty saying "that's enough," yet afraid she is offering her breast "too much" to meet her own "need to be needed" or as "bribery to shut him up." She says she gets distressed when he cries, not knowing if he is angry, hungry, or in pain. Nevertheless, in time she comes to a finely tuned ability to distinguish between "feeding and sucking," "hunger and comfort," and the baby continues to thrive as his mother increasingly enjoys him despite her self-doubts and depression, encouraged by his obvious love of her.

Finally, when an expectant mother regards her baby and herself to be *mutually dangerous for each other* or in competition over meager resources, mutual protection may be sought by ensuring autonomy and devising insulation between them (dyad V [− / −]). This may manifest itself as a refusal to engage in emotional introspection, resistance to her thoughts being "possessed" as has her body, and even antenatally, there may be a sense of mother and infant fending for themselves: "I'm damned if I'll change my lifestyle just 'cos I'm preggers—I must look after myself and if it's crafty enough, the blob will survive anyway." Postnatally, persecutory feelings may dictate geographical separation to preserve the baby from the mother's "negative" influence and to counteract her fears of contamination by the baby's infantile needs or seductive charms and competitive use of precious resources (time, energy, space). The woman may abstain from breast-feeding on the grounds of its being "cannibalistic." Indeed, she may go to lengths to avoid intimate physical contact. Enforced togetherness is likely to be accompanied by emotional detachment and phobic anxieties.

Such a sense of persecutory incompatibility may be experienced even before conception takes place. "I seem to destroy life after making love," says Ms. Z. who is referred by her doctor for "psychogenic infertility."

Joan Raphael-Leff

> It feels like a state of extreme tension exploding with aggression . . . a flash of lightning! Vitalizing but dangerous too, like handling fire. As soon as I feel there is life inside—I snuff it out. Seems like a frightening alien being in there—weird, fishlike stages. I don't know why I use my power to kill embryos when I want a baby so—perhaps I envy them their comfort or am afraid of them attacking me inside. When I got a positive result on the pregnancy test I thumped myself on the belly. Couldn't overcome my impulses. It just confirms that I'm not good enough to have a baby. My womb feels rotten, full of rubbish and yucky things inside which can't let a baby grow.

Becoming pregnant, she is convinced that her nausea is the result of fetal toxins and conversely, that vomiting means she is trying to rid herself of the baby. Restricting herself to once-weekly therapy, she continues throughout the second trimester to deliberate whether to have an abortion to rid herself of the monster growing within. At 28 weeks, she prays for the pregnancy to end so her baby can have the safety of the incubator, away from her own harmful influences. Therapy starts in earnest when the physical experience of birth sets her off screaming uncontrollably, retriggering repressed memories of childhood abuse.

To round off the chart, there are two other permutations that augur badly for future interaction and are extremely resistant to treatment. There are cases where pregnancy is psychotically denied or the fetus nonchalantly regarded as nonexistent/unreal (dyad VI [+ or − 0]). Untreated, when the prenatal position persists postnatally, measures may have to be taken to ensure the infant's safety if the mother's defensive neglect, apathetic nonresponsiveness or narcissistic ignoring of the baby persists.

Similarly, cases of compulsive separation of "good" and "bad" aspects of mother and/or baby (dyad VII [+/− +/−]), are notoriously difficult to treat. These are manifested in exquisite sentimentalized pleasure where "good" meets "good," and exquisite persecution/retaliation where "bad" meets "bad;" failure to maintain good/bad splits result in a breakthrough of obsessional thoughts or intrusive ideas, often related to violence or sexual possessiveness, and are treated by the parent as coming "out of the blue." When treatment is sought, psychological understanding is hard-won, the transference reverberates with splits (protector/prosecutor), and psychotherapy is often endangered by intractable resistance and

Pregnancy

negative therapeutic reactions. The possibility of acting on impulse cannot be ruled out.

Illustration 2

"The pregnancy was fine until I began to feel trapped. I found myself hoping that the baby would die, but I was so shocked by that thought I could tell no-one about it," says a self-referred woman in a "caring" profession, still suffering from postnatal depression a year after her baby's birth. She is worried because she has "slipped up" in her job recently. In the initial interview she tells me without any insightful connections, that having spent her childhood unsuccessfully trying to "prove her worth," in recent years she has discovered that her mother had suffered a "nervous breakdown" following the patient's birth.

> After my daughter was born it felt almost like having two babies—one lovely, the other a monster. When she was tiny sometimes these vicious thoughts intensified—I saw myself throwing her out of the window or drowning her in the bath. A thought from nowhere would just pop into my head. I'd actually have a vision of doing these things, then panic about where it came from, and feel shocked because of being capable of seeing something so horrible. Once I even put a pillow over her face, but stopped.
>
> All this time, I carried on being the perfect mother, and people all commented how good I was. Do you know, to this day my daughter has never seen me cry. I'm constantly on my guard, protecting her from my feelings. I don't want her or anyone to know what is going on in my head. I so want to try and please her. When I feel trapped, I hate her and everything I do with her seems false. At other times I love her so much—she's so sweet—but then I question whether it can be love if I am so horrible, and so I've begun to doubt everything.

During therapy, she gradually comes to recognize her "inexplicable condition" as a function of guilt and self-criticism at not living up to impeccable standards imposed by an intolerant moralizing internal mother. She even seems more aware of the split between her idealized (external) mother and the internalized rejecting and judgmental figure, who is played out in her relationship with her partner. Through extensive work, she at times acknowledges "foreign," compulsive thoughts as her own—products of the repressed

Joan Raphael-Leff

flip side of perfectionistic self-expectations and denied hatred (her own and hatred she imagined her exacting, archaic mother felt toward the "maddening" baby her).

Despite persistant ruminations and self-doubts, feeling better, she gets her doctor to begin reducing her antidepressants. Although flaring up at intervals, the violent thoughts subside, becoming "a faint voice in the background." Some three years after the beginning of her (once-weekly) therapy she spontaneously "takes stock" of her own growth, saying:

> When I first came here I had no control; I hated myself and was split between feeling and acting. I never found myself until now—I went through life trying to project the nice image of what I thought others wanted me to be without thinking what I myself wanted or that I could be acceptable as I was. It was all a balancing act of living a lie which exploded in pregnancy—I was so ashamed of myself for conceiving without marriage. I was desperately guilty and trapped. I hated my partner for treating me so badly, yet felt I had to commit myself to stay with him for my parents' sake. The first thought was: "I'm having that fucking bastard's child." Then "My God! How could I think that!" Rude words came into my mind. Terrible things I still can't say aloud. I now see that I lost all my self-esteem. I felt worthless and hated myself and hated the baby when she was born because she was his; *she* was the one who was trapping me and making me feel horrid when I'd wanted it to be wonderful. I wished she'd die and actually had visions of chopping her up. When I took her to the zoo, I thought of feeding her to the lion. Although I enjoy playing with her, it's taken me all this time to accept that she is *mine*; that she is *herself* not the horrid child I believed I was; that I have a right to be a mother; that I can be *myself* and a good mother; that I can be myself and be a good mother—don't have to play "happy families," but can be angry and complain when my partner treats me badly—and that this is not just a biochemical imbalance, a postnatal illness outside my control, but a reaction to a situation within my power. I think it really delayed my recovery that I was so helpless and handed all my responsibility over.
>
> This has been a long process of coming together and finding out who I am—for the first time being able to think about what I want, able to talk and say terrible things out loud and to accept them as part of me, not alien ideas or a shameful secret, but mine and understandable.

Pregnancy

Not long after this session, treatment ended prematurely after several missed appointments on the grounds that she was "fine now" and getting on "so well" with her partner, she did not want to be reminded of "all that."

PERINATAL PSYCHOANALYTIC TREATMENT

To sum up so far, on the basic of extensive clinical work with both expectant and new parents, I have found that when, rather than fluidly oscillating among a variety of emotional permutations, a pregnant woman's psychic reality crystallizes predominantly around one affective experience (as illustrated by any one of these *fixed* dyadic representations), her monotypic vision—whether idealized, persecutory, depressive, withdrawn, repudiating or obsessional—is cause for concern. Some seek out therapy during pregnancy or postpartum, acknowledging that something is wrong; others are referred if a professional recognizes the fetus or infant to be at risk (hence the importance of educating primary health providers to recognize symptoms of perinatal disturbance).

Often, there is some overlap between categories, but it is hoped that this simple model may help the therapist determine the nature of the core issue, the type of therapeutic treatment (developmental guidance, brief dynamic therapy, or psychoanalytic treatment), its focus (on maternal representations, family transactions, or infant reactive disorder), and the duration and frequency of treatment—whether crisis, transitional, or chronic state (for guidelines, see Raphael-Leff, 1996, p. 165) in accord with each individual's capacity and needs. Where pathological interaction is intransigent, conjoint mother-infant therapy may be necessary to free the ongoing relationship from the effects of a vicious circle inherent in precarious maternal representations and/or neonatal difficulties. Preventive treatment before the birth can preempt entrenchment of pathological patterns of exchange.

Psychoanalytical Treatment During Pregnancy

Patients who seek therapy while pregnant may be impelled by life events, or caught up in the throes of intolerable internal upheavals with insufficient ability to defend themselves. In the treatment situation, impact of a *fixed* psychic reality is often experienced by the analyst in countertransferential terms of both carrying the denied aspect of ambivalence and having to tolerate unbearable uncertainties.

An unusual feature of treatment during pregnancy is invasion of the dyadic sanctity of the analytic setting by a third—the fetus. Communication may be curtailed to evade the inner eavesdropper or protect the vulnerable ever-present witness. As with psychotic or borderline patients, archaic semiotic communications and primitive preverbal preoccupations trigger profoundly disturbing emotions in the therapist. Likewise, the pregnant woman's intense bodily preoccupations and sensory hypersensitivity may engender psychosomatic symptomatology or sympathetic bodily resonance in the unguarded therapist.

Analysts treating a woman who becomes pregnant during the course of an analysis are often caught by surprise by the emotional turbulence, dramatic changes, vivid dreams, and strange experiences occurring in a hitherto familiar patient. Therapeutic endeavors are artificially accelerated by time pressure to loosen a defensive deadlock before the "deadline" of the birth. Conversely, the pregnant patient's rapid habituation and assimilation of psychological changes, and the depth of post-birth amnesia may increase the analysts typical level of activity. Indeed, therapists who otherwise have great respect for slowly unfurling emotional processes may find themselves formulating interpretations redolent with suggestion as they champion their other "client," hidden within the folds of the pregnant patient's flesh. Likewise, the unformulated pressure of "grandparental" expectations and countertransferential envy, dread, latent anxieties, and awe often permeate the "therapeutic amnion," as containment of the pregnant woman unwittingly galvanizes the analyst's own unconscious "generative crucible."

Finally, "not knowing" and indeterminancy prevail with the very real possibilities of miscarriage, caesarean section, stillbirth, congenital abnormality, or perinatal complications. Often these anxieties reside in the analyst, partially invested in her for safekeeping by the patient who cannot tolerate exploring them, and partially by the analyst's own "press" of helplessness underscoring the lack of influence over outcome, and the desire to prepare the patient for unlikely

Pregnancy

events while avoiding undue pessimism or alarm. A similar tightrope is strung between glaring realism and the need to preserve the modicum of poetic license necessary for survival as a new mother. While respecting the raw vulnerability of pregnancy, nevertheless interpretations must explore and deflate exaggerated optimism about the birth, sanguine overconfidence regarding maternal capacities, or idealization of infancy if dashed hopes and frustrations are to be avoided. Conversely, negative feelings require acceptance and unrestricted expression. However, where these predominate, work is focused on idiosyncratic meanings of malign representations and their amelioration before the birth.

Especially during a first pregnancy, a therapist's awareness of the momentous demands of the maternal task awaiting the patient and the complex needs of the real baby to come, may join forces with internal pressures—the sense of gestating a future nursing couple and wishing to nurture the expanding patient, about to be reborn as mother. Sentimentality or its cynical converse, in either therapist or patient, is counterproductive. As with all such issues, self-scrutiny reduces the danger of acting out in the countertransference. Thus engaged in the consulting room with a pregnant patient, therapist, too, is caught up in the time strictures of that same triple stranded system of physiology, psychohistory and sociocultural matrix. The period of gestation is dominated by inexorable bodily processes, heightened sensorium and greater emotional lability with rapid changes in lifestyle, personal identity, and body image. The anticipatory period leading up to labor and birth create a natural deadline redolent with anxieties about this caesura—internal damage, intolerable pain, loss of control, alienation, humiliation, and failure. Pressure accelerates as the patient's self-doubts proliferate about revealing unknown aspects under "torture," losing her mind during labor, dying, or worst of all, remaining possessed forever and unable to return to her own singular self, the anxiety of giving birth to the "wrong one," and her body being discarded like an empty shell while the baby retains her "soul" (Raphael-Leff, 1985). Timely interpretations may prevent obstetric complications and enactments of transgenerational catastrophic pressures.

Joan Raphael-Leff

POSTNATAL PSYCHOANALYTIC TREATMENT AND MOTHER-INFANT THERAPY

For the new mother, the early puerperium is dominated by sleepless exhaustion, hormonal fluctuations, and infantile arousal due to exposure to the smell, feel, and touch of primal substances (amniotic fluid, lochia, milk, feces, urine, saliva, mucus, blood). Clinically, I have found that these inchoate experiences contribute in many patients to loss of self- and bodily cohesion, and temporary regression to an often agitated state of sensory-dominated asymbolic impressions. Unbearable anxieties may include dread of reengulfment within a womblike state of dissolution, captivation by primitive merger, terror at being whirled into the turbulent eye of the neonatal tornado, fears of being sucked dry or swallowed by the insatiably grasping mouth clamped to her breast, invasion by a malevolent, exploitative, intrusive being, becoming swamped by the compelling maternal madness of sacrificial devotion (see Raphael-Leff, 1991, 1996).

In women with a fragile sense of self, traumatic experiences during labor and preverbal reactivations during parenting may crack open ossified infantile encapsulations I have termed "geodes" (Raphael-Leff, 1994), with consequent eruptions of unprocessed primal anxieties. Released, these unmetabolized emotions, unmitigated and fresh as the original moment of trauma when they were sealed, may take therapist and patient alike by surprise, accompanied by primitive experiences of personal disintegration, fears of leaking, dissolving, or bursting open at the seams. When the mother's sense of herself as a continuous individual is thus threatened during the perinatal period, primitive manifestations of annihilation anxiety and experiences of fission and fragmentation, fusion and confusion (Hopper, 1991), and/or chaotic autistic, schizoid, or paranoid defenses akin to those depicted by Tustin (1987, 1990), Ogden (1989), and Meltzer (1992), may be in evidence.

As stressed throughout this paper, conceptualization of the baby and her own internalized maternal capacities are underpinned by a woman's unconscious representations of her internal mother and of her own benign/damaging baby self. Depending on the nature of these ideations and the degree to which rigid antenatal constructs

Pregnancy

have invaded the relationship with the infant, individual treatment or conjoint mother-infant therapy is advocated. Transference and countertransference experiences provide evidence for these archaic internal representations, which undergo sea changes in the course of treatment toward richer understanding of reciprocal dynamics and mental states of mother and baby. In cases of shared unconscious fantasies or dysfunctional family "scripts" (Byng-Hall, 1995) couple or family therapy may be the treatment of choice. An outreach program offering home visits and/or primary care support may be required for housebound depressed or agoraphobic mothers and babies at risk (see Fraiberg, 1980).

Perinatal therapy provides the (expectant) mother with a safe place to reflect about her inner life and that of her baby during this "underwater time" (as one new mother called it) when thinking is so essential but so difficult:

> Therapy makes me feel I'm appreciated for who I am, [says a mother whose second child was born during the course of therapy]. It lets me do things for other people without feeling that I get nothing from anyone . . . preserves a balance that doesn't let things get out of hand. A lot of the time these days I am seething with rage and disaffection, feeling trapped in my family, seeing myself as a failure, yet frightened of envy. Coming here has stopped me hurting my kids by helping me think before I act irrationally. I guess I can do that because I know you are thinking of me and *with* me which my parents have never had the capacity to do.

Finally, how does perinatal therapy work? To my mind, mutative effectiveness of therapy during childbearing, as at other times, is due to mutually "transformative" engagement (Bollas, 1987) generating new understanding within the common psychic reality constructed by *both* patient(s) and analyst. The product of this dialectic interplay of subjectivities within the analytic setting may be conceived of as an "analytic third" (Ogden, 1994) or, in terms of this paper, as a "metaphorical placenta" created through the joint medium of their interaction. Furthermore, therapy, like pregnancy, is a process of growth with a built-in ending. The analyst's containment offers a nurturing space for reflective development and maximization of the woman's strengths, always bearing in mind that it is she who will be caring for her baby, possibly in isolation. By attributing meaning to the woman's feelings and behavior, the analyst fosters the new mother's sensitivity to her baby's emotional states, enabling her to attribute intentionality to the neonate and to think about, understand, and interpret the infant's preverbal communications. Inevitably, through transferential arousal and countertransferential experiences, such dynamic engagement elucidates archaic familial representations of self in relation to parental figures and siblings—as self to other, fetus to placenta, baby to mother, sister to mother's babies, daughter to father, rival to mother, mother to a baby—freeing "fixed" representations of self/internal objects, engendering availability of a greater array of personal "voices" and thus providing access to fresh resources of "transpersonal exchange."

In sum, I suggest that psychoanalytic engagement with inner experience, tolerance of uncertainty, and acceptance of the simultaneous coexistence of different developmental levels and of mixed feelings, offers mothers a rich old/new *model of maternity*, metaphorically rooted not only in "containment" but in *rewarding reciprocal* ("placental") *exchange* within the therapeutic process itself.

REFERENCES

BENEDEK, T. (1970). The psychobiology of pregnancy. In *Parenthood—Its Psychology and Psychopathology*, ed. A. J. Anthony & T. Benedek. Boston: Little, Brown.

BIBRING, G. (1959). Some considerations of psychological processes in pregnancy. *Psychoanal. Study Child*, 14:113–121.

BION, W.R. (1962). *Learning from Experience*. London: Heinemann.

BOLLAS, C. (1987). *The Shadow of the Object: Psychoanalysis of the Unthought Known*. London: Free Association Books.

BYNG-HALL, J. (1995). *Rewriting Family Scripts: Improvisation and Systems Change*. New York: Guilford Press.

CHAMBERLAIN, D. (1987). The cognitive newborn: a scientific update. *Brit. J. Psychother.*, 4:30–69.

DECASPER, A.J., et al. (1987). Fetal perception and discrimination of speech stimuli: demonstrated by cardiac reactivity, preliminary results. *C. R. Acad. Sci. III*, 30:161–164.

DEUTSCH, H. (1945). *The Psychology of Women*, Vol. 2, *Motherhood*. New York: Grune & Stratton.

FRAIBERG, S., Ed. (1980). *Clinical Studies in Infant Mental Health—The First Year of Life*. London: Tavistock.

HOPPER, E.I. (1991). Encapsulation as a defence against the fear of annihilation. *Int. J. Psychoanal.*, 72:607–624.

KESTENBERG, J. (1976). Regression and reintegration in pregnancy. *J. Amer. Psychoanal. Assn.*, 24(Suppl.):213–250.

Pregnancy

MELTZER, D. (1992). *The Claustrum: An Investigation of Claustrophobic Phenomena.* Worcester, MA: Clunie Press.

OGDEN, T.H. (1989). *The Primitive Edge of Experience.* Northvale, NJ: Aronson.

——— (1994). The analytical third: working with intersubjective clinical facts. *Int. J. Psychoanal.,* 75:3–19.

PINES, D. (1972). Pregnancy and motherhood: interaction between fantasy and reality. In *A Woman's Unconscious Use of Her Body.* London: Virago, 1993, pp. 55–77.

PIONTELLI, A. (1992). *From Fetus to Child: An Observational and Psychoanalytic Study.* London: Routledge.

RAPHAEL-LEFF, J. (1985). Fears and fantasies of childbirth. *J. Pre- & Perinat. Psychol.,* 1:14–17.

——— (1986). Facilitators and regulators: conscious and unconscious processes in pregnancy and early motherhood. *Brit. J. Med. Psychol.,* 56:379–390.

——— (1991). *Psychological Processes of Childbearing.* London: Chapman & Hall.

——— (1992). Transition to parenthood in reproductive life: advances in research. In *Psychosomatic Obstetrics and Gynaecology,* ed. K. Wijma & B. von Schoultz. Lancashire, U.K.: Parthenon, pp. 115–121.

——— (1994). Imaginative bodies of childbearing: visions and revisions. In *The Imaginative Body—Psychodynamic Therapy in Health Care,* ed. A. Erskine & D. Judd. London: Whurr, pp. 115–121.

——— (1996). *Pregnancy: The Inside Story.* Northvale, NJ: Aronson.

——— (in press). Childbearing practices across the continents—reflections on pregnant metaphor and pregnant fantasies. *J. Reproduct. & Infant Psychol.,* Suppl.

TUSTIN, F. (1987). *Autistic Barriers in Neurotic Patients.* London: Karnac.

——— (1990). *The Protective Shell in Children and Adults.* London: Karnac.

WINNICOTT, D.W. (1947). Hate in the countertransference. In *Through Paediatrics to Psycho-Analysis.* London: Hogarth Press, 1982, pp. 194–203.

——— (1956). Primary maternal preoccupation. In *Through Paediatrics to Psycho-Analysis.* London: Hogarth Press, 1982, pp. 300–305.

——— (1960). Ego distortion in terms of true and false self. In *The Maturational Processes and the Facilitating Environment.* New York: Int. Univ. Press, 1965, pp. 140–152.

WOLPERT, L. (1991). *The Triumph of the Embryo.* Oxford: Oxford Univ. Press.

The Pregnant Mother and the Body Image of the Daughter

Rosemary H. Balsam

> This paper is about the place of the pregnant maternal body in the developing body image of the daughter. Adult examples from two cases are offered to demonstrate its lingering effects on the women's perceptions of their shapes, sizes, abdomens, breasts, and buttocks. Attention is drawn to its neglect in our formulations. It is suggested that the whole exterior of the body of the female is as important to her as the outer and inner genitals, and makes a vital contribution to the final shape of her gender role identity.

It is surprising that the body of the pregnant mother is so neglected in our literature about unconscious fantasies that inform the body image of her daughter. The vast belly, the bounteous breasts, the swayback posture, all create an arresting new outline for the usual form of the grown woman. This symbol of fertile maternity is a major conscious and social focus of attention for adults and children of both sexes. It requires hard work to ignore a pregnant woman in the environment. The body outline captures in a moment's glance the epitome of female biological prowess, all the more so when seen nude. The erect phallus of the grown man is a familiar, visible, similar, nude icon of biological power, promise, and destiny. This latter symbol has been granted much more focus in the minds of both female and male analysands as reported in our literature and in our clinical and developmental theory, particularly about gender differentiation. This paper will attempt to address several questions. Why is the topic of the pregnant body *per se* virtually absent from most written accounts about patients' preoccupations as they lie on the couch? What can this phenomenon mean, given the frequency of the occurrence in many peoples' early childhood? If the topic

---

Associate Clinical Professor, Department of Psychiatry, Yale University. Training and Supervising Analyst, Western New England Institute for Psychoanalysis.

has been unrecognized or glossed over, does it manifest itself in unrecognized ways? If encountered, how does it yield to interpretation? And is it indeed important in the formation of a daughter's body image? One long case example and one vignette will be offered here to suggest the place in mental life that the mother's pregnant body can assume in the analyses of adult women. Let me note that I wish to differentiate entirely all the following ideas from any implications for general "normality" or "fulfillment" of womanhood. Only an individual woman can arrive at such a judgment.

RELEVANT LITERATURE

I detect five important trends in the literature about female psychology. Because of the historical development of each, I believe that the issue of a female-to-female body comparison inherent in a woman's emotional growth has fallen by the wayside. The topic has not readily fitted into the five agendae. Mayer (1995) begins to offer a way out of the dilemma, but does not go quite far enough. She articulates *dual* developmental lines in women, one line emanating from primary femininity and one line involving phallic concern. In her case study, she demonstrated how an impasse in an adult female's analysis occurred around the patient's phallic castration attitudes, a situation that yielded to forward movement only when the analyst began to take note of an underlying but repressed primary feminine constellation. Mayer offers that this analytic work suggests evidence of an interrupted line of development from the patient's core primary femininity, which had interwoven with her more evident phallic body concerns. Mayer's consideration stops with genital comparison and the stage of anatomical distinction. I wish to extend the territory of primary femininity to include from early on, a *whole* female-to-female body comparison which would then naturally include the small girl's fascination with the pregnant female body, the breasts, abdomen, buttocks, and all body parts including skin and hair as well as genitals. I believe that this developmental trajectory provides many clues to a woman's final body image, to its pleasures as well as to the kinds

Pregnant Mother and Body Image of Daughter

of fears of inferiority that beset many females in our consulting rooms.

I shall now summarize the five trends.

1. Genital Issues

Laqueur (1990) points out that Freud's idea of the girl starting as a little boy belongs in a tradition of a "one-sex" theory of humans, i.e., " . . . woman was understood as man inverted" (p. 236) for two thousand years till about the eighteenth century. Freud therefore reintroduced an atavistic element in the sex and gender debate by separating the clitoris (male) from the rest of female genitalia. For him, the female genitals were then "an anatomical marker of woman's lack of what man has" (p. 233). Yet by suggesting a universal libido and elaborating dominance of vaginal orgasm over clitoral orgasm in adult females, Freud also demonstrated an incomplete struggle toward a two-sex model, Laqueur argues, one in which adult females are sexually capable but different from men in "every physical and moral aspect" (p. 5). Men and women were still closely compared. Freud thus collapsed the two models in his thinking and his focus remained on the genitals. Young-Bruehl (1990) contends that Freud's abiding contribution of universal bisexuality still stands. It allows for a complex concept of gender identity derived from traits of one or the other sex in patterned form in an individual woman. Early psychoanalytic dissenters to the one-sex model were Jones and Horney. Most writers, however, followed Freud in comparing the woman's sexual organs closely with those of men, but many continued also to develop and describe the female in relation to her own body. Thus there are papers over the years pointing to early vaginal awareness, infantile masturbation, a female sense of inner space, reactions to sphincter control, the introitus, e.g., Erikson (1968), Kestenberg (1982), Richards (1992). Descriptions of the adolescent girl's reactions to her rapidly changing body and onset of menses have been richly rendered (Ritvo, 1976; Shopper, 1979). But here too the focus is on the genitals and abstractions about their integration into body image; little is said about, for example, the budding breasts. After her initial confusion about comparison to males, *the girl develops more or less as girl, but the genitals and her internal awareness are the main focus of these texts.*

Rosemary H. Balsam

2. Woman as Separate

Deutsch (1944, 1945) pioneered a view of women through the life cycle. The female as menstruating, becoming pregnant and menopausal, highlights the difference of the female, even though Deutsch does not question a beginning embedded in one-sex ideas. This literature progresses, often subsequently enriched by a two-sex model. Pregnancy is a specific topic of Bibring et al. (1961), Benedek (1970), Pines (1994), Raphael-Leff (1994). Women analysts, too, were described as different from male analysts in some ways. Papers on the pregnant woman therapist belong here, Nadelson et al. (1974), Balsam and Balsam (1974), Uyehara et al. (1995). A male analysand's erotic transference, or paternal transference to a woman analyst were further explicated by Goldberger and Evans (1985).

Feminist critics contributed to a social debate toward the equality of women, decrying Freud's one-sex originary model of female development as a social construct. The biological body becomes lost in most of this writing. Chodorow (1978) discusses the mother's pregnancy importantly as part of the social oppression of the heritage of girls, but not otherwise as part of psychological development. *The fate of the woman herself is the focus.*

3. Children and Mothers

The effects of mothers on their children as the latter progress through the psychosexual phases is explored extensively in the child literature, mainly in terms of their functioning as nurturers. I find few references to the girl's specific reaction to the mother's pregnant body *per se*, but I stand to be corrected because there are so many single case histories. I think it is fair to say that the topic has not been singled out. Freud (1933) developed late an awareness of the importance of the mother to the girl child's first desire to produce a baby, and Mack-Brunswick (1940) detected the preoedipal girl's wish for a baby, antedating her awareness of her genital difference from boys. Focused here are purely the child's wishes. The child's conception theories are familiar. Anal, male-derived, and oedipal fantasies about the child's wished-for "pregnancy" are recorded. The mother's reactions to genital difference is cited as contribution to the girl's reactions to her own genitals, Lerner (1976). Much attention accrues to the new-born rival. Perhaps these complex factors overshadow the child's reaction to the maternal body. *The child's reaction to the pregnant maternal body remains slighted.*

4. Female Gender Studies

By now the concept of core gender identity is established (Stoller, 1968; Kleeman, 1971; Tyson, 1982; Tyson and Tyson, 1990). Gender role identity and sexual partner orientation are conceived as developmental additions to this basic building block. An unusual paper by Kleeman (1971) attends specifically to a two-and-a-half-year-old girl's comparisons to her pregnant mother to help her sort out anatomical difference, in addition to her comparisons to the male. My present paper belongs in this tradition for a search for detail of female comparison to female, to enrich the concepts of body image development and later to be fitted into the concepts and guidelines suggested by the Tysons in the trajectory of gender role identity formation.

5. The Kleinian and Object-Relations Tradition

Klein (1928) certainly views the mother's body as equally weighted with the father's in a child's development. Phallus, vagina, body cavity, pregnancy, breasts, and parental intercourse are of equal fascination. Attention to body surface has not drawn interest because the focus is so internally derived from originary fantasy. Body specificity, I think, requires an underpinning of an ego-psychological orientation which has not easily fit with an exclusive object-relations perspective.

None of these five kinds of studies has been attentive to female-to-female body comparison. Yet obviously, a pregnant mother is inescapable to the eye, to the touch, and to the imagination of her daughter. In order to attend to this issue psychoanalytically, one requires aspects derived from each of these five categories of contribution. Thus, an analyst needs a two-sex model, an acceptance of the girl's body as productive of its own sensation, interest, and imagined future, a view of men and women as equal but different, and an acceptance of the prime significance of the mother to a girl's development.

Rosemary H. Balsam

CASE I

Ms. A. was a forty-eight-year-old interior decorator, divorced five years previously. She had two adult, professional, single daughters in their late twenties. She turned to analysis to address a few questions that had long irked her. Why, she mulled, did she turn out to be the "spitting image" of her mother, with a short temper, a perfectionism that drove others to drink (a wry reference to her ex-husband), a need to nag her daughters about their weight, a grumbling, obsession about her own weight, and an uneasy sense that her work was never good enough? She had hated these characteristics in her mother. Ms. A. believed she was hard to live with. "I pick at people. I pick and pick. When my mother was dying and she was half-conscious, I was sitting up with her during the night. I was stroking her hand. She opened her eyes for a moment—just long enough to growl at me—'For God's sake Georgina, you're putting on weight again. Your hands are pudgy.' I felt so, so [she gasped back a sob] hurt. It was four a.m.. She died at dawn." Ms. A. did not want to continue to be enslaved to this relentless ritual of complaint.

Ms. A. was a fresh-faced, crisp little woman with a pear-shaped figure, dressed in a business suit. Her five-year analysis dealt with many issues common in the lives of women—questioning self-esteem, relationship problems, inhibition of aggression, inhibition of sexual feelings, and body image concerns.

The family history as it related to figures for identification involved this domineering and critical mother who was yet not devoid of warmth, especially for babies, and a working-class, steady father who held benign ideals of "betterment" for his two daughters and one son. My patient was the eldest. The sister, Estelle, was two years younger, and the brother, Eric, six years her junior. The patient and her sister Estelle were born during hard times in the Great Depression. The peak developmental moments of significance in the analysis of Ms. A.'s character and interwoven depression circled around the birth of each sibling—one at her anal stage, when she struggled with mother over constipation, the next at the height of her oedipal striving. Ms. A.'s marriage at eighteen years suggested an effort at a precocious push into adulthood. The figure that loomed largest in her analysis was her mother.

Pregnant Mother and Body Image of Daughter

The opening gambits in the analysis suggested a transference where I was a female friend and confidante. Excitedly, she shared with me her secrets, hopes to impress clients, disappointments. I heard about the details of her 25-year marriage, the high-school romance with the football hero, and her social success as Queen among the seniors, deteriorating to her gradual disillusion at how hard it was to have babies with a husband who was terrified that domestication would undermine his manhood. Fighting, backbiting, and his alcoholism marred their years together. Their sexual relationship was poor to nonexistent latterly. She attended art school in her thirties. As soon as she could support herself and her daughters were independent, she fulfilled a long-held promise to herself: she separated from and subsequently divorced her husband.

I watched the sting of Ms. A.'s tongue at first from a distance: this neighbor was callow in matters of taste; that co-worker lacked a sense of design; the other was laughably obese. Another was a "circus dwarf." How long, I wondered, could her contentment with me continue? Her talk to me echoed her experience with a high-school clique of nasty "popular" girls. Mutual allegiance had operated within the inner sanctum of approval. High school was her favorite time in life.

One day, about nine months into treatment, she saw me make my way toward the office, hunched against the cold, an old hat pulled over my ears, picking my path with caution over patches of ice. I preceded her, not noticing her at some distance behind me. Once established in the room, she said that I had slammed the front door in her face. What was wrong, she wanted to know. Hesitatingly at first, and with my help, though pointing out how she was holding back criticism of me, possibly sensing danger, she began to elaborate. How could I wear that old hat? The coat, too, looked worn and awful. It was too big for me. Or perhaps not, maybe I had put on weight? It was hard to get a full look at me. At the beginning of the analysis I had looked neatly dressed, she thought, more like her. I seemed bigger now—bigger and fatter than she was. I looked like a bag lady. What was I hiding?

A paradigm for the unfolding pattern of her inner conflicts was forming. Two themes will be isolated at this point. (1) "You ignored me. Then you slammed the door in my face. You hurt me and make me mad. You disappoint me." (2) "Your body looks changed. How does your body compare to mine?" The conscious level of this sequence appeared over and over in the analysis. The unconscious underpinnings belonged to the eras of both of the mother's pregnancies.

Maternal Preoccupation

At later junctures also the patient was exquisitely sensitive about my failures to see her in public places. She disliked any evidence of my preoccupation with my inner world. At these moments she described me as "dreamy and far away" and "spacey." I was "in a fog," "out to lunch," "distant," "in a world of your own."

Ms. A.'s language conjured up a transference creature adrift in internal contemplation. She denied that my actual attention to the details of her associations in the sessions had shifted. My behavior as I crossed paths outside the sessions was the stimulus. Because of her simultaneous references to my "baggy" clothes in these sightings, I asked about the connection between my look and her inference about my mental state when I failed to see her. "I can see your whole shape outside. I can tell how you're feeling when I see you from a distance," she explained. "When you're tentlike, you're too dreamy to notice me." She built many scenarios of my "troubles" and mental state based on these moments. She was worried that I was short of money. Was my husband out of work? That was the first clue to the time frame of the regressive material that began to emerge. Imaginatively, we were back in the Great Depression. The following dream also alerted us both further to the events of the time.

> I am walking in a street, and the lights are bright. It seems to be Christmas. I am very happy and expecting Santa Claus. I have on a green velvet dress. I smoothe down the front nice and flat. My parents were around someplace.
> The scene changes. Somebody in a big brown cloak has her back to me. I'm in a toilet, in a stall sitting on the toilet and feeling all swollen up. My mother turns out to be in that cloak, bears down on me and starts screaming at me. I start to cry and I wake up with my heart pounding.

The associations began with the figure in the cloak—like me, she said—turning my back. This was a symbol of my preoccupation.

Pregnant Mother and Body Image of Daughter

Given the next scene depicting the cloaked figure's screams, Ms. A. began to wonder if her urgency about my inattention "cloaked" a terror that I was in fact enraged at her. It was like sitting on the toilet before Estelle was born, trying to "poop" while mother, with her own "fat" belly, got frustrated. Her sensitivity to my preoccupation and shape were therefore especially reminiscent of her mother's pregnant state at the time of Ms. A.'s constipation. Mother, however, was always somewhat irritable about physical closeness. "You had to watch her hairstyle, or her lipstick. I did sit on her knee—it's just that I had to be very careful. I liked to sit and play with her necklaces, and touch her breasts, and I fiddled with the buttons down the front of her dresses. I used to count them and examine spaces—like I knew when her breasts were getting bigger, before Estelle's birth. And I could feel the big lump under her dress. I believe she did breast-feed me for a bit—not long. I remember her throwing me off her knee in a rage when she got so bulky, and she told me I was too heavy." We had evidence of little Ms. A.'s attempts at close physical proximity, affectionate and hostile scrutiny of the mother's body, which were nevertheless tentative due to mother's irritability and self-involvement. Ms. A. had had to curb her curious and exploratory maternal touching early. We believed that mother's pregnancy, reduced lap, plus the wrangling over the constipation added an extra blow that created more uneasy distance between them. The quality of Ms. A.'s sudden concern about my keeping her at bay because of my money worries, my unemployed husband, and the simultaneous growth of my girth reconstructively placed us in reactivated concerns from that era. "Mothers who change shape can change mood too, and get very, very mad!" she averred. "You have to watch out." Ms. A. now no longer felt safe with me.

The Changed Body and the Mother-Daughter Comparison

In the initial girl-to-girl transference, Ms. A. related to me as if I were separate but equal and possessed body similarities to herself, even if they were not brought to consciousness in analysis. The subjective realm of "shared" feeling tones, outlook, and imagined experience dominated the associative field. Others were outsiders, yet unconsciously compared to her own body as bigger than "us," uglier than "us," more grotesque than "us."

Cast out of my circle of intimacy, overt body talk was ushered in. First the clothes were the emotional trigger. These, she felt, had changed for the worse. Her own miserable feelings and my perceived ugly looks were meshed. "I feel closed out and hurt, and you are in a big, ugly coat" associatively came together. In her dream, mother's vast brown cloak ("a color I really hate"), and associated with mother's pregnant state, were featured side by side with the patient's constipated discomfort—the little girl's own enlarged, swollen belly, her weeping because her stools seemed stuck inside and would not come out. The phrase she used, "She bore down," yielded also associations of the births of Ms. A.'s own children. The patient had dreaded pregnancy and had expected her body to be ruined due to uncontrollable abdominal swelling. Her first baby had been large, and had taken many hours to deliver. She remembered vividly screaming at the midwife and cursing the doctor who had to use forceps. It was an immense relief finally to get the baby out of her body. The mother figure in the dream she was analyzing now was furious, screaming, and conveyed an image of pushing something down upon her. Ms. A. recalled her childhood fantasies about mother's screams as she gave birth to Estelle, much like Ms. A.'s own reactions to her constipation and her own subsequent childbirth experience. The dream child was overwhelmed and afraid. "It was all a nightmare," she sighed. "You shouldn't wear those baggy clothes. It makes me scared you're pregnant too. And I can't stand you not seeing me."

One can see in these sequences an interchangeability between the affects, fantasies, and body experiences of the girl child, constipated in this case, blended with her experiences of the body and affect of the adult woman, pregnant in this case. Later we understood that in part the constipation episodes, like her angry response to me at the front door, probably were designed to pull mother out of her "dreamy" pregnant states.

When Ms. A. spoke of the green dress in her dream, she used her hands to smooth down her abdomen as she lay talking, a gesture signaling the current liveliness of the topic in my presence. The velvet dress had been a precious Santa gift from her father. She looked "gorgeous" in her new dress. "Then I was so nice and thin. Not like that heap of a mother. I was so flat in those days—not like now, when I'm so lumpy." Mother, by her own self-description, was

Pregnant Mother and Body Image of Daughter

tall but always wanted to be thinner. Frequently the mother compared their bodies while taking showers together, telling the child to cherish always her slender lines. Ms. A. recalled uneasily crawling into bed beside her pregnant mother, feeling very superior to the rubbery, "lumpy" (her word earlier for her own abdomen), yet "cushiony" form that she surreptiously tried to snuggle into. She would poke mother's body and say, "Lumpy, gooey, ucky!" Mother would push her away, telling her she "couldn't help it." The patient's unconscious ambivalence toward mother's belly, echoing the mother's own ambivalence toward her increased weight, pregnant abdomen, and breasts could be appreciated in Ms. A.'s memories and her contemporary words describing her own figure. In the analysis, fears of an increase in my belly and a shift in my affect were now in focus, and guaged by comparison to hers.

Ms. A.'s mother's dresses were a theme in the analysis. There was a red polka-dot silk cocktail dress. It was slinky, with a frill around the hem—"like a mermaid." Ms. A. stressed that it was flat in front. She imagined herself, this time enviously, watching mother put it on to go out with father. "She pulled it up from the feet over her great slim legs that she said Daddy said were like a ballet dancer's. We both looked in the mirror, and thought she was gorgeous."

"That word again, 'gorgeous,' comes together with 'being flat,' or like a mermaid," I reflected. She responded, "That makes me think of another dream. I'm a grownup. I am preening in a mirror and smoothing down the front of myself, in a blood-red satin dress, and I like what I see—slender hips and abs of steel," she said longingly, "so far from this pudgy shape I'm stuck with ever since my babies came." By the elucidation of these references, we appreciated again the red dress and her body image at one with her favored internal vision of the most admired shape of her mother, the version of her body between pregnancies. The story of the red dress continued in another session.

At age ten, as punishment for fighting with both siblings, mother banished her to the parental bedroom without dinner. After her tears had dried, the child took mother's sewing shears, opened her closet, pulled out the red dress and systematically cut it into shreds. She had no memory of the repercussions. This deliberate destruction was a complex act of vengeance wreaked on both herself and mother.

Rosemary H. Balsam

"I cut up her favorite dress. It was my favorite dress of hers too. I think I was trying to destroy her thin, flat, beauty to pay her back. She could never have the satisfaction of wearing it again. I felt hopeless about ever having a figure like that myself, and I was mad about being constantly pushed away by her. I was tubby around the middle at ten, and I was scared of having periods. I knew they had something to do with being able to get pregnant. She must have so resented being pregnant with me as well as Estelle and Eric. She hated us kids fighting." One could also detect here the fear of what fate awaited Ms. A.'s enlarging prepubertal body and a dread of future body swellings.

Throughout the analysis, Ms. A. regularly noticed and spoke about my clothes. Most of these comments would be followed by references to her own wardrobe, suggesting to me ongoing scrutiny of body comparison. Often it measured who was superior and who inferior in thin/fat terms. Her own body seemed always perceived by contrast or similarity to another woman. Tent shapes on me or herself were "like haystacks." A-line dresses were "cutsey little girls playing at being pregnant." Long skirts were fine, as long as the waist was visible. If the blouse flowed to the top of the legs without definition, it was deemed "frumpy." Trouser suits were not especially noted, perhaps because she once said that her mother never wore them.

Male Influences Regarding Body Image

The male comparisons for Ms. A., as often noted in case studies, focused on the genitals. In her ex-husband's drunken, disinhibited states she had seen him late at night, in underpants, with his large, flaccid organ hanging out as he dozed in the living room. Memories of her father came back. She used to sneak peeks of him in the bathroom, in underpants, the clear bulge of his genital being her fascination. Disgust, fear, as well as excitement were registered. "They did something dirty at night. I thought he poked it into her hole," she giggled, "like poking a stick into a car tailpipe with stinky fumes ... [She sighed and nervously touched her abdomen] making damned babies again." Her emphasis was on largeness, bulge, ugliness, and a primal scene with an anal cast. I looked in vain for some connections, for awe and admiration of images of the adult phallus,

Pregnant Mother and Body Image of Daughter

perhaps leading her to an internalization of classical ideals of a "phallic" body image.

Her brother's tiny penis was the major focus for her male-oriented envy when she scrutinized their respective endowment. She thought it would be fun to play with such a dainty little stick. Secret genital play had occurred with brother. Masturbation fantasies involved "taking" his organ and putting it on her mons pubis. She admired latency-boy figures and connected her aspiration to be thin and flat also to acquiring brother's body outline. These conflicts were vivid for her at puberty. As she struggled with breast growth, growing hips, putting on weight at age twelve, and the initial horrors of menstruation, his seven-year-old body seemed enviable to her. The early adolescent closeness to peer girls, who characteristically compared their bodies, helped her to assume more comfort with breasts that were envied by other girls, and helped her appreciate her nubile body that brought excitement from peer boys. Interest in the technicalities of sexual intercourse and her female power to promote arousal and popularity with boys went side-by-side for her with temporary repression about the implications of her body for procreation and pregnancy, which, as we saw in the analysis, held a rush of horror, ambivalence, and expectation of ugliness. Adolescence was also a time of safer distance from mother. Not so, once she married. The unfinished internal work about her own body as compared to her mother's procreative body took on new life.

Ms. A.'s own experience of pregnancy and childbirth had a flavor of being "visited" upon her. At times she blamed her husband for his desire to prove his manliness by impregnating her. Once the girls were born, she was a passable caretaking parent. To say simply that she suffered from a denial of femininity did not do the situation justice. She wanted to be a mother in the executive sense. She could separate her feelings of bodily grotesqueness from her interest in the children's welfare. She recalled just "waiting out" the pregnancies, feeling depressed, and hiding from company the larger she became. Her first delivery was long and painful; she was grateful for a spinal block for the second.

A dream in which she ran through mud puddles, tearing the hem of a fancy pink dress, evoked a fantasy that she had glimpsed a torn hem on my dress the previous day. Perhaps my husband had ripped my dress off in a fit of passion, she mused. That made her think of me being torn apart giving birth. "Women aren't big enough to let out a baby," I said. "Yes . . . well I think that happens. I used to think that that must be the only way. You had a ragged and torn vagina forever after. I imagined my mother was torn inside. In fact I saw her vagina once, and it looked like a jagged black hole with fur. I thought that's what made her cross all the time with us kids. She must have been ripped when giving birth. I was certain that I would end up torn like her. I guess I still think that . . . I just said you are torn too." At one point, while working on these issues in analysis, she reported using a mirror to examine her genitalia. She detected surprise in her reaction that she still looked intact. I felt that Ms. A.'s "castration" anxiety represented much about the fear of the fate of the female vaginal canal in childbirth. Her level of association seemed to support this anxiety rather than a more classical reference to a "missing penis."

The Baby

For Ms. A., the wish to have a baby was expressed in two modes, a caretaking mode of maternal identification, which she preferred, and the bodily mode of carrying and giving birth to a baby. Envy of her mother for taking charge of the little ones, as well as a wish to join her and thus gain approval, was expressed in the former mode. We appreciated that her proclivity to criticize her children and others actually held a positive valence, and was part of a strong childhood picture of the behavior of any competent mother worth her salt. Turning out the "spitting image" of mother, in spite of contrary wishes, encoded the "spit" and "spite" of her early vision of an angry mother with three children under six years old.

The embodied mother, not surprisingly, was a largely negative construct for her. I can best show how Ms. A. reworked some of her own bodily anxiety together with her projected worries that mothers and mother/analysts hated being pregnant and delivering, by relating some unusual regressive events in my office, late in the analysis.

Consonant with her profession as an interior decorator, the patient often seemed visually compelled by the decorations on my walls. Her eyes would travel from picture to picture, while she would critique the merits and demerits of each work of art. Her gaze of me had shifted from the sightings in the street, to a closeup view of my

Pregnant Mother and Body Image of Daughter

surround. "I always feel that a person's decor is the same as their body," she said repeatedly. I understood then that her comments about the office were close displacements from her fantasies about my body. At times this was interpreted. For example, she said, "I hate that tapestry of the squirrel. People who like tapestries like dark, old, twisted things." "Perhaps something about me is dark and twisted today, and it seems easier to talk about the tapestry?" I asked, hoping to address the resistance. "What is twisted is that we both know that I'm talking about you, but I'm an artist and I just need to use this space to explore some things. Please let me do this in my own way! You have to understand that the interior of the room *is* you—as I lie here it's how I *know* your insides." She was fervent. I decided to accept her symbolism and enter into it with her, instead of insisting on secondary process.

A colorful Matisse poster from his Moroccan period particularly captured her eye. As she stared at it she reported a swelling sensation in her abdomen, "coming up like a balloon" and a tingling sensation of growing very large, extending over the end of the couch. "I feel myself inside the room in the painting, with you, looking into the distance. How can I get through the window and onto that beach below? Would I push the flowers on the windowsill aside and jump? Are there stairs hidden and leading down to the beach? The outside is sunny and there are little people on the beach below, but inside this room is blue and dark." She sighed sadly. I wondered out loud if she felt trapped. Her eyes traveled to a watercolor. "Now I am going through the woods and pushing through the black furry underbrush [I thought of her previous description of her mother's vagina]. I could swim down that brown river." Her gaze moved on. "The path down over there is hilly. The landscape is covered with little round hills. Maybe I could scramble down the bank? It's so hard," and she sighed again. I found myself in a responsive daydream. It was no accident that I, too, should have experienced my own regressive pull at those moments, for the landscapes in which she was now wandering were ones from our family place in Ireland, where I grew up. There is not an inch of the territory that surrounds me in my watercolors that I have not trodden, and there is not a "little round hill" that I have not clambered upon. I am, in effect, surrounded by my own Mother Earth, and it is the soil belonging to

Rosemary H. Balsam

my father.[1] The whole room seemed to become my own vast imagined pregnant belly. It was as if she were imagining herself as my internal fetus becoming too big for the space, as if she were viewing from the inside the obstacles of my womb, inspecting the territory and wondering how to escape into the world. At a previous point Ms. A. reported a dream where she was first in a basket of a hot-air balloon, hovering uneasily over the earth. She became transfixed with the primary colors of the balloon and, in the dream, became anxious as she was gradually sucked up into the cavity of the balloon, being first long and thin and then expanding again. In her associations she had referred to the vivid primary colors of the Matisse painting and spoke of a parallel feeling of being "sucked into" the painting. Pregnancy and birth had occupied her associations that day. More anxiety had accompanied the association then, and had been interpreted at the time. She had spoken of the balloon as a uterus, and declared a fantasy of becoming sucked into my "womb." There had been Matisse prints in her childhood home. She associated primary colors to her children's bedrooms.

Based on her own comments about how the room was symbolic of my insides, my own regressive experience, and the memory of her balloon dream, I offered an interpretation. I spoke of her wish to exist inside my body and look at it from the inside. I proposed that she feared the power of her wish because it would mean that I could suck her into myself to make me big, and she feared it would be very hard to get out. She was quiet for a bit. "I do want to become like you," she said slowly. "I want to *be* you. I want to be your baby, right inside you. I want to be part of you. And I don't want you to push me away like mother, before I'm ready myself. But I want to get out, too. . . . I want to be your big girl too . . . It will be very hard to stop coming here." She recalled days on the couch when she would sit up slowly, experiencing dizziness. "I was angry then. I didn't want to get sucked in and be dependent . . . Now that's okay . . . but I also want to be free. I can imagine you looking at me through a window now. It is sunny and I fancy you'd approve of me playing on the beach." She ultimately translated this experience as a constellation of previously repressed fantasies, embodying both her

---

[1] For a detailed description of a similar regressive transference/countertransference, see Peto (1959).

Pregnant Mother and Body Image of Daughter

desire to be inside the big belly and her desire to emerge, empowered to feel that she too could potentially become the possessor of the big form and belly. She later spoke of how important it was that I tolerate this regressive experience and not push her away as she felt mother had done when she snuggled up to her pregnant form in bed, to fantasize about her past and future as a woman, and to explore her mother's body further. It had been painful for the girl to hear her mother say about her pregnancy that she "couldn't help it." By listening to her regressive fantasy about birth, she extrapolated that I did not object to her position on the couch, in front of me, in my room, enacting a symbolic representation of being pregnant with her awaiting "delivery" (which turned out to be termination thoughts). Ms. A. was working through primitive guilt about a masturbation fantasy that involved my adult "pregnant body" (the room, the painting, and herself supine on the couch) and a fantasized trajectory of her fate as a girl infant who could also grow into a woman and be pregnant and deliver, with my blessing.

At times in the termination phase Ms. A. would wear bright blues and reds. She adopted more of a Bohemian style, "not like yours and not like mother's," with looser and flowing pants and dresses. It was an era of fashion toward the less form-fitting. But she and I interpreted her responsiveness to this shift as consonant with more ease about her underlying shape. It mattered less to appear "flat" all of the time. We terminated as she approached menopause. Her depression had lifted, and she had less fear of the physical changes she anticipated in advancing age. "Some day I hope my daughters will be pregnant and that I'll be a comfortable grandmother. I hope I'll have a granddaughter, and I suppose I'll redo the history of my body all over again." As I trudged through the snow in my old hat and coat, I hoped she would have the opportunity.

CASE 2

Ms. B. was a thirty-one-year-old loving, if anxious, mother of a two-year-old boy, and wife of a scholarly graduate student of physics. She was a high-school teacher. She suffered from "underachievement," and wanted to explore her urgent competitiveness in analysis. Compared to her academically successful husband, she felt inadequate.

Rosemary H. Balsam

It was a functional marriage with mutual encouragement and passion. They were both entranced with their little boy. Ms. B's parents were a traditional couple from the Midwest, her father a businessman. Her sister, Frances, was four years younger.

The analysis lasted four years. The first year unfolded themes about Ms. B.'s competitive feelings with her husband. She felt her father had wanted his oldest to be a boy, to keep the business in the family. A tomboy and athletic, she still enjoyed coaching field hockey. There was evidence of a classical phallic oedipal striving; she tried to become father's best boy while at the same time covertly wooing him to become his best girl. The route to a fantasy boyhood seemed more open because, as she said, "there seemed to be too many females to compete with in the household." The birth of her own boy and her marriage to a man her father admired provided an outlet for some transformation of these issues, if at times she felt rivalry with them both. She had unconscious fantasies of attempting to possess a penis, one way or another.

Male body themes became more peripheral as her specifically female body took center stage. Even from the beginning, Ms. B.'s breasts were a matter of pride and hope for body self-esteem. They did hold some phallic significance, too, for example, in such comments as, "Why should I care what the men have, when I have two beauties of my own?" All curves of her female body were of interest to her, but the breasts were predominant. Avid competition with women emerged. She was of medium height, trim and muscular, with a blonde bob. There was a bouncy air to her carriage. She had large breasts, which she talked about initially as needing special "cradling" in athletic support bras when she ran on the hockey field. Her words first attracted my ear because they were so tender, like words she used for her little boy, and they seemed offered in a slightly yearning tone: "my boobies," she called them affectionately. At menstruation, when they became engorged, she declared that the slight ache was pleasant. "My great big titties are really gigantic today," she would giggle, "I'm glad I'm on my back here—they look like they're sitting up all by themselves today. Do you look at them? I wonder what you can see from where you sit?" And she would push them up further, inviting my fuller inspection. As these moments were full of teasing giggles, one day I ventured naughtily, "All the

Pregnant Mother and Body Image of Daughter

better to see you, my dear!" entering into her playfulness. "What big eyes you have, grandma!" she flashed back. "Oh I do feel like Little Red Riding Hood with her goodies, coming to see grandma... I feel like I'm offering you my breasts—maybe to eat, but more to show them and take them away. I have something you'd like, but they're mine, and I can take them home with me." "I guess you're teasing me with your goodies," I said. This led to associations about being teased at school by "drooling" teenage boys and being lustfully stared at by older men. She agreed with my interpretation that it was a reference to her "drooling," Grandma Wolf/analyst/father. It was a response to my enactment, but with its own internal significance. We were shifting ground between male and female.

She grew sad and serious. "Big breasts and looking make me remember that I used... every excuse to watch Mother breast-feed Frances. I thought they looked luscious to suck. I envied the baby. But I urgently wanted to know what it was like to have big breasts myself. Mother's breasts were great... awesome... like the universe or something," and she sighed wistfully. Ms. B.'s flirtation and cheeriness always markedly ceased when these themes of oral desire and envy and admiration of the mother's breasts came up. Talking about women was less playful than talk about men. She was in a state of deep awe observing her mother's body.

In the last two years we spent most sessions on herself, me as woman (as opposed to me as a man), her mother, and Frances, a stereotypically "frilly" girl. Ms. B. spoke of looking at women's magazines and other women in the gym as she worked out. She searched the torsos for "boobs"—the bigger the better. She constantly compared sizes of women's "rear ends." Spandex and skin-tight workout gear were her specialty. She watched my body especially for low necklines and declivity. She declared my breasts small. Her gaze also included the lower body.

> You sit all day. Your behind is big. That reminds me of a dream. I was in a zoo. There was this mammoth kangaroo. It was like a huge pyramid, and it had a little baby in its pouch. How do they give birth anyway? Do they have a big hole under there? Ugh! Imagine they'd lose all their control—they're such athletes, jumping around usually. They must pour their "do" when they give birth—so gross! [a cloacal theory of birth, I thought]. Maybe their little Frankie, no, Joey—God, that's Frances!—comes out of their bellybuttons, right into the pouch? It

would be neat to have a pouch in front like that. You could see everything then.

Later she spoke of thoughts about her mother's body and her pregnancy with Frances. She returned to puzzles about the kangaroo. Ms. B. expressed such concern about the perineum of the kangaroo that I told her I was reminded of her telling me she had worried the nurse would forget to let her look in the mirror when she herself was giving birth. "It used to be a mystery what was hidden down under," she said. (I refrained from interpreting the meaning of the choice of kangaroo as Australian, for her "down-under" references. The mood of the moment was somber, and I felt this intervention would be distracting. I fancied that my word play would invite her back into her teasing, phallic-competitive mode.)

After a pause, Ms. B. continued: "My father used to entertain me by taking me to the zoo to make me laugh when mother was pregnant." (I realized that I may have been about to do the same thing in the analytic process, now that the child's view of the topic of pregnancy and birth was graphically in the atmosphere. I noted to myself that there really is something anxiety- and guilt-provoking about staring at a pregnant body and wondering about the birth process in a sustained way, at close quarters, through the eyes of a curious onlooker. I had wished to dilute the moment in word play. Perhaps this reticence may be more widespread among analytic couples? Perhaps this was a clue to why people do not note this kind of material very often.)

Ms. B. went on in many other sessions to recall her views of mother's pregnant body in various lingerie, in different color large dresses, in the bedroom or bathroom. She had wanted to touch her mother's belly and breasts, but instead had eyed her constantly, viewing her mother's entire body, with special attention to her huge breasts and hips. She thought the buttocks might grow out in two mountains, to match the breasts. She connected her current attraction to looking at the female behind with a hope to see varying buttock size.

> I used to look at myself when I was seven or eight and worry that I would grow big, big buns. The big boobies were okay. How I yearned for the day when my little nothing chest would grow. I waited and waited. Yet I had a very unstable sense

Pregnant Mother and Body Image of Daughter

of what it would be like to change. As Mother grew, I thought it would never stop. And then she got flat again—but she still had those big, delicious breasts for a long, long time. God, how I wanted to *be* her and have those pillows myself.

Nature was kind in at last providing little Ms. B. what she wanted. She won the competition in body contour with her analyst, and apparently her mother and Frances, too. Ms. B.'s spirited competitiveness was therefore importantly fed by her female body comparisons, in my opinion even more prominent than her male body comparisons, but they were woven together.

DISCUSSION

Does clinical material exist, in the associative process, that concerns primarily identification with the physicality of the mother? I believe that it does, and that it deserves a place in our theory of female development as it relates to psychosexuality, gender role identity, and body image. The pregnant body, for example, would seem to be a natural apex in a theory of female development which claims that "the ego is first and foremost a body ego" (Freud, 1923, p. 27). I would therefore like to separate and bring into the center for consideration specific visual, kinesthetic, and tactile perceptions of female body-to-body comparison. Such cognitive registrations of body surface can serve as an external starting point for the kernel of fantasy life integral to interiority.

I have been particularly struck by ongoing and at times insistent reference to same-sex body comparisons that are frequent in the adult female patient talking to the female analyst. A male analyst may also hear these themes, but they are inescapable with a female diad. Women like Ms. A. and Ms. B., of different ages and life experiences, are typical in their concerns as to the form and shape of their own exteriors and those of other women.

On hearing such references, which are additionally loaded with affect, such as envy or triumph, one rapidly listens on the plane of interior life and meaning. If one moves back a notch, as it were, concentrating on the description of exterior form and shape, joining the patient on the visual plane, then one begins to wonder about the origins of the heightened visual acuity for the human body that these fellow adults possess. Looking at shapes—not necessarily the detailed contents—and dressing with other women in mind seems a prominent preoccupation. The target of the eye is often other women, with a compared vision of how each appears in exterior outline. These images are often registered in comparison to the perceived outline of the subject herself.

A woman talking about another woman in analysis has often implied latent reference to "the mother." Developmentally, a diadic object relation as opposed to a triadic situation can be implied, so that the analytic listener may become taken up with expectation of more primitive material and assumption than is the case when attending to the psychic plane of triadic object relations. I suggest that if this is the case, the therapist may almost automatically be attuning for merger phenomena accompanied by primitive fantasy, and thus perhaps may listen less for the surface quality of visual and tactile registration and its mental representation. A patient's ability to verbalize these phenomena suggests a capacity for separateness in a woman when talking about her mother. It is true that Ms. A. showed primitive merger phenomena regarding the mother/analyst in her analysis, but only at one point, while deeply engaged in the analytic process prior to termination. The literature has stressed a continued internal focus on the mother, for women, as encompassing a "fixation" on her, implying a state to be hurdled if development is to proceed. This attitude could cause the analyst to try to "help" the patient too rapidly past the inevitable fascinations I dwell upon here. Mention of the same-sex body, too, is often related with alacrity to the erotic trend. Since homoeroticism is a difficult subject for patients who consider themselves heterosexual in orientation, the therapist is on the lookout for the disavowed and latent unconscious underpinnings. This listening stance could shift the attention away from granting phenomena concerning the surfaces of the body a history of their own.

"How do I occupy space as compared to other women?" seemed the underlying question as an originator of feelings, fantasies and memories that sharpened in the transference. "How do I shape up?" is a preoccupation that implies built-in comparison. "How is my body like my mother's?" is a question for a girl that encodes a present

Pregnant Mother and Body Image of Daughter

and future of changing shapes. I suggest that the questions, "Who's pregnant, who was, and who is not?" are a special unconscious dimension.

It is probably no accident that women's magazines have wide circulation in our culture. The pictures of other women in clothes of varying shapes are of endless fascination to fellow women. Tight forms, loose forms, emphasis on one curve or another concavity, colors and textures, and cosmetics draw women because of the shifting complexity of what may fit with any individual woman's visual necessity. The forms of naked women in men's magazines, which are more static, are perhaps of less interest to these manifest and latent concerns of women about fluid forms. This topic, of course, touches on the erotic response, which is a different but related question and is a complex one for women with regard to the respective visual lines of other females. I include it less here.

The attention to the analyst's clothes, the patient's own clothes and those of other women that appear in these case examples is testament to the importance of garments and their meaning to females. There is certainly a competitive element about how they will attract the male gaze.

> Mirror, mirror on the wall,
> Who is the fairest of us all?

speaks profoundly to the intergenerational as well as the cross-generational beauty contest that exists for the erotic admiration of the King and the Prince. Dressing to optimize or conceal body configuration can represent this quest. Interior oedipal themes are easy to detect when such competition is in the atmosphere. Dressing for the Queen and Princess holds a separate interest.

What emotional valences "joined in the conversation" at the exterior of the body—to quote Freud's (1896, p. 180) useful way of thinking? Ms. A. ushered in her body talk by enacting with me the scenes of feeling acutely shut out of her mother's central focus, it turned out, especially at the periods of mother's pregnancies. She was chronically frustrated in her exploratory desire to touch and feel her mother, particularly when mother was pregnant. Joining the mother in her own self-perception, she grew first to admire visually the mother's nonpregnant or "flat" state, and later to search her own body for visual and tactile signs of this ideal. The pregnant bulge, the tired body and maternal preoccupation joined forces with her anger and hurt and repulsion. It is interesting how visual and kinesthetic sense becomes amalgamated with affective response and colors the response to shapes perceived in the object. Synesthesia is a concept in cognitive psychology to capture a joining of the senses, e.g., "the taste of the smell" of something. Grammatically, the phenomenon is known as "transferred epithet," e.g., "the green joy . . . [of the pasture]." This phenomenon must happen frequently in childhood when the attachments to the continuities of body form are less fixed, less predictable, and less knowable, and the interactions with adults are so intense. Convexity of the abdomen had vehemently retained for Ms. A. a sense of ugliness, anxiety, and despair. This was projected onto other shapes of women in her environment, with constantly comparative overtones. One can appreciate also how sublimation had turned into professional virtue. As an interior decorator, Ms. A. used her visual and imaginative proclivities for comparative assessments of the shapes and forms of material objects.

Ms. B., by similar mechanism of amalgamating visual stimuli with affect, had positive associations between fantasized delights of breast-feeding and the enlarged arc and circle or oval of the breast. Convexity and largeness of the anatomical form accompanied by softness or firmness to the touch were her themes. Her focus on the buttocks seemed quite similar in quality to her focus on the breasts, but her responses were more ambivalent. Her reactions to rear ends conveyed overtones of both attractive and repulsive anal function. Her dream of the kangaroo located her body fascination with pregnancy. What a kangaroo hides under its "huge pyramidal shape" was a mystery. She admired the notion of a special pouch in front. One can hear, here, the often recorded wish of the girl to *see* the internal genital and womb, a wish often associated with envy of the boy's ability to clearly see the penis. Ms. B. seemed to have displaced upward some aspects of the swelling, growing pregnancy in the belly to her proudly held twin cupolae of the breasts. Perhaps her anxieties about the birth itself and how the babies would get out motivated her vision away from the belly toward the upper torso. Her feeling of having "nothing at all" in front, as a child, as well as comparison to mother's anatomical display arose also in comparison to her husband's and her father's sex organs. As suggested by Mayer (1995)

Pregnant Mother and Body Image of Daughter

Ms. B. could be thought of as having two interwoven developmental lines—one in consort with male body comparison, and the other in consort with the female body, including its capacity to bear children.

CONCLUSION

These are examples of women who compare themselves very closely with the mother. I think that these comparisons are probably not confined to actual experiences of mother's pregnancy, but may represent a wider scope of female preoccupation with the female body potential in general. By definition, a mother is the creature who bore the child, and the child is aware of this fact. A mother can also be pregnant or nonpregnant. It seems natural and expectable that a baby who is labeled "female" by the visual perception of her genitals by the grownups around her is going to be inculcated by virtue of mother's identified same sex and same gender with visual images of comparison. The genitals have traditionally been the main locus of definition in our literature for sorting out reactions and fantasies that build the girl's gender identity.

My material suggests that we have not sufficiently developed reactions in developmental progress about aspects of the female body other than the genital. Little has been written about the budding breasts, for example. My beginning contribution concerns the mother's pregnancy, an aspect more visible and and I contend, at least as compelling for the growing girl as her own genitals. Granted, for a growing girl, it is a futuristic image, compared to the immediacy of her genitals. Her special physical interest in the body that swells up to deliver and to feed the child that she wishes or fears too, for whatever reason, may be at least as vital to a line of primary femininity as her comparative physical interest in the male.

REFERENCES

Balsam, A. & Balsam, R.H. (1974). The pregnant therapist. In *Becoming a Psychotherapist: A Clinical Primer*. Chicago, IL: Univ. Chicago Press, 1984, pp. 265–288.

Benedek, T. (1970). The psychology of pregnancy. In *Parenthood, Its Psychobiology and Psychopathology*, ed. E. J. Anthony & T. Benedek. Boston: Little Brown, pp. 137–155.

BIBRING, G.; DWYER, T.F.; HUNTINGTON, D.S. & VALENSTEIN, A.F. (1961). A study of the psychological processes in pregnancy and of the earliest mother-child relationship. *Psychoanal. Study Child*, 16:9–72.

CHODOROW, N. (1978). *The Reproduction of Mothering: Psychoanalysis and the Sociology of Gender.* Berkeley, CA: Univ. California Press.

DEUTSCH, H. (1944, 1945). *The Psychology of Women: A Psychoanalytic Interpretation*, Vols. 1 & 2. New York: Grune & Stratton.

ERIKSON, E.H. (1968). Womanhood and the inner space. In *Identity, Youth and Crisis.* New York: Norton, pp. 261–294.

FREUD, S. (1896). Further remarks on the neuro-psychoses of defence. *S. E.*, 3.

——— (1923). The ego and the id. *S. E.*, 19.

——— (1933). Femininity. *S. E.*, 22.

GOLDBERGER, M. & EVANS, D. (1985). On transference manifestations in patients with female analysts. *Int. J. Psychoanal.*, 66:295–309.

KESTENBERG, J. (1982). The inner genital phase: prephallic and preoedipal. In *Early Female Development*, ed. D. Mendell. New York: S. P. Medical and Scientific Books, pp. 71–126.

KLEEMAN, J. (1971). The establishment of core gender identity in normal girls. 2. How meanings are conveyed between parent and child in the first three years. *Arch. Sex. Behav.*, 1(2):117–129.

KLEIN, M. (1928). Early stages of the Oedipus conflict. In *Love, Guilt and Reparation and Other Works: The Writings of Melanie Klein*, Vol. 1. London: Hogarth Press, 1975, pp. 186–198.

LAQUEUR, T. (1990). *Making Sex: Body and Gender from the Greeks to Freud.* Cambridge, MA: Harvard Univ. Press.

LERNER, H. (1976). Parental mislabeling of female genitals as a determinant of penis envy and learning inhibitions in women. *J. Amer. Psychoanal. Assn.*, 24(Suppl.):269–283.

MACK-BRUNSWICK, R. (1940). The preoedipal phase of the libido development. *Psychoanal. Q.*, 9:293–319.

MAYER, E. (1995). The phallic castration complex and primary femininity: paired developmental lines toward female gender identity. *J. Amer. Psychoanal. Assn.*, 43:17–38.

NADELSON, C.; NOTMAN, M.; AARONS, E. & FELDMAN, J. (1974). The pregnant therapist. *Amer. J. Psychiat.*, 131:1107–1111.

PETO, A. (1959). Body image and archaic thinking. *Int. J. Psychoanal.*, 40:223–231.

PINES, D. (1994). *A Woman's Unconscious Use of Her Body.* New Haven, CT: Yale Univ. Press.

RAPHAEL-LEFF, J. (1995). *Pregnancy: The Inside Story.* New York: Aronson.

RICHARDS, A.K. (1992). The influence of sphincter control and genital sensation on body image and gender identity in women. *Psychoanal. Q.*, 61:331–351.

RITVO, S. (1976). Adolescent to woman. *J. Amer. Psychoanal. Assn.*, 24(Suppl.):127–137.

SHOPPER, M. (1979). The (re)discovery of the vagina and the importance of the menstrual tampon. In *Female Adolescent Development*, ed. M. Sugar. New York: Brunner/Mazel, pp. 214–233.

Pregnant Mother and Body Image of Daughter

STOLLER, R.J. (1968). *Sex and Gender.* New York: Science House.
TYSON, P. (1982). A developmental line of gender identity, gender role, and choice of love object. *J. Amer. Psychoanal. Assn.*, 30:61–86.
——— & TYSON R. (1990). *Development: An Integration.* New Haven, CT: Yale Univ. Press.
UYEHARA, A.; AUSTRIAN, S.; UPTON, L.G.; WARNER, R.H. & WILLIAMSON, R.A. (1995). Telling of the analyst's pregnancy. *J. Amer. Psychoanal. Assn.*, 43:113–137.
YOUNG-BRUEHL, E. (1990). Introduction. In *Freud on Women: A Reader.* New York: Norton, pp. 3–47.

On Motherhood

Erna Furman

In working with mothers' responses to the total or partial loss of their child, it becomes evident that, at one level, they experience such a loss as an injury to the integrity of their body ego, which includes the child. Their capacity to invest the child as a bodily part of themselves as well as to release him and transfer bodily ownership to him in the course of personality growth necessitates flexible body boundaries. This characteristic of the female body ego is both gratifying and threatening to the mother as well as to others. It also has a profound impact on the growing boy's and girl's attempts to differentiate themselves from the mother bodily and to delineate their own sex-specific body ego. The nature and outcome of this difficult process has a significant effect on women's and men's attitudes to motherhood. These attitudes contain many defensive measures against the primitive anxieties of this early level, contributing perhaps also to the frequent neglect of motherhood in theories of female psychology.

I shall focus on an aspect of female psychology that has been sidestepped, more often than not, in analytic contributions to this topic, namely the fact that the potential for being a mother and its realization, or lack thereof, forms the genetic core of womanhood and plays a crucial role in the development of boys and girls from the very start. The widespread neglect of the central role of motherhood—exemplified, for example, by Tyson's (1994) review of contemporary contributions to female psychology—is in striking contrast to our clinical experience which has shown us that: the female and male body ego develop by differentiation from that of a mother (not just a woman); girls and boys perceive their mother as a mother first and only later as a woman; their mother (in her mothering rather than womanly function) is their first object of identification; little girls want to be a "Mommy" long before they want to be

---

From the Cleveland Center for Research in Child Development and the Hanna Perkins Therapeutic School.

Erna Furman

a "lady" and refer to their doll as their "baby" long before it is given a special name; and, not least, the conscious and unconscious feelings and concerns about being or not being a mother (and what kind of a mother) remain a crucial part of being a woman throughout every woman's—and possibly every man's—life.

In keeping with this neglect, much of the controversy about sexual phallic monism has focused on establishing a concept of bedrock femininity characterized by a sense of bodily wholeness from the start and reenforced by identification with the mother's female genitals, without reference to motherhood. The emphasis, instead, has been on showing that little girls do not define themselves as lacking or inferior, but actually feel safer and more comfortable with their female genitals than boys do with their exposed vulnerable penis. Summarizing contemporary views, Tyson (1994) points out that establishing core gender identity is easier for the girl by virtue of her anatomy as well as through identification with her mother. The girl's "genitals and associated diffuse, whole body sensations are experienced as an integral and protected... part of her body from the beginning.... Therefore, defining a sense of body integrity is normally a smoother process for the girl" (p. 452). At the same time, identification with her mother provides "an experiential sense of being female, like mother, with female genitals" (p. 454). With motherhood left out, these considerations remain limited to boy-girl comparisons and the related phallic-narcissistic question of who is "better" or "better off."

It is noteworthy that the many analytic contributions that focus on the basic role of motherhood and the "inner space" as part of it, remain as isolated and neglected as the topic itself, especially in the USA. Among these are contributions by Chasseguet-Smirgel (1976), Erikson (1956, 1964), T.-B. Hägglund et al. (1978), T.-B. Hägglund and Piha (1980), V. Hägglund (1981), Horney (1926, 1932), Kestenberg (1956a, 1956b, 1968), and Torsti (1993). In her 1976 paper, Chasseguet-Smirgel suggests that sexual phallic monism wards off the boy's double narcissistic wounds sustained in the relationship with the mother, i.e., his helplessness and dependency on her at first, and his oedipal disappointment and sexual inadequacy with her later. She finds that a powerful, envied, and terrifying maternal imago lies behind the defensive scorn of female inferiority. I do not dispute this insightful observation, but I think it does not explain everything.

Since boys *and* girls, men *and* women, find it so difficult to accept that the "psychological striving for motherhood is the core of femininity" (V. Hägglund, 1981, p. 143) and are so ready to exclude it from its role in male and female gender development, motherhood must imply additional deepseated early concerns. Over many years I have struggled to learn about these concerns and formulated some of my findings (Furman, 1982, 1984, 1992, 1993, 1994). I shall now retrace my steps in the hope of clarifying these inherently difficult issues.

THE CHILD AS PART OF THE MOTHER'S BODY EGO

In 1969 I described the parents' special investment in their child as a hallmark of their entry into the phase of parenthood. In contrast to the investment of all other object relations, that of the parents in their child is characterized by a narcissistic cathexis, the child as a part of the self, which, to start with, far outweighs the concomitant object cathexis, the child as a loved person. As the child grows, there is a relative shift in the balance between these two kinds of investment, but the narcissistic one is never fully replaced and always remains a significant factor, qualitatively and quantitatively different from narcissistic elements in other relationships. I noted at the same time that, just as the parental investment of the child differs from other object relations, so the maternal investment differs significantly from the paternal one. Both parents include the child in their own mental self, but only the mother invests him also as a part of her bodily self, i.e., he is included in the boundaries of her body ego. The physiological and biological givens of pregnancy parallel and facilitate this latter process but they do not guarantee it. Some biological mothers fail to integrate their baby into their body ego or achieve it only partially; some adoptive mothers, though by no means all, succeed in this respect.

Although, at the time, I did not appreciate the full implications of the mother's bodily investment in her child, it proved to be a crucial and most helpful concept to me in understanding motherhood and is pertinent to the present discussion.

Erna Furman

MOTHER'S RESPONSES TO THE DEATH OF THEIR BABY

My first dramatic encounter with the manifestations of the maternal bodily investment came through my work with perinatal loss, mothers who lost a newborn or very young baby through death (Furman, 1980). Along with their conscious and very understandable feelings of distress, sadness, anger, guilt, despair and unconscious defenses against them, they complained of symptoms which disturbed them but which they in no way associated with their loss or, at best, vaguely related to the aftermath of a difficult pregnancy or delivery. Most often they experienced abdominal sensations which felt to them either like a growing cancerous tumor or like a strange "hole," "like something's all wrong with my insides," "some awful illness." Quite often too, they described radiating aches in their arms, a strange heaviness and difficulty in lifting or extending them. Occasionally, they attributed the disconcerting experience of "something all wrong" to their minds, fearing they were falling apart mentally and going crazy, and sometimes they could neither localize nor find words for their worry. Since others seemed not to take their complaints seriously, did not even want to hear about them, or told them to "pull yourself together," they felt even worse. Despite the intense anxiety, some of these mothers did not seek medical help and those who did were not reassured by the negative findings.

They were, however, greatly helped by two interventions: (1) My putting into words for them that the baby had been an integral, most important part of their body; that its removal from their inside (the hole) and lack of restitution by being also unavailable on the outside (the arms intended to hold him) were therefore experienced as an amputation of a vital body part or as the loss of a vital function, such as vision. They were feeling crippled and undone and, as with a real amputation or loss of function, would take a long time to adapt to the loss and repair their sense of bodily and mental wholeness without the baby. And because this experience was different and separate from the loss of the baby as a loved person, and represented, instead, a major injury to their bodily integrity, it was something that, like the sight of cripples, disturbed others and made it hard for them to empathize or even listen to their distress. (2) A concerted effort on the part of hospital staff as well as in working with the bereaved parents to afford them postnatal contact with the baby, even the dead baby, and to enlist their active role in arranging a funeral and burial or cremation. This facilitated the process of the mother transferring her cathexis of the inside baby to the outside baby and provided some opportunity for object cathexis. The more object cathexis, the greater the opportunity to mourn the child as a separate loved one—a difficult task in itself, but much easier for others to support than coming to terms with a shattered body ego.

MOTHERS' RESPONSES TO THE DEVELOPMENTAL LOSS OF THEIR CHILD

During the subsequent years I could increasingly compare my child analytic findings with data from my work with mothers of infants and toddlers. I came to realize that the deeply shattering breach to the integrity of the maternal body ego accompanies not only the total loss of the child through death, but each developmental step in his personality growth and resulting increase in self-sufficiency (Furman, 1982, 1984, 1992, 1993, 1994).

The difference with the "ordinary devoted mother" of the living growing child is that she usually uses immediate and effective defenses against the threat of these primitive anxieties. During babyhood, turning passive into active is most commonly used. I have described some of the many instances when the mother shifts the "trauma" of weaning from herself to her baby: she responds to his signs of readiness for self-feeding and rejection of the breast by leaving him first—by going to work, going on a trip, going out one night in such a way that he wakes up to an unexpected sitter, i.e., leaving him just enough to convey the terror of abandonment (Furman, 1982). These ways of leaving him first around the time of weaning often mark the start of the many sleep disturbances during the latter part of the first year.

These sleep disturbances, however, result as often from another maternal defense, namely transferring her hold on the child's body from nursing to sleeping. While letting go of the former, mothers tighten the reins on the latter as they unwittingly interfere with the child's "not needing" them during his night or nap time (Furman, 1982). Indeed, changing the form or area of owning the child's body is as common a defense as leaving him first. For example, spoonfeeding or rigid control of the types and amounts of food offered easily nullify the child's potential independence resulting from weaning; similarly, mother's ownership of nursing (what goes in) is often transferred to elimination (what comes out) which tends to be rationalized as related to the changes in digesting new foods.

During the toddler phase, the child's second and third years, mothers face the most concentrated task of changing the balance of their investment in the child, from predominantly narcissistic to object-oriented, in keeping with the child's personality growth. For mother and toddler this process focuses on the transfer of bodily ownership from her to him. She who heretofore gauged and met all his needs is expected to yield to his demand for bodily self-care and ownership, for it is mainly through the bit-by-bit process of owning, gauging, and ministering to his own bodily needs that the child differentiates himself from his mother and defines his body ego. This includes protesting pain, learning to avoid common dangers, washing, dressing and undressing, gauging hunger and self-feeding, gauging elimination and keeping clean, recognizing fatigue and putting himself to sleep.

I have described the arduous steps by which mother and child negotiate the transfer of bodily ownership—doing for, doing with, standing by to admire, doing for oneself—and I have described how extraordinarily difficult it is for mothers to do their part (Furman, 1992, 1993). They repeatedly ignore or deny the child's signals of readiness, they prolong the first two steps and, with the third of standing by to admire, tend to turn away, feeling no longer "needed." In doing so they have passed on the skill, the knowhow of self-care, but reneged on graciously handing over the gratification they experienced in performing it. By keeping that for themselves, they deprive their child of the most valuable part of owning his body. Once again, they leave him before he can leave them. The mothers' denials, delays, and reluctance are all the more striking when contrasted with their frequently expressed wishes for the child to do for himself, complaints about the tiring job of doing for him, even pride in his achievements of self-care, and often lavish support of the

On Motherhood

child's nonbodily skills, such as his motor activities, speech, block-building, or interest in puzzles. The same child whose small muscle dexterity is praised and admired may be deemed quite incapable of learning to wipe his behind.

Some mothers avoid being "left" by taking active control of their toddler's steps toward bodily self-care. Instead of heeding and responding to his signals of readiness and self-initiative, they are intent on teaching him each skill, and insist on his doing his "chores" when they consider it the right time, i.e., their time. In doing so they both push him away and retain ownership of his body because the process proceeds at their behest, while the child feels the threat of abandonment and need to satisfy mother rather than himself by performing for her.

All these maternal defenses protect her from the threat of losing the part of her body ego that is invested in her child. Unfortunately, they also constitute considerable interference in the child's ability to differentiate and integrate his own body ego and to invest it and his caring for it in an optimally pleasurable, gratifying way.

Many mothers are well aware of the wrench caused by the child's becoming his own person, be it his weaning, dressing himself, entry to nursery school, leaving for summer camp or college, getting married. They feel and verbalize their pain and sadness and, since they are also happy with and proud of his achievements, experience it as a bittersweet time that still allows them to support rather than impede his growth. Yet their awareness, though helpful to them and their child, derives from the more mature parts of their personalities. The primitive anxieties about bodily loss and disintegration surface in the form of sudden unwarranted panic states about losing something, which they in no way connect to the current situation of loss of the child. Let me add a couple of examples to several cited previously (Furman, 1994).

Example A

Following my presentation of this topic to an analytic group, an experienced analyst confided this episode: That very morning she had looked in vain for the sweater she was now wearing. As she rummaged through her drawers a panic seized her, quite disproportionate to the value of the sweater. She feared she had lost it for good. It finally occurred to her that her married daughter and grandchild had left that morning after a nice visit, and she became convinced that her daughter, who liked the sweater, had taken it with her. She found herself quite angry at her adult child, then opened once again the drawer where the sweater was supposed to be—and there it was. She could not think how she had overlooked it, but she realized now that its presumed disappearance stood for the more profound loss of her daughter.

Example B

The mother of a two-year-old arrived to our appointment late and distraught. She had been "out of it" during the last four days because she had lost her wallet. She was without cash, credit cards, driver's license. She had searched everything in vain and spent her time telephoning around to stop misuse of the lost documents. She felt she was going crazy, could not function, and she also felt guilty for not being available to her little girl. As she retraced the events, it turned out that the night before the disappearance of the wallet the child had, at her own request, slept in a big bed for the first time, did so with pleasure, and wanted the crib removed. Mother had been pleased and appreciative of her daughter's developmental step but had reneged on removing the crib "in case she changed her mind."

Since the various effects of developmental loss on this mother had been a topic of our work in the past, I wondered with her whether perhaps, in addition to her positive feelings about her child's progress, there were also feelings of losing something very basic to her own self, so basic that it felt like she could not function without it. She connected the losses at once and cried out, "Oh my goodness, the wallet!" On returning home she called me, greatly relieved. She had found the wallet. It was where she had looked for it before.

Instances of pseudoloss are more or less effective ego measures to bind the emerging primitive experiences occasioned by body-ego loss of the child. We are alerted to them by the primitive panic the mother experiences temporarily and, often, by the accompanying anger at the child who, one way or another, is unjustly blamed for the loss or unwittingly "punished" for it, such as by mother's emotional

On Motherhood

withdrawal. It is only when mother and child reach an impasse during the transfer process or when the child reacts with symptomatic behaviors that upset the mother enough to request help that the ensuing therapeutic work reveals a glimpse of the forces that underlie mothers' manifest idiosyncracies.

Example C

One mother came for help with her eighteen-month-old's persistent sleep disturbance which manifested itself in not going to sleep, waking repeatedly, and getting up very early. It "ruined" mother's life and she was also concerned for him, fearing she was doing something wrong. She was not concerned about his still frequent nursing, lack of self-feeding, and showing no initiative in other areas of bodily self-care. We came to understand that his sleep trouble related on one hand to his total dependence on her ministrations, without any means of self-comfort (thumbsucking, transitional object, or soft toy); on the other hand, it related to her many irregular absences during the day as well as emotional withdrawals when she was physically present. With closer observation we learned that her absences often appeared to be prompted by her son's even minor steps toward independence.

When his sleep trouble improved with the help of her increased insight and changes in handling, it suddenly got worse again. It turned out she had just begun an exercise program in the early mornings which made it necessary for the father to attend to the boy on his waking up. She felt she had to exercise "to get myself in shape and put my body together"—a rather common maternal response to the loss of the child as part of her body. With further insight into their mutual conflict about bodily ownership and delineation of body boundaries, she stopped the exercises, remained available in the morning, and his sleep again improved.

Then the following episode took place which frightened mother and child: She had always carried him downstairs, considering his learning to negotiate the stairs too unsafe. He had wanted to walk on his own on several occasions, but she reneged. That morning she again carried him downstairs, stumbled under the weight, and both fell headlong, sustaining minor injuries. She found herself in a rage and lashed out at him with, "See what you've done! You are much too big and heavy to be carried. From now on you will just have to get yourself downstairs on your own." She was chagrined and puzzled about her outburst and later apologized to him. She could begin to recognize that her need to thwart his "leaving" her and to push him away instead of supporting his independent steps warded off her sense of panic and rage at being "cut off."

She was not an abusive mother. Her anger was usually in good control and she wished for and appreciated her child's achievements in many areas. His bodily independence, however, constituted such a threat to her bodily integrity that her experience of it overtook the more mature aspects of her personality and allowed primitive panic and rage to surface.

THE NATURE OF THE MATERNAL, FEMALE BODY EGO AND SOME CONSEQUENCES

Some mothers can never allow their child to delineate and own his body ego for fear of what it would do to themselves and what they would do to him. Some can, with much effort, take the necessary steps if they are helped to gain sufficient insight into the nature of their predicament and if this work takes place in the context of a containing, supportive relationship. With less vulnerable mothers, such support does not need to be available through a therapist but can come through the relationship with an emotionally available husband, grandmother, or close friend (Furman, 1994).

The mother's psychic state at the time of these shattering experiences of bodily loss resembles those of an older infant or young toddler during the period of initial differentiation from the mother when his primitive, incomplete body ego is overwhelmed from within or without, or when the still essential parts of his mother's ego have disappeared, such as through her physical or emotional unavailability. He can only reconstitute his body ego by being bodily contained within the mother's, such as through her empathic holding and soothing of him. The extent to which the early states of bodily disintegration were effectively contained and repaired will determine how quickly and well he will later be able to use his own more mature personality parts to protect himself from such overwhelmings and/or to contain and repair them when they occur.

On Motherhood

I have come to understand that the maternal body ego, and therefore motherhood itself, is characterized by never fully delineating itself. The female body ego is flexible, adapted to include a baby within its boundaries not only during pregnancy in its inside space, but also after birth when the child is physically outside the mother. This so essential extension of the mother's body ego to her child (how else could she care for him round the clock, often sacrificing satisfaction of her own bodily needs?) does, however, need to be renounced bit by bit and handed over to the child when he wants it as his own.

Graciously to surrender and even support and enjoy his taking away, as it were, now an arm, now a leg, now a need or function, renders her bodily integrity extremely vulnerable. No wonder mothers want to hold on to these outside parts of themselves or at least control the timing and form of the bodily transfer. No wonder they feel shaken to the core at times when they are not ready for it and are taken by surprise (Furman, 1994).

Many mothers experience difficulty in including the baby within their body ego when it grows inside them. Glenn's (1993) description of his pregnant patient's bodily sensations could be regarded as exemplifying this. Many avoid getting pregnant or carrying through a pregnancy because the attendant changes in their body ego are too threatening to their sense of bodily wholeness. Many experience great difficulty in letting the inside baby go (which contributes to prolonged labor). Many more find it difficult to effect the body ego changes by which the bodily self-invested inside baby becomes the bodily self-invested outside baby (which contributes to mothers' postnatal depressive or paranoidlike anxieties and is, in part, related to postpartum psychosis).

The lifelong process of "being there to be left" is, however, the hardest and most threatening aspect of motherhood (Furman, 1982). It never ends. It is repeated with each child. When one speaks of it with mothers they feel deeply understood and tend to respond with tears—not with words because these experiences predate words, predate symbolic representation, predate sexual gender experience in the usual sense of the term.

The maternal capacity to include the inside *and* outside child within her body boundaries and also to respond to his need for release by allowing him to own this most treasured part of herself constitutes the mixed blessing of motherhood—its primitive gratifications and dangers. As boys and girls, men and women, we all once were, and to a variable extent remain, a part of our mothers. Our earliest bodily unit with and differentiation from her leave us with a sense of the power and vulnerability of her flexible, undelineated body ego. This engenders awe, envy, terror, and all the defenses against them. It is a part of the way our own body ego is formed and maintained and serves as the matrix for sex-specific gender development.

DELINEATING AND INVESTING ONE'S OWN BODY EGO

Since the early seminal contributions by Winnicott (1941) and Hoffer (1949, 1950), there have been many studies of the ways infants and toddlers use their sensations and perceptions to form their own body ego, to delineate it as an increasingly complete entity, including the genitals and their sexual function, and to invest it narcissistically. Much less has been said and understood about how protracted and difficult this process of integration is and how much it depends on the role of the mother. Katan (1960) describes a thirteen-month-old offering pretend food to his penis, much as, at that age, youngsters indiscriminately feed mother and themselves. His penis, like his mother, were part self and part other, or perhaps also still part of his early narcissistic milieu and body ego which includes body parts outside his own bodily limits. Katan goes on to describe cases in which the mother's handling of the boy's body and needs interfered with his ability to own and use his penis as an adult, i.e., to integrate his penis fully within his own body ego and to delineate his body ego from that of his mother.

We know, similarly, that a mother's insistence on inserting a pacifier can interfere with hand, mouth, and ego integration, or that her attitude to the older infant's transitional object can render useless his attempts to use it as a step in self-other differentiation (Furman, 1992, 1993). At the Cleveland Center for Research in Child Development, reports of the analyses of young children who were

On Motherhood

nursed through the toddler and preschool years have repeatedly shown how such prolonged breast-feeding not only enables the mother to continue owning the child's body, but how it also allows the child to continue owning his mother's body. After weaning, these boys and girls feel depleted and dissatisfied with their own bodies. They are enraged at mother for taking away the breast they considered theirs and have difficulty in investing and delineating their body ego.

Example D

A four-year-old girl felt forever incomplete bodily and incapable mentally, with rages of irrational demandingness. She had been nursed till almost three years and had only just begun to master other areas of self-care. Early on during her analysis, she showed her underlying conflict in this episode: She tore a nipple-shaped rubber doorstop from the wall and bit it excitedly, provocatively disregarding her mother's alarmed commands to stop and hand over the doorstop. Finally she threw it across the room and, when asked to pick it up, yelled, "You can pick it up yourself. It's yours anyway!" The mother, usually patient, became uncharateristically enraged and spanked her daughter. She was puzzled and chagrined by her primitive outburst.

Tustin (1973) found autistic pathology to be caused by the rupture of the early mother-child unit which confronts the child with a traumatic sense of separateness and the lasting experience of a hole.

In the Hanna Perkins Toddler-Mother Group (Furman, 1992, 1993) we frequently observe how mother and child own each other's elimination, affecting the child's mastery of toileting and body ego differentiation. The toddler's manifest urinary and anal withholding often prompts the mother to use the toilet. For some toddlers this solves a beginning inner conflict, as if mother's mastery substituted for their own. With others, mother's going to the bathroom brings on loud, angry protests, as if her letting go interfered with their own withholding. When we can help mothers understand this, they let their child know that Mommy's going to the bathroom does not help *them* to be clean. The toddlers' responses are immediate: the relieved toddler resumes being conflicted; the protesting toddler calms down. Similarly, some mothers become quite distraught and are in tears at their toddler's trouble with toileting. They are often instantly relieved when it is pointed out that *they* achieved toilet mastery long since and it is now their child's turn. One little boy came to a mutually satisfactory arrangement with his mother: *she* used the toilet and *he* flushed it.

Anyone working closely with mothers and their toddlers can cite similar examples and ways in which the mother-child bodily unit gropes its way uneasily toward bodily differentiation and new body ego boundaries. I merely want to use these illustrative vignettes to underline that the primary mother-child joint ownership of their bodies involves flexible, unstable body ego boundaries for mother and child, that self-other differentiation implies renunciation of some parts of the extended body ego—especially for the mother, but also for the child—and that the child's progress toward owning and investigating his own circumscribed body ego depends crucially on the mother's capacity to facilitate, or at least to tolerate, this development. As noted above, it proceeds most markedly through their interactions around needs and the related impulses during the transition from mother's care to self-care.

The mother's vulnerability and difficulty in surrendering her narcissistic investment of the child's body and retracting the boundaries of her body ego accordingly have already been described. The healthy child's striving for autonomy is usually zestful (he has more to gain than to lose), but for him, too, there are satisfactions in owning mother's body and being owned by her. Being one's own separate person means relinquishing her omnipotence, having to make do with one's limited capabilities and bearing the frustrations of working toward mastery. Just as the mother never fully withdraws her cathexis of the child's body, so the child too retains a measure of his early bodily unit with the mother. Depending on the relative success of mother's facilitation and the child's self-delineation, the remnants of the primary bodily unit with its unstable boundaries of encompassing the mother and being encompassed by her, can serve boys and girls adaptively or become a lasting threat to the integrity of their basic body ego—a dread of mothers and of mothering. Such dread, primitive as it is for both sexes, is, of course, warded off by an array of defenses. This becomes incorporated in later characterological or symptomatic attitudes to mothers and women, including avoidance, denigration, idealization, and phallic monism. It affects later conflicts and compromise formations. It also plays a marked part in anorexia and bulimia and contributes to homosexual orientation in men and woman.

SOME DIFFERENCES BETWEEN BOYS' AND GIRLS' BODY EGO

In keeping with the different biological roles of men and women, boys' and girls' body egos develop along different lines. Among the several authors who have, as mentioned, studied the girl's recognition and investment of her inside genital organs, destined to become child bearing, Kestenberg (1956b) views the girl toddler's early doll play as an externalization of her internal sensations and means of mastery as well as a preparation for motherhood.

My observations of toddlers and data available through treatment-via-the-parent and the analyses of girls confirm Kestenberg's findings, and provide some additional material (Furman, 1992, 1993, 1994). Just prior to and often overlapping with the adoption of the baby doll, toddler girls tend to adopt a container—a bag, purse, little box—which they treasure and fill with precious items. Mothers vary in supporting this activity. Sometimes they give their little daughter an old purse of their own to use; sometimes they provide special items to put into it to keep. Insofar as they are comfortable with their own motherly body, they at least regard the child's behavior with bemused appreciation. I have come to view this developmental step as a sign of the inside space being integrated into the growing body ego and serving as a precursor to the doll play—the transition from the inside baby to the outside baby. Sometimes this transition is made quite explicit, for example, when the treasured container is filled with a little figure or soft toy. Sometimes all containers have to be filled with a potential baby, such as when little Mary inspected her childless aunt's pretty bowl on the coffee table and then, just before leaving, placed a little teddy in it, molding it into the concave space.

I (1994) describe elsewhere how the baby doll and the maternal caring activities performed with it become such an invested part of the girl's body ego that she spontaneously remembers it, talks about it, worries about it when they are separated, and rushes to embrace it on their reunion, such as on returning home after a walk without the doll.

In other words, in normal body ego development, given mother's facilitation and absence of bodily overwhelming (illness, abuse, medical-surgical treatments), the girl toddler's body ego integration allows for the potential of including an inside and outside baby, retains flexible boundaries and tolerates, by virtue of same, a measure of bodily interdependence with her mother. Her maternal development is part and parcel of her gender identity. As little Mary, by then a bit older, put it one day seemingly out of the blue, "Mommy, when you have your next baby, will you please give it to me." Mary had not been in the company of babies, and her parents intended her to remain the youngest. Winnicott (1964) describes the maternal capacity for changeable boundaries as woman always being also someone else, with mother, grandmother, and little girl interchangeable within her, whereas man is all unto himself.

The boy's body ego integration and related narcissistic distribution is indeed quite different. He too grows out of the joint mother-child bodily matrix, reflected perhaps in "feeding" his penis and owning mother's breast or elimination. He too includes items outside his body as part of himself as he carries around a briefcase or tool box, becomes absorbed in big machines and how they work, or feeds his soft toys. But when he takes his teddy along, he either pushes it in a stroller or holds and drags it Christopher Robin fashion, in contrast to the girl who cradles her doll tightly in her arms. And his precious items do not go into treasured boxes but into his pockets. As he assumes ownership of his bodily functions and their care, including his penis, he encloses them within the clearly delineated boundaries of his body ego. This is often reflected in his play (so different from the girl's) which focuses on creating a circumscribed space, such as the circular or oval train track or block-built corral for the toy animals. I view this as a sign of body ego integration, comparable to the girl's treasured box. One toddler showed this achievement explicitly by asking his parent to draw the outline of his body on the pavement with chalk, to which he added the outline of his penis in the correct place. His proud achievement as well as his remaining vulnerability showed in his concern that the rain might destroy his representation and in accepting his parents' reassurance that it would only affect the picture, not his body (Furman, 1992).

With the boy, as with the girl, a measure of mutual bodily investment remains part of him and of the mother-child relationship. Insofar as his body ego outlines achieve sufficient stability and narcissistic self-investment, these remnants will serve him adaptively—to be attracted to potential mothers, to allow temporary loss of ego boundaries with them in sexual intercourse, and to value, empathize with, and appreciate their mothering.

THE ROLE OF THE FATHER

Boys especially, but girls too, are greatly helped with the differentiation and boundaries of their body ego by being able to relate with their father. Among the many benefits of the father-toddler relationship, I want to underline a specific one, pertinent to this context. It is the fact that the father's body ego is clearly and stably delineated, however much he may want to include the child as a bodily part of himself and be motherly in this sense, and however much the child is tempted to effect such a bodily unit with him. It is a big help to sense that fathers are and remain physically separate, can therefore support the child's separateness and can, at the same time, relate with and tolerate mother's relative lack of separateness. I am speaking, of course, of the role of the father in addition to the mother and do not wish to imply that body ego formation is facilitated by not experiencing a bodily unit with the mother to start with (Furman, 1992, 1993).

SOME IMPLICATIONS FOR LATER DEVELOPMENT

As with all areas of personality, the development of sexual gender is made up of a series of interrelated steps. The earliest strata described above are as significant in affecting the subsequent ones as the latter are in modifying and integrating the preceding ones. To understand the relative contribution of each we have to be in feeling touch with all. Our difficulties in recognizing and appreciating the role of the bodily mother-child matrix and its effect on body ego and gender development are, inevitably, handicapped by the fact that these experiences are preverbal and preconceptual and arouse very primitive annihilation anxieties. It may therefore be easier for us to identify women by their lack of a penis or to prove that women do not lack anything, and to disregard the role of motherhood. Yet these views may owe their intensity and persistence to the fact that *women do lack something, namely, clearly delineated, stable body ego boundaries.*

Lack of a penis brings the threat of castration fear. Lack of body ego boundaries brings the much more overwhelming, primitive threat of annihilation anxiety. This danger, to an extent, is part of motherhood. It is a very immediate threat to all men and women who encountered difficulty in differentiating and investing their body ego. The greater the threat, the stronger are women's defenses against owning and using their maternal body ego and men's against empathizing with and appreciating mothers and their mothering (Furman, 1994). Inevitably, this threat also contributes to difficulty in resolving later developmental conflicts and shapes the resulting compromise formations. Colleagues who analyze adults have personally shared such findings and found it helpful to trace and interpret the early origins of these pathologies. I hope they will, in time, publish their material and that others will contribute to the further elucidation of the links between the investment and differentiation of the basic body ego and later disturbances.

REFERENCES

CHASSEGUET-SMIRGEL, J. (1976). Freud and female sexuality. *Int. J. Psychoanal.*, 57:275–286.

ERIKSON, E.H. (1956). The problem of ego identity. *J. Amer. Psychoanal. Assn.*, 4:56–121.

—— (1964). Womanhood and the inner space. In *Identity, Youth and Crisis.* New York: Norton, 1968, pp. 261–294.

FURMAN, E. (1969). Treatment via the mother. In *The Therapeutic Nursery School,* ed. R.A. Furman & A. Katan. New York: Int. Univ. Press, pp. 64–123.

—— (1980). The death of a newborn: assistance to the parent. In *The Child in His Family: Preventive Child Psychiatry in an Age of Transition. Yearbook Int. Assn. Child Psychiat. & Allied Professions,* Vol. 6, ed. E. J. Anthony & C. Chiland. New York: Wiley, pp. 497–506.

——— (1982). Mothers have to be there to be left. *Psychoanal. Study Child*, 37:15–28.
——— (1984). Mothers, toddlers and care. In *The Course of Life*, Vol. II, *Early Childhood*, ed. S.I. Greenspan & G.H. Pollock. Madison, CT: Int. Univ. Press, 1989, pp. 61–82.
——— (1992). *Toddlers and Their Mothers*. Madison, CT: Int. Univ. Press.
——— (1993). *Toddlers and Their Mothers: Abridged Version for Parents and Educators*. Madison, CT: Int. Univ. Press.
——— (1994). Early aspects of mothering: what makes it so hard to be there to be left. *J. Child Psychother.*, 20:149–164.
GLENN, J. (1993). Developmental transformation: the Isakower phenomenon as an example. *J. Amer. Psychoanal. Assn.*, 41:1113–1134.
HÄGGLUND, T.-B., HÄGGLUND, V. & IKONEN, P. (1978). Some viewpoints on woman's inner space. *Scand. Psychoanal. Rev.*, 1:65–77.
——— & PIHA, H. (1980). The inner space of the body imago. *Psychoanal. Q.*, 49:256–283.
HÄGGLUND, V. (1981). Feminine sexuality and its development. *Scand. Psychoanal. Rev.*, 4:127–150.
HOFFER, W. (1949). Mouth, hand, and ego integration. *Psychoanal. Study Child*, 3/4:49–56.
——— (1950). Development of the body ego. *Psychoanal. Study Child*, 5:18–24.
HORNEY, K. (1926). The flight from womanhood: the masculinity complex in women as viewed by men and women. *Int. J. Psychoanal.*, 7:324–339.
——— (1932). The dread of woman. Observations on a specific difference in the dread felt by men and by women respectively for the opposite sex. *Int. J. Psychoanal.*, 13:348–368.
KATAN, A. (1960). Distortions of the phallic phase. *Psychoanal. Study Child*, 15:208–214.
KESTENBERG, J.S. (1956a). Vicissitudes of female sexuality. *J. Amer. Psychoanal. Assn.*, 4:453–476.
——— (1956b). On the development of maternal feelings in early childhood. Observations and reflections. *Psychoanal. Study Child*, 11:257–291.
——— (1968). Outside and inside, male and female. *J. Amer. Psychoanal. Assn.*, 16:457–520.
TORSTI, M. (1993). The feminine self and body image. *Scand. Psychoanal. Rev.*, 16:47–62.
TUSTIN, F. (1973). *Autism and Childhood Psychosis*. New York: Aronson.
TYSON, P. (1994). Bedrock and beyond: an examination of the clinical utility of contemporary theories of female psychology. *J. Amer. Psychoanal. Assn.*, 42:447–467.
WINNICOTT, D.W. (1941). The observation of infants in a set situation. In *Through Paediatrics to Psycho-Analysis*. New York: Basic Books, 1958, pp. 52–69.
——— (1964). "This feminism." In *Home Is Where We Start From*, ed. C. Winnicott, R. Shepherd & M. Davis. New York: Norton, 1986, pp. 183–194.

Two Women and Their Mothers: On the Internalization and Development of Mother-Daughter Relationships

Anni Bergman
Maria Fahey

> This is a report from a 30-year followup study conducted by a member of Margaret Mahler's original separation-individuation research team. Based on a series of unstructured, clinical interviews with the original subjects and psychological testing of the subjects and their mothers, two mother-daughter pairs are compared from the perspective of the meaning of each daughter to her mother, how that meaning influenced the separation-individuation process, and how it influenced the unfolding of each daughter's life as a woman. Because the mother-child pairs were observed several times a week by both participant and nonparticipant observers beginning during the preverbal period, this study offers a unique opportunity to examine the influence of the earliest interactions on adult life.

This paper is based on the data collected from a longitudinal research study which has spanned 35 years. The first segment of the research was the observational study of mother child pairs which led to the formulation of separation-individuation theory (Mahler et al., 1975).[1] This study, begun in 1959 by Margaret Mahler and her associates, was based on Mahler's hypothesis of the symbiotic origin of the human infant who she thought developed a sense of

---

Anni Bergman, Ph.D., is Training and Supervising Analyst, New York Freudian Society; Clinical Associate Professor of Psychology, New York University Postdoctoral Program in Psychotherapy and Psychoanalysis; and Faculty Member of Institute for Psychoanalytic Training and Research. Maria Fahey is Research Associate to Anni Bergman, Ph.D., and Director of Studies at Friends Seminary.

The authors thank Fred Pine for his clarifying questions and enlightening comments, and John McDevitt, Wendy Olesker and Peter Neubauer for their careful reading and invaluable suggestions.

[1] This research was supported by NIMH Grant MH-08238, USPHS: Margaret Mahler, Principal Investigator; John B. McDevitt, Co-Principal Investigator.

Anni Bergman—Maria Fahey

separate identity during the period of separation-individuation. Mothers and children met in a playgroundlike setting which allowed for the comparison of the development of children the same age while each mother-child pair was studied intensively. The data were collected by a team of participant and nonparticipant observers as well as by senior clinicians who conducted regular interviews with the mothers and observed the mother-child interaction. Hypotheses about intrapsychic conflict were formulated from these observational data. While fathers were observed during occasional visits to the center, interviews, and home visits, the data on the father-child relationship are in no way comparable to data on the mother-child relationship.[2]

A brief followup study was conducted in 1973 during the children's latency period, and in 1988 the adult followup study was begun.[3] The followup study has included series of unstructured, clinical interviews with the original subjects and psychological testing of the subjects and their mothers. It needs to be emphasized that the followup data are quite different in quantity and quality from the early data which were based on daily observations collected by multiple observers and examined carefully in weekly research conferences. In contrast, the followup data have been collected by single observers, and the amount of contact with the subjects has been varied and limited according to the circumstances of each individual's life.

There is a vast time span which has not been covered by our research. Even though children and parents were seen in a brief followup study during latency, we do not have ongoing observations of the lived experience of our subjects and their parents during their later childhood, adolescence, and eventually separation from home. While there is danger in relating early material directly to adult life without observing the important developmental reorganization during latency and adolescence, it is nevertheless of interest to see if meaningful connections can be made between observed early experience and identity themes in adult life. We are looking to see

---

[2]Fortunately, a great deal of work has been done on the father-child relationship subsequently, e.g., Cath et al. (1982, 1989).

[3]Followup studies supported by The Rock Foundation: John B. McDevitt, Principal Investigator; Anni Bergman, Co-Principal Investigator.

Two Women and Their Mothers

if in the adult personality organization patterns remain that were observed early on in the mother-child interactions, and if formative early experiences can be identified.

We want to emphasize the importance of the observational data collected during the preverbal period. Since this period is usually inaccessible through memory or even psychoanalytic reconstruction, subjects in the adult followup would not be expected to remember what was observed. It is therefore of special interest to see if themes that emerge from the observation of the earliest relationship play out in adult life. The fact that we have extensive, detailed, observations, both participant and nonparticipant, of mother-child interactions during the preverbal period gives us a rare avenue for studying the influence of these earliest interactions on adult life.

Modern developmental research has shown that the infant is not a passive recipient of caretaking: from the beginning each infant brings into the world his or her own unique way of responding to and interacting with the caretaking other. These early interactions are like a *cantus firmus* upon which each person composes his or her life with endless elaboration and variation. *Grove's Dictionary of Music and Musicians* (1954) defines *cantus firmus* as "a 'fixed' song or melody... commonly adopted by a composer for contrapuntal treatment" and points out that a "tune used as a *cantus firmus* remained unaltered in one voice while the other parts proceeded independently. It was as a rule sung in long notes against quicker motion in the counterpoint, with the result that it usually moved so slowly as to become unrecognizable in performance." It is because the *cantus firmus* can become unrecognizable as the counterpoint is built around it that we choose this metaphor. While we do not expect the early interactions between mother and baby to be obviously recognizable in the life of an adult, we shall look for how the earliest mother-child relationship is internalized and wonder how the composition of each person's life is built upon the melody of the earliest relationship.

Clinicians who have worked with mother-infant pairs have shown the significance of mothers' representations of their infants (Fraiberg et al., 1975; Brazelton and Cramer, 1990; Stern, 1995). We shall examine how the mother's early representations of her baby translate into behaviors that influence the development of her child's sense of self. The original separation-individuation research was focused more on observing the developmental sequences in the infant and toddler than on the experience of the mother. Since this time, the contributions of attachment theorists have shown the importance of the mother's own attachment to her mother for the development of the mother-child relationship (Ainsworth et al., 1978; Maine et al., 1989). Our data on the nature of the mother's attachment to her own mother are not universally available since this information is drawn from what mothers revealed in unstructured interviews. The mother's representation of her child is understood better in some cases than in others, depending on how freely the individual mother shared her fantasies and how pressing these were for her. In our experience, it seemed that some mothers interpreted almost all of their children's behaviors in terms of their internal representation, whereas other mothers seemed freer to respond to even the young baby as a separate individual. However, even when mothers respond to the baby as a separate individual, often characteristics are emphasized that confirm the representation, that is, the internal needs of the mother.

One of the unique aspects of the observational separation-individuation research was the emphasis on both longitudinal and cross-sectional methods: individual mother-child pairs were observed over time, and observations of mother-child pairs were continuously compared with each other. These comparisons were a natural outgrowth of the very design of the research in its playgroundlike setting where several mother-child pairs were always present. The comparative aspects of the original research, from which patterns in the mother-child dyad emerged, allowed for the formulation of the theory of subphases of the separation-individuation process. We have found in working with the data of the followup study that comparing mother-child pairs has proven to be a fruitful method for generating ideas about the continuities between early relationship patterns and conflicts and later compromise formations.

It is important to remember that while the original study focused on the interaction between mother and child, the emphasis was always on the separation-individuation process in the child. In the adult followup, the emphasis is even more strongly on the child-now young adult. We are studying the ways in which early patterns

Two Women and Their Mothers

have been internalized and absorbed into the adult personality structure, and we are studying the continuing relationship between the child-now young adult and her mother. Our knowledge of the mother herself and the motivating forces that moved her to relate to her child in a particular way is not available with the same clinical richness. However, it should be remembered that observations of mothers and children and interviews of the mothers were conducted by psychoanalysts who were concerned always with understanding the meanings of what they saw and heard.

In examining the data collected on two mother-daughter pairs during the separation-individuation process and during the follow-up studies, we shall be guided by the following questions: (1) How is each mother's representation of her daughter internalized into each woman's own sense of self? (2) How has the mother's representation of her daughter either facilitated or interfered with the processes of separation and individuation? (3) In what way is each woman's current relationship to her family, especially to her mother, continuous or discontinuous with the relationship she had had with her mother during the first three years of life? (4) How is the way in which each woman thinks of her mother related to the relationship noted in our early observations of the separation-individuation process? (5) What part do internalization and identification play in the resolution of the rapprochement crisis and the attainment of emotional object and self-constancy?

HELEN AND HER MOTHER: FROM SEPARATION-INDIVIDUATION TO ADULTHOOD

The First Three Years

Helen and her mother started to attend the center when Helen was just over a year old. Helen was an attractive, sturdy little girl who was unusually competent for her age. She walked and climbed very well and was active but cautious. Her language development was precocious: she already said many words quite clearly. At the center Helen was very social, which her mother attributed to having taken her everywhere without Helen showing any stranger anxiety. One observer described Helen's effect on him:

Anni Bergman—Maria Fahey

I had first seen Helen when she just turned thirteen months. Her effect on me was almost immediate and very profound. I realized after some time I had surrendered a certain observational distance. Instead I felt myself captivated and in a state of great pleasure, sympathy, and almost complete admiration for this phenomenal little creature. The energy and vigor of the pretty little child's activity was indeed a joy to watch. What a contrast there was between this child and her mother, who sat almost immobile, and one could almost immediately sense her painful and self-conscious shyness.

Helen was able to let her mother know what she wanted, and her mother was responsive. Mrs. H. described Helen as an easy baby who had never slept much during the day. She had not been breast-fed, which Mrs. H. explained in a characteristically matter-of-fact way by saying that she had not been encouraged to breast-feed in the hospital. We see here a characteristic of this mother, namely to minimize issues that might be seen as a problem and to externalize them. Mrs. H. emphasized that Helen was a very independent child and had never liked to be held closely as a baby. Observers noted that Mrs. H. responded well to verbal cues. Thus, we might speculate that this mother-child pair created a holding environment in keeping with the mother's predilection that the child be competent and independent and not need much physical closeness. Mrs. H.'s wish that her daughter be self-sufficient may have been connected to her own struggles and some unconscious realization that she, in fact, could not fully fulfill herself because she was still longing for closeness to her own mother, which was not available. Mrs. H. was the oldest of three daughters; she talked far more about her father than about her mother. The wish for a caretaking mother was enacted by the way in which Mrs. H. attended the center: she came regularly four times a week and always arrived early. Arriving before the other mothers and children assured her and her daughter special attention. Her own need for attention was channeled through the needs of Helen who, she said, had difficulty occupying herself at home.

This mother's representation of her first child, a girl for whom she had wished, seemed to be an idealized version of her own self. Helen always came to our group in very pretty little girl clothes Mrs. H. made for her. In contrast, Mrs. H. always dressed herself in a manner that played down her looks. Mrs. H. may have put her own

Two Women and Their Mothers

wishes to be admired into Helen. Mrs. H. emphasized that Helen had no favorite toy or blanket; she said that she could remove any toy at home without Helen missing it. However, at the center Helen quickly attached herself to a teddy bear almost as large as herself which she liked to carry around. Was this teddy bear a representation of mother? Or, was the teddy bear a representation of herself to whom she played mother? It seems that the center, where others related to both mother and child, provided enough separation between them to allow for the creation of a transitional object (Gaddini and Gaddini, 1970).

Mrs. H. rarely talked about her husband. Later on, she told an interviewer that she had married when she first started college which was when her own parents had moved abroad. Perhaps after the abrupt separation from her own family, it was important to Mrs. H. to replace her family with a baby of her own. Mrs. H. was so gratified by her little girl, with whom she so strongly identified, that she may not have left room for another person—or even a transitional object—to become really important to Helen. An observer noted the pride this mother took in her child. It seemed to him that the child filled the mother's life and that the mother-child pair gave the impression of amazing self-sufficiency. This appearance of self-sufficiency was deceptive because it existed at the center, where they did not have to be self-sufficient. In fact, Mrs. H. had said that she liked to arrive to the center early because she found it difficult to be home alone with Helen. Through Helen, Mrs. H. was able to receive some of the mothering she had missed.

By the time Helen was fifteen months old, Helen's father's work took him abroad. At this time, Helen developed a sleep disturbance: she woke up several times each night, her mother unable to comfort her. At the center, a marked change in the child was noticed. Helen started to play bye-bye games and became very alert to people's comings and goings. During the same period Helen became listless and fatigued, a strong contrast to her former boundless energy. She began to fall more frequently and was generally irritable; she cried a lot and ran to her mother for comforting. Helen demanded food, such as cookies and pretzels, and juice. The male observer who had been so captivated by her noted that her former ability to command a response from others seemed to be replaced by an almost desperate appeal for attention, and that the feeling of pleasure and joy in her performance was no longer there. Helen became more aware of being wet or soiled, which made her uncomfortable. While Mrs. H. did not talk about her own feelings about her husband's absence, she often stated that Helen did not really miss her father. A contradiction emerges here between Mrs. H.'s feeling that she and Helen filled each other's worlds completely and Helen's strong reaction to her father's absence.

During this period, Mrs. H. talked about her own childhood, especially about her father, a brilliant and successful man who had become severely ill early in his life, after which time he had been spoiled and cared for by many people. Resentment of her father's need for caretaking by her mother and, as Mrs. H. often emphasized, by other women may have been a source of this mother's ambivalent feelings about caretaking. When Mrs. H. spoke of her college years, she said that she did not do well because she felt that nobody was there to care whether she did well or not.

When talking about her husband's absence, Mrs. H. said it was better that he should be overseas rather than in a place where they could visit easily, which would only make it more difficult to adjust to the separation. Mrs. H. seemed to defend herself from the impact of her husband's absence on herself and her child, an absence compounded by the previous times in her life when she had felt abandoned—first by her father's critical illness and then by her family leaving while she was in college. In fact, Mrs. H. also may have been particularly sensitive to separations because she was the oldest of three sisters. Perhaps the feelings about separations she would not permit herself were expressed by Helen, who began to find separation from or sharing of mother unbearable. An observer wrote at this time:

> Helen has for the first time begun to show jealousy of Mother's attention to other children. She pushed another child off Mother's lap. When the mother was taken out of the room for an interview, Helen cried a lot; it was hard to quiet her. When Mother returned, she did not go to her at once, but acted as though oblivious of Mother's presence.[4]

---

[4]Here we see an ambivalent attachment pattern in Helen, significant in light of research showing the passing on of attachment patterns from mother to child (Maine et al., 1989).

Two Women and Their Mothers

How do we interpret Helen's behavior? The avoidance of her mother may have been an expression of her anger and a way of protecting herself from the pain of renewed separation. This reaction on Helen's part was comparable to her mother's decision not to visit her husband, a decision connected to not wanting to feel repeated pain over separation.

When Helen was around sixteen months, observers noted that for the first time her mother came to the center dressed up and wearing makeup. During the following months Mrs. H. continued to give more attention to her appearance than she had when she first came to the center, when all her efforts had been spent on dressing up Helen. It is significant that her attention to her own appearance coincides with a time when she could no longer derive as much gratification from admiring attention to Helen.

When Helen was nineteen months, she was left for an afternoon with one of the other mothers who had a little boy of the same age. Helen and this little boy were bathed together, and the mother reported that upon seeing Jay's penis, Helen had said that he had two belly buttons. Later she called the penis "Jay's birthmark," perhaps attempting to undo the anatomical difference because Helen, herself, had a birthmark in the genital area. At this same time Helen suffered extreme separation distress and cried a lot when she was left by her mother. On the other hand, Helen became almost phobic of her mother's efforts to pick her up or comfort her, efforts that resulted in outbursts of rage. We saw in Helen a fairly extreme early reaction to the anatomical difference resulting in simultaneous need for her mother and rage-fear reactions toward her mother.[5]

Helen was frustrated easily, often bursting into tears. She consumed great quantities of juice, asking for it from all the adults who came into the room. Helen was happiest when she was at the center alone with her mother and the observers. Mrs. H. reported that Helen, who had begun to enjoy using the potty, now began to shun it. Helen's mother seemed very depressed and distraught, and was not very attentive to Helen. She complained that Helen was impossible at home with crying, temper tantrums, and what seemed like

---

[5]This event inspired Roiphe's conceptualizations of the early genital phase, which he further researched with Eleanor Galenson (Roiphe and Galenson, 1981). Mahler (1972) discusses the relation between castration anxiety and rapprochement.

incomprehensible behavior. But what bothered her most was, as she put it, "Helen won't let me touch her." Although she accepted help from other adults, Helen would not allow her mother to dress her or put her on the toilet; however, Helen would scream for hours if mother left her with a friend. At the center Helen asked to be taken to the toilet and then refused to sit down. She seemed miserable under urinary pressure, but would not wet herself or sit down on the toilet. She became very aggressive toward the other children, especially by pulling their hair. She was unable to share her mother or any other adult. Even on better days Helen remained extremely sensitive to any deprivation such as her mother talking on the telephone or a toy being taken from her. She broke a crayon in half, then tried to put it together. When she could not, she broke into uncontrollable sobbing for 45 minutes, during which her mother could not comfort her. While this kind of behavior is typical for children during the rapprochement crisis, it was particularly difficult for Helen and her mother. Helen's mother looked harassed and worn and at one point even asked the observers whether they considered Helen a disturbed child. This question shows that Mrs. H. was especially hard-hit by her child's rapprochement crisis, perhaps because it ended the blissful period in which Helen's precocity matched her mother's representation of her as the idealized, admired part of her own self.

As Helen came to some resolution of her rapprochement crisis, she began to internalize her mother's prohibitions by saying, for example, that she should not pull hair. She also began to play with dolls: identification with the mother emerged as both playing mother who prohibits aggression and also playing mother who takes care of the child.[6]

As the rapprochement crisis waned, Helen's mother became sensitive to Helen's asking observers to do things for her. Mrs. H. said: "Now will come the time when she will prefer her teacher to her mother. That's all right, maybe Mrs. K. [an observer] will even take her home." Was Mrs. H. hurt by Helen's turning toward other adults as she recovered from the intense conflicts of the rapprochement crisis? Did she feel rejected because she could no longer be

---

[6]McDevitt (unpublished) has shown identification in another subject from this followup study as a way to resolve rapprochement conflicts. Furer (1967) and Arlow (1982) have written on the development of the early superego.

Two Women and Their Mothers

Helen's exclusive love object? Was it an expression of her resentment that Helen could now turn to others whereas she had clung to mother when in the throws of the rapprochement crisis? Helen reacted sensitively to her mother's expression of feeling rejected by asking her to come over and join in a pretend meal. It may be that the rapprochement crisis was particularly hard for Mrs. H. not only because she had to weather it alone, without the help of the father, but also because Helen's demandingness may have evoked an unconscious memory of the abrupt ending of her own happy relationship with her father who, when he became sick, became demanding of the mother and other women.

When she was two years old, Helen's father returned, and Helen greeted him by saying, "Hi Daddy." Mrs. H. was surprised that she seemed to have remembered her father during the whole year he was gone. Mrs. H. said that she expected Helen to have difficulty in accepting him, which may have been in part a projection onto Helen of what she herself was feeling about the reunion. In fact, Helen did not want to stay with him alone. Perhaps Helen's rejection of her father was in part an accommodation of her mother's wish for an exclusive attachment.

After her father returned, Helen became particularly interested in male observers and used imaginative ways of getting attention from them. An observer noted:

> When Dr. G. came into the room, Helen looked at him for a moment. She was holding the big baby doll, and immediately dropped it on the floor and gave it no further attention. She then started to play with various toys, always with one eye on Dr. G. Also, while she had been fairly quiet until then, she now started talking in a steady stream, accompanying whatever she did with various explanations. When she did not get Dr. G.'s attention, she did not directly clamor for it. She would go and find a new activity to impress him with. In this way she went from playing with the train to playing with the push-toys. She then climbed on the window sill, made up a story about being on the roof of the house and fixing the roof. She then was painting the roof. This reminded her of the sky, and she told a story about being in an airplane and going way up into the sky, as she had done during the summer. From this she went to the active toys, such as the see-saw and the rocking boat. Being on the rocking boat set off further associations of swimming in the ocean and sailing a boat on waves.

What we seem to see here is that the return of the father gave Helen the opportunity to identify with him, both by playing out the male roles of fixing roofs and by making up stories about going overseas. It is significant that Helen needed the attention of a male observer as she played, as if this part of herself could be inspired only by the presence of her father or a surrogate, namely the male observer.

At the same time, Helen's identification with her mother continued and she became absorbed in doll play, feeding the dolls and putting them to bed. Helen played with her teddy bear, put it to bed, and wondered if its head could come off. She then tried to get into bed with the teddy bear and said it was Mommy's bed. Mother said that when she listened to Helen talking to her teddy bear, she could hear herself talk. Here we see Helen play mother to her teddy bear while she simultaneously wanted to be the baby in her mother's bed.

The return of Helen's father enriched her inner world, as demonstrated in her fantasy play where she could take both male and female roles. His return also necessitated a shift in Helen's sense of herself from being her mother's little girl to being a small child with a mother and a father (Abelin, 1975). In her play, Helen experimented with taking different roles and at the same time attempted to come to terms with the reality of the new family constellation. Not surprisingly, this transition was difficult for her, and she became increasingly sensitive to being left by mother. She refused to stay with either a baby sitter or her father, yet she wanted to walk in the street without holding her mother's hand.

Around this time, Helen's mother reported a dream in which she had to take an exam, but Helen had taken the exam instead of her and had made a few mistakes. Mrs. H. explained to her professor that it was natural for Helen to make mistakes because she did not yet know the letters. This dream reflects Mrs. H.'s identification with Helen and her fear that Helen might not be able to do well enough in school. At the time when Mrs. H. herself had expected to move out into the world to go to college, her parents moved away and she stayed behind. Mrs. H. often connected her indifference to doing well academically with having felt abandoned by her parents at this point in her life. Mrs. H.'s fears about Helen's moving out into the

Two Women and Their Mothers

world were confirmed by Helen's difficult transition to nursery school. Perhaps the combination of Mrs. H.'s feeling that she was abandoning her daughter to school, and also abandoning her exclusive relationship to Helen by having a new baby, made it difficult for her to support her daughter's transition to school.

At the time when Mrs. H. reported this dream, Helen expressed her own concerns about growing up. For example, observers heard Helen say that when she "will be a Mommy, her Mommy will be her baby." She also talked about being "a little Mommy and growing up to be a big Mommy." Helen said that when she "will be big," her mother "will be little," and that she would "grow to be a baby again." Helen expressed some resentment of her father's presence, telling him to "go away again." Thus, at the time of ever-increasing awareness of the inevitable separateness, both Helen and her mother expressed some regressive desire for exclusive attachment. Helen resisted the inevitable separateness in her omnipotent fantasies, in which she could undo who she was: she would be a baby or a Mommy, but not a little girl who had to face the world. In her play, she alternately identified with mother or with baby. For example, when mother left the room, she filled a bottle with water and said that she would give it to the baby. Then she started to drink from it herself, gurgling and cooing, lying down in the crib and drinking the water from the bottle.

When Helen was twenty-nine-and-a-half months old, her mother announced that she was four months pregnant. She was very worried about Helen and said: "This will be the end of Helen. She will be three; it will be just around her birthday. Helen won't like a new baby for a birthday present." Mother talked about the wonderful, special baby that Helen had been, already very interesting when she was only five months old. Being the first of three children herself, Mrs. H. knew how the birth of a second child forever undoes the special position of being the only one.[7]

---

[7]The powerful and lasting effect of a new sibling on the oldest child can be seen in the response of a young adolescent to the death of his dog. This boy, who was one-and-a-half years older than his younger brother, blamed the accidental death of his dog, who had been in his family for most of his life, on a visit by a new puppy of his grandparents which had occurred several days before the accident. He said that his beloved dog had run away and gotten run over because he was upset by the new puppy being brought into his house.

Anni Bergman—Maria Fahey

At the center Helen demanded the exclusive attention of observers. She was furious when other children were included in a game of ring-around-the-rosy. At story time Helen pushed away the other children and insisted on sitting on the observer's lap. Later that day, she played on the couch with a little boy, pretending it was a ferry boat. They had a big doll between them and both said it was their baby. They argued about whether the baby was a boy or a girl. Finally, when her playmate took the doll, Helen had a tantrum and cried, "He's taking my baby away." She was inconsolable for the rest of the morning. One wonders whether Helen was expressing feelings about the return of her father or whether she was expressing fear that arrival of the new baby would take her mother away from her. Perhaps she connected the return of the father with the birth of a new baby.

A few days later, Helen sang the song, "The Farmer in the Dell," but changed the words to "the hunter shot the Mommy." (Helen used to cry at the story of baby Babar being left when the hunter shoots the Mommy.) "The Farmer in the Dell" is a song about procreation and coupling, at the end of which "the cheese stands alone." What was Helen expressing by singing the tune to "The Farmer in the Dell" with words about baby Babar being left when the hunter shoots the Mommy? Was she blaming her Daddy for hunting her Mommy, which would leave her alone when the new baby arrives? This echoes Helen's distress when her little-boy playmate took the baby doll. Helen began to show marked jealousy and aggression toward all babies. The exclusivity of Helen's union with her mother during her father's absence heightened her feelings about the mother-father union, soon to produce a new baby.

Helen began to reject her father despite his special efforts to give her attention. She said, "I don't want to have a Daddy. I want to sleep in Mommy's bed and I don't want Daddy to sleep with Mommy." At the same time she said to her mother, "I will prick you with my scissors and then I won't have a Mommy any more. Will it hurt? Will you cry?" (Here she becomes the hunter.) She also told her mother to go home from the center without her: "I will stay here and then you won't have a little girl any more." We can see that Helen was struggling with oedipal conflicts, both negative and positive, and that these oedipal conflicts were strongly tinged by the

Two Women and Their Mothers

particular relationship with her mother. At the same time, Helen developed an intense conflict about giving up her bottle. Though she cried out of her sleep wanting the bottle, when her mother offered it, she refused it. Helen both wanted to remain her mother's baby and to take her mother's place.

Helen's relationship to her father began to change. Whereas earlier she had tried to send him away, one day she said: "My Daddy is a boy. He's not a man. He's a big boy." Then she said she was glad to have a Daddy and she liked him. Mother heard her say to a family friend on the telephone, "Someday my Mommy will go away, and then I will sleep with my Daddy." Helen began to develop some uncomfortable guilty feelings, demonstrated by her blaming others when she did something she was not supposed to do. Along with these advances into oedipal development, both Helen and her mother expressed longings for the earlier baby time. Helen pretended to be a baby needing her diapers changed, and her mother remarked that since toilet training, Helen missed being diapered. At home Helen was moody, which Mother thought had to do with trying to give up the bottle. Helen had some nightmares from which she woke up crying. Once she asked her mother, "Why did you break the roll?" referring to an incident the day before when Mother had broken a roll which Helen had wanted to be whole. At this time of oedipal conflict and the expecting of a new baby, the nightmare about the roll broken by the mother can be seen as a regressive recall of the rapprochement crisis, which had been exacerbated by the absence of the father and the observation of the anatomical difference. Around the time of Helen's dream, Mother remembered how possessive she had felt about Helen after she was born, not wanting anyone else to touch her, and she expressed worries about who would take care of Helen when she would have to go to the hospital for the birth of her new child.

At the age of thirty-one months Helen had given up the bottle at night, but still asked for it during the day. Her mother reported that she was very nice to her dolls, but "mean and rotten" to real babies. Helen said, "What would happen if somebody ate up all the candy in the candy store and there was none left and the candy store people would cry?" Is Helen worried about the new baby eating up everything? Or, is it she who will eat up all the candy so there won't be any left for the baby or her mother? Helen became sick with a very high fever, and her mother was worried that she might have a convulsion. She sat up with her all night. Helen had several bottles and cried out of her sleep, "I don't want the bottle. I don't want the cup. I don't want the glass." When she woke up she was very upset and rejected her mother. Finally, she got into bed with her mother and had a bottle. Helen, who still had not been told by her mother about the pregnancy, asked many questions. "Where was I when you were a little girl? Was I big when you were little?" After finally talking to Helen about the new baby, Mrs. H. said that Helen was looking forward to it and played the devoted mother to her teddy bears. Mother still would not talk to Helen about the baby being inside her body because she thought it would be disturbing to her. This demonstrates once again Mrs. H.'s own regret that she would be disturbing her perfect union between herself and her little girl through the advent of a new child.

Further Development and Adulthood

Helen's transition from the research center to nursery school was difficult for both her and her mother. Mrs. H. had just given birth to Helen's baby brother, who required a lot of attention. Helen transferred a possessive, clinging relationship she had with her mother to the nursery school teachers from whom she demanded exclusive attention, reacting to the other children as rivals. Mother was concerned that Helen was not treated well enough by her teachers; thus this first contact with the outside world of school turned out to be difficult for both mother and child. This outcome is interesting in light of Mrs. H.'s comment early on that the time would come when Helen would prefer her teachers to her mother. Did Mrs. H.'s need for Helen's exclusive attachment to her inhibit Helen's ability to become a member of her new nursery school "family"? While Mrs. H. may have unconsciously promoted this situation, it was nevertheless a disillusionment for her because it contradicted her image of Helen as the precocious, admirable child. Mrs. H. began to feel a sense of doom and failure. Helen's difficulties continued to some extent throughout her school years. They became especially exacerbated during her early adolescence when she and her family moved from the city to a small suburban community. Helen was extremely shy and had difficulty making friends. Many of

Two Women and Their Mothers

her teachers reported that she did not live up to her academic potential. The mother's sense of failure was extreme, and she became rather acutely disturbed during Helen's adolescence.

During her adult interviews, Helen did not speak about her difficult adolescence. In describing her college experience, she said that she had done well, but did not describe her experience as exciting or remarkable. After college, when Helen could not find a job she wanted, she decided to go to graduate school and entered a Master's program in rehabilitation. She described her field as one she had fallen into rather than one she had actively sought. In this way Helen was similar to her mother who always stressed her own lack of academic ambition, even though she had attended an excellent college. During the followup interviews, Helen underplayed the importance of her professional choice, but in fact she had become quite successful in her field. Helen's style of appearing casual about important decisions is congruent with her mother's style. It contrasts sharply to Helen as a child who did not easily accept disappointment and was especially sensitive to needing exclusive attention from adults. One wonders when this shift occurred and whether it was connected to leaving home. Helen chose a field in which she was able to rise to the top fairly easily—even though she did not regard this as a big success. Here we see both a defensive resignation like that of her mother and, though more hidden, an expectation to be outstanding in her surroundings.

After Helen received her Master's degree, she began to work in a program that trained people with serious disabilities to make the transition from institutional to mainstream living. This training in basic living skills was intensive, on the job, on a one-to-one basis, echoing perhaps her early desire to be in exclusive relationships with others. Helen rose quickly to become a creator and administrator of these programs, but even in this position she did not seem to appreciate fully the importance of the contribution she was making to the field. Helen was not entirely happy in her professional activities, and hoped to continue her studies. Helen's career in helping severely disabled adults learn to function in the outside world may have allowed her to play the mothering role her mother had such difficulty playing for her, namely helping her to function in the outside world.

Helen married a man she met at work. He had lost both parents early in life and had very little family of his own. By marrying a man with little family, Helen may have fulfilled her childhood longing for an exclusive relationship with her mother. She described her husband as someone with whom she got along very well, but as someone who was quite moody. She was able to tolerate and handle his moods; she said: "His moods are unpredictable. When he gets moody, I just sort of let him." Thus, Helen unconsciously played the role of mother to the moody child she herself had been. Helen made the impression of being quite stable in her own moods and not being easily upset. One might wonder if she allowed him to express the moody side of her, thereby remaining closer to being the admirable child her mother had seen her to be. While Helen described how she and her husband were good companions for each other, she did not reveal a passionate or romantic side of their relationship.

Helen talked quite a bit about the house in which she and her husband lived, an old house they had fixed up together. She described how hard they had had to work, especially stripping layers and layers of paint and wallpaper from the walls. The renovating of their old house is of particular interest in connection to her description of how the house in which her husband had grown up had been completely neglected and eventually torn down. She sounded quite burdened by all she had to do, but she liked her house and she liked gardening, an interest she shares with her mother. The theme of rehabilitation in Helen's adult life is significant because in helping people function in the outside world, Helen is doing for others what her mother could not do for her. It is of further significance that Helen shares this profession with her husband and that she shares the burden and pleasure of renovating an old house with him, as if to say it takes two to accomplish such a task.

Helen described her pleasure in her garden and how she and her mother enjoyed looking at gardening catalogs together. Helen's mother sometimes visited and helped Helen with gardening. She enjoyed her mother's visits, and described how well her mother got along with her husband. She felt it was good for her mother to get away from her father and brothers who were always making demands on her. Helen's pleasure in her garden and her sharing of this pleasure with her mother seemed to be an area of unconflicted gratification for Helen. She felt close to her mother, but much less close to her father and to her two younger brothers who, she said disapprovingly, had lived at home for a long time, allowing her mother to

Two Women and Their Mothers

continue to serve them. By working on her garden together with her mother, Helen seemed to be able to refind her early mother for whom she was the admirable little girl. She took her mother away from her father and two brothers, the rivals to the exclusive relationship.

We shall now present somewhat more briefly another mother-daughter pair for comparison and contrast.

KAREN AND HER MOTHER: FROM SEPARATION-INDIVIDUATION TO ADULTHOOD

The First Three Years

Karen and her mother first came to the center when Karen was almost one year old. Karen, an attractive, well-endowed little girl, was described by observers as listless, often sitting quietly in one place, crawling only to mother and then pulling herself up on mother's chair to be near her. Mrs. K. had difficulty taking pleasure in Karen's looks, activities, and vitality. Nonetheless, Karen responded well as soon as her mother paid attention to her: her face would light up, and she would become much more active. When Karen was a year old she actively missed her mother: she cried and crawled to the door when her mother left the room. Karen was clearly very attached to her mother but was inhibited in her capacity for exploration and autonomous functioning.

Karen was the second child; the first was a boy. Her mother had stated openly that she had not wanted a girl child because she felt that girls were fated to be unhappy, preoccupied with their looks and with the need to be thin to please men. Thus, from the beginning, Karen's mother worried about her daughter's looks and projected negative feelings about being a woman onto her little girl. Karen's mother had difficulty being a mother to her daughter, yet she longed for unconditional love from her, a love she felt she had never received from her own mother. Mrs. K. was extremely sensitive to what she experienced as rejection by her little girl. When Karen became attached to her father, Mrs. K. said, "Karen wants no part of me. On the weekend she just wants to see her father. I can't be expected to start taking care of her on Monday mornings. She can't be so fickle and get away with it." Here we see how sensitive Mrs. K. was to any sign of rejection by her daughter, for which she then felt entitled to retaliate. Mrs. K. needed Karen's love to repair the pain of not having been loved enough by her own mother.

When Karen was thirteen months old she began to walk, to point, and to say some words. She showed interest in her clothes, knew where her dresses and shoes were kept. Mrs. K. was a very well-dressed woman. Karen's early interest in clothes not only demonstrates her identification with her mother, but also her wish to please her mother. In fact, during this time, Mr. K. was able to be more responsive to Karen. Unfortunately, soon thereafter Karen had an accident in the park: she was standing right next to her mother when she slipped and fell and cut her forehead badly. Mrs. K. took her to the hospital where she had to have stitches. She described how she was very close to fainting herself and could hardly keep from crying. She feared that if she had started to cry, she never would have stopped. The mother's reaction to her daughter's accident demonstrates her overly strong need for Karen to repair Mrs. K.'s own feelings of vulnerability. It was almost as if Mrs. K. was so afraid of this vulnerability that she projected it onto her daughter and then maintained a strict distance from her. The traumatic event of this accident precipitated a crisis of separation for Karen. When her mother was out of the room, Karen was inconsolable: she could not take comfort from anything or anybody and even refused ice cream, which she usually loved. In this way Karen demonstrated an extraordinary degree of empathy for her mother's pain. Mrs. K. reacted by becoming further withdrawn from her daughter, thereby distancing herself from her overly strong identification with her little girl.

Following summer vacation, Karen was eighteen months old and in the midst of rapprochement conflicts. Her crisis took the form of clinging to her mother, seemingly in an attempt to coerce her mother to fill her emotional needs. Karen was constantly aware of her mother's presence, and any attention from the observers was experienced as a threat to the wished-for closeness with mother: even being looked at by an observer would result in Karen's running to her mother. We see here a kind of splitting in which contact with the mother is perceived as good and wished-for, whereas contact with the outside world is perceived as bad and to be warded off.

Two Women and Their Mothers

Karen's exclusive need for her mother had a tragic quality because it made her unable to take advantage of the other available resources.

One day Mrs. K. came to the center elegantly dressed, wearing jewelry and makeup, and complained that Karen had no clothes and that she would have to go shopping for her. In fact, observers often noted that Mrs. K. would attend very carefully to her own appearance while neglecting Karen's. Mrs. K. related the story of a hysterical crying attack Karen had had one night during the summer. She had been so upset that she was shaking, and Mother had been afraid that Karen was having a nervous breakdown from which she would never recover. Again, we see Mrs. K.'s projection of her own vulnerability onto Karen (just as during Karen's accident she was afraid she would have cried forever if she had let herself begin to cry). It is significant that Mrs. K. told this story on a day when she presented herself as a woman of the world, quite a contrast to a woman who needed a little girl to make her feel whole and who was so threatened by her child's needs for her.

Despite her mother's inattentiveness, Karen continued to seek closeness to her mother, and she never retaliated by rejecting her or showing open aggression. Karen would stand close to her mother, look into her face, pat her from time to time, and ask to be rocked on her foot. Whenever she got closer to Mother, she could then tolerate attention from observers. Karen could be available for attention from others when she felt more secure with her mother.

Around the age of nineteen months, Mrs. K. began to toilet-train Karen and was able to take more interest in her daughter. Typically, Karen's positive reaction to her mother's attention was almost immediate. Mrs. K. began to dress her daughter in more attractive clothes, and Karen started to look in the mirror. By the age of twenty months, Karen began fantasy play, placing dolls around a table with cups and saucers. She became more friendly to observers and was able to let her mother leave the room without clinging or crying. There seems to have been a resolution of the intense earlier crisis, helped by her beginning symbolic play in which she could enact a happy family. Toilet training proceeded well. Karen began to identify with her mother and played flirtatiously with a male observer. She liked to dress up and enjoyed putting on observers' jewelry, which she showed off to her mother. Karen also played a game she had learned from her brother. Identification with her mother and also her older brother seemed to have helped in the resolution of this rapprochement crisis. During a conversation with other mothers who were talking about the inadvisability of putting a little child on a diet, Karen's mother remarked: "If I had a fat little girl, I would put her on a strict diet and wouldn't care what it did to her personality." Thus, even during this period when things were going well between Karen and her mother, Mrs. K.'s thoughts went to a scenario in which a mother would have to harm her child in order to make her into an acceptable woman.

The relatively blissful period of positive rapprochement and sharing between Karen and her mother ended when Karen was twenty-two months old and Mrs. K. announced she was four months pregnant. Karen became demanding, asking her mother for specific things rather than just for her presence. Battles of will began. These eventually focused on the issue of toilet training, which earlier on had been a positive shared experience. Karen became frequently constipated and at times would not go to the bathroom for three to four days.

Karen began to seek her mother's attention in negative ways and actively to oppose her mother's suggestions. Of particular importance was a behavior that seems to have originated a pattern that continued into Karen's adolescence and adulthood. Karen began to be more adventurous, climbing up to dangerous places in spite of her mother's admonitions. This behavior, in which Karen would endanger herself and Mrs. K. would have to come to her rescue, assured her of her mother's attention. It also, however, can be seen as a literal enactment of Karen's intrapsychic conflict—Karen's separateness from Mother was inhibited by the simultaneous need to cling to her.

During Karen's third year, the struggles continued. When Karen was thirty months old her mother said Karen was "driving her crazy." She described a visit to the paternal grandparents during which Karen had cried, clung to her, and not allowed her to "do anything, even speak to [her] relatives." At the center Karen had difficulty staying in the toddler room without her mother, but when with her mother, continued to fight and struggle with her. This was different from the time when Karen had clung to her mother, but was always accepting of any attention her mother offered her.

Two Women and Their Mothers

At the climax of Karen's struggles with her mother, which took the form of severe constipation, Karen revealed a fantasy during a play session at the center: she said she had "a horsie in her stomach." Karen became very attached to a little toy horse which she took home from the center, kept under her bed, and did not allow anyone to touch. Earlier on, observers had noted Karen's attachment to the rocking horse in the playroom, which she often sat on for long periods and refused to let other children use. It may be that this rocking horse represented the mother from whom she did not want to separate. Perhaps sitting on the rocking horse provided her with feelings of comfort she did not get enough of from her mother, who held her only rarely. In addition, rocking on the play horse must have provided her with genital stimulation, as did the withholding of stool and urine. In taking possession of the little toy horse and not letting go of it, the horse became a kind of transitional object. It may have represented the attachment to Mother—the big rocking horse—as well as a primitive identification with Mother who had a baby in her stomach, like Karen had a "horsie" in *her* stomach. The difficulty in separating from Mother became an unconscious fantasy in which having Mother and being Mother are merged. This kind of identification with Mother could not help Karen to resolve her rapprochement struggles: if Karen's identification with her pregnant mother took the form of not wanting to relinquish her bowel movement—the "horsie in her stomach"—this identification was tainted by the conflict. Eventually Karen would have to relinquish her bowel movement and with that the fantasy that she, like Mother, could have a baby. Karen's mother's negative feelings about being a woman made it difficult for her to soften her daughter's disappointment. However, once the baby was born, Karen actively participated with mother in caring for the baby, a pleasurable activity for both of them. Karen's new identification with Mother's care for the new baby and with the cared-for baby diminished their conflicts.

Because the representation of her girl child was both negative and narrow, Karen's mother was not able to be sufficiently emotionally available during her daughter's separation-individuation process. Her unavailability had an effect on all aspects of the separation-individuation process and made it very difficult for Karen to achieve an identity separate enough from her mother to gratify her own needs. Karen, who was an intelligent and attractive girl, eventually could find satisfactions in her life apart from Mother, but carried the burden of the strong, negative bond into her adult object relations.

Further Development and Adulthood

Although the problems of her conflicted relationship with Mother continued in her preschool years, Karen was able to make a good adjustment to nursery school. Her play was rich and imaginative; her concentration was outstanding; her language was very articulate; and her ability to get along with other children and teachers was quite satisfactory. In followup school visits, observers remarked on the liveliness of Karen's expression and manner, which they contrasted to her subdued and sad mood at the center. Karen seemed to have found in nursery school a safe and enjoyable haven from turbulent family relationships. Her problem with constipation persisted in spite of medication, and it continued to be a battleground between her and her mother. In fact, Karen told an observer who inquired about why she did not go to the bathroom, that not having a bowel movement made her mother angry. The constipation was also painful to Karen. It contained layers of fantasy connected with birth and death: upon seeing a dead bird, she wondered if the bird might have died while having a bowel movement. At times Karen expressed a negative self-image, saying that nobody liked her and that she did not like herself. She identified strongly with her older brother and at times wanted to wear only boys' clothes. Karen's ability to make good use of her school experience and her identification with others enabled her to grow despite the persisting difficulties in the relationship with her mother.

When talking about her mother in the adult interviews, Karen noted how carefully and well her mother had chosen all her schools and how important her school experiences had been. While Mrs. K. could not be sufficiently attentive to Karen's needs herself, she had enough awareness of her own difficulties with Karen to know that life outside would be important and that she could provide nurturing school settings. Not surprisingly, Karen chose to become a teacher and found great satisfaction from this profession. School reports during Karen's latency and adolescent years always emphasized her intelligence and creativity. However, by the time she got to high school, Karen's personal difficulties began to interfere. She started

Two Women and Their Mothers

to drink and use drugs; she became very depressed and made a suicide attempt. During her last year in high school she became involved with a man and left home to live with him for two years. Her parents divorced during this period, which was traumatic for Karen, complicated by the fact that both parents used her as a confidante. She finally left what became a very abusive relationship with her boyfriend only to enter another one four months later. However, at this time Karen started college and began therapy. Being in therapy brought her closer to her father who also entered therapy at the time, partly because of his concern for Karen. Karen left her boyfriend who she felt was unwilling to make the relationship work. Here we see how while Mrs. K.'s negative representation of her daughter seems to have influenced her choice of partners and self-destructive behavior, Karen's experience of her mother as someone who could help her find support outside the family—as she did by choosing good schools—became an important theme in her life as she continued to find support for herself outside the nuclear family, both in relationships to extended family and in her wish to be helped by and to be helpful to others.

The year after she finished college, Karen moved away from home, supported herself doing office work, and eventually started graduate school in education. She shared a home with her younger sister who attended the same graduate program. Karen described her close relationship with her sister, and said she liked the fact that she and her sister could talk about everything and share their experiences. Then she said: "We rely on each other too much. We are always together; we always do things together, and we both feel that we need to break away because we are not helping each other get boyfriends because we just sit around and talk all the time. Maybe we have physical needs, but we don't have mental needs as much as somebody else might because we can fulfill that for each other." While Karen described this closeness to her sister, she also commented that her sister was critical of her and sometimes made fun of her for the things that she liked to do, such as reading or being outdoors. Whenever Karen did have a relationship with a man, her sister disapproved of her choice. Nevertheless, Karen derived comfort and stability from sharing her life with her sister at that time.

Karen had a great deal of difficulty thinking of herself as an attractive young woman; she was especially troubled by her tendency to be overweight. This, of course, was extremely troubling to her mother who had offered both Karen and her sister a lot of money to lose weight. Karen was very upset about this, particularly because her mother offered her no financial support for her studies. Once again Mrs. K. demonstrated her conviction that the most important thing for a girl was to be thin and beautiful.

Karen was very well aware of the destructive aspects of her relationship with her mother, but she was nevertheless always willing to spend time with her and was compassionate toward her. Eventually Karen moved away from her sister, which she experienced as a very positive step. While Karen had wanted to move away from her sister, the internal experience of the separation may still have been one of being abandoned by a maternal object. She once again became involved in a relationship with a man that turned out to be destructive to her. Even though she insisted it was the best relationship she had ever had because the man she was with was very sensitive to her feelings and very satisfying to her, he became abusive when he drank. Karen broke off her relationship with her boyfriend and refused to see him anymore unless he stopped drinking. Karen herself had started to attend AA meetings because she was worried about her own tendency to drink too much. Her boyfriend came over despite her having asked him not to and would not leave. Her mother happened to call at the time he was there, noticed something was wrong, and was able to help Karen through the immediate situation. Here we see what is perhaps the continuation of Karen's early tendency to attract her mother's attention by getting herself into dangerous situations as she had as a toddler and later on as an adolescent. We also see her mother's awareness that Karen might be in real danger. In spite of her disapproval of his actions, Karen felt a strong pull to stay with this boyfriend. This pull reflected an omnipotent fantasy that if she tried hard enough, she could make any relationship work. It also reflected a sense of being the one at fault, a continuity of Karen's old dilemma with her mother, where it was not clear to her who was to blame for the difficulties and conflicts in their relationship.

Karen's conflicts with her mother are not resolved at this point, and her burdened relationship to her mother makes it difficult for Karen to find what she longs for, namely, a satisfying relationship

Two Women and Their Mothers

with a man. However, Mrs. K.'s early representation of Karen as a little girl also contained a sense of being unable to fulfill Karen's needs. The compensation she found for this by providing good other sources for furthering Karen's development has continued to be an important asset to Karen's life. During the followup interviews, Karen was, of all the subjects, the most open and the most willing to share her internal world. She appreciated the interviews and thought they had been helpful to her. Karen's use of the followup interviews is another example of how she learned to turn to the outside world for support, though never quite enough support to help her overcome her burdens. However, it eventually became possible to help her get good therapeutic help which it seems she has been able to use well.

Karen's conflict as an adult is expressed in a response she gave to a separation-individuation test:

> A mother is going to work. She's happy the kids are old enough. She wants to be with adults and be challenged. She doesn't notice that her son can't stand the separation and is withdrawn and introverted trying to say, "Please I need your attention." She is so wrapped up she doesn't notice and never will. She'll want to be close later, but she can't and won't realize that it is because he needed her and she wasn't there when he needed her. He still loves her and is not depressed or dysfunctional, but can't give because he had to stop himself from needing her. Feeling closeness is just gone and she can't understand it.

In the light of this story, we can see that although Karen continues to be open and available to her mother, she feels that profound and irreparable harm was done by her mother's emotional unavailability. It is interesting to note that Karen's mother eventually did what Karen perceived she needed to do: she embarked on a new career, which she found fulfilling.

As an adult, Karen was still very tied to her mother. She not only reenacted negative aspects of the primary maternal relationship in other situations, but also in her adult relationship with her mother. As an adult, she still had a tendency to be willing to sacrifice too much to get the love she yearned for. Karen continues to be caught in the dilemma of her mother's representation of the burdens of femininity.

Anni Bergman—Maria Fahey

DISCUSSION

We have discussed the development of Helen and Karen during separation-individuation and early adulthood. We shall now briefly review and compare their development, keeping in mind the questions raised at the beginning of the paper.

Helen's mother saw in Helen an ideal little girl whom she could present for the world's admiration with pride. Helen and her mother were an uneven couple in which Helen was attractive, vital, and admirable, whereas her mother appeared depressed, withdrawn and colorless. They functioned well as a couple as long as the child could shine, possibly enacting the idealized and wished-for part of the mother's self-representation. In contrast, Karen's mother saw in Karen a little girl who would have to suffer her whole life the burdens of being female, which meant having to exist to please men and to deny her own pleasures and satisfactions. Karen's mother could not present her daughter for the admiration of the observers. Karen and her mother were also an uneven couple, almost the mirror image of Helen and her mother. Whereas Helen's mother seemed to receive gratification from the observers' admiration of her daughter, Karen's mother seemed in need of admiration herself and was not able to obtain narcissistic supplies from admiration of her daughter. Karen's mother's outlook on the life of a woman seemed to make her feel doomed as a mother of a girl.

While Helen's mother was able to experience fulfillment for narcissistic wishes through the birth of her baby girl, Karen's mother could not experience such satisfaction from her daughter. When Helen had difficulties, her mother tended to deny them or be overwhelmed by them. Karen's mother, on the other hand, defended against the effect of Karen's troubles on her by distancing herself. During Karen's rapprochement crisis, however, when she was confronted with Karen's intense need for her, she rallied to be more available. In contrast, the appearance of Helen's rapprochement struggles interrupted the mother's representation of the ideal mother-daughter couple, which made it difficult for Helen's mother to be emotionally available to her.

In considering how this early mother-child interaction affected Helen's self representation, we see a little girl who started out life

Two Women and Their Mothers

exuberant and confident turn into a child whose self-confidence was quite low, who became demanding, clinging, and aggressive, and who later on had difficulty getting along with people outside the family, such as teachers and peers. In addition, her father's absence further narrowed the range of people to whom Helen could relate and with whom she could identify. The birth of two brothers further strained the representation of her as her mother's special child. During her second year, the discovery of the anatomical difference between the sexes was particularly difficult for her. Helen remained vulnerable to disappointments and perceived failures.

In contrast, Karen started out depressed and lacking in motivation and confidence, and this sense of being insecure remained with her. She did, however, turn to her father and to her brother for stimulation and identification, and later on she was able to turn to people outside the family, such as teachers and school friends. In addition she benefited from identifying with her mother caring for her baby sister, and also with her baby sister as she received her mother's love and care during early babyhood. At school Karen was able to develop her interests and creativity and find appreciation for them.

When Helen and Karen were interviewed, they were close to thirty. They had both been graduated from college and were living on their own at varying distance from their parents. Helen was married, and while both Helen and Karen had professions, neither was yet completely settled in her professional life. Both women kept in fairly regular contact with their families.

As an adult Helen had made a fairly good adjustment and was able to create a life for herself that included marriage and a profession. Her relationship with her family showed appropriate concern—neither overinvolved nor uncaring. She preferred her mother to her father and was somewhat judgmental of her two younger brothers. Difficulties of her early life, particularly in the mother-child relationship, were not recalled by her: the intense envy and jealous possessiveness which had been apparent during the second and third years of life seem to have been repressed. Helen retained a special relationship with her mother which was reminiscent of her wish for an exclusive relationship with Mother early on: she liked her mother to come and visit her and her husband and enjoyed being with her. Gardening was the activity she most liked to share with her mother. Helen felt these visits were beneficial for her mother as well as for herself.

As an adult, Karen remained troubled. She had gone through a series of abusive relationships from which she had to be rescued. She was dissatisfied with her physical self, being overweight, and she struggled with unsatisfying relationships with her family, especially her mother. Karen was not satisfied with herself, but she was able to enjoy her work and activities with friends. What was striking about Karen as an adult was her energetic search and hopefulness about being able to create a healthy life for herself. Karen retained a close relationship with her younger sister, harking back to the time when Karen had been able to benefit from her mother's love and care for her new baby sister.

Helen seemed to have renounced the liveliness and outstanding potential so apparent at the beginning. She suppressed her disappointments and experienced her resentments in an impersonal way—against fate rather than anyone in particular. While at times Helen felt fate had not fairly rewarded her for her efforts, she did not express her affects very strongly, probably an identification with her mother who was always understated and undemanding. While Helen had made a better adjustment than Karen, finding a stable home and relationship, she seemed to be less open to new experiences and to reflection about herself. Karen, on the other hand, continued to go through a great deal of turbulence, but was actively searching for her place in the world, for meaningful work and for close relationships. Helen seems to have identified with a somewhat depressed mother who never quite got from life what she deserved, had to serve others, especially men, and had given up realizing her potential. It seems Helen did not find support in identification with her father or her brothers[8] or from other important relationships.

As an adult Karen continued to be burdened by the difficulties in her early relationship with her mother and by the difficulties she still experienced in getting needed narcissistic supplies from others. She suffered from her mother's negative representation of a female child and of women in general, and had difficulty taking pleasure

---

[8]Benjamin (1991) has described the importance of identification with the father for the girl's development.

Two Women and Their Mothers

being attractive or desirable. Karen continued to be involved in struggles with her mother who still could not be very generous in responding to her daughter's needs and who was herself very needy of Karen's support and attention. Karen had not given up hope that she might get emotional supplies from her mother. While Karen indeed seemed to have internalized her mother's negative representation of her, Karen also identified with her mother's search for self-realization and enrichment. Mrs. K.'s continuous search for self-realization, present already during Karen's infancy, was an obstacle to her ability to be nurturing, but also seems to have given Karen the hope that by continued searching she would find her own happiness. Karen identified with the part of her mother that was determined to have a better life. In addition, she had been able to receive strength from her identifications with her brother and her father, her father's extended family, as well as her teachers. Mrs. K. had been able to encourage Karen's relationship with the outside world and to provide environments that were enriching for her. Karen remains open to the possibility of change.

During the early observational research, what was observed most closely was the interaction between mother and child as it evolved during the course of the separation-individuation period, and the interplay between the early mother-child relationship and the child's capacity to develop her own resources, possibly in concordance with the mother's predilections as well as her unconscious needs and desires. The goal of the early research was to study the separation-individuation process, that process by which each child develops a self-representation separate from the representation of the mother. The original study did not focus on understanding the separate development of the mother through which she had arrived at her particular mothering style. During the early study, it was observed that identification with the mother was an important avenue for the development of the separate self. In examining the data from the followup study, we find that identification with the mother goes beyond identifying with her mothering. It includes identifying with other aspects of the mother's own being that might be less directly connected to the mother's interaction with the child. By the time we look at the adult subjects, important other identifications have also played a role in determining the character and lifestyle of each daughter. Helen's mother turned to the outside world in a more limited way than Karen's mother. Helen, like her mother, turned to the outside world in a limited way, evidenced in part by how she responded to the adult interviews: she treated the interviewer with a great deal of reserve. Karen, on the other hand, continued to look to the outside world, partly an identification with her mother, but also to fill a need that was present in her development from the beginning. Again, this was evident in Karen's openness in the adult interviews as an experience that might offer new understandings and directions. Thus, while Helen's development was influenced by her mother's representation of her as the wished-for baby girl, Helen also identified with a mother who had limited expectations for her own life. Karen's development was influenced by her mother's representation of her as a girl child in a world where it is burdensome to be a woman, yet Karen also identified with a mother who struggled for self-realization.

As analysts we try to reconstruct beginnings; as researchers we attempt to understand outcomes. In both cases we draw inferences from observed behaviors to internal conflicts. Psychoanalytic work, whether in the psychoanalytic situation or in psychoanalytic observations, deals with unconscious processes at which we arrive from observations of the psychic surface. In analysis the multifaceted interactions of life are funneled into and made sense of in the exclusive relationship between analyst and analysand. In observational research the original exclusive relationship is made sense of by observing how it spirals out into the multifaceted and complex interactions of later life situations.

Observational research of the kind described adds to our knowledge of intrapsychic development as it interacts with lived life, which begins with mother and infant and branches out in ever-widening circles. In the longitudinal, psychoanalytically oriented observational research presented here, we can glimpse how internal representations develop. Helen and Karen's representations of self and other had their foundation in the way in which they were originally conceived in the mind of their mother.[9] In turn, each mother's conception of her daughter influenced the ways in which she interacted

---

[9]Again, we acknowledge the importance of the father's representations and subsequent development of the father-child relationship which was not part of this particular longitudinal study.

with her daughter. These early interactions provided the ground upon which each daughter built her sense of herself in relation to others as new experiences, based on expanded capacities to perceive the world outside, broadened the world built on the first relationship. We can now return to our metaphor of the *cantus firmus*. We hope to have shown both how the earliest mother-child interactions continue to have a powerful influence on the composition of one's life, and we also hope to have shown the possibilities for unpredictable and creative use each child makes of the earliest interactions as her world widens, other voices enter in, and variations and transformations occur.

REFERENCES

ABELIN, E. (1975). Some further observations and comments on the earliest role of the father. *Int. J. Psychoanal.*, 56:293–302.

AINSWORTH, M.D.S.; BLEHARD, M.C.; WATERS, E. & WALL, S. (1978). *Patterns of Attachment*. Hillsdale, NJ: Erlbaum.

ARLOW, J.A. (1982). Problems of the superego concept. *Psychoanal. Study Child*, 37:229–244.

BENJAMIN, J. (1991). Father and daughter: identification with difference—a contribution to gender heterodoxy. *Psychoanal. Dialog.*, 1:277–299.

BRAZELTON, T.B. & CRAMER, B. (1990). *The Earliest Relationship: Parents, Infants and the Drama of Early Attachment*. Reading, MA: Addison-Wesley.

CATH, S., GURWITT, A. & ROSS, J. (1982). *Father and Child*. Hillsdale, NJ: Analytic Press.

——— ——— & GUNSBERG, L. (1989). *Fathers and Their Families*. Hillsdale, NJ: Analytic Press.

FRAIBERG, S., ADELSON, E. & SHAPIRO, V. (1975). Ghosts in the nursery: a psychoanalytic approach to the problems of impaired infant-mother relationships. *J. Amer. Psychoanal. Assn.*, 14:387–421.

FURER, M. (1967). Some developmental aspects of the superego. *Int. J. Psychoanal.*, 48:277–280.

GADDINI, R. & GADDINI, E. (1970). Transitional objects and the process of individuation: a study of three different social groups. *J. Amer. Acad. Child Psychiat.*, 9:347–365.

MAHLER, M.S. (1972). Rapprochement subphase of the separation-individuation process. In *The Selected Papers of Margaret S. Mahler*, Vol. 2. New York: Aronson, 1979, pp. 131–148.

——— PINE, F. & BERGMAN, A. (1975). *The Psychological Birth of the Human Infant*. New York: Basic Books.

MAINE, M., KAPLAN, N. & CASSIDY, J. (1989). Security in infancy, childhood, and adulthood: a move to the level of representation. In Growing points in attachment theory and research, ed. I. Bretherton & E. Waters. *Monogr. Soc. Res. Child Devel.*, 50:66–106.

ROIPHE, H. & GALENSON, E. (1981). *Infantile Origins of Sexual Identity.* New York: Int. Univ. Press.

STERN, D. (1995). *The Motherhood Constellation: A Unified View of Parent-Infant Psychotherapy.* New York: Basic Books.

V.
THE PSYCHOLOGY OF FEMALE HOMOSEXUALITY

Figure 7. Florine Stettheimer (1923) *Portrait of Myself.* Oil on canvas, 40 × 26" Gift of the Estate of Ettie Stettheimer 1967. Columbia University

Toward Further Analytic Understanding of Lesbian Patients

Eleanor Schuker

> Psychoanalytic understanding of lesbianism has been excessively welded to unitary dynamic and etiologic themes, while actual dynamics vary among lesbian patients. Clinical material will illustrate this variety. Limitations in past theories and countertransference issues will be discussed. It is proposed that dynamics in lesbian patients should not be confused with pathology, and that an object choice originally embedded in conflict can become secondarily autonomous or remain fluid.

This paper poses questions about the etiology and dynamics of female homosexualities. I propose that our understanding of female homosexualities has been excessively welded to unitary theories, while actual etiologies and psychodynamics among female homosexual patients vary. The presence of some common specific dynamics should not be universalized into quantity of pathology, etiology, or specific developmental causation for eventual homosexual object choice. I propose that there are many homosexualities, and that our thinking about this topic would be kept open if we would begin by assuming that there may be multiple developmental paths, nodal points, and conflicts resulting in homoerotic feelings, behavioral object choice, or a sense of "gay" identity. Furthermore, object choice can develop secondary autonomy, so that a compromise chosen out of conflict at a nodal point may persist with lessening or resolution of that conflict. Thus, sexual object choice may not alter with conflict resolution or clinical improvement, nor even

---

Training and Supervising Analyst, Columbia University Center for Psychoanalytic Training and Research.

This paper is a revised version of two presentations, one given at the Arden House Conference of the Columbia University Center for Psychoanalytic Training and Research, October 28–29, 1994, and another at the Western New England Psychoanalytic Society, April 22, 1995. The author is grateful to the numerous colleagues who commented on these earlier manuscripts, and to her patients who generously permitted use of their material.

with structural change. Historically, the psychoanalytic search for unitary dynamic and etiologic themes in lesbian patients may have led to overgeneralization from limited clinical material. This may account for disparate clinical descriptions in the literature.

I begin with case material to illustrate different dynamic issues in some homosexual women. These lesbian patients vary in their core dynamic issues, gender role identities, multiple functions of their erotic feelings, and conflicts along the course of development which utilized homoerotic feeling. They also vary in investment in maternal interests. Some problems with classification will be delineated. I suggest that assumptions that homosexualities are in themselves pathological may have led to confusion between dynamics and etiology, and to an equation of dynamics with pathology. We should not assume that homosexual resolutions are necessarily more pathological than are the various heterosexualities. I shall discuss the countertransference bias inherent in a view of homosexualities as pathological, thus investing in either changing or affirming sexual preferences. I shall also describe some countertransference issues related to lesbian erotic transferences.

CLINICAL MATERIAL

Case I

G. was a capable hospital administrator in her early thirties, who sought treatment when a three-year lesbian partnership with an older woman seemed to be in crisis. G. had felt frustrated as she tried to deepen the intimacy with her lover, and worried that she was becoming the caretaker of a very needy person. She felt guilty about wanting to leave, because the lover had been supportive in her "coming-out" process, and they had established a life together.

G.'s adaptive character traits as a competent, organized, nurturant rescuer were evident in her social and professional life. She was beloved by a wide circle of friends who enjoyed her social, culinary, and organizational skills. At work, G. ran her large department, nurtured younger colleagues, and was rising in her profession. (This progress was further enhanced in treatment as she confronted her own homophobia and inhibitions, so she could deal with external prejudices.)

Lesbian Patients

G.'s character structure included masochistic and obsessional traits. She was an energetic person, was sensitive to others' feelings, was vulnerable to guilt about not pleasing, and had difficulty expressing anger. G.'s appearance, body movements, and mode of dress seemed masculine, and her height, low voice, and demeanor suggested a contained, gentle, grown man. She enjoyed being seen as strong, competent, and protective of women, but longed to acquire feminine qualities she felt other women would enjoy. G. had always known she was a girl, but experienced herself as masculine. While she had engaged in doll play, she had especially enjoyed motor activity. She was better at motoric activities than her effeminate, sickly, difficult three-year-older brother. G. felt attracted to girls before age five, but kept this secret. At puberty she had few friends, and escaped into intellectual and academic achievement. As an adolescent she tried heterosexual relations, hoping to enjoy intercourse and to please her mother. She found intercourse mildly pleasant, but without deep passion, in contrast to her homosexual desires for erotic and emotional closeness with other women. Masturbation fantasies focused on wishes to give female partners pleasure, not specifically via having a phallus. She was troubled also by a maternal identification that included traits of controllingness, criticalness, and a tendency to pick partners similar to her damaged father. We later discovered that a fantasy of rescuing a damaged father hid that of restoring a depressed early mother.

G. had been the soother and source of narcissistic esteem for mother. She served as her mother's companion, active "little man," and cure for her low-keyed depressed affect. Mother's marriage to a handsome man had led to disillusionment as G.'s father became increasingly dysfunctional and withdrawn. He became overtly paranoid when the parents divorced when G. was in college, and the mother had remarried happily. Thus, G.'s early experience of her mother was of a woman depleted and strained by responsibilities. Screen memories included rescuing mother who slipped after returning exhausted from work, and of being proud at age five when left alone in an emergency room while mother took other children home. Underlying rage at these abandonments did not emerge until after considerable treatment.

Just prior to G.'s birth, grandmother came to live with the family. Grandmother was an imposing figure who fought with mother for control. Both women did agree in their idealizing of the adored child, G., and in their depreciation of men. While grandmother and mother were superficially feminine, they did not encourage femininity or romantic heterosexual daydreams in G. She became the fantasy man of the house. (No real man could be man enough; in that sense the significance of sexual difference was denied.)

Despite her father's remoteness, he accepted G., and taught her carpentry. She recalled no romantic early relationship with him. Her triadic-level fantasies and conflicts, with issues of conflicted loyalty, revolved around intense relations in the mother-grandmother-self triangle; this was a powerful triadic oedipal conflict. Issues of rivalry, erotic longing, fears of defeat and of punishment centered around relations with these two powerful adult women. They each competed for G.'s love, and G. competed with each for the other. Some element of negative oedipal victory (winning mother) was tempered by fear of loss of grandmother's love, by gradual generational disappointment, and by needs to keep homoerotic strivings hidden. She had adaptive identifications with positive aspects of both women. Thus, despite the preoedipal relation with a depressed mother, G. felt specially valued, developed a clear identity, and capacities for intimacy and love. She began having overt lesbian experiences in late adolescence, during college, feeling relief at accepting her homosexual identity.

G.'s early need to be active and lively to reach mother might be postulated to have stimulated development of homoerotic feelings. The relationship with mother lacked a sharing of pleasure in sameness or mutual joyful pride in femininity, as mother transmitted deep dissatisfaction about her own adult womanhood and devaluation of men as love objects. This reflected familial gender conflicts as well as blurring of generations. G. developed a clear sense of her own (masculinized) gender role identity, with some enduring conflicts about dependency, compliance, and aggression. Activity and homoerotic feeling helped to maintain fantasies of closeness with female figures. The relation with mother progressed to the triadic negative oedipal level, and fantasies of oedipal success with a woman partner were enhanced by her importance to both mother and grandmother. A positive oedipal relation with father was seen as hopeless or threatening, and was not developed in depth. Thus, in understanding G.'s

Lesbian Patients

sexual orientation, I hypothesize preoedipal contributions to masculine gender role identifications, a predominance of negative oedipal conflicts, familial conflicts about gender, lack of affective encouragement of femininity, and use of homoerotic feeling to achieve closeness. Genetic, prenatal, and temperamental contributions to her lesbianism are unknown, but may be significant. G. has other homosexual relatives (male and female). She was not afraid of heterosexual contact—it just was not of passionate interest—and she had male friends.

G. did not experience her lesbianism itself as conflicted. Issues in her treatment included needs to ward off passive-dependent and erotic yearnings, underlying guilty fears about aggressive feelings, dependent and erotic needs in a love relationship, and defensive controllingness and use of competence. Anger at both her mother's and grandmother's need for her to be compliant and to deny dependency emerged in the transference as she developed fears of abandonment and punishment for her yearnings. As G. became more accepting of her own dependent yearnings, for the first time she experienced wishes for a child. She left her original lover, and eventually formed a more mutual lesbian relationship. Her sexual orientation was not in question, but she became less inhibited. Working through of erotic transference feelings with their superego conflicts led to less homophobic shame and competitive guilt.

Case 2

K., a lesbian in her late thirties, had different dynamics from G. She longed to feel chosen and valued and feared being excluded from a maternal dyad. Such longings and conflicts had motivated a successful and satisfying career, and seemed the unconscious reason for seeking treatment soon after participating in the elective artificial insemination of her permanent partner. She was not yet aware of anxiety precipitated by her partner's pregnancy. A second dynamic theme for K. was her assertive inhibitions and fears of projected male aggression.

K.'s demeanor was that of a sensuous, softspoken, girlishly feminine and pretty woman. She was appealing, but also could be elusive and distant, and seemed out of touch with most of her feelings. She thought she had experienced a perfect childhood until her parents separated when she was eleven. A two-year-younger sister's chronic illness was handled "so well" by mother that everything was kept "normal." It was only after the sister's death in young adulthood that K. felt dissatisfied with her relationship with her mother, who had tried to turn to her as a substitute for the sister.

K. asked for psychotherapy to provide guidance to help her father, who was having trouble asserting himself with a second difficult wife. K.'s parallel difficulties with self-assertion were soon evident, both at work and in her love relationship. She was extremely anxious about her lover's pregnancy, using medical information to inhibit the lover's exhibitionistic pride and pleasure, and worrying whether she herself could be a parent. Like her father, she alternated between passivity and harsh attempts to control.

We tried to clarify these matters. Anxiety about the pregnancy was linked to fears of a changed relationship and to concerns about parenting. K.'s pattern of withdrawal from her partner and substitutive worrying and blaming reminded her of her father. K.'s menstrual periods stopped prematurely during this time. We came to understand how K.'s father's punitive attitude toward her as a child had led to her retreat by age seven from what had been a closer and mutually admiring early relationship with him. A final disillusionment with him came when her parents separated and she learned that the father had been having an affair. She felt unsupported by both parents at that time. After a period of depression, she shortly experienced an early adolescent homosexual attraction that reconstituted her feeling loved and special.

K. had always disparaged her mother as superficial, self-involved, and foolish, yet they shared interests in clothes and decorating. As treatment progressed, and especially after the baby was born, K. recalled her mother's controlling quality, angry neediness, and emotional unavailability, which K. had handled by keeping her distance, leaving mother and sister together. K. had retreated to substitutive relationships with father and maternal grandmother (whom mother hated), and to school achievements. Now a family "story" emerged: she and her mother had been very close until the sister was born. K. was scolded because she "acted like this baby did not exist." From this time, K. was deemed "selfish" by the mother and was seen as difficult.

Now, with the birth of the partner's child, as mother tried to get more involved, K. responded to these overtures dismissively. The

Lesbian Patients

partner protected her from mother, facilitated some interaction, and also made active efforts to include K. in the parenting. As K. felt reassured about her importance, she became less anxious.

K. discovered her homosexuality in adolescence, while distant from both parents, following a period of depression after the parents' separation. She felt freed from having to be "perfect" and from her mother's dissatisfaction with her; she used her homosexual lovers as part of an adolescent defiance. K. enjoyed her mother's distress and helplessness to control her. Sexual intimacy with women felt alluring, powerful, and worth risking mother's wrath. Later, loss of a lover's attentions was devastating. While K.'s initial choices were of narcissistic women, she gradually chose more nurturant women who could give more than mother. As an adult, K. was aware of heterosexual attractions in addition to homosexual ones, but had not acted on them. She stated that to "crave" men as mother did would be horrifying, since men are unreliable.

K.'s homosexual relations seemed to repair early narcissistic losses. They served avoidance of positive oedipal competition and fantasied male aggression and maternal retaliation. Withdrawal from feminine competition, only around maternal activities, seemed to occur before age five. K. experienced active competition with mother in matters of intellectual achievement, ceding interest in child-bearing and rearing. After the parental divorce, she also ceded heterosexuality, but not sexuality and femininity, to mother.

Case 3

P., treated by a colleague, illustrates other unique dynamic issues. From a rural family environment that included several older siblings, scant nurturing, and a remote but violent father who beat the older children, P. made a strong attachment to a favored older brother. He nurtured her in turn, and she seemed to have formed an oedipal sibling triangle (Sharpe and Rosenblatt, 1994) with him, loving him in competitive rivalry with mother. Lesbianism became P.'s adolescent solution to loss of this idealized if overstimulating older brother when he was killed in an accident when she was thirteen. This precipitated guilt about her incestuous erotic attachment to him and rage at his abandonment. P.'s lesbian identity, beginning shortly after this loss, facilitated recovery of positive aspects of the relationship with the brother by identification with him as both lost object and masculine aggressor. It protected her from feelings of guilt and abandonment, and also from fears of males' heterosexual aggression. The patient appeared as a boyish, childlike, phobic waif. In analysis, global fears of a dangerous world gradually diminished when neediness and feelings of deprivation, fantasies of aggressive revenge, and defensive projection of aggression came into interpretive view. With tolerance of her own longings for closeness with her woman analyst, she was able to enter into a lesbian relationship that was longer-term. She required being in a masochistic role for erotic arousal, and fantasized being with a man at the moment of orgasm. As the analysis progressed, her intimate relationships included more nurturance as well as experimentation with both roles in playful sadomasochistic sexual activity. P. continued an exclusive lesbian orientation and participation in the homosocial world. She developed more adaptive use of masculine and aggressive identifications with father and brother.

HISTORICAL VIEWS OF DYNAMICS OF DIFFERENT FEMALE HOMOSEXUALITIES

The psychoanalytic literature on female homosexualities is reviewed in detail elsewhere (Schuker and Levinson, 1991, Chapt. 19). The literature includes only a small number of cases. Several authors elucidate a single "central" dynamic or etiologic element in lesbianism, but these dynamics differ, so that these multiple dynamic patterns might actually reflect different homosexualities. I shall briefly review the major historical contributions.

The early literature focused on oedipal conflicts and frustrated positive oedipal longings as related to homosexual object choice. Freud (1920) describes an eighteen-year-old who falls in love with an older woman, defying her father and securing love from a mother substitute. Overt homosexual desires were precipitated by the birth of a brother at puberty, due to disappointment of her wish that her father would give her a child; she retreated from oedipal competition with mother and instead angrily identified with father. She had strong early yearnings for a mother who preferred boys and who gave birth to a brother while the girl was in her oedipal phase. She

Lesbian Patients

experienced early penis envy and believed she had been castrated. Her sexual object was a woman who seemed free, perhaps a wishful move from her own inhibition and disappointment. Freud notes that "mental sexual character" and object choice do not necessarily coincide (p. 170).

Jones (1927) views homosexuality in five women as a defensive oedipal phenomenon secondary to strong oral sadism toward mother. Fears of loss of the capacity for sexual pleasure led to renouncing incestuous wishes for father. Jones' patients regressed from oedipal disappointment and unconscious wishes to replace mother with father to preoedipal dependency. Some patients enjoyed femininity through identification with feminine women; others focused on resentment of men and envy of masculine attributes.

Deutsch (1932) describes eleven cases, emphasizing revived oedipal conflict at puberty and underlying aggression toward a preoedipal mother. Deutsch asserts that the positive oedipal phase is threatening because of sadomasochistic, passive oedipal wishes toward father and guilt over rivalry with mother. The return to love of women after an oedipal stage is distinguished from an infantile attachment to mother. Deutsch differentiates between homosexuality and physical masculinity as well. Jones and Deutsch view heterosexuality as a more successful form of development, while linking homosexuality with pathology. Later writers posit earlier origins and more severe pathology for homosexuality. Socarides (1963, 1978) views homosexual women as having primary preoedipal distortions and regression from ocdipal conflict, with primitive preoedipal fears of murderous aggression toward and from mother, making positive oedipal conflict impossible to resolve. Heterosexual intercourse is feared as disembowling and horrific, femininity is renounced, and the patients identify with father.

Khan (1979) offers clinical material from a young woman whose homosexuality was an attempt to repeat conflicts from an archaic collusion required because of the mother's depressive pathology. The child sponsored mother in a self-deception that she was good. There was a regressive idealization of early body-care experiences with mother. Treatment restored the patient to a heterosexual adaptation.

McDougall (1970, 1980) views homosexuality as a compromise maintaining a precarious sense of identity in patients with preoedipal

Eleanor Schuker

and gender identity disturbance, resulting in a specific oedipal constellation. She analyzed five homosexual women. For these patients homosexuality served as a bulwark against psychosis, via identification with a "fecal phallus," an anal father. Detached from an idealized but unconsciously feared maternal image, and identified with the paternal object who was given up libidinally but possessed symbolically by regression to an anal-sadistic identification, the homosexual woman is seen as "perverse" by McDougall in the sense that she must continually act out an internal drama in a pressured attempt to maintain ego identity. McDougall (1980) includes homosexuality as one of the perversions in which sexual overstimulation and parental pathology create an illusion that the child's pregenital sexuality is adequate to satisfy the mother. McDougall (1989) describes a case of narcissistic pathology in a homosexual woman, traced to her mother's denial of the child's father's death at fifteen months, which forced the child to be a narcissistic extension and to achieve a magical identification with the dead father. McDougall emphasizes maternal failure to help the child come to terms with sexual difference as well as with other realities.

Stoller's (1985) study of one homosexual woman delineates a central difficulty in separation-individuation. His patient's lesbian erotic choice changed a separation trauma to triumph. A central childhood story/myth about Minnie the Mermaid constituted a warning to the patient that she should not venture away from mother, for fear of abandonment. The patient retreated because of abandonment fears to a maternal "symbiotic" relationship, and to homosexual object choice. Stoller is clear that his conclusion applies to only his specific case.

Eisenbud (1982, 1986) suggests that homoerotic feeling in the preoedipal period develops either as the girl's defense against merging and engulfment by turning passive into active, or as an attempt to reach a distant mother. Siegel (1988), influenced by Socarides as well as by Kestenberg's (1968) suggestion that some homosexual women fail to sexualize the vagina, concludes that her eight analytic patients failed to schematize their vaginas. Searching to complete themselves in the mirror of the same-sex partner, they wished for merger. Siegel finds absent doll play, failure to identify with mother's femininity, and heightened olfactory incorporation and hypochondriasis. One might wonder whether her particular patients repressed

Lesbian Patients

a representation of an internal, pleasurable feminine genital in favor of a mother who was seen as intrusive, damaging, and controlling of the body, or as oedipally competitive.

Thus, these more recent writers who emphasize preoedipal pathologies in female homosexuality again find common if variant unitary themes for their group of patients. Feminist theorist De Lauretis (1994), basing her work on Lacan, states that the lesbian lacks access to her own feminine body image, so seeks to love a woman who has it. She argues that lesbianism is a search for one's own completion or for the daughter one was not, rather than for mother's body as erotic object. What follows this fetishistic split then is a normal negative oedipal line of development. DeLauretis argues further that this "reorientation" should not be understood as pathology or repair of narcissistic defect, despite its specific unitary dynamics.

In summary, the literature on female homosexual patients covers dynamics from every epoch of development—preoedipal gender disorder, problems in feminine identification and body image, need to complete a defective sense of bodily self, the warding off of a psychotic loss of identity via paternal identification, separation anxiety with continued dyadic relations, reaction formations against sadism, fixation at the negative oedipal stage, regression to a negative oedipal constellation because of fears of maternal competitive retaliation, threats of oedipal paternal sadomasochistic penetration or overstimulation, adolescent stresses reviving oedipal conflict, superego conflicts and masturbation guilt, narcissistic needs, and also, along the entire developmental span, reactions to seduction trauma and overstimulation.

This literature might lead us to conclude that lesbian patients can be found with a variety of levels of pathology, capacities for adaptation, and ego functioning. We may be misled if we conclude that object choice itself is a reflection of pathology. Rather, we should be asking what factors allow erotic object choice to serve conflict resolution in some patients, and what other factors might be involved in object choice itself. Patients with similar levels of functioning but different erotic object choices might fruitfully be compared, and common dynamics or difficulties for homosexual patients in any subgroup might help us understand the nature of object choice.

Eleanor Schuker

DISCUSSION

The three patients I described above differed in styles of expression of womanliness, gender role behavior and identity, history, pathology, and dynamics. None was psychotic, and none was perverse in the sense of requiring a driven obligatory sexual behavior for identity maintenance. They differed in preoedipal and oedipal structures, in interest in maternal activities, and in the blend of identifications with each parent. Relations with mothers had been troubled, but not in a consistent pattern; G. and P. maintained strong positive elements in these relationships. Fathers were portrayed as either having been threatening or remote during some time in each woman's development, but K., as an adult, had returned to feeling some closeness to her father. Both K. and G. had friendships with men. Gender role disturbance and early tomboyism in G. did not preclude her maternal qualities, and K. was highly conflicted about maternal activity despite enjoying being feminine and attractive, and valuing her genital. It seems clear that no specific pathology or unitary conflict provides an explanation for etiology or dynamics for all lesbians. It seems unlikely that a single developmental path exists for object choice. We can only delineate possible contributing factors and describe how object choice becomes entwined with conflict resolution in a specific case. As we understand more about erotic development, we might identify influential nodal points. Contributing factors could include constitution and temperament; preoedipal conflicts about love, hate, and separateness, from mother; vicissitudes of the development of feminine body image and reactions to sexual differences; capacity for erotic defense and the use of erotism to reach mother or father; feminine identifications (both preoedipal and oedipal); maternal feelings and wishes; oedipal conflicts including competition, submission, and resulting identifications and defenses; primal-scene experiences; relations with father (preoedipal and oedipal) and paternal identifications; adolescent resolutions, regressions, inhibitions, and experiences; familial attitudes toward femininity, sexuality, and sexual roles; sibling relations; traumatic factors including those leading to fearful images of male aggressivity; and cultural pressures (Chodorow, 1992) to conform to heterosexual behavior.

There are multiple potential meanings to the description of a woman as lesbian. We may be referring to a woman's sexual fantasies,

Lesbian Patients

to her sexual activity and responsiveness, or to her sense of self-identity and association with a social group or social role. These are not necessarily concordant. A lesbian lifestyle is not the same as having homoerotic fantasies. A same-sex object can be utilized (in reality or in fantasy) in strivings for safety, intimacy, pleasure, power, or other gratifications. Erotic fantasy itself may have been homosexual from early childhood ("primary lesbian" [Ponse, 1980]), may include varying degrees of bisexuality, may be absent, or may not be homosexual despite homosexual activity or a same-sex behavioral requirement for arousal. Should erotic fantasy itself define sexual orientation? Some women desire or need bodily intimacy with another woman for arousal, although fantasizing about being with a male body at the moment of orgasm. For these women, needs for intimacy or safety may influence partner choice more than does the sex of the fantasied erotic object. Yet other women live a heterosexual social role, coupling and reproducing as heterosexual, but cannot be emotionally close with men, may not be aroused by men, and are capable of emotional intimacy only with women. Some of this last group may be aware of lesbian fantasies, but most might abhor a lesbian social classification. This issue of behavioral vs. fantasy choice is also entwined with that of mutability vs. immutability of object choice. I argue for flexibility in our understanding and classification of individuals in their intimate and erotic lives.

Is object choice more flexible in women than in men? Conscious erotic longings and passions in women frequently follow upon the precondition or requirement for intimacy and closeness, regardless of direction of fantasy content (Panel, 1987; Kirkpatrick, 1989). Intimacy may be a common female requirement for the actual recognition of any aroused state. In evaluating reports of changes in object choice (related to trauma, treatment, opportunity, or internal shift), we have to ask whether fantasy itself or behavior were mutable. For example, do women who change the direction of their erotic life in middle age (Richards, 1996) experience a change in fantasy contents as well as in object choice, or is there merely a change in intimate behavior without a fantasy shift? Person (1980) proposes that fantasy scripts tend to narrow with development. After an experience of traumatic aggressive assault some women develop a phobic reaction toward men and toward their own heterosexual fantasies, regardless of earlier orientation. Some women seem to become lesbian because the early paternal image was charged with frightening aggression. Both these groups may retain a tendency toward heterosexual fantasy, but have homosexual activity. Women may be more open to the possibility of homosexual behavior because of reduced social approbrium for it. Many women are already comfortable with other women's bodies (related to the history of maternal child care), perhaps because of increased bisexual fantasy in women, or because a requirement for intimacy as a condition for conscious arousal or to facilitate fantasies. For many patients, object choice, once achieved, acquires fixity. In these patients, the choice may seem to evolve through conflict and remain as part of identity. This seems to have been the case for G. For P., fantasies consolidated with social identity in adolescence. For K., we might need some decades follow-up to know. We need to compare patients in whom sexual orientation becomes fixed with those in whom it is still open to change or evolution. Retrospective reports of life narratives that describe always having been aware of a given orientation may or may not be literally correct; elements of one's history might be selected so as to gain a coherent sense of identity. Consolidation of object choice is not always reported from the same developmental era. New developmental conflicts can transform and restructure earlier compromises. Some patients can use erotic feeling for conflict resolution, while others may not have this capacity (Coen, 1981).

A review of case reports describing changes in sexual orientation during psychoanalytic treatment might shed light on issues relating to the question of flexibility of object choice. Olesker (1995) describes a late adolescent girl for whom homosexual object choice had strong oedipal-conflictual determinants, where analysis led to a heterosexual orientation. The patient's homosexual fantasies and activities developed early in the analysis and were seen as multiply determined compromise formations, with mainly oedipal dynamics. A retreat from heterosexuality was hypothesized, related to fears of intense positive oedipal erotic wishes, guilt toward mother and a dead brother, reaction formations to deal with anger, a sadomasochistic conception of heterosexual relations, and harsh superego attitudes toward genital pleasure. The analysis of oedipal, aggressive, and superego conflicts led to the patient's developing heterosexual

Lesbian Patients

interests. Yet it seems possible that this particular patient, despite homosexual activity and fantasy during analysis, had a primarily heterosexual orientation, based on her early childhood fantasies. Did flexibility in erotic behavioral expression reflect an adolescent experimentation, which could have narrowed later, or a particular bisexual capacity? Although the return to predominant heterosexual behavior was in line with most of her childhood ambitions and fantasies (the homosexual behavior seen as defense), we do not know whether this evolution would have occurred without treatment. Alternatively, it is also possible that the expression of bisexual interests was facilitated by the freedom and protection of the analysis.

P. Hopkins (unpublished) reports an emergence of heterosexuality in a patient in her mid-twenties, who had begun analysis as a lesbian. The analyst believed the patient's object choice resulted from increasing accumulation of difficulties at all stages of development. As the patient experienced increased intimacy with the analyst, she seemed to develop a strong identification with the analyst's femininity. Okesker's and Hopkins' patients highlight possible ongoing fluidity in behavioral expression of object choice under some circumstances, and possible effects of treatment including conflict resolution and other factors. If behavioral expression were more acceptable, such bisexuality would be more frequent. Analytic treatment may produce transference identifications with permanent or temporary effects. Some critics might suggest common analytic countertransference pressures or biases toward heterosexuality (Blechner, 1993; Lesser, 1993; Schwartz, 1993). But not all lesbian patients in analysis change orientation. Myers (1994) gives an example of analytic change toward lesbianism. He describes a young woman's transformation from a pattern of sexual addiction with multiple male partners to intimacy with a woman partner. Here a change in erotic fantasy and behavior accompanied improved object relatedness; we do not have a long-term followup over the lifetime of the patient.

If object choice can involve multiple determining factors, we still remain ignorant about key influences that open or close off possibilities in a given individual. Are pressures cumulative, related to critical periods, or more open to change in specific epochs? Are shifts of orientation in analytic treatments the result of shifts in compromise formations alone? Is an identification with a maternal transference figure influential; for example, might intimacy with a woman analyst provide a progressive resolution, the direction of which is dependent on the patient's fantasy about the analyst's orientation?

Butler (1990) suggests that gender identity might be more fluid if social forces were less constraining. Might object choice be similar? Burch (1993b) argues that bisexual expressiveness is a sign of health, compared to exclusive or primary hetero- or homosexuality. To maintain bisexual expressiveness in the face of gender-conformist pressure may require independence, defiance, creative capacity, or internal conflictual pressures. Is comfort in same-sex physical closeness or erotic arousal in any way related to capacity for maternal feelings (McDougall, 1986)? Some heterosexual women claim that actual homosexual relationships have enhanced their femininity and maternality (Kirkpatrick and Morgan, 1980). But these hypotheses need clinical testing, and any relation between object choice and maternality is not understood. Edgecumbe et al. (1976) and Tyson and Tyson (1990) conclude that strong negative oedipal strivings can serve as substitution for a deficient maternal relationship and preoedipal problems, presaging developmental failure. Bergmann (1995) and Lax (1995) argue for the importance of an active negative oedipal phase prior to a positive oedipal direction. Since object choice can function as an individual symptom, defense, or compromise formation, we should not err by privileging only homosexual choices as subjects for analytic work.

While it is clear that early sensual pleasures underlie girls' later capacities for genital excitement (Richards, 1992), we do not yet have a complete theory of erotic development in girls. How much stimulation, frustration, or soothing leads to erotic feelings, and how are these linked to other affects and to object choice? Do good early maternal experiences for girls provide the basis for the "normal homosexual components of sexuality" (McDougall, 1986)? Is homosexual erotism repressed in heterosexual development? Kernberg (1991) leans on the French psychoanalysts Braunschweig and Fain (1971) in theorizing about the roots of erotic desire. He states that the early infant-mother relationship determines capacities for erotic desire. Her mother's subtle, unconscious rejection of a girl's sexual arousal inhibits the girl's awareness of vaginal genitality, but the girl identifies with mother's eroticism and develops an object relation with father as a loved but distant figure. This theory leaves unclear

Lesbian Patients

whether erotic arousal requires aggressive stimulus (Stoller, 1985) or whether erotic arousal is related to closeness or distance. How much pleasurable contact with each parent is the "right" amount for specific outcomes? Lesbian feelings might defend against maternal overinclusiveness, intrusion, or rejection, or may eroticize positive oedipal aggression into erotic love, or might evolve from maternal care where they have not been repressed or redirected. Through supervisory work, I have known of two daughters of a somewhat masculine, unempathic mother who could not cuddle and soothe infants and preferred active play with them. One became heterosexual, was enraged and competitive with mother, had masochistic fantasies and relations with men, and low feminine self-esteem. The other identified with the father, became homosexual, and dominated a nurturing, feminine partner. The daughters' levels of object-relatedness as adults seemed similar, and it would be difficult to argue that the homoerotic solution was more pathological.

A lesbian's love for another woman should not be assumed to reflect masculinity. Gender role is distinct from object choice (Person and Ovesey, 1983), so that gender identity differentiation, erotic development and erotic object crystallization should not be conflated (Coates et al., 1991). These elements, however, can reciprocally influence each other. Being more masculine or feminine can have meanings related to a variety of developmental issues (Burch, 1993a, 1993b), including early identifications, longed-for identifications, routes to winning an object, current needs for erotic complementarity within a given adult couple, or adaptation to cultural stereotypes. Gender role can sometimes serve as a signal for sexual preference, and masculinity may signal a wish for a female partner (Baker, 1980). But early masculine qualities in girls are not inevitably prehomosexual and masculine women may be heterosexual (McDougall, 1970). Research on gender identity disorder of childhood (GID) (Coates and Wolfe, in press) and on gender disorders (Person and Ovesey, 1983) suggests multiple influences on development of gender role, which in turn may influence sexual preference. In preliminary studies, specifically on girls, Coates (unpublished) reports that conflicts occurring at ages eighteen to thirty-six months, involving attachment, separation, aggression, and reactions to gender and genital difference, as well as the experience of a mother who has a reproductive trauma (e.g., miscarriage), can contribute to development of GID, especially if there is a base of a sufficient temperamental precondition (including sensitivity and high activity level). An individual case report of child analysis of a girl with GID (Gilmore, 1995) suggests possible reversal of outcome, thus emphasizing conflictual factors. The critical developmental periods for sexual orientation may overlap with those of GID. For example, sustained closeness and warm identifications with mother might predispose to heterosexual object choice. This could comprise not only identification with a mother's heterosexuality, but also experiences of feeling secure and protected despite rapprochement conflicts, thus enabling a view of males as erotically interesting via differentness (such as higher activity level), yet without danger. With more conflict with mother, more paternal nurturance could compensate to permit heterosexual development. Children identify not only with maternal femininity, but with both parents' conscious and unconscious images of the child as feminine (Tyson and Tyson, 1990). Just as gender role has its own developmentally vulnerable time periods and nodal points, several nodal critical periods for developing lesbian erotic fantasy may exist. The presence of biological components does not tell us how these components interact with individual developmental and cultural experiences (Freud, 1905; Friedman and Downey, 1993b; Byne, 1994; Levay and Hamer, 1994). Something immutable certainly is not necessarily biological. Disorder of core gender identity (Money and Ehrhardt, 1972; Stoller, 1968), for example, usually reflect conflictual developmental and cognitive experiences, i.e., psychological rather than biological factors.

Common countertransference tendencies to idealize heterosexuality (Stoller, 1985), indeed to idealize one's own lifestyle in all its elements (R.C. Friedman, personal communication), may have led to analytic assumptions that homosexualities *per se* are pathological. Sexual fantasies, including heterosexual fantasies, as Stoller (1985) points out, can involve feelings of rage and hatred, can be perverse, and may be used to repair narcissistic trauma, or can be used to enhance hetero- or homosexual behavior. Lifestyles accompanying each sexual orientation have inherent stresses, tragedies, and renunciations. The nonanalytic literature suggests no increased psychopathology or difficulty with parenting (Saghir and Robins, 1980; Kirkpatrick, 1989; Panel, 1987) among nonpatient homosexuals.

Lesbian Patients

Mitchell (1978) argues that it is theoretical prejudice to insist that the psychodynamic trends that have contributed to homosexuality in a given person indicate that homosexuality itself is a sign of pathology. All behavior has early developmental sources as well as current dynamic meaning. Neither psychodynamic origins nor current psychodynamic meanings necessarily imply pathology or ego deficit. Ego development and object relations are not directly correlated with sexual functioning, and genital primacy itself is not the measure of personality maturation (Ross, 1970; Person, 1980). (Consider the frequency of sexual difficulties in relatively healthy women.) Thus, homosexuality itself should not imply a specific current defect in object relatedness or ego functioning. Mitchell notes that a behavior's origins cannot be assumed to reflect its current motives, and a conflict in development that resulted in a given adaptation does not indicate that the adaptation itself has remained conflictual, i.e., object choice can become secondarily autonomous.

While analysts aim to facilitate self-exploration and understanding, they may be trapped by countertransference biases into investment in changing or affirming their patients' object choice. I feel that a patient's conflicts about orientation or about whether to "come out" always have individual meaning. Mitchell (1981) criticizes the work of Socarides (1978), Beiber (1965), and Ovesey (1969), as exploiting the transference. Isay (1989) concurs in his detailing of followup of treatments that failed to help homosexual men. Nevertheless, I believe that genuine analytic work can lead to changes in sexual orientation, and this does not mean that the original orientation should be dismissed as "defensive." This very complex issue becomes further entangled when the analyst favors "life goals," rather than analyzes central problems. A "homosexual affirmative stance" (Frommer, 1994) could foreclose exploration of inner life, producing the same unanalyzable limitations as an internally self-hating fantasy that one should change sexual orientation. "Coming out" can be an expression of healthy self-assertiveness or of masochism (Friedman, 1988). Wishes for the analyst to revolve doubts about orientation or to express personal attitudes are best explored analytically. A heterosexual patient of mine believed that I wanted her to marry in order to demonstrate the efficacy of my work. The persistent fantasy contained not only her wish, but also a transference to a maternal figure who had stifled her passions and autonomy by forcing her into social conformity. It called for analysis rather than countertransferential agreement with the social advantages she denoted. The same would be true if she had been homosexual.

Erotic transference longings can evoke uneasiness, a sense of disorientation, and a narcissistic threat in the countertransference. Heterosexual analysts need to analyze their countertransference to understand and value homoerotic yearnings, including wishes for erotic pleasure and pride different from one's own manifest interests. This may be helped by comfort with owning homosexual feelings, familiarity with adaptive homosexual lifestyles, and self-analysis about one's heterosexual narcissism. A heterosexual male analyst may erroneously assume a lesbian's erotic transference indicates budding heterosexual interest in the paternal transference, rather than erotic interest in the maternal transference. A heterosexual woman analyst may misunderstand a lesbian patient's desire to possess her sexually as reflecting erotized preoedipal desires. The analyst must be able to imagine and identify with wishes for homosexual pleasure and success, so as to help a patient to resolve inhibitions and avoid repeating past traumata of homosexually desirous persons in a heterosexual world. Although sexualized, passive, early sadistic, and identificatory yearnings can be expressed as erotic feelings by the lesbian patient (Wrye and Welles, 1989), such feelings should not be interpreted as only displaced erotizations, if they include active negative oedipal strivings. The patient herself may defend against active negative oedipal yearnings because of punishment fears or homophobic shame. Analyst and patient then might collude to avoid the homoerotic passion as part of shared homophobia, fears of active female sexuality, wishes to see lesbians as nonsexual or as really interested in men, or in a pathologizing of lesbian desire as preoedipal pathology. Wishes for homosexual pleasure and power can include deeply passionate, erotic, intimate wishes, wishes to control the object, to seduce, enslave, and excite, i.e., the mixture of erotic and aggressive feelings one sees in any erotic encounter. Erotic lesbian transferences encompass primary erotic feelings as well as wishes to express one's will, autonomy, and aggressive and sadistic assertiveness, and to elicit mutual response. Patients need help to express, accept, and

Lesbian Patients

enjoy these feelings, which are often inhibited by oedipal conflict, antihomosexual self-images, and inhibitions about female sexual assertiveness that abound in our culture. It has great importance to the homosexual patient whether her homosexual yearnings can be heard and recognized as progressive. If they are misinterpreted as merely a defensive erotization; or as regressive, pathological or immature; or as part of feminine strivings but nonerotic; or as an attempt to get the analyst in the father transference to fall in love with her, this will have different meaning. Patients with their own burden of negative attitudes toward their homoerotic feelings may have difficulty clarifying such analytic misunderstandings.

CONCLUSIONS

In summary, I have reviewed some clinical material from lesbian patients, and have suggested that no unitary dynamic or etiologic theme provides us with universal understanding of these patients. Even the meaning of classifying a patient as homosexual may vary. Lesbians show varying levels of pathology, dynamics, family histories, gender roles, and interest in maternal activity. Dynamics common to subgroups of lesbians do not indicate that homosexual orientation itself is pathological. Orientation embedded in compromise formations at one stage may achieve secondary autonomy and may serve later adaptation. Orientation may also remain fluid or flexible. Factors contributing to fixity, fluidity, change in orientation, and the development of erotic desire are still unknown. The clinical material presented illustrates a variety of dynamics. I propose that our understanding of female homosexualities has been excessively welded to unitary theories, while actual etiologies and dynamics vary. Countertransference biases and some difficulties in understanding lesbian erotic transferences have been discussed. I suggest that we are at a point in our knowledge where our understanding is incomplete, and we should continue to study case material with more awareness of our own biases. In this spirit we might learn more about problems in conceptualization and in treatment.

Eleanor Schuker

REFERENCES

BAKER, S. (1980). Biological influences in human sex and gender. *Signs* 6(1): 80–96.

BEIBER, I. (1965). Clinical aspects of male homosexuality. In *Sexual Inversion: The Multiple Roots of Homosexuality*, ed. J. Marmor. New York: Basic Books, pp. 248–267.

BERGMANN, M.V. (1995). Observations on the female negative oedipal phase and its significance in the analytic transference. *J. Clin. Psychoanal.*, 4:283–296.

BLECHNER, M.J. (1993). Homophobia in psychoanalytic writing and practice. *Psychoanal. Dialog.*, 3:623–626.

BRAUNSCHWEIG, D. & FAIN, M. (1971). *Eros et Auteros*. Paris: Payot.

BURCH, B. (1993a). Gender identities, lesbianism and potential space. *Psychoanal. Psychol.*, 10:359–376.

——— (1993b). Heterosexuality, bisexuality and lebianism: rethinking psychoanalytic views of women's object choice. *Psychoanal. Rev.*, 80:83–99.

BUTLER, J. (1990). *Gender Trouble: Feminism and the Subversion of Identity*. New York: Routledge.

BYNE, W. (1994). The biological evidence challenged. *Scient. Amer.*, May, pp. 50–55.

CHODOROW, N. (1992). Heterosexuality as a compromise formation. *Psychoanal. Contemp.Thought*, 12:267–304.

COATES, S., FRIEDMAN, R.C. & WOLFE, S. (1991). The etiology of boyhood gender identity disorders: a model for integrating temperament, development and psychodynamics. *Psychol. Dialog.*, 1:481–523.

——— & WOLFE, S. (in press). Gender identity disorders in toddlers and preschool children. In *The Handbook of Child and Adolescent Psychiatry*, ed. J. Noshpitz. New York: Wiley.

COEN, S. (1981). Sexualization as a predominant mode of defense. *J. Amer. Psychoanal. Assn.*, 29:893–920.

DE LAURETIS, T. (1994). *The Practice of Love: Lesbian Sexuality and Perverse Desire*. Bloomington, IN: Univ. Indiana Press.

DEUTSCH, H. (1932). On female homosexuality. *Psychoanal. Q.*, 1:484–510.

EDGECUMBE, R., LUNBERG, S., MARKOWITZ, R. & SALO, F. (1976). Some comments on the concept of the negative oedipal phase in girls. *Psychoanal. Study Child*, 31:35–61. New Haven, CT: Yale Univ. Press.

EISENBUD, R.-J. (1982). Early and later determinants of lesbian choice. *Psychoanal. Rev.*, 69:85–109.

——— (1986). Lesbian choice: transferences to theory. In *Psychoanalysis and Women: Contemporary Reappraisals*, ed. J. Alpert. Hillsdale, NJ: Analytic Press, pp. 215–233.

FREUD, S. (1905). Three essays on the theory of sexuality. *S. E.*, 7.

——— (1920). The psychogenesis of a case of homosexuality in a woman. *S. E.*, 18:146–172.

FRIEDMAN, R.C. (1988). *Male Homosexuality: A Contemporary Psychoanalytic Perspective*. New Haven, CT: Yale Univ. Press.

Lesbian Patients

———— & Downey, J. (1993a). Neurobiology and sexual orientation: current relationships. *J. Neuropsych. Clin. Neurosci.*, 5:131–153.

———— ———— (1993b). Psychoanalysis, psychobiology, and homosexuality. *J. Amer. Psychoanal. Assn.*, 41:1159–1198.

Frommer, M.S. (1994). Homosexuality and psychoanalysis: technical considerations revisited. *Psychoanal. Dialog.*, 4:215–233.

Gilmore, K. (1995). Gender identity disorder in a girl: insights from adoption. *J. Amer. Psychoanal. Assn.*, 43:39–61.

Isay, R. (1989). *Being Homosexual: Gay Men and Their Development.* New York: Farrar, Strauss & Giroux.

Jones, E. (1927). The early development of female sexuality. *Int. J. Psychoanal.*, 8:459–472.

Kernberg, O. (1991). Sadomasochism, sexual excitement, and perversion. *J. Amer. Psychoanal. Assn.*, 39:333–362.

Kestenberg, J. (1968). Outside and inside, male and female. *J. Amer. Psychoanal. Assn.*, 16:457–510.

Khan, M.M.R. (1979). *Alienation in Perversions.* New York: Int. Univ. Press.

Kirkpatrick, M. (1989). Lesbians: a different middle age? In *The Middle Years*, ed. J. Oldham & R. Liebert. New Haven, CT: Yale Univ. Press, pp. 135–148.

———— & Morgan, C. (1980). Psychodynamic psychotherapy of female homosexuality. In *Homosexual Behavior*, ed. J. Marmor. New York: Basic Books, pp. 357–375.

Lax, R. (1995). Motives and determinants of girls' penis envy in the negative oedipal phase. *J. Clin. Psychoanal.*, 4:297–314.

Lesser, R.C. (1993). A reconsideration of homosexual themes. *Psychoanal. Dialog.*, 3:639–642.

Levay, S. & Hamer, D. (1994). Evidence for a biological influence in male homosexuality. *Scient. Amer.*, May, pp. 44–49.

McDougall, J. (1970). Homosexuality in women. In *Female Sexuality: New Psychoanalytic Views*, ed. J. Chasseguet-Smirgel. Ann Arbor, MI: Univ. Michigan Press, pp. 171–212.

———— (1980). *Plea for a Measure of Abnormality.* New York: Int. Univ. Press.

———— (1986). Eve's reflection: on the homosexual components of female sexuality. In *Between Analyst and Patient*, ed. H. C. Meyers. Hillsdale, NJ: Analytic Press, pp. 213–228.

———— (1989). The dead father: on early psychic trauma and its relation to disturbance in sexual identity and in creative activity. *Int. J. Psychoanal.*, 70:205–219.

Mitchell, S.A. (1978). Psychodynamics, homosexuality, and the question of pathology. *Psychiat.*, 41:254–263.

———— (1981). The psychoanalytic treatment of homosexuality: some technical considerations. *Int. Rev. Psychoanal.*, 8:63–80.

Money, J. & Ehrhardt, A. (1972). *Man and Woman, Boy and Girl.* Baltimore, MD: Johns Hopkins Univ. Press.

Myers, W.A. (1994). Addictive sexual behavior. *J. Amer. Psychoanal. Assn.*, 42:1159–1182.

OLESKER, W. (1995). Unconscious fantasy and compromise formation in a case of adolescent female homosexuality. *J. Clin. Psychoanal.*, 4:361–382.
OVESEY, L. (1969). *Homosexuality and Pseudohomosexuality.* New York: Science House.
PANEL (1987). Toward the further understanding of homosexual women. A. Wolfson, reporter. *J. Amer. Psychoanal. Assn.*, 35:165–173.
PERSON, E. S. (1980). Sexuality as the mainstay of identity: psychoanalytic perspectives. *Signs*, 5:605–630.
——— & OVESEY, L. (1983). Psychoanalytic theories of gender identity. *J. Amer. Acad. Psychoanal.*, 11:203–226.
PONSE, B. (1980). Finding self in the lesbian community. In *Women's Sexual Development*, ed. M. Kirkpatrick. New York: Plenum, pp. 181–200.
RICHARDS, A.K. (1992). The influence of sphincter control and genital sensation on body image and gender identity in women. *Psychoanal. Q.*, 61:331–351.
——— (1996). Talking about lesbians: Minnie Bruce Pratt and her poetic journey. *Psychoanal. & Psychother.*, 13:109–120.
ROSS, N. (1970). The primacy of genitality in the light of ego psychology. *J. Amer. Psychoanal. Assn.*, 18:267–284.
SAGHIR, M. & ROBINS, E. (1980). Clinical aspects of female homosexuality. In *Homosexual Behavior*, ed. J.Marmor. New York: Basic Books, pp. 280–295.
SCHUKER, E. & LEVINSON, N.A. (1991). *Female Psychology: An Annotated Psychoanalytic Bibliography.* Hillsdale, NJ: Analytic Press.
SCHWARTZ, D. (1993). Heterophilia—the love that dare not speak its aim. *Psychoanal. Dialog.*, 3:643–652.
SHARPE, S. & ROSENBLATT, A. (1994). Oedipal sibling triangles. *J. Amer. Psychoanal. Assn.*, 42:491–524.
SIEGEL, E.V. (1988). *Female Homosexuality: Choice Without Volition.* Hillsdale, NJ: Analytic Press.
SOCARIDES, C. (1963). The historical development of theoretical and clinical concepts of overt female homosexuality. *J. Amer. Psychoanal. Assn.*, 11:386–414.
——— (1978). *Homosexuality.* New York: Aronson.
STOLLER, R.J. (1968). *Sex and Gender, Vol. I: On the Development of Masculinity and Femininity.* New York: Science House.
——— (1985). *Observing the Erotic Imagination.* New Haven, CT: Yale Univ. Press.
TYSON, P. & TYSON, R. (1990). *Psychoanalytic Theories of Development.* New Haven, CT: Yale Univ. Press.
WRYE, H.K. & WELLES, J. (1989). The maternal erotic transference. *Int. J. Psychoanal.*, 70:673–684.

VI.
WOMEN AND TRAINING AND RESEARCH

Figure 8. Deborah Kass (1992) *Triple Silver Yentl (My Elvis)*.
Deborah Kass

Hearing What Cannot Be Seen: A Psychoanalytic Research Group's Inquiry into Female Sexuality

Harriet I. Basseches et al.*

> Advances in the theoretical understanding of female psychology are not easily integrated into psychoanalytic practice. This paper reports on a study of female psychology and clinical practice by a group of seven female psychoanalysts. Through discussing the literature and case vignettes, we discovered a lag between current theoretical ideas and our clinical practice. The group identified an anachronistic emphasis on penis envy functioning as "bedrock." This report addresses how the group facilitated individual members' integration of theory and practice, and how this integration affected work with patients. We found that as we became open to considering a wider range of potential dynamic meanings of penis envy and female bodily concerns, we were able to explore a richer, and often surprising unfolding of vicissitudes. The discussion highlights some technical issues with this approach.

While Freud's ideas about feminine psychological development are often debated, they have had a profound impact on psychoanalysts as well as on the culture at large. Freud (1925, 1931, 1933, 1937) portrays the female as imprisoned and propelled by her envy over the superiority of the male genital. From this perspective, the analysis of a female will inevitably uncover penis envy and culminate with the view that penis envy is "bedrock."

A burgeoning body of literature rejects this classical Freudian picture as phallocentric.[1] These writers propose that early on, little girls experience genital sensations and develop a narcissistically valued sense of femininity. They also form psychic representations of

---

*Paula L. Ellman, Susan S. Elmendorf, Elizabeth Fritsch, Nancy R. Goodman, Fonya L. Helm, and Shelley Rockwell. Members, New York Freudian Society.

[1] Freud constructed working hypotheses that were not always aligned with others of his ideas. His powerful metaphor of "the first ego as a body ego" (1923) supports the notion of a central female bodily sense as the organizational core for the female.

the female genitalia and generate fantasies and anxieties about them. This literature emphasizes concepts associated with primary femininity, often challenging Freud's view that penis envy is "bedrock."

Mayer (1995) observes that while primary femininity represents a significant theoretical advance, it has not been "adequately incorporated into everyday clinical work" (p. 35). By discussing concepts from the literature side by side with case material, our research group was surprised to discover the extent of the lag in our work. This study represents an attempt to bridge theory and practice.

In a brief review of the early and recent literature, this paper documents that more than sixty years ago, some analysts anticipated contemporary ideas of female development. The report then presents the research findings: identification of the lag, exploration of the difficulties in changing technique, and subsequent shifts in the analytic work. Vignettes from two cases illustrate these changes. The discussion addresses the tenacity of the lag, the role of the group in integrating theory and practice, and the implications of the shift for technique.

LITERATURE REVIEW

Early Literature

Although Freud's view of the centrality of penis envy and the castration complex dominated the early writings on female sexuality, some analysts tried to present another perspective. On December 3, 1924, Abraham wrote to Freud: "... I have recently wondered whether in early infancy there may be an early vaginal awakening of the female libido, which is destined to be repressed and which is subsequently followed by clitoral primacy as the expression of the phallic phase..." (Abraham and Freud, 1965, p. 375). Freud (in 1924) replied, "... According to my preconceived ideas on the subject, the vaginal share would tend to be expressed anally. The vagina ... is a later acquisition by separation from the cloaca..." (Abraham and Freud, 1965, p. 377). Nine years later, Freud (1933) stated, "... It is true, that there are a few isolated reports of early vaginal sensations as well, but it cannot be easy to distinguish these

Hearing What Cannot Be Seen

from sensations in the anus or vestibulum; in any case they cannot play a great part..." (p. 118). In 1937 Freud declared, "... [W]ith the wish for a penis... we have... reached bedrock, and thus our activities are at an end.... [T]he biological field does in fact play the part of the underlying bedrock..." (p. 252).[2]

While analysts agreed about the importance of penis envy in women, Horney (1926) and Jones (1927) pointed out that penis envy can serve as a defense against oedipal wishes. A number of early analysts concurred with Abraham's view that the little girl develops an early female identity and body image based on her kinesthetic knowledge of an interior genital (Brierley, 1932; Horney, 1926; Jones, 1927; Klein, 1928; Muller, 1932; Muller-Braunschweig, 1926). And some clinicians observed "female" fears and fantasies about the inner genital: fear of penetration (Horney, 1924); fear of the destruction of internal organs and the capacity for motherhood (Klein, 1928); anxiety about violation by an overpowering father (Muller-Braunschweig, 1926); and dread of the "masochistic triad... castration-defloration-parturition" (Deutsch, 1930). Brierley (1932) posited "... two lines or directions of displacement of cathexis, namely, a nipple-penis-faeces-child line and a mouth-anus-vagina line" (p. 435). The seeds were sown for what was later to become a significant revision in Freud's hypotheses about women.

Recent Literature—Expanding Ideas of Primary Femininity

Recent writings about female development and conflict do not disregard the presence of penis envy, but emphasize the centrality of primary femininity, a concept articulated by Stoller (1976). From this perspective the little girl draws on early body experiences to create psychic representations of her body ego. These images, in turn, have an impact on her drive/defense constellations. Over the last two decades, there has been an elaboration of these ideas. Writings have focused on the girl's awareness of both inner and outer genital sensations, representations of the female genitalia, and associated anxieties.

Some clinicians describe the little girl's early bodily experiences. Girls become aware of inner and outer genital sensations through

---

[2]Freud is using the word "biological" loosely here to mean unanalyzable. Freud was influenced by the idea of the inheritance of acquired characteristics (Ritvo, 1965) and seems to have believed that the clitoris was a vestigial penis.

masturbation (Lax, 1994), the flexing of perineal muscles (Richards, 1992), and closely linked urethral and anal feelings (Bass, 1994; Kestenberg, 1982; Lax, 1994). Delineation of these kinesthetic experiences adds new dimensions of what girls want—that is, the wanting of their own pleasure.

Psychoanalytic observations of children also confirm the little girl's knowledge of her genitalia. Galenson and Roiphe (1976) document genital awareness in boys and girls between 15 months and 19 months. Kestenberg (1982) designates an inner-genital phase of development for girls between infancy and the phallic phase. Characteristic of this period is the young girl's interest in distinguishing inside from outside. Erikson's (1950, 1974) and Mayer's (1991) observations of girls' building of and responses to block designs also suggest that from an early age girls are grappling to form representations of their inner genital. There is evidence that adult women do form mental representations of the inner genital. Kalinich (1993) proposes that adult female analysands displace representations of their inner genital onto mental functioning. Krausz (1994) and Lerner (1976) report on female analysands who defend against awareness of their inner genital through fantasies of being invisible and diffuse.

Lerner (1976) claims that the mother's failure to label her daughter's genitalia contributes to the girl's denial, resulting in a conviction that "[t]he vulva (including the clitoris) is not important, must not be spoken of or thought about, or should not exist" (p. 276). By not naming what the girl has, the mother deprives her daughter of "permission" to be "a sexually operative and responsive female" (p. 270). Lerner argues that the traditional castration complex results more from the mother's failure to label what the girl has, than from "the fact that the clitoris is a smaller (and thus inferior) organ compared to the penis" (p. 277).

Recognition that girls get pleasure from genital sensations and form mental representations and fantasies about their genitalia makes it possible to conceptualize women as having uniquely female genital anxieties. As punishment for libidinal strivings, girls fear threats to their inner space, i.e., that it will be violated, taken away, or sealed off (Kulish, 1991; Mayer, 1995; Richards, 1992, 1996; Wilkinson, 1991). Clinicians point out that the little girl's confusion over vaginal, urethral, and anal sensations fosters anal-stage regressions, and concomitant anxieties about loss of control and incapacity to hold on to contents (Barnett, 1996; Kalinich, 1993; Shaw, 1995).

The model of female development set forth in these writings presents the girl as having knowledge and conflicts about "what she isn't and hasn't [as well as about] . . . what she is and what she has" (Mayer, 1995, p. 32). These dual anxieties play off each other and contribute to rich and varied movements within and between compromise formations.

FINDINGS: IDENTIFYING THE LAG AND MAKING A SHIFT

The research group, comprised of seven female psychoanalysts, met weekly over one year. The group reviewed literature on female development and sexuality, and discussed vignettes from each analyst's psychoanalyses with women, twenty-five in total. Reading the more recent literature solidified the group's theoretical thinking and dramatized the extent of the lag between theory and clinical technique. Early on, we discovered our collusion with Freud's phallocentric perspective in concert with our patients' self-assessments.[3] There is always the question to what extent the patient's associations are influenced by the analyst's bias. In clinical vignettes we were experts at identifying the female castration complex. We documented two familiar constellations of the female body self. First, patients suffered from a sense of shame about being defective or damaged. Using concrete images, female analysands complained that their body parts were too big, too small, or misshapen. They spoke of defective mouth, waist, breasts, or genitals. In displacements, analysands viewed themselves as incompetent in their careers, academic work, or in relationships with spouses, lovers or children. Second, patients tended to view activity as masculine. When they perceived and expressed bodily urges in an active way, they talked about "having a

---

[3]Grossman and Stewart (1976) point out that the patients who have a narcissistic character disorder tend quickly to concur with interpretations of penis envy which "confirm their worst fears of being worthless" (p. 208).

penis" or "penetrating a boyfriend." Even specifically female functions, such as pushing out a baby, breast-feeding or managing a household, were often imbued with phallic meaning.

As discussions of the literature and vignettes evolved, the group realized that at times images of damage and activity might not be simply evidence of the castration complex and penis envy, but also serve defensive functions. As already noted, Horney (1926) and Jones (1927) had set forth this idea in the 1920's. Almost fifty years later, Grossman and Stewart (1976) emphasized the importance of treating penis envy as "manifest content, the significance of which will only emerge in the analysis" (p. 207). Also elaborating on these ideas, Tyson (1994) stated, ". . . penis envy represents a complicated compromise formation involving aspects of gender identity, pathological object relations, defenses, narcissism, and self-esteem" (p. 456).

Yet, participant analysts' theories and identifications with their own personal analysts and clinical supervisors did not yield easily to integrating the newer ideas of primary femininity into clinical practice. They felt uneasy about "moving away" from these "inner authorities" (Grossman, unpublished). Buttressed by the recent literature and the group's interest in expanding their horizons, they began to try out different ways to intervene. One member of the group reported her dream, a dream full of joy (and conflict about the joy) at the discovery of an exquisite new flower with a beautiful inside shape. The group resonated to this image and the difficulty in accepting its obviously feminine message. The dreamer revealed not only her delight in the dream, but also the punishing way she began to use interpretations of penis envy to diminish her discovery. The "new flower" came to represent a broader understanding of the participating analysts' female patients and their own feminine identities and conflicts.

Analysts reported somewhat timidly on early attempts to experiment with new types of interventions. Over time, they became more comfortable giving language to what had now been analyzed into consciousness. Yet, seeking new ways to address patients' feminine fantasies and conflicts continued to stir up both excitement and anxiety. One analyst reported feeling "knocked off her analytic position" as she shifted from focusing on her patient's wish to deny

Hearing What Cannot Be Seen

penis envy to looking at the patient's wish to deny interest in her feminine space.

The following clinical vignettes illustrate the efforts of group members to intervene in ways more consistent with current theories of female psychology.

Case 1. Ms. Q., a thirty-five-year-old single woman, entered treatment with an inability to establish a satisfying partnership with a man. She saw men and women as having hopelessly irreconcilable differences. As her analysis progressed, she developed a viable relationship with a man, but remained fearful of being overwhelmed by him.

She began the following session with a mild complaint that the analyst had been "bossy" in the previous session:

> *P.* You think I should want a relationship and be living with my boyfriend in six months. You don't know how much I like my splendid isolation. I love my apartment. My boyfriend is the one who brought up the idea of living together.
>
> *A.* Perhaps we could understand more about the importance of having your own place. What is it that your apartment reflects of you?
>
> *A.* It reflects my love of travel, fine things, style.
>
> *A.* And what do you think a place you shared with your boyfriend would reflect?
>
> *P.* I would get diluted—like having paintings on the walls that are not me. That is disconcerting. My boyfriend even said, "I am really beginning to like your photographs. If we lived together, I might sell some of my paintings," and I replied, "Oh no, you have worked so hard to acquire them."
>
> *A.* Your thoughts remind me of your fantasy that to share a place with a man means you would be "overwhelmed." And you are seeing me right now as a man who would overwhelm you. You felt I didn't understand you or your viewpoint in the session yesterday.
>
> *P.* I feel so relieved. That is the first feeling of relief I have had. [She becomes tearful and falls silent.]
>
> *A.* In your view, perhaps a man shouldn't give up his things.
>
> *P.* That was why I thought my boyfriend was gay. He wanted help in redoing his office. My boss never asks for direction. He is never collaborative. The connection with a man leaves me diminished....
>
> *P.* [Nearing the end of the hour] This is a chock-full session. I'm extremely anxious. I have the feeling somehow this is

something I've never gotten to with you before—how difficult is it to think about being in a relationship.

The analyst understood Ms. Q.'s associations to her apartment as referring to her inner feminine space. Previously, when the patient had spoken about her apartment and her pleasure in its museumlike quality, the analyst had thought of the apartment as a phallic equivalent. Certainly one of this patient's conflicts involved her wish to be like father. In this hour, the analyst heard the associations of the apartment differently. Recalling recent readings on the female's narcissistic investment in her genital (e.g., as described by Krausz, 1994, and Kubie, 1974), the analyst encouraged the patient to elaborate on protective feelings about her "inner space."

Ms. Q.'s concerns about her space, whether and how it would be filled, were at the center of her feminine identity concerns. She felt strong and invulnerable in her determination not to yield or share her space. But her "splendid isolation" within her apartment/body was threatened by the paternal transference. When misunderstood by the analyst, she felt overwhelmed. The patient seemed relieved when the analyst interpreted the paternal transference: "You are seeing me right now as a man who would overwhelm you." The patient's view that the session seemed "chock-full" reflected her evolving capacity to open herself to a man.

In a session a few weeks later, Ms. Q began by recounting her fury with her boss who refers to women in demeaning ways. She then observed her difficulty holding on to her sense of outrage.

> P. With my boss, I feel humiliated because I don't have a penis. I remember Dad would go in the bathroom and be peeing and talking to me at the same time. I felt curious about what he was doing.
>
> A. You speak about your curiosity about your father in the bathroom. I wonder what happened to your awareness and curiosity about your body and what you have. You have a vulva, a vagina, a urethral opening. . . .
>
> P. When I was a little girl, I remember asking my mother, "What is this blister next to my vagina?" My mother said that once she had left me in diapers too long and it was "an ammonia burn." She said, "Hair would grow over it and you won't see it anymore." I remember seeing a blue stain on my mother's underwear. I used to wonder if blood was blue in your body and then became red. I think she douched and that caused the

Hearing What Cannot Be Seen

blue stain. I'm suddenly remembering being at my grandfather's house and a black woman came up to the porch with a knife wound in her arm. And Grandfather said, "You're bleeding like a stuck pig." That makes me think of my boss and his comments about women. I felt curious about this black woman and seeing her blood and what color it was. And I remember thinking my Grandfather was upset she was getting blood on his porch.

In this example, the analyst's intervention focused on repressed aspects of the girl's bodily experience *vis-à-vis* her father. The patient shifted from an initial feeling of humiliation in relation to the man, due to her penisless condition, to a state of excited curiosity. The patient's heightened interest in what her father was doing in the bathroom appeared to involve a defense against her awareness of a matching interest in her own body. The analyst's inquiry elicited in the patient a flood of speculations about the female body, tinged with anal and urethral concerns. In previous sessions, the analyst had interpreted the patient's fixed voyeuristic interest in men from the viewpoint of penis envy. Now, influenced by the study, the analyst felt freer to explore the defensive use of this focus and to experiment with explicit language to delineate the female genital.

The analyst's intervention led to an important piece of reconstruction. On several occasions the patient had told the analyst about this "memory" of discovering a "blister" on her vulva. Up to this point, the patient had used this "memory" as confirmation of her mother's neglect. In this session, the "memory" was illuminated in a new way. It appeared that Ms. Q. was recounting a question to her mother about her clitoris and her mother's failure to label this part of her anatomy. Clitoris, thus, had become "blister," something to be covered by hair and forgotten. On reflection, the analyst realized that when she had named parts of the female genitalia, she also had omitted any reference to the clitoris. Her intervention may well have triggered the memory of the mother's omission. This screen memory seemed to contain an element of experience with the mother (the clitoris remaining unnamed) as well as the accompanying sense that her mother forbade her to find pleasure in this part of her body (Lerner, 1976; Tyson, 1994). Confirmation of this hypothesis in subsequent sessions supports Lerner's (1976) theory that "incomplete, undifferentiated, and often inaccurate [naming] . . . of female genitals prevents the growing girl from achieving pride in femininity, and may lead to anxiety and confusion regarding her sexuality" (p. 282).

Although the analyst's intervention referring to the female genitalia was abrupt and interrupted Ms. Q.'s further associations to her father, the patient's pressured responses demonstrate a deep connection between her feeling of being demeaned/castrated and her mother/analyst's inadequate "naming" of her clitoris. The most important castration for Ms. Q. as it emerged in this session was the misnamed clitoris. The bloody images and memories that followed give a hint of her primitive anxieties about her genitalia. The preoccupation with male demeaning behavior may help Ms. Q. contain the equal if not greater anxiety about what her body actually possesses. If she can complain about the devaluation by men, she can express some of the fear and disappointment in herself without fully grappling with it, a compromise formation. Here is an example of the phallic castration complex as a symptom, defense, and gratification. In addition, this symptom serves to ward off a more intimate relationship with her analyst.

Case 2. Ms. T. is a twenty-five-year-old woman in the fourth year of her analysis. She began to speak of a fantasy of having malformed genitals. In one hour, she spoke of conflicts over her exhibitionism.

> P. You think I'm provocative? I worry about being sexy, strong and hurtful. . . . I remember telling you I'm anxious. Having something valuable and showy is not okay. Something is wrong with my genitals. When I look at myself I always see a bump. It does not look feminine. . . . Other women don't have a bump. It's too much. I try to hide it. It doesn't look feminine enough. I feel humiliated not having a penis and not having an adequate vagina. . . .
> A. Your vagina, your labia, and your clitoral bump are not adequate?
> P. Labia and vagina are fine. I don't know all these words. It's all unclear to me, what's what. I'm the one who keeps it unclear. I touch the bump and it's like a penis, a not adequate penis, and then my vagina is not adequate.
> A. You can't feel good about whatever you have.
> P. I remember when I was a young girl and I dressed up and my Dad took me out. That felt good. [She then recalled childhood memories of feeling ashamed of her genitals.]

In a following hour Ms. T. began questioning her professional and interpersonal capacities.

Hearing What Cannot Be Seen

    P. I'm anxious about my adequacy. I have talked before about the adequacy of my female genitals. Yesterday I looked at myself and was embarrassed. If I had a boyfriend, would he be pleased or would I disappoint him?
    A. What did you see?
    P. A bump, a bump protruding. It's inadequate, not feminine . . . I notice now how large my hips are . . . I like that, but I wish I didn't care. I don't like the fact that larger is more feminine.
    A. Larger genitals, larger clitoris, is not more feminine?
    P. It pushes out, like a penis.
    A. If you have something, it must be a penis. It can't be feminine. If it is more than other women have, it must be masculine.
    P. I believe men prefer voluptuously big women.
    A. And so with your genitals, you can't look at yourself as more femininely developed.
    P. I worry that I will disappoint a boyfriend. I enjoy telling my father, not my mother, about my dates. My mother seemed especially distant last night, and I asked if she was okay. She's not happy with her job, and I love working at the newspaper. I felt I was hurting her feelings by telling her of my happiness. I don't want to lose her.
    A. Especially to your success.

On one level, Ms. T.'s fantasy of the "bump" is an expression that something is "wrong" with her genital. She feels defective and wishes for a penis. Ms. T.'s inaccurate naming of the clitoris as a "bump" appears to reflect her belief that this pleasurable organ is "unfeminine" (Lerner, 1976, p. 270).

In this vignette, the analyst listened to the patient's associations with an ear toward the material that "penis envy" might be keeping obscure. Rather than assist Ms. T. in accepting her lot in life as a "castrated man" and her ineffectual pursuit for compensation, the analytic work moved toward uncovering the layers of her experience.

In the second hour the analyst interpreted the defensive nature of Ms. T.'s penis envy. After Ms. T. had stated her belief that men prefer "voluptuously big" women, the analyst pointed out that Ms. T. cannot seem to look at herself as femininely developed. The threat of her oedipal longings emerged both in displacements and more directly (Richards, 1996; Shaw, 1995). Shaw writes, ". . . resolution of . . . symptoms . . . hinged on an integrated understanding of the ways . . . [the patient's] . . . sense of genital damage not only expressed her phallic envy . . . but also defended against her guilt and anxiety about having a pleasurable and valued genital that could be aroused and penetrated . . ." (p. 325). Ms. T.'s wishes to gain her father's love and usurp her mother's place were accompanied by fears of losing her mother.

For Ms. T. there is an uncertainty about the nature of her genitalia. The fantasy of the bump is a symptom that substitutes for a piece of disavowed reality. Bass (1991) notes, "The study of disavowal continually demonstrates a partial detachment from reality marked by a non-synthesizeable oscillation between absence and presence" (p. 322). Mrs. T.'s bump fantasy represents a regression from the acknowledgment of anatomical differences between the sexes. It keeps alive her omnipotent wish to be both male and female (Fast, 1979; Kubie, 1974), and thereby contributes to her "worry about being sexy, strong, and hurtful." By labeling the genitalia, the analyst interfered with the patient's omnipotent wish. Yet, in spite of the analyst's intervention, Ms. T. was invested in maintaining her disavowal of the reality of anatomical differences: "I don't know all these words. It's all unclear. . . . I'm the one who keeps it unclear."

Earlier in the work, the analyst had been frustrated with the immobility of the patient's "penis envy" construction. Exploration of the patient's defensive use of penis envy facilitated the patient's awareness of both oedipal strivings and fantasies of omnipotence.

DISCUSSION

The identification of the lag between theory and clinical practice raises questions. Why has there been such a tenacious lag? Once participants in this study recognized the problematic position they had maintained, how did the group facilitate their new integration of theory and practice? And what are the technical implications of this shift?

The persistence of the lag arises from powerful identifications that shape psychoanalytic thinking. While Freud's "masculine" perspective about the female body and experience has been disputed, his ideas about feminine development have been a mainstay in the

Hearing What Cannot Be Seen

identity of psychoanalysts. Not only do analysts have strong identifications with Freud, but also with their personal analysts and clinical supervisors. It is difficult to scrutinize and revamp these highly invested ideas without intensive self-examination. Through discussion of the literature and clinical material, the group project facilitated this process. It is persuasion of a scientific community that produces changes in its tenets and language (Kuhn, 1964).

The reification of Freud's phallocentric theory (a boy's version of femininity characterized by the absence of a penis) may have occurred because it lessens anxiety about anatomical differences for analysts and patients of both sexes (Bass, 1991; Bernheimer, 1991; Young-Bruehl, 1994). Bass (1991) points out, "The unacceptable reality is not the absence of the penis, but the genital distinction" (p. 313). Indeed, both Bass and Bernheimer argue that the psychoanalytic theory of female development based on the phallic castration complex "disavows" sexual differences and therefore functions as a fetish. The fetishist's "fundamental fear is that women are intolerably, uncannily other" (Bernheimer, 1991, p. 3). To enable the female analysand to come to terms with what she "has" and "has not" requires the analyst and patient to lift the fetishistic veil hiding her mental representations and conflicts about her genitalia.[4]

We observed our patients' tendencies to form explanations in very concrete terms. Upon reflection, we realized it had been easy to join them in this kind of literalism to reduce complex layers of material to a traditional view of penis envy and the castration complex. In exploring the female's sexual fantasies and conflicts, we were aware of the temptation for analysts to overlook Waelder's (1936) principle of multiple function as well as the principle of synecdoche (Sharpe, 1937).[5] In addition, the analyst can lose sight of the idea that images and metaphors have many meanings (Grossman and Stewart, 1976), and that body images can become embedded in the context of object relations, which appear in psychoanalyses as transferences.

---

[4]Many societies show evidence of difficulty in acknowledging girls and women as sexual beings with female fantasies and conflicts. Resistance to seeing and accepting anatomical differences between the sexes is reflected in such religious and cultural practices as the hiding and covering of women, especially their heads and hair.

[5]The part stands for the whole.

We wondered whether our reluctance to give up relying on penis envy interventions might be because this focus can function as a phallic equivalent with its clear, penetrating interpretations. Our struggle to allow space for a new theory seemed to echo our female analysands' difficulty opening their minds to the discovery of a feminine space. Young-Bruehl (1994) notes that there is a tendency to choose either "feminine" or "masculine" to describe particular images or fantasies (p. 390). In adding a lens of primary femininity through which to view the patient's material, we were cognizant of the danger of substituting a feminine theory for a masculine theory. Young-Bruehl cautions, "If Freudian psychoanalysis is phallocentric, any theory aimed at correcting for its bias runs the risk of bias in the opposite direction, a compensatory bias" (p. 384). We were also aware that just as a phallocentric theory might influence the patient's material, so might a primary femininity perspective, especially if the analyst were riveted to this position.

How did the group facilitate a shift in our thinking? Once research participants became convinced of the considerable lag between current theory and their clinical practice, the group functioned to encourage experimentation and confront resistance. Similar to our work with patients, we challenged each others' reluctance to exploring material relating to primary femininity, i.e., to "looking," acknowledging, and giving words to "what was there." We interpreted the ways that one or another of us seemed "fixed" on an idea or avoided hearing something. The group supported disclosure in a nonjudgmental way. As we gradually integrated concepts of primary femininity along with the paradigm of penis envy and the phallic castration complex, the group offered new ego ideals and alternative identifications. The study also stimulated further self-analysis, for investigating female psychology was as important personally as it was clinically and professionally to this group of women analysts.

This paper demonstrates the value of drawing on the theoretical constructs of primary femininity, as well as of penis envy and the phallic castration complex. In each case presented, the analyst's shift in focus to a primary femininity perspective facilitated the emergence of oedipal themes that had previously remained unanalyzable. This approach also elicited memories and fantasies of early body experiences and early object relations in the transference. In the work with Ms. Q., the transference intensified as the analyst began to use her thinking about primary femininity. There was a struggle (i.e., the analyst's "bossiness") over who would yield to whom, who would provide the feminine holding space. The analyst's acceptance of the patient's criticism enabled Ms. Q. to reveal more of her anxiety about sharing her "splendid isolation." Ms. T. had been caught in an impasse formerly understood as intractable penis envy. With the added dimension of primary femininity, the analyst was able to hear the more complex situation of her oedipal conflicts as well as the primitive confusion about her genitalia.

By naming the female genitalia the analyst addressed each patient's defense of disavowal, and as Lerner (1976) suggests, gave the patient permission to "look," to elaborate on mental representations and fantasies about "what she does have." This labeling may also have facilitated the patient's capacity to lift into consciousness formerly repressed representations and fantasies about her genitals. Freud (1915) states that "a presentation which is not put into words . . . remains therefore in the *Ucs.* in a state of repression" (p. 202). In *The Words to Say It*, an autobiographical account of her analysis, Cardinal (1983) recognizes the importance of words for bringing into consciousness and claiming "unnamed" parts of her body.[6] The analyst's words enabled Ms. Q. to gain access to heretofore hidden fantasies about her female anatomy. The analyst's naming of the genitals led Ms. T. to renewed efforts to disavow delineation of her female parts in order to maintain a fantasy of being both male and female.

Participant analysts observed a tendency to make more active and challenging interventions when exploring issues of gender identity and sexuality with their female analysands. At times patients felt directed and pursued. They often appeared startled by the analyst's labeling of the female genitalia, and occasionally experienced this naming as seductive, thereby heightening the homosexual transference. The analyst's increased activity may reflect an eagerness to

---

[6]Referring to her anus, she writes, "Then I understood there was an entire area of the body which I had never accepted and which somehow, never belonged to me. The zone between my legs could be only expressed in shameful words, and had never been the object of my conscious thought" (p. 240).

correct an earlier, masculine bias. As analysts more fully integrate concepts of primary femininity along with penis envy, there may be a decrease in the level of activity, as well as a refinement of interventions to encourage patients to oscillate more freely between perspectives.

CONCLUSION

The findings of this study demonstrate the usefulness of expanding the analyst's listening to include two theoretical paradigms: penis envy and the phallic castration complex, and primary femininity and its derivatives. All psychoanalysts face the challenge of integrating new ideas into technique each time they read or hear a stimulating paper, receive consultation, or develop new insights. Relinquishing the narrow view of penis envy as "bedrock" and the traditional understanding of the phallic castration complex enables the analyst to gain a more analytic stance from which to explore the metaphoric and defensive layers of the patient's material. While patients were often surprised by the change in focus, several analytic impasses were broken, demonstrating that penis envy is not "bedrock." The idea that something, anything, can be "bedrock" and therefore unanalyzable is essentially unanalytic. We join writers such as Grossman and Kaplan (1988) in stressing that clinical work be grounded in technical concepts that are psychoanalytic in nature. The recognition of the ever unfolding and multilayered vicissitudes of compromise formations is as essential to understanding female sexuality as it is to all psychoanalytic discovery.

REFERENCES

ABRAHAM, H.C. & FREUD, E.L., Eds. (1965). *A Psycho-Analytic Dialogue. The Letters of Sigmund Freud and Karl Abraham 1907–1926.* New York: Basic Books.
BARNETT, M.C. (1966). Vaginal awareness in the infancy and childhood of girls. *J. Amer. Psychoanal. Assn.,* 14:129–141.
BASS, A. (1991). Fetishism, reality, and "The Snow Man." *Amer. Imago,* 48:295–328.
——— (1994). Aspects of urethrality in women. *Psychoanal. Q.,* 63:491–517.
BERNHEIMER, C. (1991). "Castration" as fetish. *Paragraph,* 14:1–9.
BERNSTEIN, D. (1990). Female genital anxieties, conflicts and typical mastery modes. *Int. J. Psychoanal.,* 71:151–165.

BRIERLEY, M. (1932). Some problems of integration in women. *Int. J. Psychoanal.*, 13:433–448.
CARDINAL, L. (1983). *The Words to Say It.* Cambridge, MA: Van Vactor & Goodheart.
DEUTSCH, H. (1930). The significance of masochism in the mental life of women. *Int. J. Psychoanal.*, 9:48–60.
ERIKSON, E.H. (1950). *Childhood and Society.* New York: Norton.
——— (1974). Once more the inner space: letter to a former student. In *Women and Analysis,* ed. J. Strouse. New York: Grossman.
FAST, I. (1979). Developments in gender identity: gender differentiation in girls. *Int. J. Psychoanal.*, 60:443–453.
FREUD, S. (1915). The unconscious. *S. E.,* 14.
——— (1923). The ego and the id. *S. E.,* 19.
——— (1925). Some psychical consequences of the anatomical distinction between the sexes. *S. E.,* 19.
——— (1931). Female sexuality. *S. E.,* 21.
——— (1933). Femininity. *S. E.,* 22.
——— (1937). Analysis terminable and interminable. *S. E.,* 23.
GALENSON, E. & ROIPHE, H. (1976). Some suggested revisions concerning early female development. *J. Amer. Psychoanal. Assn.,* 24(Suppl.):29–57.
GROSSMAN, W.I. & KAPLAN, D.M. (1988). Three commentaries on gender in Freud's thought: a prologue to the psychoanalytic theory of sexuality. In *Fantasy, Myth, and Reality,* ed. H.P. Blum, Y. Kramer, A.K. Richards & A.D. Richards. New York: Int. Univ. Press, 1990, pp. 339–370.
——— & STEWART, W.A. (1976). Penis envy: from childhood wish to developmental metaphor. *J. Amer. Psychoanal. Assn.,* 24:193–212.
HORNEY, K. (1924). On the genesis of the castration complex in women. *Int. J. Psychoanal.,* 5:50–65.
——— (1926). The flight from womanhood. *Int. J. Psychoanal.,* 7:324–339.
JONES, E. (1927). The early development of female sexuality. *Int. J. Psychoanal.,* 8:438–451.
KALINICH, L.J. (1993). On the sense of absence: a perspective on womanly issues. *Psychoanal. Q.,* 62:206–228.
KESTENBERG, J. (1982). The inner-genital phase—prephallic and preoedipal. In *Early Female Development: Current Psychoanalytic Views,* ed. D. Mendell. New York: Spectrum.
KLEIN, M. (1928). Early stages of the Oedipus complex. *Int. J. Psychoanal.,* 9:167–180.
KRAUSZ, R. (1994). The invisible woman. *Int. J. Psychoanal.,* 75:59–72.
KUBIE, L.S. (1974). The drive to become both sexes. *Psychoanal. Q.,* 43:349–426.
KUHN, T. (1964). *The Structure of Scientific Revolutions.* Chicago: Univ. Chicago Press, 1970.
KULISH, N.M. (1991). The mental representation of the clitoris: the fear of female sexuality. *Psychoanal. Inq.,* 11:511–536.
LAX, R. (1994). Aspects of primary and secondary genital feelings and anxieties in girls during the preoedipal and early oedipal phases. *Psychoanal. Q.,* 63:271–296.

Lerner, H. (1976). Parental mislabeling of female genitals as a determinant of penis envy and learning in women. *J. Amer. Psychoanal. Assn.*, 24:269–283.

Mayer, E.L. (1991). Towers and enclosed spaces: a preliminary report on gender differences in children's reactions to block structures. *Psychoanal. Inq.*, 11:480–510.

——— (1995). The phallic castration complex and primary femininity: paired developmental lines toward female gender identity. *J. Amer. Psychoanal. Assn.*, 43:17–38.

Muller, J. (1932). A contribution to the problem of libidinal development of the genital phase in girls. *Int. J. Psychoanal.*, 13:361–368.

Muller-Braunschweig, C. (1926). The genesis of the feminine super-ego. *Int. J. Psychoanal.*, 7:359–365.

Richards, A.K. (1992). The influence of sphincter control and genital sensation on body image and gender identity in women. *Psychoanal. Q.*, 61:331–351.

——— (1996). Primary femininity and female genital anxiety. *J. Amer. Psychoanal. Assn.*, 44(Supp.):261–281.

Ritvo, L.B. (1965). Darwin as the source of Freud's neo-Lamarckianism. *J. Amer. Psychoanal. Assn.*, 13:499–517.

Sharpe, E.F. (1937). *Dream Analysis.* New York: Brunner/Mazel, 1978.

Shaw, R.R. (1995). Female genital anxieties: an integration of new and old ideas. *J. Clin. Psychoanal.*, 4:297–314.

Stoller, R.J. (1976). Primary femininity. *J. Amer. Psychoanal. Assn.*, 24(Suppl.): 59–78.

Tyson, P. (1994). Bedrock and beyond: an examination of the clinical utility of contemporary theories of female psychology. *J. Amer. Psychoanal. Assn.*, 42:447–467.

Waelder, R. (1936). The principle of multiple function. In *Psychoanalysis: Observation, Theory, Application,* ed. S.A. Guttman. New York: Int. Univ. Press, 1976, pp. 65–80.

Wilkinson, S.M. (1991). Penis envy: libidinal metaphor and experiential metonym. *Int. J. Psychoanal.*, 72:335–346.

Young-Bruehl, E. (1994). What theories women want. *Amer. Imago*, 51:373–396.

CAN WE BE BOTH WOMEN AND ANALYSTS?

Sallye Wilkinson et al.*

> The authors, candidates at a psychoanalytic institute that has not had a woman training analyst for more than 20 years, have a unique vantage point from which to examine the woman's development as an adult female and as a psychoanalyst. Our group has engaged in a series of discussions asking: Can we be both women and analysts? Comparing and contrasting our experiences with feedback from colleagues across the United States and abroad, we had to accept that our unique situation could not be a foil for the training dilemmas facing women. Our insights into the challenges involved with training, expression of sexuality, family ties, formation of an analytic identity, creative contributions to the field, and career progression have caused us to arrive at some sobering observations and hard-hitting questions which we present here. We hope that as we describe our discussions about the woman analyst's experience an active dialogue will arise within the reader's mind, and subsequently with colleagues.

Women's experiences of becoming analysts have received little attention in the burgeoning psychoanalytic literature on primary femininity and female psychology. When discussed, the analyst's femaleness tends to be woven into formulations concerning erotic and preoedipal transferences, perhaps with attention to the effects of her pregnancy on the analysis (Bassen, 1988; Fenster et al., 1986), or to specific difficulties in cross-gender supervisory processes (Goldberger and Evans, 1985; Lester, 1985; Mendell, 1986). But attention to the effects of femaleness on patients and colleagues prevents appreciation of the analyst's personal experience as a woman who provides psychoanalysis. It is as if her femaleness is distinct from her analytic skill. Is this a desirable conclusion for women? For the

---

*Mary Jo Peebles-Kleiger, Bonnie Buchele, Alice Brand Bartlett, Sharon Nathan, Regine Benalcazar-Schmid, Michelle Mintzer, Deborah Everhart. From the Topeka Institute for Psychoanalysis.

field of psychoanalysis? The authors—candidates at a psychoanalytic institute that last appointed a woman training analyst 33 years ago and has not had a woman training analyst available for more than 20 years—have a unique position to examine the juxtaposition between developing as a woman and developing as an analyst. We have discussed and debated the challenges around training, expressing sexuality, maintaining family ties, forming an analytic ego ideal, contributing to technical and theoretical advances, and achieving career progression that face women analysts. Over and over we have returned to the question: "Can we be both women and analysts?"

We paused to consider whether our question was idiosyncratic to our institute. However, as we described our situation on an Internet bulletin board[1] and invited comments, we received encouraging responses from women and men in Seattle, Chicago, Los Angeles, Pittsburgh, Washington, San Francisco, and London. Past Presidents of both the American Psychoanalytic Association and International Psycho-Analytical Association commented on the important influence of women mentors. An earlier version of this paper was read at the International Psychoanalytic Studies Organization meeting (San Francisco, July 29, 1995). There women candidates from around the country and Latin America discussed their experiences in institutes that provide varying degrees of access to female training and supervising analysts. We also presented this material at a meeting of the Topeka Society for Psychoanalysis (June 1, 1995). There our male colleagues asked questions, offered counterpoints, and shared their own struggles with gendered expectations and limitations. We wholeheartedly encouraged them to pursue their own examination of their male subjectivity so that we could eventually share and learn from each other. Thus enriched by comments from local and international colleagues, we shall examine here the dilemmas arising from a series of choices women analysts must make between internal and external aspects of their lives.

GROWING UP FEMALE IN A MALE INSTITUTE

Two years into her psychoanalytic training, one of the authors had the following dream:

[1]The Psychoanalytic Virtual Bulletin Board is sponsored by the American Psychoanalytic Association; Robert M. Galatzer-Levy, M.D., SYSOP.

Can We Be Both Women and Analysts?

> I am in a great hall with long tables. It is the dining hall of a prestigious boys' school like Eton. Rows and rows of boys are there, smiling, joking, spontaneously enjoying each other. I watch and listen apart from it all. They begin singing their "school song" and I want to join in, but I do not know the words.

The meaning seemed to be understood immediately by this woman who was the only female and only nonphysician in her Institute class. She must be envious of her male peers who seemed to "know the words" while she felt only a sense of loss and outsideness. She associated to her personal awareness of penis envy as a partial interpretation, but remained stirred by questions of, "Why can't I be happy with my femaleness? Why don't I know the words? Why is it a boys' school?" She had scotomized the fact that there were no women training analysts available in her "school."

As her training continued, she told her first analyst, "I know what it takes to be an analyst. I have to bring back three golden apples, kill the Wicked Witch of the West, and have a sex change operation." Only in her second analysis could she understand that three golden apples represented three patients [the number required for graduation] in the "pure gold" of analysis. The Wicked Witch symbolized working through her oedipal relationship with her mother.

But the "sex change operation" eluded understanding. Could only men be analysts? Surely she did not mean that! Was it penis envy again? A reading of Harriet Lerner's (1976) paper on parental mislabeling of female genitals was eye-opening. Lerner persuasively described how labeling only the girl's internal genital organ—the vagina—without naming her external genitalia—the vulva, labia, and clitoris—led to an incomplete, poorly differentiated, and anatomically incorrect picture of the girl's own body. Lerner writes, "In Freud's time, the words clitoris, vulva, and labia were not included in the dictionary and, in this country, the only word in Webster's dictionary to refer to female genitals was vagina" (p. 277). She adds, "Because neither sex is informed that the clitoris is part of 'what girls have,' this organ will be cathected as a small and inadequate penis rather than as a valid and feminine part of the girl's sexuality" (p. 276). Unacknowledged and not validated, her prime source of sexual stimulation and gratification would be inevitably experienced

531

as "unfeminine" (i.e., only boys have *something* on the outside; only boys have *permission* for sensitive external genitals). Was it that our dreamer did not know the words to the school song? Or did the school song not have words for her? Extrapolating from Lerner's contribution, could this candidate's unresolved questions revolve around the valuing of the something that she had, rather than an attenuation of what she lacked? Was her struggle less one of envy and more one of needing permission?

She began to notice a pattern in her attendance at presentations given at the American Psychoanalytic Association meetings. Although at first believing that she attended workshops and readings of papers according to topic, she later realized that she had consistently and exclusively attended presentations by women! When a researcher from the Committee on Issues in Training Women asked her to distribute a questionnaire to the Topeka candidates, she found herself defending against the attitude toward our institute which ran something like, "Poor Topeka—there are no women there!" Reflexively, she parroted the local comment: "It takes a long time to grow one!" In retrospect, she still had not fully appreciated the yield of her dream.

Now, years later, she realizes that contact with women mentors at the American Psychoanalytic Association meetings had provided her with *something that was female, exciting, expert, and authoritative*. Those women provided another context for knowing herself as analyst, which could be used to challenge the familiar ways in which she viewed herself as analyst in her home institute. In many ways her perspective was unique among her fellow candidates, as well as among her instructors, who were immersed in the home institution. Only through her growing awareness of an absent something and a differentness could she speak the words: "There has been no woman training analyst for more than 20 years!" No one had earnestly said that before. No one truly had noticed. This candidate was not looking for a penis. Her joke about a sex change operation was reflecting her anxiety that somehow her femaleness would have to be castrated as she tried to become an analyst within her milieu—a milieu that was male-dominated.

As a result of this woman's journey, our group of authors joined together. Together we became able to ask the questions stated here.

Can We Be Both Women and Analysts?

Coming from different professional disciplines, some of us were radicalized by years of wrangling with the waiver process. Some never had to consider making waiver applications. Others were shaped by the rigors of postgraduate education, especially in medical school, where women had to fight to retain their well-deserved positions. Still others benefited from training when the old-boy network was not so entrenched and rigid. Some of us are richly experienced while others are at the beginning of our careers. Some have been candidates for a matter of months, others for 19 years.

We immensely value learning from our nurturing, challenging, creative, and bright male analysts and supervisors. They have touched our lives. But, like our co-author with the dream of the exclusive boys' school, we need to lay claim to the awareness that a woman needs to internalize a sense of acceptance—even admiration—of her femaleness. Lerner's (1976) observations about the developmental need for giving the girl permission to value both her inside and her outside became a metaphor for examining our psychoanalytic training and practice. Just as the little girl benefits from an internalized acceptance from both her mother and her father, so does the budding woman analyst need to internalize acceptance and pride in her femaleness as an analyst from both male analysts and female analysts, as well as from supervisors and colleagues.

MINORITY STATUS OF WOMEN CANDIDATES: HARMONY, POLYPHONY, OR CACOPHONY?

Each of the candidate classes represented by the eight authors was predominantly male, although the trend is clearly shifting. The changing ratios of men to women within our institute roughly parallel those within the membership of the American Psychoanalytic Association. In 1993, an American Psychoanalytic Association survey of psychoanalytic practice reported that 18% of the graduated members were women (L. Brauer, personal communication). Of these, 68 women, amounting to 4% of the membership, were training analysts.[2] The emotional impact of these figures is cogently described

---

[2]The 1570 respondents included 1280 men and 290 women. Four hundred seventy-two of the 1280 men, or 37%, were training analysts; and 68 of the 290 women, or 23%, were training analysts. Brauer points out that the percentages differ

Sallye Wilkinson et al.

by an Internet colleague in Chicago who, in her word, made a "stunning" discovery (which she had known all along) that only three out of 100 training analysts in her institute were women. The minority status of women at all levels in the field is a statistical fact.

The numbers would seem to speak for themselves. But the implications are not easily received. We are, in essence, offering an interpretation about gender issues within the practice of our profession that may not be conscious. Clearly the timing of an interpretation must be optimal for the listener to accept the insight. Because we have the benefit of being without a female training analyst for 20 years, we are especially primed, perhaps urgently so, to articulate the implications of such statistics. But the understanding we may shed could well meet with the reaction we have heard for years: "Poor Topeka!" In our experience, if we stand firm and do not take on the mantle of victim, those feeling sorry that we do not have what they do begin to reconsider perceptions of their own situations. For example, our co-author on the "Committee on Issues in Training Women" heard the "Poor Topeka!" condolence meeting after meeting of the American Psychoanalytic Association, until one day it dawned on other Committee members that their institutes, like that of our colleague in Chicago, lacked sufficient women mentors. This sympathetic, yet dismissive, reaction also met us at the International Psychoanalytic Studies Organization presentation. When we asserted that our collaboration on this paper was an effort to offer much more to them (through the sharing of our experiences) than a bid for recognition and support for us, the discussion never returned to our unique situation and ranged freely on how women managed issues of competition with women colleagues, competition with women mentors, competition with men, competence, ambition, family responsibilities, and cultural norms. The situation in Topeka is not categorically different from that in other institutes, only relatively so. Thus we question the degree to which our institute has

---

between the sexes, in part due to age since there are more younger women who would be less likely to have become training analysts than the older men. This fact, in itself, is worthy of attention. But more to the point, what appears to have been overlooked by focusing on the intrasex percentages is that women and men vie together for training analyst positions. Four hundred seventy-two male training analysts out of 1570 respondents yields 30%. Sixty-eight female training analysts out of 1570 respondents yields a stark 4%.

Can We Be Both Women and Analysts?

served as a token to contain feelings or conflicts about the minority status of women nationwide.[3] The answer to that question, it is hoped, will be facilitated by an examination of this contribution.

On the local level, we have had to contend with the experience that the "school song" has yet to fully include words for us. Two general options for managing our minority status have emerged: we can sing in unison by harmonizing with the prevailing school melody and by becoming another voice in the chorus, or we can find the contrapuntal line that provides a polyphonic richness. Group theory highlights how individuals must negotiate a balance between affiliation through conformity to group expectations and personal commitment to their individuality. Within our group, this concept was illustrated by heated discussions about the extent to which we should "sing in unison." How different could we sound before we were dismissed as a harping cacophony? To what extent did we have to conform to traditional stylistic and theoretical conventions to enable this paper to be published in a mainstream psychoanalytic journal? As we began to articulate this tension *among* us (and thus *within* each of us) between conformity and personal expression, we recognized that the tension was not new; for years, we had struggled silently with various definitions of what was acceptable to voice about our experience as women in class, in supervision, and even in analysis. The pressures, both internal and external, we keenly felt underscore the liabilities facing minorities.

Minority status can also confer special privileges. There are advantages to being able to sing the counterpoint. To the extent that minority members are discounted and excluded, we tend not to be viewed as true competitors. Implicitly, the contrapuntal opportunity

---

[3]Reference to a social psychology perspective on organizations proves a useful reference. Kanter (1977) describes several kinds of groups differentiated by the ratios within. In the *skewed group* the ratio of the dominant subgroup to the minority is 85:15. In such groups the minority tends to be treated as token. Rather than respond to members individually, there is a pull to respond to them symbolically. In this manner they are encapsulated. Pressure to conform allows everyone to be less anxious. With approximately 18% of the membership of the American Psychoanalytic Association women and about 4% of the membership female training analysts, the dynamics of Kanter's skewed group must be considered. In fact, these dynamics must be considered across all institutes where, with few exceptions, women mentors are a significant minority. Kanter also describes a *tilted group*, one where the ratio is 60:40. Here minorities have formed coalitions and the status quo is being questioned. This is the situation in Topeka. A *balanced group* is 50:50.

provides greater freedom to be creative, both in our navigation of the system and in our conceptualization of the psychoanalytic enterprise. With outsider status, we must be creative to fit in and to succeed. But this observation bifurcated our group. Those at the beginning of their careers felt strongly compelled to establish themselves as competitors. They pursued awesome caseloads and carefully crafted relationships with mentors. Others, more seasoned, found relief in their awareness of less pressure to conform to training and practice expectations. They considered themselves freer to combine competing interests such as clinical work, family responsibilities, professional writing, and personal passions in more distinct and nonconforming ways than male colleagues. Several men underscored this point when we presented this paper to the Topeka Society. They acknowledged a fresh awareness of their tendency to passively conform to expectations about career progression, and spoke of envy regarding our freedom to collaborate in the writing of this paper. Even with such comments, we could arrive at no consensus on how to understand the so-called freedom. For some of us, the freedom to negotiate the tasks of becoming an analyst came at the heavy price of accepting a perpetual minority status. For others, the creation of alternative routes to success was a regrettable, but pleasurable, challenge.

Because of the relatively small numbers of women in classes, local societies, and the American Psychoanalytic Association, our voice within the power structure of psychoanalysis has been limited. We suspect that historically the female figure most consistently present at analytic discussions has been embodied in the clinical vignette as the female patient with a male analyst. To the extent that this is true, the pull to view women as maternal, seductive, coquettish, and lacking in intellectual rigor has found no immediate checks or balances. Such portrayals, although not intended by instructors and advisers, cause women in training to feel not fully legitimate, and so their self-esteem as analysts suffers. A conflict emerges between demonstrating to the majority that we can sing in harmony and acting on our internal desires to sing our own song. Never resolved, this conflict remains a constant companion.

These gender distinctions are complicated by generational issues. For example, our training and supervising analysts are all men.

Can We Be Both Women and Analysts?

In many cases, the male analyst is a generation older than the female candidate. Thus one transference, facilitated by age differences, emerging on the group level is that of little girls relating to their fathers. While this compromise clearly serves both sides by eliminating other kinds of tensions, the result for women is a sense of being perpetually in training. We can never grow up, neither for ourselves nor in relation to these fatherlike men. That many women do take longer to progress through their training because of family responsibilities serves as reinforcement. Sometimes older candidates feel marginalized when described as "good clinicians." Such praise, when coupled with their later completion of analytic training, stirs questions about whether the intended message is that these women cannot fully contribute to advances in theory and technique. Yet among our group of "good clinicians" are women nationally recognized for their expertise in various areas of the mental health field. Despite this dichotomy, the rut of wise father/good little girl is difficult to leave behind.

Given the impact of gendered and generational issues on our minority status, the ambitious woman in this situation must be very comfortable with both self-assertion and management of angry frustration. This partnership with her growth-promoting aggression may make her a better analyst, but she pays a price for such competency. After all, within our culture, assertive, ambitious, and competitive women are commonly described as castrating. Our training programs and psychoanalytic societies do not and cannot offer pristine sanctuaries from such societal notions. Thus different standards for what is an acceptable level of ambition and competitiveness are applied by male and female colleagues. The ambitious woman must learn to tolerate her hurt and rage over attributions of ruthlessness when she steps out of her shadowy minority role.

A number of survival strategies may be employed. There may be a tendency to avoid being seen as "wild," so as not to be marginalized. But the dilemma then becomes how to avoid being seen as "mild," so as not to be overlooked. To be acknowledged as a candidate of substance the woman must wear a vest of conformity. Toward this end, she may exert disproportional efforts to carry vast caseloads, secure publication, or devote extra hours to largely invisible and thankless low-level administrative jobs. Or, she may achieve success as the result of a professional partnership with an influential male analyst. Finally, as with the authors, women also have adapted by moving toward one another and affiliating more strongly in times of stress.

In anticipation of presenting this paper to the Topeka Society, there were massive amounts of transference projections to be managed. Some of us had completed training analyses and some of us were in the midst. Would our analysts and mentors feel attacked? Were we being too wild? Were we worrying too much? After all, our milieu was generative enough for our group to form. The discussion after the formal paper presentation had some tension, but the ground was fertile enough to yield a dialogue which continues. The dilemmas were not yet resolved, but the path was open. We felt affirmed in using our voice to talk about our experiences as women and have since felt increased respect within ourselves and from the men in our institute for our efforts at individuation. Perhaps most important, we discovered that the men at our institute shared our discontent. It seems the determination, perseverance, and creativity of our outsider status were prerequisites for these dissatisfactions to be articulated.

WHAT DOES *WOMAN* ANALYST MEAN?

For decades, Freud's ideas on the development of female sexuality held full sway. His was the theory to refute or uphold. According to Freud, at about four years of age, girls recognize the inferiority of their genitalia then clamor psychologically for a penis (Freud, 1908, 1924, 1925, 1931, 1933, 1937). Neurotic women settle into patterns ranging between passive, compensatory wishing or aggressive, castrating revenge (Abraham, 1922). Other women adapt more readily to their developmental experience of penis envy and look forward to attachment to a man who will provide a compensatory phallus in the form of a baby. Although these latter women become fully feminine in Freud's view, no woman is understood to have a superego "so inexorable, so impersonal, so independent of its emotional origins as [would be required] in men" (Freud, 1925, p. 257). In the last

Can We Be Both Women and Analysts?

three decades, Freud's ideas about female development and psychology have been systematically challenged and, for the most part, reworked. Today, psychoanalytic thinkers generally understand Freud's blindspots to be rooted, literally, in the point of view of how little girls must look to little boys.

Despite recent advances, we have wondered incredulously how the few yet noteworthy women analysts who were practicing, writing, and teaching up until the 1970s could avoid challenging Freud's formulations. The prescient ideas of Horney (1924, 1926), Jones (1927, 1935), Klein (1928, 1932) and others concerning primary femininity, maternal identifications, female sexuality and the vicissitudes of penis envy were all but forgotten. Freud (1935) himself acknowledges these authors by noting that their work "seems in itself proof that something is missing, undiscovered or unsaid at this point" (p. 329). Yet the debate on female sexuality was silenced when Freud died without having attained further clarity (Fliegel, 1973).

Chodorow's (1989) description of "seventies questions for thirties women" (p. 199) provides an intriguing perspective on how this lapse in the psychoanalytic dialogue on women may have occurred. The early women analysts she interviewed did not experience gender in the same absolute terms as Chodorow and her contemporaries did in the 1970s, nor as we do in the 1990s. As Chodorow describes, their lack of interest in changing Freud's theories has continued to guide contemporary analysts to

> look at gender as a situated phenomenon, both in itself, as it can be more or less salient in different arenas or at different times of life, and in relation to other aspects of social and cultural categorization. Social, historical, and cultural context—on the one hand a social situation of low gender-salience and a relative lack of feminist politics, or a politics that assumed natural differences between the sexes, on the other a social, professional, and political situation that stresses high gender-salience—served to create what I considered to be normative patterns of gender-blindness in early women psychoanalysts, and what I came to see as normative patterns of hyper-gender-sensitivity in contemporary feminists like myself. . . . An examination of interpretations of gender, and of the dialogue between those with different interpretations, informs our

Sallye Wilkinson et al.

understanding of the social, historical, and cultural context that these interpretations help to produce and that help to produce them [p. 218].

The dialogue that Chodorow invites about our gendered theories, gendered training, and gendered technique has proceeded in fits and starts. One leap occurred during the 1970s when Chodorow formulated her questions. That period had extraordinary importance for the subsequent psychoanalytic understanding of women.

With the emergent counterculture of the 1960s, women's voices had begun to be raised and heard in a different way. Feminist writers dared to write about female homosexuality, sexual politics, rape, and the myth of the vaginal orgasm (Friedan, 1963; Koedt, 1971; Millet, 1973). Masters and Johnson (1966) explicated the human sexual response, and Roe v. Wade became the law of the land. For the most part, these shifting perspectives on gender occurred outside the field of psychoanalysis. Parenthetically, the resemblance between this growing awareness of woman's experience outside psychoanalysis and our dreamer's growing awareness after traveling outside our institute may be coincidental. But what if it is not?

In the 1970s, psychoanalytic literature began to reflect changes in social attitudes toward women. In fact, the literature on female psychology mushroomed and the powerful writings touched our generation of future analysts. Heralded by the 1976 supplement to the *Journal of the American Psychoanalytic Association* devoted to female psychology, the 1970s were the decade in which primary femininity was finally affirmed within mainstream American psychoanalysis.

Perhaps these long overdue developments in the psychoanalytic understanding of women can be attributed to the use of apprenticeship and identification to transmit knowledge (Morris, 1992). Despite the best of intentions on both sides of the couch, theories about what constitutes female psychology may have repeatedly foreclosed further exploration of femaleness. In retrospect, too many years passed as mainstream psychoanalysis foundered on the blindspots in Freud's theory on the psychology of women.

These observations form the backdrop for our questions. Can we, as women, embrace psychoanalysis with all its troubling blind spots? If we subscribe to classical theories that the femininity of our women patients is likely to be influenced by a sense of inferiority,

Can We Be Both Women and Analysts?

then what are we ascribing to ourselves as women analysts? Is the answer to this question truly compatible with the simultaneous, long-held belief that the gender of the analyst is inconsequential? Although a compelling trend toward questioning how the analyst's gender affects the transference is emerging in the psychoanalytic literature (Kulish, 1984, 1986; Kulish and Mayman, 1993; Lester, 1993; Mendell, 1986; Welles and Wrye, 1991; Wrye and Welles, 1989), disturbing vestiges of Freud's notions about the inferiority of women remain in practice. Before this assertion is rejected as unfounded, we must ask why referral patterns to women analysts diverge from what would be expected based on clinical theory. Mayer and DeMarneffe (1992) found that women analysts receive relatively few adult male referrals, thereby making that requisite clinical experience more difficult to complete. Furthermore, they found that adult referrals, including those made by analysts, were greatly influenced by the issue of an analyst-patient gender match.

Given these observations about actual practice, what are the implications of choosing a designation of *woman* analyst? Does not *analyst* identify and describe the clinical capabilities of a woman clearly enough? We do not specify a *woman* mother. Nor do we say a *woman* nurse. But we do say *woman* analyst, much as we say *woman* physician, or *male* nurse. The gender specification in front of the noun suggests an anomaly in identity, if not incompetence, as in, "this is not a *regular* (man) analyst; this is a *woman* analyst." We infer from the survey by Mayer and DeMarneffe that this implicit anomaly has a palpable impact on a woman's analytic practice. Thus, to borrow from Chodorow (1989), the increased understanding of gender-salience within the transference-countertransference paradigm continues, ironically, to be accompanied by a qualitative gender blindness to anomalies within clinical practice. A male colleague commented on this inference. He offered that awareness of gender issues has been heightened in recent years by contributions such as that of Mayer and DeMarneffe's, and that the use of *woman* analyst may also reflect gender sensitivity. We hope so. But, in our clinical practices such enhanced sensitivity has yet to be translated into consistent referral of male patients. Once again, something is missing. Like the all-male school song, the words of theory and the words in practice seem not quite right.

Sallye Wilkinson et al.

DO PARENTAL IDENTIFICATIONS DETERMINE ANALYTIC IDENTITY?

One of our co-authors found herself dramatically torn between her very serious professional responsibilities and her longing for a child. She had to take much time away from work for procedures in a fertility clinic, and in the process observed that "the enormity of my commitment to patients and to the institute became apparent. Clearly, I have not chosen a career path where my work is something to dabble in as a secondary consideration to family needs. If I were a male, the enormity of my commitment to my work would not be conflictual. But as a female analyst, this tension is prominent."

Becoming analysts requires that we continually reexamine ourselves as women. Demands requiring reflection and choice fly at us constantly from external sources and from our inner worlds. For example, training necessitates extraordinary commitments of time, money, and personal devotion that repeatedly affect choices between career and family, self and other. In search of guidance, we may turn to an exploration of our identifications and counteridentifications with our mothers' and fathers' definition of femaleness vis-à-vis such choices. But this attempt to resolve our questions about how to be both women and analysts is dauntingly complex. We are not little girls, although we are shaped by our earliest experiences. Clearly we have to examine those early experiences to further our own self-definition and differentiation—but with what measure? For example, our co-author's fantasy of "killing of the Wicked Witch of the West" to secure graduation was likely much more complex than simply resolving her conflicts about competing with and surpassing mother. Could an additional interpretation have been that the Wicked Witch represented conflicts concerning being a woman and an analyst? Was there a wish and a fear that black magic was needed to resolve these dilemmas? To what degree was her oedipal drama recalled within her analyses as a communication about analytic training experiences? Or, more broadly speaking, are there misrecognitions of our femaleness both in our past and in our present that threaten our potential to consolidate a viable analytic identity?

The mothers we remembered varied in their appreciation of their femininity, schooling, occupation, mothering, and sexuality.

Can We Be Both Women and Analysts?

For example, one mother wanted to work. In fact, she kept her marriage secret so that she would not be fired. That mother's pleasure became her daughter's permission. Another mother moved to a distant town for two years when her work was transferred, leaving her daughter and husband behind. For her, being the primary wage earner meant that she was not a good woman. Her daughter discovered in the course of her own training analysis that she understood her mother better than her mother understood herself. Her mother was proud of her work, but deceived herself into believing that this was not the case. As her daughter achieved greater and greater successes, this mother counseled her to cut back so that her husband would not feel threatened. One mother delighted in raising her children and providing a warm home for the family. Another mother returned to work when her daughter was in high school. Proud and relieved that her mother had taken on other projects besides herself, the daughter was disappointed when her mother quit because the professional arena had changed too much for her to keep up over the years she had spent rearing her children. Yet another mother had given up a prestigious scholarship to stay home to care for an ill grandmother. Bitter over her lost opportunities, she stressed the importance of choosing a career that allowed her daughter to "put the family first."

In a similar vein, the fathers we remembered varied in their appreciation of women's femininity, schooling, mothering, and sexuality. They, too, had attitudes about women's employment that were shaped by the traditions of the times. One father encouraged his daughter's education so that she could "stay busy" until she could marry and rear a family. Another father delightfully debated with his daughter the implications of business decisions in a manner that fully supported her own professional development. In contrast, another intellectually erudite father consistently and subtly devalued his daughter's academic successes. When she had achieved proficiency as a pianist at the age of sixteen, he announced that he would stop playing, which he had done with gusto and talent for years, "since you are now playing much better than I." For her, the writing of this paper was both threatening and joyous.

Her joy grew from a *fresh awareness* that she was no longer that sixteen-year-old girl struggling to separate from her parents. She is

Sallye Wilkinson et al.

a mature, competent clinician, administrator, mother, and wife. For these pages, she thought as an analyst and wrote as an analyst. While her writing inhibitions remain, they are lessened because she has accomplished some internal work that she previously could not. What is different may be that our group is sufficiently powerful, nurturant, competitive, and containing for her to develop alternatives to the inhibiting identifications of her childhood. Thus, although it is tempting to look to our internal mothers and fathers for clues and cues, developmentally and retrospectively, to help sort our current training dilemmas, we must recognize simultaneously that we are no longer little girls. Our development of a healthy, viable analytic identity grows as much from our adult development as from our childhood development.

At the risk of being reductionistic with very complicated developmental processes, we can make the following comparison: Just as little girls build from identifications with both parents toward separation, individuation, and differentiation, so we as adult analytic candidates build from identifications with mentors and training analysts toward differentiated, autonomous analytic identities. Although recent analytic writers (Colarusso and Nemiroff, 1981) have proposed a model of adult development based on an understanding that sense of self and defensive strategies change during the life course, few others have discussed the healthy consolidation of professional identity as an adult developmental milestone for women. What has been written tends to circle back to preoedipal and oedipal conflicts, which are thought to impede achievement (Applegarth, 1976; Moulton, 1986). Although early experiences are of utmost significance in the formation of character structure, the very nature of psychoanalytic treatment and training assumes that desirable changes are made in adulthood. Toward this end, we devote an extraordinary degree of energy to training analyses and coursework.

What are the factors that go into consolidating the identity of the woman analyst? McGoldrick (1988), writing from a systems theory point of view, emphasizes:

> ... women have always played a central role in families, but *the idea that they have a life cycle apart from their roles as wife and mother is a relatively recent one,* and still is not widely accepted in our culture. *The expectation for women has been that they would take care of the needs of others, first, men, then children, then the elderly.* Until

Can We Be Both Women and Analysts?

> very recently, "human development" referred to male development and women's development was defined by the men in their lives. They went from being daughter, to wife, to mother, with their status defined by the male in the relationship and their role by their position in the family's life cycle. *Rarely has it been accepted that they had a right to a life for themselves* [p. 29; italics added].

McGoldrick's ideas are amply portrayed by over 60 years of American cinema, in which women analysts are consistently smitten by a countertransference love that causes them to become sexually or romantically involved with male patients, and to surrender their career (Gabbard and Gabbard, 1989). But, unlike these Tinsel Town caricatures, we do have a life cycle apart from our traditional roles, and being an analyst is but one aspect, not a mutually exclusive role, of that life cycle.

There are some distinct differences between the sexes that require very sensitive mentoring to encourage growth. More often than not, women struggle with numerous conflicts about how to create a bridge between their public, professional lives and their private, family lives. Women's private concerns about becoming analysts could be subdivided further into mothering and sexuality. Our struggles to feel fulfilled as mothers, or to feel comfortable and accepted with our mature sexuality, provide the hooks on which to hang perceptions of women analysts as erotic stimuli or containers for preoedipal deficits. However, an important differentiation must be made. The woman candidate values and wishes to integrate an increasingly enriched identity as lover, wife, mother, and analyst. Drives toward synthesis and growth are quite different from perceptions of the woman analyst that question her sexuality as being too stimulating and presume that her femininity will somehow absorb primitivity. Such perceptions strip personal identity rather than enhance it. After all, we are not movie starlets who obsessively disavow feelings and sensuality, avoid "female domesticity" (Gabbard and Gabbard, 1989, p. 1043), and become pathologically devoted to the practice of psychoanalysis.

Another aspect of women forming an analytic identity is illustrated by the example of a woman candidate who chose her training institute due to the availability of women training analysts. That woman struggled with conflicting role models presented by two different women supervisors. One was "very maternal and emphasized the holding aspects of the analytic situation; the other was very cerebral and competitive." In contrast to our predominant experience of needing to individuate ourselves from male mentors and analysts, this woman had a different kind of conflict in establishing a feminine analytic identity. Perhaps another variation is represented through the poignant description by a colleague from Los Angeles who repeatedly found herself discounting the teachings of her well-known and widely respected female training analyst in favor of anything a male analyst might say. How a woman (or a man) comes to view herself as an analyst will be affected by gender whether the training pair is same sex, cross-sex, or triangulated.

These vignettes serve to illuminate our point that a candidate's analytic identity is most fruitfully encouraged by a diverse sampling of mentors. The false dichotomy that women feel and men think can be challenged as experience accrues with cerebral men, maternal women, cerebral women, and maternal men. As a result, femininity in men and masculinity in women may become available to enhance the psychoanalytic enterprise without being politicized. A woman candidate in Seattle amplified this point through her observation that the recent addition of two women training analysts at her institute was a welcome shift from many years without women mentors. She added that both sexes could benefit from the different points of view noting that her own experience of being in analysis with both a male and female analyst had been valuable, although in different ways. She had been told by male faculty that they also had derived benefit from being in two analyses: one with a man, and one with a woman.

Perhaps now the words needed for the "school song" become a bit clearer. The choices that must be made between attention to self and other, career advancement or family, financial security or children, recognition or relationship all have a unique slant for women (just as there is a uniquely different slant for men). Solutions based on identification and counteridentification with parents, or analysts, or mentors simply limit our choices to theirs. For this reason the Topeka situation will not be resolved when the next training analyst appointed is a woman. With such assumptions that individual is stripped of her identity as she is reified into some sort of representation of femininity. What is needed instead is a diverse sampling of

Can We Be Both Women and Analysts?

women. We need women who can "sing" of a variety of analytic career choices while still keeping their femaleness intact: for example, women who have never married; women with young children; women with grown children; women who are homosexual; women who followed the "immersion" model; and women who took decades to complete their training, taking sequential cases as a solution to their wish to put family first. Men candidates need such women mentors, too.

CAN WE BE SEXUAL?

It has been our experience that the woman analyst's mature sexuality, denoted by acknowledging her as a sexual subject rather than as a sex object, is inconsistently addressed in psychoanalytic training. Only rarely does healthy female sexuality appear within course readings (where, along with the extant literature on both sexes, writings tend to be devoted to psychopathology), and dialogues about it are often absent from supervision. More frequently, theory and clinical formulations portray women as mothers, with the focus on preoedipal issues. The taboo dictating that one does not have sex with one's mother, or even thoughts about it, is suspect here. What must be defended against within the field of psychoanalysis in this manner? In the absence of consistent and forthright dialogue, we must infer that female sexuality threatens the institution of psychoanalysis.

Freud's treatment of women's sexuality in his technique papers and personal correspondence emphasizes the importance of maintaining boundaries (Blum, 1994; Freud, 1915). For example, he wrote in a letter of his concern regarding Ferenczi's technique:

> We have hitherto in our technique held to the conclusion that patients are to be refused erotic gratifications.... A number of independent thinkers in matters of technique, will say to themselves: "why stop at a kiss?" Certainly one gets further when one adopts "pawing" as well, which after all doesn't make a baby. And then bolder ones will come along, will go further to peeping and showing—and soon we have accepted in the technique of psychoanalysis the whole repertoire of demi-viergereie and petting parties, resulting in an enormous increase of interest in psychoanalysis among both analysts and patient....

father Ferenczi gazing at the lively scene he has created will perhaps say to himself: "Maybe after all I should have halted my technique of motherly affection before the kiss" [Jones, 1957, p. 164].

Freud's emphasis on abstinence and objectivity presumably grew out of concern for the boundariless behavior of his disciples Jung, Jones, Ferenczi, Tausk, Stekel, and Gross (Gabbard and Lester, 1996; Gay, 1988). His attitude about sexual relations between analyst and patient, however, was not as clear-cut as implied in the above passage and in his technique papers. For example, Freud was surprisingly conciliatory toward Jung regarding his disastrous liaison with Spielrein and, like Jung, he appeared to blame female patients for the transgression of analysts: "The way these women manage to charm us with every conceivable psychic perfection until they have attained their purpose is one of nature's greatest spectacles" (McGuire, 1974, p. 231; see also Gabbard and Lester, 1996). Adumbrated within this comment is Freud's view that the female superego is more lax, and that the male analyst must be skilled enough to avoid the seduction (Eissler, 1983). Freud's ambitendent communications about sexual relations between analyst and patient raise the question: Was there, or more immediately relevant, is there such a profound anxiety about the analyst's sexuality that it has yet to be fully articulated? Articles specifically addressing the analyst's erotic countertransference feelings are fairly recent developments in the psychoanalytic literature, and the topic sparks controversial discussions at analytic meetings (Davies, 1994; Gabbard, 1994; Hirsch, 1994; Tansey, 1994).

To a person, the co-authors received messages growing up that women had to be in control of their sexuality because, after a point, men could not be expected to exercise restraint. Thus Freud's pessimistic warning to males about the weaknesses of the female superego is ludicrously, insanely, turned topsy-turvy into a warning to females about the weaknesses of the male ego. One dynamic among many underlying this confusion over who does want to whom is that the fearful, terrifying, and wondrous aspects of sexuality may be displaced by persons of either sex onto women. Women are then viewed as dangerous seductresses. Contrivances like this limit everyone's capacity to experience mature sexual agency. Consider the experience of one co-author whose male psychotherapy supervisor, an analyst, asked her if she wore her V-neck blouse when seeing a male

Can We Be Both Women and Analysts?

patient. The implication was that she was unnecessarily exposing herself. Confident that she was not, she replied that she wore this blouse only when she came to see him, thus divesting herself of his sexual stirrings. Her audaciousness prevented her mature sexuality from being reduced to the status of erotic stimulus for her patient—or her supervisor.

Men and women may also bind sexual anxieties by perceiving women as asexual. Given this perception, perhaps the goal of our dreamer's sex-change operation was to become neuter rather than transsexual. Such efforts cast new light on the charming little girl role, which denies the excitement and joy of being full sexual human beings. Oddly, the illusion of sexual immaturity may coexist with an expectation that women are the moral arbiters of sexual expression. Thus when an impropriety is perceived, the woman may be blamed for having perpetrated "one of nature's greatest spectacles," thereby perpetuating a cycle in which attributions of having childlike innocence are replaced by those of being a whore. Can we be sexual without the risk of triggering such dynamics?

The relative silence within the field of psychoanalysis about these issues has unfortunate consequences. The woman psychoanalyst may quietly inhibit her sexuality so as not to be considered seductive. But our collusion with this silence prevents both men and women, patients and analysts, from exploring their views of mature, healthy female sexuality. Aspects of womanhood continue to be perceived as mutually exclusive. An opportunity to appreciate the many facets of female homosexuality is shunted aside. Better understanding of psychopathology in women—for example, adding to the literature on perversions (Kaplan, 1991; Richards, 1990; Welldon, 1991)—is essentially foreclosed. If we have no model for appreciating and integrating our own mature sexuality, then what healing aspects uniquely accessible through the experience of women analysts, and thereby available to men analysts, are never fully realized? Without attention to these questions, the psychoanalytic enterprise runs the risk of perpetuating a psychological, social, and cultural status quo. Could it be that our dreamer had to kill off the Wicked Witch because the Witch's apparent frigidity, or barenness, or lasciviousness blocked her path to mature sexuality?

Sallye Wilkinson et al.

CAN "GOOD ENOUGH" MOTHERS WORK?

Although the majority of the men in our institute are psychiatric residents or freshly out of their postgraduate training, recently married, and with young families, there is far greater diversity among the women candidates regarding training, work, and motherhood. For example, one of our colleagues dropped out of training after finishing classes, to raise her four children and work half-time as a child psychiatrist. One of our co-authors stays home with her young children, except to carry one analytic case. These choices are built on strong convictions of both a personal and a professional nature that our children need their mothers. Thus juggling part-time work, parenting, and analytic training is a constantly guilt-inducing challenge for those of us with young children. Although our candidate or analyst husbands also struggle with finding time for career development as well as for family, the bulk of childrearing responsibilities tend to fall to us. Priorities tend to be given to our husbands' career needs and they may be saddled with financial responsibilities as a result. At the same time, if a child is sick, we almost always are the parent to stay home thereby disrupting our analytic practice. Are we being "good enough" analysts? Are we being "good enough" mothers? The balance between the number of courses, the number of analytic cases, and the amount of professional work is calculated and adjusted, and then recalculated and readjusted throughout our children's development.

Others among us have waited to begin full training until their children were adolescents or young adults. With the struggles of postgraduate schooling, career building, and parenting behind them, they approached analytic training with more energy and enthusiasm, and their progress occurs more quickly and with less conflict than it does for colleagues with younger children. Still, they well remember the earlier strain between professional development and parenting and may deal with their residual guilt over choices and compromises by suggesting analytic treatment for their grown children. By comparing these different routes (as well as by observing other working women with whom we regularly have contact, such as our secretaries, nonanalyst colleagues, and children's teachers), we are reminded that balancing work and family is never easy. In what

Can We Be Both Women and Analysts?

ways, then, do the demands of analytic training and practice create special pressures?

The tripartite model of psychoanalytic training involves the simultaneous experience of a personal analysis, coursework, and supervised analyses, ideally with "immersion" in which three or more cases are seen concurrently (Morris, 1992). Often the control cases carry a reduced fee, which necessitates a double-time pace to reap the same financial rewards as noncandidate colleagues. How can we keep a straight face when considering these expectations in light of efforts to earn a living, advance professionally, raise young children with less than live-in help, engage in intimate relationships, and keep a household running? During the last decade, many institutes have become more flexible in allowing women to spread out the coursework and take cases sequentially (Morris, 1992). This "mommy track" has enabled training for women who would not have been able to have it otherwise. But those of us taking advantage of this opportunity still do not find it easy. The very slow progression makes us even more of a minority. More important, we continue to spend hours, over the span of months and years, brooding about when to take courses, how much income-producing professional work to take up or forgo, how many cases to accept, and how many, or which, hours will be left for our husbands and children.

We have painfully observed that once decisions about the external aspects of balancing analytic training, professional practice, and parenting have been made, the internal repercussions confront us. Like all working mothers, those of us choosing to do full training must cope with guilt about time spent away from young children. The intimate nature of analytic work, though, gives this guilt a unique complexion. To put this emotional conflict in bold relief, it is difficult to spend four hours a week thoughtfully playing games with a child analytic patient and then to rush through meals, play, homework, chores, and bedtime rituals with one's own children. It gets worse when our own children catch on to this discrepancy and ask pointed questions about it. Further reverberations come when child patients complain about their own day care arrangements, or adult patients report memories of separation or parental neglect. How can we not worry about our own mothering choices?

On the other hand, those of us choosing to train more slowly face the internal challenge of integrating insights about dynamics, transference, technique, countertransference, and analytic identity over the course of many years instead of just a few. Although there can be a richness in seeing analytic skills mature as we pass through our own and our children's developmental phases, the lost opportunity to compare and contrast reactions to several patients at once is not a trivial one (Morris, 1992). Those candidates who take cases sequentially are inevitably faced with countertransference fears that the patient will quit, and careful attention must be given to urges to keep the analysand happy. The difficult task of integrating analytic experience over many years can be amplified over time by changes within one's institute. As training analysts, teachers, and supervisors retire and age, we have noticed a sense that parts of our own clinical training can be lost as well. Aside from the symbolic implications of having a training experience of an "immersion" rather than a "sprinkling," the kind of analyst one becomes through these two paths is bound to be different.

But is that differentness rendered an inferior training experience? We believe it to be an achievement to develop and maintain a sense that the relative influence of "sprinkling" can be positive. Being "immersed" in the lives of our children and their friends can make us appropriately skeptical about established theories of development and the analytic relationship. Appreciating the complexities of children's real lives and the extent and subtlety of everyday interactions, encourages caution about too readily interpreting the unconscious and the impact of particular early experiences. At the same time, despite all the brooding and guilt, being an analyst can positively infuse our mothering. Our mastery of the balancing acts stokes confidence in capacities to problem-solve, integrate, work, and relate meaningfully. Acceptance of compromises and adjustments fuel flexibility in responding to our children's struggles with achievement and disappointment. And, of course, we do manage to teach what we know; it can be a joy when, after all the struggle, we find that our kids have become empathic, introspective individuals who make great dream interpretations and sometimes express a fleeting wish to become analysts themselves.

Can We Be Both Women and Analysts?

CONCLUSION

Through examining the juxtaposition between developing as women and developing as analysts, we have repeatedly arrived at the importance of synthesizing identities that are complex and generative. This is easier said than done considering the challenges of training, minority status, differentiating from parental identifications, expressing sexuality, maintaining family ties, forming an analytic identity, contributing to technical and theoretical advances, and achieving career progression. Each of these aspects of our experiences as women who provide psychoanalysis has the potential to pull us into mutually exclusive roles that fragment our sense of agency and relatedness. Our efforts to resolve both internal and external conflicts in these spheres of our lives may provide hooks on which to hang common perceptions of women analysts as erotic stimuli or containers for preoedipal deficits. But we feel that it is very important to realize that such attributions are clinical constructions about transference projections that fail to represent the intricacy of our efforts to build from our rich experiences as females, lovers, mothers, wives, and analysts. From this point we can look back to our dreamer and see in a different way her lonely plight, for as we reach to know ourselves as women analysts, the singing becomes our own.

REFERENCES

ABRAHAM, K. (1922). Manifestations of the female castration complex. *Int. J Psychoanal.*, 3:1–29.

APPLEGARTH, A. (1976). Some observations on work inhibitions in women. *J. Amer. Psychoanal. Assn.*, 24:251–268.

BASSEN, C. (1988). The impact of the analyst's pregnancy on the course of analysis. *Psychoanal. Inq.*, 8:280–298.

BLUM, H.P. (1994). The confusion of tongues and psychic trauma. *Int. J. Psychoanal.*, 75:871–882.

CHODOROW, N. (1989). *Feminism and Psychoanalytic Theory.* New Haven, CT: Yale Univ. Press.

COLARUSSO, C.A. & NEMIROFF, R.A. (1981). *Adult Development: A New Dimension in Psychodynamic Theory and Practice.* New York: Plenum.

DAVIES, J.M. (1994). Love in the afternoon: a relational reconsideration of desire and dread in the countertransference. *Psychoanal. Dial.*, 4:153–170.

EISSLER, K.R. (1983). *Victor Tausk's Suicide.* New York: Int. Univ. Press.

FENSTER, S., PHILLIPS, S.B. & RAPOPORT, E.R.G. (1986). *The Therapist's Pregnancy: Intrusion in the Analytic Space.* Hillsdale, NJ: Analytic Press.

FLIEGEL, Z.O. (1973). Feminine psychosexual development in Freudian theory: a historical reconstruction. *Psychoanal. Q.*, 42:364–384.
FREUD, S. (1908). On the sexual theories of children. *S. E.*, 9.
——— (1915), Observations on transference-love (Further recommendations on the technique of psycho-analysis III). *S. E.*, 12.
——— (1924). The dissolution of the Oedipus complex. *S. E.*, 19.
——— (1925). Some psychical consequences of the anatomical distinction between the sexes. *S. E.*, 19.
——— (1931). Female sexuality. *S. E.*, 21.
——— (1933). New introductory lectures on psychoanalysis. *S. E.*, 22.
——— (1935). Letter to Dr. Carl Müller-Braunschweig. *Psychiatry*, 34:329.
——— (1937). Analysis terminable and interminable. *S. E.*, 23.
FRIEDAN, B. (1963). *The Feminine Mystique*. New York: Norton.
GABBARD, G.O. (1994). Commentary on papers by M.J. Tansey, I. Hirsch, and J.M. Davies. *Psychoanal. Dial.*, 4:203–213.
——— & GABBARD, K. (1989). The female psychoanalyst in the movies. *J. Amer. Psychoanal. Assn.*, 37:1031–1049.
——— & LESTER, E. (1996). *Boundaries and Boundary Violations in Psychoanalysis*. New York: Basic Books.
GAY, P. (1988). *Freud: A Life for Our Time*. New York: Norton.
GOLDBERGER, M. & EVANS, D. (1985). On transference manifestations in male patients with female analysts. *Int. J. Psychoanal.*, 66:295–309.
HIRSCH, I. (1994). Countertransference love and theoretical model. *Psychoanal. Dial.*, 4:171–192.
HORNEY, K. (1924). On the genesis of the castration complex in women. *Int. J. Psychoanal.*, 5:50–65.
——— (1926). The flight from womanhood: the masculinity-complex in women, as viewed by men and by women. *Int. J. Psychoanal.*, 7:324–339.
JONES, E. (1927). The early development of female sexuality. *Int. J. Psychoanal.*, 8:459–472.
——— (1932). The phallic phase. *Int. J. Psychoanal.*, 14:1–33.
——— (1935). Early female sexuality. *Int. J. Psychoanal.*, 16:203–273.
——— (1957). *The Life and Work of Sigmund Freud*, Vol. 3. New York: Basic Books.
KANTER, R.M. (1977). *Men and Women of the Corporation*. New York: Basic Books.
KAPLAN, L. (1991). *Female Perversions: The Temptations of Emma Bovary*. New York: Doubleday.
KLEIN, M. (1928). Early stages of the Oedipus conflict. *Int. J. Psychoanal.*, 9:167–180.
——— (1932). *The Psychoanalysis of Children*. New York: Norton.
KOEDT, A. (1971). The myth of the vaginal orgasm. In *The Radical Therapist*. New York: Ballantine Books, pp. 127–138.
KULISH, N.M. (1984). The effect of the sex of the analyst on transference: a review of the literature. *Bull. Menninger Clin.*, 48:95–110.
——— (1986). Gender and transference: the screen of the phallic mother. *Int. Rev. Psychoanal.*, 13:393–404.

———— & MAYMAN, M. (1993). Gender-linked determinants of transference and countertransference in psychoanalytic psychotherapy. *Psychoanal. Inq.*, 13:286–305.

LERNER, H.E. (1976). Parental mislabeling of female genitals as a determinant of penis envy and learning inhibitions in women. *J. Amer. Psychoanal. Assn.*, 24(Suppl.):269–283.

LESTER, E.P. (1985). The female analyst and the erotized transference. *Int. J. Psychoanal.*, 66:283–293.

———— (1993). Boundaries and gender: their interplay in the analytic situation. *Psychoanal. Inq.*, 13:153–172.

MASTERS, W. & JOHNSON, V. (1966). *Human Sexual Response.* Boston: Little Brown.

MAYER, E.L. & DE MARNEFFE, D. (1992). When theory and practice diverge: gender-related patterns of referral to psychoanalysts. *J. Amer. Psychoanal. Assn.*, 40:551–583.

MCGOLDRICK, M. (1988). Women and the family life cycle. In *The Changing Family Life Cycle*, ed. B. Carter & M. McGoldrick. New York: Gardner Press, pp. 29–68.

MCGUIRE, W., Ed. (1974). *The Freud/Jung Letters: The Correspondence between Sigmund Freud and C.G. Jung.* Princeton, NJ: Princeton Univ. Press.

MENDELL, D. (1986). Cross-gender supervision of cross-gender therapy: female supervisor, male candidate, female patient. *Amer. J. Psychoanal.*, 46:270–275.

MILLET, K. (1973). Sexual politics: a manifesto for revolution. In *Radical Feminism.* New York: Quadrangle, pp. 365–267.

MORRIS, J. (1992). Psychoanalytic training today. *J. Amer. Psychoanal. Assn.*, 40:1185–1210.

MOULTON, R. (1986). Professional success: a conflict for women. In *Psychoanalysis and Women: Contemporary Reappraisals.* Hillsdale, NJ: Analytic Press, pp. 161–181.

RICHARDS, A.K. (1990). Female fetishes and female perversions: Hermine Hug-Hellmuth's "A case of female foot or more properly boot fetishism" reconsidered. *Psychoanal. Rev.*, 77:11–23.

TANSEY, M.J. (1994). Sexual attraction and phobic dread in the countertransference. *Psychoanal. Dial.*, 4:139–152.

WELLDON, E. (1991). Psychology and psychopathology in women—a psychoanalytic perspective. *Brit. J. Psychiat.*, 158:85–92.

WELLES, J.K. & Wrye, H.K. (1991). The maternal erotic countertransference. *Int. J. Psychoanal.*, 72:93–106.

WRYE, H.K. & WELLES, H.K. (1989). The maternal erotic transference. *Int. J. Psychoanal.*, 70:673–684.

Name Index

Aarons, E., 404
Abelin, E. L., 151, 460
Abelin, G., 277
Abelin-Sas, G., 208
Abraham, H. C., 512
Abraham, K., 182, 246, 253, 307, 308, 538
Abraham, R. D., 312
Abrams, S., 201
Adelson, E., 451
Adler, A., 36, 40
Aeschylus, 310
Agnati, L., 106
Ainsworth, M. D. S., 452
Akhtar, S., 147
Alavi, A., 109
Ames, D. W., 311
Amsterdam, B., 100
Andreas-Salomé, L., 243
Antony, L. M., 198n
Anzieu, D., 51, 53
Appignanese, L., 46, 51, 59
Applegarth, A., 147, 217, 544
Arlow, J. A., 210n
Arnold, S., 109
Aronson, M., 106
Atwood, G., 101
Austin, L., 312
Austrian, S., 404

Baker, S., 501
Balint, E., 119
Balsam, A., 404
Balsam, R. H., 404
Barglow, P., 150
Barnett, M. C., 146–147, 246, 285, 515
Bass, A., 241, 275, 337, 514, 522, 523
Bassen, C., 529
Bassin, D., 120, 175, 178, 274
Baudry, F., 26, 184
Beatty, W., 107

Bégoin, J., 124
Beiber, I., 503
Belenky, M. F., 218
Bell, A. I., 185
Bem, S., 223, 226
Benedek, T., 208n, 354–355, 375, 404
Benjamin, J., 25, 27, 99, 100, 101, 103–104, 161, 174, 175, 179, 182, 183, 218, 478n
Benveniste, E., 23
Berger, L. S., 24
Bergman, A., 100, 449, 450n
Bergman, M., 159, 173, 182
Bergmann, M. V., 211, 263, 275, 500
Berlin, S., 95
Bernheimer, C., 523
Bernstein, D., 120, 121, 122, 123, 174, 175, 208, 241, 246, 256, 257, 263, 290, 291, 330
Bernstein, I., 276
Bernstein, J., 108
Berry, J., 96
Bettelheim, B., 310–311
Beyene, Y., 353n
Bibring, G., 375, 404
Bion, W. R., 207, 376–377
Birksted-Breen, D., 124, 208
Blass, R., 103
Blatt, S., 103
Blechner, M. J., 499
Blehard, M. C., 452
Blier, R., 95, 98
Blos, P., 159, 185
Blum, H. P., 3, 11, 13, 52, 121, 135, 147, 150, 200, 262, 276, 355, 547
Boehlich, W., 24
Boehm, F., 173
Bollas, C., 397
Bonaparte, M., 73, 276, 308
Bornstein, B., 146

Name Index

Brabant, E., 204
Brakel, L. A., 201
Brambilla, E., 352
Brash, J. C., 243
Brauer, L., 533–534n
Braunschweig, D., 500
Brazelton, T. B., 451
Breen, D., 13, 16, 17, 123, 176, 278
Brenner, C., 135, 262, 292–294, 334
Breton, A., 73
Breuer, J., 54
Brierley, M., 513
Brill, A. A., 72
Brodie, K., 108
Bronson, E., 108
Brooks-Gunn, J., 100
Brown, L. M., 218
Brown, N., 174n
Brunswick, R. M., 41
Bullfinch, T., 304
Bullock, C., 147
Burch, B., 500, 501
Burgner, M., 119
Burton, A., 275–286
Butler, J., 25, 26, 500
Bygott, J., 97
Byne, W., 502
Byng-Hall, J., 397

Cardinal, L., 525
Cassidy, J., 452, 456n
Cath, S., 450n
Chamberlain, D., 377
Chasseguet-Smirgel, J., 25, 37, 39, 56, 120, 124, 206, 207, 217, 242, 246, 252, 256, 430
Chehrazi, S., 147, 288
Chertoff, J. M., 180
Chodorow, N., 27, 41, 71, 75, 77–79, 99, 101–103, 160, 161, 182, 216, 217, 220, 221, 223, 226, 229, 234, 277, 404, 496, 539–540, 541
Cintra, A., 106
Cixous, H., 71, 81, 84–85

Clark, C., 106, 108
Clinchy, B. M., 218
Clower, V. L., 99, 285, 335
Coates, S., 501
Coen, S., 498
Colarusso, C. A., 544
Constable, R. T., 109
Contratto, S., 221
Cournut, J., 120
Cournut-Janin, M., 120
Cramer, B., 451

Damasio, A., 274
Davies, J. M., 548
de Marneffe, D., 231
DeCasper, A. J., 377
De Lauretis, T., 495
DeMarneffe, D., 541
Desjardins, C., 108
Deutsch, H., 221, 262, 274, 308, 351, 352, 353, 375, 404, 493, 513
Devereux, G., 266
Dewald, P. A., 147
Dewey, J., 278
Dimen, M., 176, 216, 218, 226
Dinesen, I., 311–312
Dinnerstein, D., 101
Divale, W., 98
Dodge, A., 107
Doering, C., 106
Dove, R., 261
Downey, J., 112, 502
duBois, P., 275
Dwyer, T. F., 404
Dyk, R., 96

Eckstein, E., 52
Edgecumbe, R., 119, 500
Ehrhardt, A., 136, 148, 502
Eisenbud, R.-J., 494
Eissler, K. R., 548
Elam, D., 87
Eldredge, C. C., 133
Ember, C., 96
Emde, R., 100

Name Index

Erikson, E. H., 100, 120, 158, 159n, 171, 184, 274, 403, 430, 514
Evans, D., 404, 529

Fain, M., 500
Fairbairn, W. R. D., 101, 106
Faludi, S., 79
Falzeder, E., 204
Fast, I., 105, 158, 179–180, 224, 289, 290, 522
Faterson, H., 96
Feldman, J., 404
Fenster, S., 529
Ferenczi, S., 46, 55, 72, 204–205, 253–254, 547–548
Fine, B. D., 283–284
First, E., 177
Firth, R., 312
Flax, J., 101, 102, 103
Fliegel, Z. O., 25, 30, 34–35, 134, 539
Fliers, E., 106
Fliess, R., 53
Fliess, W., 51, 52–54, 55, 57, 58, 62, 203–204
Fonagy, P., 159
Formanek, R., 359
Forrester, J., 46, 51, 59
Foucault, M., 176
Fraiberg, S., 146, 285, 397, 451
Freedman, N., 186, 187
Freidan, B., 74, 540
Frenkel, R. S., 142, 144, 149, 150
Freud, A., 14, 33–34, 37, 46, 53
Freud, E. L., 54, 512
Freud, S., xi, 3, 5, 8, 12–19, 23–41, 45–66, 71–91, 94, 96, 99, 119, 120, 121n, 122–123, 133–134, 135, 136, 145, 149–151, 153, 172, 174–177, 179, 185, 191, 202–205, 206, 219, 221, 225, 226, 232, 242, 243, 247, 253, 256, 262, 274, 276, 285, 287, 288, 298, 305–307, 308, 329, 353, 356, 403, 404, 421, 423, 492–493, 502, 511–513, 515, 523, 525, 538, 539, 547–548
Friedman, L., 276
Friedman, R. C., 112, 501, 502, 503
Friedman, S. S., 65
Frommer, M. S., 503
Frye, M., 226
Furer, M., 458n
Furman, E., 431–435, 438–441, 443, 445, 446
Fuxe, K., 106

Gabbard, G. O., 545, 548
Gabbard, K., 545
Gaddini, E., 455
Gaddini, R., 455
Galatzer-Levy, R. M., 530n
Galenson, E., 100, 121, 122, 217, 219, 241, 254–255, 277, 286, 457n, 514
Gallop, J., 161, 183, 185
Garai, J., 95
Gardiner, M., 308
Gay, P., 548
Gerall, A., 107
Giampieri-Deutsch, P., 204
Gibeault, A., 122, 124
Gillespie, W. H., 119
Gilligan, C., 71, 75, 79–80, 96, 101, 105, 218
Gilmore, K., 275–286, 502
Gimbutas, M., 275
Glenn, J., 58, 276, 439
Goldberger, M., 263, 404, 529
Goldenberger, N. R., 218, 277
Goldfoot, D., 107
Goldner, V., 183, 218
Goodenough, D., 96
Gorski, R., 95, 106, 107
Goy, R., 107
Grand, S., 178
Green, A., 16
Greenacre, P., 241, 242, 254, 255, 276
Greenson, R. R., 101, 102
Grossman, L., 100

Name Index

Grossman, W. I., 27, 34–35, 120, 147, 173, 176, 183, 200, 206, 210, 273, 287, 515n, 516, 523, 526
Grunberger, B., 251n
Gunsberg, L., 450n
Gur, R. C., 109
Gur, R. E., 109
Gurwitt, A., 450n
Gustaffson, J.-A., 106

Haber, S., 107
Hägglund, T.-B., 430
Hägglund, V., 430, 431
Haladay, J., 108
Hamburg, D., 97
Hamer, D., 502
Hamilton, E., 275
Hanson, A. E., 304
Harfstrand, A., 106
Harris, A., 176, 185, 218
Harris, H., 352
Hartmann, H., 17
Heiman, M., 208n
Hershey, D. W., 182
Hielbrun, C. G., 223
Hirsch, I., 548
Hoffer, W., 440
Hoffman, I., 100
Hoffman, L., 276
Hopper, E. I., 396
Horney, K., 25, 27, 32, 34–35, 52, 72, 77, 94, 100, 123, 134, 143, 175, 210, 220, 263, 274, 285, 286, 287, 308, 330, 403, 430, 513, 516, 539
Hrdy, S., 97, 100, 102
Huntington, D. S., 404

Ikonen, P., 430
Irigaray, L., 25, 27, 71, 81, 85–88, 175, 217
Isay, R., 503

Jacklin, C., 95, 96, 98, 106, 223
Jacobsbon, E., 262

Jacobson, E., 159, 241, 248, 256–257, 283
Jaffe, D. S., 326
Jakobson, R., 80
Johnson, C., 95
Johnson, V., 136, 540
Jones, E., 25, 27, 32, 36, 40–41, 72, 123, 134, 172, 173, 175, 176, 181, 210, 263, 285, 289, 403, 493, 513, 516, 539
Jordan, J., 218
Joselyn, W., 108
Jung, C. G., 29–30, 36–37, 40, 548

Kaess, W., 96
Kagan, J., 95
Kahlo, F., xi, 2
Kakar, S., 234
Kalinich, L. J., 40, 201, 208, 514, 515
Kanter, R. M., 535n
Kanzer, M., 258
Kaplan, A., 218
Kaplan, D., 173, 176, 181, 184, 210, 526
Kaplan, L., 549
Kaplan, N., 452, 456n
Kapp, S., 96
Karlp, J., 109
Karme, L., 147, 287
Kass, D., xii, 510
Katan, A., 440
Keiser, S., 208n
Keller, E. F., 98, 101–105
Kemp, P., 312
Kernberg, O. F., 182–183, 200, 271, 500
Kestenberg, J. S., 100, 122, 146, 158, 175, 185–186, 208n, 217, 241, 245, 246, 253, 255–256, 285, 375, 403, 430, 443, 494, 514
Khan, M. M. R., 493
Kirkpatrick, M., 497, 500, 502
Klar, H., 147
Kleeman, J. A., 134, 136, 285, 405
Klein, M., 37, 40–41, 88, 104, 119–

Name Index

120, 121–122, 124, 180, 207, 263, 405, 513, 539
Koedt, A., 540
Kohlberg, 79
Kohut, H., 101
Kopala, L., 106, 108
Korner, A., 95, 98
Kotelchuck, M., 95
Kramer, P., 146
Kramer, S., 121, 147, 276, 287, 289
Krausz, R., 201n, 514, 518
Kris, E., 200
Kristeva, J., 71, 81, 85, 88–90
Kubie, L. S., 159–160, 192, 211, 290, 518, 522
Kuhn, T., 523
Kulish, N. M., 25, 327, 514, 541

Lacan, J., 18, 25, 27, 35, 39, 73, 80–86, 88, 120, 161, 177, 185, 207, 275, 495
Lamb, M. E., 148, 151
Lampl-de Groot, J., 30, 64
Lang, M., 106, 108
Laqueur, T., 24, 198, 403
Lasky, R., 159, 174, 183
Laufer, M. E., 119
Lax, R., 147, 193n, 201, 211, 263, 275, 283, 291–292, 351, 354, 500, 514
Lederer, W., 312
Lehmann, H., 45, 46
Lerner, H. E., 120, 299, 308–309, 404, 514, 519–520, 521, 525, 531–532, 533
Lesser, R. C., 499
Lester, E. P., 529, 541, 548
Levay, S., 502
Levenson, E., 100–101
Leventhal, B., 108
Levine, D. N., 312
Levine, H. B., 147
LeVine, R., 95
Levinson, N., 285, 492
Lévi-Strauss, C., 80

Lewin, B. D., 201, 245
Lewis, M., 95, 100
Lewis, S., 352
Loewald, H. W., 171, 174, 181
Lord, 175, 183
Lunberg, S., 500
Lupton, M. J., 327
Luquet-Parat, C., 276
Lynn, D., 101

MacArthur, R., 96
Maccoby, E., 106, 223
Maccoby, R., 95, 96, 98, 107
Mack-Brunswick, R., 404
MacLean, P., 107
MacLusky, N., 106
Mahler, M. S., 100, 101, 102, 200, 449–450, 457n
Maine, M., 452, 456n
Makari, G. J., 135
Malinowski, B., 312
Markowitz, R., 500
Martin, E., 234
Martin, J. R., 218
Masson, J. M., 52, 54, 57, 58, 62, 203
Masters, W., 136, 311, 540
May, R., 184
Mayer, E. L., 26, 100, 121–122, 135, 153, 202, 217, 223, 235, 241, 263, 274, 275, 290, 291, 326, 330, 333, 334, 352, 355, 402, 424–425, 512, 514, 515, 541
Mayman, M., 541
Mazur, A., 108
McClintock, M., 109
McDevitt, J. B., 200, 450n, 458n
McDougall, J., 39, 175, 192, 217, 493–494, 500, 501
McEwan, B., 106, 107
McGoldrick, M., 544–545
McGuire, W., 548
McKinlay, J., 352
McKinlay, S., 352
Meaney, M., 106, 107
Meltzer, D., 396

Name Index

Meluk, T., 206
Mendell, D., 175, 529, 541
Miller, J. B., 71, 75–77, 78, 79, 80, 95, 99, 101, 218
Miller, N. E., 359
Millet, K., 540
Mitchell, J., 25, 41, 119, 172, 217
Mitchell, S. A., 503
Money, J., 136, 148, 502
Montessori, M., 278
Moore, B. E., 206, 283–284
Mor, B., 305
Morgan, C., 500
Morris, J., 540, 551, 552
Moss, H., 98
Moulton, R., 544
Mozley, D., 109
Mozley, L., 109
Mueller, J., 285
Muller, J., 513
Muller-Braunschweig, C., 513
Myers, W. A., 499

Nadelson, C., 96, 98, 404
Naftolin, F., 106
Nemiroff, R. A., 544
Notman, M., 96, 98, 404
Notman, N., 352
Novey, S., 182
Noy, P., 180
Nunberg, H., 206, 326

Ogden, T. H., 103, 160, 180, 396, 397
O'Keeffe, G., xi, 133
Olesker, W., 264, 277, 498
Oliner, M., 73, 251n, 252
Oppenheim, M., xi, 22
Ovesey, L., 100, 175, 501, 503
Ovid, 309

Pappenheim, B., 54
Parens, H., 121, 276, 287, 288, 289
Park, R., 95
Partridge, E., 304

Paskauskas, R. A., 40
Penman, S. K., 303
Person, E. S., 100, 147, 175, 217, 223, 274, 497, 501, 503
Peters, E. L., 311
Peto, A., 416n
Phillips, A., 221
Phillips, S. B., 529
Phoenix, C., 107
Piaget, J., 278
Piha, H., 430
Pine, F., 100, 449
Pines, D., 119, 375, 404
Piontelli, A., 377
Poe, E. A., 304, 325, 360
Poland, W., 173
Pollock, L., 121, 276, 287, 289
Ponse, B., 497
Poulin, P., 106
Pugh, K., 109

Quinodoz, J., 262–263

Rado, S., 262
Rangell, L., 135, 151, 200, 292, 294–295, 298, 334
Rapaport, D., 179
Raphael-Leff, J., 374, 375, 377, 379, 381t, 386, 393, 395, 396, 404
Rapoport, E. R. G., 529
Rees, K., 276
Reich, A., 277
Reich, W., 159
Renik, O., 193, 333, 334, 356, 359
Resnick, S., 109
Richards, A. D., 200
Richards, A. K., 123, 149, 153, 201, 241, 242, 246–247, 274, 288–289, 330, 337, 403, 497, 500, 514, 521, 549
Ritvo, L. B., 513n
Ritvo, S., 403
Riviere, J., 36, 39
Robbins, M., 110, 112
Robins, E., 502

Name Index

Rogers, A. S., 218
Rogow, A. A., 61n
Roiphe, H., 100, 121, 122, 217, 219, 241, 254–255, 277, 286, 288, 356n, 457n, 514
Rose, G., 158, 180, 206
Rose, J., 27, 119, 217, 304
Rose, R., 108
Rosenblatt, A., 491
Rosenthal, M., 351
Ross, J., 101, 450n
Ross, N., 182, 503
Rossetti, C., 310

Saghir, M., 502
Salo, F., 500
Sampson, E., 101
Sappho, 309–310
Saussure, F. de, 80
Schaefer, M., 150
Schafer, R., 25, 55, 56, 59n, 220, 221, 223, 287
Schenfeld, A., 95
Schilder, P., 178
Schuker, E., 285, 492
Schwartz, D., 499
Seeman, M., 106, 108
Segal, H., 167, 180
Serebriany, R., 206
Shakespeare, W., 65–66
Shapiro, V., 451
Sharpe, E. F., 523
Sharpe, S., 491
Shaw, R. R., 193, 515, 521–522
Shaywitz, B., 109
Shaywitz, S., 109
Shea, J., xi–xii, 70
Shengold, L. L., 47, 201, 223, 246, 247
Sherwin, B., 108
Shopper, M., 403
Siegel, E. V., 494
Silver, D., 25
Simon, B., 147
Sissa, G., 304, 305

Sjoo, M., 305
Skudlarski, P., 109
Slaby, R., 95
Slap, J. W., 201
Smith, K., xii, 240
Socarides, C., 493, 494, 503
Soll, M. H., 193
Spelke, E., 95
Steele, B. F., 148
Stepansky, P. E., 36
Stern, D., 103, 216, 451
Stern, J., 121, 276, 287, 289
Stettheimer, F., xii, 484
Stewart, J., 106
Stewart, W. A., 120, 147, 273, 287, 515n, 516, 523
Stiver, I., 218
Stoller, R. J., 15, 16, 17, 100, 101, 121, 135, 136, 263, 287, 334, 355, 405, 494, 501, 502, 513
Stolorow, R., 101
Stone, L., 63
Streisand, B., xii
Sullivan, H. S., 100
Surrey, J., 218
Swaab, D., 106

Tansey, M. J., 548
Tarule, J. M., 218
Tawney, L., xii, 372
Thompson, C., 72, 77, 94, 220, 285
Ticho, E. A., 200
Tobias, C., 352
Tolman, D., 218
Torok, M., 287
Torsti, M., 208, 430
Trevarthan, C., 216
Turkle, S., 86
Tustin, F., 396, 441
Tyler, I., 96
Tyson, P., 14, 18, 100, 110, 121, 147, 151, 153, 217, 277, 286, 288, 289–290, 330, 334, 405, 429, 430, 500, 502, 516, 519
Tyson, R. L., 14, 147, 151, 153, 277,

Name Index

334, 405, 500, 502

Upton, L. G., 404
Uyehara, A., 404

Valenstein, A. F., 404
van Lawick-Goodall, J., 97
Vygotsky, 278

Waelder, R., 523
Wall, S., 452
Warner, R. H., 404
Waters, E., 452
Weinraub, M., 95
Welldon, E., 274, 549
Welles, J. K., 504, 541
White, R., 179
Wilkinson, S. M., 289, 514
Williamson, R. A., 404

Winnicott, D. W., 25, 103, 105, 172, 174, 175, 177, 178, 185, 216, 220, 381–382, 388, 440, 444
Wisdom, J. O., 173, 185, 198
Witelson, A., 107
Witkin, H., 96
Witryol, S., 96
Witt, C., 198n
Wolfe, S., 501
Wolfflin, H., xii
Wolfson, A., 497, 502
Wolpert, L., 378
Wrye, H. K., 504, 541

Yates, S. L., 307, 308, 326
Young-Bruehl, E., 25, 33–34, 47, 71n, 90, 403, 523

Zelazo, P., 95
Zoli, M., 106

Subject Index

Access
 concept of, 263, 291
 fear of losing, 291–292
Active, renunciation of, 32–34
Active/passive polarity, 28–31
 sexual pleasure and, 31–36
Addiction, masturbation as, 57
Adolescence, female, 77
Aggression
 gender differences in, 95–96
 of girl toward mother, 49–50
 hormonal control of, 107–108
 male versus female, 97–98
 in oedipal situations, 41
 oral, 49–50, 194–195, 493
 in primate cultures, 97
 renunciation of, 38–39
 role in mental life of, 36–39
 variances in, 219
Aggressive drive derivatives, 28
Agoraphobia, 142–143
Altruistic surrender, 33–34, 35
American Psychoanalytic Association, women analysts in, 530–553
Amphimixis, 253–254
Amygdala, 107–108
Anal conflict, 138–139
 talion fears from, 256–257
Anal/genital function, 241–258
Anal-vaginal connection, 244–258
Analysts
 gender of, 540–541
 women's experience becoming, 529–553
Analytic dyad
 boundaries in, 547–548
 invasion of, by fetus, 394
Analytic process, defloration as metaphor for, 329
Anatomy. *See also specific bodily parts*
 as destiny, 14, 122–123
 in ego functions, 120–121
 incomplete knowledge of female, 308–309
 sexual, 232–234
 sexuality and, 177–178
Androgens, 108
Anna O case, 54
Anthropological studies, 97
Anxiety
 erotization of, 340–341
 over bodily sensations, 348–349
Archaic maternal enigma, 88–89
Art, women's image in, xi–xii
Assertiveness, gender differences in, 95–96
Attachment, failure of, 148–149
Autistic pathology, 441
Autonomy
 defensive, 171
 dynamic and static, 104
 goal of, 76
 primary, 17

Baby. *See also* Infant; Mother-infant unit
 conceptualizations of, 396–397
 fantasy, 380
 good enough, 381–382
 including in mother's body ego, 439–440
 incorporation of, 380–381
 response to death of, 432–433
 second, 461–462
 wish for, 414–417
Baby dolls, 443–444
Baby envy, 149–150
Beating fantasy, 33
Behavior
 differences in, 97–98
 hormonal effects on, 107
Being-in-relationship, 76–77
Biological essentialism, 84

Subject Index

Biological reductionism, 94–95
Bisexual core, 191
Bisexual fantasy, 191, 192, 290–291
  in genital phase, 182–183
  universality of, 203–204
Bisexuality, 159–160
  creativity and, 192, 500
  current understanding of, 7–8
  dichotomizing of, 175
  metaphors of mind and, 191–212
  mourning loss of, 180–181
  need to renounce, 179–180
  of parental couple, 6, 7
Bleeding. *See also* Menstruation
  from broken hymen, 321–324
  in life cycle, 357
Bodily functions, ownership of, 434–435, 444–445
Bodily sensation
  in early female development, 347–349
  masturbation fantasies and, in prelatency girl, 334–349
  role in mental functioning, 274
Body
  activity of, 179
  changing with pregnancy, 409–412
  in female gender identity, 334
  imaginative elaboration of, 177
  mastery over, 249
  in sexual development, 232–234
  as source of pleasure, 278–279
  specificity of, 405
  transfer of ownership from mother to child, 434–435
Body ego. *See also* Female body ego; Maternal body ego
  boys' versus girls', 443–445
  child as part of, 431
  containing function of, 178–179
  delineating and investing one's own, 440–443
  father in development of, 445
  implications for later development of, 445–446
  as origin and container for symbolization, 177–180
  overinclusive representation of, 158–159, 160, 186–187
  relation to body, 177–178
  symbolic transformation of, 157–187
Body image. *See also* Female body image
  male influences regarding, 412–414
  pregnant maternal body in, 401–425
  role in mental functioning, 274
Boundaries
  in analytic relationship, 547–548
  body ego, 443–446
  changeable, 443–444
Bowel control, 244
Brain
  gender differences in, 105–111
  hemispheric functioning of, 109
  organization of, 105–107
Breast(s)
  envy of, 149–150
  fantasy of, 225
  in gender identity, 233

Caesarean section, 394
Cantus firmus, 451
Castration
  acceptance of, 173–174
  as central conflict, 298
  confusion in meaning of, 290–291
  definition of, 283
  fantasy of, 5
  memorial to, 181
  theme of, xii
Castration anxiety, 219, 257, 277
  bisexuality and, 159–160
  in boys, 151
  definition of, 283–284
  versus feminine genital anxiety, 283–300

Subject Index

in femininity, 262
in girls, 293–294
hymen and, 314–315
in menopause, 352
Castration complex, 120, 516
  cultural significance of, 81–82
  in feminine development, 34, 121
  phallic versus female, 355–360
  remobilized, 366
Castration loss, 263
Castration shock, 276
Central nervous system, sex-specific differentiation of, 105–106
Child. See also Mother-child unit
  developmental loss of, 433–438
  as part of mother's body ego, 431
  response to death of, 432–433
Childbearing capacity, loss of, 358
Childbirth, blood of, 323–324
Circumscribed space, in boys' body ego, 444–445
Clitoris, 134, 153
  denial of, 519
  importance of, 274
  shape of, 243
Cloacal genital fantasy, 253–254, 321
Cognitive development levels, 179–180
Collective identity models, 100–105
Completeness, longing for. See Bisexuality; Cross-sex representations
Compromise formation, 284
  psychic function of, 293
Conflict-free sphere, 17
Conformity, 172–173
Congenital abnormalities, 394
Connectivity, 220
Constitutional factors
  versus cultural factors, 97
  gender differences and, 110–111
Containers, filling, 443
Containment, procreative, 376–379
Core gender identity, 109–111, 121, 334, 405

in female development, 148–149
as frame for self-identity, 175
for girls, 430
polarization of, 186–187
in psychoanalysis, 100
Counterculture, 540
Countermode, 160, 171–172
Countertransference bias, heterosexual, 502–504
Couple, dynamics of, 182–183
Covering up, xi–xii
Creativity
  bisexuality and, 192
  transcending difficulty, 166–167
Critical periods, 106
Cross-gender transference, 180–181
Cross-sex representations, 158–159
  complexities of, 161–187
  in genital phase, 182–183
  integration and reconciliation of, 157–158, 174–177
  mastery and symbolic use of, 186–187
Cultural bias, 94–95
  in behavioral studies, 98
Cultural norms, 172
Culture
  assumptions about women of, 220–223
  versus constitutional effects, 97
  in gender, 222–223
  relating to gender, 95–96
  sexual differences in founding of, 81–82

Defloration
  anxiety about, 329–330
  of bride, 305
  classical-literary and anthropological writings on, 309–312
  in clinical material, 312–324
  masochistic character of, 308
  meaning for men versus women, 326–328
  menstruation and, 307

Subject Index

psychoanalytic literature on, 305–309
psychological meaning of, 303–330
rituals representing, 306n, 307
symbols of, 306
taboo of, 306–307
triggering aggression, 38–39
Demeter myth, 309
Depression
  fear of, 124
  with menopause, 351–352, 353, 354–355, 364–366
Depressive affect, 292–293
Depressive stage, 180–181
Desire, polymorphic nature of, 86
Development
  female. *See* Female development
  male model of, 5
  maternal role in, 429–430
In a Different Voice (Gilligan), 79
Differentiation, separation-individuation and, 103–105
Diffusivity, 291
Dora case, 38, 46
  Freud as phallic woman in, 203n
  Freud's analysis of, 56–62
Dreams, mystery of, 198–199
Duty, 79
Dyadic relationship, 99. *See also* Mother-infant unit

Early life experience, female, 6–7
Ego
  anatomy and physiology in function of, 120–121
  boundaries in girls versus boys, 78–79
  homosexuality and, 503
  primary autonomy of, 17
Ego psychology, 16–17
Electra complex, 37
Engagement, permeability to, 373
Erotic masturbation fantasy, 335–337

Essentializing, 219–220
Estrogen, 106
Exhibitionism, 520–521
External world/body ego relationship, 178–179

Fairy tales, defloration theme in, 310–311
Family relationships, gendered meanings in, 230–231
Fantasy. *See also* Masturbation fantasy; Unconscious fantasy
  body ego and, 179
  in menopause, 357–358, 361–362
Father
  absence of, 456–457
  anal, 494
  death of, 46–47
  in developing own body ego, 445
  gender identity from, 231
  gestation and, 378
  girl's bodily experience and, 519
  of homosexual girl, 488, 490, 491–492
  identification with, 459–460
  rejection of, 462–463
  of women analysts, 543
Female bodily experience, 519–520
Female body comparisons, 418–421, 422–425
Female body ego, 175–176. *See also* Body ego; Maternal body ego
  nature of, 438–440
Female body image
  genital issues in, 403
  literature related to, 402–405
Female characteristics, 99–100
  maturity and, 101
Female development, 4–5
  body image in, 402–405
  challenge to Freudian theory of, 355–356
  core gender identity and primary femininity in, 148–149
  evolution of theory of, 285–286

Subject Index

Freud's theory of, 538–539
 phallocentric view of, 133–134
Female embodiedness, 219–220
Female eroticism, 500–501
Female gender identity, 16
 core, 100–105
 primary, 99
Female gender studies, 405
Female genital anxiety. *See also* Genital anxiety
 versus castration anxiety, 283–300
 versus penis envy, 285–286
 types of, 291–292
 underpinnings of, 291
Female genitality, 181–184
Female genitals
 in body image, 403
 denial of, 514
 early interest in, 519–520
 fantasies about, 227
 fear of damage to, 273, 283–284, 513, 516
 functions of, 274
 male fear of, 275–276
 "missing," 129–130
 naming, 525
 parental mislabeling of, 531–532
 shapes of, xi
 uncertainty about, 521–522
Female homosexuality
 historical views of dynamics of, 492–495
 multiple meanings of, 496–497
Female life cycle, 404
Female psychology
 cultural assumptions in, 220–223
 early literature on, 512–513
 early theories of, 3–4
 epistemology of, 215–236
 versus female sexuality, 4, 13–14
 feminism and, 540
 Freud's theory of, 538–539
 genital anxiety in, 261–279
 interest in, 11–12
 introduction to, 11–19
 mother-daughter relationship in, 229–230
 progress of, 3–9
 recent literature on, 513–515
 women's liberation movement in, 286–287
Female sexuality
 blaming mothers for ignorance about, 324, 327
 versus female psychology, 4, 13–14
 Freud on, 12, 13–14, 47–66, 71–72, 134
 penis envy in, 204–205
 pleasure-oriented, 34–35
 in theory versus clinical practice, 511–526
 in topographical framework, 16
Feminine
 nature of, 87
 repudiation of, 45–66
The Feminine Mystique (Friedan), 74
Feminine subjectivity, 23–41
Feminine-passive equation, 287
Femininity
 aggression in, 37–39
 anatomy and physiology in, 121–123
 associated with object and passivity, 29–31, 40
 bedrock, 430
 British psychoanalytic theory on, 119–120
 dual aspect of, 123–130
 essence of, 219–220
 French psychoanalytic theory on, 120
 genital anxiety and, 261–279
 lack of sexual pleasure in, 31–36
 male fear of, 276–277
 personal constructions of, 224–235
 positive, 176
 in postoedipal female mind, 157–187

Subject Index

primary, 6–7, 26, 121–122, 148–149, 219–220, 261–279, 333–349, 355–356, 513–515, 524–526
repudiation of, 123–124
secondary, 25–26
sense of, 15–16
theories of, 17–18
in transference-countertransference, 234–235
transitionality of, 181–184
unconscious representation of, 119–130
U.S. psychoanalytic theory on, 120–121
Feminist critique, 216
Feminist movement, 74
Feminist psychoanalytic theory, 71–91
in France, 80–90
in United States, 74–80
Fertility, xii
power of, 275–276
Fertility goddesses, 11
Fetus, influence of, 377
Folklore, female psychology in, 11
Freud-Jones debate, 119
Friendship, fending off intimacy, 270–272
Frigidity, 308
factors in, 305–306
fear of, 262
Fusional maternal presence, 84–85

Gender
categorizations of, 231
as character, 184
constructing subjective, 228–235
data relating culture to, 95–96
essentializing about, 219–220
false universalizing about, 219–220
generalizations about, 218–219
inner object world in, 229–232
language and culture in, 222–223
observed versus subjective, 224–228
prevalent animations of, 234–235
sexual anatomy in, 232–234
sexuality and genitals in, 221–222
theoretical and clinical, 215–236
universalistic claims about, 216–217
variances in, 219
Gender differences
in body ego, 443–445
cultural influences in, 97–98
feminist view of, 75–77
generalizations about, 218–219
linguistic, 81–84
in moral development, 79–80
neurobiology of, 105–109
psychoanalytic studies of, 98–105
variations in, 223
Gender identity, 7–8, 17–18. *See also* Core gender identity; Female gender identity; Femininity; Masculinity
core, 109–111, 121
cultural assumptions about, 221–223
female, 16
fluidity of, 500
genital sensation and sphincter control in, 288–289
lines of development in, 333–334
nature versus nurture in, 93–112
personally constructed sense of, 15–16
polar, 183–184
polarization of, 186–187
renunciation of overinclusiveness and, 179–180
Gender identity disturbance, 494
influences of, 501–502
preoedipal, 495
Gender overinclusiveness, 176–177
Gender role, 405
cultural normative, 172–173
flexibility of, 173
rigid, 184

Subject Index

versus sexual object choice, 501–502
Gendered theories, 539–540
Gender-prejudicial model, 102
Generalizations, 218–219
Genital anxiety
versus castration anxiety, 283–300
future research on, 276–278
hymen and, 318–319
manifest fears in, 263–264
primary femininity and, 261–279
types of, 291–292
upward displacement of, 320
Genital injury
fear of, 278, 294–295
in oedipal fantasy, 342–343
Genital pain, 278
Genital pleasure
body as source of, 278–279
in female self-esteem, 277–278
loss of, 268–273
renunciation of, 278
Genital sensation
in female gender identity, 288–289
girls' awareness of, 513–515
role in mental functioning, 274
Genital sexuality, guilt over, 154
Genital stage
classical conception of, 181–182
early, 122
male, 184–186
Genital structures
inner versus outer, 185–186
integration of, 7
Genitality
female, 181–184
in terms of life tasks, 159n
Genitals. *See also* Female genitals; *specific organs*
denial of differences in, 523
in female body image, 403
fused male and female, 198
in gender, 221–222
hormonal effects on, 105–106

infantile, 253, 287–288
inner, 122, 200–201
mother's reaction to differences in, 404–405
in subjective gender, 232–234
Genitourinary organs, 242–243
Geodes, 396
Gestation. *See also* Pregnancy
fetal influence in, 377
parental input on, 378
Gestation drive, 85
Greek mythology
female psychology in, 11–12
Hymen in, 304
Guilt, 138
hymen and, 321
incorporation, 120
over genital sexuality, 154

Hermaphrodite, 203
Hermaphroditic omnipotence, 160
Heterosexual drive, 120
Heterosexuality
idealization of, 502–503
variety of, 160
Hilda Doolittle case, 65–66
Homosexual wish, 165
Homosexuality. *See also* Lesbian patients
in Dora case, 62
female, 32–35, 62–65, 485–505
mother-child relationship in, 64–66
Hormonal effects, 105–109
Hormonal feedback loops, 107
Hormone replacement therapy, 360
Humanism, lyrical, 89–90
Husband
abusive, 264–265
hostility toward, 248–249
Hymen
bisexual meaning of, 326
blood from breaking of, 311–312
castration anxiety in men and, 314–315

Subject Index

genital anxiety and vulnerability and, 318–319
in Greek myth, 304
knowledge of, by ancient scholars, 304–305
loss of virginity and, 303–330
masturbation guilt and, 321
meaning of, for women versus men, 326–328
menstruation and childbirth blood and, 323–324
mother role and, 321–323
positive oedipal themes and, 313–314
protection and thresholds in women and, 319–321
in psychoanalytic literature, 306–307
sadomasochism in men and, 315–318
Hypothalamus, development of, 107–108
Hysteria, 137–142
bisexual nature of, 191
Freudian theory of, 12–13

Identity fusion, 103–104
Incorporation fantasy, 244–258, 248–249
Infant. *See also* Baby; Mother-infant unit
early interactions of, 451
fusion by, 383, 384
mother's representations of, 451–452
Infantile genital stage, 158–159
Infantile genitals
cloacal/anal shadowing of pleasure in, 253
organization of, 287–288
Infantile sexuality, 40–41
Infertile couples, 376
Inner genitals
in psychosexual development, 200–201

sensations of, 122
Inner object world, 229–232
Inner space
fear of damage to, 196–197
protective feelings about, 518
in role of motherhood, 430
Instinctual drive
in changing object choice, 152–153
importance of, 136–154
vicissitudes of, 144–146
Integration, new models of, 174–177
Internal agency, 24–25
Internalization, early mother-daughter relationship, 453–481
Intersubjectivity, 100–105
mature, 103
Intimacy, fending off, 270–272
Intrapsychic conflict, infant, 147–148
Introitus, denial of, 245
Irma dream, 50–54

"Jane Eyre" fantasy, 225
Joissance, 83
Jones-Horney-Freud debates, 134

Kore, 309

Language
defensive use of, 210
in gender, 222–223
in gender identity, 231
in learning, 278–279
poetic, 89
semiotics of, 88–89
sexual differences in, 81–84
Learning, language-mediated, 278–279
Lesbian(s)
analytic understanding of, 485–505
character structure of, 486–487
father and, 488, 490, 491–492
gay identity of, 485

Subject Index

lifestyle of, 496–497
mother and, 487–489
primary, 497
Libido
 female, 5, 512–513
 feminine and, 31–32
 masculinity and, 28, 31
 menopause and development of, 353–354
 psychic life and, 14–15
 theory of, 135, 136
Life tasks, 159n
Linguistic signifiers, 82
Linguistic theory, 81–84
Literature, defloration theme in, 309–311
Little Hans case, 30, 46
 phobia in, 36
Love loss, 151

Male dominance, mothering and, 78–79
Male gender identity
 genitality and transitionality in, 184–186
 primal conflict in, 102
Male genitalia, metaphorical representation of, 191–212
Male institute, females in, 530–533
Male-dominated society, 94
Masculine characteristics, 99–100
Masculine psychology, 25–26
Masculine sexuality
 acceptance of female aspects of, 185
 genitality and transitionality in, 184–186
Masculine-active equation, 287
Masculinity
 associated with subject and activity, 28–31, 40
 essence of, 219–220
 libido and, 28
 personal constructions of, 224–235

 in postoedipal female mind, 157–187
 primary nature of, 25
 sense of, 15–16
 sexual pleasure and, 31–36, 40
 transitionality of, 181–184
Mastery model, 174
Masturbation
 beating fantasies and, 33
 in girls, 133–134
 hymen and guilt with, 321, 327
 as "primary addiction," 57
Masturbation fantasy, 145
 erotic, 335–337
 in prelatency girl, 333–349
Maternal body ego
 child as part of, 432–446
 defense against loss of, 432–438
 nature of, 438–440
Maternal enigma, 88–89
Maternal imago, powerful, 430–431
Maternal-phallic stage, 256
Mature event-centered thought, 180
Men
 generalizations about, 218–219
 repudiation of feminine in, 45–66
Menarche, 357–358
Menopause
 in clinical example, 360–368
 depression in, 364–366
 depression with, 351–352, 353, 354–355
 dream themes during, 362–365
 emotional effects of, 359
 mourning loss in, 364–368
 psychoanalytic view of, 351–368
 puberty and, 353–354, 356–357
 reluctance to discuss, 359–360
 sexual fantasy in, 361–362
 theoretical basis of revised view of, 355–360
 traditional view of, 352–355
Menstruation
 defloration and, 307
 hymen and, 323–324

Subject Index

hymeneal blood and, 312
Mental life, aggressive, 36–39
Mentoring, 545–546
Merging, defense against, 494
Metaphorical placenta, 397
Metaphors, bisexual fantasy and, 192–212
Mickey and the Night Kitchen, 261
Mind
  metaphors of, 192–212
  as mirror of genital anatomy, 200
  normal, 172–174
Minority status, 533–538
Mirroring relatedness, 102
Miscarriage, 394
Moral development, female, 79–80
Mother
  attachment of, to own mother, 452
  bad, 387
  betrayal by, 296
  blaming, for lost sexuality, 324, 327
  bodily integrity of, 439
  bodily investment in child, 432–446
  capacity for changeable boundaries of, 443–444
  child as part of body ego of, 431
  conflicting images of, 328
  cultural assumptions about, 221
  death of, 45–46
  domineering, 406
  effects on children, 404–405
  emotional unavailability of, 471–472
  empowered, 275–276
  fear of destruction by, 138–139
  as first object of identification, 429–430
  gender identity from, 231
  girl's attachment to, 48–49
  good enough, 381–382, 550–553
  of homosexual girl, 487–488
  hymen and role of, 321–323
  identification with, 460
  intensified identification with, 358
  interfering with development of own body ego, 440–443
  joissance of, 89
  latent reference to, 422
  narcissistic investment in child's body, 442–443
  oral aggression toward, 49–50, 493
  phallic, 275, 315
  physicality of, 421
  pregnant, 401–425
  preoccupation of, 408–409
  preoedipal relation to, 48–49
  projecting negative feelings about child, 467–468, 469
  representation of child, 454–455
  repudiating, 102, 123–124
  response to death of baby, 432–433
  response to developmental loss of child, 433–438
  retiring in favor of, 63
  role of, 78–79
  smothering love of, 388–389
  symbolic phallic penetration of, 51
  of women analysts, 542–543
Mother-child unit
  developing body ego and, 441–443
  in homosexuality, 64–66
Mother-daughter bond, 12
Mother-daughter comparison, 409–412
Mother-daughter relationship, 261
  destructive, 474–475
  in female psyche, 229–230
  of homosexual girl, 488–489
  internalization and development of, 449–481
  loss of, 364–366
  as primary, 7
Motherhood, xii, 274
  central role of, 429–446

Subject Index

innate wish for, 34
Mother-infant bond
  physiological system in, 374–375
  systems in, 374
Mother-infant therapy, 396–398
Mother-infant unit
  good-bad split of, 390–391
  mother's representations in, 451–452
  mutually dangerous, 389–390
  symbiotic, 450
Mothering, 78–79
Mourning
  in menopause, 364–368
  with menopause, 354
Mythology
  defloration in, 309–311
  female psychology in, 11–12
  Hymen in, 304

Narcissistic loss, 491
Narcissistic pathology, 494
Narcissistic-genital stage, 277
Neurobiology, of gender difference, 105–109
Neuroconstitutional factors, 110–111
Nothing, concept of, 201–203
Nurturing, lack of, 491–492

Object choice. *See also* Sexual object choice
  difficulties with, 142–144
  exclusive homosexual, 55n
  instinctual drives in, 152–153
  in oedipal phase, 150–151
  in women, 133–154
Object loss, memorials to, 180–181
Object relations
  homosexuality and, 503
  in modifying instinctual drives, 144–146
  mother's body in, 405
Oedipal anxiety, 328
Oedipal configuration, universality of, 206–207
Oedipal conflict, 462–463
  in early female development, 347–349
  female homosexuality and, 492–493
  positive, 60
Oedipal fantasy, unresolved, 294
Oedipal phase
  object choice in, 150–151
  perineal sphincter in, 257
  resolution of, 161
Oedipus complex, 40
  bisexuality and, 8, 175
  centrality of, 88
  in girls, 37
  hymen and, 313–314
  origin in girls, 134
One-sex theory, 403
Openness
  breaking of hymen and, 318–319
  fear of loss of, 275
Oral aggression
  female homosexuality and, 493
  of girl toward mother, 49–50
  representations of, 194–195
Oral conflict, 138–139
Orestes, 310
Organizational models, new, 174–177
Orgasm, capacity for in girls, 146–147
Other
  discovery of repressed in, 182–183
  imaginative elaboration of, 158–159
Overinclusive body-ego representation, 158–159, 160, 176–177, 186–187
Overinclusive gender representation, need to renounce, 179–180

Parents. *See also* Father; Mother
  gender identity from, 231

Subject Index

identification with, in women analysts, 542–547
influence on gestation, 378
Passive fantasy, 29
Passivity, struggle against, 55–56
Penetration, 291
  fear of, 513
  painful, 262–263, 264–267, 273, 308
Penis
  aggressive, destructive attitude toward, 265–266
  in gender identity, 233
  illusory, 284, 292
  in inner sexual development, 201
  in masturbation fantasies, 344–345
  missing, 341–342
Penis envy, 5, 119, 219, 220, 227
  as bedrock of female sexuality, 204–205, 262, 286, 511, 513
  in boys and girls, 149–150
  as compromise formation, 293
  defensive, 521–522
  definition of, 283–284
  denial of, 516–517
  in female object choice, 133–154
  in feminine development, 120–121
  versus feminine genital anxiety, 285–286
  integrating with primary femininity, 525–526
  as pathological, 147
  phallic identification and, 289–290
  as phallus envy, 124
  reluctance to give up, 523–524
  as secondary defense, 134, 142–144
  social reinforcement of, 285
Perceptual-spatial abilities, 96
Perforation complex, 308
Perinatal complications, 394
Perinatal therapy, 393–395, 397

Perineal activity, 241–258
Perineal sphincter fantasy, 246–247, 251–258
Persephone myth, 12, 309
Personality
  cultural influence on, 95–96
  female versus male, 93–112
  modal female, 93
  modal male, 93
  relationship model of, 100–105
Phallic castration complex, 290
Phallic identification, 289–290
Phallic monism, 120
  controversy over, 430
  defensive, 430–431
Phallic order, 160–161
Phallic phase, 26, 290
Phallic symbol, 195
Phallic woman, 6, 290
Phallicism, 85
  as denial of sexual differences, 86
Phallocentric theory
  reification of, 523
  rejection of, 511–512
Phallocentrism, 5, 75
Phallus, 124
  as anatomic term, 208n
  castration of inner, 320–321
  fear of loss of, 283–284
  fecal, 494
  as linguistic signifier, 82
  penis and, 85
  as power, 207–208
Phallus envy, 124
Placental exchange, 376–379
  in therapeutic process, 398
Placental paradigm, 373, 379–393
Pleasure
  fear of losing, 263, 268–273
  indirect, 33–34
  renouncing direct, 32–34
Pluto, 309
Poetic language, 89
Poetics, 88
Postoedipal psyche, masculinity and femininity in, 157–187

Subject Index

Powers of Horror (Kristeva), 88–89
Pregnancy
  ambivalence toward, 380–381
  in analysis, 8
  denial of negative feelings about, 382–383
  emotional turbulence during, 379–380
  in gender identity, 233
  hymenal bleeding and, 323–324
  "illness" with, 51–52
  monotypic vision during, 393
  perinatal psychoanalytic treatment and, 393–395
  placental paradigm and, 379–393
  postnatal psychoanalytic treatment and, 396–398
  procreative containment and, 376–379
  procreative systems in, 373–376
  self-doubts during, 394–395
  symbolic representations of, 196–197
Pregnant mother
  in body image of daughter, 401–425
  literature related to, 402–405
Prelatency masturbation fantasies, 333–349
Preoedipal conflict, 149
Preoedipal phase
  homoerotic feeling in, 494–495
  unconscious conflicts of, 136–154
Primal scene
  enactment of, 346
  identification of members of, 54–55
Primal-scene couple, fused, 207
Primary femininity, 6–7, 26, 121–122, 148–149, 219–220, 261–279, 355–356
  acceptance of, 333
  expanding ideas of, 513–515
  female body fantasy conflicts and, 333–349

shifting to focus on, 524–526
Primary maternal persecution, 386–387
Primary maternal preoccupation, 381–382
Primate society, 97
  same-sex relationships in, 102
Procreative container, 373
Procreative containment, 376–379
Procreative systems, 373–376
Progesterone, 108
Psyche, art trends and, xi–xii
Psychic conflict, 25–26
Psychoanalysis
  birth of, 54–55
  development of, 8
  of expectant couples, 376
  feminist critique of, 216
  in France, 73, 80–90
  gender differences in models of, 98–105
  perinatal, 393–395
  postnatal, 396–398
  of pregnant women, 375–376
  in United States, 72, 74–80
Psychoanalytic constitutionalists, 94
Psychoanalytic theory
  American and French traditions of, 71–91
  feminist, 71–91
  menopause in, 351–368
Psychosexual development
  of girls versus boys, 242–244
  perineal activity in, 241–258
Puberty, 353–354, 356–358

Rapprochement, positive, 470
Rapprochement crisis, 458–459, 468–469, 476
  regressive recall of, 463
Rectal-vaginal sensations, 244–255
Relational psychoanalysis, 217–218
Relationships. *See also* Mother-child unit; Mother-daughter relationship; Mother-infant unit

577

Subject Index

in femininity, 220
moral development and, 80
need for, 77–79
orientation toward, 76, 77, 96, 100–105
same-sex, 102
The Reproduction of Mothering (Chodorow), 77–78
Reproductive function, fear of losing, 263–264
Responsibility, 79
Rituals, 11–12

Sadomasochism
  hymen and, 315–318
  perineal sphincter control and, 244–258
Schizophrenia, genetic factors in, 110–111
Science, masculine bias of, 98
Scientific change, 94–95
Self-centrism, 93, 105
Self-in-relation theory, 218
  essentialism in, 220
Self-representation
  earliest, 76
  early mother-child interactions and, 476–481
  in women, 76–77
Semiotics, 88–89
Sensory development, gender differences in, 95, 110
Sensory experience, 278–279
Separation, 76
  painful penetration and fear of, 265–267
  protection from pain of, 456–457
Separation-individuation process
  female homosexuality and, 494
  gender differentiation and, 103–105
  mother-daughter relationship and, 449–481
  in women, 101

Separation-loss, 180–181
Sexual abuse, 147
  generational transmission of, 148–149
Sexual characters, physical versus mental, 14
Sexual identity, conflictual, xi
Sexual intimacy, fending off, 270
Sexual object choice. *See also* Object choice
  flexibility of in women, 497–499
  versus gender role, 501–502
  of lesbians, 485–486
  multiple determining factors of, 499–500
Sexual orientation, changes in during treatment, 498–499
Sexual pleasure
  active/passive and subject/object polarities and, 31–36
  clitoris as locus of, 153
  in girls, 133–134
  renunciation of, 32–34
  value of, 262
Sexual relations, impossibility of, 86–87
Sexuality, 4. *See also* Female sexuality
  anatomy and, 177–178
  Freud's theory of, 14
  in gender, 221–222
  infantile, 40–41
  paradoxes of, 40
  studies of, 15
  of women analysts, 547–549
Siblings, effect of, on oldest child, 461–462
Social collectivity, 100–105
Sociocentrism, 93, 105
Sociocultural environment, 374
Speech, preverbal beginnings of, 88
Sphincter control, 345
  in female gender identity, 288–289
  "inner sphinx" fantasy and, 241–242

Subject Index

in masturbation in girls, 337, 340–341
psychic meaning of, 244–258
Sphinx, riddle of, 257–258
Stillbirth, 394
Structural psychology, 14
Subjective gender
　constructing, 228–235
　versus observed gender, 224–228
Subjectivity
　definition of, 23–24, 39–40
　feminine, 23–41
　gendered, 224–235
　as masculine, 24–25
　nature of, 27
　sexual pleasure and, 35
Subject/object polarity, 28–31
　sexual pleasure and, 31–36
Sublimation, oedipal sensual aims, 33
Superego
　development in boys versus girls, 151
　early harsh female, 256–257
　female, 5, 256–257
　formation of, 37
　gender differences in development of, 96
　in girls, 79–80, 288
　pathways to, 256–257
　super-rigid, 168
Symbolic process, 157–187
Symbolization
　body ego and, 177–180
　female body ego and, 175–176
　linking to lost objects, 180–181

Taboos, defloration, 311–312
Testosterone, 106, 108
Theoretical reversals, 74–75
Threshold of immunity, 380–381
Thumb-sucking, 60
Toddler
　body ego development in, 441–442, 443–445

mother's response to, 434
Toilet training, 338, 469
　anxiety over, 339
Topographical theory, 14–15
Toward a New Psychology of Women (Miller), 75–76
Transference
　in Dora case, 60–61
　fluidity of, 235
　gender role in, 216
　maternal, 64–65
　theoretical versus clinical role of gender in, 216
Transference-countertransference
　femininity in, 234–235
　focus on, 221–222
Transitional object concept, 105
Triangular play, 339–340
Triangular relationship, 65–66, 342
　aggression in, 41
　during pregnancy, 378
Two-sex theory, 405

Unconscious
　femininity in, 119–130
　topographical theory and, 14–15
Unconscious fantasy, 121n
　of "inner sphinx," 241–258
　in subjective gender, 224–232
Universalism, 216–218
　false, 219–220
Unpleasure, fear of, 262

Vagina
　awareness of, 146–147, 297–298, 403
　congenital absence of, 276
　early valuation of, 257, 512–513
　ignorance of, 134, 153
　infantile awareness of, 299
　as inner powerful organ, 241–258
　as "nothing," 201–203
　as potential space, 243
　primary nonrecognition of, 130

Subject Index

in psychosexual development, 200–201
rectal sensations and, 244–258
unawareness of, 294–295
unconscious knowledge of, 120
Virgin, 305
Virginity
  cross-cultural images of, 312
  loss of, 38–39, 303–330
  psychoanalytic literature on, 305–309
  vulnerability and loss of, 318–319
Vulnerability, hymen and, 318–319
Vulva, 274–275

Weaning, trauma of, 433
Western metaphysics, 86–87
Wolf Man case, 30, 46
Woman
  as absence of man, 83
  acting as subject, 35
  aggression in, 37–39
  as asexual, 549
  as castrated men, 56
  contemporary images in women's art, xi–xii
  cultural assumptions in thinking about, 220–223
  dangerous aggressions of, 38–39
  Freud's observations on, 71–72
  generalizations about, 218–219
  as genitally defective males, 94
  homosexuality in, 62–65
  hymen and genital anxiety and vulnerability in, 318–319
  hymen and thresholds in, 319–321
  lack of subjectivity, 24–25
  in male institute, 530–533
  masculine desires in, 32–33
  masturbation guilt in, 321
  meaning of perineal activity in, 241–258
  as mentor, 532
  mother role and, 321–323
  motherhood as central role of, 274
  need for relationships in, 77–79
  object choice in, 133–154
  passions of, 25, 27
  pathologizing of, 84–85
  sense of self in, 76–77
  as separate, 404
  in training as psychoanalysts, 529–553
Woman analyst(s)
  as good enough mothers, 550–553
  meaning of, 538–541
  minority status of, 533–538
  parental identification of, 542–547
  sexuality of, 547–549
The Woman That Never Was (Hrdy), 97–98
Womb
  envy, 5–6
  primary nonrecognition of, 130
Women's movement, 286–287, 540
Working mothers, 550–552
Writing
  as indirect pleasure, 33
  in masculine versus feminine mode, 84